The Black Experience in America

SECOND EDITION

Edited by

Edward Ramsamy, PhD

Rutgers University

and

Gayle T. Tate, PhD

Rutgers University

Kendall Hunt
publishing company

Front cover image © Library of Congress, Prints & Photographs Division,
U.S. News & World Report Magazine Collection, LC-DIG-ppmsca-03128

Back cover image © U.S. Army photo by D. Myles Cullen

Kendall Hunt
publishing company

www.kendallhunt.com
Send all inquiries to:
4050 Westmark Drive
Dubuque, IA 52004-1840

Copyright © 2006, 2011 by Edward Ramsamy and Gayle T. Tate

ISBN 978-0-7575-9414-4

Printed in the United States of America
10 9 8 7 6 5 4 3 2 1

CONTENTS

Section 4   The Civil Rights and Black Power Movements   235

Contributors

Donna A. Auston is a PhD student in the department of Anthropology at Rutgers University, where she also received her BA in Linguistics and Africana Studies. In addition to her academic work, she has been an activist and organizer American Muslim community for nearly 15 years, having worked with a wide variety of local and national Islamic organizations over the years. She has spent many years researching and documenting the history and experiences of American Muslims, with particular focus on the African American Muslim community, and has organized several seminars and conferences on the topic, including "Forgotten Roots: Black Atlantic Islam and the Legacy of African Muslims in the Americas" and "Fish, Grits, and Couscous: Islam and the African American Experience." She has published articles on African American and Latino Muslims, and has several forthcoming essays, including an examination of African American Muslim women's service and community activism in Newark, New Jersey via their work as professional undertakers, and a study of the Nation of Islam in the 1975 Transition era. Both of these works will appear in edited volumes of Africana studies. Her other research interests include examinations of race, ethnicity, identity, and culture, most particularly in areas where these phenomenon intersect with language, religion, social structures and institutions. She is currently working on a study of the process of conversion to Islam in African American communities.

Cheryl Clarke is the Dean of Students (Livingston Campus) at Rutgers University. She is the founding director of the Office of Diverse Community Affairs and LGBT Concerns and has specific responsibility for lesbian, gay, bisexual, transgender, queer, and questioning student life at Rutgers University, New Brunswick campus. She is also a member of the graduate faculty of the Department of Women and Gender Studies. She has been a member of the campus community since 1969. She received her BA from Howard University and her M.A. and PhD in English from Rutgers. She is a poet and the author of four books of poetry since 1983: *Narratives: Poems: In The Tradition Of Black Women, Living As A Lesbian, Humid Pitch,* and *Experimental Love.* Her poetry and prose have appeared in numerous publications since 1981. She was an editor of *Conditions* from 1981–1990. Clarke's poetry is distinguished by its direct explorations of the poetics and politics of sexuality. Her book, *After Mecca: Women Poets and the Black Arts Movement* was published by Rutgers University Press (2005).

Gloria Harper Dickinson (late) was Associate Professor and chair of the Department of African American Studies at The College of New Jersey in Ewing, New Jersey. Her academic areas of interest include Africana women and religion, black popular culture, and women writers of Africa and the African Diaspora. She co-authored the 1990 and 1991 editions of the *Tougaloo College (Mississippi) Mission Involvement Program Textbook,* and contributed biographies of Police Officer Margaret Creswell Hiawatha, AME Zion pastor Rev. Elizabeth Randolph and novelist Helen Jackson Lee to the 1990 publication *Past and Promise: Lives of New Jersey Women.* She has also authored a chapter on Africana Women's Studies in *Creating an Inclusive College Curriculum: A Teaching Sourcebook from the New Jersey Project* (Columbia University Teachers College Press, 1996).

Thomas Edge is a visiting professor of African American studies at Northwestern University. He completed his undergraduate education at Rutgers University where he majored in Africana Studies and History. He earned his PhD from the University of Massachusetts at Amherst. His dissertation was on the life and career of Mordecai Wyatt Johnson. His research interests include Black higher education, African American leadership, and the Civil Rights Movement.

Paul J. Edwards graduated from Wesleyan University with a BA in Music with honors. While at Wesleyan, he facilitated an educational course, "American Popular Culture" at York Correctional Institute. A bass player, he has performed at Lincoln Center and Newport Folk Festival and has music featured in the web series, *Gray Matters*. Mr. Edwards has released several independent albums and produced from his studio located in Brooklyn, New York. A licensed sound engineer, Mr. Edwards currently works as a Director for Audible Inc./Amazon.com in Newark, New Jersey.

Susan S. Fainstein is Professor of Urban Planning at Harvard University. Her teaching and research have focused on comparative urban public policy, planning theory, and urban redevelopment. She has authored and edited several groundbreaking books on comparative urban political economy are *The City Builders: Property, Politics, and Planning in London* (2001); *The Tourist City* (1999); *New York, Divided Cities: New York and London in the Contemporary World* (1992) and *Urban Political Movements: The Search for Power by Minority Groups in American Cities*. Her numerous articles have appeared in a wide variety of geography, urban planning, and public policy journals.

Donald C. Heilman is a 1976 graduate of Rutgers University and 1983 graduate of the Seton Hall University School of Law. Admitted in both New Jersey and Washington, D.C., he was certified by the New Jersey Supreme Court as a Certified Civil Trial Attorney from 1990–2010. He earned his Master's Degree in the Social and Philosophical Foundations of Education from the Rutgers University Graduate School of Education in 2007 and is a doctoral candidate in the same field. His research is in the field of Transformative Learning and its place in higher education. His studies have included the topics of law and society; apartheid and segregation; and, the Civil Rights movement and the law. Mr. Heilman currently serves as the Director of the Office of Student Legal Services at Rutgers University. His background also includes the facts that he played football and ran track at Rutgers from 1972–1976, and was a sports writer for several New Jersey daily newspapers from 1976–1983 covering college football, professional basketball, and track and field.

Rajani Iyer completed her undergraduate education at Rutgers College in 1998 majoring in English and subsequently enrolled for graduate studies at the University of Pennsylvania. Specializing in Victorian literature, she earned her PhD in 2004. Her dissertation titled *My Soul Was Singing at a Work Apart: Female Victorian Poets Achieving Voice* focused specifically on Victorian poetry.

Regina Jennings is Assistant Professor in the Department of Africana Studies. She obtained her PhD in Africana Studies from Temple University. She is author of *Midnight Morning Musings*, "The Malcom X Muse" (in Haki Madhubuti's *Poetic Vision*), and *Race, Rage and Roses*. She teaches courses on African American folklore, Black social and political development, and Black profiles. She is founder of the *Journal of Black Poetry* at Rutgers.

Rhett S. Jones (late) was Professor of Afro American Studies and Research Director of Rites and Reason Theatre at Brown University. He is the author of "Mulattos, Freejacks, Cape Verdeans, Black Seminoles and Others" (for anthology edited by James L. Conyers); "One Africanity or Many? Researching the Deep Structural Location of Blackness" (in *The International Journal of Africana Studies*); and "Sub-Africanity in Africa and the Americas" (in the *Western Journal of Black Studies*.) He has published over 70 essays over the last three decades.

Haki Madhubuti is Distinguished University Professor, founder and Director Emeritus of the Gwendolyn Brooks Center for Black Literature and Creative Writing, and Director of the Master of Fine Arts and Creative Writing Program at Chicago State University. Over the years, he has published 24 books (some under his former name, Don L. Lee), including *Black Men: Obsolete, Single, Dangerous: The African American Family in Transition* (1990) and *Claiming Earth: Race, Rage, Rape, Redemption* (1994), *GroundWork: New and Selected Poems 1966–1996* (1996), and *HeartLove: Wedding and Love Poems* (1998) and *Tough Notes: A Healing Call For Creating Exceptional Black Men* (2002). Professor Madhubuti is the founder, publisher, and chairman of the board of Third World Press.

Allison McGevna graduated from Douglass College, Rutgers University, in 2005 with a major in History and a minor in Spanish. Her research interests include the study of gender roles and femininity of black women during the Civil Rights Movement. Her senior honors thesis was a biography of the late Ruby Hurley as the Southeast Regional Director of the NAACP. She received the Helen Prager Miller Prize in History which enabled her to study abroad at the University of Sao Paolo in Brazil. She currently works for the Rutgers University Ronald E. McNair Program, which seeks to enable low-income, first generation, and/or underrepresented students to pursue a higher education.

Olubayi Olubayi is an associate professor of microbiology and the chair of the biotechnology program at Middlesex County College in Edison, New Jersey. He is also a lecturer in Africana Studies at Rutgers University. He earned his PhD in plant biology from Rutgers University in 1995. His research focus was on the biology of bacteria-plant-cell interactions. He holds a United States research patent on the flocculation of bacteria, and he has published on bacterial physiology, the biology of plants, and the place of science in Africana studies. He is the co-founder and president of the Global Literacy Project, Inc., a nonprofit organization that ships books and computers to economically disadvantaged countries in Africa, the Caribbean, and Asia.

Melanye Price is assistant professor of Africana Studies and Political Science at Rutgers University—New Brunswick. Her research and teaching interests include black politics, public opinion, political psychology, and social movements. Dr. Price completed her BA in geography with a political science minor at Prairie View A&M University in 1995 and her MA (1998) and PhD (2003) in political science with a specialization in the field of American politics at The Ohio State University. Her next research project examines the construction of a "Katrina evacuee" identity around race and class and its impact on political preferences in the city of Houston following Hurricane Katrina. Her most recent book is *Dreaming Blackness: Black Nationalism and African American Public Opinion* (New York University Press, 2009.)

Anitha Ramachandran is a lecturer in Africana Studies at Rutgers University and PhD Candidate in the Department of English at Princeton University. Her fields of research include 19th and 20th century American and British literature, African American literature, postcolonial literature, and literary and critical theory. She has taught undergraduate courses in 19th and 20th century African American literature, Victorian fiction, postcolonial literature, children's literature, modern American drama, and English composition. She has received the Andrew W. Mellon Fellowship for Humanistic Studies from the Woodrow Wilson Foundation, the Hyde Fellowship from the Four Oaks Foundation, and the John E. Annan Class of 1855 Prize for Excellence from Princeton University. She is also a Fellow of the Cornell University School of Criticism and Theory, and *American Quarterly*. Prior to completing an MA degree at Princeton University, she received an MA from Georgetown University, where she specialized in literary theory and African American literature. She received her BA from Johns Hopkins University, where she majored in Molecular Biology.

Kavitha Ramachandran is a lecturer in Africana Studies and PhD candidate in Geography at Rutgers University. Her research pertains to theorizing comparative diaspora; feminist geographies of race, culture, and identity; cartography and geographic information systems (GIS); and theories of space, nature, and society. Her teaching interests include Indian African relations in a global context; Black migration and urbanization; Black Asian relations in the United States; race, class, and gender in urban economic development; and cultural pluralism and democracy. In addition to her writings in these areas, she has an active interest in developing educational media. She has written a manual for ESL (English as a Second Language) instruction, and produced a DVD with workbooks for children in rural India to learn English as a second language.

Edward Ramsamy, PhD is Associate Professor of Africana Studies and a member of the graduate faculty of Geography at the School of Arts and Sciences, and a member of the graduate faculty at the Edward J. Bloustein School of Urban Planning and Policy Development at Rutgers University. He is the author of the book *The World Bank and Urban Development: From Projects to Policy* (Routledge, 2006). In addition to his research in international development planning and the geographies of globalization, Dr. Ramsamy's fields of study include the political economy of transition and nation-building in post-colonial/developing societies; and the comparative politics of identity and race relations in South Africa and the United States. He is editor of *Science, Culture and the Politics of Knowledge: Contexts and Conversations* (forthcoming, Rowman and Littlefield), and co-editor of *The Black Experience in America* (with Gayle T. Tate, 2006, Kendall Hunt). He has published numerous articles on regional integration in southern Africa, as well as on racial, ethnic, and national identity in post-apartheid South Africa. Dr. Ramsamy is the recipient of numerous honors and awards, and a fellow of the Social Science Research Council, the Center for the Critical Analysis of Contemporary Culture, the Institute for Research on Women, and the Rutgers Center for Historical Analysis.

Lewis A. Randolph was Professor in the Department of Political Science and the Public Administration Program at Ohio University. His areas of research specialization include urban politics, black conservative theory, race, class and gender, presidential politics, urban development, black politics, social movements/civil rights, and domestic political economy. His publications have appeared in the *Western Journal of Black Studies*, *Proteus-Journal of Ideas*, and *The Urban Affairs Review*, and he has reviewed books for *The Journal of Black Studies* and *Women & Politics*. He recently completed a three-book series with Dr. Gayle Tate of Rutgers University-New Brunswick: *Made In America: Dimensions of Black Conservatives in the U.S.* (St. Martin's Press, June 2002) and *Rights for A Season: Race, Class, and Gender in Richmond, Virginia* (UT Press, May 2003) and *Black Urban Communities: From Dusk to Dawn* (Palgrave, 2006).

Louis Ray is an assistant professor at Fairleigh Dickinson University. He obtained his PhD in History of Education from New York University. His teaching interests include the history of Blacks in education in the United States; multicultural education and the Black experience; and higher education in the United States. His research interests encompass the history of education; Charles S. Thompson; graduate school preparation for first generation, low-income and underrepresented students; and access and opportunity in higher education.

James W. Reed is Professor of History at Rutgers University and former Dean of Rutgers College (1985–1994). He is published widely in the fields of social and medical history and is the author of *From Private Vice to Public Virtue : The Birth Control Movement and American Society Since 1830* (Princeton University Press). He was the Schlessinger Fellow at Harvard University. His current project *The Road to Viagra: Sex, Science and Medicine in the United States* is on the history of biomedical sex research in the United States.

Ibram H. Rogers is an assistant professor of African American history at SUNY College at Oneonta. He earned his doctoral degree in African American Studies from Temple University. He has received several research grants and fellowships including from the Library of Congress, Rutgers Center for Historical Analysis, Lyndon Baines Johnson Library and Museum, Chicago's Black Metropolis Research Consortium, UCLA, University of Chicago, and Duke University. His primary field is twentieth-century African American History, and his research and teaching interests include American social history, civil rights and black power studies, student activism and the Long Sixties, and intellectual history. His first book will be published by Palgrave MacMillan and it is titled *The Black Campus Movement*, a historical analysis of the black students' struggle to diversify and make higher education relevant in the late 1960s and early 1970s.

Gayle T. Tate is an Associate Professor of Political Science in the Africana Studies Department and a member of the Graduate Faculty of the Department of Women's and Gender Studies. She is a past and current Chairperson of the Department of Africana Studies. Her published work has appeared in numerous scholarly journals including the *Western Journal of Black Studies, Women & Politics, the National Political Science Review, Urban Affairs Annual Review, Third World in Perspective, Black Women's History at the Intersection of Knowledge and Power*, and the *Journal of Black Studies*. Her work has also appeared in several encyclopedias including *Black Women in America: A Historical Encyclopedia*. She was an associate editor for *Africana: An Introduction & Study* (1999); the co-editor of *Dimensions of Black Conservatism in the United States: Made in America* (2002); *The Black Urban Community* (2006). She is the author of *Unknown Tongues: Black Women's Political Activism in the Antebellum Era, 1830–1860* (2003) and co-author of *Rights for a Season: The Politics of Race, Class, and Gender in Richmond, Virginia* (2003). Dr. Tate's book, *Unknown Tongues* was a Choice recommendation in 2004 and her book, *Rights for a Season* was the 2004 Winner of the Best Book Award for Urban Politics from the American Political Science Association

Ivan Van Sertima (late) was Professor of Africana Studies at Rutgers University. He is author of *They Came Before Columbus*, which won the Clarence L. Holt Prize, an honor awarded every two years "for a work of excellence in literature and the humanities relating to the cultural heritage of Africa and the African Diaspora." He founded the *Journal of African Civilizations* in 1979 to explore the contributions of African people to the civilizations of the world. The *Journal* publications include *Blacks in Science, Nile Valley Civilizations, African Presence in Early America, Black Women in Antiquity, Egypt Revisited, Egypt: Child of Africa, African Presence in Early Europe, Golden Age of the Moor, African Presence in the Art of the Americas, Great Black Leaders, Great African Thinkers* (co-edited with Larry Obadele Williams), and *African Presence in Early Asia* (co-edited with Runoko Rashidi). His latest work, *Early America Revisited* was published in 1998. On July 7, 1987, he appeared before a Congressional Committee to testify against the Columbus doctrine and defended his thesis in an address to the Smithsonian Institute in 1991.

Janice Warner is a board-certified Diplomate in Clinical Social Work. She is on the staff of the Faculty/Staff Assistance program, Rutgers University and is in private practice in psychotherapy and couples counseling in Plainfield, New Jersey. She is also a faculty member of the Continuing Education and Professional Development Program of the Rutgers School of Social Work in New Brunswick, New Jersey. She is a graduate of the Columbia University School of Social Work, the Post Masters program in Advanced Clinical Social Work, The Pastoral Counseling Program and the Group Therapy Training program of the Postgraduate Center for Mental Health. In addition to her professional work she has a long history of activism in Native American struggles for social justice and a member of a number of organizations promoting Native American culture and history.

Robert E. Weems, Jr. is Professor of History and Interim Associate Vice Chancellor for Equity at the University of Missouri-Columbia. His areas of academic specialization are African American history, African American Studies, and United States history. He is author of *Black Business in the Black Metropolis: The Chicago Metropolitan Assurance Company, 1925–1985* (Indiana University Press, 1996); *Desegregating The Dollar: African American Consumerism in the Twentieth Century* (New York University Press, 1998); *The African American Experience: An Historiographical and Bibliographic Guide*, co-edited with Arvarh E. Strickland (Greenwood Publishers, 2001). His most recent book is *Business in Black and White: American Presidents and Black Entrepreneurs in the Twentieth Century* (NYU Press, 2009).

Randall Westbrook is an instructor in Africana Studies at Rutgers University, and lecturer in the School of Education of Fairleigh Dickinson University. His areas of academic interest include early 20th century African American political thought, the history of African American Education, the life and work of Paul Robeson and the early work of W. E. B. Du Bois. He is presently at work on a book of essays about race and education, a number of biographical efforts, and editing works by Du Bois for publication.

Ben Wisner holds a PhD in Geography. He began his academic career as a lecturer at the University of Dar es Salaam (Tanzania) in the late 1960s. He has held academic appointments in universities in Africa, Europe, and the United States. Prior to his recent retirement he was the Henry R. Luce Professor of Food, Resources and International Policy at Hampshire College and Director of International Studies and Professor of Geography at California State University at Long Branch. At present he is engaged in full-time research and writing. He has just completed a four-year project for United Nations University on defining and managing urban social vulnerability to disasters in six megacites (Johannesburg, Tokyo, Manila, Mumbai, Mexico City, and Los Angeles). He is currently a research fellow at the Development Studies Institute at the London School of Economics (DESTIN). He also serves as vice-chair of the Earthquakes and Megacities Initiative, vice-chair of the International Geographical Union's Commission on Hazards and Risks, and a research coordinator for the United Nations University's project on urban disasters. He is known for his book *At Risk: Natural Hazards, People's Vulnerability, and Disasters* (London: Routledge, 1994) and numerous other publications on disaster and social vulnerability.

Preface to Second Edition

"The problem of the 20th century is the problem of the color line," wrote the great intellectual Dr. W. E. B. Du Bois, one of the architects of the Modern Civil Rights Movement in the United States. His prophetic statement captured the decisive and controlling role played by race in social, political, and economic relations in American society. In fact, so frustrated and disillusioned was Du Bois toward the end of his life, with what he deemed to be an unchanging racial status quo, that he felt compelled to renounce his U.S citizenship and resettle in the newly independent African nation of Ghana. "I just cannot take anymore of this country's treatment," he declared. "We leave for Ghana October 5th and set no date to return. . . . Chin up, and fight on, but realize that American Negroes can't win."[1] American race relations seemed to be in such a stalemate to Dr. Du Bois during his lifetime that he could not have foreseen that a person of African descent would be elected into the most powerful political office in the nation, and indeed the world, the Presidency of the United States of America. Yet, forty-five years after the great Professor's death, in 2008, that is exactly what came to pass.

The presidential campaign and election of President Barack Obama in 2008 was a historical moment that may redefine the future American political landscape. Unfailingly, historical moments produce dramatic changes, major shifts in the economic structure, and even greater movement in the ideological moorings of the populace as they search for political and social policy advantages. Historical moments are each distinctive in character, typified by the emergence of new leadership in the national discourse, with local leaders coalescing around community initiatives that have direct tie-ins to emerging social policies. Women occupy organizing roles as well as moving to the forefront of the freedom struggle with an agenda of inclusion. As female activists gain momentum in the public arena, they shift the ground beneath their feet, and their community-based efforts are cross-fertilized with national policies that impact family, children, education, and community. This historical moment is a global one, with capitalism out of control, and an extreme conservative agenda gaining sway. At the center of this moment is President Barack Obama, an African-American president. People struggle to identify and locate his blackness to coincide with their political sentiments and beliefs, either by critiquing his race neutral policies or by seeking to stymie his agenda entirely, thus ensuring that the white power structure remains steadfast.

A historical moment has a plethora of forces. Ronald Walters acknowledges in his essay, "Obama's Edge: Understanding Nation Time" that historical moments combine charismatic leadership, the disaffection of American voters, and broad-based political participation into the potential for a social movement.[2] But this historical moment, with all of the flaws, global crises and profound uncertainties precipitated by runaway capitalism, carries with it larger-than-life expectations for political leadership, including the presidency of the United States, that no one, including President Barack Obama, could possibly scale. Alice Walker was prophetic when she noted during the presidential campaign of Senator Barack Obama that if he won the presidency "our country is in such ruin it may well be beyond his power to lead us toward rehabilitation."[3]

The election of President Barack Obama caused many to believe that America was moving into a post-racial society. Some saw this momentous event as a new day dawning in America where race would no longer be a factor in the equality of opportunity and continuously stunt black progress. Others saw this election as an emerging vehicle for opportunities for Blacks that have long been denied. Still others saw this election as a victorious end of the four hundred year black struggle for freedom, justice, and equality. Yet, none of these could be further from the truth. After much of the emotion and optimism surrounding the presidential campaign and election have now dissipated, the realities of daily life are being freshly confronted. Poverty, gender discrimination, unemployment, substandard housing, meager educational opportunities, inadequate health care for those without means, all will take billions of dollars of reinvestment at the local, state, and federal levels to resuscitate communities. These challenges must be joined in concert with the President's initiatives, with community residents all participating, to propel the country forward.

In an effort to link his presidency symbolically with struggles against slavery and the Modern Civil Rights Movement, President Obama displays the original Emancipation Proclamation Act and a bust of Dr. Martin Luther King, Jr. in the Oval Office. Indeed, the African American struggle for freedom and the Modern Civil Rights Movement created the political spaces that made President Obama's election possible. It is, however, important to remember that increasing Black representation and electing Blacks to political office were only part of the Modern Civil Rights Movement's agenda. For example, prior to his assassination, Dr. King had dedicated the last years of his life mobilizing the Poor Peoples' Campaign, speaking out against American imperialism in Vietnam, supporting sanitation workers' strikes, and embracing the great Professor's call for social justice. Reflecting on King and the Civil Rights Movement, Cornel West observes that President Obama's election represents "a fulfillment of Martin Luther King's dream, not THE fulfillment of King's dream."[4] Thus, poverty, inequality, militarism, and need for social justice, both domestically and internationally, remain fundamental challenges in the age of President Barack Obama. As President Obama's first term in office nears completion, it remains to be seen whether his policies will bend to the pressures of Wall Street or respond to the call made by Du Bois and King on behalf of the poor and working classes of America.

The second edition of this book is released three years into the Obama Presidency. It features eight new chapters on topics ranging from Barack Obama's ascendancy to the White House, LGBT (Lesbian, Gay, Bisexual, and Transgender) struggles for rights and recognition, Islam in the Black experience, sports and the struggle for desegregation, music during the Civil War era, and a chapter synthesizing W. E. B. Du Bois' monumental contributions to the Black struggle for freedom and justice. Together with material from the first edition, these chapters attempt to chronicle the experiences of African Americans as they strove to create spaces of meaning and hope in a hostile land.

Edward Ramsamy, PhD
Gayle T. Tate, PhD

Endnotes

1. Quoted from Cornel West, *The American Evasion of Philosophy: A Genealogy of Pragmatism* (The University of Wisconsin Press, 1989), 149.
2. Ronald Walters, "Obama's Edge: Understanding Nation Time," *The Black Scholar: Journal of Black Studies and Research*, 38, no. 1 (Spring 2008): 24–25, 32–33.
3. Alice Walker, "Lest We Forget: An Open Letter to my Sisters," *The Black Scholar, Journal of Black Studies and Research*, 38, no. 1 (Spring 2008): 46.
4. Reported on moxnews.com, http://www.youtube.com/profile?annotation_id=annotation_845996& feature=iv&user=CSPANJUNKIEd0tORG#p/search/0/PFxyHNau7jQ (accessed July 1, 2011).

Preface to First Edition

The Black experience in America unfolded in what the noted historian John Hope Franklin (1993:36) has characterized as "the theater of the absurd." Americans of African ancestry created spaces of meaning and hope in a deeply hostile, alienating, and irrational environment. The specificity of the Black cultural experience, according to philosopher Cornel West (1996:79):

> lies in both the African and American character of Black people's attempts to sustain their mental sanity and spiritual health, social life and political struggle in the midst of a slave holding, white supremacist civilization that viewed itself as the most enlightened, free, tolerant and democratic experiment in human history.

African Americans' indefatigable will to survive is captured in Henry Ossawa Tanner's classic painting *The Banjo Lesson* (1893), which depicts an old man, perhaps a grandfather, imparting the gift of music to his young protégé. The stark, bare setting ominously suggests that the lesson and the precious time the two share together could easily end the very next moment, given the bizarre conditions of life in the South at the time. Yet, wisdom was transmitted from one generation to another as these two people managed to live out their own purpose in spite of the bleak circumstances under which they lived.

This book is an attempt to document the social and political history of a courageous people and their perseverance over adversity. While Blacks have played an integral role in the making of the nation and the modern world economy, their contribution has been rendered invisible in mainstream accounts. As Columbia University literary critic Edward Said (2000) recalls:

> I received my entire education between 1953 and 1963 in English and American literature, and yet all we studied were works written and done by white men, exclusively. No Du Bois, no slave narratives, no Zora Neale Hurston, no Langston Hughes, no Ralph Ellison, no Richard Wright. I recall asking a distinguished professor at Harvard, who lectured 30 more or less consecutive weeks during the academic year on 250 years of American literature, from the 17th-century preacher Jonathan Edwards to Ernest Hemingway, why he didn't lecture on Black literature. His answer was, "There is no Black literature."

The distinguished Africana Studies scholar John Henrik Clark recounts a similar experience. As a high school student, Clark had a part-time job with a local lawyer who had an impressive personal library. When Clark asked to borrow a book so that he could "learn about the history of my [Black] people," the lawyer curtly replied, "your people have no history" (WBAI, October 15, 1999). Clark's enthusiasm was temporarily diminished, but the remark taught him that his life's quest would be to prove the lawyer wrong.

The claim that Blacks have no significant history arose during the age of European empire. This theme is explored in detail in the first section of the book, *Conceptualizing Race: Empire, Modernity, and Representation.* As economic and political power began to concentrate in and shift within Europe from the 1500s to the end of World War II, European conquest, culture, and knowledge systems began to change the world in profound new ways. While there were some important and even liberating breakthroughs during this time in science, philosophy, technology, medicine, transportation, and other fields, there was also a tragic aspect to the European empire. These very same marvels of Europe produced and maintained some of the most heinous atrocities the world had ever seen, affirming cultural theorist Walter Benjamin's observation that "every document of civilization is also a document of barbarism" (cf: Said, 2004:23). The contradiction between the Enlightenment, on one hand, and slavery on the other remains unaddressed to this day. European settlers in the Americas fought for their own independence yet turned to Africa to meet their labor needs. They invented the ideology of African inferiority to justify the largest forced migration in human history, which is estimated to have transported 10 to 60 million enslaved Africans to various destinations outside of Africa. For more than 250 years, slavery sustained the economies of the Western hemisphere. Thus, no critical history of slavery is complete without an account of the ideological structures that rationalize that "peculiar institution."

The second section of the book, *Slavery, Resistance, and Freedom* pays particular attention to the strategies employed by enslaved persons to resist and survive their oppression. Sociologist Orlando Paterson defined slavery as a form of "natal alienation" in which enslaved persons are born with no rights to a past or a future. Yet, even in this deeply alienated state, African Americans struggled to reclaim their past and author their own future. They created psychic and material spaces that sustained the spirit and community by organizing networks of resistance that kept the vision of freedom alive through posterity. Thus, persistent faith, in spite of adverse conditions, is a recurrent theme of the Black experience in America.

Although the aim of the Civil War was to preserve the Union, not to end slavery *per se*, the North's victory in the war technically marked the end of the institution that had undergirded Black life in the South from the mid-1600s. During the next two decades, the country briefly grappled with the incorporation of newly freed slaves as citizens. However, in spite of the ratification of three major amendments to the Constitution, the promises of freedom, citizenship, and franchise remained unactualized as reconstruction of the war-torn South ascended in priority. The eminent intellectual W. E. B. Du Bois characterizes the post-bellum period as a time "when the slave went free; stood for a brief moment in the sun; then moved back towards slavery again," as the country calculated that it could not do without Black labor on Southern plantations. The third section of the book, *Freedom, the Resurgence of White Supremacy, and Strategies for Transforming the Status Quo* examines how African Americans pursued empowerment after the demise of Reconstruction. This was a particularly challenging period for Blacks. The rhetoric of inclusion in the nation's civic culture faded as lynching escalated and segregation became law. Blacks were disfranchised, and the system of sharecropping kept most of them in deep poverty. In this section, the contrasting views of key individuals like Frederick Douglass, Booker T. Washington, W. E. B. Du Bois, and Ida B. Wells are explored, especially their strategies for Black empowerment during these difficult times.

The 1950s and 1960s were important decades in the Black struggle for civic inclusion in American society. The 1954 *Brown v Board of Education* Supreme Court decision reversed *Plessy v Ferguson*, arguing that the doctrine of "separate but equal" was inherently unequal. The *Brown* decision was the culmination of decade-long pressure from the NAACP on the legal pillars of segregation. However, that monumental legal victory did not immediately translate into tangible gains for Blacks. Rosa Parks' arrest on December 1, 1955, ignited the Civil Rights Movement that fought to translate the legal gains of the *Brown* decision into a reality for African Americans. The fourth section of the book, *The Civil Rights and Black Power Movements*, focuses on the role of social activism in transforming American democracy. In addition to providing an overview of the movement, this section concentrates on the important role played by women in civil rights activism, since, all too often, historical accounts of the Civil Rights Movement fall prey to the assumption that history is "driven by the will of great men." Women's activism was vital to the organizational successes of the Civil Rights Movement. The Black Power Movement, an outgrowth of the Civil Rights Movement, stressed Black self-sufficiency and self-reliance. Malcolm X emerged as a powerful spokesperson for this movement as young people, in particular, were attracted to his militant and candid rhetoric. The presence of Malcolm X made Martin Luther King's message more palatable to White America.

The final section of the book, *Identity, Globalization, and Contemporary Struggles*, presents some contemporary challenges facing African Americans. There have been some remarkable changes in race relations since the Civil Rights Movement of the 1960s. Racial segregation in public education was outlawed, and Congress passed the groundbreaking Civil Rights and Voting Rights Acts of 1964 and 1965, respectively. A few African Americans enjoyed unprecedented success in the public and private sectors. However, the color line continues to haunt Black America in the 21st century as structural inequalities remain unaddressed. King's vision of the "beloved community" continues to elude America in spite of important strides made by African Americans. The end of the Cold War, the restructuring of the U.S. economy, and a conservative ideological shift have transformed African American political, economic, and social life in the United States. More recently, the Katrina disaster has served as a painful reminder that the more times change, the more things remain the same. As leading disaster expert Ben Wisner concludes in an essay in this collection, "What America needs are not more levees, but another Civil Rights Movement."

Edward Ramsamy, PhD
New Brunswick, NJ

References

Franklin, John Hope. (1993). *The Color Line: Legacy for the 21st Century.* Columbia: University of Missouri Press.

Said, Edward. (2000). "Reflections on American Injustice," *Al-Ahram Weekly* (February 24– March 1). Available online at *http://weekly.ahram.org.eg/2000/470/op3.htm.*

Said, Edward. (2004). *Humanism and Democratic Criticism.* New York: Columbia University Press.

West, Cornel. (1996). "Black Strivings in a Twilight Civilization," in *The Future of the Race.* Cornel West and Henry Louis Gates (eds.). New York: Alfred A. Knopf, 53–112.

Section 1

Conceptualizing Race, Empire, Modernity, and Representation

Chapter 1

Conceptualizing Race, Empire, Modernity, and Representation: An Introduction

Edward Ramsamy

Race is a powerful cultural, economic, and political axis of division in modern society. Anthropologist Ashley Montagu called it "Man's most dangerous myth," and the scholar W. E. B. Du Bois regarded it as the defining "problem of the 20th century." The primary aim of this section of the book is to examine the importance of race to the United States and explore its implications for the Black experience in the United States. The essays in this section explore how the Black "other" is constructed in history, science, ethnography, literature, and art.

Samir Amin (1989), the noted development economist, remarked that "history is a weapon in the ideological battle between those who want to change society and those who want to maintain its basic features." In his view, history is not simply a value free, politically neutral recollection of the past. Instead, it is a contested terrain in which the power relations of society are inscribed. Racial identities are the products of particular courses of history, leading philosopher Cornel West (1993:39) to reason that "Blackness has no meaning outside a system of race-conscious people and practices." While discrimination, prejudice, stereotypes, and socio-economic hierarchies have existed throughout human history, the association of skin pigmentation and other markers of racial difference with inferiority is largely a product of the age of European empire. In explaining the rise of modern racism, philosopher Hannah Arendt (1950:180) writes:

> Imperialism would have necessitated the invention of racism as the only possible explanation and excuse for its deeds, even if no race thinking existed in the civilized world.

Racist ideologies sought to justify oppressive practices that accompanied the rise of Christian Europe. Christian beliefs in the equality of humans, who were supposedly created in the image of God, co-existed with slavery and colonialism by claiming that subject populations were not part of the same human community. For instance, the German philosopher Hegel (1956:91–99) expounded on the nature of Africa and Africans in history:

> Africa proper as far as history goes back, remained for all purposes of connection with the rest of the world, shut up. It was a land of gold compressed within itself—the land of childhood, which lying beyond the day of self-conscious history, is enveloped in the dark mantle of the night. The peculiarly African character is difficult to comprehend, for the very reason that in reference to it we must quite give up the principle that accompanies all ideas—the category of universality. In Negro life the characteristic point is the fact that consciousness has not yet reached the realization that any substantial objective existence—as for example God or Law, in which the interest of man's volition is involved, and in which he realizes his own being.

> The Negro, as already observed, exhibits the natural man in his completely wild and untamed state. We must lay aside all thought of reverence and morality—all we can call feeling—if we would rightly comprehend him; there is nothing in this type of character.

These words were written contemporaneously with France's establishment of a settler colony in Algeria, north Africa. Hegel's racist ideas provided intellectual and moral justification for unjust and exploitative economic and political practices by appealing to value and knowledge systems that placed the blame for oppressive practices on the supposedly inferior status of those experiencing the oppression. Western intellectual discourse is replete with ethnocentric statements such as those of Hegel. In surveying key Western intellectuals' views on race, West (1982:47) observes that:

> The notion that Black people are human beings is a relatively new discovery in the modern West. The idea of Black equality in beauty, culture, and intellectual capacity remains problematic and controversial within prestigious halls of learning and sophisticated intellectual circles. The Afro-American encounter with the modern world has been shaped first and foremost by the doctrine of White supremacy, which is embodied in institutional practices and enacted in everyday folkways under varying circumstances and evolving conditions.

As a result of the dominant status of Eurocentrism, the agency and achievements of non-European people were marginalized from the narrative of history as written by Europeans. European progress was regarded as owing nothing to the outside world, somehow resulting from intrinsic inventiveness and rationality that were apparently lacking in other peoples. Artificial binaries were created between Western and non-Western societies, which were said to be paralyzed by traditionalism and barbarism. Much of contemporary Western thought is still characterized by a deep parochialism, especially with respect to the contributions of non-Western societies. India, for example, is frequently seen as a society steeped in mysticism. Nobel laureate Amartya Sen (1997:3) observes that "Western approaches to India have encouraged a disposition to focus particularly on the religious and spiritual elements in Indian culture. There has also been a tendency to emphasize the contrast between what is taken to be 'Western rationality' and the cultivation of what 'Westerners' would see as 'irrational' in Indian intellectual traditions." This artificial dichotomy ignores the fact that India is the source of vast atheistic, rationalist, and materialist traditions in addition to its famed spiritual tradition. The decimal system and other mathematical inventions of India were transmitted by Arab mathematicians to the West around the 10th century. Contrary to Eurocentric claims, Indian mathematics subsequently played an "important part in the scientific revolution that helped to transform Europe" (Sen, 2002).

If Asian societies were regarded as superstitious and despotic, Africa was seen as the "the heart of darkness" itself. In a footnote to his essay "Of National Characteristics," Scottish philosopher David Hume writes:

> I am apt to suspect the Negroes, and in general all the other species of men (for there are four or five different kinds) to be naturally inferior to the whites. There never was a civilized nation of any complexion than white, nor even any individual eminent either in action or speculation. No ingenious manufactures among them, no arts, no sciences. . . . In Jamaica indeed they talk of one negroe as a man of parts [sic] and learning, but 'tis likely he is admired for very slender accomplishments, like a parrot, who speaks a few words plainly. (cf: West, 1982:62)

American founding father Thomas Jefferson expresses similar sentiments in his *Notes on Virginia*:

> Comparing them by their faculties of memory, reason, and imagination, it appears to me, that in memory they are equal to whites; in reason much inferior . . . and that in imagination they are dull, tasteless and anomalous. Never yet could I find that a black had uttered a thought above the level of plain narration; never see even an elementary trait of painting or sculpture. (cf: West, 1982:62)

These are examples of a concerted effort to deny that Africa contributed anything substantial to human progress in spite of overwhelming evidence to the contrary. Unfortunately, this trend continues into the present. For example, when it was evident that Africans developed iron smelting techniques approximately 1500 to 2000 years ago (Van Sertima, 1983; Schmidt and Avery, 1978; Schmidt and Childs, 1985), historians went to great lengths to claim that the knowledge must have been received from elsewhere. In his work, *The Making of the Past: The Kingdoms of Africa*, Peter Garlake (1978:10) claims that "iron working is so complex a process that the technology must have reached tropical Africa from other areas." The historian Kevin Shillington (1995:39) initially concurred with Garlake "Because of the specialized nature of iron smelting, it is generally assumed that its techniques could not have been independently invented in more than one place in the ancient world. . . . The knowledge almost certainly originated from western Asia." However, in the 2005 edition of his book, Shillington (2005:37) conceded that Africana scholars like Van Sertima had always been correct and that "the argument of diffusion from only one source of invention is now widely accepted among African archaeologists and historians as no longer valid . . . there is no reason to suppose that ancient Africans were not capable of using the techniques of copper-smelting and independently applying them to the problem of smelting iron."

Mainstream European accounts maintain that Copernicus and Galileo were the first to discover that the earth revolves around the sun. However, there is much evidence that Africans knew of this fact long before Copernicus and Galileo. The Dogons of central Africa, for example, possessed a sophisticated understanding of the solar system hundreds of years before European astronomers. In his popular television science documentary *Cosmos*, the astronomer Carl Sagan, author of the spirited defense of scientific reason *A Demon Haunted World*, observes that "in contrast to almost all pre-scientific societies, the Dogons held that the planets as well as the earth rotate about their axes and revolve around the sun. They further held that Jupiter has four satellites and that Saturn is encircled by a ring." However, instead of giving the Dogons any credit for developing this knowledge, Sagan speculates that it must have been derived from a "Gallic [European] visitor to the Dogon people . . . [who] may have been a diplomat, an explorer, an adventurer or an early anthropologist." Ironically, for someone who deeply believed in the power of reason over superstition, Sagan fell prey to his own demon of Eurocentrism when he assumed that Europeans must have imparted the knowledge to the Dogons, who then must have simply parroted the information to visiting European anthropologists. Others go further to suggest that "extraterrestrials" must have left their charts with the Dogons (Temple, 1975). The real question is, Why was it inconceivable for Sagan and others that the Dogons made and recorded their own observations of the heavens?

Eurocentrism also pervades the way in which African politics is represented in the popular media. African political conflicts are frequently portrayed as "tribal" while similar conflicts in Europe are regarded as "national," "ethnic," or "religious." This can be no coincidence, given the history of Eurocentric accounts of Africa mentioned previously, and the fact that the word *tribe* connotes a primitive people who have no social or political history. This incongruity has led Mamdani (1992:316–317) to ask, "What makes eight million Swedes a 'nation' . . . and millions more Hausa a 'tribe'? Why are four million Norwegians a 'nation' and eight million Baganda 'a tribe'?" In a similar vein, there is a decided difference in the way significant events in Europe and Africa are treated in historical accounts. The French and American Revolutions, for example, are seen as important historical moments in the advance of democracy, whereas the Nat Turner slave revolt in the United States and the "Mau Mau" struggle in Kenya are seen as eruptions of savagery. Violence, death, and disorder were, sadly, outcomes of both the European and African uprisings but in the former, the accompanying violence is always situated in its socio-historical context, whereas African rebellions are represented as incoherent outbursts of rage, lacking aim or purpose.

Correcting the distorted histories and representations of Africa and peoples of African descent is a key component of the struggles of African Americans. Central to the Black experience in America is the development of a narrative to counter dominant ethnocentric views. This section of the book begins with an interview with Ivan Van Sertima, an important force in challenging Hegel's thesis of African under-achievement. In the late 1970s, Van Sertima advanced the controversial argument that the African presence in the Americas precedes the age of European "discovery." bell hooks (1994:199) views the significance of Van Sertima's works as follows:

> Thinking about the Columbus legacy and the foundations of white supremacy in the United States, I am drawn most immediately to Ivan Van Sertima and his groundbreaking book *They Came Before Columbus*. Documenting the presence of Africans in this land before Columbus, his work calls us to rethink issues of origins and beginnings.

Not surprisingly, Van Sertima's views have been met with resistance by mainstream scholarship. However, Franklin and Moss (1998:30) argue that "Although most scholars have not yet accepted these [Van Sertima's] claims, it is not so much that the arguments are not convincing, as it is their refusal to deny claims that had become deeply entrenched conventional wisdom for more than four centuries."

In his interview with Edward Ramsamy, "The Place of Africa in History and Scholarship," Ivan Van Sertima disputes Eurocentric constructions of history that deny the technological, intellectual, and cultural contributions of Africans. He presents extensive evidence that points to an African presence in the Americas long before Columbus's voyage in 1492, including eyewitness accounts of Europeans who describe distinct

Black societies in the Americas, such as the Jamassi of Florida and the Charruas of Brazil. Van Sertima argues that Africans traveled to the Americas in the pre-Christian era, and that their influence is evident in both material culture of the Americas, such as art and sculpture, as well as the linguistic traditions of the region. He discusses various advances in science, agriculture, and metallurgy attributable to Africans long before Europe's Age of Exploration. According to Van Sertima, Africans also brought back to Africa their own discoveries from the "New World," such as cotton, which is indigenous to South America, not Africa, as is commonly believed.

When challenging the racism of Eurocentric scholarship and history, it is important to interrogate the idea of "race" itself. In his essay "Thinking of Race in the Age of DNA," biologist Olubayi Olubayi ponders the scientific basis of race. He argues that the popular notion of race as a biological category is erroneous and unscientific because it is based on only a few visually observable features while ignoring the far more numerous biological similarities between people of different races. He then poses a number of intriguing scenarios that challenge conventional views on race and queries the human impulse to place objects and events into groups. Olubayi concludes that "DNA codes are a reminder that our shared humanity forms a complex set of continuums that do not fit into simple separate groups called races."

The policy and practice of paternalism has been central to the development of imperialism and modern racism. The idea that those in power "know" what is best for subjugated peoples has been the cornerstone of the justifications of modern slavery as well as the European conquests of Africa and elsewhere. In one of the most famous examples of paternalistic thought in the English language, "White Man's Burden," Rudyard Kipling exhorts fellow whites to "Take up the White Man's burden—Send forth the best ye breed" while, at the same time, categorizing subjugated non-whites as "Your new-caught sullen peoples,—Half devil and half child." In his chapter "The Paternalizers and the Paternalized": A Genealogy of Justifying Exploitation Through the Ideology of Paternalism," Ibram Rogers traces the origins of modern racism. Arguing that "racism as a deed occurs when a privileged race uses its power to discriminate against another race to maintain or extend its power," Rogers shows how "paternalism is the conceptual adhesive" for racism.

In her essay, "Race, Gender, and Nineteenth Century Ethnography: Mary Kingsley's *Travels in West Africa*," Anitha Ramachandran observes how the myth of the "scientific" basis of racial difference is utilized in Eurocentric scholarship to justify the colonization of peoples around the world. She argues that the work of Mary Kingsley, a Victorian ethnographer who traveled extensively in Western Africa to study its peoples and cultural practices, needs to be interrogated not only for the racist ideology that undergirds its "scientific" claims, but for the power it wields as a scientific work to give force to imperialist theories of racial difference. Ramachandran stresses the importance of recognizing ethnography's epistemological power and points out its role in the machinery of imperial domination and control.

Racism also permeates much of Western literature. In her essay "Racism and Sexism in Works for Children," Rajani Iyer explores how Robert Moore, Roger Andersen, and other literary critics have identified the pervasiveness of racist and sexist thought in the English language, and the way it is spoken in America today. Languages create their own cultural hierarchies; for instance, Iyer points out that the use of such words as "non-white" and "minority" are indicative of America's White "aristocracy," in which whiteness is the norm to which other identities are compared. Iyer critiques several "classic" works for children that propagate stereotypes about the racial "other," and considers the ways in which Blacks, Native Americans, Asians, women, and other marginalized groups are represented in these texts.

The idea of "otherness" is also the focus of James Reed's essay, "Columbus and the Making of American Identity," but from the perspective of American history. Reed examines how the figure of Columbus has, over the years, become a contested symbol for various ethnic and racial groups in America. For American Roman Catholics seeking inclusion into Protestant dominated mainstream culture and politics, Columbus was a Catholic hero who preceded the English Protestant explorers, and to whom the existence of the United States was owed. According to Reed, the establishment of Columbus Day in the 1930s may be seen as a symbol of Roman Catholic acculturation in the United States. Yet, as the 20th century progressed, people of color protested the celebration of the holiday, which, in their view, commemorates the colonization, genocide, and exclusion of Native peoples. In her essay, "The Legacy of 1492," Jan Warner points out that while the meaning of Columbus Day may have changed over the years, the legacy of 1492 remains and is borne by Native Americans to this day, who still have difficulty accessing their traditional worship grounds, and whose dispossession continues in both North and South America.

In his interview with Edward Ramsamy, "Scientific Racism and the Culture Wars," James Reed outlines the history of determinist theories of race, class, and intelligence that have prevailed in Western scholarship since the 19th century. He demonstrates how *The Bell Curve*, a popular work of scientific racism by Richard J. Hernstein and Charles Murray, resurrects these theories for the contemporary age. Reed points out the fallacies in *The Bell Curve's* arguments and situates its racist reasoning within the larger system of American racial stratification that has existed since colonial times, when racial markers were first used to form a racial caste system to ease class conflict between poor Whites and rich White landowners. However, in spite of this history, Reed has faith in the ability of Americans to overcome the injustices of bigotry.

While works like *The Bell Curve* demonstrate the power of White supremacy to construct racist theories of Blackness, African Americans have always consciously and subversively proclaimed their own idea of what it means to be Black, culturally and politically. In her essay "Representing Blackness: The 'New Negro' Art of the Harlem Renaissance," Kavitha Ramachandran describes how "Blackness" is not only a "visual marker of a social and cultural 'other'" but also "a metaphor of exclusion and resistance for a dispersed peoples with a common predicament." She argues that while the "New Negro" Art participated in an ongoing struggle for the representation of Blackness in a specific American context, it also offered diasporan, Pan African conceptualizations of Black consciousness and resistance.

References

Amin, Samir. (1989). *Eurocentrism*. New York: Monthly Press Review.

Arendt, Hannah. (1950). *The Burden of our Times*. London: Secker and Warburg Publishers.

Franklin, John Hope and Alfred Moss. (1998). *From Slavery to Freedom: A History of African Americans*. New York: McGraw-Hill.

Garlake, Peter. (1978). *The Kingdoms of Africa*. Oxford: Phaidon Press.

Hegel, G. W. F. (1956). *The Philosophy of History*. London: Daner Publications Inc.

hooks, bell. (1994). *Outlaw Culture: Resisting Representations*. New York: Routledge.

Mamdani, Mahmood. (1992). "Africa: Democratic Theory and Democratic Struggles." *Dissent* (Summer) 312–390.

Schmidt, P., & Avery, D. H. (1978). "Prehistoric Culture and Complex Iron Smelting in Tanzania." *Science*, 201, 1085–1089.

Schmidt, P., & Childs, S. Terry. (1985). "Innovation and industry during the Early Iron Age in East Africa: the KM2 and KM3 sites of northwest Tanzania." *African Archaeological Review*. 3(1), 53–94.

Sen, Amaryta. (1997). "Indians Traditions and the Western Imagination." *DÆDALUS* (Spring 1997), 1–26.

Sen, Amartya. (2002). "How to Judge Globalism." *American Prospect*, available at *http://.prospect.org/print/V13/1/sen-a.html*.

Shillington, Kevin. (1995). *History of Africa*. New York: St. Martins Press.

Shillington, Kevin. (2005). *History of Africa*. New York: Palgrave McMillan.

Temple, Robert. (1975). *The Sirius Mystery*. New York: St. Martins Press.

Van Sertima, Ivan. (1983). *Blacks in Science: Ancient and Modern*. New Brunswick, NJ: Transactions Publishers.

West, Cornel. (1982). *Prophesy and Deliverance: an Afro-American Revolution*. Philadelphia: The Westminster Press.

West, Cornel. (1993). *Race Matters*. New York: Vintage Press.

Chapter 2

The Place of Africa in History and Scholarship:
A Conversation with Ivan Van Sertima

Edward Ramsamy

Africa's history and contributions to human development have been grossly misrepresented in Western portrayals of the continent. German philosopher Hegel's view that "Africa is the land of unredeemable savagery" unfortunately still pervades the popular mindset on Africa. As Cornel West, professor of Religion and African American Studies at Princeton, observes, "The notion that Black people are human beings is a relatively recent discovery in the Western world." Ivan Van Sertima has dedicated his life to counteracting Hegel's irrational and erroneous caricature of Africa. In 1977, he published *They Came Before Columbus: The African Presence in Ancient America*, now in its 10th printing. The book advanced the controversial thesis that Africans traveled to the Americas long before Christopher Columbus' voyage in 1492. In *Blacks in Science: Ancient and Modern*, among other works, he examines the technological and scientific legacies of ancient Africa.

Some of Van Sertima's critics argue that Van Sertima presents a romanticized view of ancient Africa and subjects knowledge to chauvinistic Afrocentric nationalism. In the following interview, Van Sertima discusses how he developed an intellectual interest in his field and responds to his critics. Ivan Van Sertima teaches in the Africana Studies department at Rutgers and is the editor of *The Journal of African Civilizations*.

Ramsamy: How did you develop an interest in the contributions of ancient Africa to various human civilizations?

Van Sertima: It was an accident. I was invited by the Prime Minister of British Guiana to read poetry during the celebration of our independence. So I flew from Britain, where I was living and working on a novel at the time, to Guyana (our name after independence) for Republic Day. There, a friend asked me to stop off in the United States on my way back to Britain. I arrived on a Saturday and that Sunday morning, while he was asleep, I went through his library and noticed a strange book, *Africans and the Discovery of the Americas*, by Leo Wiener. I read the book because it was very exciting, but I dismissed its argument that Africans had "discovered" the Americas. I felt that although Wiener's case for linguistic evidence was impressive, he had not really proven his case. I didn't think he had enough upon which to build such a thesis. So, I actually attacked this thesis 25 years ago. I wrote an essay arguing that even though this is an interesting thesis, it was not properly probed; it was built on fragile pillars of philology. I concluded my essay by saying, "If anyone can show me at least one convincing image of an African in the Americas before Columbus, I would believe."

A week later, Charles Harris, an editor at Random House, called me and said that something unusual has happened. He told me that John Williams, the novelist, had been to Mexico and met a strange German there who had spent many years of his life collecting pieces of pre-Columbian sculpture and art. I rushed off to Mexico that very next weekend to see this man. Alexander Von Wuthenau was really an extraordinary individual. Hitler's government had initially put him in charge of the German embassy in Argentina. The Nazis then decreed that all ambassadors have to sign a document swearing that they were pure Aryans. He wrote an essay arguing that there was no such thing as a "pure Aryan" and, as a result, had to flee Argentina. He went to Mexico and got very involved in studying pre-Columbian culture in the Americas. Von Wuthenau was the last of the royal house of Germany, the son of Count Charles Adam Von Wuthenau and Countess Marie Antoinette Chotek. He spent a lot of time excavating artifacts and eventually wrote a book called *The Art of Terra Cotta Pottery in Pre-Columbian South and Central America*. In this work, he presented the argument of an African influence in pre-Columbian American crafts. After talking with him, I realized that he knew nothing of the linguistic evidence, just as I knew nothing about the art evidence. It occurred to me that the only way that one can investigate the idea of an African presence in pre-Columbian America was through a multidisciplinary approach. So, I investigated within various disciplines. In botany, I discovered that there were some unsolved mysteries. For instance, some African plants were found in the Americas that could not have come by themselves. As I delved into the issue, I found much evidence to support this thesis.

My first attempt at a book on this topic dealt strictly with the Africans' 14th and 15th century journeys, commissioned by the Mandingo King Abu Bakari II of Mali. One captain actually returned from an expedition and Abu Bakari then abdicated the throne and commanded another expedition himself. It was during this period that there were reports by Europeans, including Columbus himself, of seeing Blacks in America. Columbus himself suggested that there were Blacks in America before him. For instance, it is recorded in his *Journal of the Second Voyage*, and quoted in many places, that when he was in Haiti (then called Hispaniola), the Native Americans told him that Black-skinned people had come from the south and southeast in boats, trading in gold-tipped spears made of a metal alloy called "guanin." It is recorded in *Raccolta Part I* that Columbus wanted to find out whether what the Indians of Hispaniola had told him was true. He had samples of the spears sent to the king and queen of Spain for assay and they were found to have 18 parts gold, 6 parts silver, and 8 parts copper, of 32 parts. The proportion of gold, silver, and copper alloys were not just identical to spears in African Guinea; the words used by the Caribbean people for these spears were similar to the words used in Africa by Africans.

In addition to the metallurgical and linguistic evidence, there were at least a dozen Europeans who wrote on the African presence in the Americas. Ferdinand Columbus, one of the sons of Columbus, reported that his father told him about seeing Blacks north of a place we now call Honduras. In September 1513, Vasco Nunez de Balboa wrote that as he was coming down the slopes of Quarequa, near Darien (which we now call Panama), he saw two Black men who were captured by Native Americans. These men were not only exceedingly Black; they were also of different stature than the Native Americans and had different hair texture. Peter Martyr, a prominent historian, has said that these Blacks must have been shipwrecked in the area and taken refuge in the mountains. Alphonse de Quatrefages, author of *The Human Species*, speaks of distinct Black tribes among the Native Americans, like the Jamassi of Florida, and the Charruas of Brazil. Quatrefages presents a map made by a French captain, Kerhallet, showing independent Black settlements along South American coasts. Fray Gregoria Garcia reports a Black presence off Cartagena, Colombia and says that these are the first Negroes in the Indies. One can go on citing other eyewitness accounts.

There are other kinds of evidence as well, such as the important corroborative evidence by botanists. The Portuguese were in West Africa before 1450. They found cotton growing plentifully in West Africa and introduced it into the Cape Verde islands in 1462, assuming that cotton was indigenously African. In the 20th century, it was found that cotton was not African at all. *Gossypium hirsutum var punctatum*, which was grown in the pre-Columbian Caribbean and in parts of South America, is not African. Thus, there is also evidence of people returning to Africa from the Americas long before Columbus. The Arabs have also documented these travels by Africans.

There is also evidence of pre-Christian voyages that we don't have time to discuss now. Let me just mention one aspect of it. We found a stone head at a place called Tres Zapotes that not only had African features but also had seven braids. Similar heads have also been found at La Venta but made of wood. The La Venta heads are very important because wood, an organic material, can be dated easily. The platform at La Venta was dated to 814 BC, plus or minus 134 years. I have been misrepresented often by my critics as saying that Africans founded the cultures of the Americas. I have never said this. I am talking about Africans influencing a culture in the Americas.

Ramsamy: Why is there a reluctance to accept your thesis, in spite of the evidence you present in your books?

Van Sertima: My own earlier reluctance may help to explain it. We were trained to despise ourselves and all of Africa. We felt that Africans were either primitive or semi-primitive, that they had no science and made no significant contribution to civilization. We did not realize that we were looking at a looted Africa, a shattered Africa. We did not realize that there were two Africas, Africa before and after the holocausts. We did not know then what American, French, and German scientists have discovered within the last 25 years, that Africans had steel smelting machines. Peter Schmidt and Donald Avery from Brown University have shown that African machines were producing steel in the 5th century along the lakes of Tanzania and Uganda, where the Africans had built an industrial site. Africans were manufacturing steel at temperatures of 2600 degrees Fahrenheit! No machine anywhere else in the world at the time produced steel at temperatures achieved in the African blast furnaces. The Africans had a single-stage process while the Europeans had a two-stage process of making steel. So, the Africans were using less fuel.

This puzzled me more than anything else. I kept asking why Africans would be driven into fuel-saving technology when Africa was said to be "full of jungles." I turned to scholars who were investigating Africa's physical geography through a United Nations study. The study found that Africa has less jungle than any other continent in relation to its area. So, Africa had always been mismeasured. The new Peterson projections show that Africa is much larger than it was represented in the older McCarter projections. Recent maps from NASA also show that Europe has more forestation than Africa. (I am talking about Europe, proper, not "Eurasia.") The Arabs have also described the vastness of Africa. The empire of Mali was apparently larger than all the states of Western Europe put together and in that empire there was no jungle. It was bordered on the north by desert, on the south by the jungle, on one side by the Atlantic, and on the other side by another African empire, the Songhai.

My point is that Europeans constructed this myth of "jungle Africa." Once this idea was popularized, it became impossible to conceive of Africans crossing oceans or inventing things. Chinese records show that Africans brought elephants in ships to China 200 years before Columbus. We did not know that Africans had made significant advances in astronomy or that they had astronomical observatories. Lynch and Robins of Michigan State University uncovered an observatory from 300 BC in northwest Kenya. This supposedly primitive area also had one of the most accurate pre-historic calendars. We did not know that Africans had domesticated cattle earlier than any other people. When I was attending university in London, I was told that Africans were "dull-witted agricultural Negroes." Dr. Charles Nelson from the University of Massachusetts and his research team have found evidence that Africans began domesticating cattle about 15,000 years ago. Yet "conventional wisdom" would have us believe that Africans contributed nothing to advances in agriculture, that they were just "dull-witted."

There is also evidence that Africans had first domesticated fire in Kenya about 1 million 400 years ago, not the Chinese, as always assumed. All of our fantasies about Africa, all of the anthropology that portrayed Africans as one step above the monkey, and all "conventional history" come from Europe, which gets all the credit for human civilization as if everything occurred in one little place called Europe and nothing of any significance happened elsewhere.

Ramsamy: Why were you invited to testify before Congress on the controversy surrounding the celebration of Columbus' Quincentennial? Did you influence public attitudes towards Columbus Day in any way?

Van Sertima: I was a little mystified about why I was called at first. It appears that my various lectures have had an effect on how people regarded the Quincentennial. The desire to make Columbus out to be some great hero, a "great discoverer," fell down badly. I had been called to address the issue of why we should not refer to Christopher Columbus' accidental stumble into the Caribbean as a discovery. I pointed out to the Congressional Committee that I was not the first person to suggest that there were Africans in the Americas before Columbus, that Columbus himself was the first person to suggest that. In fact, as I said earlier, most of the evidence comes from European narratives. There were no Blacks trying to prove that they had come to America. This whole idea of "discovery" is absurd. We have evidence in Roman Chronicles of Native Americans being shipwrecked in Europe and nobody claimed that Americans "discovered" Europe! Columbus' appearance in the Caribbean was purely accidental because he intended to go to India. When he found "India" in the West, he started calling the Caribbean Sea the "Gulf of the Ganges." He called Cuba a continent and South America an island. When he set out, he did not know exactly where he was going and when he got there, he did not know exactly where he was. When he got back home, he did not know where he had been. How can we make a hero out of someone like that? Even the word "Carib," given to the region and its peoples, reflects Columbus' ignorance of linguistics. *Car-e-ib* meant "foreigners" and it was used by the Native Americans to describe the Europeans! However, since the Europeans conquered the indigenous people, the word became associated with the region.

My testimony led the chairman of the Congressional Committee to advise the Quincentennial Commission that it would not be wise to use the word *discovery* because it is insulting. It also led the Bahamas to be included in the celebration and led to the "discovery" that there were no Native Americans in the Commission and just one or two Blacks. The whole racial constitution of the Commission was called into question. As a result of my testimony, the emphasis was shifted away from "Columbus' discovery of America" to a celebration of the extraordinary meeting and mixing of the peoples of the world. What we were celebrating here in the Americas, the New World, was the creation of a New World people. This is a significant date for Latinos because it is the birth date of "Latino" identity, a distinctively New World identity. We have to transcend the absurd idea that one person discovers another and lifts them to greater heights because various peoples of the world have made advances at various times and in various places.

Ramsamy: You are frequently called a "nationalist" and an "Afrocentric." How do you respond to these characterizations?

Van Sertima: You can have a plural society in which various races take pride in their achievements without losing sense of their shared humanity with others. I am not a "nationalist" in the sense of one who goes around saying that my people or race is the "superior" race. Europeans have a history of that; they have invented all sorts of myths to justify their supposed superiority. First of all, race, as it is currently used to describe phenotypes, is a social construction, not a biological fact. Secondly, we cannot expect a people who have been treated as inferiors for centuries, because of the Eurocentric constructions, to destroy those myths by meekly pleading, "I am just as good as you." That makes no sense. There is a certain militancy that comes with a revolution in thinking and certain excesses, unfortunate as they may be, are to be expected. But those excesses don't come from me. My thought and perspectives are informed by having lived on four continents. I was born in South America, and I have spent much time in North America, Eastern and Western Europe, and in Africa. I am not stuck within a narrow perspective based on a particular locality. My scholarship is about recovering and reconstructing the best in African history so that we can resist that Eurocentric vision which dominates everything. While it is true that in any revolution there is an extremist element, it is also true that if you try to wipe out new ideas because they challenge your earlier, false conceptions of the world, there will be trouble.

"Afrocentricity" is a strange word. It can be understood only in the context of "Eurocentric," which refers to the belief that Europe is the be-all and end-all of the world, that Europeans created the world, and that only Europeans can re-create the world. Afrocentricity, taken to extremes, would lead to the same sort of conceit and fantasy. What I may have is an Afrocentric perspective that points to African achievement in an effort to correct the distortions of Eurocentricity. I hope that as a result, there will no longer be an "Afrocentricity" or "Eurocentricity," but a new, balanced consciousness. There would be no need for Afrocentricity once Eurocentricity has been corrected. In revolutions, it is difficult to avoid extremes, although that is our hope. A person may be reacting to being treated in the most abominable manner and, as a result, may be forced to make certain emphases in order to gain a new, positive self-image. I emphasize things African in order to bring about a balanced world view and to deflate Europeans' exaggerated pride in their achievements without realizing how much credit they owe the rest of the world. For example, most people think that the Industrial Revolution is purely a European development. Were it not for the Moors, for instance, both African and Arab

Moors, Europe would not have become the head of the Industrial Revolution. Were it not for the Moors, Europe would not have had cotton, which entered Europe around the 9th or 10th century. Europe would not have rice and various other agricultural products. Important commodities in Europe were brought by the Moors. The Moors had a profound effect on European classical music and the first major books used in European universities were the books of the Moors. Of course, the numbers that we use today—0,1,2,3—are not European. I don't think pointing these things out necessarily makes me an "Afrocentric" or a "nationalist."

Ramsamy: Critics such as Gross and Levitt argue that your work *Blacks in Science* is a flagrant falsification of science in the service of Afrocentric chauvinism. How do you respond to this?

Van Sertima: It is amazing that educated people can read a book without checking out its authors. Almost half of the authors in my book are European. Are these European scientists Afrocentric? Are Lynch and Robbins, who I referred to earlier, Afrocentric? Schmidt and Avery actually tested the iron smelting machines in Tanzania and verified that they were achieving temperatures higher than any European machine. Are they Afrocentric? This is nonsense! These people haven't even read my work! John Pappademos, a Greek who has seriously studied Greek and Egyptian history, has shown the interaction between the two civilizations. How does Pappademos become Afrocentric? I am surprised at the audacity of people to lie about works they haven't read properly and call themselves scholars. These prejudices, masquerading as scholarship, freeze the intellect and the capacity for vision. These people want to put everything in a box. What I and the Afrocentrists say can easily be dismissed by putting it in a Black box. My objective is to show that the African is no fool. I am not here to show that he is some kind of superman, as the European believes himself to be. However, if I say, "But look here, we did certain things too," they react by saying, "Oh my God, these guys are becoming presumptuous; let me remind them that they are fundamentally inferior." That is why books like *The Bell Curve* are received so well by White society and why any attempt to emphasize African achievement is so viciously criticized or inhibited.

Ramsamy: Some critics claim that there is a paradox in your school of thought, in that Black Africa played a role in European development and yet blames Europe for the ills of Africa. How would you respond to that?

Van Sertima: It's a very stupid argument. If you gave me shoes to walk on and I caught a germ in my toe, are you to be blamed because you gave me the shoes? It is as absurd as saying that if the Japanese were to take the computer and the radio from European scientists, then the ills of Japan somehow must be visited on European scientists. That is so silly!

Ramsamy: In *Black Athena* (Volumes I and II), published by Rutgers University Press, Martin Bernal addresses some issues similar to the ones that have occupied you over the years. What do you think of his work?

Van Sertima: Bernal's main contribution is in showing that the Greeks recognized Africans' important contributions to the development of human civilization. Later on, Europeans created an "Aryan" model that assumed the Greeks did it all when, in fact, the Greeks paid homage to the early Egyptians, who were African. Egypt is no longer African because there have been massive movements of people. Syrians, Greeks, Romans, Persians, and Arabs have all interacted with Egypt and integrated with the African population.

Apart from those who criticize Bernal because they wish to maintain the Aryan model, he is also criticized for assuming that the Egyptian civilization was a mulatto, or mixed-race civilization. Of course, there are no totally homogeneous civilizations, but the mixing of races did not occur until later. Many Blacks live in Britain today and there are Blacks in China now but nobody says these are mixed English or Chinese civilizations! The problem with Bernal, although it is not really his fault, is that he did not know that Africans have at least six phenotypes. There is the elongated variant, the Nilotic variant, and the so-called "true Negro," which accounts for less than 50% of pure-blooded Africans. When archaeologists went into the graves of ancient Egypt and found someone with a narrow nose, they assumed Egyptians were "Caucasoid" even though the hair was "Negroid." As far as they were concerned, a narrow nose meant "Euro-Asiatic." They didn't realize, however, that a dry, hot climate gives rise to a narrow nose, not just cold, icy climates. They went on to argue that if people with dark skins or kinky hair had great achievements, it is because of their fusion with "superior" races. That way, credit would be given to the "superior" race. In order to justify the European myth of the fundamentally "inferior" African, they had to show that any African achievement is because of the blending with "superior" blood and brains. Others have tried to argue that African achievements weren't really achievements at all.

Ramsamy: In 1991, you were invited to deliver an address at the Smithsonian. How important was that lecture to the wider recognition of your work?

Van Sertima: Well, I don't want to embarrass the Smithsonian. They have produced a book, in which my essay appears, which sells for $42. This book is not made of glossy pages, most of the photographs in the book are mine, and none of the writers have asked the Smithsonian for money. Yet they are selling the book for $42. It is not well advertised; I would not accuse them of anything but it seems strange to me that the Smithsonian is not making any effort to distribute it. Are they embarrassed by the book's ideas? Most of the scientists that appeared at the forum were quite surprised at the amount of evidence I was able to produce on the African presence in the Americas; they had thought it was all just fantasy. The organizers of the lecture told me I had 45 minutes to speak. I got up there and told everyone that is was impossible to present such a controversial thesis in 45 minutes and that I was going to speak for an hour and a half, and that I would like anyone in this building to try and stop me. There comes a time when it is very difficult not to take up an aggressive attitude when you find that you are not dealing with equals, with people who want to fight you on a fair ground. You are dealing with people who appear to be intellectually competent but are really in stages of emotional idiocy. Many of my critics have not read my work and they are not prepared to read them. It is upsetting because I am prepared to read and contest their ideas. They lump me with every Tom, Dick, and Harry, so that I am portrayed as belonging to the lunatic fringe. I remember, for example, the year after *They Came Before Columbus* was published, someone inside the Smithsonian told me they had about four meetings to decide whether to invite me to speak at the Smithsonian. At the fourth meeting, an Englishman apparently got up and said, "Now, now, now! We have got to put a stop to all this nonsense. First, flying saucers and now, transatlantic Negroes." It took about sixteen years before they invited me to speak.

Ramsamy: What are your current intellectual pursuits?

Van Sertima: I have edited 18 issues of the *Journal of African Civilizations*. Twelve of these are anthologies and I have 10 of them in permanent circulation. I have had to drop *Nile Valley Civilizations* because most of the essays are being carried in other works I have done. I have just selected two essays, from *African Presence in the Art of the Americas*, for my present volume. I now want to produce study guides. Teachers and students need study guides so that they can know how best to use this material and question it with intelligence. I spent a week with 350 teachers in St. Louis, most of them White. I am not racist, but my critics think I talk only to Blacks, from within my "Black box." But I am not in any Black box; I am in the human box! We have to take into account more seriously what Africans have done. One way is through responsible scholarship, drawing upon the best that has been discovered and not just by shouting slogans. I am not a person who shouts but I am interested in rebellion—intellectual rebellion. I am interested in the revolution of ideas. Rebellion has often been defined as strictly protest. Intellectual revolutions involve a change of thinking, a change of structures. That is how I see my enterprise. I can't be simply confined to a racial or racist attitude. I don't want changes with just different faces. I am involved in the change of the human being. This change can only come about by looking closely over the centuries of myths, looking closely at what people have done, and not just concentrating on one race or group and its achievements.

Chapter 3

Thinking of Race in the Age of DNA

Olubayi Olubayi

What most people think of as race is a purely visual category that is based on what we see with our naked eyes and is guided by the dominant assumptions in each country or region. One specific individual, let us call her Maria, can be classified as Black/African American in the United States, and classified as Colored in South Africa, and classified as White/European in Brazil, and as Mzungu/White/European in rural East Africa. Maria's race will depend on which particular country or region is judging her. Each region or country has invented its own idea of what constitutes race, and these inventions change over time. Four hundred years ago, the English and the Irish belonged to different races, now they are both European. Four hundred years ago, Zulus and Amharic-Ethiopians thought of themselves strictly as Zulus or Amharas. They did not see themselves as Africans, but now virtually all of them consider themselves as belonging to the same "racial" group, the African race.

Whether a country or region assumes that there are four racial groups (as the United States and South Africa do) or 12 racial groups (as Brazil does) is really a historically determined social-political decision. In the United States, for example, race is based on a combination of both visual appearance and reported or known recent ancestry; in Brazil, alternatively, visual appearance is usually separated from reported recent ancestry and, therefore, two sisters from the same two parents can be assigned to two different racial groups based on the visual characteristics of skin color, hair texture, eye color, and so on (see *http://www.teachersparadise.com/ency/en/wikipedia/r/ra/race.html*). Similar assignments of race were made in the Republic of South Africa before their independence in 1994 whenever an individual was to be classified as either being of the Colored race or of the African race.

Visual characteristics are what we actually see with our eyes when we look at a person. Invisible characteristics cannot be seen with our naked eyes. Examples of invisible biochemical characteristics are the ability to digest milk-sugar, the shape of hemoglobin molecules in red blood cells, the quantity of insulin in a person's body, and the presence of lysozyme enzyme in tears. There are less than 50 visual characteristics that a careful observer can discern. By comparison, there are more than 100,000 biochemical characteristics in the body of every human being, and most of them are types of proteins, and the activities and collaborations of those proteins. In comparing the rational significance that we should assign to various characteristics, it is important to note that some visual characteristics that have been given great value or weight or significance in the past, such as nose shape and hair texture, are really structures that a person can actually live without. You can live without your hair, and you can live without your nose. But, by comparison, invisible biochemical characteristics that have been ignored in our past socio-political groupings of humans into races such as presence of insulin in the body are so important that a person can NOT live without them. There is no reason, other than the ease of seeing the nose and the difficulty of "seeing" insulin, why we have historically put more weight on the presence and shape of the nose than we put on the presence and quantity of insulin. Our assignment of great value to visual characteristics is arbitrary and fails to predict essential biochemical characteristics. For example, if I am presented with two very black Black men (Hakim and Zuma), their shared blackness of skin does not tell me which one of them cannot produce insulin and must depend on daily injections of insulin.

DNA is beginning to play the same role that visual characteristics like skin colors and noses played in the past. The presence of a particular set of DNA markers and/or genes in say 90% of a "racial" group tells us nothing about the presence of that particular set of genes or DNA markers in a person that we visually place in that same "racial group." It also does not predict that a different color group will not have the same gene set. For example, the fact that approximately 20% of Black Nigerians carry the gene for sickle cell anemia (an often fatal disease) would lead most people to predict that these genes will be more likely to be present in a similar percentage among Black Zulus, than among White Greeks, but the reality is that the gene is common in Mediterranean populations like Greeks, but virtually absent among Black Zulus in South Africa. The external nonessential visual characteristic does not predict the internal essential or deleterious characteristic. And even if it did, we are still left with the question of what to do with the INDIVIDUAL who belongs to the subgroup of that same "racial group" but does not have a particular gene or DNA marker that we associate with that particular "racial group." For example, the FDA may approve the BiDil drug as a treatment for African American heart patients. Because the drug worked well in a non-random sample of 1050 patients who self-identified themselves as African American or Black and who had cardiovascular disease, and who, presumably, carry the gene mutations that allow them to benefit from BiDil in a way that the White "racial" group presumably does not, what happens to the rest of the African Americans who do not carry the gene and cannot benefit from BiDil? Should cardiologists simply treat such heart patients with BiDil simply because some members of their "racial group" are known to benefit from BiDil? The answer to this problem is obvious to me—we should drive the future of genetic DNA-based medicine towards individuals not towards "racial" groupings. Genetic medicine will work best and most reliably when we analyze the DNA of each individual and determine what treatments will work for that particular individual. The obvious model for decision making here is the ABO blood group one: you do not transfuse blood from Peter to John because Peter looks like John or because Peter is presumed to belong to the same race as John. You transfuse blood from Peter to John only if the two belong to the same blood group (or if Peter is type O) regardless of what "races" Peter and John belong to. One cannot assume the blood type by looking at the person visually or asking them to self-identify, as in the BiDil drug case; one actually performs a biochemical test for blood type for each individual in order to determine compatibility. And it should be noted that blood-type compatibility is in fact a genetic DNA-based compatibility that exists despite visual "race" differences: a very Black man will have the same ABO blood type as a very blonde man whose own biological brother may have a different ABO blood type.

DNA analyses are scientific and attractive but open to abuse and misinterpretation just the way that visual characteristics were abused and misinterpreted in the last few centuries. The classification of Africans as inferior Negroes was part of the justification for the enslavement of Africans. And the classification of Jews as an inferior race, different from the German race, was Hitler's justification for killing Jews in the Jewish holocaust. The questions and scenarios in this chapter are designed to encourage the reader to think carefully about "races" of human beings regardless of whether claims are traditional and based on visual characteristics or modern and based on identification of genes or sections of DNA with unique sequences that are referred to as DNA markers. Readers should realize that even though a scientist may announce the discovery of new DNA markers that are found in most Africans but missing in most Europeans, this does not mean that we have established a new strong criterion for classifying people into Africans or Europeans. What do we do with the European individuals who happen to have these "African" DNA markers? And why should we assume that a DNA marker that usually does not code for any proteins and is part of the intron, or junk, DNA is more important than say the Y-chromosome, which is missing in all women even though we classify women and men as belonging to the same race. If we choose to use the DNA sequences of the Y-chromosome as a basis for classifying humans into races, then women and men would belong to two different races. Likewise, if we choose to use the gene for sickle cell anemia as the criterion for our "racial" grouping, then the Black Nigerians and White Greeks would belong to the same race to which the Black Zulus would not belong. If we choose to use the frequency of lactose intolerance (which has a clear genetic basis), then we would group Black Nigerians (most of whom are lactose intolerant) with Yellow Japanese (most of whom are also lactose intolerant) into the same race to which Black Kenyans would not belong because most Kenyans are not lactose intolerant. And if we choose to use the ABO blood group system as the primary criterion then we shall have to place White Germans and Black Papua New Guineans into the same race (http://anthro.palomar.edu/vary/vary_3.htm).

Criteria for placing individuals into "racial groups" should remain open to thought, debate, and discussion regardless of whether the criteria are merely visual or DNA based. The main problem with thinking of "race" as a biological category as opposed to thinking of race as a socially constructed category is that biological categories presume that characteristics (both visual and biochemical) come in sets that allow us to assume or predict that if characteristic Q is present, therefore, characteristics P and R will also be present. For example, since men and women are biological categories, we can assume or predict with great confidence that if a human individual is a man (characteristic Q), therefore he has a penis (characteristic P) and a high ratio of testosterone to estrogen (characteristic R); and if a human individual is a woman (characteristic Q), therefore she has a uterus (characteristic P) and a low ratio of testosterone to estrogen (characteristic R). These kinds of categorical statements cannot be made for socially constructed races, even if one chooses to use visual characteristics. One cannot say that ALL Africans are black-skinned (because most African Zulus or African Ethiopians, for example, have skins that are browner than those of most Caucasian Indian Dravidians). And also saying that all Africans are black-skinned does not mean that the reverse is true. It is not true to say that all black-skinned people are African because black skin colors are found among Dravidians in South India, Aborigines in Australia, and Melanesians. Knowing that someone is of the "Black race" does not allow me to predict with confidence which distinguishing characteristics they will have; I have to perform biochemical tests and physical exams before I can determine if, for example, they are lactose intolerant, diabetic, or hemophiliac.

The aim of this chapter is to introduce the reader to the idea that even though races exist historically and socio-politically, most of what we have historically assumed about races is not true and is not the same from global region to global region. People have been and are enslaved or murdered or oppressed because of the race or caste that they are placed into within their society or region. Depending on which country one lives in, one's presumed race or caste is still a very strong determinant of economic opportunity, political freedom, social status, and lifespan. Race matters. But this is not to say that race is a fixed biological category. DNA analyses are providing us with strong scientific evidence of the heterogeneity, or hybridity, or mixedness, of being human. Human genotypes (DNA) and human phenotypes (visual and biochemical characteristics) are on a continuum that is not discrete and does not break up easily into the finite "racial groups" or castes that many societies have preferred in the past. Using DNA analyses and essential biochemical characteristics we find that we have all kinds of "brothers" and "sisters" in many regions of the world and that some people that we thought were just like us (same race) are genetically different, while those that we thought were very different from us (different race) are just like us in essential characteristics like blood type. Whether we choose to use DNA markers or to use visual characteristics as criteria for placing individuals into races, we should be fully aware that we have never known what to do with the millions of individuals that have the intermediate visual phenotypes, between Black and White, or between European and Asian, or between African and European—likewise we won't know what do with the millions of individuals that have the intermediate DNA markers or gene mutations. These situations will continue to convince careful thinkers that we should regard humans as individuals not as races. Our humanity sits on a continuum of genotypes and phenotypes.

A. The Impulse to Place Objects and Events into Groups

Human thought requires categories or classes or groups, and so we are always placing objects and events into categories or classes based on perceived characteristics; and most of the time we are quite satisfied with simple classifications as answers to our questions about the identities of objects and events. Here are some simple examples of this kind of virtually automated human response to questions about the identities of objects and events:

- Peter: "Maria is taking me to dinner tonight."
  Jane: "Who is Maria?"
  Peter: "Maria is a student (at Rutgers University)."

- Gabriella: "I hate George."
  Selvan: "Who is George?"
  Gabriella: "George is a teacher (at my school)."

- Yuri: "What is Salsa?"
  Natasha: "A dance."

- Suraj: "Who is Condoleeza Rice?"
  Mike: "An African American."
- Ngugi: "Who is Mandela?"
  Chao: "A Zulu."
- Marjorie: "What is a kiwi?"
  Joseph: "A fruit."

With a little reflection you will agree with me that too many complex questions in which we seek to know the identity of an object or event, we tend to be quite satisfied with simple groupings, categorizations, or classifications as sufficient responses. Most of us are culturally programmed to accept the idea that once we know the group or category to which an object or event belongs, therefore we know what the object is—this process allows us to transfer all the believed or assumed or perceived characteristics of the group to the object or event that we are told belongs to that group. The intellectual problem here is that we tend to stop the process of inquiry and thought at the level of grouping—most of us fail to realize that the grouping process leaves the following questions open:

1. Do all the characteristics of the group belong to the specific object or event?
2. Are the characteristics themselves really accurate?
3. What is the origin of our faith in the accuracy of the group's characteristics?
4. Is what is true for a part of a group automatically true for the whole group?
5. Are we using enough characteristics in our grouping or classification?
6. Does possession of characteristic A automatically mean possession of characteristic B?
7. If both C and D belong to the same group, does this fact make C and D identical in characteristic A?
8. How much does knowing the group to which C belongs tell us about C?
9. Is there a better way of knowing C than merely finding the group to which C belongs?
10. Do objects and events belong to several groups simultaneously?
11. Have we chosen our criteria or characteristics for grouping based on mere convenience (e.g., easy to see), or have we used a rigorous basis for selecting a few diagnostic criteria out of thousands of existing chemical and physical characteristics that individual objects possess? Do we, for example, put more weight arbitrarily on what we see than on more essential characteristics that we cannot see with our naked eyes?

B. Placing the Daughters of the Same Woman into Two Different Races in the United States

1. Ivan is a White Russian man from Russia.
2. Michelle is a White American woman of Norwegian parentage.
3. Hakim is a Black American man of African descent.
4. Michelle sleeps with Ivan and has a baby by the name of Lucy.
5. Michelle sleeps with Hakim and has a baby by the name of Lisa.
6. To what race does Lucy belong? White/Caucasian.
7. To what race does Lisa belong? Black/African American.
8. Lila is a White American woman of Irish descent.
9. Lila and Lucy belong to the same race—they are both White—but Lucy and Lisa do not belong to the same race, even though they are sisters, daughters of the same woman—what is wrong with this picture? Why is it acceptable in the United States to group sisters (Lucy and Lisa) into different racial groups?

C. Blood and Race: When a Black Man Belongs to the Same Race as a White Man

1. In all human cultures blood is used as a metaphor of kinship (i.e., close biological relatedness, and by extension membership in the same "race").
2. Max is a White American soldier with blood group A+.
3. Martin is Max's brother (same parents), a soldier, and has blood group B+.

4. Malcolm is a Black American soldier with blood group A+.
5. Max is injured in the field during battle, and immediate blood transfusion is needed.
6. Based on our "traditional" thinking about blood, whose blood should be given to Max [Malcolm's or Martin's]? Martin's
7. Based on scientific knowledge, whose blood should be given to Max? Malcolm's
8. Who is more closely related to Max using blood-transfusion compatibility as a characteristic for grouping? Malcolm
9. Who belongs to the same race as Max if one uses naked eyes only? Martin, of course.
10. Who belongs to the same race as Max using blood type as the criterion? Malcolm, of course.
11. What does race tell us about the blood type of INDIVIDUALS? Not much.

D. Chromosomes, DNA, and Race

1. Chromosomes are made up of DNA, and genes are actual segments of chromosomes (i.e., genes are sections of DNA that carry information that codes for chemical and physical characteristics).
2. Human cells have approximately 25,000 genes sitting on 23 pairs of chromosomes.
3. The Y chromosome has 251 genes, and all of these 251 genes are missing in women.
4. The genes and/or the gene-expression for "femaleness," including genes that regulate the construction of the uterus, are missing in men.
5. There is currently a drug (BiDil) that is targeted for treating heart patients who belong to the African American racial group because the drug works well for a higher percentage of African Americans than for the "general population." See *http://evolgen.blogspot.com/2005/07/more-bidil-news.html.*
   for the commercial explanation for re-patenting BiDil as a racial drug, even though there was no control non-Black group in the study, and the patients were self-identified as African American.
6. BiDil targets the nitric oxide pathway that is regulated by less than 20 genes [less than the 251 on the Y chromosome that is missing in women].
7. What happens to the African American heart patient whose response to BiDil is more like that of the "general population" than that of the few African Americans who respond well to BiDil?
8. How many genes should we use for racial grouping? Should we use 251 or the less than 20 in the BiDil racial drug story? Or the less than 20 that directly regulate skin color and hair texture?
9. Keita is a Black African man from Mali, and all his body cells contain chromosome Y.
10. Joseph is a White American of German descent, and all his body cells contain chromosome Y.
11. Joy is Joseph's sister, and all of Joy's body cells DO NOT contain chromosome Y.
12. Using only the genes that are sitting on chromosome Y for grouping humans, who is more closely related to Joseph? [is it Keita or Joy?] Keita, of course.
13. Are there genes that are present in Keita and in Joseph that are completely missing in Joy? Yes, all the 251 genes on the Y chromosome.
14. Are there physical structures in/on Keita's body that are present in/on Joseph's body but missing in/on Joy's body? Yes, male sexual organs.
15. Is there a major biological organ that is present in Joy, but missing in both Keita and Joseph? Yes, the uterus, the ovaries, and the vagina.
16. Then why don't we classify Joy and Joseph (siblings) as belonging to different races, the way that we are willing to classify Lucy and Lisa (siblings) as belonging to different races—Lucy is White, and Lisa is Black (see section B).

E. A List of 40 Common Human Characteristics That Are INVISIBLE to the Naked Eye and That the General Public Does NOT Use in Grouping Humans into Races (these are 40 out of a total of about 100,000 human characteristics)

1. Presence and quantity of insulin (the hormone without which you are a diabetic)
2. Presence and quantity of amylase (enzyme for starch digestion in mouth and intestines)
3. Presence and quantity of lactase (enzyme for breakdown of the milk sugar lactose)

4. Amount of pepsin enzyme in the stomach (initiates protein digestion)
5. Amount of lysozyme enzyme in tears (protects eyes from bacteria)
6. Amount of hydrochloric acid in the stomach (destroys microbes in food; initiates digestion)
7. Amount of bile produced by the liver (emulsifies fats; makes fat digestion possible)
8. Quantity of hemoglobin proteins in each red blood cell (carries oxygen)
9. Shape of hemoglobin molecules (determines shape of red blood cells; normal or sickled)
10. Quantity of red blood cells per mL of blood (reflects condition of your health)
11. Quantity of white blood cells (determines strength of your immune system and reflects condition of your health)
12. Types of relative quantities of antibody classes in your body (protect the body from infections)
13. Potential for over-production of class E antibodies (development of allergies)
14. Quantity of testosterone (degree of maleness; and sex drive in females)
15. Quantity of estrogen (degree of femaleness)
16. Ratio of testosterone to estrogen (determines degree of masculinity and sex drive)
17. Ratio of LDL cholesterol to HDL cholesterol (determines risk for blocked arteries)
18. Quantity of total lipases in intestines (for digestion of fats and oils)
19. Quantity of alcohol dehydrogenase (determines how quickly you get drunk)
20. Blood group on the ABO system (whom you can donate blood to or receive from)
21. Blood group on the Rhesus system (whom you can donate blood to or receive from)
22. Quantity of the neurotransmitter acetyl choline (effectiveness of your brain and memory)
23. Quantity of cortisol hormone (determines level of stress in your body)
24. Quantity of epinephrine and norepinephrine (control excitement and alertness, etc.)
25. Quantity and quality of dopamine receptors (how easily you will be addicted to drugs)
26. Presence and quantity of nicotine receptors (determines your rate of cigarette addiction)
27. Quantity of endorphins (determines intensity of your happiness or depression)
28. Quantity and quality of mucus in the respiratory tract (symptoms of cystic fibrosis)
29. Presence of the gene for Huntington's disease (caused by single autosomal dominant gene; uncontrolled body movements plus depression plus mental degeneration)
30. Presence of gene for hemophilia (X-linked recessive gene; failure of blood clotting)
31. Presence of gene for Duchenne Muscular dystrophy (X-linked recessive gene, the presence of which leads to degeneration of muscles and loss of ability to walk)
32. Absence of hexosamindase enzyme due to gene mutation (causes Tay-Sach disease, i.e., neural degeneration and death before age 5)
33. Presence of the mitochondrial gene for Leber's Hereditary Optic Neuropathy (LHON)
34. Presence of gene combinations for diabetes
35. Presence of gene combinations for epilepsy
36. Presence of gene combinations for hypertension
37. Presence of gene combinations for manic depression
38. Presence of gene combinations for cleft palate
39. Presence of gene combinations for schizophrenia
40. Presence of gene combinations for congenital heart defects

F. A List of 10 Common Human Characteristics That Are Easily SEEN and That the General Public USES in Grouping Humans into Races (these are only 10 out of a total of about 100,000 human characteristics)

1. Skin color (black, white, yellow, brown, olive, other)
2. Hair texture (rough, smooth, silky, thin, thick, curly, straight)
3. Hair length (long, short)
4. Nose shape (flat, raised, hooked, thin)
5. Nostrils (flared, small)
6. Angle of forehead and angle of cheek bones

7. Shape of eyes (round, oval, other)
8. Type of eyelid (presence or absence of the epicanthic fold—Usually seen in Khoisan Africans, Xhosa Africans, Chinese, Japanese, Koreans)
9. Eye color (black, brown, blue, grey, green)
10. Shape of lips (thick, thin, other)

G. A Question on Racial Grouping

Dorothy and Tabitha are very similar based on the 10 visual characteristics listed in section F.
Dorothy and Tabitha are different in all the 40 non-visual characteristics listed in section E.
Dorothy and Sidney are approximately the same in all the 40 non-visual characteristics listed on
    section E, but approximately different in all the 10 visual characteristics listed in section F.
Dorothy has dark brown skin, curly short hair, brown eyes, a flat nose, and wide nostrils.
Tabitha has dark brown skin, curly short hair, brown eyes, a flat nose, and wide nostrils.
Sidney has pinkish white skin, long silky hair, grey eyes, a thin hooked nose, and narrow nostrils.
Why will most Americans group Dorothy and Tabitha into the same race (i.e., Black/African American)
    but group Sidney, who shares more characteristics with Dorothy than Dorothy does with Tabitha,
    into a different racial group (i.e., White/Caucasian)?

Conclusions

Based on the questions and scenarios presented in this chapter, it should be clear to the reader that race is a category that we human beings construct. We decide socially and politically which criteria to use in our classifications and how many races to recognize. The United States recognizes four, and Brazil recognizes about 12. Maria is a Black/African American in the United States, but the same Maria is a White/Mzungu in rural East Africa. And in almost all historical choices of criteria, all human societies or countries or regions have used visual characteristics plus presumed ancestry as the basis of their "racial" and/or caste classification systems. The choice of visual characteristics like nose shape or hair texture over biochemical characteristics like insulin is arbitrary, socially significant, but scientifically irrational. There is no serious rational basis for declaring an easy visual characteristic that humans can live without like cranial hair as being a more significant determining or diagnostic criterion than is a more essential but difficult-to-see characteristic like the quantity of insulin, without which a person will die. Our grouping exercises are always complicated by the fact that our human genotypes (DNA) and our phenotypes (visual and biochemical characteristics) form a continuum instead of the separate groups that we have historically preferred. Societies have never been very good at knowing what to do with the intermediate genotypes and the intermediate phenotypes.

DNA analyses are giving useful information about individuals and about clusters of individuals who share the same genetic mutations or genetic diseases or genetic advantages, but DNA analyses do not and will not tell us anything about ALL individuals that we historically placed into a particular "racial" group *apriori* (i.e., by ignoring intermediate phenotypes and using only convenient visual characteristics and before doing the DNA analyses). DNA analyses and understanding the invisible essential biochemical characteristics that DNA codes for will actually help in convincing careful thinkers that our old convenient ideas about race need serious revision because our humanity sits on a complex continuum that has little to do with our ancient non-scientific assumptions about race. Think of human height, for example. We do not have simply short humans and tall humans—we have every height between 4 feet and 7 feet. The same type continuums exist in most of our phenotypes and genotypes. And to enhance the natural confusion, individuals that appear different in skin color, for example, can be virtually the same in some particular set of essential biochemical traits. DNA and the thousands of biochemical characteristics that DNA codes for are really a warning that our unaided eyes use very limited criteria and that we should continue to strive to judge individuals as Martin Luther King Jr. said "by the content of their character," and not by the color of their skins or the shapes of their noses or the DNA markers of their "race." The future of health care, and of forensic science, and of our notions of who we are, will be informed more by the "content" of each individual's DNA sequences than by the visually based "racial groupings." Research into DNA and into the thousands of essential biochemical characteristics that DNA codes are a reminder that our shared humanity forms a complex set of continuums that do not fit into simple separate groups called races.

References

Lewin, Benjamin. (2003). *Genes VIII*. Saddle River, NJ: Prentice Hall.

Luca Cavalli-Sforza, L., Menozzi, Paolo, & Piazza, Alberto. (1996). *The History and Geography of Human Genes*. Princeton, NJ: Princeton University Press.

Ridley, Matt. (2002). *Genome: the autobiography of a species in 23 chapters*. New York: Perennial.

Wells, Spencer. (2002). *The Journey of Man: A Genetic Odyssey*. New York: Random House.

http://www.nature.com/genomics/index.html

http://www.worldcommunitygrid.org/projects_showcase/human_proteome.html

http://www.ornl.gov/sci/techresources/Human_Genome/project/info.shtml

http://www.nsti.org/publ/MSM2002/330.pdf

http://www.borg.com/~lubehawk/hdigsys.htm

http://ghr.nlm.nih.gov/condition=cysticfibrosis

http://en.wikipedia.org/wiki/Genetic_disease

http://evolgen.blogspot.com/2005/07/more-bidil-news.html

http://www.americanheart.org/presenter.jhtml?identifier=180

http://www.ninds.nih.gov/disorders/huntington/huntington.htm

http://www.mdausa.org/publications/fa-dmdbmd-what.html

http://www.newsreel.org/guides/race/whatdiff.htm

http://web.mit.edu/racescience/in_media/what_dna_says_about_human/

http://www.teachersparadise.com/ency/en/wikipedia/r/ra/race.html

http://sickle.bwh.harvard.edu/scd_inheritance.html

http://www.nslc.wustl.edu/sicklecell/part3/biogeography.html

http://anthro.palomar.edu/vary/vary_3.htm

Chapter 4

The Paternalizers and the Paternalized: A Genealogy of Justifying Exploitation through the Ideology of Paternalism

Ibram H. Rogers

Modern racism grew from the ideological tree of paternalism that had long spawned a branch of ethnocentrism (as well as sexism).[1] In order to understand the theoretical components of racism and its application in modern social systems, a historical understanding of the ideology of paternalism is essential. Racism as an ideology contends one race is fundamentally superior to another. Racism as a deed occurs when a privileged race uses its power to discriminate against another race to maintain or extend its power. Paternalism is the conceptual adhesive that has fused racism as an ideology, and racism as a deed. Said differently, when challenged racist deeds are often substantiated on the basis of racist ideas. This substantiation is usually saturated with paternalistic idioms.

Many scholars have examined the use of racist and ethnocentric paternalistic rhetoric to legitimize slavery, colonialism, and imperialism. However, they have focused on particular systems of exploitation, time periods, or locations. This paper provides the first examination of this paternalistic rhetoric across time and space, allowing scholars to further understand these substantiations, and the historical connections between pre-modern ethnocentrism and modern racism and ethnocentrism. It delineates a genealogy of paternalistic thought linking many of these diverse systems of exploitation, time periods, and locations. I show the clear genealogy of paternalistic ideas that connects (with mild refinements) the theorists who justified slavery in Greco-Roman antiquity, the European Middle Ages, and the Southern United States with those who justified colonialism and other forms of exploitation in the modern era. The paper consists of two sections—slavery and imperialism. In the initial section on slavery, I examine the ethnocentric justifications of Aristotle, St. Paul, and St. Augustine in Greco-Roman antiquity. The ethnocentric paternalistic pro-slavery arguments of St. Thomas Aquinas during the Middle Ages in Europe are then reviewed followed by the racist positions of Thomas Bacon and Henry Pattillo in colonial America, and Thomas Roderick Dew and George Fitzhugh in antebellum America. I end the section exploring the racist arguments of Lewis H. Blair of Virginia and W. M. Cox of Mississippi—who sought to justify the exploitation of African Americans in the decades after emancipation, which one scholar described as another form of slavery (Blackmon 2008).

The second section on imperialism is further divided into three parts: European paternalizers, Pan-African paternalizers, and American presidential paternalizers. In the first, I examine the racist European paternalizers, some of Britain's most popular justifiers of colonialism—Rudyard Kipling, Joseph Conrad, and Sir Frederick Lugard. I discuss the ethnocentric Pan-African ideas of Martin Delany and Edward Blyden, who paternalized continental Africans by describing them as backward and needing civilizing assistance from African America. I conclude reviewing journalist John O'Sullivan's concept of America's manifest destiny and the ethnocentric paternalism within aspects of the foreign policies of U.S. Presidents James Monroe, William McKinley, Theodore Roosevelt, Woodrow Wilson, and Harry Truman. Paternalism came full circle, beginning with ethnocentrism, traversing into racism (with an embedded ethnocentrism) and back to ethnocentrism (with an embedded racism). Before I present the paternalistic thoughts of these presidents and their Western ideological predecessors, I offer a conceptual framework for this genealogy of ideas.

Conceptual Framework

Genovese opened his text insisting on the 'centrality of class relations as manifested in paternalism,' which 'like every other paternalism, had little to do with Ole Massa's ostensible benevolence, kindness, and good cheer . . . It grew out of the necessity to discipline and morally justify a system of exploitation' (Genovese 1976, p. 4). This need for paternalism can be generalized, as Genovese did, to several systems of exploitation—not just slavery—in which paternalism has been used for discipline and as a moral justification. The centrality of class (or group) relations as manifested in paternalism is a phenomenon that has existed across time and space in slavery, colonialism, and other systems of exploitation.

In order to legitimate the exploitative relationship of colonialism, and show the need for the colonial situation, there is a continuous articulation and demonstration of the merits of the colonizers and the demerits of the colonized to show the colonized benefit from being exploited, Memmi (1991) theorized. This creates the need for a paternal relationship in which the colonizers have been sent to the colony to care for the colonized. The most often cited merit and demerit is the 'taste for action' of the colonizer or paternalizer and the laziness of the colonized or paternalized, respectively, Memmi (1991) asserted (p. 79). The paternalizer further describes the paternalized as 'a wicked, backward person with evil, thievish, somewhat sadistic instincts.' Ultimately, the description of the colonized is a 'series of negations,' Memmi (1991) noted. 'The colonized is not this, is not that' (pp. 82–83). In comparison, the colonizer is always propagandized in a positive light.

Genovese theorized primarily on the need for the ideology of paternalism—to discipline and morally justify a system of exploitation—while Memmi explained the praxis of it—a series of affirmations for the paternalizers and negations for the paternalized, and the call for a paternal relationship so the advantaged can provide for the disadvantaged. Together, the two sets of ideas form a general theory for an ideology of paternalism used by Western paternalizers for thousands of years—the primary exposition of this paper. In order to settle on a working definition of the amalgamation of Genovese's and Memmi's ideas, I started with John Kleinig's (1984) explanation of paternalism as involving 'an imposition, the exercise of freedom-diminishing control by one person over another' (p. xii).[2] I eliminate the notion of it being an 'imposition' since that is inferred, as an imposition—whether realized or unrealized—must occur in order to diminish the freedom of another. Also, freedom is not only diminished in the case of colonialism, but it is eliminated in the case of slavery. And, as Memmi noted, there must be a clear delineation between the paternalizer—the exploiter, slaveholder, or colonizer—and the paternalized—the exploited, enslaved, or colonized in any definition of paternalism through the paternalizers articulations of the suggested privileged essence of one and the deprived essence of another. Furthermore, the crux of the paternal relationship is there is not just an over/under relationship, as Kleinig said. But an epistemic balance is sought in which the privileged control the deprived for their benefit—the rich in being providing for the poor in being—creating the ultimate cover for exploitation, as Genovese (1976) explained. Ultimately, building off of Kleinig's definition and with these concepts and the work of Genovese and Memmi in mind, I define the ideology of paternalism as *the exercise of articulating the need for freedom-diminishing or eliminating control by one privileged and benevolent person or group for the benefit of another deprived person or group.*

As I show in the thoughts of St. Paul, St. Augustine, and Aristotle, the genealogy of paternalism can be traced to Greco-Roman antiquity. In justifying systems of exploitation, there are two trajectories of thought emanating from this era—civil paternalism and Christian paternalism. In civil paternalism, articulated by Aristotle with his natural slave theory, there is a paternal dialectic based on the judgment of civilization. Some persons or groups are naturally civilized and serve as paternalizers to those who are by nature uncivilized—the paternalized. Civil paternalism may be defined *as the exercise of articulating the need for freedom-diminishing or eliminating control by one supposedly civilized person or group for the benefit of another supposedly uncivilized person or group.* In Christian paternalism, first articulated by St. Paul and St. Augustine, there is a paternal hierarchy with Father/God/Master at the top, Child/Slave/Father/Master in the middle, and Child/Slave at the bottom. God is the supreme paternalizer. The slaveholders are at the same time paternalizers in relation to the enslaved and paternalized in relation to God. The enslaved are paternalized in their relation to God and their 'earthly masters.' Therefore, Christian paternalism may be defined *as the exercise of articulating the need for freedom-diminishing or eliminating control by one divinely privileged person or group for the benefit of another divinely deprived person or group.*

System of Exploitation: Slavery

Greco-Roman Antiquity

Aristotle, a native of Thrace and pupil of Plato, sought to justify slavery by articulating an ideology of civil paternalism. He was the foundational thinker of this ideology, the driving force of which has been called his 'natural slave theory.' He posited the ethnocentric idea that some people are naturally fit to be free or civilized, while others are naturally fit to be enslaved or uncivilized (Garnsey 1996, p. 11). The core of this theory was differentiating between the two groups. Aristotle (1944) described the paternalized as 'an article of property . . . strong for necessary service' (pp. 1254b28–34). They participate 'in reason so far as to apprehend it but not to possess it' (pp. 1254b21–24). And they are 'serviceable for the mere necessaries of life,' as their 'usefulness' is 'little from that of animals' (pp. 1260a33–b5, 1254b25–34). They are 'incapable of reasoning and live a life of pure sensation, like certain tribes on the borders of the civilized world' (Aristotle 1953, pp. 1149a9–12). And they are 'a living tool' that is dependent—a part of something, Aristotle (1953) claimed (pp. 1161a30–b6). Meanwhile, he characterized the slave owners or the paternalizers as civilized, reasoned, 'serviceable for a life of citizenship,' the hand or soul that coordinates the living tool, and independent (Aristotle 1944, pp. 1254b28–34; Aristotle 1935, pp. 1241b18–24).

A secondary mission of Aristotle's theory was to emphasize that the paternal relationship is a result of these different qualities, as the 'household in its perfect form consists of slaves and freemen,' Aristotle (1944) wrote. 'The investigation of everything should begin with its smallest parts, and the primary and smallest parts of household are master and slave, husband and wife, father and children' (pp. 1253b1–18). These two groups of naturally free and naturally enslaved relate to each other in a paternalistic way. 'There are by nature various classes of rulers and ruled,' Aristotle posited in *Politics*. 'For the free rules the slave,' and it is 'advantageous' for the naturally enslaved 'to be governed by this kind of authority,' Aristotle (1944) argued (pp. 1260a7–14, 1254b16–21).

While Aristotle articulated a civil paternalism through his natural slave theory, which focused more on describing the subjective human qualities of what it means to be civilized or uncivilized, St. Paul in several passages in the Bible introduced a theory of Christian paternalism with a three-tiered hierarchy of paternal relations—heavenly master (top), earthly master (middle), enslaved (bottom). 'For he who was called in the Lord as a slave is a freedman of the Lord,' Paul declared. 'Likewise he who was free when called is a slave of Christ.'[3] Also, Paul instructed the 'slaves' to 'obey in everything those that are your earthly masters, not with eyeservice as men-pleasers, but in singleness of heart, fearing the Lord.'[4] And he advised the earthly 'masters' to 'do the same to them, and forbear threatening, knowing that he who is both their Master and yours is in heaven, and that there is no partiality with Him.'[5] Throughout his writings in the Bible, Paul described the paternalized or the enslaved as submissive, obedient, hearty workers with the ability to suffer unjust treatment without revenge. In contrast, Paul saw the paternalizers as worthy of all honor since they are the true leaders of human beings with the leadership quality God bestows upon them. As a result of their qualities, his argument continued, slaves should submit to their earthly and heavenly masters, while their earthly masters submit only to their heavenly masters. So, according to Paul, the paternalism exists in three relations: God to Master, Master to Slave, and God to Slave.

St. Augustine also articulated a Christian paternalism with a new wrinkle, which shall be described as his 'sin theology.' In this sin theology, St. Augustine made the paternalized (or slaves) synonymous with sinners or pagans and indirectly made the paternalizers (or slave owners) synonymous with non-sinners or Christians. Case in point, Augustine once simply declared, 'We are, willy nilly, slaves,' meaning that everyone is a slave of either God or sin (Garnsey 1996, p. 206). And if one is a slave to sin, then one can be a slave to man since sinners are synonymous with slaves. Thus, the paternalistic hierarchy is as follows: God at the top, non-sinners/Christians/slave owners in the middle, and sinners/enslaved people at the bottom. 'The primary cause of slavery is sin, so that man was put under man in a state of bondage; and this can be only by a judgement of God, in whom there is no unrighteousness, and who knows how to assign divers punishments according to the deserts of the sinners,' St. Augustine said (p. 206).

European Middle Ages

Sicilian St. Thomas Aquinas, one of the greatest of the Christian theologians of the Middle Ages, was heavily influenced by Aristotle, 'reducing all knowledge to a system intelligible on Aristotelian lines' (Roberts 1993, p. 234). But he did articulate a Christian paternalism derived from St. Augustine's sin theology. Thomas saw it not as a correction or punishment for being a sinner, but instead a correction of morals, which is related to sin and some could argue is sin, 'so that the wicked may be coerced to perform the actions of virtue' (Brett 1994, p. 68). Moreover, for St. Thomas there are two types of slavery:

> One is . . . in which the ruler manages the subject for his own advantage, and this sort of subjection came in after sin. But the other kind of subjection is domestic or civil, in which the ruler manages his subjects for their advantage and benefit. And this sort of subjection would have obtained even before sin. For the human group would have lacked the benefit of order had some of its members not been governed by others who were wiser (p. 69).

Thomas builds on Aristotle's natural slave theory and forms what can be called a 'practical slave theory,' which is entrenched in his civil paternalism. The basis of Aristotle's ethnocentric theory was projecting the qualities that make some naturally free or civilized and others naturally slaves and uncivilized—differentiating between the two groups, or like Memmi did so eloquently, describing the paternalizers visa vie the paternalized. However, for St. Thomas, this differentiation between the paternalizers and paternalized is an afterthought—a basic assumption to his theory. Said differently, by the time of the European Middle Ages, Aristotle's natural slave theory had become generally accepted—at least by St. Thomas—such that he did not have to focus on arguing how and why some are naturally civilized and others are naturally uncivilized. Instead, St. Thomas focused on the paternal relationship itself that is necessitated by the superior and inferior qualities of the two groups. In order to maintain the social good, or an epistemic balance, the civilized must manage and govern the uncivilized, St. Thomas postulated, forming the core of the practical slave theory. 'Many people cannot live a social life together unless someone is in charge to look after the common good,' he argued. And if 'one man greatly surpassed another in knowledge and justice, it would be all wrong if he did not perform this function (of being principal or director) for the benefit of others' (p. 72).

Colonial America

Thomas Bacon, a preacher in Maryland who first compiled Maryland's laws in 1765, justified slavery with ideas drawn directly from Paul's Christian paternalism. By now though, the ethnocentric connotation had transformed into a racist implication based on the new modern conception of races, which determined your sovereignty in eighteenth century America. Bacon (1749) constructs the hierarchy and even the paternal relationships, preaching to the enslaved African Americans that 'it was Almighty God, therefore, who made you, and all the World, that sent you here, as he had sent your Fathers and Mothers, your Masters and Mistresses before you, to take Care of you, and provide for you, while you take no Care of, or help, or provide for yourselves.' Bacon described the world as 'but one large Family, of which Almighty God is the Head and Master' who 'takes care of all' (p. 13). The paternalized have dual duties, those toward their heavenly master and those toward their earthly masters, Bacon theorized just as Paul did before him. In terms of their heavenly master, their duty is to look up to 'him as your Great and chief Master, to whom you are accountable for all your Behavior' (p. 21). Continuing to echo the sentiments of Paul, Bacon said there is one general rule that they should follow in terms of their earthly masters—'to do all Service for Them, as if you did it for God himself' (p. 30).

Henry Pattillo of Virginia, a Presbyterian minister born in Scotland, also tried to justify slavery through an ideology of Christian paternalism, emanating from St. Paul's three-tierd hierarchy. 'My servant has offended me; but my master is in heaven, whom I offend every day of my life,' Pattillo (1787) once noted (p. 24). And, like St. Thomas centuries before him, the practical slave theory of civil paternalism is also evident in Pattillo's justifications for slavery. A slave's lack of agency is beneficial, he noted, because agents have many more worries, than those who are wholly dependent. Pattillo characterized the paternalized as 'among the happiest of human beings' since they are wholly dependent objects who are 'void of all the distressing cares of life' (pp. 22–23). These paternalized slaves need to be ruled because they have 'real or pretended ignorance'; they are lazy, liars, 'heathen,' 'unenlightened,' and 'backward.' In comparison, the paternalizers are very patient and 'fit . . . to command' the paternalized (pp. 24–29).

Antebellum America

A slaveholder, intellectual, and social commentator, Thomas Roderick Dew of Virginia first published 'Abolition of Negro Slavery' in 1832 in the *American Quarterly Review*, which became one of the first major pieces of the notorious post-1830 pro-slavery intellectual movement. Dew, a civil paternalizer, articulated a practical slave theory like St. Thomas. He argued that the enslaved, from an 'economical and moral point of view, are entirely unfit for a state of freedom among the whites' (p. 228). Because, he said, 'if we were to liberate the slaves, we could not, in fact, alter their condition—they would still be virtually slaves; talent, habit, and wealth, would make the white master still' (p. 227). The paternalized are not fit for freedom because they are ignorant, 'unaccustomed to guiding and directing themselves,' 'void of all the attributes of free agents,' the type that will only work by compulsion and are 'vastly inferior in the scale of civilization' (pp. 189, 222, 230). Meanwhile, the paternalizers are civilized, unselfish, talented, and concerted with great habits and therefore it is their job to care for those 'poor' creatures, Dew said (pp. 242, 250, 255–256).

Like Dew, George Fitzhugh was a native Virginian, who published *Slavery Justified, by a Southerner* in 1851, followed by a flood of articles and two famous volumes on slavery, *Sociology for the South; or the Failure of Free Society* in 1854 and *Cannibals All! Or Slaves Without Masters* in 1857. He branded the enslaved or the paternalized as inferior to their superior masters or paternalizers. Then, like Aristotle before him, he claimed this was a natural order in a slave society. There is 'a series of subordinations' that 'is consistent with Christian morality—for fathers, masters, husbands, wives, children, and slaves, not being equals, rivals, competitors, and antagonists, best promote each other's selfish interests when they do most for those above and beneath them' (Fitzhugh 1857, p. 452). This concept of 'Christian morality,' as first communicated by St. Augustine, is used to describe why the paternalizers should care for the paternalized since 'to protect the weak, we must first enslave them,' Fitzhugh said. 'Slavery educates, refines, and moralizes the masses by separating them from each other, and bringing them into continual intercourse with masters of superior minds, information and morality' (p. 454).[6]

Post-slavery U.S. South

Southern pro-slavery intellectuals did not discontinue their ideology of paternalism when slavery was abolished. They just had to re-articulate it. After the chains were removed from African Americans, the intellectuals and segregationist leaders were no longer able to use the slave hierarchy of Christian paternalism or the natural or practical slave theories. Scientific racism became the dominant feature of their argument to now justify their subjection of the Southern African Americans. The southern paternalizers argued that 'the superior white race, with its roots deep in the experiences of law and government, had the obligation of teaching the inferior Negro race, with its history of four thousand years of barbarism, the precious knowledge of citizenship,' Johnson (1957) found (p. 484). Along with colonial paternalizers, they turned the practical slave theory that had been espoused for centuries into a practical race theory. It was now the task of the civilized and Christian White race to take care of and protect the uncivilized and pagan non-White races in order to maintain the social good, the colonial paternalizers argued through their refined theory (Christian paternalism moved under the banner of civil paternalism since being Christian became a primary measure of civilization). There was no need to first create a natural race theory to serve as the theory's predecessor, as Aristotle's natural slave theory had served, because the inferiority of Africans and non-Whites was generally accepted among Western paternalizers by the nineteenth century (Clarke 1991).

Lewis H. Blair (1889), a member of Virginia's planter aristocracy, articulated the practical race theory, describing the paternalized as 'depraved and degraded human beings' whose 'self-respect is feeble, his hope faint, and his intelligence slight' and 'must economically, morally, and socially be born again,' under paternal tutelage (p. 47). Also, W. M. Cox of Mississippi described the paternalized African Americans as lacking in 'preparation for freedom and citizenship' with 'brutish instincts and propensies' whose lot is to be 'submissive' to their paternalizers (Galloway 1904, pp. 14–15).[7]

System of Exploitation: Imperialism

European Paternalizers

Europe most notoriously used the practical race theory during the Berlin Conference in 1884–1885 where European statesmen convened to distribute parcels of African land. The conference formalized Europe's colonial grip on practically all of Africa.[8] Its conveners desired to, among other things, 'increase the oral and material well being of the indigenous population' (Clarke 1991, p. 194). Great Britain led the way in theorizing and publicizing the ideas of colonial paternalizers. It was Britain's 'imperial responsibility or the obligation to expand British territorial boundaries in order to provide 'just' rule for those 'less fortunate' peoples of the earth,' a justification for empire continually professed by the British, Bass (1995) explained (p. 208). Like the U.S. southern paternalizers, they justified colonialism through the practical race theory. Some of the British thinkers who articulated the practical race theory, Raskin (1971) listed, included novelists' Rudyard Kipling, Joseph Conrad, E. M. Forster, D. H. Lawrence, and Joyce Cary.[9]

Kipling most famously championed the theory in his 1899 poem "The White Man's Burden." Whites were burdened with the task of maintaining the common good by taking care of and protecting the world's non-White children—the crux of the practical race theory, which Kipling expressed in his literature. In the poem, Kipling begins each stanza with 'Take up the White Man's burden,' urging his fellow Whites to become paternalizers. He characterized the paternalized in the poem as 'sullen peoples' and 'Half-devil and half-child.' He therefore advised Britain to take up this so-called burden 'to seek another's profit, and work another's gain,' and to 'fill full the mouth of Famine and bid the sickness cease' (pp. 4–6).

Conrad also, like Kipling, described Britain's colonial exploits as a necessary burden using the practical race theory in his literature. In his book of essays, *The Mirror of the Sea*, Conrad has a section entitled, 'The Weight of the Burden.' According to Robert F. Lee, Conrad further defined this burden of the paternalizers in three main works: '*The Nigger of the Narcissus*, as the "burden" itself; "Karain: A Memory," as a depiction of the courage of responsibility necessary to assume the "burden"; and *Heart of Darkness*, as a contrast powerful enough in the negative to strongly stress the positive aspect' (Lee 1969, p. 56). With the burden of trying to maintain a good world, British colonialists are scattered all over the globe serving 'as a beacon on the road towards better things,' Conrad asserted (p. 43). The main characteristic of these British men 'spread all over the world is not the spirit of adventure so much as the spirit of service,' Conrad argued as paternalizers have for ages (p. 20). The paternalized need these British servants to voyage to their locales because they are villains or failures, as most of the non-British characters in Conrad's works are described. The paternalized are also repeatedly characterized as savage and primitive—essentially uncivilized by nature—who need the altruistic British to care for them (Lee 1969).

Several other British statesmen utilized paternalism to justify empire. Nowhere was the practical race theory more posited to justify its colonial presence than in Africa. One of the chief articulators of African paternalism was Sir Frederick Lugard. He served as Britain's representative on the League of Nations' Permanent Mandates Commission, which supervised some of Europe's colonial territories, from its inception until 1936. To justify colonialism, Lugard coined the famous theory of the 'dual mandate,' clearly a derivative of the practical race theory. It was a bold theory, as previously the maintenance of social good—the feature of the practical race theory—was based on the deprived paternalized needing the privileges of the paternalizers. The paternalizers stayed away from addressing economic advantages to ensure it would not be seen as a relationship of exploitation. But Lugard (1929) did not shy away from speaking about the economic returns, saying there were two aspects to the dual mandate: those economic advantages for the paternalizers or the civilized, and the moral advantages of the paternalized or uncivilized.[10]

Pan-African Paternalizers

The most understudied of the colonial paternalizers are the African American leaders and preachers in the nineteenth century who supported African American emigration back to Africa.[11] Alexander Crummell, Edward Wilmot Blyden, Henry Highland Garnett, James Holly, Henry McNeal Turner, and Martin Delany supported (in varying degrees) this idea using Pan African justifications that emanated from the colonial union of civil and Christian paternalism. I classify them as 'Pan African paternalizers.' Unlike St. Paul, Bacon, and other Christian paternalizers who used a tri-tiered hierarchy, the Pan African paternalizers' ideology of Christian paternalism had a four-tiered hierarchy: God/Teacher, Teacher/Slave Owner/Europeans,

Teacher/Slave/African Americans, Student/Continental Africans. God, who stood at the top, charged the European slave owners to bring civilization and Christianity to African Americans through slavery who in turn would bring these lessons to their long lost uncivilized sons and daughters in Africa. In the civil paternalistic aspect of their ideology, they changed the racial make-up of the practical race theory, positioning African-Americans as the paternalizers and continental Africans as paternalized. It was a basic ethnocentric assumption that African-Americans were superior, so they spent most of their time calling for African American paternalizers to care for and develop their paternalized children abroad.

Martin Delany (1992) of Virginia, a journalist, novelist, and doctor, fought for 'the civilization and enlightenment of Africa' (p. 73). Delany found that only 7,000 or 8,000 of the 300,000 inhabitants of Liberia 'may be regarded as civilized' and a 'large part of them are actually expecting and demanding civilization' to be brought to them from the African American paternalizers (p. 77). Delany (1861) believed the European grandfathers had done all they could to develop the childlike and uncivilized afflictions of continental Africans, so it was now the job of their African American fathers. What can the African American paternalizers (who are enlightened, Christian and civilized) now bring to the paternalized who he described as degenerates? They can introduce the social, political, and cultural aspects of civilized life, which 'go hand in hand in aiding of the missionary efforts which are purely religious in character and teaching,' Delany (1861) stated (p. 53).

Edward W. Blyden (1992a), a long-time educator and missionary in Liberia, also used his life urging African-Americans to emigrate. Blyden believed that God had given African Americans a 'providential' call to 'go up and possess' Africa to 'help raise the land of their forefathers from her degradation' (pp. 115, 125). This directive set up a paternalistic relationship, placing the African Americans as the paternalizers and the continental Africans as the paternalized, who according to Blyden, were 'earnestly inviting all to come' and help (p. 117). But how exactly should the African American paternalizers help the paternalized continental Africans? 'It is theirs to betake themselves to injured Africa, and bless those outrageous shores, and quiet those distracted families with the blessings of Christianity and civilization,' Blyden said (p. 114). In 1890, Blyden (1992b) even wrote admirably about Belgium's King Leopold II who 'has expended fortunes recently in opening the Congo and in introducing the appliances of civilization' and could serve as a model for African American paternalizers (p. 134).[12]

God not only charged African Americans with this duty, but God gave them (through the White slave master) the social and cultural tools to perform this obligation effectively, Blyden claimed. Like the Jews of Biblical Egypt who God placed into slavery for 400 years 'that they might be fitted, both by discipline and numerical increase, for the work that would delve upon them,' so too had African Americans been preserved and fitted through slavery in America. 'Slavery would seem to be a strange school in which to preserve a people; but God has a way of salting as well as purifying by fire,' Blyden (1992b) added (p. 130).

American Presidential Paternalizers

In articulating their foreign policy, American presidents, from the first decades of the nineteenth century to the present, used ideas from the storied ideology of civil paternalism, refining the practical race theory into a practical nation-state theory riddled with ethnocentrism. Instead of saying it was imperative for the White race to maintain the social good by caring for non-Whites, these presidents argued it was the role of the nation-state of America to protect and care for other nation-states with a basic assumption that America was preeminent. The paternalizer was America, and the paternalized became other countries around the world. This paternalism 'used to describe much of American foreign policy in Hispanic America,' according to Weischadle (1970), began officially in 1823 with President James Monroe's protective doctrine for Latin America—generally known as the Monroe Doctrine (p. 263). Through this doctrine, he shared in a message to Congress on 2 December 1823, President Monroe intimated that America would protect free countries in the Western Hemisphere from the European colonialists (Monroe 1999). What he did not say directly, but what became policy, was 'the establishment of a subordinate role for the Latin American countries in their relations with the United States' and 'an almost complete control over the direction of this relationship by the United States,' Weischadle (1970) maintained (p. 264).

A corollary to the Monroe Doctrine, according to McDougal (1997), became the concept of 'Manifest Destiny' (p. 74). Journalist John L. O'Sullivan first used the term in 1845 when he claimed it was the United States' 'manifest destiny to overspread and to possess the whole of the continent which Providence has given us for the development of the great experiment of liberty and federated self-government entrusted to us' (p. 5). However, U.S. presidents had been using the concept to justify taking Native American and Mexican land since 1812 and would continue until 1860 during an era one analyst called the 'Age of Manifest Destiny' (Stuart 1988). It was the 'destiny' of the paternalizer, America with its virtuous institutions, this wrinkle of the nation-state theory posited, to expand to the coast of the Pacific Ocean and the Gulf of Mexico to bring 'happiness' and 'peace and prosperity,' to the paternalized Mexicans and Native Americans, said President John Quincy Adams (McDougal 1997, p. 78).

Presidents William McKinley, Theodore Roosevelt, and Woodrow Wilson also expressed this practical nation-state theory, in which the inferiority and dependency of Latin America (and to a lesser extent Asia) and the supremacy of the U.S. were prevailing assumptions. It was best for the common good if America protected and cared for these countries, these presidents said or implied. In actuality though, these civil paternalistic sentiments were used to justify American imperialism. In an 1899 interview at the White House, to defend the American colonization of the Philippines, President William McKinley said the United States 'could not leave (the Filipinos) to themselves—they were unfit for self-government—and they would soon have anarchy and misrule' (Olcott 1916, p. 110). Just like slaveholders and colonizers had been arguing for centuries that the enslaved and uncivilized, respectively, could not be left to themselves, now an American president was using the same argument to justify American imperialism. Uttering a mix of civil and Christian paternalism, which had been fused by paternalizers after emancipation, President McKinley explained 'there was nothing left for us to do, but to take them all, and to educate the Filipinos, and uplift and civilize and Christianize them' (Olcott 1916, p. 110).

A few years later, President Roosevelt, who succeeded President McKinley, used McKinley's principle to relegate the entire Western Hemisphere through evoking what became known as his Roosevelt Corollary to the Monroe Doctrine. 'In the adherence of the United States to the Monroe Doctrine may force the United States, however reluctantly, in flagrant cases of such wrongdoing or impotence, to the exercise of an international police power,' President Roosevelt (1904) stated. This concept of America being the 'international police' forms the basis of Roosevelt's ideology of civil paternalism. What was the U.S. policing? To make sure, Roosevelt (1904) continued, that other nation-states 'obey the laws of civilized society . . . It is a mere truism to say that every nation, whether in America or anywhere else, which desires to maintain its freedom, its independence, must ultimately realize that the right of such independence can not be separated from the responsibility of making good use of it.' This is an argument paternalizers have used for ages—that they are protecting the paternalized, even from themselves, instead of objecting them to exploitation. But they are not only protecting them. Due to the paternalizers' presence, 'prosperity is sure to come to them,' President Roosevelt (1904) asserted like so many paternalizers before him. President Wilson continued to justify American imperialism in the Western hemisphere, this time during the Mexican Revolution. In 1915, he told an emissary of the British foreign secretary his Mexican policy was one of service. 'I am going to teach the South American republics to elect good men,' President Wilson said (Smith 1994, p. 60).[13]

President Harry S. Truman espoused to Congress in 1947 what became known as the 'Truman Doctrine' in which he labeled America as the 'leader of the free world.' After World War II, America became not just the parents of nation-states in the Western Hemisphere, but the paternalizers of the entire world. This evolution of the nation-state theory has been espoused by U.S. presidents ever since. Instead of gaining control of these nation-states to civilize or Christianize them, American presidents have argued it was the grand paternal responsibility of America during and after the Cold War to bring 'freedom' and 'democracy' to the paternalized unfree and undemocratic nation-states. America, the paternalizer, was/is 'exceptional,' a construct known as 'American exceptionalism' scholars have long debated. Meanwhile, it is the calling of America to bring this freedom and democracy (which used to be called civilization) to the world.[14]

This ideology President Truman articulated stretches back to Greco-Roman thought. In antiquity, Aristotle articulated the natural slave theory, which became the foundational theory of civil paternalism, while both St. Paul and St. Augustine articulated a Christian paternalism with the latter adding a sin theology to his articulations—all to justify slavery. St. Thomas used St. Augustine's sin theology to rationalize slavery during the European Middle Ages and refined Aristotle's natural slave theory into a practical slave theory. Centuries later in colonial America, Henry Pattillo articulated this civil paternalistic practical slave theory along with Paul's Christian paternalism, which Thomas Bacon also used to validate slavery during this period. Decades afterward in antebellum America, both Thomas Roderick Dew and George Fitzhugh continued to use the practical slave theory to defend slavery with the latter also employing St. Augustine's sin theology.

With the dawn of colonialism and the demise of slavery in the nineteenth century, the practical slave theory became inoperable, so the paternalizers created a new theory of civil paternalism—the practical race theory. European paternalizers and the Pan African paternalizers used this new theory and the American presidential paternalizers refined it into the practical nation-state theory—all to justify imperialism.

In actuality, the paternalized were never inferior to the paternalizers whether they were enslaved, colonized, sharecroppers, continental Africans, or nation-states. But many slaveholders (or paternalizers) across time and space have necessitated an 'ideological inversion of reality,' Patterson (1982) argued (p. 338). Through transposing reality, instead of viewing the slaves as active agents being held in servitude primarily by brute force, 'almost all masters, in fact, genuinely believed that they cared and provided for their slaves and that it was the slaves who, in the word of one southern ex-slave owner, had 'been raised to depend on others' (p. 338). Racist and ethnocentric deeds—be it slavery, colonialism, or imperialism—were justified through paternalism not only to encourage the exploiter, but to pacify the exploited. However, the paternalizers' need to continue to identify the paternalized as submissive, provided the paternalized with a glimmer of being, albeit slight. As Genovese (1976) explains, 'Paternalism's insistence upon mutual obligations—duties, responsibilities, and ultimately even rights—implicitly recognized the slaves' humanity' (p. 5). Consequently, for thousands of years, the paternalized racial and cultural groups, who had to face the exploitation of Western paternalizers, were able to latch onto this glimmer of being, this sparkle of humanity. They continuously fought against the dominant ideology of paternalism—the primary conceptual benefactor of racist and ethnocentric measures throughout human history.

Endnotes

1. This essay's title was inspired by the title of Memmi's (1991) book.
2. For more definitions of paternalism, see Clarke (2002), Husak, (1981), and Lee (1981).
3. 1 Cor. 7:22.
4. Col. 3:22.
5. Eph 6:8.
6. For more studies on paternalism in slavery, see Young (1993), McMichael (1991), and Szasz (2002).
7. For more studies on paternalism after emancipation in the United States, see Alston and Ferrie (1999), Tone (1997), and Ochiltree (1998).
8. For more information on the Berlin conference, see Forster, Mommsen, and Robinson (1988).
9. For a more general study of paternalism in British history, see Thornton (1996) and Hetherington (1978).
10. For more studies on paternalism in colonialism, see Hetherington (1978), Blaut (1993), Crush (1996), Ngidang (2005), and Murphy (1986).
11. For one take on this phenomenon, see Appiah (1992).
12. So in effect, Blyden was advising (unknowingly) African Americans to model themselves after someone who became one of the most notorious murderers of African people in human history, who forced his soldiers to cut off Congolese hands for every bullet used to repress them, and robbed $1.5 million a year from the Congo (Jackson 1970).
13. For paternalism of U.S. presidents, see Green (1971).
14. For the latest study of the American foreign policy since World War II and the dynamic of American exceptionalism, or what I am calling the latest form of the nation-state theory, see Hook and Spanier (2009). See also Papandreou (1972).

References

Alston, Lee J. and Ferrie, Joseph P. (1999). *Southern Paternalism and the American Welfare State*. Cambridge: Cambridge University Press.

Appiah, Kwame A. (1992). *In My Father's House: African in the Philosophy of Culture*. New York: Oxford University Press.

Aristotle. (1935). *The Athenian Constitution; Eudemian Ethics; Virtues and Vices*, trans. Harris Rackman. Cambridge: Harvard University Press.

Aristotle. (1944). *Politics*, trans. Harris Rackman. Cambridge: Harvard University Press.

Aristotle. (1953). *The Ethics of Aristotle: Nicomachean Ethics*, trans. James A. K. Thompson. Harmondsworth: Penguin Classics.

Bacon, Thomas. (1749). *Two Sermons, Preached to a Congregation of Black Slaves at the Parish Church of S. P. in the Province of Maryland*. London: John Oliver.

Bass, Jeff D. (1995). 'The Perversion of empire: Edmund Burke and the natural of imperial responsibility.' *Quarterly Journal of Speech* 81(2): 208–227.

Blackmon, Douglas A. (2008). *Slavery by Another Name: The Re-Enslavement of Black Americans from the Civil War to World War II*. New York: Doubleday.

Blair, Lewis H. (1889). *The Prosperity of the South Dependent upon the Elevation of the Negro*. Richmond: E. Waddey.

Blaut, J. M. (1993). *The Colonizer's Model of the World: Geographical Diffusionism and Eurocentric History*. New York: The Guilford Press.

Blyden, Edward W. (1992a). 'The call of providence to the descendants of Africa in America.' In Howard Brotz (Ed.). *African-American Social & Political Thought, 1850–1920*. New Brunswick: Transaction Publishers, 112–126.

Blyden, Edward W. (1992b). 'The African problem and the method of its solution.' In Howard Brotz (Ed.), *African-American Social & Political Thought, 1850–1920*. New Brunswick: Transaction Publishers, 126–139.

Brett, Stephen F. (1994). *Slavery and the Catholic Tradition*. New York: Peter Lang Publishing.

Clarke, John H. (1991). *Africans at the Crossroads: Notes for an African World Revolution*. Trenton: Africa World Press.

Clarke, Simon. (2002). 'A definition of paternalism.' *Current Research in Social Psychology* 5(1): 81–91.

Crush, Jonathan. (1996). 'The culture of failure: Racism, violence and white farming in colonial Swaziland.' *Journal of Historical Geography* 22(2): 177–197.

Delany, Martin R. (1861). *Official Report of the Niger Valley Exploring Party*. London: Thomas Hamilton.

—— (1992). 'The condition, elevation, emigration, and destiny of the colored people of the United States.' In Howard Brotz (Ed.) *African-American Social & Political Thought, 1850–1920*. New Brunswick: Transaction Publishers, 37–101.

Dew, Thomas R. (1832). 'Abolition of Negro slavery.' *American Quarterly Review* 12: 189–265.

Fitzhugh, George. (1851). *Slavery Justified, by a Southerner*. Fredericksburg: Recorder Job Office.

—— (1854). *Sociology for the South; or the Failure of Free Society*. Richmond: A. Morris.

—— (1857). *Cannibals All! or Slaves Without Masters*. Richmond: A Morris.

—— (1857). 'Southern thought again.' *De Bow's Review* 23: 449–462.

Forster, Stig, Mommsen, Wolfgang J., and Robinson, Ronald. (1988). *Bismarck, Europe, and Africa: the Berlin Africa conference 1884-1885 and the Onset of Partition*. Oxford: Oxford University Press.

Galloway, Charles B. (1904). *The Negro and the South*. New York: The Trustees.

Garnsey, Peter. (1996). *Ideas of Slavery from Aristotle to Augustine*. New York: Press Syndicate of the University of Cambridge.

Genovese, Eugene D. (1976). *Roll, Jordan, Roll: The World the Slaves Made*. New York: Vintage Books.

Green, David. (1971). 'Paternalism and profits: The ideology of U.S. aid to Latin America, 1943–1971.' *Historical Papers* 7(1): 335–372.

Hetherington, Penelope. (1978). *British Paternalism and Africa 1920–1940*. Totowa: Frank Cass and Company Limited.

Hook, Steven W. and Spanier, John. (2009). *American Foreign Policy Since World War II*. Washington DC: CQ Press.

Husak, Douglas. (1981). 'Paternalism and autonomy.' *Philosophy and Public Affairs* 10(1): 27–46.

Jackson, John G. (1970). *Introduction to African Civilizations*. New York: Kensington Publishing Corp.

Johnson, Guion G. (1957). 'Southern paternalism toward Negroes after emancipation.' *The Journal of Southern History* 23(4): 483–509.

Kipling, Rudyard. (1899). 'The white man's burden.' *McClure's Magazine* 7: 4–6.

Kleinig, John. (1984). *Paternalism*. Totowa: Rowman & Allanheld.

Lee, Robert F. (1969). *Conrad's Colonialism*. The Netherlands: Mouton.

Lee, Steven. (1981). 'On the justification of paternalism.' *Social Theory and Practice* 7(2): 193–203.

Lugard, F. D. (1929). *The Dual Mandate in British Tropical Africa*. Edinburg: William Blackwood & Sons.

McDougal, Walter A. (1997). *Promised Land, Crusader State: The American Encounter with the World Since 1776*. New York: Houghton Mifflin.

McMichael, Philip. (1991). 'Slavery in the regime of wage labor: Beyond paternalism in the U.S. cotton culture.' *Social Concept* 6(1): 10–28.

Memmi, Albert. (1991). *The Colonizer and the Colonized*. Boston: Beacon Press.

Monroe, James. (1999). 'The Monroe doctrine: Excerpts from Monroe's original message, December 2, 1823.' In D. W. Dent, *The Legacy of the Monroe Doctrine: A Reference Guide to U.S. Involvement in Latin American and the Caribbean*. Westport: Greenwood Press, 379–380.

Murphy, John F. (1986). Murphy, 'Legitimation and paternalism: The colonial state in Kenya.' *African Studies Review* 29(3): 55–65.

Ngidang, Dimbab. (2005). 'Deconstruction and reconstruction of native customary land tenure in Sarawak.' *Southeast Asian Studies* 43(1): 47–75.

Ochiltree, Ian D. (1998). '"A just and self-respecting system" black independence, sharecropping, and paternalistic relations in the American South and South Africa.' *Agricultural History* 72(22): 352–380.

Olcott, Charles S. (1916). *The Life of William McKinley*. Boston: Houghton Mifflin Company.

O'Sullivan, John L. (1945). 'Annexation.' *United States Magazine and Democratic Review* 17(1): 5–10.

Papandreou, Andreas G. (1972). Paternalistic Capitalism: A Powerful Critique of American Capitalism and its Relationship to Government and Foreign Policy. Minneapolis: University of Minnesota Press.

Patterson, Orlando. (1982). *Slavery and Social Death: A Comparative Study*. Cambridge: Harvard University Press.

Pattillo, Henry. (1787). *The Plain Planter's Family Assistant; Containing an Address to Husbands and Wives, Children and Servants*. Wilmington: James Adams.

Raskin, Jonah. (1971). *The Mythology of Imperialism: Rudyard Kipling, Joseph Conrad, E. M. Forster, D. H. Lawrence, and Joyce Cary*. New York: Dell.

Roberts, J. M. (1993). *A Short History of the World*. New York: Oxford University Press.

Roosevelt, Theodore. (1904). 'Annual message to Congress for 1904.' House Records HR 58A-K2, Records of the U.S. House of Representatives, Record Group 233, Center for Legislative Archives; National Archives.

Smith, Tony. (1994). *America's Mission: The United States and the Worldwide Struggle for Democracy in the Twentieth Century*. Princeton: Princeton University Press.

Stuart, Reginald C. (1988). *United States expansionism and British North America, 1775–1871*. Chapel Hill: University of North Carolina Press.

Szasz, Thomas. (2002). *Liberation By Oppression: A Comparative Study of Slavery and Psychiatry*. New Brunswick: Transaction Publishers.

Thorton, A. P. (1996). *The Habit of Authority*. Toronto: The University of Toronto Press.

Tone, Andrea. (1997). *The Business of Benevolence: Industrial Paternalism in Progressive America*. Ithaca: Cornell University Press.

Weischadle, David E. (1970). 'Paternalism: A view of the Latin American foreign policy of the United States, 1823–1934.' *Social Studies* 61(6): 263–270.

Young, Jeffrey R. (1993). 'Ideology and death on a Savannah river rice plantation, 1833–1867: Paternalism amidst "a good supply of disease and pain."' *The Journal of Southern History* 59(4): 673–706.

Chapter 5

Race, Gender, and Nineteenth Century Ethnography: Mary Kingsley's *Travels in West Africa*

Anitha Ramachandran

Contemporary theories of racial essentialism owe much to the long traditions of ethnography and anthropology that flourished during the course of Western imperialism, especially in the late 19th century. During this period, the study of these exotic racialized "sciences" drew unprecedented numbers of European intellectuals to the colonies, such as the English ethnographer and public speaker Mary Kingsley (1862–1900). One of the most intriguing figures of 1890s England, Kingsley was a self-educated Victorian woman whose remarkable work and experiences provide a rich entry point for analyzing the intertwined politics of race, gender, and scientific inquiry that were integral to Victorian ethnography. Her life and work bespeaks the impossibility of considering gender identity in isolation from racial identity, or vice versa.

The daughter of Charles Kingsley and his servant Mary Bailey, Mary was born into both a prominent middle-class intellectual family, as well as an obscure working class family. Kingsley's life prior to her West African travels was restricted to the domestic sphere, where she spent most of her time caring first for her ailing mother, and then her father. When her parents passed away and her brother no longer needed her domestic help, Kingsley, for the first time in her life, "found [herself] in possession of five or six months which were not heavily forestalled."[1] Thus freed, Mary Kingsley made two journeys to West Africa between 1893 and 1895 in order to "complete her father's anthropological work"[2] and engage in her own study of "fish and fetish."[3] Upon her return to England, Kingsley published two books, *Travels in West Africa* (1897) and *West African Studies* (1899), both of which brought her extraordinary fame and caused the British public to marvel at how a "sheltered, middle-class Victorian spinster lady"[4] could possibly have written them.

Indeed, within the patriarchal intellectual environment of 1890s England, the spectacle of Kingsley's "eccentric" travels was perceived primarily as a transgression of gender identity, winning her titles such as the "lone she-wolf."[5] According to Laura Ciolkowski, much of the critical work on English women's travel literature from the imperial period continues to focus on "powerful rhetorics of ideological freedom and sexual liberation," in which the "repressed bodies of Victorian angels can leave their English homes, . . . burst the sexual restraints that define proper ladies, and thereby challenge . . . the ideals and principles of bourgeois womanhood."[6] Arguing against Dea Birkett and Katherine Frank, two critics who have studied Kingsley from this perspective, Ciolkowski suggests a different view, that Kingsley's *Travels in West Africa* actually works to *establish*, or at least to reaffirm, constructions of Victorian bourgeois womanhood.

While both of these perspectives are equally valid and necessary for understanding Kingsley, they work best, I would argue, when contextualized within an analysis of the racial, political, and scientific fabric of imperialism and 19th century ethnographic "science." I would argue that Mary Kingsley's identity as an imperialist ethnographer enabled her both to burst *and* to establish the restraints of her bourgeois womanhood, and thereby simultaneously challenge and reinforce Victorian gender roles. Not only did this subject position afford Kingsley the authorizing mechanisms of racial superiority and rights of "scientific" scrutiny,[7] it also gave her the authority to travel. Her travels afforded her *spatial* movement between and within the patriarchal and imperial discourses of both colonized periphery and colonizing center.[8]

Various theorists have provided insights regarding the spatial positioning of European colonizing women. Alison Blunt and Gillian Rose write that imperial women are simultaneously positioned both inside and outside colonial discourses by virtue of their gender and race.[9] Similarly, Birkett points out that the racial stratification of the colonies offered an opportunity for the "intermingling" of patriarchal and imperial discourses, resulting in a new, hybrid subject position for white women, who were simultaneously marginalized by the former and empowered by the latter.[10] As Sara Mills writes, within the colonial context, "constructions of racial superiority could overcome those of gender inferiority, and thus colonizing women could share in colonial discourses of power and authority" without necessarily suffering from gender oppression in that discourse.

One such colonial discourse of power and authority is that of the scientist, specifically, that of the imperial ethnographer. As ethnographer, Kingsley repeatedly describes her activities in the language of hunting. For example, she writes:

> Stalking the wild West African idea is one of the most charming pursuits in the world. Quite apart from the intellectual, it has a high sporting interest; for its pursuit is as beset with difficulty and danger as grizzly bear hunting. . . . Personally, I prefer it to elephant hunting . . . I shall never forget the pleasure with which, in the forest among the Fans, I netted one reason for the advantage of possessing a white man's eye-ball, and . . . I wrote it down in my water-worn notebook. . . .[11]

Most of Kingsley's "scientific" and "ethnological" activities actually amount to "netting reasons" (Kingsley's phrase) for the superiority of European civilization, and her "scientific findings" are rarely more than biased conjectures, stereotypes, and generalizations about the "African mind." That such a highly evaluative log of one individual's perception of Africans was lauded as a landmark work of "science" in 1890s England highlights the fact that any analysis of Mary Kingsley requires the deconstruction of the terms *science* and *ethnography.*

Rather than the impartial, neutral, and detached activity of cataloging facts that the term *science* often suggests, 19th century ethnography, like any science, was coded with the historical and cultural ideologies of its day. For example, one of the most popular scientific ideologies of Kingsley's time was the belief that a polygenetic difference existed between the races;[12] one of the ways in which 19th century medical science sought to prove this erroneous belief was through the exhibition and (upon death) dissection of the African woman Saartje Baartman, known in Europe as the "Hottentot Venus." Baartman's anatomy was believed to be bodily, and thus, "scientific," evidence of racial "primitivity"; as Sander Gilman points out, the Victorians believed that if Baartman's anatomy could be shown to be intrinsically different from the anatomy of White women, her display could be used as "sufficient sign that blacks were a separate . . . race, as different from the European as the proverbial orangutan."[13]

The example of "The Hottentot Venus" illustrates how the relationship between science and racist ideology is a mutual one; while ideology influences how science is conducted, science in turn has the power to strengthen, justify, and give voice to particular ideologies. Throughout *Travels,* Kingsley's ethnography wields this discursive power of science. Kingsley's work endorses the polygenetic theory of racial evolution and attempts to fix the bodily signifiers of race to biologically rooted moral, psychical, and evolutionary equivalences; it presents race as incontrovertible scientific evidence of what is actually a socially constructed difference between human beings. Truly a product of her time, Kingsley and her contemporaries did not recognize that the outward bodily signifiers of race perform what Stuart Hall has called racism's "arbitrary discursive operation—arbitrary because race is a sliding signifier with equivalences that cannot be fixed outside of discourse."[14] As Hall argues, "The evidence of racial difference, which appears to be figured so obviously on the surface of the body, is capable of carrying its negative connotations only because of the power of science to fix and stabilize racial difference."[15]

Additionally, critical to any discussion of Kingsley's ethnography is an examination of its epistemological power *as* a science. Nineteenth century ethnography of the kind Kingsley conducted provided the imperial powers with intimate knowledge of the "subject races"; as Edward Said writes in *Orientalism,* "knowledge of subject races . . . is what makes their management easy and profitable; knowledge gives power, more power requires more knowledge, and so on in an increasingly profitable dialectic of information and control."[16] Elsewhere, in "Representing the Colonized: Anthropology's Interlocutors," Said reiterates the role that ethnography and its descendant, anthropology, have played in the "manipulation . . . of native societies for imperial purposes."[17] The "science" of ethnography has also sought to consolidate the representation of "the native" as primitive and inferior, and thus in need of colonialism's "civilizing mission." Abdul JanMohamed's insights on colonialist discourse are particularly useful in this context; although his focus is primarily on colonialist literature, his analysis can be extended to ethnography as well: "If literature [or ethnography] can demonstrate that the barbarism of the native is irrevocable, or at least very deeply ingrained, then the European's attempt to civilize him can continue indefinitely."[18]

Mary Kingsley's activity as ethnographer contributed to this dialectic of information, racism, and the civilizing mission; she was quite self-conscious about her status as "scientist," and hoped that the knowledge she collected would be beneficial to the maintenance of the British Empire. As Julie Early writes, "Kingsley was always concerned to make her information matter: by reconfiguring the processes of science . . . and by showing the fundamental importance of scientific understanding to the practical workings of the British Empire."[19]

While this statement is true of Kingsley, Early's essay, "The Spectacle of Science and Self," endorses Kingsley's work as "science" without the ideological and political critique of ethnography advanced by Said. Furthermore, Early praises Kingsley's "scientific technique," although it is neither methodological, rigorous, nor consistent enough to be called a "technique"; Kingsley's "scientific" observations and conclusions are based upon little more than conjecture or preconceived notions. Third, even if one subscribes to the notion that Kingsley is a *scientist*, the fact that Early positions Kingsley only along the discursive lines of gender is problematic. While noting that "the qualities needed to practice science were also the qualities that Kingsley demanded of an audience that would watch a woman work,"[20] Early does not pay adequate attention to Kingsley's racial subject position, which in an imperial racial hierarchy, provided her the authority to do this work: to conduct "scientific" studies of colonized populations.

Last, Early's essay does not problematize Kingsley's politics. For instance, Early offers admiration for Kingsley's belief that the "scientific understanding . . . of West African practices . . . must be brought to bear on devising political and economical policies that . . . would least interfere with West Africans,"[21] but does not critique Kingsley's support of imperialism and "benevolent rule" of West Africans. Also, the following statement from Early's essay requires elaboration: "Kingsley refused the categorization and hierarchical charting of [West African] practices . . . and instead pointed to a plurality of culture."[22] While Kingsley did point to the local differences between West African cultures in her ethnography, her conclusions about "the African" homogenize West African pluralism into a general racial Other, in contrast to "the European." Also, while she might not have ordered *West African* practices into a hierarchy, Kingsley did categorize the colored "races" as evolutionarily distinct from the white "race."[23]

Just as Kingsley refused to question England's dominant and exploitative relationship with its colonial possessions, neither did she question the patriarchal oppression of women in her own society of Victorian England. Puzzlingly, Kingsley was a staunch opponent of women's suffrage.[24] Some historians have postulated that Kingsley had much to gain politically by her antifeminism. By aligning herself with imperialism, but refusing to align herself with any of the feminisms of her day, Kingsley was able to gain far more acceptance and support from the existing patriarchal order than many of her contemporaries. Like other Victorian women travelers, Mary Kingsley might have sojourned "for personal reasons linked to a desire to escape the confinement of domesticity"[25] and the "ideals and principles of Victorian bourgeois womanhood"; however, when the popularity of her work thrust her into the public sphere, Kingsley, like many other traveling women, found it necessary to "legitimate [her] motives in terms of scientific [or] professional interests."[26] According to Blunt, many traveling women expressed a "desire to be distanced from suffragists" as part of their desire for success in the "masculine, public realm of scientific research, professionalism, and politics that arose from their construction as feminine on their return 'home.'"[27]

In conclusion, traveling abroad as an imperial ethnographic scientist enabled Mary Kingsley to break free from traditionally feminine gender roles; her travels and studies, however, did not automatically put her in sympathy with feminist claims for equality, but rather, revealed her support for British imperialism. Ironically, although Kingsley had longed for a formal education in childhood and for readier acceptance by her male intellectual peers, her politics ran in sharp contrast to *fin de siecle* feminists who struggled against "social policies which denied [women] higher education, alternative roles, professional opportunities, and votes."[28] According to Blunt, "Kingsley correlated a lack of power with femininity," but did not "perceive the need for structural change in gender relations."[29] Kingsley's anti-feminist and imperialist stance makes more sense in light of such a correlation. Entering the imperialist and masculine worlds of 1890s travel, publishing, and politics as a woman brought Kingsley extraordinary fame, but this acceptance was probably due to her inoffensiveness to the existing power structures of Victorian society. Though Kingsley may have crossed gender boundaries by practicing science, her ethnographic work served to reinforce the racial boundaries that were so essential to England's colonial regime. Unlike many of her anti-imperialist peers, who were rapidly growing in numbers both in England and the rest of Europe by the late 19th century, Mary Kingsley neither questioned racial or gender oppression, nor the "scientific" assertions that sustained them.

Endnotes

1. Mary Kingsley, *Travels in West Africa*, Abridged ed. (J.M. Dent, Orion Publishing Group, 1993), 11. (1st ed: Macmillan, 1897).
2. Alison Blunt, *Travel, Gender and Imperialism: Mary Kingsley and West Africa* (Guilford Press, 1994), 64.
3. Kingsley, 15.
4. Elspeth Huxley, "Editor's Introduction," *Travels*, 4–9.
5. Huxley, 5.
6. Laura Ciolkowski, "Travelers' Tales: Empire, Victorian Travel, and the Spectacle of English Womanhood in Mary Kingsley's *Travels in West Africa*," in *Victorian Literature and Culture* (Cambridge University Press, 1998), 338.
7. Blunt and McEwan both discuss this. See Alison Blunt, "Mapping Authorship and Authority: Reading Mary Kingsley's Landscape Descriptions," and Cheryl McEwan, "Encounters with Western Women: Textual Representations of Difference by White Women Abroad," in (eds.) Alison Blunt and Gillian Rose, *Writing Women and Space: Colonial and Postcolonial Geographies* (Guilford Press, 1994).
8. Alison Blunt and Gillian Rose, *Writing Women and Space: Colonial and Postcolonial Geographies* (Guilford Press, 1994).
9. Alison Blunt and Gillian Rose, "Introduction," *Writing Women and Space*, 13–14. Ibid., 13.
10. Dea Birkett, *Spinsters Abroad: Victorian Lady Explorers* (Oxford University Press, 1989).
11. Kingsley, 160–161.
12. Sander Gilman, "Black Bodies, White Bodies: Toward an Iconography of Female Sexuality in Late Nineteenth Century Art, Medicine, and Literature," *Critical Inquiry* 12 (Autumn 1985), 210–216.
13. Ibid., 216.
14. Stuart Hall, "The After-life of Franz Fanon," *The Fact of Blackness: Frantz Fanon and Visual Representation* (Bay Press, 1996), 21.
15. Stuart Hall, "The After-life of Frantz Fanon," *The Fact of Blackness: Frantz Fanon and Visual Representation* (Bay Press, 1996), 21.
16. Edward W. Said, *Orientalism* (Vintage, 1978), 36.
17. Edward Said, "Representing the Colonized: Anthropology's Interlocutors," *Critical Inquiry* 15 (Winter 1989), 205–223, 207.
18. Abdul JanMohamed, "The Economy of Manichean Allegory: The Function of Racial Difference in Colonialist Literature," *Critical Inquiry* 12 (Autumn 1985), 62.
19. Julie English Early, "The Spectacle of Science and Self: Mary Kingsley," in (eds.) Barbara T. Gates and Ann B. Shteir, *Natural Eloquence: Women Reinscribe Science* (University of Wisconsin Press, 1997), 215–236, 229.
20. Ibid., 228.
21. Ibid., 229.
22. Ibid., 229.
23. Blunt, 100–110.
24. Blunt 154–157.
25. Blunt, 157.
26. Ibid., 157.
27. Ibid., 157.
28. Elaine Showalter, *Sexual Anarchy: Gender and Culture at the* Fin de Siecle (Viking Press, 1991), 20.
29. Blunt, 156.

Chapter 6

Racism and Sexism in Works for Children

Rajani Iyer

I really didn't notice that he had a funny nose.
And he certainly looked better all dressed up in fancy clothes.
He's not nearly as attractive as he seemed the other night.
So I think I'll just pretend that this glass slipper feels too tight.

> *". . . And Then the Prince Knelt Down and Tried to Put the Glass Slipper on Cinderella's Foot"*—Judith Viorst[1]

This version of the famous fairy tale "Cinderella" is certainly not the one most children hear. It is usually concluded with the line, "And so the Prince married the beautiful Cinderella, and they lived happily ever after." The attractive, passive heroine is rewarded for her continual self-sacrifice with marriage to a prince; marriage in this situation precludes any possible quest by Cinderella for fulfilled selfhood while continuing to accord the prince the power of choice. Cinderella must subjugate herself to the stranger she has married, who is interested in her only because he thought her beautiful while she was under her fairy godmother's spell. But why is that the acceptable ending of this story that millions of young girls read or have read to them? Why is Judith Viorst's ending, which grants Cinderella both power over and choice of her fate, not more widely circulated? Viorst's conclusion challenges the strongly hierarchical power structure that fairy tales present, and is therefore dangerous to those that formerly manipulated words for their own purposes.

This chapter will examine racism and sexism in works for children—why they exist, how widespread they are, and the ways in which they influence children. Children's literature will be the medium most emphasized, but some salient examples from movies and television have been included to emphasize certain aspects of the danger posed. American works will be the primary focus; the portion of the chapter that deals with racism will concentrate on Native Americans and African-Americans. The first objective of the chapter is to explicate the power inherent in everyday language, but a few definitions are necessary for a foundation. Racism is "the systematic oppression and exploitation of human beings on the basis of their belonging to a particular racial group or people. 'Systematic' indicates that we must look at the status of the group as a whole, and not at those few who may have climbed a 'ladder of success' in the white society. The word 'systematic' also connotes practices and policies which are pervasive, regardless of whether they are intentional or unintentional. Racism is different from individual prejudice because it requires the possession of genuine power in a society. . . . So racism is not merely prejudice, but prejudice plus power."[2] Sexism is defined as "any attitude, action or institutional structure which subordinates or limits a person on the basis of sex."[3]

Robert B. Moore's "Racism in the English Language: A Lesson Plan and Study Essay" considers various instances of "everyday racism." His thesis is that "[l]anguage not only *expresses* ideas and concepts but actually *shapes* thought";[4] the connection between language and thought, or language and values, upon which Moore bases his work, has been well-documented by studies conducted by Edward Sapir and Benjamin Lee Whorf, Kenneth B. Clark, Mary Ellen Goodman, Judith Porter, and many others.

The piece achieves its resonance because everything Moore points out is something that the reader has tacitly accepted through her or his use of the English language; Moore demonstrates how traditional, accepted uses of everyday language can be instrumental in spreading racism and are therefore particularly insidious. For example, the symbolism the colors black and white have assumed can do nothing but further the existence of racism. It is important to note, however, that the words black and white themselves do not inherently mean anything except the absence of color and the combination of all colors, respectively. But the connotations have grown; "white," according to the *Oxford English Dictionary*, can be (besides the well-known denotations): ". . . [m]orally or spiritually pure; innocent . . . free from malignity or evil intent; beneficent, harmless . . . truthful . . . Highly prized, precious; dear, favourite . . . auspicious, happy . . . Honourable, decent, fair." However, "black" is very different; it can mean: ". . . blackmail . . . A serious mistake or blunder . . . Deeply stained with dirt, soiled, filthy . . . Characterized by the absence of light; dusky, gloomy; overcast . . . Foreboding or threatening; angry, sulky; dismal; melancholy . . . Foul, atrocious; wicked; hateful . . . Malignant, deadly; sinister . . . Macabre . . . Disgraceful, deserving censure, illegal . . . Bruise or discolour . . . Defame, speak evil of."[5] Why have these words been saddled with these meanings? More importantly, who has been providing these connotations? How have these meanings been allowed to become an integral part of the English language, appearing in words and phrases such as "denigrate," "a black day," and "black sheep"?[6] Indeed, why have these terms been applied to individuals who are actually brown and pink; why are colors acceptable classifications of human beings?

Moore continues his explication with a demonstration of how the passive voice can be in its own way as damaging as out-and-out racist remarks. The passive voice, if a subject is not provided, can hide the doer of the verb; if the action is one that elicits disapproval from the reader, the reader has no way of knowing who is responsible or who is to blame. For example, a history text may state, "'slaves were *brought* to America.' Not only does this omit the destruction of African societies and families, but it ignores the role of northern merchants and southern slave holders in the profitable trade of human beings."[7] Also, if the action is laudable, the reader does not know who to commend; by using the passive voice, the achievements of many victims of prejudice can be minimized, especially those of slaves.

Blaming the victim is the next trend Moore attacks; terms to classify people that depend upon a pre-supposed value system are invalid. Often these terms, such as "culturally deprived," make the people they describe seem responsible for their own situation, or, at best, they are hopelessly skewed in favor of those who are in power, regardless of the truth. The previous term "assumes that the dominant whites are cultured and all others without culture. In fact, third world children generally are bicultural, and many are bilingual, having grown up in their own culture as well as absorbing the dominant culture. In many ways, they are equipped with skills and experiences which white youth have been deprived of, since most white youth develop in a monocultural, monolingual environment."[8] Therefore, what the term "culturally deprived" really means is unclear; the peoples it refers to usually have both their own culture and that of the group making the value judgment. In what sense, then, are these peoples deprived? Another sign of America's white "aristocracy" is the fact that words such as "non-white" and "minority" are commonly used. The former sets up whiteness as the standard by which judgment must occur. The latter, as used within the United States, is highly fallacious; the groups dubbed "minorities" in America are actually the majority of the world's population and within this country too.

Equally pernicious is the causal use of what Moore terms "loaded words." As the black/white examples proved earlier, there is more to a word than just its definition; synonyms can be very difficult to find. So when people speak about European political and cultural units as "countries," but about those of Africans or Native Americans as "tribes," another value judgment has been made, because "tribe" has generally been taken to signify primitive, temporary, rather artificial divisions. In reality, the distinctions between African and Native American units has been as complex as those of the Europeans; they were political, social, linguistic, cultural, and religious. Consider also how infrequently the European colonizers are described in textbooks as raping, ravaging beasts seizing land that was not theirs; brutal "Indian attacks" on "defenseless white settlers," however, are a staple of many history books for children. The insider/outsider divisions create the pattern upon which language is formed.

Roger Andersen's *The Power and The Word: Language, Power and Change* approaches the problem of the power struggles inherent in every language in a more scientific manner. The insider/outsider conflict apparent in the structure of language is elucidated when he quotes *The German Ideology* of Karl Marx and Friedrich Engels: "'. . . the class which is the ruling material force of society, is at the same time its ruling intellectual force. The class which has the means of material production at its disposal, has control at the same time over the means of mental production, so that thereby, generally speaking, the ideas of those who lack the means of mental production are subject to it. . . . during the time that the aristocracy was dominant, the concepts loyalty etc. were dominant, during the dominance of the bourgeoisie the concepts freedom, equality, etc. . . . each new class which puts itself in the place of the one ruling before it, is compelled, merely in order to carry through its aim, to represent its interest as the common interest of all the members of society, that is, expressed in ideal form: it has to give its ideas the form of universality, and represent them as the only rational, universally valid ones.'"[9]

But the problem goes deeper than that. It is not just that the people who are in power can create a language suited to meet their needs and prejudices, but that language itself becomes reified; Peter Berger and Thomas Luckmann, authors of *The Social Construction of Reality*, define the dangerous process thus: "Reification is the apprehension of products of human activity as if they were something other than human products—such as facts of nature, results of cosmic laws, or manifestations of divine will. . . . [it] implies that man is capable of forgetting his own authorship of the human world. . .".[10] The result of reification is that people utilize existing words that are harmful (because they reflect the influence of people in power) rather than try to create a language that is acceptable to all the peoples who must make use of it. An excellent example of reification is the persistence of the words "slave," "slave owner," and "master." The word "slave," although it means a captive person subjected to forced labor, has as part of its dynamic a sense of property; the seizure and rape of "slaves" does not have the same impact upon the reader as does the seizure and rape of "African men and women torn from their homelands and families and brutally abused into forced labor." The word "master" implies that the people who owned slaves were in some way superior to the Africans. Even "slave owner" expresses the thought that the slaves were only property anyway. As Andersen says, "Knowledge is created when consciousness becomes structured and articulated through language."[11] Reification is a phenomenon threatening to those who wish to reshape language to include a wider group of people.

Andersen is also concerned with the roles language assigns to women, especially because the terms are virtually ubiquitous; "[i]f the language that we use constantly encourages us to think of women and men in particular ways its cumulative effect is likely to be persuasive. This effect will be even stronger if we are offered no equally persuasive alternative."[12] Some of the problems he cites are the incessant attention to the attractiveness and marital status of women, the use of their first names alone, the lack of women's surnames, the relationship frequently established between women and food (things men can devour), and the belittling of their work. He relates these problems to conditioning of children by society; "[t]he differences between women and men are taken to be based mainly on biology, and therefore to be 'natural'. Too often this allows men to continue naming women as they want and controlling women's reality."[13] The lack of continuous female surnames makes it difficult to trace the achievements of women in the world; even those who fought for women's rights are generally referred to as Mrs. _____. Andersen astutely compares the tradition of wives taking males' names with a more overtly power-based relationship: "The use of names will reflect where power lies in society. It is difficult to build a sense of identity if your name is always taken from others and your history is wiped out. . . . [many slaves were] forced to take on the names of their owners. . .".[14] While there is clearly a difference between marriage (which is often voluntary) and slavery, the two institutions do have common practices.

The terms that language assigns to certain jobs defines them as specifically, rightfully male; this problem is only exacerbated when people refer to a professional (such as a doctor) who happens to be female as a "woman doctor," as if being a doctor were a purely masculine prerogative that this particular woman has usurped. The true meanings of words (what they are understood to mean) are more important than dictionary definitions. Andersen unequivocally states, "It is not possible to find the 'real' meaning of a word by looking at its history: the meaning of a word is established by how it is used today," taking as his example "man," which is derived from a word that meant human (man or woman)[15]; some feminists have been fighting the use of this word on the grounds that its practical use excludes women despite its etymology. Also, derision for female accomplishments is the norm. Domesticity (which is all many women are allowed to do) is often scorned as not real work; Andersen points out that if men were "housewives," the job would be defined as including the roles of "financial controller, store supervisor, expert chef, psycho- and sex-therapist, medical attendant, child psychologist, pre-school educationist, entertainer, as well as permanent trouble-shooter."[16] But this is the traditional female role, and it is the only one with which many men are comfortable.

Although Moore and Andersen are actually concerned with the effects of language on people in general (not just children), their conclusions have even more resonance when applied to children. The mind of a child is a remarkably impressionable thing; children learn better and more quickly than adults. What is to prevent them from learning the meanings of "black" that are damaging to their peers and themselves as well as the innocuous ones? In addition, since children do not distinguish, as adults often do, between didactic literature and literature produced for the purpose of entertainment only, awareness of how flexible language can become within the confines of a story needs to be raised: "Arthur Applebee has shown conclusively how story characters become part of a child's 'real world' and form part of their cultural heritage. Thus, tales play an important role in early socialisation. For instance, upon hearing a fairy tale, children of four and five will 'assimilate the story to their past expectations about such things as types of characters, patterns of behaviour, and suitable endings. . . . As a key agent of socialisation, the fairy tale enables the child to discover his or her place in the world and to test hypotheses about the world.'"[17] It is patently clear that children's literature must be very carefully constructed; there is too much at stake to allow an author's ignorance or prejudices to affect the readers. Whatever a child reads is true in her or his mind.

Children's literature is more instrumental than many people are willing to admit in forming children's ideas, because the stories are often reflections of popular contemporary beliefs; the ubiquity of certain notions renders them unassailable in the eyes of most children and many adults. In addition, "[s]ince in our society children tend to be isolated from others unlike themselves—culturally and economically—books provide one of the few ways to shatter the myths about Black people [or any other group that is often stereotyped within literature] on which racist attitudes flourish."[18] However, children's literature has been notoriously racist and sexist; many books awarded the status of children's "classics" are nothing more than demonstrations of the author's deep-rooted prejudices. *The Story of Little Black Sambo* and *The Matchlock Gun* are examples of brazen racism against African-Americans and Native Americans respectively, and yet these books are still widely available on the shelves of libraries across the nation. The stereotypes these works perpetuate have been proven several times over to be false and degrading; why then can these books be so much more easily accessed than books that respect all cultures and both sexes? It is through books, which are always praised as good and educational tools (as opposed to the "boob tube" or "idiot box," the television), that children learn many of their own prejudices; elementary school libraries in particular usually do not have the funding to be able to update their resources, and so harmful works stay on the shelves. Moreover, parents often read their own favorite children's books to their children; nostalgia can easily keep them from recognizing the flaws in the book that could have a major impact upon their child's mind.

> *We must move beyond the idea that integrated books are needed only by Black children. While the Black child needs to have books that include him for his own self-confirmation, it is crucial that the white child be exposed to integrated literature. It is impossible for the Black child to grow up unaware of the experiences of the dominant white culture. He is immersed in that culture through literature, the mass media and all the institutions he comes in contact with in the course of his life. But it is possible for the white child to grow up unaware of the experience of Black people.[19]*
>
> "Starting Out Right: Choosing Books About Black People for Young Children"—
> Children's Literature Review Board, Bettye I. Latimer, ed.

Black people have been subjected to many forms of literary racism. There is, first of all, the disconcerting trend of "blaming the victim." African-Americans, so the familiar story goes, were childlike and/or bestial. They not only needed slavery to discipline them, but they actually thrived under it and came a little closer to becoming human. Now that they are free, it is their responsibility to prove to "us" that they are truly human beings, and thereby win "our" acceptance (and, it can be inferred, true success). A complete disregard of the obstacles in their path, often those that "we" have put there, is the norm. There is an alarming paucity of realistic black characters in children's literature. They are often thrown pell-mell into a story to present a multicultural façade, to help the spiritual growth of a white character, or even just to "prove" the stereotypes with which they are burdened. Sometimes, however, they are romanticized to such a degree that these African American characters are no longer credible; they have become superhuman ideals. More often, they are simply avoided in the children's books that are published and widely disseminated. It is this pattern of avoidance, along with the other ridiculous trends, that can lead to racism in the children that read these books.

Black children are often put into children's books for quite worthy reasons, but the final effect is marred by the author's (often unconscious) racism. *Bright April* and Theodore Taylor's *The Cay* are two of the many examples of failed attempts to be completely prejudice-free. In each of the two novels, "[t]he white child learns to accept the Black as 'just like me.' . . . In both, the Black person is finally accepted *by* whites. But what about a Black person's acceptance *of* the white? That is just automatically assumed. This aspect of the relationship has no importance; white is the norm, the standard that counts. . . . It blames the victims of racism for their long history of oppression. If it is up to the third world person to win 'acceptance,' then by implication they are defective until they prove themselves worthy of white approval. . . . Personal virtue or strength may have worked for many white people but not for the vast majority of not white—not for any third world people *as a group*."[20] Thus the purpose of the books, to demonstrate that, deep down, all people(s) are the same, is wasted, because they instead foster the notion that it is only black children who need to be explained; whiteness is still the correct standard, and white children's questions are more important than those of other children. Token integration (also known as the Oasis Syndrome) is the other major problem of these books; the single black child is expected to represent every emotion of all African-Americans. Token inclusion of black children in the white-dominated world of children's literature often ends in the integration of the child into the white world that represents the norm, the real world; no trace of her or his black heritage is left. The implication, of course, is that white culture is truly necessary, but black culture is not; it is at best a means to an end. In animation, the erasure of a character's race once s/he is accepted into dominant (in America, white) society can be shown literally. One episode of *The Smurfs*, a cartoon about a band of tiny blue men, was clearly based on the ideas of token integration. Gargamel, the evil foe of the benevolent, happy-go-lucky Smurfs, decided to shatter the Smurfs' fraternal harmony by making a female Smurf for whom they would all fight. He duly made Smurfette, an evil creature with rough, shaggy, dark hair and clad in a dark and dingy dress; Papa Smurf, however, saw that her evil was Gargamel's doing, and transformed her into a good woman. The new Smurfette emerged from the spell blonde, wearing a white, lacy dress, high heels, and a string of pearls. She was integrated with a vengeance.

Furthermore, the inclusion of only one black child necessarily puts her or him into a decided numerical minority, often incapable of effectively solving her or his problems. No matter—hordes of benevolent white people are waiting with their hands stretched out to catch and comfort the poor black child. The black child becomes the recipient of charity that is frequently patronizing. This trend of white people solving black people's problems for them is so widespread that it strengthens the belief that these "minority" groups need to be helped or guided.

Black characters, overall, are seldom portrayed realistically enough. Ignorance of circumstance is often a factor in perpetuating racism. An angry black character definitely has some semblance of reality, but the racism s/he reacts to with anger is often missing from the book; the reader can easily be left with the notion that all black people are unjustifiably angry. Someone who has never experienced racism cannot know how truly damaging it can be, but many of these authors seem to expect that knowledge of their youthful audience. Insight into the mind of a black person is not often offered, as it usually is for the white characters. "Too often, we write books about how whites felt about Blacks, how whites treated Blacks and why it was necessary for whites to develop certain attitudes. However, we do not write history books that show how Blacks felt about whites, what Blacks did for the progress of whites, what Blacks did for themselves, and how Black Americans have protested enslavement through today."[21] Do black people, then, think at all? Or is whiteness such a universally accepted state of being that no one questions it at all anymore? The inquisitive child will think of these questions and search in vain for answers.

Many books do not share the same ideals as the books that at least attempted (however well or poorly) to portray black people as the equals of white people. For example, speaking only of a black child's "white eyes" or "white teeth" enforces the belief that whiteness is the best asset s/he possesses. Primitive, backwards black people abound in the realm of children's literature, and misuse of "black slang" often reinforces this image; these authors ignore the fact that many African languages had a richness that was at least the equal of that of English. Illustrations of black people often makes them look like dirty or smudged white people, and the behavior assigned them by some authors does nothing to dispel that horrible notion. In Helen Bannerman's *The Story of Little Black Sambo*, for example, the father, Black Jumbo, sees a pool of butter lying on the ground and scoops it up so that his wife, Black Mumbo, can cook dinner with it.

Bannerman's familial trio (Black Jumbo, Black Mumbo, and Little Black Sambo) has other problems as well; their names are patently ridiculous, for no one would ever name herself or himself thus. A person's true name is what s/he calls herself/himself; labels (such as "black") are false because they are bestowed by outsiders. Bannerman, an Englishwoman living in India, "where black children abound and tigers are everyday affairs," wrote and, "being extremely talented,"[22] also illustrated *The Story of Little Black Sambo*. But not only is her story guilty of portaying black people as dirty and childlike, her illustrations depict thick-lipped, ridiculously dressed, animalistic figures; Black Mumbo looks like a bear in profile, and Little Black Sambo has feet resembling hooves. And yet this book, initially published in 1899, is still remarkably accessible and widely praised; May Lamberton Becker, a prominent critic of children's literature, gave this advice to parents: "I cannot imagine a childhood without it. For it has fun—hilarious, rollicking fun. . . . Never let yourself be misled into getting this blessed book with any other illustrations but the author's: indeed, once you let your child see them, he will 'accept no other.'"[23]

Mary Poppins, another children's "classic," was written in 1934 by P. L. Travers; also widely available, it contains derogatory references and words. Her next book, *Friend Monkey*, is equally discriminatory against Africans. In *Mary Poppins*, Travers included references to the stereotypes associated with African characters ("'Ah bin 'specting you a long time, Mar' Poppins,' [the black woman] said, smiling. 'You bring dem chillun dere into ma li'l house for a slice of watermelon right now. My, but dem's very white babies. You wan' use a li'l bit black boot polish on dem'"),[24] but she insisted that the book was not at all racist, because she herself was not.

Racism, she implied in an interview, is a purely American phenomenon, for she encountered it only there; "'I have no racism in me. I wasn't born with it,'"[25] she told the interviewer. However, when she wrote the novel, she knew no black people; her only experience with them was through *Uncle Remus* and one of her favorite books, *The Story of Little Black Sambo*, which she knew by heart. It is clear that they formed her racist image of black people which she has been unable to dispel, largely because she is unaware of (or refuses to acknowledge) her racism. Travers continues the cycle with her own books and words. When asked why she used the word "picaninny" and left it in the revised (to mitigate its racism) edition, Travers responded, "'To me, even now the word "picaninny" is very pretty. I've used it myself time and time again to children. Not to Black children because life hasn't brought me very much in contact with Black children, but I've used it time and again to small children.'"[26] Furthermore, the "picaninny" is not described as human; "'[i]t [the picaninny] smiled at the children as its Mother spoke.'"[27] Travers refuses to allow for the possibility that her use of the word "picaninny" (defined as "a Negro baby or child: a patronizing or contemptuous term"[28]) to young, non-black children, she is fostering racism in them; teaching a child a derogatory term for another child can lead only to deeply-rooted racism, much like Travers's own. The scene in the book in which Michael steals the compass is equally appalling. Expecting to be punished for his theft, he sees four familiar faces: "'the Eskimo with a spear, the Negro lady with her husband's huge club, the Mandarin with a great curved sword, and the Red Indian with a tomahawk'"[29] whom he befriended earlier that day. But they are now giants, and they loom threateningly, vengefully over the guilty boy; they are close enough that he can feel their breath on his face and see their terrible anger. "This racist nightmare in which Third World people turn—without the slightest provocation—into monsters to punish a white child remains unaltered in the new version of *Mary Poppins*. Viewed as . . . an expression of racist fears of retribution, this scene may make perfect sense; but . . . it is clearly irresponsible to teach children to identify their fears of punishment with Third World people. . . ".[30] Weapon-wielding, personality-shifting characters such as these can scare a child into believing that non-white peoples are not to be trusted.

In Travers's *Friend Monkey* (1971), a deaf black child is left on the riverbank to be eaten by crocodiles; the implication is that black parents are unfeeling and evil. Travers insisted that the incident was based upon truth, but the rest of her story is clearly not. The nadir comes when Stanley Livingston Fan (the deaf African child, rescued by a white woman, and named after two of the British explorers who "conquered" Africa) encounters a monkey that has escaped from the zoo; Travers writes, "The black and the brown hugged each other as though they were long lost brothers.'"[31] Later, as the two play together, onlookers cannot visually differentiate between Stanley and the monkey. The notion that Africans are incorrigibly animalistic (even being raised by a white woman could not truly change what was important about Stanley) is explicit in this work. Travers, however, was correct that she was not born with racism; she was taught effectively by books such as *The Story of Little Black Sambo* to believe in the innate superiority of white people. Her writings alone should be enough proof that children's literature does dramatically influence young minds.

> *Native American stereotyping occurs when particular characteristics are treated as distinguishing Native people from other people. What children learn from these books is: Native people always wear feathers or headdresses; they frequently brandish tomahawks; they live in tipis; the women usually have babies on their backs; the men are fierce and violent; they lurk behind trees; they spend much time dancing on one leg; and their existence is dependent on the proximity of cowboys. Native people are not men, women and children but 'braves,' 'squaws' and 'papooses.'*[32]
>
> *Unlearning "Indian" Stereotypes: A Teaching Unit for Elementary Teachers and Children's Librarians*—Racism and Sexism Resource Center for Educators

While most American "minorities" have been virtually ignored by the author's of widely available children's books, Native Americans are almost ubiquitous in children's literature and other reflections of popular culture. The widespread images of them are patently false, but they were created to justify the more powerful white people's demands for land belonging to the Natives. That these ludicrous images have persisted so long is a tribute to the force of language and its power to persuade.

Many of the "syndromes" that affect the characterization of African-Americans apply to Native Americans as well. The noble savage, the childlike figure, the warrior-brave, the bestial brute, and the sadistic scalp-hunter are all familiar to readers of books featuring Native Americans. But many images belong to the Native Americans alone: the headdress, the tipi, the peace pipe, and the tomahawk; each of these Native symbols is recklessly misused by Native characters in children's literature, because the (non-Native) authors wrote purely for the purpose of entertainment, not education.

One of the major problems Native Americans encounter in characterizations of themselves in children's literature is objectification. Native Americans are portrayed all too often as objects to be counted or defined. Children's dictionaries often define "Indian" as casually as they define "ice cream" or "igloo." But "[n]o other group is similarly treated: the 'I—Indian' is never followed by a 'J—Jew' or a 'P—Puerto Rican.' . . . Rather, the 'I—Indian' co-exists . . . with Insects. . .".[33] Illustrations for these "reference" books necessarily follow the lead of the text, and the "Indian" in the full (and often wildly inaccurate), stereotypical "Indian" attire is frequently shown eating an ice cream cone. What is to prevent a child from believing that all Native Americans existing today wear outdated outfits like the one the illustrator invented? The objectification of Native Americans as illustrated in the verse "Ten Little Indians" has a much more horrifying manifestation; it is important to make children realize that Native Americans are not things to be counted, especially since they are not all alike. The popular children's rhyme "romanticizes the genocidal destruction of Native nations from the time Columbus arrived in the Americas. . . . In order to better understand why many Native people object to this rhyme, consider present-day German youth reciting, 'Ten little, nine little, eight little Jews. . .'. This comparison is significant, since Hitler not only was fascinated by 'cowboys and Indians' as a child, but told associates that his genocidal plans against the Jewish people were molded in part on his admiration of the practices of the United States against Native people, particularly in forcing them onto reservations and starving them."[34] *Hailstones and Halibut Bones,* a children's book of colors, asks what red is, and answers, "Red is an Indian."[35] No other people is thus portrayed in the book. The individuality and humanity of Native peoples is constantly denied.

Objectification often is replaced with animalistic characterizations of Native Americans, especially when contrasted with white people. The image of Indians, stealthily creeping or crawling toward peaceful white settlers, brandishing sharp tomahawks (the better to scalp you with, my dear) and finally uttering fierce warwhoops as they close in for the kill, must be replaced with a more accurate one that reveals that the Native Americans overwhelmingly fought in self-defense, and that the white settlers were often anything but peaceful. "Undoubtedly it is accurate that settlers were threatened by, and afraid of, Indians, but Indians were equally, if not more, threatened by the settlers and they had much more to lose. The history books . . . seldom make it clear that Native Americans in fighting back, were defending their homes and families and were not just being malicious."[36] But the storybooks, even less constrained by the limitations of truth than history books, usually ignore this fact altogether and indulge wantonly in stereotypes and falsehoods.

In *Indian Summer,* Indians inexplicably attack the McCallum household. When the family cleverly burns goose feathers to smoke out the Indian trying to sneak down the chimney, *"Ugh! Ugh!* coughed the Indian."[37] Later, the McCallum boys discover that the Indians took the bells off of their cows; their neighbor, old Mr. Harrod, explains, "'They [the Indians] wanted you to follow the cowbells deep into the woods. Then they could have scalped you a long way from your cabin. That's an old Indian trick.'"[38] However, *Indian Summer* does not make clear the fact that "scalping was not a wide-spread custom among American Indian tribes . . . research shows that it was not a very old practice on the American continent, and was originally confined to an area limited to the eastern United States and the lower St. Lawrence region, excluding New England and much of the Atlantic coast region. . . . 'The spread of the scalping practice over a great part of central and western United States was a direct result of the encouragement in the shape of scalp bounties offered by the colonial and more recent governments'. . . . The Puritans offered rewards for Indian heads. As early as 1641 New Amsterdam (New York City) paid bounties for Indian scalps, as did other colonies."[39] *Indian Summer* names each of the white characters, no matter how minor, but the Native Americans (pictured, of course, with feathered headdresses and tomahawks) remain nameless; continuous anonymity has the effect of denying humanity.

The Matchlock Gun by Walter D. Edmonds was awarded the Newberry Medal for the most distinguished contribution to American literature for children in 1941. Remarkable only for the depth of the author's anti-Native American sentiment, it utilizes several of the common misconceptions about Native Americans. The scalp-bearing Indians once again attack inexplicably, and their bestiality is emphasized: "[t]here were five of them, dark shapes on the road, coming from the brick house. They hardly looked like men, the way they moved. They were trotting, stooped over, first one and then another coming up, like dogs sifting up to the scent of food."[40] The Indians attack a defenseless woman, throwing a tomahawk into her shoulder. The hero of the story, ten-year-old Edward, kills three of the Indians with his great-grandfather's unwieldy gun while his father is away, serving in the militia. "'You've killed more than all the rest of us [the militia men] put together!'"[41] his father's best friend tells young Edward admiringly. Once again, there is no mention of the massacres white settlers unleashed upon the Native Americans to get their land.

The very domestic household of the Dutch settlers, complete with loving young parents, son, and daughter, is presented as the norm by which the Native Americans must be judged, and must, inevitably, be found wanting; the Native Americans as depicted have no close-knit families or circles of friends. In William O'Steele's *Tomahawks and Trouble*, Laird must fight off a brutal Indian attack: "'Laird's fingers tightened on his rifle. It was hard to believe there could be varmints as mean as Indians in this world. He'd heard folks say the only good Indian was a dead Indian, and he believed it.'"[42] Stereotyping of Native Americans (in children's books and on television) is so successful that the following could occur: "St. Louis, Mo., 1976: A white family is telling their five-year-old son about his adopted one-year-old sister's Native American heritage. She is a Winnebago and they tell him about her people and culture. Suddenly he interrupts and nervously asks if his baby sister 'will kill us when she grows up?'"[43]

By incessantly exploiting the traditional symbols of some Native nations and making them apply to all, children's authors are guilty of lumping all Native Americans together into one homogenous group. "Generalized reference to 'the American Indian' or to 'Indian culture' obliterates the enormous diversity of ceremonies, world views, political and social organization, lifestyles, language, and art among the Chickahominy, Navajo, Menominee, Ojibway, Mohawk, Choctaw, Osage, Ute, Hopi and other Native peoples, both in the past as well as today."[44] Many times this ignorant grouping stems from the fact that the accepted word for Native units is "tribe" and not "nation." The divisions between Native peoples are seen as artificial, or even as unimportant; also, few of these writers are willing to acknowledge the richness of the Native cultures. *The Young Riders*, a television drama about riders for the Pony Express, had a Native American man, Gregg Rainwater, in its cast; he was amazed at how ignorant the writers were about Native diversity. He said that they were joining various aspects of different Native cultures to make a hodgepodge culture whose ceremonies and rituals would keep the viewer interested. Rainwater compared this to making a film about Norway and including flamenco dancing, which is patently ludicrous, but if European distinctions are acknowledged, why are Native ones not accorded the same respect? Books such as *Red Fox and His Canoe* ignore even distinctions that common sense can recognize. The protagonist, Red Fox, is an "Indian boy"; "[l]ike all Indian boys, Red Fox had a canoe to go fishing in."[45] But why would the Native Americans who lived in the southwestern part of the United States have canoes? Obviously, they would not need them, nor would they have the resources to build them. By disregarding such basic distinctions, writers once again deny the full humanity of Native peoples.

Another false image this homogeneity projects is that Native cultures were in continual stasis; they never developed past the time Columbus "discovered" America. Jack Forbes rightfully argues, "'. . . it is technically incorrect to speak of "Navaho culture," "Quechan culture," or "Sioux culture" without a reference to a particular time period unless it is fully understood that one is speaking about a fluid, changing "tradition" which has only one basic, unifying element, that is, that it is associated with a particular people. "Navaho culture" before 1000 was very different from that of 1700, which in turn was different from 1890, which in turn was very different from 1960.'"[46]

Another means of dehumanizing Native Americans is "playing Indian," for it ignores not only their differences but also their humanity. Thousands of children's books describe the protagonist dressing up for Halloween or a costume party as an Indian, and usually becoming violent as s/he puts on the feathers and war-paint, while her/his friends dress up as astronauts, doctors, and so on. "There is nothing harmful in children dressing up to play clowns, witches, cowboys, or pilots. These are *roles* that can be taken on by people of any racial, religious or national group. *But being a Native American is not a role.* Native people are human beings with diverse cultures and distinctive national identities. Being Lakota (Sioux), Hopi, Navajo, etc., is an integral aspect of their human condition. To suggest that other people can *become* 'Indian' simply by donning a feather is to trivialize Native peoples' diversity and to assault their humanity."[47]

Even schools often present plays in which religious rituals of Native peoples (once again a hodgepodge) are portrayed. There is often no serious learning of correct Native practices; it is all for fun. No other religion could be thus exploited. Also found in schools is the trend of not mentioning Native Americans in history texts unless their presence was too great an obstacle to America's "manifest destiny." Then "Indian attacks" galore come flying off the page into the young reader's mind; were Native Americans only significant in relation to white people? According to most of American children's literature, the answer (for all "minorities") is an emphatic "yes."

> *Oppression of whatever kind does not go away simply by shutting the door and proclaiming this room as your 'reality' into which the oppressor may not enter. All too often the oppressor holds a duplicate set of keys and the lease on the building as well. Of course, some women may exclude men from most of their personal lives, but they cannot avoid the effects of sexist practices in their public lives.*[48]
>
> The Power and The Word: Language, Power and Change—Roger Andersen quoting Anne Beezer

Women have been consistently oppressed (or at least suppressed) in children's literature, even when the authors are enlightened enough to write in a non-racist manner. The rationalization that boys will not read "girls' books" has led to the virtual imprisonment of female characters in minor, passive roles while boys take the lead; subsequent complaints—often from girls—that these books are boring has caused a further decline in female-oriented works, especially for children. But women are very seldom completely marginalized; that fact alone should indicate that women have power, enough to create a literature of their own.

Too many authors of children's books seem to subscribe to the beliefs set forth in Otto Jaspersen's *Language*. The chapter entitled "The Woman" says, "'Men will certainly with great justice object that there is a danger of the language becoming languid and insipid if we are always to content ourselves with women's expressions . . . the vocabulary of a woman as a rule is much less extensive than that of a man . . . a woman's thought is no sooner formed than uttered.'"[49] Andersen points out that "[t]he problem with this and the work of many other men writers is that it assumes that male language is the norm, while female language is an additional oddity that can be examined along with the language of primitives, foreigners, children, imbeciles and madmen."[50] Often, women are allowed (in literature) no role other than one of secondary importance; in society, many are allowed only one role, that of domestic manager. And while that role is vital to the family, society, and the world, it also feeds into sexist thought patterns. Little girls are trained almost from birth to be passive, caring, self-sacrificing, nurturing, and domestic. Hence, when they grow up and become housewives, their domesticity seems to be an innate part of their nature; they are not truly working as men work: "They ["women's work": cooking , sewing, mothering] demonstrate no special accomplishment, since they come 'naturally.' Men are the real doers."[51]

But despite the fact that women almost inevitably have had to take the backseat, women are still ubiquitous in children's literature; the general ratio in the publishing industry was, for many years, three males for every female. But even women's consistent presence is not a boon if the female characters are reduced to two-dimensional figures in the background. It is important to note that "[s]exism has not resulted in many books with *no* female characters at all, but this is only because of another sexist concept. To leave out the mother would put the father in uncomfortable 'female' roles (while a family without a father would have the woman assuming 'male' responsibilities). Therefore, two women—mom and sis—usually make it into children's books. But they might as well not be there because they only play roles: baking a pie, setting their hair, welcoming Daddy home from work."[52] On the popular and highly influential children's television show *Mr. Rogers' Neighborhood*, viewers were sometimes taken by trolley to the Land of Make-Believe, which was ruled over by King Friday and Queen Tuesday. Queen Tuesday, despite her status and power, uttered (in most episodes) only one line: "Right as usual, King Friday!" What is the lesson to be learned from the queen's behavior?

Books with female protagonists are sorely needed, but only if the girls are as active, creative, and real as many fictional boys are. But compensation is not really what is required of the next generation of writers; books with heroes should not be rewritten so that the hero's name is changed into a girl's name. Books that are truly *about* women, that occur in a female-oriented setting, that demonstrate understanding of the lives and conditions of females, are necessary: ". . . we have no desire to see children's books that would solely help the dominated get a bigger piece of the pie. We don't like the pie, period. We are not interested in seeing certain people win a place in the status quo, the present social structure; we are challenging the structure itself. Very often, for example, the study of 'women's accomplishments' in history has a give-me-more-pie approach and fails to question the very definition of 'accomplishments.' We should not study merely the few women who have overcome sexist barriers, but examine the very standards that have excluded other women's actions from being considered 'accomplishments.'"[53] Society, in short, needs to be dramatically overhauled in order for women to claim what is rightfully theirs.

The roles women usually take in children's books are: mother, sister, sidekick who unwittingly leads the protagonist into trouble, romantic interest, and prize for a brave man. This last, of course, was made prevalent by the most popular form of children's literature, the fairy tale. Typical fairy tales feature a valiant prince and the passive, beautiful girl he will eventually win. He usually frees her from a spell or a place of evil; what is not told, however, is that he liberates her from one form of bondage only to enslave her anew with the shackles of sexism. There is no opportunity for Cinderella, Snow White, Sleeping Beauty, or any of the other heroines to speak their minds; silent for so long, they never recover their capacity for speech and therefore thought. The effects their stories can have is astounding. In her book *Woman Hating*, Andrea Dworkin explicates: "[t]he point is that we have not formed that ancient world—it has formed us. We ingested it as children whole, had its values and consciousness imprinted on our minds as cultural absolutes long before we were in fact men and women. We have taken the fairy tales of childhood with us into maturity, chewed but still lying in the stomach, as real identity. Between Snow White and her heroic prince, our two great fictions, we never did have much of a chance. At some point the Great Divide took place: they (the boys) dreamed of mounting the Great Steed and buying Snow White from the dwarfs: we (the girls) aspired to become that object of every necrophiliac's lust—the innocent, *victimized* Sleeping Beauty, beauteous lump of ultimate, sleeping good. Despite ourselves, sometimes knowing, unwilling, unable to do otherwise, we act out the roles we were taught."[54]

But fairy tales are being reexamined and rewritten. Female protagonists (now "sheroes" instead of "heroines") do not wait for men to ride up and rescue them; they take the initiative and start on the path to self-actualization. Harmony with others, not power over them, is usually the goal of the female protagonist. What were once regarded as flaws are turned into assets by clever and creative women; many sexist staples are questioned thereby. In Jeanne Desy's "The Princess Who Stood On Her Own Two Feet," the Princess's handsome new suitor cannot stand the fact that she is taller than he; in her confusion, she asks her pet why the Prince must be taller: "The dog struggled to explain. 'They think if they're not, they can't . . . train falcons as well. Or something.' Now that he thought for a moment, he didn't know either."[55] The Princess, forced by the Prince to ride sidesaddle, is thrown from her horse. She pretends that her legs are too badly injured for her to walk; seated, she is the same height as the Prince. When the Prince is jealous of her superior intellect (manifested by her witty words), she gives up her voice. The dog, the only being that truly loved her as she was, dies for her sake; the Prince despises him. Then the Princess realizes that she is as much of a person as the Prince, that she has rights as well. She calls off her wedding to the Prince: "'It is not necessarily my duty to sacrifice everything,' the Princess interrupted. 'And I have other duties: a Princess says what she thinks. A Princess stands on her own two feet. A Princess stands tall. And she does not betray those who love her.'"[56] The Princess then meets a man (really the enchanted dog who loved her in his proper human form) who accepts her as she is; he, shorter than she, tells her, "'It is a pleasure to look up to a proud and beautiful lady.'"[57] The Princess's words are the theme of many of the new fairy tales. Women are just as individual and important as men. Even though the tall and wise Princess marries her lover, marriage in these tales is no longer a requirement but an option; the "shero" may choose to wed, or she may choose to stay single, but her individuality is sacrificed in neither case. She is no longer a prize to be won by the prince who can scale a glass mountain. She is a human being with worth and dignity.

Conclusion

Readers seek their reflections in books. For people who find themselves marginalized because of race, religion, ethnicity, class, gender or age, the book as a mirror reaffirms their existence, and confirms the legitimacy of their attempts to be 'decent people' in their own society.[58]

—Emrys Evans, *Reading Against Racism*

The more one uses a term or phrase with unfavorable connotations to describe a certain group of people, the more likely it is that the audience will begin to think of the group in that way. By constantly thinking of the group in a negative fashion, the willingness and ability to recognize that group's humanity diminishes; there is nothing left to preclude the utter destruction of the marginalized group because "[k]nowledge is not just a passive reflection of the world out there, and the ideational function of language is embedded in social practices where some people maintain power over others."[59] Language and values are inextricably linked; the creation of new words and a new literature will gradually change the existing imbalance of power and right many wrongs.

Endnotes

1. Judith Viorst, ". . . And Then the Prince Knelt Down and Tried to Put the Glass Slipper on Cinderella's Foot," in *Don't Bet on the Prince: Contemporary Feminist Fairy Tales in North America and England*, edited by Jack Zipes. (New York: Routledge, Chapman and Hall, Inc., 1989).
2. Council on Interracial Books for Children, *Human (and Anti-Human) Values in Children's Books: A Content Rating Instrument for Educators and Concerned Parents*. (New York: Racism and Sexism Resource Center for Educators a division of the Council on Interracial Books for Children, Inc. 1976), 4–5.
3. *Human (and Anti-Human)*, 11.
4. Robert B. Moore, "Racism in the English Language: A Lesson Plan and Study Essay," 5.
5. Lesley Brown (ed.), *The New Shorter Oxford English Dictionary on Historical Principles*. New York: Oxford University Press, 1993.
6. Moore, 6.
7. Moore, 9.
8. Moore, 9.
9. Roger Andersen, *The Power and The Word: Language, Power and Change*. (London: Paladin Grafton Books), p. 88.
10. Andersen, 87.
11. Andersen, 85.
12. Andersen, 185.
13. Andersen, 194.
14. Andersen, 188.
15. Andersen, 191.
16. Andersen, 190.
17. Jack Zipes (ed.), *Don't Bet on the Prince*, xii.
18. Bettye I. Latimer (ed.), "Starting Out Right: Choosing Books About Black People for Young Children." Prepared by the Children's Literature Review Board, 112.
19. Latimer, 129.
20. *Human (and Anti-Human)*, 7.
21. Latimer, 113.
22. Helen Bannerman, *The Story of Little Black Sambo*. (Harper Collins Publishers).
23. May Lamberton Becker, *First Adventures in Reading*, quoted in *The Story of Little Black Sambo*.
24. Albert V. Schwartz, "*Mary Poppins* Revised: An Interview with P. L. Travers" in *Cultural Conformity in Books for Children: Further Readings in Racism*. Donnarae MacCann and Gloria Woodard (eds.) (Metuchen, New Jersey: The Scarecrow Press, Inc., 1977), 136.
25. Schwartz, 138.
26. Schwartz, 135.
27. Schwartz, 136.
28. Joseph H. Friend and David R. Guralnik (eds.), *Webster's New World Dictionary of the American Language*. (Cleveland: The World Publishing Company, 1951).
29. Schwartz, 137.
30. Schwartz, 137.
31. Schwartz, 137.

32. Racism and Sexism Resource Center for Educators, a Division of the Council on Interracial Books for Children, *Unlearning "Indian" Stereotypes: A Teaching Unit for Elementary Teachers and Children's Librarians.* (New York: Racism and Sexism Resource Center for Educators, 1977), 7–8.
33. *Unlearning "Indian" Stereotypes*, 16.
34. *Unlearning "Indian" Stereotypes*, 19.
35. Mary O'Neill, *Hailstones and Halibut Bones: Adventures in Color.* Garden City, (New York: Doubleday & Company, Inc., 1961), 44.
36. Mary Gloyne Byler, "American Indian Authors for Young Readers" in *Cultural Conformity*, 33.
37. F. N. Monjo, *Indian Summer.* (New York: Harper & Row, Publishers, 1968), 41.
38. Monjo, 57.
39. Byler, 34.
40. Walter D. Edmonds, *The Matchlock Gun.* (New York: Dodd, Mead & Company, 1941), 39.
41. Edmonds, 50.
42. *Unlearning "Indian" Stereotypes*, 37.
43. *Unlearning "Indian" Stereotypes*, 5.
44. *Unlearning "Indian" Stereotypes*, 6.
45. Nathaniel Benchley, *Red Fox and His Canoe.* (New York: Harper & Row, Publishers, 1964).
46. *Unlearning "Indian" Stereotypes*, 6.
47. *Unlearning "Indian" Stereotypes*, 13.
48. Andersen, 207.
49. Andersen, 196.
50. Andersen, 197.
51. *Human (and Anti-Human)*, 12.
52. *Human (and Anti-Human)*, 13–14.
53. *Human (and Anti-Human)*, 2.
54. Zipes, 5.
55. Jeanne Desy, "The Princess Who Stood On Her Own Two Feet," in *Don't Bet on the Prince*, 41.
56. Desy, 46.
57. Desy, 47.
58. Emrys Evans (ed.), *Reading Against Racism*, 19.
59. Andersen, 91.

References

Andersen, Vicki. (1994). *Cultures Outside the United States in Fiction: A Guide to 2,875 Books for Librarians and Teachers, K–9.* Jefferson, McFarland & Company, Inc.
Balibar, Etienne. (1991). *Race, Nation, Class: Ambiguous Identities.* London: Verso.
Bannerman, Helen. *The Story of Little Black Sambo.* New York: Harper Collins Publishers.
Barnett, Louise K. (1975). *The Ignoble Savage: American Literary Racism, 1790–1890.* Westport, CT: Greenwood Press.
Barthelemy, Anthony Gerard. (1987). *Black Face, Maligned Race: The Representation of Blacks in English Drama from Shakespeare to Southerne.* Baton Rouge: La State University Press.
Bate, Barbara Ann. (1976). *A Rhetorical Approach to the Nonsexist Language Controversy: An Exploratory Study Using Interviews with Selected University Faculty.* Thesis.
Benchley, Nathaniel. (1964). *Red Fox and His Canoe.* New York: Harper & Row, Publishers.
Bettelheim, Bruno. (1977). *The Uses of Enchantment: The Meaning and Importance of Fairy Tales.* New York: Alfred A. Knopf, Inc.
Bibliography of Nonsexist Supplementary Books (K–12). (1984). Phoenix, AZ: Oryx Press.
Blauner, Bob. (1992). "Talking Past Each Other," *The American Prospect.* Summer, 1992: n. 10.
Booklist and Subscription Books Bulletin. (1970). *Books for Children: Preschool through Junior High School, 1968–1969.* Chicago: American Library Association.
Caywood, Cynthia L. (ed.) (1987). *Teaching Writing: Pedagogy, Gender, and Equity.* Albany: State University of New York Press.

Cole, Jim. (1990). *Filtering People: Understanding and Confronting Our Prejudices.* Philadelphia: New Society Publishers.

Council on Interracial Books for Children, Racism and Sexism Resource Center for Educators. (1976). *Human (and Anti-Human) Values in Children's Books: A Content Rating Instrument for Educators and Concerned Parents: Guidelines for the Future.* New York: The Center.

Craig, Terrence L. (1987). *Racial Attitudes in English-Canadian Fiction, 1905–1980.* Waterloo, Ontario, Canada: Wilfrid Laurier University Press.

Davis, James E. (1990). *Dealing with Censorship.* Urbana, Il: National Council of Teachers of English.

Dijk, Teun Adreianus van. (1993). *Elite Discourse and Racism.* Newbury Park, CA: Sage Publications.

Dowling, Colette. (1981). *The Cinderella Complex: Woman's Hidden Fear of Independence.* New York: Pocket Books.

Edmonds, Walter D. (1941). *The Matchlock Gun.* New York: Dodd, Mead & Company.

Essed, Philomena. (1990). *Everyday Racism: Reports from Women of Two Cultures.* Claremont, CA: Hunter House.

Evans, Emrys (ed). (1992). *Reading Against Racism.* Buckingham and Philadelphia: Open University Press.

Fontenot, Chester J. (1979). *Frantz Fanon: Language as the God Gone Astray in the Flesh.* Lincoln, NE: University of Nebraska.

Freedman, Monroe H. and Eric M. (eds). (1995). *Group Defamation and Freedom of Speech: The Relationship Between Language and Violence.* Westport, CT: Greenwood Press.

Gates, Henry Louis. (1994). *Speaking of Race, Speaking of Sex: Hate Speech, Civil Rights, and Civil Liberties.* New York: New York University Press.

Gilligan, Carol. (1982). *In a Different Voice: Psychological Theory and Women's Development.* Cambridge, MA: Harvard University Press.

Gillespie, John T. (ed). (1991). *Best Books for Junior High Readers.* New Providence, NJ: R. R. Bowker.

Gounard, Jean-François. (1992). *The Racial Problem in the Works of Richard Wright and James Baldwin.* Westport, CT: Greenwood Press.

Gunderson, Doris Virginia. *Sexism in Reading Materials.* Cassette #598 (Alexander Library, Rutgers University, New Brunswick, NJ).

Harris, Joel Chandler. (1948). *The Favorite Uncle Remus.* Boston: Houghton Mifflin Company.

Haupt, Carol Magdalene. (1984). *The Image of the American Indian Female in the Biographical Literature and Social Studies Textbooks of the Elementary Schools.* Thesis, 1984.

Herrmann, Claudine. (1989). *The Tongue Snatchers.* Lincoln, NE: University of Nebraska Press.

Hirsch, S. Carl. (1972). *The Riddle of Racism.* New York: Viking Press.

Jones, Eugene H. (1988). *Native Americans as Shown on the Stage 1753–1916.* Metuchen, NJ: Scarecrow Press.

Klein, Gillian. (1985). *Reading into Racism: Bias in Children's Literature and Learning Materials.* London: Routledge & Kegan Paul.

Kristeva, Julia. (1993). *Nations without Nationalism.* New York: Columbia University Press.

Lang, Andrew (ed). (1978). *Blue Fairy Book.* New York: The Viking Press.

Langone, John. (1993). *Spreading Poison: A Book About Racism and Prejudice.* Boston: Little, Brown and Company.

Leonard, J. S. (1992). *Satire or Evasion? Black Perspectives on Huckleberry Finn.* Durham, NC: Duke University Press.

MacCann, Donnarae. (1977). *Cultural Conformity in Books for Children: Further Readings in Racism.* Metuchen, NJ: Scarecrow Press.

MacCann, Donnarae. (1980). *Black Americans in Books for Children.* Metuchen, NJ: Scarecrow Press.

MacKinnon, Catharine A. (1993). *Only Words.* Cambridge, Ma: Harvard University Press.

Maggio, Rosalie. (1991). *The Dictionary of Bias-Free Usage: A Guide to Nondiscriminatory Language.* Phoenix, AZ: Oryx Press.

McConnell-Ginet, Sally, Ruth Borker, and Nelly Furman (eds). (1980). *Women and Language in Literature and Society.* NY: Praeger Publishers.

McPhail, Mark Lawrence. (1994). *The Rhetoric of Racism.* Lanham, MD: University Press of America.

Miller, Casey. (1976). *Words and Women.* Garden City, NY: Anchor Press.

Monjo, F. N. (1968). *Indian Summer.* New York: Harper & Row, Publishers.

Moore, Robert B. (1976). *Racism in the English Language: A Lesson Plan and Study Essay.* New York: The Racism and Sexism Resource Center for Educators.

Nielsen, Aldon Lynn. (1988). *Reading Race: White American Poets and the Racial Discourse in the Twentieth Century.* Athens, GA: University of Georgia Press.

O'Neill, Mary. (1961). *Hailstones and Halibut Bones: Adventures in Color.* Garden City, NY: Doubleday & Company, Inc.

Pascoe, Elaine. (1985). *Racial Prejudice: Issues in American History.* New York: Franklin Watts.

Philip, Marlene Nourbese. (1992). *Frontiers: Selected Essays and Writings on Racism and Culture, 1984–1992.* Stratford, Ontario, Canada: Mercury Press.

Racism and Sexism Resource Center for Educators, A Division of The Council on Interracial Books for Children. (1977). *Unlearning "Indian" Stereotypes: A Teaching Unit for Elementary Teachers and Children's Librarians.* New York: Council on Interracial Books for Children.

Robinson, Forrest G. (1986). *In Bad Faith: The Dynamics of Deception in Mark Twain's America.* Cambridge, MA: Harvard University Press.

Smith, Tom W. (1992). "Changing Racial Labels," *Public Opinion Quarterly* Winter 1992: v. 56.

Smitherman-Donaldson, Geneva (ed). (1988). *Discourse and Discrimination.* Detroit: Wayne State University Press.

Stevenson, Robert Louis. (1905). *A Child's Garden of Verses.* New York: Charles Scribner's Sons.

Vetterling-Braggin, Mary (ed). (1981). *Sexist Language: A Modern Philosophical Analysis.* Totowa, NJ: Rowman and Littlefield.

Wetherell, Margaret. (1992). *Mapping the Language of Racism: Discourse and the Legitimation of Exploitation.* New York: Columbia University Press.

Williamson, Judith. (1986). "Woman Is an Island: Femininity and Colonization" *Studies in Entertainment: Critical Approaches to Mass Cultures,* ed. Tania Modleski. Bloomington, IN: Indiana University Press.

Wilson, J. *Multimedia Guide to Non-Racist Children's Literature.*

Wright, Nathan. (1970). *Let's Face Racism.* Camden, NJ: T. Nelson.

Young, Joseph A. (1989). *Black Novelist as White Racist.* New York: Greenwood Press.

Zipes, Jack (ed). (1987). *Don't Bet on the Prince: Contemporary Feminist Fairy Tales in North America and England.* NY: Routledge, Chapman and Hall, Inc.

Chapter 7

Columbus and the Making of American Identity

James W. Reed

Christopher Columbus is an extremely obscure person, since the details of his life have mostly been lost. Nevertheless, Columbus is still an important figure because he represents events that transcend his own personal biography. Columbus' enterprise ought to be situated within the context of his time, which is early modern European history. Columbus, who emerged on the stage fairly early during the expansion of Europe, is one of 500 to 600 important figures in the development of the modern world system. He was one of the many blue water sailors who were learning how to travel on the Atlantic Ocean and were gradually "discovering" the islands and lands that border the Atlantic.

I am of the opinion that Columbus was part of the historical context of exploration and conquest along the Mediterranean coast and down the coast of West Africa that was going on for a hundred years or more. I like very much the arguments advanced by Alfred Crosby in his book, *Ecological Imperialism: The Biological Expansion of Europe*, where he argues that the discovery and conquest of the Canary Islands was a prototype for European imperialism. Crosby demonstrates that the experience of the Canary Islands is very similar to the story of the Caribbean. There were approximately 80,000 inhabitants in the Canary Islands prior to European conquest of these islands with cultures very similar to those of the peoples in the Americas. The Spanish explored and eventually conquered the islands. Ecological disasters followed the arrival of the Spanish. Disease played a major role in the conquest of the natives, giving Europeans the ability to use certain kinds of technology to their advantage, especially horses ridden by armed men. These events have to be seen in the context of a need to gather things that were of great value in Europe and the search for an alternative sea route to the wealth of the East.

Let us now turn to the relationship between Columbus and American culture. Most Americans don't know or have forgotten that at one time, Roman Catholics were regarded as a subversive minority in American society, a clear threat to the integrity of American Republican culture. In the early 19th century, Americans believed that freedom was associated with the Protestant religion, and they also thought it was associated with a particular ethnic group. They created the myth of an Anglo-Saxon race that had become Protestant and had developed Republican values. To them, the history of the United States was the expansion of this great Anglo-Saxon Protestant culture across North America and then across the world. Then large numbers of Roman Catholic immigrants, fleeing from their troubles in Ireland and Germany, started showing up in the United States and later, the Southern Germans came. The Protestants were extremely upset and some of the most important and interesting episodes in the history of ethnic bigotry and nativism in America involved, on the one hand, Protestants organizing to drive away the Catholics or minimize their influence, and the Catholics counter-attacking on the other hand. When the Irish came, the majority of Americans hoped they would just die or go away, but they remained. The Irish survived and Americans learned that they had to live with one another.

This was not a particularly attractive choice, but they simply learned that co-existence was the way. In the process, American Catholics wanted to prove their patriotism to this country and did so by fighting in the Civil War. During the Civil War, Harvard University gave the Archbishop of Boston, a Roman Catholic, an honorary degree. This was a gesture of reconciliation between the Protestant and Catholic cultures in recognition of the fact that the Irish enlisted in large numbers in the Union Army and fought heroically. Thus, they were slowly, but not completely, accepted by the Yankees. During this process, Catholics who wanted to be part of American culture worked very hard to create symbols that portrayed them as good Americans, and one of these symbols was Columbus. The Knights of Columbus was established in the late 19th century by Jesuits and other Catholic leaders, almost all of whom were Irish, who were looking for a Roman Catholic who could be seen as a great American, who came before the Puritans, and who came before all those great English Protestants. Thus, they celebrated Columbus as the great man who introduced Christianity to the Americas, although they knew very little about Columbus. At that time, it wasn't very important to them that Columbus was an Italian, although later it became an important issue. What mattered to them was that he came before the English-speaking people and was a symbol of Christianity, which they wanted to emphasize as the common characteristic of the Protestants and Catholics. It was important to them to show that Christianity was the American Way, not Protestantism. This was a good way to overcome a long history of bigotry and hostility towards Roman Catholics and, at that time, it was successful. Long before Columbus Day was made a national holiday, individual states began adopting it as a holiday, and surprisingly, the first state to do it was Colorado in 1907 because there was an Italian-American there who had enough political influence to get this issue on the docket. In 1908, the New York State Legislature voted to make Columbus Day a holiday, but it was vetoed by Governor Charles Evans Hughes, the high WASP, who said that a state holiday cannot be trivialized like this. However, Big Jim Sullivan, a state senator representing the Italian district in New York City, led an override, which eventually passed over the Governor's veto.

Thus, Columbus Day became a holiday in New York State and, during the period before World War I, state after state recognized Columbus Day as a holiday. To me, this is a symbol of the acculturation of Roman Catholics, their arrival in American culture, and their ability to demand that they be recognized and given a place. Soon afterward, Roman Catholics began to occupy positions such as district attorney, state legislator, and soon aspired to higher office. When did Columbus Day become a national holiday? It is no coincidence that it took place in the 1930s under Franklin Roosevelt. What is the symbolic meaning of that proclamation? Essentially, it meant that the Democratic Party became the majority party over the Republicans because they recognized the importance of the ethnic votes of the Eastern and Southern Europeans. So Democrats began to play to this vote. They began to give patronage to Italians, Jews, Poles, and others.

Incidentally, it is ironic that just as Americans were beginning to accept that Columbus was a great hero because he introduced Christianity to the Western Hemisphere, the Jews began arriving in America in large numbers. A similar story unfolds: Americans wished they would go away, treated them very badly, but the Jews persisted, survived, and were eventually accommodated. Gradually mainstream politicians stopped talking about America as a Christian society. They increasingly talked about the Judeo-Christian tradition in order to be inclusive. I would submit to you that anyone who is staking his or her political future today on some kind of litmus test of allegiance to the Judeo-Christian tradition will not have a great future in American politics. Today, this tradition is played down because, as you know, it is no longer adequate to encompass all the groups in America today. It has become very clear that today's Americans can only be brought together under an umbrella that is greater than Christianity or the Judeo-Christian tradition.

Chapter 8

The Legacy of 1492

Janice Warner

I think as I was growing up, I would not have expected to see some of the headlines that are in today's papers. One of my friends, who is a teacher, gave me a *Weekly Reader* that said "In the past century, most people saw Columbus as a super hero. Today, people realize that while Columbus was a brave, endearing man, he was dishonest and dealt in slavery, which was common and accepted in the 15th century." Even on the advertising page, *The New York Times* said, "Columbus' voyage is a hard sell after five hundred years. This time, Columbus readers seem to have fallen off the edge of the earth. There were expectations a year or two ago that the hoopla over the 500th anniversary of his arrival would be so wide spread, it would be inescapable. Instead, as Americans hedge into this Columbus Day weekend, one must search as assiduously as any explorer to find promotion or advertising with Columbus themes."

I think it has been a year when maybe Americans have discovered the real Columbus, which partly may have been due to the publication of some of his logs. He didn't have a tape recorder to get him into trouble, but in his logs, he recorded, "How well-formed and muscular were the men and women who he first encountered in this country, with no bellies and good teeth." He noted, too, "What good servants they would make, reminding King Ferdinand that slavery had been justified historically many times." He wrote in his log, "Many other times, this has already happened to men who were brought from Ghana." He thought "these men would make excellent servants" and speculated that "a few Spanish soldiers could easily capture them because they were naked and didn't possess weapons nor knew how to use them and thus very well-fitted to be governed and set to work to till the land and do whatever was necessary. They may also be taught to build houses and wear clothes and adopt our customs. With fifty men, all could be subdued and made to do what is desired." He also noted what a beautiful country this was, how healthy the people looked, how well they treated the Spanish, and then made the conclusion that they would make good slaves. I know that if I found new lands that were beautiful and people who were healthy, I would figure that maybe they knew something unknown to me and try to learn from them. Columbus and his men did not realize or did not want to realize that they came to a land that had many rich cultures and civilizations, with advanced techniques of agriculture, much knowledge of medicine, and a much healthier group of people than those who lived in the dirty cities of Europe. They even had universities throughout South America. All of this was negated when they were labeled as savages, primitive, and sub-human. Of course it is very helpful to label people in order to justify one's actions toward them, like taking their land.

One hundred years ago, on the 400th anniversary of Columbus Day, there was a huge hoopla in this country that was centered in Chicago, called the World Columbian Exposition. It was a huge World's Fair that brought the President, the Cabinet, and dignitaries from all over the world to celebrate the civilization brought to this country by Columbus. Statues of Columbus were erected everywhere during this time. Missing from these festivities was any thought or mention of Native American cultures. Native Americans began working over 5 years ago to make certain that things would be different this year and that we do not repeat what happened in Chicago.

In 1990, Native Americans from North America, South America, and the Caribbean met in Ecuador at one of their first international meetings. The theme of the conference was "Five Hundred Years of Indigenous Resistance." The group committed itself to international solidarity in confronting the quincentennial of

Columbus' arrival in the Americas. If one reads Native American newspapers, one will notice that there is much inclusion of news from the various indigenous populations of the Americas. Native Americans thought of 1992 primarily as an opportunity to mobilize North American Indian communities for long-range, constructive, political action. An example of this is in Minnesota where native Americans are raising funds, pursuing legal strategies, and employing the media in their campaign to recover tribal lands that federal, state, and county governments currently hold. A number of Native American groups have organized around issues of religious freedom, protection of sacred sites, and economic development.

The Columbuses of our day still exist. Native Americans are still having trouble getting to their religious sites to practice their religion because modern bureaucrats are not allowing them into the sacred areas. Modern roads are being built through traditional Indian sites of worship. We have changed its forms, but the prejudice toward Native American religion still exists. A year ago, some of the traditional leaders were able to work out informal arrangements with federal agencies to allow access to these places, but the new generation of bureaucrats are more difficult to deal with. In many parts of South America, there are traditional tribal groups that are still not affected by modern civilization. Most of their lands are still being taken away these days. In Brazil, just in the last six months, these lands were raided and the natives were killed.

The difference now is that news of these events gets out, but still, governments in many parts of South America are not receptive to the Native American's rights or needs. I think what is important now in the discussion of Columbus Day is how we are treating people of different cultures today. It is easy to look back and criticize Columbus for his prejudice and slavery, but how do we treat other people from other countries today? Do we value their cultures and learn something from them, or do we make fun of them and negate their cultures? If that is our attitude, then we have accepted Columbus and what he represents. Is there a Columbus in us?

Chapter 9

Scientific Racism and the Culture Wars:
A Talk with James Reed

Edward Ramsamy

Since its publication, phenomenal attention has been given to *The Bell Curve*. Written in 1994 by Richard J. Herrnstein and Charles Murray, this book revisits the disputes surrounding race, class, and intelligence that have raged for over a century, through a revised theory of biological determinism: that social and economic differences among different races, classes, and sexes are a result of inherited, inborn distinctions that reflect differences in biology. The authors use this argument to assert that there exists "a decisive correlation between a high incidence of social problems and the low intelligence of those who suffer from them."

The viewpoints presented in *The Bell Curve* echo in many ways of "Social Darwinism," a 19th century theory of class stratification that claimed the existence in industrial society of a genetically inferior poor underclass. In the authors' own words, the purpose of *The Bell Curve* is "to reveal the dramatic transformation that is currently in process in American society that has created a new kind of class structure led by a 'cognitive elite,' itself a result of concentration and self-selection in those social pools well endowed with cognitive abilities. This transformation, sadly, has its opposite: the perpetuation of a class of people deficient in these endowments and abilities and increasingly doomed to labor, if they find any work at all, outside the information economy."

James Reed is former dean of Rutgers College, professor of history at Rutgers, and a leading historian on the American birth control movement. In the following, he discusses how this reopening of the debate over group intelligence reflects the historical and political moment in which we live, a moment of unprecedented attack on social programs and the welfare state. He shares his views on how scientific racism has been used to justify the status quo in the United States.

Reed also criticizes the view propagated in the *Bell Curve*, that educational standards have declined since the 1960s. What has caused the sudden panic among certain intellectual circles who have accused American institutions of "dumbing down"? He explores possible answers to this question, and raises yet others: What were some of the political or socioeconomic agendas behind the opening of institutions of higher education to Blacks and women?

Reed addresses these issues and others pertaining to the multiculturalism and racial pluralism of American society. His optimism and faith in the ability of Americans to overcome the realities of bigotry and injustice are as refreshing as they are insightful—in the interview, Professor Reed shares his thoughts on these topics.

Ramsamy: Why is there a receptive ear today to the arguments advanced by Murray and Herrnstein that intelligence is mostly inherited, immutable, and distributed unequally among various ethnic groups?

Reed: The tradition of linking socio-political inequality to biological factors goes back further than Galton. Stephen Jay Gould, in his book *The Mismeasure of Man,* has a long section on the American school of ethnographers in the 19th century who tried to prove that there is a racial hierarchy based on differences in cranial capacity. They collected skulls of different groups of people, and tried to show that Anglo-Saxon skulls held more material than other skulls. Gould demonstrated in his book that the data was fabricated. Even by their own standards, they did not prove their case.

The reason this tradition of work exists is that our society depends upon a rigid hierarchy in which great numbers of people are degraded so that a privileged minority can enjoy the benefits. Of course, these privileged are often ethical and good people who are deeply concerned about the degradation of others. They would be disturbed if it turned out that this hierarchy was humanly created. So they comfort and assure themselves that there is really nothing wrong in our society. It is just a reflection of nature, not something that is socially constructed or capable of change.

For me, the beginning point of any discussion of this sort is W. E. B. Du Bois. Du Bois, a Harvard man and a Yankee, went south to Atlanta to teach. When he arrived there, he saw things that were unacceptable to him, such as the fingers of lynched Black men displayed in shop windows. He knew many good White people in Atlanta—fellow educators, ministers, industrialists. Some of these people were even kind to him. What Du Bois could not understand was how these good White people could accept the systematic degradation of masses of his people. In one of his autobiographical essays, he notes that when he saw those fingers, he realized that people can ignore almost anything as long as it does not intrude on their own personal lives and fundamental interests.

The Bell Curve is part of a long history of racial thinking and science. It is part of the process by which White people have convinced themselves that they are not part of an evil conspiracy, process, or system that must be changed. It is no accident that *The Bell Curve* appears at a time when the welfare state is under attack. The welfare state was constructed during the New Deal in the 1930s and escalated rapidly in the 1960s. This trend actually continued into the Nixon years. This social safety net has come under attack by those who believe that our society really is a meritocracy.

Charles Murray's first pot-boiler book tried to demonstrate that aid programs to women with dependent children encourage illegitimacy and really do not save anyone from anything. If anything, they made matters worse, according to Murray. The people to whom Murray speaks desperately want to believe that our problems are caused either by nature or these social welfare programs. We know that in reality, these programs don't eat up the resources as people like Murray claim. They are such a small part of our budget. Even if these programs are abolished, we will still be in a mess; the middle classes would then have to start looking at some of their own welfare programs.

Ramsamy: What are the backgrounds of Herrnstein and Murray?

Reed: Herrnstein was a behaviorist by training. He was one of B. F. Skinner's students at Harvard. He was an expert on operant conditioning and learning in animals, not in the area of intelligence testing in people. Skinner himself believed that the world could be transformed if the environment of human beings could be transformed. I see some irony in that an individual trained in behavioralism under Skinner got involved with genetic determinism. The concerns of *The Bell Curve* were a sideline for Herrnstein, but he invested a lot of time, emotion, and energy and believed deeply in the operational definition of intelligence, X. He devoted his life to the worship of X and to proving that X was real. I think it was a waste of his intellectual ability. That work is puerile; there are other scholars at Harvard who have demonstrated at great length that there were fundamental errors in his "scientific method" that Herrnstein should have been able to avoid. For instance, the population biologist Richard Lewontin has devoted serious attention to this issue.

Charles Murray, on the other hand, is one of those opportunistic (perhaps well meaning—I don't know) persons who in time will be characterized as a dupe of the society in which he lived. This man is either intellectually mediocre himself, or simply an intellectual whore; I don't know what the judgment will be. I don't know of any good thing that Murray has done that would give him a claim on our sympathy. He is certainly not a scholar; he works in a think-tank dedicated to assuring low-brow suburbanites that they shouldn't have to pay for the welfare state and that only their concerns are important. That is my reading of him. Murray stands on the shoulders of better intellectuals, including Herrnstein, who had earned a reputation as a scholar in the narrow, technical field of conditioning animals.

In their book, Herrnstein and Murray cited suspicious works to support their arguments. They used the works of outspoken racists in an indiscriminate way and disguised what they were doing. One of the articles that impressed me was a review by Charles Lane in *The New York Review of Books* on the tainted sources of *The Bell Curve*. Lane shows just how shoddy *The Bell Curve's* scholarship is. The sources used in *The Bell Curve* are militant defenders of a very hard brand of scientific racism. Many of them defended apartheid in South Africa.

Ramsamy: How should a university accommodate divergent viewpoints on the issues of heritability and intelligence?

Reed: I don't think there is an easy way to resolve this dilemma. All curriculum reform is local. Grand plans that come from on high don't translate very well into action. You have to hire good people for whom learning is a calling and a vocation and then hope for the best. I don't think that the university is a place where anyone should be denied a forum. The best model we have is that the university is a marketplace of ideas. Much of intellectual progress comes from an outright war of ideas between people. The good news is that it is a war of words, not a war of clubs and rocks.

The people who say that they want relief from the Charles Murrays of the world have to understand that the university cannot give them that relief. The fact of the matter is that the future is undetermined, and it is going to be decided by struggle. I am an optimist, and I think that the human race has a decent chance. We can't really protect people from the fact that they live in a competitive society, where competition often takes on the form of unfair practices like racism. You fight this by getting your act together and having faith. And it wouldn't hurt to have some luck sometimes.

The trouble with all of this, however, is that if people want to understand these issues, they will have to invest a lot of time and libido and read a lot of boring stuff. For years I taught a course on the IQ controversy. I quit because I was tired of it. I hated having to work through Jensen. If you're going to teach a course on the IQ controversy, you are going to have to assign Jensen's article in the *Harvard Educational Review*. There's no way around it. This is the article which said that "Head Start" cannot work and that compensatory education will fail. If you want to deal with this issue you will have to read 120 pages of dense argument. No one enjoys this. If you are motivated to understand and refute scientific racism, you will have to do it.

While I am open to discussion about human differences, and what we can and cannot learn from multivariate factor analysis of all kinds of social trends, I don't think this body of literature has anything to do with "nature" *per se*. It has to do with the rationalization of social prejudices that are essential to social order. William Tucker's book, *The Science and Politics of Racial Research*, is a good summary of what I would regard a reasonable position on this issue. According to Tucker, "the truth is that although the war is waged with scientific weapons, the goal has always been political. Indeed, the debate has no strictly scientific purpose or value. The question of genetic differences between races did not arise purely out of scientific curiosity, or to solve some significant scientific problem; it arose only because of the belief, explicit or implicit, that the answer has political consequences." I think Tucker is correct on this point.

Another book that I like is a work by Raymond Francher, titled *The Intelligence Men: Makers of the IQ Controversy*. Francher tries to be fair; he recognizes the contributions that some of these characters have made, like Galton. According to him, the bell curve is a powerful and useful statistical tool, although many of the men who developed it were bent on showing the power of hereditary factors. It can be useful if it can be removed from its political origins. People like Lewis Terman sometimes did good things with it. Terman was a big defender of the rights of highly precocious children. If you have been through public schools, as I have, you know that exceptionally smart kids are at risk. They are a tiny minority who are savagely repressed by their peers. Terman was the champion of identifying these kids and giving them the support they need in order to achieve as much as they can. Terman did this multi-generational study of smart kids and showed that they were not "geeks"; they were healthier than other children. He said that we could predict success in these instances but that these bright kids needed special attention. Therefore, some people working within the Galtonian tradition did produce some good stuff.

Ramsamy: The section on education in *The Bell Curve* echoes the position held by Alan Bloom and others, that institutions of higher education are "dumbing down." What are your thoughts on this?

Reed: Historically, the American university was non-selective until the 1920s. Harvard, Stanford, and so on admitted people who could pay. They took the children of graduates, people aspiring to certain professions, and people who could pay their tuition. Sometimes they let in a few poor boys when they had no one to fill the slots. America in the 19th and early 20th century was a profoundly business-oriented culture in which there was great hostility to abstract learning. So you can't "dumb down" American schools, because they were "dumb" to begin with. In 1900 they were filled with "dumb boys" who were there not because they wanted an education but because they were supposed to do it and could afford it. They spent most of their time in student life, fraternities, athletics, rituals, and things of that nature. Michael Moffatt does a wonderful job documenting this in his *Rutgers Picture Book*. American schools became selective in the 1920s, only because they were very concerned that pretty soon their student bodies would become 95% Jewish, which they wanted to avoid.

The hysteria of "dumbing down" had to do with the paralysis of the lower middle class. People who have no capital can only give education to their children. Those are the people whose interests are most often sacrificed by affirmative action programs. However, we blame the people below us for this situation, not the people above us who created it in the first place. It is much easier for us to get angry at the relatively powerless people below us than to take on the people above who can hurt us if their positions are challenged.

I think the notion of "dumbing down" is silly. What happened was an enormous expansion of admission to higher education. This was America's answer to all the contradictions of our class system: "We may be unequal now, but everybody has a fair chance in the future." Without this opening-up called "dumbing-down," we would not have been able to accommodate our GIs after World War II. There would have been considerable social unrest. After you train someone to use a gun, it's hard to tell him that he has a fixed place in life, and that he has to cheer-up even if he has a dead end job. Our answer to the Civil Rights Movement in the 1960s was to expand educational opportunities for Blacks. Institutions of higher education were opened up because society wanted to avoid the challenges of addressing the socioeconomic disparities in American society. This is what we have to understand before we say universities are dumbing down.

The fact of the matter is, honors theses written today in American liberal arts colleges are certainly equal to or superior to the ones that were written in the 1930s or 1960s. In fact, due to the development of knowledge, it is a lot harder now, in some respects, to write a good thesis. There has been no degradation of higher education but, rather, a tremendous expansion and opening up.

As a result, higher education has assumed many burdens that it is not well fitted for. The university is a socialization agent for half of the youth between 18 and 22 years of age. We try to help them figure out who they are, keep them out of the labor market, and keep them from burning down our cities. This has little to do with the university's function as creator and transmitter of knowledge. Nevertheless, the people that talk about "dumbing down" are the same people that are fervently in favor of our football and basketball programs, all of which have very little to do with the transmission and creation of knowledge. Modern universities are complex institutions that serve many purposes and functions.

We paid Alan Bloom an obscene amount of money to come to Rutgers. Bloom was in love with the 18th century philosophers and the founding fathers, whom he may or may not have read. I don't want to slander a dead man. In a conversation with him, I said, "The Constitution was a covenant with death." He was outraged at this remark. He was foaming at the mouth! He thought I was a crazy radical. What he didn't know was that William Lloyd Garrison said this in the 1800s. Bloom did not understand United States history. Bloom reified these great books and lived in an imaginary world that was satisfying to an aging man alienated from young people who no longer sat at his feet listening to him. So he made up this elaborate story of how Nietzsche has poisoned the wells of learning.

Many people who present themselves as great scholars defending the great books haven't read a lot of books that I think they should read. Alan Bloom did not know who William Lloyd Garrison was, and for me, that is a serious criticism of him. Don't tell me about Montesquieu, Madison, or the Federalist Papers, and then tell me you don't know who Frederick Douglass was. You've read Sartre, but you haven't read Richard

Wright. This is not acceptable to me. The leaders of any great university, like Rutgers, need to know who W. E. B. Du Bois was. They need to have read him, and if they haven't, they are at peril and face great difficulty in defending some canon that does not include people who were crucial to the making of our world.

I am willing to defend the Constitution in that it has within it the seeds of its own redemption. The redemption is not complete yet, and it may never be realized, but I look to the future with hope. It is not evil or subversive to say that the Constitution was a covenant with death. Some interests had to be sacrificed so that other interests could flourish. That is a fact. The sooner the Lynn Cheneys and the Alan Blooms of this world get a good education and start doing the tough job of real intellectuals, the better off we will all be.

Ramsamy: Why is the United States so deeply divided on racial lines?

Reed: First, the popular perception of race as phenotypic difference is not scientifically valid. Races are breeding pools that in evolutionary terms are notoriously plastic and flexible. No sophisticated biologist uses race in the way it is used in this debate, as stable categories. However, notions of racial difference have taken on a social and political life that has little to do with genetics.

In American history, racial markers were very important in the stabilization of colonial society. The first English speaking colonies of North America, in the Chesapeake region and in the South, produced the export values that kept everybody going. These successful regions produced the political and social elite that would lead society in the late 18th and early 19th centuries. They developed that way because they were based on slave labor. America was able to have a republic for White men because it had slavery for Black men. Edmund Morgan's work, *American Slavery, American Freedom*, argues that without the mud-sill of slavery, American history may have been different. We might have had a much more authoritarian government. We would not have had the commitment to the Enlightenment and republican values.

There were many crises in this colonial society stemming from the fact that this was a poor man's country. Compared to Europe, poor people in America got land and freedom. When they got land, the poor challenged the authority of rich landowners. Jamestown was burned down in Bacon's rebellion; crops were destroyed, and so on. The west country gentry's utopia was at stake. The solution to this crisis was the creation of a racial caste system that would mitigate class divisions in U.S. society. It wasn't planned that way; it happened over a long period. And it was a hellishly good system for maintaining the consensus among Whites and the stability of the society.

The United States grew, developed, and prospered as the most dynamic market economy in the history of the world because of the bedrock of export values provided by plantation society and slavery. The ruling class at this time were the Whigs, liberals who believed in "equality." What they really meant was the relative equality of White men, but in the context of 19th century history, they were progressive. They spoke about liberal nationalism, which was a radical idea in its time. Compared to the regimes in Europe, they really were at the cutting edge of struggles for popular democracy. However, while we should be aware of the positive side of this equation, we also have to deal with the negative side.

Ramsamy: Why are you optimistic about race relations in America, in spite of the pessimist wave sweeping the country at present?

Reed: I am optimistic because I don't think the future is determined. I don't deny the realities of bigotry and injustice, but as an historian, I am not impressed by arguments that things are worse now than they were in the past. Jim Crow is a 20th century thing. The creation of this insidious system of physical segregation of the races was a response to the populist movement in the South, an effort to create another mud-sill to maintain stability after the abolition of slavery. I have no idea how much further we have to go, but I am not impressed by the idea that things are getting worse. I think we have a fighting chance of making things better.

The United States has a good chance to become a multiracial democracy. I don't know of any others. In other countries you have 20% set aside for one group and 52% for another group, but those are not societies in which people are treated as individuals, the way we would like to be treated. I think some of our ideas have enormous potential and appeal. I am not afraid of the future, although there are no guarantees. When I was a little kid, schools were segregated and Black people were routinely murdered for trying to register to vote. The White kids that I went to school with had rotten teeth and were in miserable health, covered with sores for a good part of the year. Men were shot dead for trying to organize the oil fields.

In my experience, things have gotten better. What people of good will are trying to do in our society is quite audacious and hard to pull off, but I would rather have hope and do my little part than retreat into a self-indulgent pessimism, or let anger become my main oracle. I believe that human beings have a tremendous capacity for cooperation, empathy, and love. I respect the position of those who say we have a long way to go, but I don't think that there is historical evidence to demonstrate that the past was a lot better. I think it would be unbearable for someone from the present to go back and live in the past.

Ramsamy: Why do you believe that the metaphor of the "melting pot" is still appropriate to describe cultural relations in America?

Reed: Well, part of it is empirical fact. Robert E. Park, the man who invented assimilation theory, was George Washington Carver's press agent at the Tuskegee Institute. He was a card-carrying multiculturalist of the first order who was simply trying to figure out what was happening. There is a well-documented process that groups go through in which they are first mistreated and abused. Then they develop a certain amount of economic clout. They become acculturated and are able to survive in the society. Then they develop self-consciousness.

We had a Civil Rights Movement in the 1940s and 1950s because a Black property-owning class emerged which benefitted from New Deal programs. They survived the share cropping system and got their land. The Civil Rights Movement was not about a bunch of northern liberals going down south and shaking things up; rather, it was a mass movement of property-owning Blacks who had reached that point in time when they could fight back. When groups achieve self-consciousness, they challenge the establishment. While society resists, they make incremental gains, which leads to assimilation. It seems that groups which maintain separate identities maintain a separate language as well, which is lost usually within three generations as the group assimilates.

I am not saying that this is a rule that every example fits; rather, most of the examples can be explained through this process. The universal marketplace dissolves these group identities. I don't mean to reify that marketplace, but it is a powerful social force on this planet at present. People get sucked into it. Assimilation is a reality. You can deny it, brow-beat some professor at school and thrash somebody who wrote a book that you don't like, but the fact is that this process is going to continue.

Culture formation is a dynamic process. People who want to capture a cultural moment in order to preserve it in the name of an ethnic group are usually fated to be unhappy. The world is going to change, and people that are getting the most out of their lives are changing with the world. They are learning, growing, and meeting challenges. They are not convinced that the only good music in the world is jazz, for example. At one time, listening to jazz was an act of rebellion. Today it is something everyone ought to be familiar with. You can't know American culture or history without knowing anything about jazz. But if jazz is the end of your world, I'd feel sorry for you, as I would if you thought that 19th century Romantic music was it, and that it all ended after Beethoven. The good news is, there is more to come. A major source of creativity in our society has been marginalized people.

People have to realize that race and ethnicity are not innocent. Bad things are done to individuals in the name of group identity. One reason why I like today's society is that our right to be individuals is respected along with our right to be part of a group. I would like to maintain that in the future. Yet these two things are often at war with one another. I am very glad that I escaped my roots. I go back to survey the ruins and to help my poor relatives who are not competent to function in the modern world, but I don't go back to be sustained. I agree with Richard Wright; the action is in the city and I'm glad I headed north. The ideals of the Enlightenment and the French Revolution are my choice. I believe in life, liberty, and the pursuit of happiness for everyone, not just *herrenvolk* men. However, implementing these ideals will never be easy.

Chapter 10

Representing Blackness:
The "New Negro" Art of the Harlem Renaissance

Kavitha Ramachandran

Introduction

Dating back to the "voyages of discovery," the signifier "Black" at once refers to the visual encounter between Europeans and darker-skinned peoples as well as the condition of economic exploitation and cultural domination resulting from that ongoing relationship. "Black" is simultaneously a White supremacist marker of racial difference as well as a state of consciousness that peoples of various pigmentations have, at different times, experienced, struggled with, and proudly proclaimed. It is the result of an attempt to arrest the multiple meanings of race with a rigid nomenclature based on the visual perception of differences in human phenotypes. Race collapses into a single color the variety of physical characteristics and a range of complexions found in all the human populations of the world. Its myopic gaze identifies "Black" not only as a distinct color, but also as the visual marker of a social and cultural "other." "Black," is the name of the peoples who inhabit the segregated and unequal spaces that characterize both the real and imaginary geographies of the world.

As a social condition arising from a spurious, "biological" definition, "race" involves an ingrained way of thinking that has been difficult to overcome for all those who live with it. Yet, for peoples of African descent, "Blackness" is about more than color; it is simultaneously the metaphor of exclusion and resistance for dispersed people with a common predicament. Africans in the diaspora have had to come to terms with mass subjugation by Europeans under slavery and capitalism. By the beginning of the 20th century, "Black," despite its deep, unstable, and often contradictory meanings, had become a fitting term for a Pan-African, diasporan solidarity that extended from Africa to Europe and across the Atlantic. The aim of this chapter is to interpret the art produced during the New Negro Movement through an understanding of "Blackness," both as a signifier and as a social consciousness, that embraces a range of experiences across national borders, but in historically and geographically specific ways.

The intrinsically hybrid nature of "Blackness" has meant that art and other forms of Black cultural production have always had to wrestle with claims of racial quintessence, from both within the Black communities and without. Reflecting on the deeply problematic nature of 'Blackness,' sociologist Hall (1992) writes that while an understanding of Black popular culture needs to avoid the ideological pitfall of defining "Black" in absolute terms, it should nevertheless acknowledge the strategic necessity of the concept:

> *It is this mark of difference inside forms of popular culture—which are by definition contradictory and which therefore appear as impure, threatened by incorporation or exclusion—that is carried by the signifier "black" in the term "black popular culture." It has come to signify the black community, where these traditions were kept, and whose struggles survive the persistence of the black experience (the historical experience of black people in the diaspora), of the black aesthetic (the distinctive cultural repertories out of which popular representations were made), and of the black counternarratives we have struggled to voice.*

Hall is wary of the often insular and essentialist positions espoused by many Black nationalist activists and thinkers, maintaining that the reality of "Blackness" is not negated by the acknowledgment of its social construction, but, rather, augmented by it.

With roots in earlier, Pan-African-informed political and cultural movements, cultural theorist Gilroy (1993) has revised the idea of "Blackness" and regards Africa's many dispersed peoples as historically grounded yet modern entities, products of socio-political change and cultural self-affirmation in Black communities worldwide. According to Gilroy, the African diaspora moves toward an open-ended, "Black political culture" in the face of European cultural hegemony and Western technocracy. For art historian Thompson (1993), following Gilroy, a "transatlantic" visual tradition indicates that the African diaspora is not so much a monolith as an "infinite process of identity construction." Upon surveying Black art in the 20th century, he argues that multiple worlds of meaning are opened up by a diasporan perspective on art and its role in the social production of Black identities.

When the art of the New Negro Movement is seen in a diasporan frame, it is possible to identify some tensions, both within and between the works. One may ask whether a work of art is intellectually bound by the perceived racial identity of its creator, or whether it speaks for itself as an art object. One may also ask whether it is part of a historical discourse that is limited to a specific national context or one that spans across national boundaries. This chapter will argue that New Negro Art had always contended with these issues, which constitute the socio-political and cultural context in which that art was produced. Specifically, this body of art was a response to the concurrent processes of disfranchisement and physical violence toward Blacks in the United States; the mass migration and urbanization of Black people, as a result of accelerated industrialization, especially to New York City; segregation and other inequalities precipitated by racism and wage labor under capitalism; cultural domination and subordination through artistic and literary tropes that represented the Black "other" as alternatively ridiculous, sensual, and sinister; and an emerging, modern Pan-African consciousness that compelled New Negro artists to engage with their own traditions as well as a broader diasporan discourse. To support that argument, the chapter will examine some art from the Harlem Renaissance and discuss its role as cultural propaganda for "the Race." Some socio-political and cultural circumstances will be explored in order to contextualize New Negro Art within the scopic regime of its time but also to trace the visual ideologies inherent in these works of cultural propaganda. An iconology of these works shows that they were signifiers that collectively constituted a visual argument for a specific course forward in American race relations. In this light, the rhetorical role of New Negro Art may itself be interpreted as a particular response to hostile circumstances, not unlike those experienced in other parts of the diaspora under colonialism and imperialism. Black culture in the United States is informed by West and Central African cultural sensibilities and has in common with other Black diasporan cultures the experience of the Transatlantic Slave Trade. For example, Black styles of religious worship, performance, and verbal, musical, and literary expression find resonance in their diasporan counterparts. Thus, New Negro Art participates in a struggle against racial and cultural discrimination, segregation, disfranchisement, and dehumanization as part of an evolving Pan-African consciousness and resistance.

Contextualizing the New Negro Movement

The early 20th century was an unprecedented time for consciously redefining and creating a new image for Black culture in the United States. It was a period of intense disfranchisement and violence toward Blacks within the United States as well as a period of political and cultural imperialism in other parts of the Black diasporan world. In the American South, lynching became a grotesque "festival of racist violence" for Whites after the Reconstruction, complete with anatomical souvenirs and keepsakes, presented to sweethearts and showcased in homes (Beck and Tolnay, 1995). It was simultaneously a spectator sport and political strategy; it both amused and exalted Whites to "discipline" newly franchised Blacks through murder. In the half-century spanning 1880 through 1930, lynching was nothing less than an all-American pastime, with the number of Black men, women, and children killed in 10 southern states exceeding 2500; in other words, one Black person was murdered nearly every week of every year during that period (Brundage, 1993).

Mass migration also characterized the period. Blacks moved from rural settings in the South to Northern cities that were deep in the throes of industrialization. The Great Migration, which began early in the 20th century, represents for African Americans an exodus from the South in search of independence and freedom from violence, segregation, disfranchisement, and economic bondage. Regardless of the final destination, the significance of the Great Migration is that it transformed African Americans into a predominantly urban people, profoundly changed their cultures, their new urban home base, as well as the national racial consciousness.

In every Northern city, as old racial fears were revived among Whites, the Black migrants found themselves in separate residential areas, facing a severe shortage of services such as housing and health care (Grossman, 1989). However, migration and urbanization also encouraged the development of Black institutions and organizations that served a Black urban population, such as hospitals, banks, and legal services. To the migrant, there were numerous other advantages in the urban ghetto: comparatively higher incomes, a chance to obtain an education, as well as the cultural ambiance of the city. As Black workers were increasingly incorporated into an urban, industrial economy, the nation began to feel their presence in everything from politics and culture to struggles over labor and citizenship (Drake and Cayton, 1993).

New York City was one of the major destinations for Southern Black migrants in search of opportunities in the North, where factories recruited them in large numbers, especially during the years of the Great War when immigration from Europe temporarily abated. Harlem's large and growing Black population numbered about 175,000 in 1925. By 1930, with continued migration from the South and some immigration from the Caribbean and elsewhere from the Black diaspora, Harlem's Black population had expanded to over 200,000, making it the largest African American urban community in the country (Watson, 1995). New arrivals found support for their collective interests among several major Black organizations with headquarters in Harlem, such as the NAACP, the National Urban League, the Universal Negro Improvement Association, as well as scores of churches, social clubs, weekly newspapers, and businesses who had established themselves during the previous two decades (Lewis, 1979). In the words of Locke (1974), a Harlem intellectual, the migrants saw in the ghetto "a spiritual emancipation," a chance for "group expression and self-determination," and an opportunity "to convert a defensive into an offensive position, a handicap into an incentive."

As a destination full of opportunities for immigrants and as a city that thrived on everything extraordinary and new, the reputation and status that New York enjoyed at the turn of the 20th century was increasingly shared with Harlem. Black poet laureate Langston Hughes (1940) first used the phrase "Manhattan's Black Renaissance" in his autobiography to describe the artistic scene whose center of gravity lay in the predominantly African American community of Harlem. However, it is important to note that the "Harlem Renaissance" actually represents only a phase of African American folk life rather than a distinct Harlem topography. While Harlem was extremely important as a cultural center for many African American artists, it was hardly the sole cradle of the New Negro Movement. Other metropolitan centers like Chicago and Philadelphia produced their own counterparts to the Harlem arts scene. Harlem, then, was a racial motif, a literary and artistic conceit that artists and writers drew upon and worked with, a placeless place that became a crucible of Black modernity. The regional connotations of Harlem and hence "Harlem Renaissance" and "New Negro" became incorporated into a metaphoric racial landscape.

The "New Negro" idea was conceived amidst several circumstances. Beginning with the 1919 Palmer Raids, the New Negro Movement's momentum increased in the aftermath of the Raids, named after President Woodrow Wilson's attorney general, A. Mitchell Palmer. The raids were Palmer's solution to what he saw as the cause of a national crisis brought on by strikes and economic unrest: foreign-born, bomb-throwing anarchists, socialists, and communists. Palmer's plan was to simply "terrorize those he could not deport and deport those who, because they were aliens, were *ipso facto* terrorists" (Lewis, 1979). On the whole, the average African American was indifferent toward the Palmer Raids and the "Red Scare" of 1919. Blacks were generally suspicious of and disapproved of socialism as an ideology. In fact, during this time, most Blacks supported bills in Congress that aimed to limit immigration because they naively believed that socialism was an immigrant scheme to insure that Blacks continued to be the "last-hired and first-fired." Blacks also believed that the Red Scare was a White issue exclusively, with the exception of a couple of notable Black socialist labor organizers, Chandler Owen and A. Philip Randolph, who believed otherwise. Nevertheless, there was a fear among Blacks that they would become scapegoats as the government scoured the land for tangible villains. That fear was augmented and justified by the fact that the number of lynchings was rising sharply (Lewis, 1979).

More popular among Blacks than socialism was Black Zionism, or the "Back to Africa" movement, which sought to redefine Africa as a symbol of pride and accomplishment for African peoples. The movement's main vehicle was the Universal Negro Improvement Association (UNIA), founded by the charismatic and visionary Jamaican activist Marcus Garvey. For the racial militants who followed Garvey, the same historical "facts," found everywhere in the diaspora—the shared African origin, the social dissolution which afflicted peoples who underwent the Middle Passage, the futility of universal emancipation, and the socio-economic stagnation resulting from Western imperialism and racism—suggested that the world's African peoples had more in common with one another than with Whites. Such an interpretation created, in its own way, particular stereotypes and perceptions of Black people and their cultures, albeit dramatically different from other representations that existed at that time. Black Harlem was the base from which Garvey ambitiously proposed to repatriate Africa's scattered peoples back to their homeland, demanding "Africa for the Africans." Although Garvey's rhetoric presented images of a despotic Black world (Garvey and UNIA called for Black capitalism and considered themselves the first fascists) its message of Black pride and economic self-sufficiency was embraced by Black communities throughout the northeastern United States and the English-speaking Caribbean (Lewis, 1979).

The prevailing White belief at the time with respect to race, as affirmed by contemporary ethnography, was that the "lowly" status of Black peoples worldwide, and their "primitive" cultures, were "evidence" that the policies of White paternalism and social control were necessary for order and progress. This mentality among Whites always produced certain representations of Blacks. One tendency borrowed from the extremely popular African American performance tradition with its roots in the slave plantations. Parodies of this culture by White "black-face" minstrels in the post-bellum decades spawned a whole industry in comic, music-and-dance-oriented, racist representations of Black people. Characterizations of Blacks as backward, shiftless, ridiculous, childish, criminals, and "coons" dominated European and American theatrical productions, popular literature, advertisements, children's toys, and so on as numerous graphic artists, illustrators, writers, and actors thrived in lucrative careers. Ironically, the Black *vaudeville* performer and composer Ernest Hogan was among the most responsible for popularizing the derogatory word *coon*. His notorious song "All Coons Look Alike to Me" launched the "coon" craze onto the world stage. Years later, Josephine Baker and others would follow in this controversial tradition. In film, D. W. Griffith's scathing portrayal of Blacks in *The Birth of a Nation* (1915) transformed verbal insults into larger-than-life, moving stereotypes for eager and receptive White audiences. Even President Wilson endorsed the film, saying that it was "like writing history with lightning."

In light of these circumstances, Locke (1974) wrote that "neither racial militancy nor socialist nostrums could improve the current conditions of Afro-Americans." Instead, he argued, "the more immediate hope rests in the revaluation by white and black alike of the Negro in terms of his artistic endowments and cultural contributions, past and prospective." James Weldon Johnson (1959), another prominent figure in the movement, shared Locke's view that "nothing will do more to change the mental attitude and raise his status than a demonstration of intellectual parity by the Negro through his production of literature and art." With these aims in mind, they joined forces with other Black intellectuals, like W. E. B. Du Bois, to form and lead the "New Negro Movement"as Black America's Talented Tenth. The movement was their carefully orchestrated effort to place African American social issues at the forefront of the national agenda.

At the time, intellectuals like Du Bois were inspired by the first Pan-African Conference in 1900 and even helped to organize the two subsequent meetings in 1919 and 1924 (Lewis, 1979). The pervasive cultural, economic, and psychological colonization of African peoples worldwide, rampant racism, violence, and genocide were seen as proof that all Black people had certain concerns, fears, aspirations, and values in common. Also, just a few months prior to the Conference, the Exposition Universelle in Paris had attracted many Black visitors to see and take pride in its "American Negro Exhibit." Comprising of various media, the display demonstrated what was possible for an oppressed people, once they had a chance to "do something for themselves." Therefore, the idea to use African American arts and culture as the principal vehicle for promoting "the Race," and "Pan-Africanism" was neither new nor unique to the Harlem Renaissance. It did, however, present an alternative to the racial militancy of Marcus Garvey, who was a great champion of Pan-Africanism in his own right.

The Harlem Renaissance, then, as an elitist response from a small group of educated and affluent African Americans, was literally "made to happen." In other words, it was institutionally encouraged and shaped by the leaders of the Black establishment of Harlem for the stated purpose of improving "race relations" in America. At a time of extreme national reaction to economic gains won by African Americans during the Great War, the elite wished to steer clear of racial militancy, on one hand, and socialism on the other, should Blacks be scapegoated during those unpredictable times (Lewis, 1979). Yet the individuals who conceptualized the movement, made the necessary political and philanthropic connections with wealthy White patrons and humanitarians, scouted out and recruited the artists, and staged the interracial awards banquets, were not vulgar propagandists; their campaign was more sophisticated. The Black literati of Harlem genuinely believed, for a time, that they were promoting a "culture of understanding" between Blacks and Whites that would transform a racist nation. However, Zora Neale Hurston, a major Black author of the period, was not so sure about this alliance between the "Niggerati" and "Negrotarians." (Watson, 1995).

The Art of the Harlem Renaissance

The New Negro Movement in the arts drew extensively upon existing traditions in Black art as a way of demonstrating continuity in the midst of the "new" and the "modern." The work of Henry Ossawa Tanner is part of a tradition that existed before the New Negro Movement, which employed realism in order to represent Black people and everyday life more "truthfully," given the prevailing White assumptions of Black inferiority. The tenets of this school of art are exemplified in Tanner's *The Banjo Lesson* (1893). Most educated Blacks of this period shunned those aspects of Black culture that perpetuated notions of Black servility, reveled in racial jokes and crude images and other derogatory characterizations. To them, these attributes were seen as base reminders of a shameful past that was embarrassing to "the Race." According to literary critic Gates (1988), the Black elite's rejection of the so-called "Old Negro" and their eagerness to embrace the "New Negro" often prevented them from confidently articulating a broader and more subtle African American self. One exception among the conservative Black elite was the sociologist, historian, and activist W. E. B. Du Bois, who introduced cultural metaphors such as a "double consciousness" and "the Veil" through his writings to describe the experiences of inequality, rejection, and racial segregation that could not be denied. Nevertheless, in a climate of ridicule and slander, the African American elite, especially in the Northeast, began to defend itself with literary societies, industrial fairs, and art exhibitions featuring the best creative talents of "the Race" (Lewis, 1979). For example, sculptors Isaac Scott Hathaway and Meta Warrick Fuller waged their own campaigns by creating larger-than-life-size commemorative plaster busts of Black leaders and achievers (Hathaways's *Frederick Douglass*, 1919) or allegorical depictions of history and racial consciousness (Fuller's *The Awakening of Ethiopia*, 1914).

In contrast, representations of Black soldiers reveal the conflict inherent to their position as well as the ambivalence of many artists toward the times. Edwin A. Harleston's portrait of *The Soldier* (1919), proud, Black, brave, but unsettling, conveys the disappointment and disillusionment that African Americans felt about their wartime service. Harleston's soldier expresses the frustration of many for whom the promise of racial equality, symbolized by the triumphant February 1919 parade up Fifth Avenue by the all-Black 369th Regiment, was negated by a wave of lynchings, violence, and riots across America that very year, during what came to be known as the "Red Summer of 1919." Interestingly, the mood is similar 15 years later in Malvin Gray Johnson's *Negro Soldier* (1934).

Although the "New Negro" concept mainly emphasized urbanity, progress, and youth, there is an often-overlooked message of rediscovery, growth, and tradition that informs much of the movement's subject matter, as seen in Doris Ullman's ethereal photograph, *Baptism in River, South Carolina* (1929). According to Campbell (1987), the representational extremes of the "New Negro" are present in two of the period's better known African American portraits. Philadelphia-based artist Laura Wheeler Waring's portrait of *Anna Washington Derry* (1927), the elderly mother of one of her friends, employs a conservative painting style to create a sentimental tribute to a proud Black matriarch. William H. Johnson's *Self Portrait* (1929), on the other hand, is a less nostalgic presentation of the artist as a "New Negro" bohemian. Other portraits from this period include Archibald Motley Jr.'s *Octoroon Girl* (1925), Edgar Eugene Phipps' *Ready for School* (1927), and Lois Mailou Jones' *Negro Youth* (1929).

Art historian Smith (1993) traces the American obsession during the 1920s and 1930s with the creation of modernism as a contemporary aesthetic. It was a sensibility that he described as "polished, efficient, progressive, democratic, and pure," which functioned with "only the newest structures" in mind. Smith's investigation of modernism reveals a deliberate construction of the "modern" out of an American marketplace of ideas and dreams that produced distinct winners and losers. For Black artists and intellectuals, the "Negro Renaisssance" was a new and auspicious moment in American cultural life that presented African Americans with an unprecedented opportunity to fashion their modern selves. For the first time, Blacks had access to, and an active role in, the mass media, the venues of mainstream entertainment, and other cultural institutions, through which they intended to make winners of themselves (Watson, 1995).

For many Whites, on the other hand, the "New Negro" was less of a movement, a moment, or an actual person, than it was a mood, or a sentiment, in which Black culture and its practitioners were seen as an important part of a larger cultural scene of careless abandon. In a society that had recently suffered a world war and was transforming into an impersonal, urban, industry-driven machine, Black culture was viewed as exactly the opposite: it was an antidote for *ennui* as a ubiquitous symptom of the modern world, a sexual escape, a sanctuary for the spiritually seeking. It was a call back to nature, waiting there in Harlem, just a subway ride away. Whites could leave their fast-paced, ordered, modern way of life and plunge into that timeless pool of Black *élan* called Harlem, where every ailment of the body and soul was cured.

A stop-over along this journey that is seldom discussed is the New Negro underworld, where the stereotypically familiar terrain of Black sexuality was surveyed and explored with manifest delight. Josephine Baker, a Black dancer and performer, was the apotheosis of the "primitivist" genre of Black culture popularized by Whites and a few Blacks in the Paris "New Negro" scene. Baker, as a willing subject and participant in this venture, was joined by other cultural primitivists for whom, unfortunately, the peoples and cultures of Africa were the principal objects of caricature. These explorations often took place in the representational space of the Black female body. In Paul Colin's lithograph *Le Tumulte Noir* (1927), Josephine Baker, a Black woman, appears in a cage, like an animal, as if to mock the "Hottentot Venus." A Khoi-San woman from South Africa named Saartjie Baartmann, or "the Hottentot Venus" as she was called, was actually likened to a simian and displayed in a cage before the salon set of Paris in the 18th century. Baartmann eventually ended up on the dissecting table of the esteemed anatomist Georges Cuvier who was finally able to clear up a great mystery of the day: Did she refuse to display her private parts, when touring, because she was indeed concealing a secret sex organ that was fabled among her people? While Josephine Baker did not meet Baartmann's fate, she nevertheless participated in an enterprise that exploited African peoples, did little to dispel the widespread ignorance about Africa, and perpetuated the view of Africans as exotic, passionate, and bestial. The participation of the Black artists and subjects in this mode of representation remains a source of controversy today, nearly four decades after the Civil Rights and Feminist movements.

While some people were still looking for the New Negro as "the primitive," "the noble savage," (see *Feral Benga* or *The African Dancer* by Richmond Barthe, 1935) or "the urban sophisticate," (Samuel Joseph Brown Jr.'s *Smoking My Pipe*, 1934), others had long given up the search and begun to explore socioeconomic issues such as class. By the mid 1920s, as seen in his editorials for *Crisis* magazine, Du Bois became increasingly disillusioned with a sensational and commercial arts scene that was divorced from the day-to-day issues of race solidarity and labor. Du Bois did not denounce the exploration of Black identity in art, but did demand that art, in turn, did not forget the fact that African Americans were "full-fledged Americans, with all the rights of other American citizens" (Lewis, 1979). Even Locke came to believe that the so-called "Renaissance" was succeeded by a "Reformation" of sorts, characterized by "more penetrating," "even handed," and "less illusioned" portrayals of Black life. As if sensing the coming Depression and the dispossession it threatened, the movement's advocates increasingly began to adopt more altruistic icons of "the people," "the worker," and the "folk."

For example, James Lesesne Wells' book jacket for Lorenzo J. Greene and Carter G. Woodson's *The Negro Wage Earner* (1930) anticipated the Black worker theme that would preoccupy artists and intellectuals through the next two decades. Class as a concern was already germinating a decade earlier in the midst of the "New Negro" movement itself. Wells' Black worker is a waiter who serves up the city on a platter, while bridging ancient pyramids and modern skyscrapers. By 1930, as the New Negro Movement's momentum was ebbing, Wells had clearly taken its quest for racial upliftment to another level, where the superficial indicators of success and class-based privileges were rejected in favor of Black economic development across class lines. The "Everyman" was gaining importance, as can be seen in Malvin Gray Johnson's *The Postman* (1934). Similarly, Sargent Johnson's *Negro Woman* (1933) drew from the Black vernacular tradition which, during the Depression, people found not only relevant to and expressive of their own experiences, but also marketable at a time when working-class images were idealized. The tendency toward class consciousness was ever present but latent during the New Negro Movement but the Great Crash of 1929 and the ensuing world economic depression created an atmosphere in which the concerns of working class people, and the austerities they faced, began to dominate the scene.

Conclusion

In a very self-conscious way, the New Negro Movement attempted to avoid, as much as possible, art that was suggestive of the agitation that was all around even during the prosperous decade of the 1920s. Political activism at the time was often combined with economic activism, as seen in labor unionism. The battles fought in the United States by labor leaders like Randolph, over such issues as full employment, optimum on-the-job environmental conditions, and union representation, were frequently associated with political efforts to combat racism and job discrimination. Yet the New Negro Movement did not involve itself directly with these issues; instead, it sought to draw attention to an aesthetic of "Blackness" and affirm "Black" identity in its own right, whose dignity and destiny had to be restored through extra-political means. In light of this consideration, it is possible to argue that the New Negro Movement's agenda was an alternative strategy to navigate through a political landscape that was growing restless in spite of the opulence of the "Roaring '20s." New Negro leaders sought to direct the movement's trajectory clear of censure and censorship by yoking it to the world of White art criticism, philanthropic sponsorships, and endorsements (Watson, 1995). In its own way, the Movement engaged with the notion of "art for art's sake" that many members of the European and Euro-American art community espoused. As Locke (1974) affirmed, for New Negro artists and intellectuals, Black subjectivity was a world in which Black peoples and their cultures could be seen and represented without always being filtered through the White supremacist gaze. When the poet Claude McKay expressed his disappointment that a "true" artistic impulse was being corrupted by the propaganda of racial upliftment, Du Bois retorted that he did not "care a damn for any art that is not used for propaganda," because he was equally disappointed by "the displacement of legitimate polemics and propaganda by art devoid of political content" (Lewis, 1979).

It is also important, however, to avoid the opposite temptation of grouping together the complex and varied Black cultural products under the heading of a monolithic "Black aesthetic," in the eagerness to capture some primordial essence of "Blackness" that supposedly resides in "Black" genes and in the African soil. Instead, a "Black aesthetic" might be seen as the oppositional stance adopted by post-Emancipation, post-colonial, hybrid Black identities, which, from Harlem to Rio, London to Cape Town, thrive in communities where creativity is seen as the desire to articulate and bear witness to the political condition of Blackness.

References

Beck, E. M., & Tolnay, S. E. (1995). *A Festival of Violence: An Analysis of Southern Lynchings, 1882–1930,* Chicago: University of Illinois Press.

Brundage, F. (1993). *Lynching in the New South: Georgia and Virginia, 1880–1930,* Chicago: University of Illinois Press.

Campbell, M. S. (1987). *Harlem Renaissance: Art of Black America,* New York: Abrams.

Drake, S., & Cayton, H. R. (1993). *Black Metropolis: A Study of Negro Life in a Northern City,* Chicago: University of Chicago Press (orig. published in 1945).

Gates, H. L. (1988). "The Trope of the New Negro and the Reconstruction of the Image of the Black" in *Representations* 24, (Fall), 129–155.

Gilroy, P. (1993). *The Black Atlantic: Modernity and Double Consciousness,* Cambridge, MA: Harvard University Press.

Grossman, J. R. (1989). *Land of Hope: Chicago, Black Southerners, and the Great Migration,* Chicago: University of Chicago Press.

Hall, S. (1992). "What is this 'Black' in Black Popular Cuture?" in G. Dent (ed.) *Black Popular Cuture,* Seattle: Bay Press.

Hughes, L. (1994). "The Big Sea," in D. L. Lewis (ed.) *The Portable Harlem Renaissance Reader,* New York: Penguin. (orig. published in 1940).

Johnson, J. W. (1959). *The Book of American Negro Poetry,* New York: Harcourt and Brace (orig. published in 1922).

Lewis, D. L (1979). *When Harlem Was in Vogue,* Oxford: Oxford University Press.

Locke, A. (1974). "Harlem, The Cultural Capital" in *The New Negro,* New York: Atheneum (orig. published in 1925).

Smith, T. (1993). *Making the Modern: Industry, Art, and Design in America,* Chicago: University of Chicago Press.

Thompson, R. F. (1993). *Face of the Gods: Art and Altars of Africa and the African Americas,* New York: Museum for African Art.

Ullman, D. (1974). *The Darkness and the Light: Photographs by Doris Ullman,* Millerton, NY: Aperture.

Watson, S. (1995). *The Harlem Renaissance: Hub of African American Culture, 1920–1930,* New York: Pantheon.

Section 1—Study Questions

1. What evidence for the African presence in the Americas does Ivan Van Sertima discuss in his interview?

2. Does Ivan Van Sertima consider himself an Afrocentrist or a nationalist? Why? Explain.

3. What is the difference between a phenotype and a genotype? Which one provides information about people's visually observable characteristics?

4. Why is it unscientific to place humans in racial categories based purely on visually observable criteria?

5. What is the relationship between "paternalism" and "racism" according to Ibram Rogers?

6. Cite three examples of paternalistic thought and practice as mentioned by Rogers in his chapter.

7. Why does Reed see the establishment of Columbus Day as a state holiday during the period before World War I as a symbol of Roman Catholic acculturation in the United States?

8. According to Reed, how does Alfred Crosby describe the conquest of the Canary Islands? Is this history similar to that of the Caribbean?

9. Describe the phenomenon of "token integration." Why is this a problem in children's literature?

10. How is Robert B. Moore's critique of "everyday racism" relevant to children's literature?

11. According to Jan Warner, how have Native Americans responded to the 500th Anniversary of Columbus's arrival in the United States?

12. How did Columbus describe the indigenous people of the New World in his writings?

13. How did Mary Kingsley's ethnography represent West Africans?

14. Briefly describe Kingsley's gender politics within the context of the European feminist struggles of her day.

15. List some historical examples of scholarship linking socio-political inequality to biological factors that James Reed discusses in his interview.

16. According to Reed, why is *The Bell Curve's* argument scientifically unsound?

17. Which two competing conceptualizations of "Blackness" did the New Negro Movement wrestle with in attempting to define a "Black Aesthetic"?

18. Name a few artists from the Harlem Renaissance and describe how they attempted to represent "Blackness" within the framework of the New Negro Movement.

Section 2

Slavery, Resistance, and Freedom

Chapter 11

Slavery, Resistance, and Freedom: An Introduction

Gayle T. Tate

Slavery proved to be an encounter between Africans and the Europeans that would simultaneously depopulate Africa as it provided laborers for the New World, transform free Africans in Africa to chattel property in America, and recast Africa as a labor source for slave cargoes into the European geopolitical orbit. Slavery might have begun slowly as the desire and greed increased and the mechanics were put in place, but it built momentum so that by the 18th century slave ships had become commonplace. Thus, the journey of the enslavement process began, from the chaos that captured the Africans in Africa, through the horrors of the Middle Passage, to the breaking in of these slave laborers in the American colonies and would mark the 17th, 18th, and 19th centuries. Developed primarily out of greed and profit, slavery was an institution that subjugated African peoples, forcing them to create a great deal of the riches of the New World. The trappings of the systems, the beatings of the slaves, the raping of slave women, daily psychological intimidation, dismemberment, and backbreaking labor offered little reprieve and a lot less hope that slaves would live to see freedom in their lifetime.

The counterpoint of slavery was the spirit of resistance, which began in Africa to meet the onslaught of the slave trade, was continued aboard slave ships in the form of mutinies, and was reorganized in a multitude of ways in slave communities. Here, principally, resistance was covert—the sabotaging of crops and farm equipment, torching the master's property, poisoning the master's food, and malingerers—and overt—consisting of dramatic uprisings and rebellions. Survival, the cornerstone of resistance, was critical in shaping both modes of undermining the slave system. Female slave networks were instrumental in forging an intergenerational resistance among the slaves. Some children were encouraged to escape by their mothers. Additionally, spontaneous acts of individual rebellion were not uncommon and despite their rhetoric that slaves were content with their lot, Southern Whites believed that Blacks were a troublesome presence in the region. But "slave fever" and dreams of wealth from slave labor supplanted the apprehensions of the planters.

Resistance did not end as free Blacks migrated North during the antebellum era nor did it stop with emancipation. As free Blacks or escaping fugitives migrated to northern cities, principally Philadelphia, New York City, or Boston, they found that they were quasi-free at best, meaning that while they were free they did not have any legal rights of citizenship. Thus, they occupied an ambiguous legal status of second-class citizenship and were relegated to the bottom of the economic ladder. With emancipation in 1863, and the bright hopes of Reconstruction that faded rapidly, African Americans were once again stymied, this time by social segregation and disfranchisement in the South and racial discrimination and circumscribed job mobility in the North. De jure segregation was a fact of life in the South and de facto segregation was the Northern reality. As an aggrieved population, African Americans organized to protest against their material conditions and legal status. Resistance became a way of life and Blacks organized churches, mutual benevolent societies, the Black press, community ad hoc, and were militant abolitionists before the Civil War as they fought to abolish slavery. Following slavery, their organizational impetus continued as they sought group solidarity to combat the racism engulfing their lives.

Anitha Ramachandran's, "The Ghost of Slavery in Toni Morrison's *Beloved*," explores the psychological scars of slavery through the memory processes and personal narrative of Sethe, the protagonist. Morrison uses the ghost of Sethe's daughter to awaken the memory of her enslavement, to give her the power to mourn over her slave experiences, and finally begin the process of healing. Thomas Edge's "Black Women in the

Abolitionist Movement" and Gayle T. Tate's "The Political Thought and Abolition of Maria W. Stewart" examine the role of Black female abolitionists as they sought to fulfill the twin goals of abolitionism—improve the lives of free Blacks and the immediate emancipation of the slaves. Both chapters look at the nature and complexities of free Black women's resistance in northern cities. Despite their organizational influence and activism, many of these women have lived in the shadows of history. Edge highlights those female activists that fought alongside of Black and White men and women to free the slaves, and Tate examines the intellectual and philosophical thought that shaped Maria W. Stewart's militant abolitionism. Adopting unconventional gender traditions, in challenging slavery, these women had to also challenge the racism and sexism that was organically related to the slave institution and the nature of oppression in American society.

Rhett S. Jones, in his chapter, "Zambo Histories: Studying Afro-Indians" departs from the "master narrative of American history" and explores the racial relations and tensions in America's past between African Americans and native Americans. In part, some of the dynamics of those tensions pivot upon the nature of racism toward each of these groups in society and some were the inherent tensions between the groups themselves. Zambos, those of mixed heritage of these two groups, seeking a more acceptable racial category, either denied their African heritage or found themselves excluded from several native American tribes. As both of these groups, the African Americans and Zambos, are integrated into American history, the interpretations and historical perspectives on race and racism will be reinterpreted.

The excerpts by Olaudah Equiano, David Walker, and Nat Turner speak to the yearning for freedom and resistance by both slaves and free Blacks during the enslavement period. Equiano offers a sharp contrast between freedom in Africa and enslavement in Barbados, which was the beginning of his slavery in the New World. In this excerpt of "The Interesting Life of Olaudah Equiano," also known as Gustavus Vassa, Equiano was born in 1745, in the kingdom of Benin, was captured while he was a child and shipped to Virginia via Barbados. David Walker, a militant abolitionist in Boston, Massachusetts, printed his incendiary 76-page pamphlet, *Walker's Appeal, In Four Articles, Together With a Preamble, To The Colored Citizens of the World*, to galvanize the free Blacks and those in bondage to speak out against oppression. But Walker saw an armed resistance struggle, a righteous divine struggle if you will, that would overturn slavery in America. It was his strident criticism of American society and his clarion call for violent retaliation that threatened the planter elite and put a bounty on his head. This excerpt is Walker's analysis of the causes of the oppression of African Americans.

Nat Turner, a slave, also walked the path of resistance. Known to some as "Prophet Nat" for his gifts of prophecy, Nat Turner would grow up believing he had been especially anointed by God with a mission to right injustice. On August 22, 1831, Nat Turner and his resistance fighters went from plantation to plantation killing Whites who were involved with slavery. Eventually captured and sentenced to death on November 11, 1831, he remains a symbol for those slaves who fought against slavery.

The excerpt, "What if I am a Woman" by Maria Stewart, a passionate plea for women's rights, predates the early Women's Rights Movement by almost two decades. Stewart argued that Black women must position themselves as leaders in the abolitionist movement and in the cause for women's rights as well. She encouraged them to become economic producers so that they could gain their independence and educate their children. Maria W. Stewart and Sojourner Truth saw the rights of Black women as critical to the overall Black liberation struggle. Truth, with her legendary oratorical skills, came of political age at a time when the abolitionist and Women's Rights Movements were, in many respects, cojoined in struggle. In this excerpt, "Ar'n't I a Woman," Truth, a champion of both causes, identified racism and sexism as the twin evils of oppression.

The *Dred Scott Decision* (1857) and *Plessy v. Ferguson* (1896) were legal decisions determined to keep Blacks in subordinate positions in society. Dred Scott sued for his freedom on the grounds that his residence in free territories, first free Illinois and then Fort Snelling, in the northern part of the Louisiana purchase, entitled him to his freedom. Chief Justice B. Taney's majority opinion for the Court refused to acknowledge Blacks as citizens, citing that they were property and had no legal standing in the courts, and, moreover, had "no rights which the White man was bound to respect." The *Plessy v. Ferguson* case was to solidify the disfranchisement of African Americans on public conveyances and accommodations—that is, virtually to uphold the segregation that had spread across the South since 1875. *Plessy* upheld social segregation in its separate but equal doctrine that would remain the law of the land until the *Brown Decision* in 1954. Supreme Court Justice John Marshall Harlan offered a strong dissent (excerpt) against the majority opinion of the Court in *Plessy v. Ferguson*. He argued that African Americans had rights of citizenship guaranteed by the Fourteenth Amendment to the Constitution. They were also entitled, the same as everyone else, to their personal liberties. Harlan foresaw that the decision in *Plessy* would set a dangerous precedent by fostering "race hatred to be planted under the sanction of law."

Chapter 12

The Ghost of Slavery in Toni Morrison's *Beloved*

Anitha Ramachandran

Introduction

Toni Morrison's *Beloved* (1987) is a richly textured fictional, historical, and theoretical exploration of slavery, the Middle Passage, and the aftermath of both. A deeply nuanced and poetic text, *Beloved* performatively explores spaces between the traditionally rigid binaries of past and present, existence and nonexistence, living and dead. The sheer complexity of *Beloved*, however, beckons readers to utilize a variety of theoretical approaches simultaneously and put these in dialogue with each other. Using a variety of critical approaches such as psychoanalysis, deconstruction, and performance theory, this essay hopes to explore how the figure of the ghost functions in *Beloved* to articulate the psychological and historical experiences of slavery—a history that largely has been "disremembered and unaccounted for" (*Beloved*, p. 275) in dominant discourses.

The study of *Beloved* from these perspectives invites the reader to examine the relationship between African American literature and "theory." Studying this juncture is necessary in light of existing controversies surrounding the use of "Western" theoretical paradigms for the analysis of African American texts. Many prominent African American critics have debated the role of theory in the study of Black culture, art and literature. Some critics, such as Barbara Christian, have asserted that theory maintains a hegemonic but largely irrelevant position in academic discourse, and, as a function of its Western cultural and logical paradigms, is inappropriate for the analysis of African American texts. Other, more post-structurally oriented critics such as Michael Awkward, Hortense Spillers, Claudia Tate, Cornel West, and Houston A. Baker, Jr. support the position that Western theoretical paradigms can be "appropriated" (to use Awkward's phrase) for the productive analysis of Black art forms and can be employed to study Black literature's historical, political, social, psychological, and cultural contexts. For instance, Claudia Tate, in her landmark study, *Psychoanalysis and Black Novels*, broke the boundaries of both traditional psychoanalysis and traditional African American literary criticism through such a gesture of theoretical "appropriation."

Thus, in approaching *Beloved* through the "Western" methodologies of psychoanalysis, deconstruction, and performance theory, this essay seeks to consciously "appropriate" the critical and theoretical tools of the "West" to perform close readings of Morrison's text.

* * *

At the opening of *Beloved*, life for Sethe consists of "work[ing] hard to remember as close to nothing as was safe" (*Beloved*, p. 6), and "the future was a matter of keeping the past at bay" (p. 42). During the 18 years between the murder of her "crawling already?" baby and the arrival of Paul D at her doorstep, Sethe desperately tries to avoid the "rememory" of her lost baby—memories that conjure up an enslaved past unaccounted for, unmourned for: "Counting on the stillness of her own soul, [Sethe] had forgotten the other one: the soul of her baby girl" (p. 5).

Morrison uses the figure of the ghost to simultaneously literalize and metaphorize the haunting quality of Sethe's unmourned memories of slavery. Initially, Sethe is frozen in a state of melancholia, unable to mourn her child and everything the child psychically represents for her. As Sethe's relationship with Paul D grows, the narrator leaves it up to the reader to make the link between two things that occur simultaneously: Sethe's growing defenses against remembering and the growing manifestation of her baby's ghost. Early on, when Paul D kisses the "tree" (p. 17) on her back, Sethe wonders if she could "trust and remember things" (p. 18) now that the "last of the Sweet Home men was there to catch her if she sank" (p. 18). At this moment the baby ghost buckles the house, in impatient agreement[1] and in desire for acknowledgment. A few days later, the ghost is manifested further: it visibly appears, its invisible body clothed in a white dress which "holds on" (p. 35) to Sethe's waist. The next morning, Sethe thinks about "what Denver had seen kneeling next to her, and thought also of the temptation to trust and remember as she stood before the cooking stove in [Paul D's] arms. Would it be alright?" (p. 38) she wonders again.

Despite these gestures toward remembering, however, Sethe continues to avoid rememory as much as possible, seeking to keep her enslaved past away from herself and her daughter. As the narrator explains, "the 'better life' [Sethe] believed she and Denver were living was simply not the other one. The fact that Paul D had come out of 'that other one' into her bed was better too; and the notion of a future with him, or for that matter without him, was beginning to stroke her mind" (p. 42). Later on, when Paul D asks her, "What about inside?" She firmly responds, "I don't go inside" (p. 46). On the day of the carnival, Sethe's desire to mourn the past becomes even more over- "shadowed" by the possibility of Denver, Paul D, and herself forming a family: "on the way home, although leading them now, the shadows of three people still held hands" (p. 49). Waiting for her at home, however, is the ghost of 124, fully manifested now as a young woman who is exactly the age the crawling-already baby would have been had she lived.

Although Sethe is unaware of it at the time, Beloved the ghost has "come" because she was conjured, both consciously and unconsciously, by each of the characters. " . . . If she'd only come," Sethe tells Denver at the beginning of the novel, "I could make it clear to her" (p. 4). Even Paul D challenges the ghost, "You want to fight, come on! God damn it!" (p. 18) Identifying Paul D as the distraction that prevents Sethe from fully mourning her, Beloved materializes to secure her maternal attention.

Beloved's ghostliness, her simultaneous absence and presence between life and death, situate her in an ambiguous space; Derrida's deconstructive theory of hauntology is useful in understanding this power. In *Specters of Marx: The State of the Debt, the Work of Mourning, and the New International*, Derrida writes:

> *The production of the ghost . . . is effected . . . only . . . [when] the ghostly moment comes upon [it], adds to it a supplementary dimension, one more simulacrum . . . Namely, a body! In the flesh! For there is no ghost . . . without at least the appearance of flesh, in a space of invisible visibility . . . For there to be a ghost, there must be a return to the body, but to a body that is more abstract than ever. (p. 126)*

Thus, Beloved's flesh and blood appearance is, contradictorily, a necessary feature of her invisible visibility, her ghostliness.

Reading Beloved's ghostliness through the lens of the Kleinian psychoanalytic theory of object relations, one can argue that Beloved is a reflection, both literally and metaphorically, of the "phantastic nature" (Klein, 1940, p. 346) of Sethe's inner world. Sethe's haunting rememories are so strong that they imbue the inaccessible inner object of her lost child with a ghostly reality that is simultaneously metaphorical, literal, and material. Beloved is the double of a previously inaccessible inner object, the living "crawling-already?" child, as well as a newly recovered lost external object, both of which provide Sethe the key to her repressed memories of slavery.

Beloved's new visibility as a ghost functions in a manner similar to the visibility of the external object in Kleinian object relations theory. For the Kleinian infant, for whom the mother is the external object, "the visible mother provides continuous proofs of what the 'internal' mother is like," (Klein, 1940). In a psychoanalytic reversal of roles between infant and mother, Beloved the ghost performs, for Sethe, the role of the visible external object; this visibility provides Sethe the "continuous proof" of Beloved's flesh and blood existence which, attaining a life of its own, refuses to be "disremembered and unaccounted for" (*Beloved*, p. 275).

> [Sethe]"Some things you forget. Other things you never do . . . the picture of it stays, and not just in my rememory, but out there, in the world. What I remember is a picture floating around out there outside my head. . . . "
>
> "Can other people see it?" asked Denver.

"Oh yes. Oh, yes, yes, yes. Someday you will be walking down the road and you think you hear some-thing or see something going on. So clear. And you think it's you thinking it up. A thought picture. But no. It's when you bump into a rememory that belongs to somebody else. . . . Where I was before I came here, that place is real. . . . It's never going away." (Beloved, p. 36)

As this passages shows, Sethe's rememory is not mimetic to the actual experiences that generate mem-ory, but instead, is the active performance by which her enslaved past, with all its embodied and witnessed acts, sites, and scenes, repeatedly breaks into her present. Beloved is the impetus that prompts Sethe to revisit what "she and Baby Suggs had agreed . . . was unspeakable" (*Beloved*, p. 58). Sethe fully responds to Beloved's insistent questions, like "Where your diamonds?" and "your woman she never fix up your hair?" (p. 58). In her attempt to satiate Beloved's incessant desire, and later demands, to hear her confessions, expla-nations, and apologies, Sethe "began to talk, explain, describe how much she had suffered, been through, for her children, waving away flies in grape arbors, crawling on her knees to a lean-to" (p. 241). Beloved's pres-ence in her life again is the catalyst for these powerful, extended rememories that emerge out of her uncon-scious.

The impact of Beloved's ghostliness extends far beyond Sethe's personal psyche; as the conjured ghost of personal and collective rememory, Beloved is an ongoing performance that represents and re-presents all the experiences, memories, and rememories of trauma sustained by "sixty million and more" during the Middle Passage, slavery, and its aftermath. It is Beloved's dual ontology between substantiality and insub-stantiality that enables this immense representational power. She provides the "continuous proof" of their flesh-and-blood bodies; her indisputable material substance signifies the onerous weight and material expe-rience of slavery, an institution that enacted, in the words of Hortense Spillers, "high crimes against the flesh" (1997). In her essay "Mama's Baby, Papa's Maybe," Spillers writes, "before the 'body' there is the 'flesh,' that zero degree of social conceptualization that does not escape concealment under the brush of discourse, or the reflexes of iconography" (p. 67). Beloved's flesh-and-blood ghostliness is necessary in understanding "the 'flesh' as a primary narrative . . . its seared dividedness, ripped-apartness" (p. 67). Beloved's ghostly lack of substance is equally crucial; it stands for the haunting void of the unspeakable and of the absent, that which "was not a story to pass on," of "loneliness that roams," of the "disremembered and unaccounted for" who "have claim" but are "not claimed" (*Beloved*, pp. 274–275).

As a ghost, Beloved's presence is verified by her visibility, not only to Sethe, but to others around her, such as Denver, Paul D, and Sethe's community. According to Derrida, ghosts necessarily possess this inde-pendent reality:

. . . the critique of the ghost or of spirits would thus be the critique of subjective representation and an abstraction, of what happens in the head, . . . what stays in the head, even as it has come out of there, . . . and survives outside the head. But nothing would be possible, beginning with the critique, without this autonomy . . . outside the head. (1994, p. 171; italics in original)

Thus, as a ghost, Beloved is autonomous, in much the same way that Sethe, in her dialogue with Denver, describes rememory as autonomous of the thinking subject:

"Some things you forget. Other things you never do . . . the picture of it stays, and not just in my remem-ory, but out there, in the world. What I remember is a picture floating around out there outside my head . . . Someday you will be walking down the road and you think you hear something or see some-thing going on. So clear. And you think it's you thinking it up. A thought picture. But no. It's when you bump into a rememory that belongs to somebody else . . . " (Beloved, p. 36)

Beloved thus represents rememories which are so haunting that they literally and allegorically come to life to "survive outside the head" (Derrida, 1994, p. 171).

Beloved the ghost yearns to be remembered, confronted, and mourned not just by Sethe, but by the entire ex-slave community. Like Sethe, Paul D is so wounded by slavery that he refuses to mourn, instead making sure that the contents of his heart, the "tobacco tin"—which includes "Alfred, Georgia, Sixo, school-teacher, Halle, his brothers, Sethe, Mister, the taste of iron, the sight of butter, the smell of hickory, notebook paper" (*Beloved*, p. 113)—remains tightly locked. Of Paul D, the narrator writes, "By the time he got to 124, nothing in this world could pry it open" (p. 113). Indeed, it takes something outside of this world: a ghost.

"SHE MOVED HIM" (p. 114), writes the narrator; Beloved physically moves Paul D from place to place, and emotionally moves him toward the process of rememory. He realizes this much later, when he tells Stamp Paid, "She reminds me of something. Something, looks like, I'm supposed to remember" (p. 234). Beloved's seduction of Paul D, in which she asks him to "touch [her] on the inside part" (p. 116) and "call [her] by [her] name" (p. 117), is in effect her plea for Paul D to "touch the inside part" of his own self and acknowledge what will be found there: his own vulnerability, pain, and beauty. In calling her "Beloved," he also calls her "beloved"; uttering "Beloved" is a long-avoided endearment that enacts for Paul D a state of self-acceptance, a rememory of his own self during a more vulnerable time. Indeed, in *"call[ing] her beloved which was not beloved* (ital. in original)" (*Beloved*, p. ix),[2] he begins to rememory his own past as an enslaved person, as well as the collective past of the ex-slave community.

> . . . *[Paul D] didn't hear the whisper that the flakes of rust made either as they fell away from the seams of his tobacco tin. So when the lid gave he didn't know it. What he knew was that when he reached the inside part he was saying, "Red heart. Red heart," over and over again. Softly, and then so loud it woke Denver, then Paul D himself. "Red heart. Red Heart. Red Heart." (p. 117)*

Like "Beloved," the words "Red heart" enable Paul D to will his red heart's capacity to love back into existence and initiate his process of remembering, which continues until the end of the novel. Pried open, the contents of Paul D's tobacco tin heart—the repressed traumas of slavery—are shared by Beloved, who carries it in the form of a literal and allegorical "child" conceived by their union. Like Beloved herself, this ghostly pregnancy is a testament to the power of collective memory for the ex-slave community, seen not only by Paul D, but also by Sethe, Denver, and all those who see "the pregnant woman, naked and smiling in the sun" (*Beloved*, p. 261).

Of the women who come to Sethe's home to exorcize Beloved, Morrison writes: "The first thing they saw was not Denver sitting on the steps, but themselves . . . Younger, stronger, even as little girls lying in the grass asleep. . . . They recognized Sethe at once and surprised themselves by the absence of fear when they saw what stood next to her. . . ." (p. 258). Everyone who sees Beloved and her pregnancy "bumps into a rememory which belongs to someone else" (p. 36), to use Sethe's earlier phrase. The women of the community experience Beloved collectively and allow her to stand in for their own sense of absence and loss. This appropriative gesture enables the women to transform their individual pain into collective experience and agency.

Beloved possesses the representational power to stand in for the millions whose untold stories and anguishes she figuratively embodies, signifying the irretrievable loss of flesh-and-blood family and ancestry whose biological genes were "passed on" without memories or stories to retrieve them. Yet, she also represents the idea and feeling of personal, communal, and historical belovedness; the figure of the ghost in *Beloved* not only foregrounds and politicizes the intimate link between the living and the beloved dead, but also the living individual's connection and sympathy with others who are living. As Hortense Spillers reminds:

> *It must be conceded that African-Americans, under the press of a hostile and compulsory patriarchal order, bound and determined to destroy them, or to preserve them only in the service and at the behest of the "master" class, exercised a degree of courage and will to survive that startles the imagination even now. . . . Time and again, certain ethical and sentimental features . . . tied him or her, across the landscape to others, often sold from hand to hand, of the same and different blood in a common fabric of memory and inspiration. (1997, 71)*

These "powerful ties of sympathy" maintained by diasporized African peoples in the face of catastrophe, Spillers writes, is what "historians have long identified as the inviolable Black Family, [a] . . . structure which remains one of the supreme social achievements of African Americans under the conditions of enslavement" (Spillers, 1997, p. 71). *Beloved* highlights the central role that these "ties of sympathy" have in enabling each character's journey toward healing.

Conclusion

Beloved carries on African American literature's long and rich tradition of using the ghost story as a medium for political, psychological, and spiritual expression. Its development in Black literature can be traced to the oral traditions and narratives of the enslaved in the Americas, and to the cultures of Western Africa (Smith-Wright, 1991, p. 142). Also, the nonlinear chronology of the text and the nesting of stories within stories, two strategies of storytelling often called postmodern, can be traced to oral slave narratives and folk tales. Through such narrative techniques, the novel enacts and performs the fragmentation of slavery. The reader of *Beloved* becomes aware of multiple perspectives, each fragmented but equally important toward the reconstruction of the characters' histories. The histories of each character are revealed through rememories, recollections, and embedded stories; piecing together the different parts of stories, the reader can ultimately arrive at only a partial understanding of each character's thoughts and experiences. By telling and retelling the novel's multiple stories from different viewpoints, Morrison acknowledges not only the uniqueness of each character's individual experience of mutually shared history but highlights the inability and impossibility to know every possible dimension of that history, which, like slavery, ultimately must be remembered in its fragmented state.

In sum, *Beloved* is a unique achievement in American letters that is simultaneously a work of fiction; of political, social, and psychological theory; of history; of poetry; of spirituality; of testimony; and of historical and social commentary. It clearly points to the inadequacy of narrow definitions of form that can trap such a dynamic, multifaceted work within a particular genre or discipline. This feature of *Beloved* highlights the necessity of studying literary texts from many different critical and theoretical approaches, and the importance of contextualizing texts within history. Some of these approaches, however, are often unnecessarily kept apart from one another in critical discourse and engagement. In her book, *"The Changing Same": Black Women's Literature, Criticism, and Theory*, Deborah McDowell voices concern regarding this forced separation, stressing the importance of resisting "the theory/practice dichotomy, which is too broad, abbreviated, and compromised by hedging definitions to capture the range and diversity of contemporary critical projects . . . " (1995, p. 558) This dichotomy often separates the historical and cultural analysis of African American literature from a purely "theoretical" analysis; the former, according to McDowell, is "termed 'contextual' by theoreticians [and] is often frowned upon if not dismissed entirely by critics who insist exclusively upon textual analysis" (1995, p. 558). I agree with McDowell in that a truly productive study of African American literary texts should seek to bridge this divide.

Endnotes

1. Or in impatient disagreement with Sethe's desire, as Angelyn Mitchell has suggested.
2. See the dedication of *Beloved*, p. ix: "I will call them my people which were not my people, and her beloved, which was not beloved." (Romans 9:25)

References

Awkward, Michael. "Appropriative Gestures: Theory and Afro-American Literary Criticism," in *Gender and Theory: Dialogues on Feminist Criticism*. Linda Kauffman (ed.). Oxford: Basil Blackwell.

Baker, Houston A. (1991). "Theoretical Returns," in *Working of the Spirit: The Poetics of Afro-American Women's Writing*. Chicago: University of Chicago Press.

Blassingame, John W. (1979). *The Slave Community: Plantation Life in the Antebellum South*. New York: Oxford University Press.

Christian, Barbara. (1997). "The Race for Theory." *Cultural Critique 6* (Spring), 51–63.

Derrida, Jacques. (1978). "Structure, Sign and Play in the Discourse of the Human Sciences, " in *Writing and Difference* (1967, trans. 1978 by Alan Bass). Chicago: University of Chicago Press.

Derrida, Jacques. (1994). *Specters of Marx: The State of the Debt, the Work of Mourning, and the New International*. New York and London: Routledge.

Douglass, Frederick. (1987). *My Bondage and My Freedom*. 1855. William L. Andrews (ed). Urbana: University of Illinois Press.

Douglass, Frederick. (2001). *Narrative of the Life of Frederick Douglass, as American Slave, Written by Himself.* 1845. John W. Blassingame, John R. McKivigan, and Peter Hinks (ed). New Haven: Yale University Press.

Freud, Sigmund. (1989). "Mourning and Melancholia." *A General Selection from the Works of Sigmund Freud.* John Rickman (ed). New York: Anchor Books.

Gutman, Herbert G. (1977). *The Black Family in Slavery and Freedom, 1750–1925.* New York: Vintage Books.

Holloway, Karla F. C. (2000). "Cultural Narratives Passed On: African American Mourning Stories," in Napier, Winston (ed). *African American Literary Theory: A Reader.* New York, NY: New York UP.

Klein, Melanie. (1940). "Mourning and its Relation to Manic Depressive States." *International Journal of Psychoanalysis* 21: 125–153.

McDowell, Deborah. (1995). "Transferences: Black Feminist Thinking: The Practice of Theory," in *The Changing Same: Black Women's Literature, Criticism, and Theory.* Bloomington and Indiannapolis: Indiana University Press.

Mitchell, Angelyn. (2002). *The Freedom to Remember: Narrative, Slavery, and Gender in Contemporary Black Women's Fiction.* New Brunswick: Rutgers University Press.

Morrison, Toni. (1987). *Beloved.* New York: Signet.

Rawick, George. (1972). *From Sundown to Sunup: The Making of the Black Slave Community.* Westport, CT: Greenwood Pub. Co.

Smith-Wright, Geraldine. (1991). "In Spite of the Klan: Ghosts in the Fiction of Black Women Writers." *Haunting the House of Fiction: Feminist Perspectives on Ghost Stories by American Women.* Lynette Carpenter and Wendy K. Kolmar (ed.). Knoxville, TN: University of Tennessee Press.

Spillers, Hortense. (1997). "Mama's Baby, Papa's Maybe: An American Grammar Book." *Diacritics.* (Summer): 65–81.

Tate, Claudia. (1998). *Psychoanalysis and Black Novels.* New York: Oxford University Press.

West, Cornel. (1991). "Theory, Pragmatisms, and Politics." *Consequences of Theory (Selected Papers from the English Institute 1987–88).* Jonathan Arac and Barbara Johnson (eds). Baltimore and London: The Johns Hopkins University Press.

Chapter 13

Beyond Tubman and Truth:
The Unsung Heroes of the Black Female
Abolitionist Movement

Thomas Edge

The period of American history from approximately 1828 until the dawn of the Civil War marked a time when Blacks forced their own issues of equality into the public consciousness. These crusaders saw the contradictions inherent in a democratic society that preserved slavery. Critics of this system knew that America could not experience true liberty while millions of potential citizens languished in the nation's slave quarters. It is only natural to assume that such divisive issues and heated debates triggered an incredible politicization of the Black population, a trend that knew no boundaries due to class or gender. Nothing demonstrates this notion better than the role played by Black women in the abolition movement. Black women from every social station participated in this struggle—from the working-class poor to the wealthiest elites. Despite harsh opposition from all walks of life—Blacks and Whites, men and women, rich and poor, clerical and secular—these women vehemently fought for the rights of their enslaved brothers and sisters with a passion and dignity to match their most revered male counterparts. They knew that the treatment of Blacks on the plantations of South Carolina dramatically affected the rights and privileges of Black citizens in New York City and, indeed, throughout the nation. Combating the stereotypical images that hounded their every movement, Black women used a variety of methods, from petitions to abetting runaway slaves, in their efforts to undermine this system. In doing so, they established a solid political connection between the destinies of Black men and women in the United States, irrevocably linking the liberties and struggles of each group to one another.

These ideas raise a very pertinent question regarding the role of Black women in the abolition movement: why is it important to study the contributions of this particular subgroup? What is it about their experiences in the anti-slavery battles that warrants special consideration? More than any other faction, Black women represented the inherent contradictions posed by American republicanism—the political, social, and economic oppression of women and Blacks. "Black in a white society, slave in a free society, woman in a society ruled by men, [they] had the least formal power and were perhaps the most vulnerable group of antebellum Americans."[1] Consequently, Black women were in a unique position to critique the status quo from a perspective shaped by this triple specter of race/sex/class. And, more than any other group in 19th-century America, their experiences offered tangible evidence against the arguments used to justify this three-tiered social stratification.

In order to understand the role that Black women played in this movement, it is necessary to first examine the stereotypical images that shaped public opinions of Black womanhood. Each of these portrayals established a prevailing zeitgeist that placed power firmly in the hands of White males. Thus, Black women were caught in a double-bind: Black in a White world, female in a male-dominated society. As a result of their unique position in this power dialectic of race and gender, Black women had a chance to view their oppression and shape opposition to it as no other group in American society could. Indeed, the study of their actions in antebellum reform movements, including abolition, is important because from this very position in society, they could offer a unique critique of the status quo. They managed to combine the creation of a "Black" identity through the institution of slavery with society's depiction of women to form a synthesis reflecting their dual personalities. In some cases, however, these images severely limited the arguments that

Black women utilized on behalf of the slave population and in favor of their own activism. Often, they had to consider the prevailing views of Blackness and womanhood when constructing their appeals in order to avoid alienating their supporters. As women like Harriet Jacobs demonstrated, it was easier to form strategies within existing societal parameters regarding race and gender than to attack them and elicit the wrath of would-be sympathizers.

The views that established this hierarchy fell into three essential categories: the portrayals of Blacks in general, of Black women specifically, and of White middle-class women. Such ideas invaded both the exclusive realm of the rich intelligentsia and the hovels of the poorest wage earners, thus providing a large popular base for the labeling (and libeling) of these groups. Not only did these three classifications shape the way Americans generally viewed Black women in the larger society, but they had profound implications on American views of Black women in the public domain.

By the time that abolitionist forces truly began to gather steam in the late-1820s, the racist defenders of slavery already established a series of stereotypes about Blacks that favored their cause. In one form or another, many of these ideas survived well into the 20th century. In 1918, Ulrich B. Phillips, the leading "expert" on slavery at the turn of this century, described the African American slave as follows:

> *[They have] an eagerness for society, music and merriment, a fondness for display . . . , a not flagrant sensuality, a receptiveness toward any religion whose exercises were exhilarating, a proneness to superstition, a courteous acceptance of subordination, an avidity for praise, a readiness for loyalty of a feudal sort, and last but not least, a healthy human repugnance toward overwork.[2]*

Other pro-slavery forces took a more scientific approach to the problem. Dr. Samuel Cartwright and Dr. Josiah Nott were two of the leading men in the movement to prove that Blacks had a limited mental capacity due to their inferior physical make-up. While historians debate the appeal of such scientific arguments within the Southern masses,[3] they effectively demonstrated the prevailing belief that Blacks essentially had a simple nature. In the minds of many Whites, slaves embodied four distinct characteristics: docility, childishness, laziness, and stupidity. To the pro-slavery elements, these facts alone stood as hard evidence that Blacks needed slavery as a means of protecting themselves from a cruel world in which they had little chance to survive, let alone succeed.

At the same time that Black women confronted these racial stereotypes, they also had to face the "cult of true womanhood," which determined acceptable modes of behavior for White, middle-class women. "According to the 'experts' of the day, the 'true woman,' who would also be a 'true wife,' was characterized by piety, purity, domesticity, and submissiveness."[4] Women were, in the eyes of the larger society, the standard bearers of the nation's morality. This was a period in American history when "the home and family began to accumulate new social and political significance . . . [,] to support important new emotional functions . . . ," and society expected women to act as the moral barometer within this family unit.[5] The concept of the "Republican wife" soon came into existence, as a woman's "place" was in the home exerting her moral influence over the rest of the family. Wives needed to provide a fundamental education for their children (thus encouraging them to one day act as noble citizens) while also establishing a "spiritual and virtuous environment" that protected the entire family from the ravages of the outside world.

As a result of this view, the family confined women to the home, frowning upon those White women who worked for wages outside of its "safe" confines. While it is true that more factory and industrial jobs became available to women during this period, such positions typically went to young, single women who promptly left the factory upon finding the right husband. Teaching was the only option available to most White, middle-class women seeking employment outside the home, and even this opportunity flew from their grasp at the moment they recited their wedding vows. People viewed the emerging market economy as "an arena of conflict increasingly identified with men and dominated by base self-interest." To them, it was only natural that women should thus remain in the home, which benefited from their moral influence and preserved their sense of purity. Black women, however, typically *needed* to work outside the home in order to support the family financially. Most of them could not uphold this ivory-tower view of womanhood because their families might otherwise starve.[6]

Finally, Black women had to deflect criticism directed specifically towards their own position in American society. Whereas Southern Whites characterized most male slaves (and free Blacks) as "docile" and "lazy," Black women often fell under the opposite end of the sociological spectrum. Many of these ideas born in the mid-19th century persist to this very day: "The image of the 'bad' black woman, in particular, which has persisted into the twentieth century, portrays her as sexually promiscuous and, because of her hard work as a laborer, physically powerful."[7] Her integral role in providing financial support for the family, combined with her "physical strength" from years of hard labor, reflected negatively upon the Black family. Critics seized upon these images to portray the Black family as "matriarchal and, hence, pathological." In turn, such ideas about the Black family led many to paint the picture of the domineering Black woman, trying to control her husband and ultimately "keeping him down" to assert her own authority.[8]

Shirley Yee went to great lengths to stress the fact that "stereotypes of black and white women were mutually reinforcing images, not simply opposites; the assumption that black women were sensual and physically strong served to buttress the notion that white women were delicate and passionless." In effect, this led to the debasement of both groups. White women who did not live up to their status as "true women" feared reprisal from their peers and categorization with women of ill repute (i.e., Blacks, poor Whites, etc.) And Black women, both free and slave, continued to suffer the indignities of their positions in society, which was used to justify everything from the raping of female slaves to the economic role of free women as washerwomen and domestics. In the end, regardless of the inherent difficulties White women faced from this "cult," Black women sustained far greater indignities, both from a racial and a gender standpoint.[9] With the "cult of true womanhood" standing as the marker for White female virtue, and slavery proclaiming White superiority, it is no wonder that:

> Black women—described by English slave traders as "hot constitution'd ladies," possessed of a "lascivious temper," who had an inclination for White men—would be impaled on the cutting edges of this race/sex dialectic.[10]

Rather than allow the "cutting edges" of racism and sexism to "impale" them, Black women attempted to use the words of their oppressors as keys to entering the abolitionist ranks. Within this framework of social, political, and economic oppression, Black women found several key justifications for their work in the abolitionist struggle. First, they utilized one of the primary arguments of the inchoate women's rights movement, which in turn sought justification through the "cult of true womanhood" itself. Women, they argued, carried the moral torch for the nation as a whole. They provided, according to the "experts" of this period, the fundamental lessons and guidance for the family unit and served as a stabilizing force in an ever-changing world. Why, then, should they not exert this influence on society as a whole? Would it not be beneficial for the most moral members of the Republic to exercise their judgments on a larger scale? Many women saw the inherent contradictions in using their positive attributes to maintain a high sense of morality within the home while lacking the ability to do likewise in the political realm. They simply could not see why it was "unnatural," as many clergymen argued, for a women to attack society's immorality from the lectern, when a chorus of voices told her that a woman's "natural" place was attacking vice in her own backyard. Black women in the educated middle- and upper-classes were no different: they knew that they had the necessary tools to shape the Black liberation struggle, and all they needed was a chance to place these talents on display.[11]

Black women in the lower classes cited another justification for their service in the public sphere. To them, it was no different than the services they provided for the Black community by earning their daily bread to support the family. Unlike the White (and some Black) women to whom the "cult" applied, Black working-class women did not face as much resistance to their role in the workplace. While those people occupying a higher station in society might look down upon these underlings, they voiced no opposition when these same women washed their clothes and cooked their meals. Thus, many Black women were quite accustomed to playing a crucial role in the Black community and saw no reason why it should be limited to the financial realm. If anything, their pecuniary contributions to the Black family reinforced, if only in their own minds, the rights of Black women to share their opinions in the struggle ahead.[12]

The early rumblings of Black feminism provided a third justification for service to the community. Black women viewed the abolition movement as a struggle for the *entire* African American community, one in which men and women, free Blacks and slaves, were equally degraded by an oppressive slave system. They viewed the resulting politicization of Black men as a call-to-arms for women as well. After all, how could Blacks argue for their equality with Whites if, within their own movement, they sought to distinguish between the potential contributions of men and women? Since their arrival on American shores, Black women helped to provide the spiritual, social, and economic backbone for the African American experience; why should they be now excluded from those pressing political concerns affecting the entire race? Black women saw, in the struggles for the race as a whole, a chance to publicly assert their own power and authority—not in an effort to dominate, as the stereotypes dictated, but to benefit the community as a whole.[13]

As each of these justifications demonstrated, Black women always remained mindful of the popular portrayals that affected their public standing. Some of them took advantage of their activism to soundly attack these images, while others used them as a context for developing justifications for their own liberation. Sojourner Truth's oft-quoted speech from the 1851 Akron Women Right's convention offers a rousing summary of this point:

> *Dat man ober dar say dat woman needs to be lifted ober ditches, and to have de best place every whar. Nobody eber helped me into carriages, or ober mud puddles, or gives me any best place and ar'n't I a woman? Look at me! Look at my arm! I have plowed, and planted, and gathered into barns, and no man could head me—and ar'n't I a woman? I could work as much and eat as much as a man (when I could get it) and bear de lash as well—and ar'n't I a woman? I have borne thirteen chilern and seen em mos' all sold off into slavery, and when I cried out with a mother's grief, none but Jesus heard—and ar'n't I a woman?*[14]

Perhaps more than any other single accomplishment or speech, this oration attacked the fundamental notions that girded the American social hierarchy and established the "place" of Black women within it. Faced with allegations of Black docility and laziness, her accounts indicated a strong work ethic and a burning desire to confront the evils of the slave system. To the charge that women needed to be shielded from the evils of a cruel world, Truth was a living testament demonstrating women's ability to work alongside men and not only survive, but excel. She and other Black women in the movement knew that they had to "bear de lash" of oppression more than the average activist. In everything they did, in all of the goals they set for themselves, Black female abolitionists ultimately wanted to change these fundamental relationships in order to facilitate growing democratic desires among the "outcasts" of American society. More than any other reformers from this period, they recognized (and experienced) the dire consequences of this developing caste system and sought to institute change on a dramatic scale.

Just as their position in society and their political message suggested grounds for recognition, these factors also contributed to a unique style that provided a moving human quality to the movement. In doing so, they often used the prevailing images of womanhood to strengthen their messages. Take the last line of Truth's speech as an example: "I have borne thirteen chilern and seen em mos' all sold off into slavery, and when I cried out with a mother's grief, none but Jesus heard—and ar'n't I a woman?" Given the popular beliefs of the time regarding women and their role in promoting a stable home environment, this solitary line had to strike a sore spot in the hearts of men and women, Blacks and Whites, rich and poor. This sentence changed the way that people viewed the institution of slavery. It was no longer simply an economic system that treated its workers inhumanely. Slavery also took children away from their mothers, not only depriving the young of their mother's love, but also stripping the woman, in the eyes of 19th-century Americans, of her "duty" to raise these children properly. While such views tended to reinforce existing notions of gender roles, they also added a cogent ethical argument to the existing political debates. Such perspectives infused the movement with an almost religious moralism that appealed to humanistic concerns instead of dry political discourse.

Often, Black women used their status *as women* to demonstrate the specific evils inflicted by the institution of slavery. The narratives of runaway slaves provide excellent examples of the differences that arose between Black men and women who used these slave experiences as a foundation for their activism. Perhaps the two most prominent slave narrators from this period were Frederick Douglass and Harriet Jacobs. Each served on a plantation; each struggled to endure the vicious torments of the Whites in power. Yet they provided two separate ways of looking at the slave experience and, thus, two ways of approaching the abolition movement.

Douglass' *Narrative of the Life of Frederick Douglass, An American Slave, Written by Himself* leaves the audience with a prevailing vision of resistance to slavery. Having lived for a period of seven years in Baltimore, he knew to some extent what it meant to be free and never forgot this feeling upon returning to the plantation as a field hand. One day, the tremendous physical strain caught up with him. He collapsed in the field, only to be whipped by his overseer, Mr. Covey, for failing to complete the task at hand. Douglass then walked seven miles to register a complaint with the master, finding that the latter had no sympathy for his plight. Several days later, Douglass returned to his home, but the overseer did not confront him. The very next day, however, Covey cornered Douglass in the barn and tied him up in an attempt to whip him for his insubordination. But Douglass was not about to let this happen, not without a fight:

> *Mr. Covey seemed now to think he had me, and could do what he pleased; but at this moment—from whence came the spirit I don't know—I resolved to fight. . . . My resistance was so entirely unexpected, that Covey seemed taken all aback. He trembled like a leaf. . . . He asked me if I meant to persist in my resistance. I told him I did, come what might; that he had used me like a brute for six months, and that I was determined to be used so no longer.*[15]

This undoubtedly struck a nerve in the reader, as s/he pictured this struggle for not only independence, but for life itself. Slaveholders and their minions came across as unseemly cowards who faltered at the first sign of resistance, while the slave retained a large degree of nobility in spite of his dehumanizing plight.

Harriet Jacobs, while providing another example of someone who rebelled against the system and eventually escaped to the North, also deals with aspects of slavery specific to the female experience—namely, sexual abuse. Her struggles for freedom (under the pseudonym of Linda Brent) were no less heroic than those related by Douglass, nor did they inspire less admiration in the reader. But Jacobs wrote quite candidly on the subject of sexual advances, detailing the innuendoes her master proposed when she first reached puberty: "But I now entered on my fifteenth year—a sad epoch in the life of a slave girl. My master began to whisper foul words in my ear. Young as I was, I could not remain ignorant of their import."[16]

Douglass, on the other hand, does not make this issue the primary focus of his work. He does cite a specific example of sexual abuse by making vague references to the master's treatment of "Aunt Hester" and his ensuing jealousy when she had a relationship with another slave. Douglass also gave direct references to the dozens of mulatto children running around the slave quarters—including himself—and indicated what their presence meant to the slaves and the slaveholder. In the great scheme of his work, however, these were relatively minor points, while Jacobs presented these ideas as part of her overriding theme.[17] This is not to say that Black men were ignorant of such abuses or that it had no bearing on their standing in society. Yet it *does* demonstrate that there were vast differences in the approaches taken by Black men and women within the movement—differences that were rooted in their respective experiences and which arose strictly along gender lines.

Jacobs took an interesting approach to addressing the subject of sexual abuse in the slave quarters. She appealed to the popular notions of the period regarding gender and sexuality. Pleading to the White, middle-class activists who still adhered to the "cult of true womanhood," she constantly asked for forgiveness from the readers:

> *"But, O, ye happy women, whose purity has been sheltered from childhood, who have been free to choose the objects of your affection, whose homes are protected by law, do not judge the poor desolate slave girl too severely! . . . I wanted to keep myself pure; and, under the most adverse circumstances, I tried hard to preserve my self-respect. . . . "*[18]

Throughout the book Jacobs not only pleaded for the pity of the readers, but she also asked them to imagine a loved one—a mother, wife, daughter, or sister—faced with such demoralizing circumstances. In doing so, she not only painted herself as a noble heroine struggling against the cruel nature of slavery, but as a woman trying to uphold her high sense of morality. Both of these objectives instilled an emotional and deeply personal quality into the words of the female abolitionists. The moral outrage engendered in defending their sense of "womanhood," combined with the appalling stories of slavery itself, created a visceral reaction against the institution that may not have otherwise existed. Granted, it is difficult to effectively gauge the impact of Jacobs' book as compared with the narratives of Douglass, but history points to a strong connection between defense of womanhood and militant action. Just as the White Southerners in the post-bellum period used this rationale to defend mob rule and lynchings, abolitionists could rally behind such a cause in attacking the "peculiar institution." Thus, Jacobs' characterization of Linda Brent (representing Everywoman) as the ultimate defender of female purity, combined with her courageous image of the fugitive slave, probably had a broader appeal than the narratives of Douglass.

The varied testimonials, methods, and images employed by Jacobs and Truth suggest an important point regarding their activism. Although Black women participated in the abolition movement as a "group," they were not a homogenous bloc with one set of ideas, methods, and experiences. Each of the women and families involved in this strain of activism came from widely varying backgrounds. While White female activists tended to be financially secure, Black women from all walks of life participated in the abolitionist struggles. Consequently, their diverse experiences in society gave the movement a greater sense of fluidity, allowing women of all social standings to contribute what they could in the way of both ideas and methods. More than any other reform effort of this period, abolition called for widespread action on behalf of an entire community, instead of the wealthy elites with too much time on their hands. Slavery affected the entire Black community by placing the stigma of inferiority upon the race as a whole. As a result, Blacks from every station needed to contribute to the defense of the Black perspective and experience. Within this context, Black women representing each social class contributed substantially to the growing movement.

Class did not represent the only difference between many of the Black female activists. Nonetheless, it provided the best example of the heterogeneity present within their movement:

> Black women abolitionists came from all walks of life; most were wage-earners who struggled to make a decent living and worked for the cause when they could; others came from prosperous families, and a few from wealthy households.[19]

Although this last group—Black women from wealthy households—comprised the smallest percentage of Black female activists, they represented an important part of the movement.

> These women came from the few northern free black families that had amassed considerable wealth and were well-known and respected in their communities for their activism and philanthropy. The high social and financial position of their families instilled in some of the women a self-consciousness about their social responsibilities both to aid the less fortunate of their race and to maintain female respectability and prescribed sex roles.[20]

The Forten-Purvis clan of Philadelphia was the most famous and influential of these wealthy Black households. James Forten, Sr., the great-grandson of an African slave, established their family fortune as a sailmaker. He served as a powder boy on a ship during the American Revolution before starting his apprenticeship to a local sailmaker. Within 12 years he took control of the business, and "[t]hrough his invention of a device which made it possible to handle sails more easily, he made a hundred thousand dollars, a fortune in those days. He became a distinguished leader of the Negro population of Philadelphia."[21] One of the distinguishing characteristics of the Forten-Purvis men was their own sense of feminism. They not only supported a fierce sense of activism in the women of their family but actively promoted it. During a speech in April 1836, Forten's son, James Forten, Jr., stated:

> It has often been said by anti-Abolitionists that the females have no right to interfere with the question of slavery or petition for its overthrow; that they had better be at home attending to domestic affairs, etc. What a gross error—what an anti-Christian spirit this bespeaks! Were not the holy commands: "Remember them that are in bonds, as bound with them," and "Do unto others as ye would they should do unto you," intended for women to obey as well as men? Most assuredly they were.[22]

Thus, the Forten-Purvis women were in an environment much more conducive to and accepting of female activism than most other women in their social strata. Indeed, they took advantage of this fact, leaving their own indelible print upon the abolition movement. James Sr.'s wife, Charlotte Forten, along with her three daughters (Margaretta, Harriet, and Sarah Louise), helped to found the Philadelphia Female Anti-Slavery Society. This followed her lifetime as a "competent manager who presided over a large household with ease and grace . . . [and] brought up five children." Margaretta was not only an officer and founder of the Female Anti-Slavery Society (she served as either recording secretary or treasurer from its founding to its dissolution), but later became active in the Women's Rights Movement. Harriet married Robert Purvis, another wealthy and successful Black like her father, and both of them became extremely active in various anti-slavery societies and in the Pennsylvania branch of the Underground Railroad. Sarah married Robert Purvis's brother,

Joseph, and served on the Female Anti-Slavery Society's Board of Managers. As part of her duties, she worked on annual fundraising fairs, organized abolitionist sewing circles, and submitted "over a dozen creditable poems and essays" to several well-known abolitionist publications.[23]

James Forten, Sr.'s granddaughter, Charlotte Forten, helped to carry the torch for yet another generation of activists. Charlotte followed in the others' footsteps by joining the Salem Female Anti-Slavery Society at the age of 17. Craving to have a direct impact upon the efforts to uplift her people, she journeyed to Sea Island off the coast of South Carolina in October 1862. Her mission there was to offer the newly-freed slaves of the island a rudimentary education. She found herself in an awkward position—caught between the Whites on the island who were closer to her station in life (many, in fact, knew her family in Pennsylvania) and the Blacks who never saw a member of their own race with such a high degree of education and sophistication. To her credit, she tried to understand the slave culture, but still found it "strange" and "barbarous." Charlotte left after a year-and-a-half of work when her physical condition deteriorated to the point where she could no longer teach. She spent 6 years working for the Teachers Committee of the New England Freedmen's Union Commission before returning South to teach at Shaw Memorial School in Charleston, S.C. Later in life, she taught in Washington, D.C., worked as a clerk for the Treasury Department, and eventually married Francis Grimke, another member of a prominent abolitionist family.[24]

Though not nearly as wealthy as the Forten-Purvis clan, the Shadd family was fairly well-off and extremely active in abolitionist circles. Abraham D. Shadd, the patriarch of the family, built his fortune as a shoemaker in Wilmington, Delaware, before moving to Chester County, Pennsylvania. He was a founding member and a delegate to the Board of Governors for the American Anti-Slavery Society and served as a leading agent in the promotion of abolitionist newspapers. Shadd's home in West Chester served as a station on the Underground Railroad; such actions, in turn, served as a vivid example of activism to the next generation of Shadd abolitionists.[25]

Abraham's daughter, Mary Ann Shadd Cary, became an important voice in the emigrationist movement during the 1850s. This idea caught the attention of several prominent Blacks in the 1810s and 1820s, but quickly lost its momentum because many of the Whites supporting it did so out of self-interest and racism, not for the improvement of the Black condition. In the 1850s, however, the idea took root again with the passage of a stronger Fugitive Slave Law that threatened not only those Blacks who escaped from slavery, but those who were born free.

Cary and one of her brothers traveled to Canada West shortly after the passage of the Fugitive Slave Law to investigate the conditions in the territory for Black emigrants. Finding them to her liking, she brought the rest of the Shadd family to Canada, eventually settling in the town of Chatham. It was here that she began her zealous campaign to convince other Blacks to follow her lead. First, Cary wrote and distributed a popular pamphlet entitled *Notes on Canada West*, giving details to prospective Black emigrants on the conditions of the region. From 1854 to 1858, with funding from other Blacks in Toronto, she published *The Provincial Freeman*, "the first anti-slavery paper in Canada West." Over the next few years, she made various speaking engagements throughout the North, soliciting funds for her cause and warning Blacks of the inherent dangers in staying in America. After the Dred Scott decision and its declaration that Blacks had no civil rights which Whites were required to respect, she warned African Americans, "Your ship is rotten and sinking, why not leave it?" The situation in Canada, however, was not always as bright as Cary described it; against her wishes, many Blacks formed their own communities in the territory for fear of racism from Whites or to prove that Blacks could indeed survive on their own. Despite her status as a naturalized British subject, she returned to the United States in 1863 to recruit Black men for the Union army after President Lincoln called for an additional 500,000 troops. After the war was over, she moved to Washington, D.C., where she eventually earned a law degree from Howard University.[26]

Middle-class activists faced a special series of hurdles that these upper-class reformers never confronted:

> *The Remonds, Chesters, Douglasses, and Pauls, for example, maintained a comfortable lifestyle as long as all adults in the family brought home a steady income. The women of these families found employment in the only jobs then available to women, regardless of race: teaching, running small businesses, and domestic-related work as laundresses, seamstresses, and servants.[27]*

Consequently, they could not afford to devote as much time to abolitionist causes as the "professional reformers" in the well-to-do families. They realized that if a sudden tragedy struck their family (i.e., death, sudden illness, fire, economic downturn, etc.), their fortunes could quickly take a turn for the worse and the family could soon fall on hard times. Furthermore, the rise of vandalism and violence against Black-owned businesses prior to the Civil War increased the chances of encountering an unexpected catastrophe to uncomfortable levels. In light of such conditions, the Remond women ran a cake-making business and a wig factory in order to maintain the style of living to which they grew accustomed, and Jane Marie Chester helped her husband run a successful restaurant and catering business. While trying to preserve their middle-class position, the Remond women "frequently participated in the activities of the Salem Female Anti-Slavery Society, which began as a black female organization in 1832 and was later reorganized into a racially-mixed society." Jane and George Chester, meanwhile, "were well-known supporters of the anti-colonizationist activities in Harrisburg, Pennsylvania." They instilled this sense of activism into their children, including their daughter Charlotte, the first Black teacher in Harrisburg.[28]

Other families did not experience the same strokes of good luck that blessed the Remonds and the Chesters. In terms of the struggles they faced and the accomplishments they still produced, the Douglasses offered a prime example of such a family. Grace Bustill Douglass came from an activist Quaker family in Burlington, N.J., and worked throughout her life with the Black communities of South Jersey and Philadelphia. Yet when she died in 1842, the loss of income that she provided through her millinery shop hurt the family. Sarah Mapps Douglass, her only daughter, became the primary wage earner for the family, working as a teacher in Philadelphia. All of this, according to Sarah Grimke, took its toll on Sarah: "[Her] health is so precarious that her physician tells her it will be almost the certain sacrifice of life for her to continue school-keeping . . . yet their circumstances render it necessary for her to do something for a living."[29]

These physical and financial strains, however, did not prevent Sarah Mapps Douglass from assailing that which she considered unjust. In 1832, the state of Pennsylvania introduced a bill that called for all Blacks to carry passes. This was the event that propelled Douglass into political activism:

> *One short year ago, how different were my feelings on the subject of slavery! It is true, the wail of the captive sometimes came to my ear in the midst of my happiness, and caused my heart to bleed for his wrongs; but, alas! the impression was as evanescent as the early cloud and morning dew. . . . But how the scene changed when I beheld the oppressor lurking on the border of my own peaceful home! . . . I started up, and with one mighty effort threw from me the lethargy which had covered me as a mantle for years; and determined, by the help of the Almighty, to use every exertion in my power to elevate the character of my wronged and neglected race.*[30]

Douglass, like the Fortens and other prominent Black women in Philadelphia, threw her support behind the formation of the Philadelphia Female Anti-Slavery Society. Until the Civil War, she was one of its most active members, serving at various times as librarian and recording secretary or serving on the Board of Managers and the Fair Committee. As an educator, she used her connections in the Society to fund the nation's first academy offering a high school education to Black women. Later, "[i]n 1853 she assumed responsibility for running the girls' department of the Institute for Colored Youth"; when she relinquished control to Fannie Jackson Coppin in 1869, she remained on staff as a teacher. Throughout this period, Douglass pioneered in attacking both racial and gender biases. She not only denounced the segregated benches of the Quaker churches, but taught young women courses in anatomy when science was still considered a taboo subject for them. In doing so, she provided many activists with a clear link between the two movements at a time when friction between these forces often threatened what should have been a natural alliance.[31]

Susan Paul provided another example of a woman faced with economic difficulties and an activist heart. Her father, Thomas Paul, was a prominent Baptist minister in Boston, and an active abolitionist until his death in 1831. Following his death, Susan spent the better part of the next decade working as a seamstress and teacher to support both her widowed mother and the children of her late sister. At the same time, she tried to remain active in the Boston Anti-Slavery Society; she served as a delegate to the 1837 Anti-Slavery Convention in New York, organized a "Garrison Junior Choir, which sang at abolitionist gatherings and gave concerts for the benefit of the Mashpee Indians and similar charities," and in October 1833 paid her lifetime membership fee of $15 to the newly-formed New England Anti-Slavery Society.[32] Paul spent the last four years of her life depending upon the help of close abolitionist friends and the Black community in Boston to support her family and to find them a place to live. She contracted consumption during her trip to New York (the segregated policies of the steamship forced her to stay in the damp lower deck) and died in 1841 at the age of 34:

Warren Weston wrote of Paul's death . . . : "Miss Paul died the day I came out of town. . . . Everything was done by Mrs. [Hannah] Southwick, Henrietta [Sargent] & others for her comfort. The family will now be broken up & the children taken by sundry friends." Thus, even in death, Paul relied primarily on the assistance and friendship of white abolitionists.[33]

Black women of the lower classes often had difficulty balancing the economic strains of their social position with their desire to aid the abolitionist cause. With both the men and the women of the household confined to menial employment (when jobs were indeed available), their position was even more precarious than that of the middle class reformers. For some, like Harriet Hayden, the burden was too much to bear; in a letter to Maria Weston Chapman, she wrote, "I have been spending the last week in working for the Mass. Fair, I want very much to do a great deal but time & circumstances forbid." Others, such as Eliza Ann Dixon Day, faced incredible odds in remaining active in the movement. Widowed in 1829 and left to raise four children by herself, Day regularly attended both church and abolitionist meetings, including one broken by an unruly mob. Like many Black women of this period, she plunged her limited funds into educating the children, while her activism provided an example that they eventually followed.[34]

Among the ranks of these lower-class Black women were former slaves. In some ways, these women had little choice but to join the movement for their own protection or else risk capture and return to the South. All of them realized that the tortures they endured under the "peculiar institution" were more than any human being should bear, and thus, devoted their lives to combating the evil influences of slavery. In doing so, these women provided some of the most famous names to come out of the abolitionist camps, not to mention the few examples of Black female activism that receive proper recognition from most history textbooks.

Harriet Ross Tubman is arguably the most famous Black woman in the history of 19th-century America. Born in approximately 1823, she became associated with the plight of the runaway slave more than any single person. Throughout her life she suffered "sleeping seizures and dizzy spells," results of an episode during her time in slavery: "[a]t about fifteen years of age, she intervened to protect another slave and was struck in the head by a two-pound weight hurled by the overseer." Persevering in spite of such abuse, she eventually married a freedman, John Tubman, and decided to venture forth to take her own freedom. John, however, was too frightened of the consequences of abetting a fugitive slave, as were Tubman's two brothers who began the journey with her but soon returned to the plantation. Not only did she survive the ordeal on her own, but she went on to make 19 more trips into the South to rescue slaves—including her own mother and father. Armed with a pistol and a driving sense of courage, Tubman led over 300 Blacks to freedom, warning each of them that they would either "be free or die." Sarah Bradford quoted her in her biography as saying:

There was one of two things I had a right to, liberty, or death; if I could not have one, I would have the other; for no man should take me alive; I should fight for my liberty as long as my strength lasted, and when the time came for me to go, the Lord would let them take me.[35]

Tubman traveled widely through the Northern states, Canada, and Great Britain to spread her anti-slavery message, disarming many people with her sense of militancy. In 1859, she supported John Brown's raid on Harper's Ferry, but could not participate because of illness. She later served as a scout and spy in the Union Army; Tubman led several army raids (with both Black and White soldiers) into the South and, on one particularly daring excursion, returned with 756 newly-freed slaves. Even as the years advanced, she remained as active as ever, especially in the emerging women's suffrage campaigns. Eventually, the federal government granted her a pension for her work in the U.S. Army, which she used to fund an old-age home for elderly Blacks. Tubman remained active in this pursuit until her death in 1913.[36]

In the eyes of one historian, "Few black women combined abolitionism and feminism as effectively as Sojourner Truth. . . . "[37] Born a slave in 1797, in Hurley, Ulster County, New York, her experiences with slavery differed greatly from those of Tubman. While she grew up performing "men's" work in the fields of the Dumont family farm, she never experienced the same terror that Tubman faced in Maryland, or that other Black women endured in the Deep South. Still, she suffered enough beatings and degradations to take her own freedom in November or December of 1826, several months before the state of New York freed all slaves on July 4, 1827. The next 15 years of her life featured a whirlwind of events, as she eventually joined Elijah Pierson and Robert Matthew on a utopian settlement called Zion Hill. When Pierson was murdered under suspicious circumstances, Truth spent 8 or 9 years as a domestic worker in New York City before hearing "the call" to preach in 1843.[38]

This "call from God" effectively began a public career that spanned the next three decades. Truth spent the first few years of her "sojourn" lecturing on religion wherever she could find an audience. During one of her trips through New England, she met an abolitionist, George Benson, who brought her into the anti-slavery fold. Over the next few years, she not only published her slave narrative but became one of the most popular speakers on the abolitionist circuit. Audiences raved at her fiery style and her fearlessness when faced with opponents who displayed a better education and higher social standing than she. Her travels to the "west" (i.e., Ohio, Illinois, etc.) brought her into contact with the Women's Rights Movement and led to her oft-quoted, "Ar'n't I a Woman?" speech in Akron, Ohio, in 1851. Between then and her retirement in 1875, she spoke about issues such as women's rights, abolition, and the procurement of western lands for freed slaves. In each of these movements, activists across the country knew of her blunt, simple style, which evoked as much power and emotion as any other speaker from this era.[39]

These tales of activism, while demonstrating the class mechanisms behind the general workings of the abolitionist movement, also indicate the various methods of resistance set forth by women of color. They attacked slavery with an overwhelming sense of zeal in every conceivable sphere. Their actions took advantage of both the existing institutions within the Black community (such as the Black Church) and those within the larger face of American society. Working within the political system and around it (when necessary), the actions of Black women left an indelible mark upon a movement that often attempted to limit their participation.

As previously mentioned, anti-slavery societies provided a cornerstone for Black female participation. Like their male counterparts, these female abolitionist groups served as a base of operations for every other aspect of the movement, organizing disparate groups and activities under the common rubric of an organization. In addition to their tangible actions against the institution of slavery, they served a crucial role in developing social networks within the abolitionist struggle. Not only did they link people within a given geographical region through the abolitionist cause, but the separate abolitionist groups throughout the country helped to maintain communications between activists nationwide. Black women, in particular, found themselves at the crux of a vast and "dynamic" series of social networks that became crucial to their work:

> The connections that free black women formed, through either their own initiative or the influence of relatives, provided many of them with important resources for both financial and emotional support, forging a network that proved particularly valuable in light of increasing hostility from white society and the relatively poor economic condition of the free black community.[40]

Such connections provided Black women with a number of advantages that could not exist under different circumstances. Many of the activists who faced financial difficulties relied on their newfound friends in the movement to avoid dire economic straits. Elizabeth and Charles Lenox Remond, for example, relied heavily upon the generosity of Wendell Phillips while Charles was active within the movement. While Elizabeth's work as a seamstress kept the family solvent when Charles was away, his return brought further financial difficulties to the family. During the Civil War, he spent most of his time continuing his abolitionist work and, later, attempting to recruit Black soldiers; thus, his regular income was next to nothing. Phillips arranged a loan to the family to help them survive, but several years later Elizabeth remained worried about their financial situation: "'I have been overwhelmed with care and anxiety over two years but I have good friends now who stood by me in my poverty & of course I shall retain them if I succeed in getting my money back. . . . I think I am very fortunate.'"[41]

Black women gained other forms of assistance from their network of abolitionist friends. Many of them benefited greatly when attempting to spread their message overseas. Sarah Parker Remond utilized her American connections, including Samuel J. May and Maria Weston Chapman, to secure speaking engagements and companionship during her sojourns to Great Britain in 1858–1859. Chapman, in particular, tried to use her name within abolitionist circles to aid Remond, offering letters of introduction to facilitate a smooth journey through the British Isles. Coming from a particularly active anti-slavery family, Remond acknowledged the importance of her ties to other abolitionists: "without their 'influence and money' she could 'not have done the antislavery [work].'" Remond and other women also used these tight-knit circles to form lasting friendships with both Black and White activists. Although these friendships often crossed racial lines and remained strong for decades, there was a common ground among the Black female abolitionists that White women could not truly understand. While women like the Grimke sisters offered a great deal of sympathy and a listening ear, Black women such as Sarah Forten and Sarah Mapps Douglass could not expect them to truly comprehend the implications of race in their daily lives. Indeed, White women such as Anne Warren Weston occasionally indicated that despite their good intentions, they too succumbed to the prevailing notions of stereotypical Black behavior:

> *[She] once described a visit to her home by Charles and Sarah Remond. While she expressed admiration for Charles's "high breeding" and "talk to Shakespeare," she noted that "Miss R on the contrary has many of the manners & ways supposed to be peculiar to her race. She is not in the least like the pretty one we saw at the N[ew] E[ngland] Convention."*

Thus, Black women took advantage of these groups to form lasting friendships within their own community. At the same time that abolitionist groups created contacts between the Black and White worlds, they also granted Black women an open forum to discuss their racial/gender plight with others in similar circumstances.[42] Often, this was not the case in the company of White women, despite the abolitionism and/or feminism which they espoused. These White female activists sometimes failed to see those connections between gender, race, and class that perpetuated Black female activism. Some women, like Frances Ellen Watkins Harper, heatedly debated these issues with "sympathizers" such as Susan B. Anthony and Elizabeth Cady Stanton in the 1850s and 1860s. Such tensions made friendships between Black female abolitionists more practical than interracial relationships, as Black women sought a chance to examine their own status in society among others who related to the tensions unique to their experiences.[43]

Not all Black women, however, benefited from such associations. In forming such strong bonds to the abolitionist community, some women, like Elizabeth Brown, found that swift retribution fell upon those people who did not uphold the movement's moral standards. While her husband, William Wells Brown, lectured on the abolitionist circuit, Elizabeth allegedly had an affair with another man. William took the children and left, leaving her with little money to support herself. "When she appealed to the Massachusetts Anti-Slavery Society for financial support from William, the committee appointed to investigate the matter sided with him. . . . For Elizabeth Brown, her associations with the movement, however tangential, had resulted in a life of economic hardship, loneliness, and frustration." Forced to choose between one of its leading activists and the damaged credibility of his wife, the Society opted to protect one of its own, and in doing so left Elizabeth out in the cold for the final three years of her life.[44]

While the abolitionist circles cultivated a crucial network of friendships and communication, they served the much more important function of fostering other direct attacks against the institution of slavery. Their promotion of abolitionist speakers within the lecture circuit, for example, provided an integral link between the activists of the movement and the mass audiences to whom they hoped to appeal. Nobody exemplified the impact of the lectern better than Maria Stewart.

Born in Connecticut in 1803, Stewart's little formal education primarily came from Sabbath school. After the death of her husband in 1829, she experienced a "religious conversion" that triggered her desire to awaken the Black masses. Unlike the vast majority of famed abolitionists, Stewart came to prominence immediately before the rise of mass abolitionist groups in the 1830s. Yet she served not only as an important example of Black women who graced the lecture circuit, but as a forerunner to the militant Black female activists who succeeded her during the following decades. In 1831, she began her career as a lecturer, becoming "the first native-born American woman to engage in a public speaking career, and to leave extant texts of her addresses." This fact in itself is enough to secure her place in the annals of abolitionist history. But it was her charisma on the podium, combined with her uncompromising stands on issues facing Blacks *and* women, that warrants closer attention.

An interesting example of her ideologies appeared in excerpts from an 1831 speech in Boston, Massachusetts. Like David Walker before her, Stewart predicted that violence would play an integral part in the liberation of Blacks from their existing conditions: "'Many will suffer for pleading the cause of oppressed Africa . . . and I shall glory in being one of the martyrs." In this same speech, a full 17 years before the Seneca Falls Convention, she expressed the necessity of unifying Black women in order to promote both their families and themselves:

How long shall the fair daughters of Africa be compelled to bury their minds and talents beneath a load of iron pots and kettles? Until union, knowledge and love begin to flow among us. How long shall a mean set of men flatter us with smiles, and enrich themselves with our hard earnings; their wives sparkling with rings, and they themselves laughing at our folly? Until we begin to promote and patronize each other. . . . We have never had an opportunity of displaying our talents; therefore the world thinks we know nothing. . . . Possess the spirit of men, bold and enterprising, fearless and undaunted. Sue for your rights and privileges. Know the reason that you cannot attain them. Weary them [men] with your importunities.[45]

Here we see the earliest signs of an emerging Black feminist movement. Stewart laid the foundations for Black women to justify an equal position with male abolitionists on the grounds that they indeed deserved full equality in every aspect of life. Not only was she one of the earliest purveyors of Black nationalism through her emphasis on racial unity, but she managed to combine this with a militant feminism unparalleled even within the emerging Women's Rights Movement. Throughout the decade, supporters of gender equality such as Lucretia Mott found few listeners willing to lend a sympathetic ear. Yet Stewart took advantage of the relative popularity of abolitionism to stress her ideas on the war between the sexes, inextricably linking the two causes under one banner.

Stewart strove to motivate action within her audience, particularly in her Black listeners. She had no qualms whatsoever with criticizing the free Black community for what she perceived to be a lack of direct action against slavery. "'Most of our color,' she said, 'have been taught to stand in fear of the white man from their earliest infancy, to work as soon as they can walk, and call "master" before they could scarce lisp the name of "mother."'" In this same speech, Stewart expressed to her audience the need for political activism. She encouraged them to send a petition to Washington calling for an end to slavery; within several weeks, a petition of 1200 Providence Blacks asked for emancipation in Washington, Arkansas, and Florida. Similarly, she asked "several women" to hire young Black girls, stressing the need for Blacks to seek employment and an economic stake in society. Despite the abuses towards Blacks by the American system, Stewart remained determined to find success on these shores, spurning emigrationist attempts and stating that "'the bayonet shall pierce me through'" before she departed for Africa.[46]

Stewart's short career as a public speaker ended approximately two years after it began. Yet in her "farewell address," she resurrected her famed militancy one last time:

What if I am a woman; is not the God of ancient times the God of these modern days: Did he not raise up Deborah to be a mother and a judge in Israel? Did not Queen Esther save the lives of the Jews? And Mary Magdalene first declare the resurrection of Christ from the dead? . . . What if such women as are here described should rise among our sable race? And it is not impossible; for it is not the color of the skin that makes the man or the woman, but the principle formed in the soul.[47]

Characteristic of her entire career, Stewart employed Biblical references in defending her positions. And once again, she linked her assertions about women to the racial situation in America. It was her success in achieving this dual consciousness, in fusing the ideas at the heart of future Black female activism, that established her place in history. Having said her piece, she soon went back to school for several years, becoming a teacher for the rest of her life and seeking to use education to uplift the Black community.

As Stewart's call to action indicated, petitions served as another focal point for Black female activism. They provided one of the few political outlets for Blacks to voice their concern about the issue of slavery. Voting was out of the question; "[b]y 1860 equal suffrage existed only in New England, excluding Connecticut. In the remaining states the Negro was barred outright from the polls or, as in New York, faced with a property requirement."[48] It goes without saying that this restriction extended to women as well. Yet the right to petition, as one Black speaker said in Alton, Illinois, in November 1856, was "'the only constitutional guarantee now inviolate from the ruffianism of American Slavery.'"[49]

Women served as key players in the petition movement on both the state and federal level. Abolitionists flooded the 25th U.S. Congress with a petition of 67,000 names, of whom some 45,000 were women. "By the end of 1838, the petitions had become so numerous that they presented storage problems in Washington. 'If the ladies and school children would let us alone,' commented Senator Robert Walker of Mississippi, 'there would be but a few abolition petitions.'"[50] Hundreds of these petitions opposed the annexation of Texas, as abolitionists across the country feared that it would enter the Union as a slave state (or several, if Congress decided to divide the territory). Others joined the howling choruses protesting the "gag rule" instituted by Congress in May 1836 to prevent members of the House of Representatives from debating the slavery issue on the floor. An 1839 petition led by Black women in the state of Massachusetts attacked racial discrimination in the law and sought to end the restrictions on interracial marriage; four years later, they were indeed successful in striking the marriage law from the books. Future petition drives assailed discrimination in other areas, including the segregated school systems. In these cases and hundreds of others, Black women took advantage of the few constitutional rights they still possessed and told government officials exactly where they stood on the issues of slavery and racial discrimination.[51]

Perhaps the most spectacular and radical form of Black female abolitionism came in direct assaults on the institution itself—that is, the freeing of slaves and violence against slaveholders. Harriet Tubman is the most obvious example, freeing over 300 slaves through her work with the Underground Railroad. But she was far from the only one active in this aspect of abolitionism. Mary Ellen Pleasant was born a slave on a Georgia plantation in the early 1800s. Price, a local planter, bought Pleasant from her master and granted her freedom. She traveled to Boston in search of an education before meeting and marrying Alexander Smith, an active member of the Garrison Anti-Slavery Society. When he died, Smith forced Pleasant to promise that she would use his fortune ($50,000 in gold) to support abolitionist causes. In 1851, she settled in San Francisco with a number of other abolitionist families. There, she invested his fortune in the silver and gold markets, using local political contacts to determine which markets offered the best returns.

Pleasant used this wealth to support the abolitionist cause, in keeping with her husband's dying wish. She used her investments to purchase a number of slaves from their Southern owners; in several cases, according to her biographer Helen Holdridge, she actually traveled into the South a la Tubman to secure their freedoms. Once they made it to free soil, Pleasant often "provided them food, clothing and, in some cases, start-up money for their own businesses." Moreover, she funded the defense's efforts in the Archy Lee Case of 1858, a decision that "led to the repeal of the law banning Black testimony in California." These activities earned her the nickname "Mother of the Civil Rights struggle in California."

Her most daring exploits, however, occurred in 1859. Pleasant heard of John Brown's attempts to free the enslaved people of the South and hoped to fulfill the deathbed promise she made to her husband. She allegedly met with Brown in Chatham, Canada to give him $30,000 to prepare for his raid on Harper's Ferry, Virginia. When responding soldiers captured him, they found a note with the initials "M.E.P," but misread it to say "W.E.P." Nonetheless, Pleasant still did all she could with her fortune to build a strong Black community among the growing African American constituency in the West. Despite her own Catholic beliefs, she funded the building of the AME Church, the AME Zion Church, and the Baptist Church of San Francisco. In 1866, Pleasant sued the San Francisco Trolley Company for refusing her a seat on one of its cars.[52]

In hindsight, it is much easier for historians to examine the roles of Black women in the abolition movement and attest to their indispensability. During this period, however, they faced a great deal of opposition to their participation by other members of the anti-slavery struggle. The arguments against Black female activism came from people of all colors, genders, and social institutions. Generally, resistance to Black female participation had its roots in the defense of contemporary gender roles. To be more precise, these activists wanted to uphold the "cult of true womanhood," which stood as a benchmark for White middle-class women and, consequently, dictated acceptable modes of behavior for *all* American women. One of their overriding motivations was the establishment of a new Black female identity; instead of the negative stereotypical images, members of the movement "described women of their race in terms usually used to represent middle-class white women."[53]

By painting Black women in these terms, fellow abolitionists attempted to subdue their strong reformist urges as part of the quest for respectability. This trend was especially apparent in the writings of the Black Press. Samuel Cornish, editor of *Freedom's Journal*, wrote that Black women could not risk losing their tempers in public:

> *A man, in a furious passion, is terrible to his enemies; but a woman, in a passion, is disgusting to her friends; she loses all that respect due to her sex; she has not masculine strength and courage to enforce any other kind of respect. . . . The happiness and influence of women, both as wives and mothers, and indeed, in every relation so much depends on the temper, that it ought to be most carefully cultivated.*[54]

Even a prominent male feminist such as Frederick Douglass succumbed to the "cult" in *The North Star* when describing proper behavior for women: "There is certainly something in the ordinance of human affairs, in the organization of society, that demands from the female sex the highest tone of purity and strictest observance of duties pertaining to the woman's sphere."

Other members of the Black Press criticized women who took an active role in anti-slavery actions. The *Colored American* attacked a group of Black women who tried to rescue several fugitive slaves. "Everlasting shame and remorse seize upon those females that so degraded themselves yesterday. We beg their husbands to keep them at home and find some better occupation for them." Letters to Black newspapers called for higher morality among women of color in order to promote the advancement of the race as a whole; some of these letters included female signatures, although nobody can prove whether women indeed authored these critiques.[55]

Often, the opposition did not go so far as to assert that Black women should have no role whatsoever in the preservation and uplift of the race. Many of them, however, wanted men to initiate activities in the abolition movement, with women occupying a supporting role behind the scenes. Male abolitionists, both Black and White, deemed certain activities "proper" for the women's sphere. Fundraising, for instance, served as an activity that was not only crucial to the movement as a whole, but in which women played an important role with the full blessing of men. While these activities were most likely difficult due to the financial constraints levied upon the Black community, Black women had the opportunity to participate in this aspect of the movement with little fear of reprisal. Through existing female organizations and even traditional institutions like the Black Church, Black women used charitable fairs and other methods to financially support the abolitionist cause.[56]

Many of the prominent Black institutions, however, did not accept the full-fledged activism espoused by a number of famous Black women. For example, the Black Upper- and Middle-Classes wanted to assert their own position in society, preferably on an equal par with Whites of the same strata. They believed, as part of this "initiation" process, that Blacks had to adopt the same social mores as Whites—including the role of women within the home, acting as a moral barometer for the community. Thus, to prove that they were indeed equal to the task at hand (and to Whites of the upper- and middle-classes), Blacks sought to institute the "cult of true womanhood" within their own community. In redefining the way that society viewed Blacks as a whole, they placed a special emphasis upon reshaping the image of Black womanhood.

The Black Church, as one might expect, also maintained a conservative stance on the role of Black women in political activism. There are several known cases of religious leaders expelling female members for "failing to maintain harmonious marriages" or refusing to "submit to her husband as a dutiful wife." This submission to male rule extended not only to the family and the political realm, but to the Church hierarchy as well. While some women held powerful positions on Church committees, few invaded the "male" realm of preaching. Reverend J. W. C. Pennington argued against female participation in the ministry:

> on account of their supposed inferiority, maintaining that the ministry, like the army, navy, and "all the learned professions, where mighty thought and laborious investigation are needed," was clearly a masculine calling that "the weaker sex is incapacitated for, both physically and mentally."[57]

At the same time, two White women, Angelina and Sarah Grimke, endured a storm of criticism from both the Black and White clergy on account of their public speaking tours. Clergymen felt that the lectern, regardless of what Maria Stewart said six years earlier, was an exclusively male realm. Any women who practiced otherwise, the argument went, not only violated their social sphere as a women, but defied the Scriptures themselves.[58]

Finally, the Black education system tried to instill a sense of "difference" between men and women. In some cases, educators separated Black students by gender. While this was not always the case, there were certainly different levels of expectations for the males and females attending Black schools:

> For boys, formal education was intended to prepare them for their future roles as heads of households, in which they controlled the family finances, to train them as learned 'gentlemen' in their own communities, and to prepare them for the few professions that did not exclude them, such as the ministry. For girls, however, 'book learning' prepared them for lives as educators of their children and as interesting companions for their husbands.

Black abolitionist Charles B. Ray summed up this point concerning the education of Black women when he said that "Daughters are destined to be wives and mothers—they should, therefore, be taught how to manage a house, and govern and instruct children." While many schools did indeed teach women the rudiments of a traditional education, they still impressed upon them the expectation that their primary role in the future would be in the home.[59]

At the same time that these institutions promoted Black female participation in the "cult of true womanhood," they unwittingly provided Black women with an escape clause. Black schools, for instance, prepared women for jobs as teachers, domestics, and washerwomen, thus perpetuating their role outside the home. Their economic importance to the Black community served as a focal point for their service in the public sphere. It gave them both an opportunity to gain power outside the home and a justification for it through pecuniary reward. Likewise, the Black Church gave women a degree of power through their participation in fundraising and church committees. Just as the schools prepared them for life outside the home, Church functions whetted the appetites of Black women for work in a public sphere traditionally reserved for men. As members of the upper- and middle-classes strove to establish their class identities, White women from these same social classes emerged from the home to participate in a variety of reform movements. At a time when Black men wanted women of color to follow the examples of their White counterparts, Black women were only too happy to step into the reform movements that benefited their race as a whole.[60]

Debates over the "proper" role of Black women in the movement polarized the abolitionist forces. At the First and Second Anti-Slavery Conventions of American Women in 1837 and 1838, "one of the most hotly debated issues was whether Black women should be allowed to participate. . . . After much heated discussion Black women were finally seated at the convention[s]." Similarly, an 1835 meeting of the Fall River Female Anti-Slavery Society nearly destroyed the organization when a commotion arose over the attendance of Black women.[61]

In 1839, the clash between the abolitionist forces and the Women's Rights Movement finally occurred during the annual meeting of the Massachusetts Anti-Slavery Society. Anti-Garrison factions, seizing upon the issue of women's rights to attack his leadership, sought to deny women their voting rights within the organization. Garrisonian supporters, however, defeated the amendment; its backers promptly withdrew from the group to form the Massachusetts Abolitionist Society. Garrison's stand on this issue, however, endeared him to many of the Black female activists. While they did not agree with his proposal that abolitionists should distance themselves from mainstream politics, Grace and Sarah Douglass "sent Garrison a supporting letter that was couched in religious and moralistic tones."[62]

More than anything else, the Garrison debates and others like them indicate the large degree of risk that Black female abolitionists endured. Within their own movements, people refused to see their potential contributions, focusing instead upon the "traditional" roles society expected for members of their race and gender. Black women stood at an interesting crossroads, at the very point where these two estranged components of society met in one flesh. Yet through it all, the overwhelming concern of Black women in the abolitionist movement was to uplift the race as a whole and, in doing so, find their own niche in the panorama of American society. Women like Maria Stewart and Mary Ellen Pleasant took different routes through their lifetimes, but they had the same destination in mind when they embarked upon their respective journeys.

To Black women, their status as the "pariah" class in American society was not a hindrance but an asset. Slavery helped to create a mindset that stressed the inferiority of Blacks, while male dominance portrayed women as a servant class whose entire existence revolved around maintaining the family and home. Black women, however, understood the dynamics at play here. Before many White women and Black men fully comprehended the ramifications of this oppressive system, Black women realized that the mechanisms controlling American society tried to empower White men above all other societal groups. In coming to this realization, they stressed the importance of denouncing both racism and sexism wherever they might dwell—for at the crossroads between Blackness and womanhood, they created a unique position from which to denounce the injustices of American society.

While many of the history books ignore their contributions as a whole, Black women effectively overcame widespread opposition to their activism and left a lasting mark on American history. They not only succeeded within the realm of male-dominated organizations and movements, but they created their own outlets to express the unique perspective they developed regarding this society. Black women participated in every facet of the struggle—from public speaking engagements to armed opposition—with the same courage and determination that marked male contributions to the movement. In doing so, they not only combated images of

Black inferiority, but of the "proper" place for women within the home. Even those who used prevailing notions of "womanhood" to further their own ideas unwittingly advanced feminist principles. For in their sheer desire and ability to participate in mass abolitionist struggles, they offered the most cogent arguments against the oppression of both Blacks *and* women. As representatives of each group, Black women used the oppression that marked both experiences as a tool for attacking the injustices of American society. Despite all efforts to dampen their shouts of protest, Black female abolitionists served as a constant reminder of how far America had to venture before consummating its proposed marriage with democracy.

Endnotes

1. White, Deborah Gray. (1985). *Ar'n't I a Woman?: Female Slaves in the Plantation South.* New York: W. W. Norton and Company, 15.

2. Kolchin, Peter. (1993). *American Slavery, 1619–1877.* New York: Hill and Wang, 134.

3. Ibid., 192–3. Kolchin pointed out that "the ridicule to which some 'scientific' racists subjected the biblical story of creation raised serious questions about their credentials. Far more widespread within pro-slavery propaganda than detailed ethnological analyses were brief, unscientific, and vaguely supported assertions that blacks were by nature different, inferior, and thereby unsuited for freedom."

4. Hersh, Blanche Glassman. (1978). *The Slavery of Sex: Feminist-Abolitionists in America.* Urbana, IL: University of Illinois Press, 208–9.

5. Conway, Jill K. (1982). *The Female Experience in Eighteenth- and Nineteenth-Century America: A Guide to the History of American Women.* New York: Garland Publishing, Inc., 40.

6. Norton, Mary Beth et al. (1994). *A People and a Nation: A History of the United States, Volume I: To 1877.* Boston: Houghton Mifflin Co., 346–7.

7. Yee, Shirley J. (1992). *Black Women Abolitionists: A Study in Activism, 1828–1860.* Knoxville: The University of Tennessee Press, 41–2.

8. Ibid., 42.

9. Ibid., 42–3.

10. Giddings, Paula. (1984). *When and Where I Enter: The Impact of Black Women on Race and Sex in America.* New York: William Morrow and Co., 35.

11. Hersh, 206.

12. Yee, 51–5.

13. Davis, Marianna W. (ed.). (1982). *Contributions of Black Women to America, Volume II.* Columbia, SC: Kenday Press, Inc., 42–3.

14. Ibid., 14. Nell Painter's biography of Truth raises some doubts as to whether Frances Dana Gage's traditional account of Truth's speech in Akron, OH, is accurate. Despite this controversy, Painter and others still admit that Truth represented the ideas of this speech throughout her life as an activist. This, more than the authenticity of the Akron convention accounts, is important to the workings of this essay. See Painter, Chapter 18 for a more detailed discussion.

15. Douglass, Frederick (edited by Benjamin Quarles). (1960). *Narrative of the Life of Frederick Douglass, An American Slave, Written by Himself.* Cambridge: The Belknap Press of Harvard University Press, 103–4.

16. Jacobs, Harriet A. (edited by Jean Fagan Yellin). (1987). *Incidents in the Life of a Slave Girl, Written by Herself.* Cambridge: Harvard University Press, 29.

17. Douglass, 29.

18. Jacobs, 54.

19. Yee, 12.

20. Ibid., 12–3.

21. Chittenden, Elizabeth F. (1973). *Profiles in Black and White: Stories of Men and Women Who Fought Against Slavery.* New York: Charles Scribner's Sons, 108.

22. Aptheker, Herbert. (1989). *Abolitionism: A Revolutionary Movement.* Boston: Twayne Publishers, 86–7.

23. Sterling, Dorothy (ed.). (1984). *We Are Your Sisters: Black Women in the Nineteenth Century.* New York: W. W. Norton and Company, 119–21.

24. Ibid., 279–86.
25. Quarles, Benjamin. (1969). *Black Abolitionists*. New York: Oxford University Press, 25, 33, 149.
26. Davis, 48–50; and Quarles, 217–8.
27. Yee, 15.
28. Ibid., 15–7.
29. Ibid., 17–8.
30. Sterling, 126–7.
31. Lerner, Gerda. (1972). *Black Women in White America: A Documentary History*. New York: Pantheon Books, 85–6; and Sterling, 126–33.
32. Quarles, 30–1.
33. Yee, 18–9.
34. Ibid., 19–21.
35. Lerner, 65.
36. Ibid, 63–4.
37. Ripley, C. Peter (ed.), et al. (1991). *The Black Abolitionist Papers, Volume IV: The United States, 1847–1858*. Chapel Hill: The University of North Carolina Press, 81.
38. Painter, Nell Irvin. (1996). *Sojourner Truth: A Life, A Symbol*. New York: W. W. Norton and Company, 5–31; and Ripley, 81–2.
39. Painter, 113–31; and Ripley, 82.
40. Yee, 37–8.
41. Ibid., 32–3.
42. Ibid., 34–7.
43. Painter, 223–9.
44. Yee, 31–2.
45. Davis, 41–2.
46. Quarles, 7, 50, 192.
47. Lerner, 563–5.
48. Quarles, 169.
49. Ibid., 191.
50. Davis, 45.
51. Quarles, 192–3, and Yee, 130–2.
52. Davis, 47–8, and Giddings, 73, 262.
53. Yee, 44.
54. Ibid., 45.
55. Ibid., 45–7.
56. Sterling, 117–9.
57. Yee, 57.
58. Ibid., 56.
59. Ibid., 47–50.
60. Ibid., 51, 55–6, 58–9.
61. Davis, 43–4.
62. Ibid., 45–6.

Chapter 14

The Political Thought and Abolition of Maria W. Stewart

Gayle T. Tate

Black female abolitionists, whether they were on the national or international abolitionist lecture circuit, were in open defiance against American society with their challenges regarding slavery, racism, and sexism. Their lectures, as Black female activists lodging criticism against the White power structure, caused them to fly in the face of the conventional trappings of gender. Part of their criticism was to illuminate the position of slave women, and by this focus, also mirror the plight of free Black women as well. As Black female abolitionists traveled around the country, sometimes alone or in the company of others, it frequently made them vulnerable, subject them to harassment on various modes of transportation or in the city streets. In this secular sphere, where they experienced the daily taunts of White men and women, Black female abolitionists needed fortitude, courage, and tremendous resolve to champion the cause of freedom. Although most confined themselves to the North, the Mid-West, and the international lecture circuit, the antipathies of racial prejudice and the desire on the part of both the North and the South to maintain slavery was a daily presence in their lives.

Black female activism evolved in two complementary directions. The most overt and popular were the traditional abolitionist course of participating in community associations, ad hoc collectives, church organizations, and predominantly Black or biracial antislavery organizations. This traditional course of action also raised monies for William Lloyd Garrison's abolitionist journal, *the Liberator,* and Frederick Douglass's weekly, *The North Star.* The other side of the abolitionist movement was the subversive activities. "This covert direction was the illegal participation of Black female activists in dramatic slave rescues, vigilance committees, protests, raising monies, and the multifarious operations on the Underground Railroad."[1] Maria W. Stewart was an early Black female abolitionist and while her overt activities are documented, there is some speculation that her husband, James W. Stewart, who had some business ties with David Walker, might have granted some assistance in placing Walker's pamphlet, the *Appeal, In Four Articles; Together With A Preamble, To The Coloured Citizens Of The World, But In Particular, And Very Expressly, To Those Of The United States Of America,* aboard ships.[2] The couple admired David Walker and the work he was doing, both as one of the more active members of the Massachusetts General Colored Association, a Black abolitionist society founded in 1826, and in his more subversive activities assisting runaways.[3]

Maria W. Stewart was an abolitionist that came of political age as the antebellum phase of the abolitionist movement was gathering steam. Indeed, before modern abolitionism had gained its sway, Maria W. Stewart was already a committed abolitionist by the early 1830s, and distinguished herself by being one of the first American women to speak publically before mixed audiences of both sexes. The growing militancy of Black abolitionists was very different from White abolitionists. Most Black abolitionists, like Stewart, utilized a two-prong approach to abolitionism: the improvement of free Black communities and the immediate emancipation of the slaves.[4] A fiery abolitionist, some scholars have noted Stewart's revolutionary zeal akin to David Walker, and his societal criticism was to have quite a profound influence on her political thought. Following his mysterious death in 1830, Stewart declared, "Though Walker sleeps, yet he lives, and his name shall be had in everlasting remembrance."[5] Stewart became, in a sense, a public intellectual, and although she appeared on the public stage for a short time, actually, "a public career in Boston of barely three years' duration," she left an indelible impression on the movement.[6] Her lectures, essays, articles, tracts, and speeches—which embodied a large part of her vision, and were published from time to time in the abolitionist weekly,

The Liberator—contribute to a lasting legacy of her role as a Black female activist in the liberation struggle to emancipate the slaves.

Like many other Black female activists, Stewart saw her mission as being the quest for social justice. It is not hard to realize that these activists would adopt this mission since approximately 90% of African Americans were enslaved in the 1830s and the lives of free Blacks were circumscribed by nascent capitalism, as well as racial and sexual discrimination. Despite the illusionary sense of freedom for free Blacks and their racial constraints, they were building Black communities and attempting to lay an economic foundation for all of the community residents. Northern Black communities, in particular, embodied the founding of several Black churches, the establishment of the Black press, and the organizing of multi-faceted mutual benevolent societies. For Black people, these venues became places where the political and social issues of the day were debated and men and women could participate in community activities. For women, like Maria W. Stewart, their talents and mission were honed through community activism; indeed, other women who heard the call disseminated their philosophy in newspapers, journals, public lectures, sermons, books, tracts, and oral histories; and still others became a part of the larger national and international abolitionist struggle. Some female activists engaged in all these initiatives as a way to express their political and social commitment.

In so many ways, Maria W. Stewart's philosophy, which shaped her abolitionism, set astride evangelical Christianity, early Black feminism, and the rising tide of Black nationalism growing in Black communities. Evangelical Christianity would create the moral anchor that Stewart used to shape her political thought, vision, and strategies of Black liberation. Her critique of early Black feminism, and legitimizing the struggle of Black women for their rights and critical necessity for political leadership, placed Stewart in the early pioneering efforts of the Women's Rights Movement. And her mission of pragmatic Black nationalism, based on human virtue and divine power to build the infrastructure for Black communities, made her an avowed Black nationalist. The outgrowth of her political thought was her militant abolitionism and a relentless campaign to elevate the free Black community and to emancipate the slaves. Viewing slavery, racism, and sexism as inextricably linked to each other, Stewart did not shrink away from violence or the need for uprisings, believing that in the cause of freedom such acts were a critical necessity.

The Influences of Evangelical Christianity

All three components of Stewart's political thought offer a composite of the times in which she lived. Although she peered beyond her age, particularly in her understanding of the material plight of Black women and the role that they must play as leaders in the struggle to free Black people from oppression, she remained tied to her time in some of the conventional gender norms and the impact that evangelical Christianity had upon her thought. Deeply pious, some of her early religious influences came from growing up in a minister's house, where she was "bound out" as a servant girl when she lost her parents at 5 years of age.[7] Staying in his home for at least a decade, Stewart not only received religious instruction, directly or indirectly, but also became acutely aware of the impact that material conditions have upon the human spirit. This tedious labor, in many cases numbing work, gave Stewart some of her later comparisons of Northern Black laborers and slaves:

> During that period, characterized by the influence of religion and the search for knowledge and intellectual growth, Stewart gained the first-hand experience that enabled her to write so compellingly of the effects of endless toil and drudgery on the minds and spirits of those Blacks in the North she would come to consider only nominally free.[8]

Stewart typified many early Black female evangelists of her day, like Jarena Lee, Zilpha Elaw, Elizabeth, and Julia A. J. Foote, with her message of the liberation of Black women and the emancipation of the slaves, which was viewed through a moral prism. Most of these early Black female evangelists became gospel pioneers for the social and moral regeneration of society. Viewing their divine mission in universal and humanist terms, they carried the gospel to homes, churches, communities, and wherever people wanted to hear the word of God. Some heard a more distant call and went to foreign lands to spread the Word. Believing that God determined who was anointed to preach the gospel, these evangelists challenged ecclesiastical sexism in the churches. Forming interracial spiritual ties to the larger evangelical community, they used those opportunities to speak out against slavery, racism, and sexism that dominated the lives of Black people. Empowered by their religious resolve, evangelists spoke out against the social inequities that oppressed them as Black women. Most of these early Black evangelists became abolitionists and used their sermons to large interracial audiences to lodge a strident criticism against slavery and other societal injustices. "Female converts to the cause later became some of the most outspoken social reformers of the age."[9]

Stewart had a religious conversion experience in 1829 following the loss of her husband. This conversion experience enabled her to seek a higher spiritual calling and fortify an inner sanctum of power. In her spiritual journey of purifying her soul, Stewart was searching for the inner peace that comes after conversion. Being "born again" for these evangelists, the "walk with God" was a powerful healing force, and it empowered them to rectify the world using the moral barometer upon which they based their lives. For Black female evangelists, in particular, once they had been spiritually renewed with God's blessings, they were able to defy conventional mores and standards, challenge racism and sexism, take issue with proslavery supporters, and follow the righteousness of their social cause. Thus, Stewart was in keeping with her spiritual sisters, and she was able to use her inner source of power for her individual and societal transformation. "Fueled with the same Christian zeal that propelled Zilpha Elaw and Jarena Lee, Maria Stewart felt called upon to address the earthly problems of her people."[10] Frequently, evangelists bonded together, prayed together, and brought down the spirit of the Almighty. For Stewart, she saw Black feminism and morality as one cause.

In 1831, following two years in which she experienced the loss of her husband and David Walker, Maria W. Stewart penned *Religion and The Pure Principles of Morality, The Sure Foundation on Which We Must Build*, her political manifesto in which she identified her overarching themes of the Black liberation struggle. Stewart saw the Black struggle of liberation tied to their spiritual redemption as a people. Their journey toward freedom would be a journey of self-discovery and spiritual renewal. Their deeper piety, which Stewart believed would require constant prayer, would allow them to defy the conventional trappings of both race and gender. "Oh turn your attention to knowledge and improvement; for knowledge is power. And God is able to fill you with wisdom and understanding, and to dispel your fears. Arm yourselves with the weapons of prayer."[11] Although Stewart saw the freedom struggle where male and female activists would participate, many of her remarks and pragmatic plans were for the empowerment of Black women to become equal partners in Black activism. Women could empower themselves by defining their political space and claiming their rights of political leadership. What Stewart saw was that Black women could claim the moral authority over the struggle in concert with Black female evangelists who were charting the same cause in both community activism and the abolitionist movement. To pave the way for their role in the struggle, Black women had to mobilize the community and unite in sisterhood. Stewart reminded Black women that victory would be assured only when "we become united as one, and cultivate among ourselves the pure principles of piety, morality, and virtue."[12]

The evolution of Black women's political consciousness was intertwined with a journey of spiritual redemption. Stewart believed that the urban influences had caused many Blacks to fall under negative influences and abandon their sense of morality. To claim their rights to political leadership, Black women had to begin their journey of spiritual redemption. For Stewart, this would be the reconnection to God by African peoples and would be their sure path to redemption. "Return again unto us, O Lord God, we beseech thee; and pardon this the iniquity of thy servants. Cause thy face to shine upon us and we shall be saved."[13] But morality and virtue were also critical to the active struggle against oppression, and this righteous struggle would cause God to slay their enemies. "You may kill, tyrannize, and oppress as much as you choose, until our cry shall come up before the throne of God; for I am firmly persuaded, that he will not suffer you to quell the proud, fearless, and undaunted spirits of the Africans forever." Stewart delivered her spiritual redemptive message with an urgency that sometimes made her audience chary of her lecture style.

Early Black Feminism

Maria W. Stewart departed from David Walker in her analysis of the Black women's role in revolutionary struggle and, instead, sought to expand their political consciousness as combatants in struggle. In some sense, Stewart, in advocating progressive political, economic, and social development for Black women, was also cognizant of her own life and material circumstances. Stewart, as Marilyn Richardson notes in *Maria W. Stewart, America's First Black Woman Political Writer: Essays and Speeches*, was occupying a safe middle ground in conventional gender standards because she was a widow.[14] While this made her acceptable to the community, simultaneously it gave her the freedom to develop her education, career, mission, and lifestyle. Similar to some of the early female evangelists, Stewart placed herself and her message on a transcendental plane, above the dictates of men and thus could defy the conventional trappings of gender in antebellum society. Having found God, and having experienced a religious conversion, it was the divine power that was guiding her mission. In pragmatic realities, most evangelists came into their definition of womanhood and their own divine power when they became widows and had opportunities to pursue and shape their life's work. The trappings of marriage, children, and household production would not have been conducive for Stewart to develop as an abolitionist or political thinker.

In Stewart's political essay, *Mrs. Stewart's Farewell Address To Her Friends In The City of Boston*, delivered September 21, 1833, she argued for the education of Black women. Stewart believed that education was paramount for Black women if they were to assume their role as moral and political leaders in Black communities. Initially, she had to dispel the notion that was pervasive in the Black Boston community that she, herself, had no right to give public lectures. Her rhetorical question sets the stage for that query: "What if I am a woman; is not the God of ancient times the God of these modern days? Did he not raise up Deborah, to be a mother, and a judge in Israel (Judges 4:4)? Did not (Q)queen Esther save the lives of the Jews?" Having shown that women in the Bible played major roles in political affairs of their people, Stewart also cited women's role in history:

> *Among the Greeks, women delivered the Oracles, the respect the Romans paid to the Sibyls is well known. The Jews had their prophetesses. The prediction of the Egyptian women obtained much credit at Rome, even under the Emperors. And in the most barbarous nations, all things that have the appearance of being supernatural, the mysteries of religion, the secrets of physic, and the rites of magic, were in the possession of women.*[15]

Stewart saw higher learning for women as a necessary role to challenge the inherent racial bias of Whites who supported the notion of Black inferiority. Stewart proposed a high school for women and the women themselves were responsible for collectively mobilizing their resources to make it a reality.

> *Let every female heart become united, and let us raise a fund ourselves; and at the end of one year and a half, we might be able to lay the corner stone for the building of a High School, that the higher branches of knowledge might be enjoyed by us.*[16]

Stewart argued that just as women took their places at the centers of learning in other periods in history, they could do so in the contemporary period as well. "Why cannot a religious spirit animate us now? Why cannot we become divines and scholars?" Once education was obtained as an initial stage, Stewart saw the development of economic initiatives by Black women as a way to demonstrate their skills and talents. Black women were encouraged to cultivate business and social enterprises to enhance their business acumen and enrich Black community life. Since the majority of Black families depended on the wages of both men and women, this was a practical plan that received a great deal of support. The fact of the matter was that most, if not all, Black women worked anyway. The idea, however, of promoting business acumen, becoming self-employed, and promoting Black women's economic independence would not only enrich the economic life of the family but the community as well. Stewart encouraged women "to pool their economic resources" and to "promote and patronize each other" for financial success.

Stewart believed that Black women had to be educated, have a sound business plan for economic development, and lead moral, exemplary lives. Once this plan was in place, Stewart saw Black women as primary caretakers of the home, children, and family. In the notion of family, Stewart adhered to the conventional mores of gender of the time. She emphasized that Black women were responsible for the future of the race and it was critical that they educate their children. "It is you that must create in the minds of your little girls and boys a thirst for knowledge. . . ."[17] But Stewart believed that an educated woman could best imbue that "thirst for knowledge" in her own children. For Stewart, women had to play a primary role in the education and socialization of their children.

Despite Stewart's support of some of the conventional trappings of the time, she also dealt with the material conditions of Black women in urban spaces. While she embraced motherhood and placed the full responsibility of child rearing upon the shoulders of Black women, she, simultaneously, moved beyond the traditional boundaries of gender norms to create Black economic independence for Black women. Clearly,

Stewart, who herself had experienced hard labor as a child, understood the vital necessity of Black women's economic initiatives and that these economic initiatives would be a venue for Black women's economic independence as well as a linchpin to Black women's political activism.[18]

Arguably, Stewart was seeking to transform and reconstruct Black women's lives and, in so doing, the lives of their children, family, and community. Thus, her catalyst for the spiritual redemption of the Black community was viewed through the moral rearmament of Black women. The economic enterprises of Black women would change the material circumstances of their lives. Stewart was giving Black women the power over their own lives and placing their political activism above the place of mere mortals. Empowered with God's providential care, Black women were fortified in this program of political and social development. To Stewart, this was critical in demonstrating those talents that Black women possessed. "O, ye daughters of Africa, awake! Awake! Arise! No longer sleep nor slumber, but distinguish yourselves. Show forth to the world that ye are endowed with noble and exalted faculties."[19]

Black Nationalism and Militant Abolitionism

Maria W. Stewart's political thought was driven by the growing Black nationalism in northern Black communities with its major tenets of racial solidarity, spiritual redemption, and self-determination, all of which she fully supported. Nationalism focused on the racial unity of Blacks throughout the diaspora, initially starting in urban areas where Blacks were migrating to in the 1830s, and a strident criticism of slavery, racism, and sexism that was inextricably linked to their oppression. In many ways, with early Black female evangelists and others like Maria Stewart finding their voices, Black women were attempting to reposition nationalism's masculine emphasis and place women in political leadership positions for the freedom struggle. Thus, they tied the early Black feminism to the nationalist ethos in Black communities and positioned themselves for leadership. This pragmatic face of nationalism emphasized Black women's collective strategies, mobilization of Black communities, spiritual regeneration, and political protest, all of which Maria W. Stewart saw as the developing political praxis for Black women. Although most Black female activists initially shaped their political consciousness with their community activism, many became active in the larger abolitionist movement as well. Active Black nationalists, who espoused the same struggles of freedom from slavery, the degradation of racism, and the crippling economic and psychological forces of sexism were all militant abolitionists as well. As many female activists moved into the broader political arena that abolition afforded, the context for the Black community improved and the emancipation of the slaves expressed their nationalism.

As most nationalists, like David Walker and Robert Alexander Young, Maria W. Stewart saw the divine power of God shaping the freedom struggle. "I am a strong advocate for the cause of God and for the cause of freedom."[20] Having identified the righteousness of the freedom cause, Stewart attributes part of this divine empowerment process to Africa's historical greatness:

> History informs us that we sprung from one of the most learned nations of the whole earth, from the seat, if not the parent, of science. Yes, poor despised Africa was the resort of sages and legislators of other nations, was esteemed the school of learning, and the most illustrious men in Greece flocked thither for instruction.[21]

But Africa's greatness was marred by the global slave trade that went on for centuries depopulating Africa and stripping people of their homeland, heritage, and history. Stewart argued that the oppression of African peoples started with the enslavement process and the transplantation of African peoples to New World societies. Native Americans were also caught in this enslavement process and were stripped of their homes:

> The unfriendly Whites first drove the Native American from his much loved home. Then they stole our fathers from their peaceful and quiet dwellings, and brought them hither, and made bond-men and bond-women of them and their little ones.[22]

While slavery in the South was the primary cause for the abolitionist movement, Black abolitionists saw the material conditions of Northern Blacks to be only slightly better than that of the Southern slaves. White abolitionists shied away from any focus on northern racial discrimination and their own inherent biases, instead focusing on slavery because it was far away. One traveler, examining the condition of Blacks in the northern states, noted that "chains of a stronger kind still manacled their limbs, from which no legislative act could free them; a mental and moral subordination and inferiority, to which tyrant custom has here subjected all the sons and daughters of Africa."[23] Black abolitionists, like Maria W. Stewart, understood that Southern slavery and Northern racial discrimination were two sides of the same coin, and both had to be assailed together. Stewart united both of these political issues in her speeches. "Tell us no more of southern slavery; for with few exceptions, although I may be very erroneous in my opinion, yet I consider our condition but little better than that."[24]

Stewart, like most activists of her day, derided the colonizationists who wanted free Blacks to be transported to Africa. Even those who favored emigrationism were skeptical of the American Society for Colonizing the Free People of Color in the United States, a group of White men attempting to colonize Blacks on the West Coast of Africa. While many Blacks did not doubt Robert Finley's integrity as the founder of the organization, they believed that the rest of the members were interested in quelling political protest against slavery in this country. Slaveholders who were members of the organization were particularly suspect. Free Blacks believed this was a scheme that would quell the voices of free Blacks who were protesting against slavery and leave the slaves powerless.[25] Stewart, in declaring her opposition, noted that ". . . if the colonizationists are the real friends to Africa, let them expend the money which they collect in erecting a college to educate her injured sons in this land of gospel, light, and liberty . . ."[26]

The urgency of Stewart's lectures conveyed that Black people were in a crisis state. Stewart believed that emancipation of the slaves would require violence as a necessary part of the freedom cause. She pointed to the Haitian Revolution, a 13-year struggle that Black people celebrated, as a sign of a victorious slave uprising that could bring about freedom and independence for slaves. And in characteristic fashion, she also made the point that while America celebrated other valiant struggles across the globe, there was no celebration of the Haitian victory. Yet, ". . . Hayti, the glory of the Blacks and terror of the tyrants," was a symbol of collective struggle. Like Walker, she did not shy away from violence and saw violence being done to Blacks everyday. She insisted that Blacks had to mobilize their collective strength as a people and struggle as a group. Political protest against injustice by an aggrieved population was Stewart's clarion call. "O ye sons of Africa, when will your voices be heard in our legislative halls, in defiance of your enemies, contending for equal rights and liberty?"[27] Stewart also advocated shoring up the Black community's infrastructure and urged that Blacks focus on "mental and moral improvement" and use monies for "schools and seminaries of learning for our children and youth." For the adults, she insisted that they become "the promoters of temperance . . . and useful and scientific knowledge."[28] This critical community development would also pave the way for community activism by creating an expanding consciousness in their quest for freedom.

A Concluding Note

Although Stewart was a deeply committed abolitionist, her urgent delivery and strident oratorical style frequently aroused the ire of her audiences, particularly the men in the audience, whom she accused of not exercising due diligence in the emancipation struggle. Although she followed the tradition of David Walker, with his upbraiding of Black men, this upbraiding was not seen in the same vein when it came from a woman. "Walker, citing armed struggles for liberty around the globe, could dramatically bemoan the failure of manhood among American Blacks as a spur to inciting rebellion. It was much less likely that accusations of cowardice, ignorance, and lack of ambition hurled by a woman would rally Stewart's listeners, male or female, to the barricades of social activism."[29] Stewart's fiery critique was not received well by Black men in the Boston community, and she also caused some uneasiness in Boston's Black middle-class community as a whole.

But Maria W. Stewart was one of the early political thinkers who understood that the treatment of the material conditions of African American people had to be dealt with systematically by Black people themselves. In her essays and lectures, she helped illuminate the political issues of the day. She was not afraid to speak on the issues of slavery, racism, and sexism and understand that the plight of impoverishment for Northern Blacks was organically related to these factors. While she placed herself under God's protection and divine source of energy, her analysis was of the material conditions that were crippling the lives of African Americans in American society. Undoubtedly, she did much in gaining female adherents to social causes and enabled them to construct their own definitions of womanhood. In encouraging Black women to play leading roles in community activism and in the national political arena, she helped them refine and broaden their growing political consciousness. It may be well within the mark in acknowledging that Stewart helped define a Black feminist protest tradition.

Endnotes

1. Tate, Gayle T. (2003). *Unknown Tongues: Black Women's Political Activism in the Antebellum Era, 1830–1860.* East Lansing: Michigan State University Press, 189.

2. Richardson, Marilyn (ed.). (1987). *Maria Stewart, America's First Black Woman Political Writer: Essays & Speeches.* Bloomington: Indiana University Press, introduction, 6–7.

3. Ibid; Foner, Philip S. (1983). *History of Black Americans: From the Emergence of the Cotton Kingdom to the Eve of the Compromise of 1850.* v. 2. Westport, CT: Greenwood Press, 360–367.

4. Quarles, Benjamin. (1969). *Black Abolitionists.* New York: Oxford University Press, 49.

5. "Religion and the Pure Principles of Morality, The Sure Foundation on Which We Must Build," in Marilyn Richardson. (1987). *Maria W. Stewart: America's First Black Woman Political Writer, Essays & Speeches.* Bloomington: Indiana University Press, 40.

6. Richardson, Marilyn. (1987). *Maria W. Stewart, America's First Black Woman Political Writer.* Bloomington: Indiana University Press, preface, xiv.

7. Richardson, Marilyn. (1980). *Black Women and Religion, a bibliography.* Boston: G. K. Hall & Co., xix.

8. Richardson, Marilyn. *Maria W. Stewart, America's First Black Woman Political Writer,* preface, xv.

9. Elaw, Zilpha. (1986). *Memoirs of the Life, Religious Experience, Ministerial Travels and Labours of Mrs. Zilpha Elaw, an American Female of Colour; Together with Some Accounts of the Great Religious Revivals in American,* in William L. Andrews, ed., *Sisters of the Spirit: Three Black Women's Autobiographies of the Nineteenth Century.* Bloomington: Indiana University Press, 137.

10. Coleman, Willi. "Architects of a Vision: Black Women and Their Antebellum Quest for Political and Social Equality," in Ann Gordon with Collier-Thomas, Bracey, Avakian, and Berkman, *African American Women and the Vote, 1837–1965.* Amherst: University of Massachusetts Press, 1997, 27.

11. *Religion and The Pure Principles of Morality,* 41.

12. Ibid., 30.

13. Ibid., 34.

14. Richardson, Marilyn. *Maria W. Stewart, America's First Black Woman Political Writer,* introduction, 19.

15. "Mrs. Stewart's Farewell Address To Her Friends In The City of Boston," delivered September 21, 1833, in Marilyn Richardson, *Maria W. Stewart America's First Black Woman Political Writer,* 69.

16. Ibid., 37.

17. Ibid., 35.

18. Tate, Gayle T. (2003). *Unknown Tongues: Black Women's Political Activism in the Antebellum Era, 1830–1860.* East Lansing: Michigan State University Press, note Chapter 4 on free black women's economic development, 100–127, 198–201.

19. *Religion and The Pure Principles of Morality,* 30.

20. "An Address Delivered Before the Afric-American Female Intelligence Society of America," Spring 1832, in Marilyn Richardson's *Maria W. Stewart, America's First Black Woman Political Writer,* 52.

21. "An Address Delivered At The African Masonic Hall," Boston, February 27, 1833, in Marilyn Richardson's, *Maria W. Stewart, America's First Black Woman Political Writer,* 58.

22. Ibid., 63.

23. Duncan, John M. (1823). *Travels through Part of the United States and Canada in 1818 and 1819.* New York , v. 1, 60.

24. "Lecture Delivered At The Franklin Hall," Boston, September 21, 1832.

25. Quarles, Benjamin. (1969). *Black Abolitionists.* New York: Oxford University Press, 1–8.

26. "An Address Delivered at The African Masonic Hall," Boston, February 27, 1833, 61.

27. Ibid., 59.

28. Ibid., 60.

29. Ibid., 16.

Chapter 15

Zambo Histories: Studying Afro-Indians

Rhett S. Jones

In his careful exploration of the evolution of ideas about race in colonial Virginia, Edmund S. Morgan, after first noting that Englishmen have always had their fair share of xenophobia and national consciousness, writes:

> But something more than nationalism or xenophobia seems to have affected English relations with the Indians from the beginning. When Englishmen at Roanoke react to the alleged theft of a silver cup by burning a village, we suspect that more than meets the eye is involved. And when Englishmen at Jamestown throw Indian children into the water and shoot out their brains, we suspect that they might not have done the same with French or Spanish children.[1]

Sorting out why they might not have done the same thing to White children takes Morgan most of his critically acclaimed book as he also grapples with why White Virginians gradually became (or already were) equally indifferent to the sufferings of enslaved Black children. The study of the roots of anti-Black racism has a long history, though Frank Tannenbaum's *Slave and Citizen; The Negro in the Americas*[2] is widely regarded as kicking off the formal, long-lasting and sometimes acrimonious debate among scholars trained in a number of disciplines as to why Black slaves were treated better in some parts of the New World than in others. Study of the causes of anti-Native American racism has a somewhat shorter but equally complex history, though unlike its anti-Black counterpart, its exploration was initially carried on by anthropologists, not by historians and sociologists. The evolution of racist thought in the Americas, complicated enough if focused only on Amerindians or Black Americas, becomes even more difficult to sort out if concerned with both. Most scholars have focused on one or the other, though a number[3] grappled with how the conquest of the Native peoples and the enslavement of Africans, in very different ways, fed into the New World's long love of Whiteness. Not surprisingly, these studies—useful as they are for an understanding of American ideas about race—have mostly focused on what Whites have thought of, and how they have behaved toward, Indigenous people and Afro-Americans. Not much attention has been given to what Indians and Blacks believed about race, much less—to use the Spanish term for persons or individuals of mixed Native American/African American heritage—to zambos.

This paper first examines how, from what perspectives, and with what consequences, Blacks and Indians have been studied. It then briefly examines what is necessary if the study of zambo history is to be expanded. A quick discussion of terminology is necessary. In this paper the terms Amerindian, Indian, Indigenous peoples, Native American, and Native peoples are used interchangeably, as are the terms African American, Afro-American, Black, and Black American. The terms Afro-Indian, Black Indian, and zambo are also used interchangeably, as are Africanity and Blackness. The use of a name and the power to force it onto persons who do not accept it as descriptive of themselves runs as an important thread in the fabric of race relations in the Western Hemisphere. Under Euro-American pressure, influence, and power, Native peoples of the Americas became Indians, while the ethnic identity of enslaved Africans transported across the Atlantic was erased and they became simply Blacks. The use of a few interchangeable terms to facilitate discussion and avoid fatiguing repetition should not obscure the fact that Americans forcefully named (a better term would be re-named) Amerindians and Afro-Americans. The fact that the colonists of British North America never developed and agreed upon an equivalent to the Spanish North American term zambo is also significant.[4]

Three, not two, races met during America's colonial period; until recently only the history of Whites received much scholarly attention and when Indians and Blacks were considered it was generally in terms of their relationship to Whites. Indians were typically approached as barriers to the expansion of White civilization, while Blacks were studied in terms of evolving Euro-American debates concerning the morality of slavery and the meaning of Blackness. As they interacted with Whites in different ways, the two non-White peoples were almost never studied together, in any systematic comparative sense, or in terms of their relationship to one another.[5] Despite a wide range of ideas about race, this exploitation of Indigenous peoples and Black Americans[6] held true not just in British North America, but elsewhere in the Americas as well. The conceptualization of Native peoples and Blacks as very different folk may have made sense later in the history of the New World when the two peoples were separated from one another. In the newly independent United States, for example, Native peoples were forcibly removed west of the Mississippi River and then later forced onto reservations, while Blacks were isolated from one another on separate plantations. Early on, Blacks began to see cities as not only places where fugitive slaves might pass as free, but where Afro-Americans could establish churches, self-help societies, schools, and other organizations aimed at serving Blacks.[7] While Black Americans were fleeing to Euro-American cities, Native Americans were trying to escape from these centers of White power. By the end of the 19th century, Native Americans and African Americans were so geographically isolated from one another that it was possible to study one group without giving much attention to the other. In the 20th century this separation continued so it was a rare scholarly study of indigenous people that made any mention of Blacks and vice versa.

But scholarly neglect of the initial period of Indian/Black contact is more difficult to explain. In the first three centuries of European dominance of the Western Hemisphere, Indians and Blacks were not so separated from one another either by the efforts of Whites or by their own choice. It is true that virtually all the colonizing powers feared a Black-Indian alliance and therefore sought to separate the two peoples, but they were not always successful.[8] Much of the complex history of these attempts is only recently being recovered and even then it is largely cast as White attempts to control non-Whites. Carter G. Woodson, regarded by many as the founding father of African American History, understood the importance of understanding Afro-Indian relations in their own right: "One of the longest unwritten chapters in the history of the United States is that treating of the relations of the Negroes and the Indians. The Indians were already here when the White men came and the Negroes brought in soon after to serve as a subject race found among the Indians one of their means of escape."[9] Woodson himself did not always celebrate Native peoples, he belittled them for their lack of literacy, while admonishing Blacks that if they did not read and write their own history they would wind up like the Indians.[10] Still, *The Journal of Negro History*, founded by Woodson, published a number of articles on Native/Black relations, particularly by Kenneth W. Porter who began to research and write on these relations in the 1930s.[11]

Black Histories

Porter's work and that of a number of others who wrote in the pages of *The Journal of Negro History* generally approached Black/Indigenous relations from the perspective of Blacks as they sought to demonstrate that Afro-Americans had contributed far more to American civilization than had Indians. One scholar wrote of those who contributed to this kind of Native American/Afro-American study:

> They have little respect for Native American life, are prone to construct and accept negative stereotypes concerning Indians, and view the Indians as weak and incapable of hard, disciplined labor. To this negative conception of Indians they add a vicious kind of black chauvinism which denigrates and simplifies the complexities of Indian societies and insists that those of West Africa were far superior. Finally, they insist that African laborers were far stronger and more civilized than Indian workers and hence contributed more to the creation of New World societies.[12]

This approach to Black/Indian relations fits comfortably within the master narrative constructed by the European American scholarly establishment.

The master narrative of American history consists, according to John Sensbach, of a "litany of praise for the European immigrants who founded a model society and whose descendants created a new nation of liberty out of the chaos of revolution. Put most simply it is a celebration of the achievements of White people in North America. A good deal of the scholarship on Native/Black relations continues to operate within this framework, aligning Blacks with Whites against Indians and seeking to show that Afro-Americans also had an important role in the development of America. Those who write within the framework of the narrative demonstrate its continued hold on all Americans. Daniel Richter argues, "the hoary 'master narrative' of American history seems distressingly tenacious. Much scholarship remains trapped in what Vine Deloria, Jr. calls the 'cameo' theory of history, which "takes a basic manifest destiny . . . and lovingly plugs in a few feathers, wooly heads, and sombreros into the famous events without really changing the story line."[13] When applied by researchers approaching Afro-Indian studies from a Black perspective, this strategy enlists Blacks in the army of Whiteness; Blacks become a few wooly heads in the willing service of the expansion of White America westward.

This Black-oriented strategy for study of Native/Black American peoples rests on three assumptions. First, it accepts the European American ideology that Indians were outsiders, and as such played no meaningful role in the evolution of the United States. Second, stubborn Indian military resistance, Indian refusal to adopt civilized ways, and Indian rejection of Christianity—as these scholars see it—made it difficult for the United States to develop. Third, the approach insists that while both Native peoples and Blacks suffered under White hegemony, Blacks suffered most.

The sense that Native peoples were outsiders, a barrier that needed to be overcome, is most clear in the fulsome celebration of the Buffalo Soldiers by some in the African American community. These Black men served in the United States army in the years after the Civil War in the battles that finally defeated the plains Indians.[14] Black Americans are rightly proud of their Buffalo Soldiers' courage as well as their determination to serve their country despite the racist practices of the Army and what was then called the Department of War. This pride has impacted scholarship so that John Hope Franklin's widely used, periodically revised, and oft-reprinted survey text, *From Slavery to Freedom: A History of Black America* makes little mention of Indians.[15] Indeed "Indians" do not appear in the index of the 1994 edition. The index does include, however, a heading for "Indian Wars," which when followed back into the text one reads, "there were four African-American [military] outfits, all of which had been used in actions against the Indians of the West." There is no systematic discussion in Franklin, or for that matter in any other textbook on Afro-American History of such Indian nations as the Cherokee, Creek, or Seminole, all of which played not only an important role in American history, but in Black American history. Nor is there any discussion of the mixed-race communities, termed by some scholars tri-racial isolates, though exploration of their history would reveal much about Afro-American ideas about race in general and the one-drop rule in particular.[16] In sum, much—not all—of this sort of scholarship on Afro-Indian relations has centered around demonstrating that Blacks were insiders, part of a nation proud of its democratic, egalitarian, Christian traditions to say nothing of its many material successes. In this viewpoint Blacks, like Whites, are determined to overcome Amerindian resistance to progress. Indians are people to whom things happen as they are acted upon by Whites and Blacks together as a part of an expanding civilization. Native peoples are incidental to the study of Afro-Americans, who are best understood in terms of the culture(s) they created, despite slavery, on this side of the Atlantic, and in terms of their relations to Euro-Americans.

From this perspective, Blacks also suffered far more than Indians. It acknowledges that Amerindians were forced off their lands, killed without justification, pressured to renounce their ancestral religions in favor of Christianity, subjected to vicious stereotypes, and otherwise maltreated and exploited. But, as this school of thought generally sees it, Indians never had to endure slavery, the impact the peculiar institution had on Black families, or the way Black women and men defined themselves. In this, the school ignores the fact that the enslavement of Indians in British North America continued until late in the 18th century with all the negative impact on Indians that the institution had on Afro-Americans. Slavery was also a divisive force among Native peoples as members of some nations willingly enslaved members of others. From this Afro-Indian perspective it is important to demonstrate that Blacks, though fully committed to the American way and thinking of themselves as American, were more cruelly treated than were the Indians who stood outside the nation and were opposed to its basic beliefs.

Within Black thought, there are two major alternatives to the idea that zambos are best understood by approaching them from the perspective that Afro-Americans were full (and often eager) participants in aggressive expansion of Euro-America. These alternatives are Marxism and Afrocentrism, but neither has devoted much attention to Black/Indian relations. Despite the fact that one of the most useful explorations of Blacks during the pre-industrial and industrial period was undertaken by a Marxist,[17] the Marxian approach to slaves and the cultures they created was constrained by the attempt to apply constructs originally developed to understand European workers to American slaves. The results have often been clumsy and not very persuasive to the various schools of Marxism (of which there are many), to other scholars, or to Black Americans. When, in the 1960s, Black history emerged as a discipline in major (read: White) research universities of the United States, it focused on the slave communities of the plantation south. There was little here that Marxists found compatible with their conceptual schema so that their best studies of Black life in North America had to wait until studies of the emergent Black urban communities of the late 18th century and beyond appeared.[18] Hard at work trying to fit slaves into their Eurocentric theoretical framework, Marxist scholars had little time to spare for consideration of how Blacks and Indians might have related to one another. Almost without exception they focused on White/Black relations.

Afrocentrists, at least most of those writing in the United States, have a curious and large gap in their approach to the history of persons of African descent. They begin with Africa itself, then having established the existence of a culture of which all Black peoples are members, discuss the slave trade and 19th century American slavery. They then move on to the 20th century and from there to current events. As most Afrocentrists, while interested in knowledge itself, seek to use it to liberate black peoples, this orientation toward the present is understandable. Afrocentrists believe it is necessary for Black people to develop their own conception of the Black past, but as texts representative of the approach demonstrate,[19] they seem to think knowledge of ancient Africa and Black American history from 19th century slavery forward is sufficient. In this research agenda, there is little room for the study of 17th and 18th century Black Americans. Yet it is in the 18th century that Africans became African Americans, both physically and culturally. At the beginning of the 18th century the majority of Black people living in the 13 colonies of British North America were born in Africa, but by the end of the century most of them were born in the New World. This cultural transformation— with a focus on how, why, and to what extent the African mind was lost, retained, or modified—ought to lie at the very center of Afrocentric study, but it has not, and as a result the 18th century has received little attention from Afrocentrists. The theoretical orientation and resultant research concerns of Afrocentrists have directed its scholars away from this period. This is unfortunate, as it was in the 1700s that African/Indigenous contact was initiated and important to both peoples.

A notable exception to this Afrocentric neglect is Barbara A. Faggins' work, *Africans and Indians: An Afrocentric Analysis of Contacts between Africans and Indians in Colonial Virginia.*[20] Faggins, a student of Molefi Asante, one of the leading Afrocentric scholars, while sympathetic to Native peoples (she prefers the term First Americans) writes, "Clearly the conditions under which the Indians existed were similar to those of Americans—although the First American's total experience was nowhere comparable to Africans.[21] Her insistence that Blacks suffered more under Whites than did Indians is like that of scholars who take the position that Blacks are part of Euro-American civilization. In exploring the relationship between Native peoples and Blacks in colonial Virginia, Faggins acknowledges problems resulting from the Eurocentric approach to Virginia's history, the resultant bias in sources, and the difficulty of using these sources to develop an understanding of Black/Indian relations. She also devotes a number of pages to the Afrocentric paradigm itself and urges future scholars to apply it to the study of Amerindian/African American relations. Yet Faggins' findings and the lack of other Afrocentric studies of Native peoples and their relations with Blacks (on which her work might have been modeled), demonstrates that for Afrocentrists, Black/Indigenous relations are not an important area of concern.

Yet, in terms of the ongoing Afrocentric project itself there is no reason why Native peoples ought to be any less important than Whites. In each case the single African culture (according to Afrocentrists) that unites all folk of African ancestry encounters other cultures. Black/Indian contacts and the emergence of zambo peoples should provide Afrocentrists with an exciting laboratory for the exploration of interaction between the African mind and the mind of other peoples. Study of Black/Indian contact would be of special importance because Native peoples clearly evolved in their conception of and relations with Black peoples.[22]

Native Histories

The approach of Indians and non-Indian scholars, who have adopted a Native perspective on Black/Indigenous relations, often parallels the approach of Blacks and non-Black scholars who take a Black perspective on these relations. First, this approach demonstrates that Natives resisted accepting White ideas about race and a sense of themselves as "Indians." As a number of researchers have shown Native peoples, like Blacks, and for that matter like Whites, had no conception of race prior to European colonization of the New World.[23] Native peoples had, of course, a sense of difference among themselves sometimes reflected in tribal conflict and feelings of superiority over their neighbors. While these differences were rooted in a clear sense of lineage—many indigenous peoples were matrilineal—they were also centered on belief. So, for example, virtually every Indian nation had rituals of adoption whereby persons born into one tribe could become fully-fledged members of another. But as the power of racism grew among New World Whites, Indians were pressured to accept it. Two of the most distinguished scholars in the study of Indigenous peoples, William McLoughlin and Theda Perdue, argue that, at least in the United States, Natives accepted European American ideas about race because they feared being lumped with Blacks.[24] As Indians, ever watchful of Whites, monitored the Euro-American debates over race, they realized that it was important to distance themselves from Blacks. From the first quarter of the 19th century on, as most Native peoples saw it, Whites were at the top of the system and Blacks at the bottom. By accepting Euro-American racist ideologies, which argued God—or the forces of nature—had created the races with different abilities, Indians could force White people to acknowledge that while Indians were not the equal of Whites, they were superior to Blacks.

It took some time, however, for most Indians to accept the racist ideologies promulgated by White folk. According to Gregory Dowd, the pan-Indian alliance pieced together with considerable difficulty by the great Shawnee leader Tecumseh fell apart after his death, but it was a weak alliance at best.[25] Tecumseh sought to get Indians to stand together, pointing out the relentless push westward of British colonists, the seizure of Indian lands, and the maltreatment of Native peoples that fell under English control. But even in the late 18th century, with nearly 200 years of contact with Europeans, most Indians continued to think of themselves as Cherokee, or Seneca, or Narragansett. That is, they conceived of themselves as members of individual nations with their own languages and traditions, and even when some Indians urged that they unite against the Europeans, were unable to do so. In part this may have been because neither Europeans nor Africans, the non-Native people with whom they were in regular contact from the 17th century on, had a clear idea about race. As the scholarship[26] demonstrates, the European settlers who had powerful reasons to create racism as a justification to deprive Amerindians of their lands and to justify Black slavery, were for much of the North American colonial period fumbling about with the concept of race. Only in the last quarter of the 18th century did they begin to reach agreement on its meaning.

Even as Native peoples came to understand what race meant to most Whites (and some Blacks), it was not simply something they could accept as an isolated ideological construct. It was as part of the Euro-American culture that many Natives resisted the concept of race. Practicing racism was White, not Indian. Much scholarship has divided the Native response to European American culture into two camps. There were traditionalists who sought to retain and maintain pre-contact beliefs, behavior, and customs, and there were the accomodationists who sought to adjust traditional culture to the ways of White folk. Most who use these two terms admit they are inadequate oversimplifications and ought to be viewed as merely suggestive. There are, in fact, two additional groups, the assimilationists—who were willing to abandon Amerindian ways and completely accept European ways—and the neo-traditionalists—who sought to maintain the old ways by consciously confronting the challenges of Euro-American lifestyles. Accepting the idea of race was part of larger Indian approval of White American culture, an action with which assimilationists and accomodationists were comfortable. Neither traditionalists nor neo-traditionalists could accept race. Race had not existed in pre-contact indigenous cultures and was clearly not part of the Amerindian way.

As if this schema of assimilationists, accomodationists, neo-traditionalists, and traditionalists was not itself complex, a second parallel to the Black and Native approaches to zambo history is that Amerindians themselves were divided over the meaning of race. There were divisions between the tribes. So, for example, the Cherokee and the Seminole had very different ideas about race and the proper treatment of African Americans, and there were differences within the tribes. After removal, Cherokee accomodationists advocated and were generally successful in the passage of laws that treated Blacks—whether slave or free—much as they were treated in the neighboring slave states of Arkansas and Texas. But there was Cherokee opposition to these laws, and when they were passed, they were ignored by Cherokee neo-traditionalists who argued that they were not part of the Cherokee way. Those who study Afro-Indian relations—from the Indian perspective—can either ignore these complexities and present Indians as a monolithic people, with a single agreed-upon perspective on Blacks, or they can address them. A number of recent dissertations, some since published as books, written by both Indians and non-Indian scholars, are promising in the sense that they begin where the Indians begin—with a sense of tribe.[27] They then move to carefully examine how Blacks were treated within the nations and how the acceptance by some Indians of the idea of Black inferiority worked itself out within the framework of particular native cultures.

For example, Tiya Alicia Miles shows how the zambo daughters of Shoeboots, a Cherokee leader, were regarded by the tribe after they were kidnapped. The Cherokee sent men to recapture the girls who, it was assumed, had been kidnapped for the purpose of being sold into slavery. They were successful and the girls were returned, but this account is important for two reasons. First, the girls would not have been seized in the first place if they were not of part-African ancestry. Otherwise, it would have been impossible to sell them. After all, many Cherokee themselves held slaves at the time. Second, the Cherokee described the youngsters as mulattos—apparently meaning that they were of mixed Cherokee and Black ancestry[28]—and not as Cherokee. They were regarded as residents in the Cherokee nation, but not as Cherokee.[29] Discussion of whether persons of Afro-American ancestry should be regarded as tribal members became an issue among the five "civilized"[30] tribes—Cherokee, Chickasaw, Choctaw, Creek, and Seminole—who were removed to Oklahoma after the Civil War. The United States government required each of the tribes to accept as members and give full civil rights to Black residents, whether they had been slave or free at the beginning of the War. The government declared that as the tribes had been in rebellion and had sided with the Confederate States of America, they should be treated similarly to the CSA. In point of fact, while some tribes such as the Choctaw and the Chickasaw had been overwhelmingly Confederate, and others such as the Cherokee, had been more inclined toward the Union, all the tribes had been divided. Each of the five tribes included persons who were pro-Confederacy, pro-Union, and those who sought to stay out of the White man's war. While the government took advantage of the fact that each nation included some supporters of the CSA, it allowed the Indians themselves some leeway to determine how the Black residents of their nation were to be accorded civil rights. As Daniel Littlefield, one of the leading students of these Indians found, Indigenous peoples handled the situation in different ways.[31]

Toward Zambo Histories

Blacks also differed in their response both to the idea of race and to the idea of Blackness, and like Native peoples their responses varied over time and space. The obvious difference between the two peoples is that African Americans had to figure out the meaning of race at the same time they were constructing Black communities under the cruelties of the peculiar institution. Race as an idea came into Native communities with longstanding traditions, the members of which had then to decide how they would handle it. But among Afro-Americans, the idea of race confounded and made more difficult the construction of their new communities. Indeed, they would not have had to construct separate communities in the first place had it not been for race and its ugly, evil twin—slavery. In a sense the first Afro-American communities were similar to Native communities in that they were geographically isolated from one another and on their own in figuring out the meaning of race. Even those who had much in common were often unable to formulate a shared strategy based on a sense of racial identity that transcended geography.[32] Some scholarship demonstrates that there were links among enslaved Africans adrift in a strange new world, cultural survivals from Africa that helped to shape a united response to emergent ideas of Whiteness and Blackness.

Islam may have provided common ground for some slaves, though if African born Muslims were able to maintain a sense of community, their sense of being distinct and privileged separated them from non-Muslim Africans, preventing a sense of pan-Africanity from emerging, just as the mid-18th century pan-Indian movement failed among Indigenous peoples. John K. Thornton[33] suggests that the Stono Rebellion of 1739 was organized by Catholic Africans from the Kingdom of the Kongo, and in a sense was both oppositionist and rooted in the religious and cultural beliefs of the slaves. Thornton makes clear that, as Catholics, the slaves were doubly burdened by their English masters who were Protestant and oppressive, so an emergent sense of Afro-Catholic self led to the rebellion and to the determined efforts of the rebels to reach fellow Catholics in Florida. While it is clear that African slaves in such places as Brazil, Cuba, and Haiti were able to retain a conscious sense of ethnicity within a Catholic framework,[34] in British North America even if those who write of Muslims and the Kongo are correct, it was much more difficult for slaves to construct an organized, culturally based response to ideologies of race than it was for Native peoples.

A sense of Blackness was first worked out in the cities of British North America,[35] which housed fugitive slaves, slaves, free Blacks, as well as persons who, while formally slaves, were hired out and pretty much lived lives independent of their masters. Most of North America's first cities were coastal ones, so Black sailors were almost always present. As William Jeffrey Bolster clearly demonstrates, these men brought with them a sense of how Black peoples lived not just in the various port cities of North America, but in the Caribbean, South America, Africa, and Europe.[36] As a consequence of their experiences urban Black communities gradually developed ideas about Blackness. In no sense were these ideas always in agreement—even while some Blacks were resisting slavery others held slaves[37]—but all Afro-Americans gradually accepted the idea of race.

Scholars seeking to understand Afro-Indian relations from the standpoint of Native peoples and those seeking to understand these relations from the standpoint of Black peoples must therefore understand that each group was divided into a number of sub-groups. And while men such as David Walker and Tecumseh sought to cultivate a sense of unity among their respective peoples, many of those they sought to unify were not convinced. Indigenous peoples retained many of their traditional rivalries, while Afro-Americans busily created new ones of their own. Tecumseh apparently made no mention of Blacks, while Walker merely used Native peoples as examples as to what African Americans ought and ought not to do.[38] Scholars who have studied Black/Indian relations have often followed the Tecumseh/Walker lead both in suggesting that each of the two groups of people—not yet clearly races—were monolithic. This was not the case. Indians and Blacks were each divided over a number of cultural issues, primary among them how to respond to an emergent Euro-American culture powerfully backed by wealth, politics, military force, and racial arrogance. The very existence of zambo peoples demonstrates that at least some Amerindians and Black Americans were at least as interested in one another as they were concerned with White Americans.

For the most part, the scholarly literature has not given much attention to Amerindian/Afro-American relations as, whether written by Indians, Blacks, those supportive of Indians, or those supportive of Blacks, it has generally focused on relations with Whites and not on relations between these two peoples of color. When this literature examines zambo peoples and their origin, it almost always approaches them by choosing either the side of Blacks or the side of Indians. An example of this is the recent literature on Afro-Indians written by persons who have been raised in Black communities and regarded as Black, but now wish to publicly acknowledge their Native ancestry. Perhaps they have always thought of themselves as Indian, perhaps they were told they were Indians by older family members, perhaps they were told by family members that they were really Indian but had to conceal this fact from outsiders, or perhaps they were persecuted by Blacks when they declared themselves as Indian. The grounds for this persecution was that they were "really" Afro-American but only pretending to be Indian so as to escape the stigma of Blackness. In her Epilogue to the anthology on the 2000 Black Indian Conference at Dartmouth College, Valerie J. Phillips addresses many of these issues but notes at the beginning of her essay, "Growing up in Chicago, I learned to live in fear. Black youth seldom saw me for who or what I was. Instead, they saw me through the White man's eyes, deciding at the height of the Black is Beautiful era that all that mattered was my relatively light skin and 'good' hair, both of which made me a target, a substitute for the White man they never dared to touch."[39] While Phillips' essay elegantly and often poignantly touches on the many complicated issues in Indigenous/Black relations, she clearly takes an Indian perspective in arguing that Black people "never dared to" attack White people. As she is obviously a well-read person, to suggest that African Americans have never dared to physically confront European Americans is a willful and deliberate misreading of American history. Like the Black authors discussed previously who denigrated Indians, Phillips denigrates Blacks (at least those in Chicago), denouncing them as cowards willing to attack a defenseless child but physically afraid of White people.[40]

In an essay in the same collection, Ron Welburn examines many of the same issues but argues that persons of Indian ancestry, like himself, living within Black communities hid their Native ancestry under Blackness.[41] This sense of being a race within a race was sometimes confusing for children, as some of their elders insisted they were Black, others that they were Indian, and still others that they were "colored" people, thereby fudging the issue. Like the essay by Phillips, Welburn usefully examines Black Indians from both a social structural and a personal perspective, but he shares with Phillips a sense that Indians were superior to Blacks, writing, "Though I knew I was also part Black, as a youngster I assimilated a kind of sovereignty of the spirit that paid allegiance to my indigenous ancestry."[42] Just as Phillips perceives Blacks as cowardly bullies, Welburn attributes his "sovereignty of spirit" to his Native ancestry, not to his Black one. From his perspective, Afro-Americans have no such spirit. While depressing, this is all understandable. In their denigration of Afro-Americans, zambos such as Phillips and Welburn accept the racial categories created by Euro-Americans, despite the fact that Phillips herself warns, "Blacks and Indians who uncritically persist in looking at each other through the White man's eyes only undermine themselves.[43]

These zambos also fail to acknowledge that in the racial hierarchy of the United States Native peoples were always ranked above Blacks. While Thomas Jefferson and others early began to argue that Africans were an inferior people, many of those involved in the early government of the United States, as well as leaders of the major Protestant denominations, believed the Native peoples were much like Whites. With a little effort, these men often declared, Indians could become Americans and important contributors to the United States. Despite the fact that Amerindians were perceived as being outside the nation and Afro-Americans as being within its borders, Indians were viewed as superior to Blacks. By the 1830s, racism had gained such a hold on the American mind that Indians, like Blacks—because they were not White—were regarded as outsiders. Removal provided a geographic dimension to this ideological assumption. But prior to removal, and even thereafter, few White Americans felt a need to deny or conceal their Native ancestry. Indeed, many of the men who led the Cherokee and other nations into "civilization" were persons of mixed Indian and European ancestry, full members of Native societies, while accepted as White men by most Euro-Americans. This group had no Afro-American counterpart. Indians themselves, for reasons already noted, confirmed this hierarchy by allowing mestizos to lead their nations while passing laws to deny zambos membership in their tribes.

Given that Whites and Indians agreed on placing Blacks at the bottom of their respective societies, it is strange to find scholars such as Phillips and Welburn writing of their oppression at the hands of Blacks. Even before there was a United States of America, Indians were more highly regarded than were Blacks, a reality that was frequently written into law in both independent Indian nations and the United States. In both, for example, intermarriage with Blacks was often forbidden, but there were few laws among Indians forbidding intermarriage with Whites and, many of the states that made it illegal for White people to marry Black people placed no barrier between Indians and Whites.

In a sense the accusations of Black oppression of Afro-Indians is part of a larger assault on Blackness.[44] The one-drop rule, which asserts the Blackness of all persons of any known African ancestry, wherever they may live and whatever their physical appearance, exists only in the United States. F. James Davis provides a useful overview of how this rule came into existence, and other scholars have also tackled this vexing issue.[45] While zambos in other parts of the New World confronted a wide range of cultural, religious, economic, and racial challenges, they did not have to grapple with the one-drop rule. The rules of race in most of the rest of the Americas allow persons to admit that they are of mixed heritage. In most parts of the New World there has historically been little to gain by declaring oneself a zambo. Outside the United States, Afro-Indians, while they have not denied their African ancestry, have when possible, promoted themselves into a more highly regarded racial category. In other words, they could and can acknowledge African ancestry without being Black.

The one-drop rule makes it impossible for zambos in the United States to follow this strategy. This hard racial reality has created numerous problems for Native peoples in the United States where persons of mixed Native/European ancestry are accepted into tribes while those of mixed Native/African ancestry are queried, questioned, and barred. In general, North America's Native peoples appear to have accepted North America's one-drop rule. It is possible to be part White and yet be an accepted as an Indian, but if one is part Black then one is Black not an Indian.

Conclusion

Until the last quarter of the 20th century, the study of Native American/Black relations was a kind of sideshow in the master narrative of American history. Amerindians and Afro-Americans figured in this discourse only as persons who interacted with, were uplifted by, and sought to be a part of, an emergent Euro-American civilization. Some Blacks and Native peoples were studied as persons who resisted Manifest Destiny and its various ideological forerunners and successors. Near the end of the 20th century Indians and Blacks increasingly demonstrated both determination and ability to write their own histories, as well as an aggressive willingness to confront the master narrative and expose its many inadequacies. But the demonstrated ability of Indians to tell their own stories did not result in any special respect for the story of Blacks, any more than did the ability of Blacks to tell their own stories led to any particular respect for the story of Native peoples. Each of the non-Native, non-Black scholars who wrote in support of these emergent perspectives still organize their works around the master narrative. As a consequence they can find little room for the study of zambos.

While those who work within the master narrative of White supremacy can pretend that current racial politics do not matter in interpretations of the American past, Indian and Black scholars, as well as those who write in support of a non-racist history, cannot. Once they emancipate themselves from the master narrative and its racist support system, Zambo History will be right there ready to be uncovered.

Endnotes

1. Morgan, Edmund. (1975). *American Slavery American Freedom: The Ordeal of Colonial Virginia.* New York: Norton, 130.
2. Tannenbaum, Frank. (1946). *Slave and Citizen: The Negro in the Americas.* New York: Vintage Books.
3. See, for example, Jones, Rhett S. (2001). "Native American/African American Relations: An Overview of the Scholarship," *Transforming Anthropology* 10 (1); McLoughlin, William G. (1984). *The Cherokee Ghost Dance.* Mercer, GA: Mercer University Press; Nash, Gary B. (1995). "The Hidden History of Mestizo America," *Journal of American History* 82 (December): 941–964; Perdue, Theda. (1979). *Slavery and the Evolution of Cherokee Society, 1540–1866.* Knoxville, TN: University of Tennessee Press.
4. The best discussion of racial terminologies and their consequences remains Forbes, Jack D. (1993). *Africans and Native Americans: The Language of Race and the Evolution of Red-Black Peoples.* Urbana, IL: University of Illinois Press. Forbes has been about the examination of the links among racial intermixture, racial labels, power, and culture in the Americas for nearly a generation. All of his work is useful.
5. Notable exceptions are Bateman, Rebecca. (1990). "Africans and Indians: A Comparative History of the Black Carib and Black Seminole," *Ethnohistory* 37 (Winter): 1–24; Berry, Brewton. (1945). "The Mestizos of South Carolina," *American Journal of Sociology* 51 (1): 34–41; Gonzalez, Nancie. (1969). *Black Carib Household Structure.* Seattle, WA: University of Washington Press; Mandell, Daniel. (1988). "Shifting Boundaries of Race and Ethnicity: Indian-Black Intermarriage in Southern New England, 1760–1880," *Journal of American History* 75 (September): 466–501; and Willis, Jr., William S. (1963)."Divide and Rule: Red, White and Black in the Southeast," *Journal of Negro History* 48: 157–176.
6. Cope, R. Douglas. (1994). *The Limits of Racial Domination: Plebian Society in Colonial Mexico City, 1660–1720.* Madison, WI: University of Wisconsin Press; Morner, Magnus. (1967). *Race Mixture in the History of Latin America.* Boston: Little Brown; Olien, Michael D. (1967). *The Negro in Costa Rica: The Ethnohistory of an Ethnic Minority in a Complex Society.* Ph.D. dissertation, University of Oregon, Eugene, OR; Rout, Leslie B. (1976). *The African Experience in Spanish America.* New York: Cambridge University Press.
7. See Piersen, William D. (1988). *Black Yankees: The Development of an Afro-American Subculture in Eighteenth Century New England.* Amherst, MA: University of Massachusetts Press.
8. Willis, "Divide and Rule." Also Mulroy, Kevin. (1993). *Freedom on the Border: The Seminole Maroons.* Lubbock, TX: Texas Tech University Press.
9. Woodson, Carter G. (1920). "The Relations of Negroes and Indians in Massachusetts," *Journal of Negro History* 5 (January): 45.
10. Woodson, Carter G. (1925). "Ten Years of Collecting and Publishing Records of the Negro," *Journal of Negro History* 10 (October): 598–606. Nor was Woodson alone in his inclination to criticize Native peoples as a means of emphasizing how much more Blacks had contributed to the development of the United States than had Indians. See Jones, Rhett S. (1977). "Black over Red: The Image of Native Americans in Black History," *Umoja* I (September): 13–29.
11. A number of Porter's essays were collected and published as *The Negro on the American Frontier.* (1971). New York: Arno Press.
12. Jones, "Black over Red," 24.
13. Cited in Sensbach, Jon F. (1993). "Charting a Course in Early African-American History, *William and Mary Quarterly* 3rd Series 50 (April): 394–405.

14. Katz, William (1986). *Black Indians: A Hidden Heritage.* New York: Atheneum; places the Buffalo soldiers in context.

15. Franklin, John Hope, and Moss, Jr., Alfred A. (1994). *From Slavery to Freedom: A History of Black America.* New York: McGraw-Hill.

16. An informative overview of tri-racial isolates—for its time and still useful—is: Berry, Brewton. (1963). *Almost White.* New York: Macmillan.

17. Cox, Oliver Cromwell. (1959). *Caste, Class, and Race.* New York: Monthly Review Press.

18. These include Piersen, *Black Yankees;* Cottrol, Robert J. (1982). *The Afro-Yankees.* Westport, CT: Greenwood Press; Winch, Julie. (1988). *Philadelphia's Black Elite.* Philadelphia: Temple University Press; Levesque, George. (1994). *Black Boston.* New York: Garland; Melish, Joanie P. (1998). *Slavery Disowned.* Ithaca, NY: Cornell University Press.

19. Representative Afrocentric texts, such as Kete Asante, Molefi. (1988). *Afrocentricity.* Trenton, NJ: Africa World Press; and Karenga, Maulana. (1993). *Introduction to Black Studies.* Los Angeles: University of Sankore Press, pretty much ignore Black life in the Americas during the 17th and 18th centuries.

20. Faggins, Barbara A. (2001). *Africans and Indians.* New York: Routledge.

21. Faggins, 71.

22. Perdue, *Slavery and the Evolution of Cherokee Society,* especially chapter 3. Also Holland-Braund, Kathryn E. (1991). "The Creek Indians, Blacks and Slavery," *Journal of Southern History* 57 (November): 601–636.

23. Perdue, *Slavery and the Evolution of Cherokee Society.* Also Shoemaker, Nancy. (1997). "How Indians Got to be Red," *American Historical Review* 102 (June): 625–644.

24. Perdue, *Slavery and the Evolution of Cherokee Society.* McLoughlin, William G. (1974). "Red Indians, Black Slavery and White Racism," *American Quarterly* 26 (October): 367–385.

25. Dowd, Gregory. (1992). *A Spirited Resistance: The Indian Struggle for Unity, 1745–1815.* Baltimore: Johns Hopkins University Press; especially chapter 2.

26. Morgan, *American Slavery American Freedom.* Also Jordan, Winthrop D. (1968). *White over Black.* Chapel Hill, NC: University of North Carolina Press; and Fredrickson, George M. (1982). *White Supremacy.* New York: Oxford University Press.

27. See, for example, May, Katja Helma. (1994). *Collision and Collusion: Native Americans and African Americans in the Cherokee and Creek Nations.* Ph.D. dissertation, University of California, Berkeley, CA; Micco, Melinda. (1995). *Freedmen and Seminoles.* Ph.D. dissertation, University of California, Berkeley, CA; Krauthamer, Barbara. (2000). *Blacks on the Borders.* Ph.D. dissertation, Princeton University, Princeton, NJ; and Naylor-Ojurongbe, Celia E. (2001). *"More at Home with the Indians."* Ph.D. dissertation, Duke University, Durham, NC.

28. Miles, Tiya Alicia. (2000). *"Bone of My Bone:" Stories of a Black Cherokee Family.* Ph.D. dissertation, University of Minnesota, Minneapolis, MN.

29. Miles, *"Bone of my Bone,"* see especially chapters 4 and 5.

30. Discussion of these demands and the decisions made by the nations in response to them is found in Littlefield, Jr., Daniel F. (1977). *Africans and Seminoles.* Westport, CT: Greenwood Press.

31. Littlefield, *Africans and Seminoles.*

32. Boles, John B. (1984). *Black Southerners, 1619–1869.* Lexington, KY: University Press of Kentucky; especially chapter 2. Race, of course eventually came to trump geographic isolation, class and culture among Blacks as well as among Whites and Natives.

33. Thornton, John K. (1991). "African Dimensions of the Stono Rebellion, *American Historical Review* 96 (October): 1101–1113.

34. For discussion of the interaction between Roman Catholicism and African religions in three Catholic colonies, compare Deren, Maya. (1970). *Divine Horsemen.* New York: Delta Books; Bastide, Roger. (1978). *The African Religions of Brazil.* Baltimore: The Johns Hopkins University Press; and Murphy, Joseph M. (1993). *Santeria.* Boston: Beacon Press.

35. Jones, Rhett S. (2002). "Black Creole Cultures," in Gayle T. Tate and Lewis A. Randolph (Eds.), *Dimensions of Black Conservatism in the Americas.* New York: Palgrave.

36. Bolster, William Jeffrey. (1997). *Black Jacks: African American Seamen in the Age of Sail.* Cambridge, MA: Harvard University Press.

37. Koger, Larry. (1985). *Black Slaveowners: Free Black Slave Masters in South Carolina.* Jefferson, NC: McFarland Press. Also Landers, Jane. (1999). *Black Society in Spanish Florida.* Urbana, IL: University of Illinois Press.

38. *David Walker's Appeal to the Coloured Citizens of the World.* (1965). New York: Hill and Wang, 63.

39. Phillips, Valerie J. (2002). "Seeing Each Other Through the White Man's Eyes," in James F. Brooks (ed.), *Confounding the Color Line: The Indian-Black Experience in North America.* Lincoln, NE: University of Nebraska Press, 371.

40. Jones, "Black over Red."

41. Welburn, Ron. "A Most Secret Identity: Native American Assimilation and Identity Resistance in African America," in James F. Brooks (ed.), *Confounding the Color Line,* 292–320.

42. Welburn, "A Most Secret Identity," 293.

43. Phillips, "Seeing Each Other," 383.

44. Jones, Rhett S. (1994). "The End of Africanity? The Bi-Racial Assault on Blackness," *The Western Journal of Black Studies* 18 (Winter): 201–211.

45. Davis, F. James. (1991). *Who Is Black?* University Park, PA: Pennsylvania State University Press. See also van den Berghe, Pierre. (1967). *Race and Racism.* New York: Wiley; and Hoetink, Harmannus. (1967). *The Two Variants in Caribbean Race Relations.* New York: Oxford University Press.

Chapter 16

The Interesting Life of Olaudah Equiano (Excerpts, 1789)

That part of Africa known by the name of Guinea to which the trade of slaves is carried on extends along the coast above 3,400 miles, from the Senegal to Angola, and includes a variety of kingdoms. Of these the most considerable is the kingdom of Benin, both as to extent and wealth, the richness and cultivation of the soil, the power of its king, and the number and warlike disposition of the inhabitants. It is situated nearly under the line and extends along the coast about 170 miles, but runs back into the interior part of Africa to a distance hitherto I believe unexplored by any traveller, and seems only terminated at length by the empire of Abyssinia, near 1,500 miles from its beginning. This kingdom is divided into many provinces or districts, in one of the most remote and fertile of which, called Eboe, I was born in the year 1745, situated in a charming fruitful vale, named Essaka. The distance of this province from the capital of Benin and the sea coast must be very considerable, for I had never heard of white men or Europeans, nor of the sea, and our subjection to the king of Benin was little more than nominal; for every transaction of the government, as far as my slender observation extended, was conducted by the chiefs or elders of the place. The manners and government of a people who have little commerce with other countries are generally very simple, and the history of what passes in one family or village may serve as a specimen of a nation. My father was one of those elders or chiefs I have spoken of and was styled Embrenché, a term as I remember importing the highest distinction, and signifying in our language a *mark* of grandeur. This mark is conferred on the person entitled to it by cutting the skin across at the top of the forehead and drawing it down to the eyebrows, and while it is in this situation applying a warm hand and rubbing it until it shrinks up into a thick *weal* across the lower part of the forehead. Most of the judges and senators were thus marked; my father had long borne it. I had seen it conferred on one of my brothers, and I was also *destined* to receive it by my parents. . . .

We are almost a nation of dancers, musicians, and poets. Thus every great event such as a triumphant return from battle or other cause of public rejoicing is celebrated in public dances, which are accompanied with songs and music suited to the occasion. The assembly is separated into four divisions, which dance either apart or in succession, and each with a character peculiar to itself. The first division contains the married men, who in their dances frequently exhibit feats of arms and the representation of a battle. To these succeed the married women, who dance in the second division. The young men occupy the third and the maidens the fourth. Each represents some interesting scene of real life, such as a great achievement, domestic employment, a pathetic story, or some rural sport, and as the subject is generally founded on some recent event it is therefore ever new. This gives our dances a spirit and variety which I have scarcely seen elsewhere. We have many musical instruments, particularly drums of different kinds, a piece of music which resembles a guitar, and another much like a stickado. These last are chiefly used by betrothed virgins who play on them on all grand festivals.

As our manners are simple, our luxuries are few. The dress of both sexes is nearly the same. It generally consists of a long piece of calico or muslin, wrapped loosely round the body somewhat in the form of a highland plaid. This is usually dyed blue, which is our favourite colour. It is extracted from a berry and is brighter and richer than any I have seen in Europe. Besides this our women of distinction wear golden ornaments, which they dispose with some profusion on their arms and legs. When our women are not employed with the men in tillage, their usual occupation is spinning and weaving cotton, which they afterwards dye and make into garments. They also manufacture earthen vessels, of which we have many kinds. Among the rest tobacco pipes, made after the same fashion and used in the same manner, as those in Turkey.

Our manner of living is entirely plain, for as yet the natives are unacquainted with those refinements in cookery which debauch the taste: bullocks, goats, and poultry, supply the greatest part of their food. These constitute likewise the principal wealth of the country and the chief articles of its commerce. The flesh is usually stewed in a pan; to make it savoury we sometimes use also pepper and other spices, and we have salt made of wood ashes. Our vegetables are mostly plantains, eadas, yams, beans, and Indian com. The head of the family usually eats alone; his wives and slaves have also their separate tables. Before we taste food we always wash our hands: indeed our cleanliness on all occasions is extreme, but on this it is an indispensable ceremony. After washing, libation is made by pouring out a small portion of the drink on the floor, and tossing a small quantity of the food in a certain place for the spirits of departed relations, which the natives suppose to preside over their conduct and guard them from evil. They are totally unacquainted with strong or spirituous liquors, and their principal beverage is palm wine. This is got from a tree of that name by tapping it at the top and fastening a large gourd to it, and sometimes one tree will yield three or four gallons in a night. When just drawn it is of a most delicious sweetness, but in a few days it acquires a tartish and more spirituous flavour, though I never saw anyone intoxicated by it. The same tree also produces nuts and oil. Our principal luxury is in perfumes; one sort of these is an odoriferous wood of delicious fragrance, the other a kind of earth, a small portion of which thrown into the fire diffuses a more powerful odour. We beat this wood into powder and mix it with palm oil, with which both men and women perfume themselves.

In our buildings we study convenience rather than ornament. Each master of a family has a large square piece of ground, surrounded with a moat or fence or enclosed with a wall made of red earth tempered, which when dry is as hard as brick. Within this are his houses to accommodate his family and slaves which if numerous frequently present the appearance of a village. In the middle stands the principal building, appropriated to the sole use of the master and consisting of two apartments, in one of which he sits in the day with his family. The other is left apart for the reception of his friends. He has besides these a distinct apartment in which he sleeps, together with his male children. On each side are the apartments of his wives, who have also their separate day and night houses. The habitations of the slaves and their families are distributed throughout the rest of the enclosure. These houses never exceed one story in height: they are always built of wood or stakes driven into the ground, crossed with wattles, and neatly plastered within and without. The roof is thatched with reeds. Our day-houses are left open at the sides, but those in which we sleep are always covered, and plastered in the inside with a composition mixed with cow-dung to keep off the different insects which annoy us during the night. The walls and floors also of these are generally covered with mats. Our beds consist of a platform raised three or four feet from the ground, on which are laid skins and different parts of a spungy tree called plantain. Our covering is calico or muslin, the same as our dress. The usual seats are a few logs of wood, but we have benches, which are generally perfumed to accommodate strangers: these compose the greater part of our household furniture. Houses so constructed and furnished require but little skill to erect them. Every man is a sufficient architect for the purpose. The whole neighborhood afford their unanimous assistance in building them and in return receive and expect no other recompense than a feast.

As we live in a country where nature is prodigal of her favours, our wants are few and easily supplied; of course we have few manufactures. They consist for the most part of calicoes, earthenware, ornaments, and instruments of war and husbandry. But these make no part of our commerce, the principal articles of which, as I have observed, are provisions. In such a state money is of little use; however we have some small pieces of coin, if I may call them such. They are made something like an anchor, but I do not remember either their value or denomination. We have also markets, at which I have been frequently with my mother. These are sometimes visited by stout mahogany-coloured men from the southwest of us: we call them *Oye-Eboe*, which term signifies red men living at a distance. They generally bring us firearms, gunpowder, hats, beads, and dried fish. The last we esteemed a great rarity as our waters were only brooks and springs. These articles they barter with us for odoriferous woods and earth, and our salt of wood ashes. They always carry slaves through our land, but the strictest account is exacted of their manner of procuring them before they are suffered to pass. Some times indeed we sold slaves to them, but they were only prisoners of war, or such among us as had been convicted of kidnapping, or adultery, and some other crimes which we esteemed heinous. This practice of kidnapping induces me to think that, notwithstanding all our strictness, their principal business among us was to trepan our people. I remember too they carried great sacks along with them, which not long after I had an opportunity of fatally seeing applied to that infamous purpose.

Our land is uncommonly rich and fruitful, and produces all kinds of vegetables in great abundance. We have plenty of Indian corn, and vast quantities of cotton and tobacco. Our pineapples grow without culture;

they are about the size of the largest sugar-loaf and finely flavoured. We have also spices of different kinds, particularly pepper, and a variety of delicious fruits which I have never seen in Europe, together with gums of various kinds and honey in abundance. All our industry is exerted to improve those blessings of nature. Agriculture is our chief employment, and everyone, even the children and women, are engaged in it. Thus we are all habituated to labour from our earliest years. Everyone contributes something to the common stock, and as we are unacquainted with idleness we have no beggars. The benefits of such a mode of living are obvious. The West India planters prefer the slaves of Benin or Eboe to those of any other part of Guinea for their hardiness, intelligence, integrity, and zeal. Those benefits are felt by us in the general healthiness of the people, and in their vigour and activity; I might have added too in their comeliness. Deformity is indeed unknown amongst us, I mean that of shape. Numbers of the natives of Eboe now in London might be brought in support of this assertion, for in regard to complexion, ideas of beauty are wholly relative. I remember while in Africa to have seen three negro children who were tawny, and another quite white, who were universally regarded by myself and the natives in general, as far as related to their complexions, as deformed. Our women too were in my eyes at least uncommonly graceful, alert, and modest to a degree of bashfulness; nor do I remember to have ever heard of an instance of incontinence amongst them before marriage. They are also remarkably cheerful. Indeed cheerfulness and affability are two of the leading characteristics of our nation.

Our tillage is exercised in a large plain or common, some hours walk from our dwellings, and all the neighbours resort thither in a body. They use no beasts of husbandry, and their only instruments are hoes, axes, shovels, and beaks, or pointed iron to dig with. Sometimes we are visited by locusts, which come in large clouds so as to darken the air and destroy our harvest. This however happens rarely, but when it does a famine is produced by it. I remember an instance or two wherein this happened. This common is often the theatre of war, and therefore when our people go out to till their land they not only go in a body but generally take their arms with them for fear of a surprise, and when they apprehend an invasion they guard the avenues to their dwellings by driving sticks into the ground, which are so sharp at one end as to pierce the foot and are generally dipped in poison. From what I can recollect of these battles, they appear to have been irruptions of one little state or district on the other to obtain prisoners or booty. Perhaps they were incited to this by those traders who brought the European goods I mentioned amongst us. Such a mode of obtaining slaves in Africa is common, and I believe more are procured this way and by kidnapping than any other. When a trader wants slaves he applies to a chief for them and tempts him with his wares. It is not extraordinary if on this occasion he yields to the temptation with as little firmness, and accepts the price of his fellow creatures liberty with as little reluctance as the enlightened merchant. Accordingly he falls on his neighbours and a desperate battle ensues. If he prevails and takes prisoners, he gratifies his avarice by selling them; but if his party be vanquished and he falls into the hands of the enemy, he is put to death: for as he has been known to foment their quarrels it is thought dangerous to let him survive, and no ransom can save him, though all other prisoners may be redeemed . . . .

* * *

The first object which saluted my eyes when I arrived on the coast was the sea, and a slave ship, which was then riding at anchor, and waiting for its cargo. These filled me with astonishment, which was soon converted into terror, when I was carried on board I was immediately handled, and tossed up, to see if I were sound, by some of the crew; and I was now persuaded that I had got into a world of bad spirits, and that they were going to kill me. Their complexions too differing so much from ours, their long hair, and the language they spoke (which was very different from any I had ever heard) united to confirm me in this belief. Indeed such were the horrors of my views and fears at the moment, that, if ten thousand worlds had been my own, I would have freely parted with them all to have exchanged my condition with that of the meanest slave in my own country. When I looked round the ship too and saw a large furnace or copper boiling, and a multitude of black people of every description chained together, every one of their countenances expressing dejection and sorrow, I no longer doubted of my fate; and, quite overpowered with horror and anguish, I fell motionless on the deck and fainted. When I recovered a little I found some black people about me, who I believed were some of those who had brought me on board, and had been receiving their pay; they talked to me in order to cheer me, but all in vain. I asked them if we were not to be eaten by those white men with horrible looks, red faces, and long hair. They told me I was not; and one of the crew brought me a small portion of spirituous liquor in a wine-glass; but being afraid of him, I would not take it out of his hand. One of the blacks therefore took it from him and gave it to me, and I took a little down my palate, which, instead of reviving me, as they thought it would, threw me into the greatest consternation at the strange feeling it produced, having never tasted any such liquor before. Soon after this the blacks who brought me on board went off, and left me abandoned to despair. I now saw myself deprived of all chance of returning to my native country, or even the least glimpse of hope of gaining the shore, which I now considered as friendly; and I even wished for my former slavery in preference to my present situation, which was filled with horrors of every kind, still heightened by my ignorance of what I was to undergo. I was not long suffered to indulge my grief; I was soon put down under the decks, and there I received such a salutation in my nostrils as I had never experienced in my life: so that with the loathsomeness of the stench, and crying together, I became so sick and low that I was not able to eat, nor had I the least desire to taste any thing. I now wished for the last friend, death, to relieve me; but soon, to my grief, two of the white men offered me eatables; and, on my refusing to eat, one of them held me fast by the hands, and laid me across, I think the windlass, and tied my feet, while the other flogged me severely. I had never experienced any thing of this kind before: and, although not being used to the water, I naturally feared that element the first time I saw it, yet, nevertheless, could I have got over the nettings, I would have jumped over the side, but I could not; and, besides, the crew used to watch us very closely who were not chained down to the decks, lest we should leap into the water: and I have seen some of these poor African prisoners most severely cut for attempting to do so, and hourly whipped for not eating. This indeed was often the case with myself. In a little time after, amongst the poor chained men, I found some of my own nation, which in a small degree gave ease to my mind. I inquired of these what was to be done with us? they gave me to understand we were to be carried to these white people's country to work for them. I then was a little revived, and thought, if it were no worse than working, my situation was not so desperate: but still I feared I should be put to death, the white people looked and acted, as I thought, in so savage a manner; for I had never seen among any people such instances of brutal cruelty; and this not only shown towards us blacks, but also to some of the whites themselves. One white man in particular I saw, when we were permitted to be on deck, flogged so unmercifully with a large rope near the foremast, that he died in consequence of it; and they tossed him over the side as they would have done a brute. This made me fear these people the more; and I expected nothing less than to be treated in the same manner. I could not help expressing my fears and apprehensions to some of my countrymen: I asked them if these people had no country, but lived in this hollow place (the ship)? they told me they did not, but came from a distant one, "Then," said I, "how comes it in all our country we never heard of them!" They told me, because they lived so very far off. I then asked where were their women? had they any like themselves? I was told they had: "And why," said I, "do we not see them?" they answered, because they were left behind. I asked how the vessel could go? they told me they could not tell; but that there were cloth put upon the masts by the help of the ropes I saw, and then the vessel went on; and the white men had some spell or magic they put in the water when they liked in order to stop the vessel, I was exceedingly amazed at this account, and really thought they were spirits. I therefore wished much to be from amongst them, for I expected they would sacrifice me: but my wishes were vain; for we were so quartered that it was impossible for any of us to make our escape. While we stayed on the coast I was mostly on deck; and one day, to my great astonishment, I saw one of these vessels coming in with the sails up. As soon as the whites saw it, they gave a great shout, at which we were amazed: and the more so as the vessel appeared larger by approaching nearer. At last she came to an anchor in my sight, and when the anchor was let go I and my countrymen who saw it were lost in astonishment to observe the vessel stop; and were now convinced it was done by magic. Soon after this the other ship got her boats out, and they came on board of us, and the people of both ships seemed very glad to see each other. Several of the strangers also shook hands with us black people, and made motions with their hands, signifying I suppose, we were to go to their country; but we did not understand them. At last, when the ship we were in, had got in all her cargo, they made ready with many fearful noises, and we were all put under deck, so that we could not see how they managed the vessel. But this disappointment was the least of my sorrow. The stench of the hold while we were on the coast was so intolerably loathsome, that it was dangerous to remain there for any time, and some of us had been permitted to stay on the deck for the fresh air; but now that the whole ship's cargo were confined together, it became absolutely pestilential. The closeness of the place, and the heat of the climate, added to the number in the ship, which was so crowded that each had scarcely room to turn himself, almost suffocated us. This produced copious perspirations, so that the air soon became unfit for respiration, from a variety of loathsome smells, and brought on a sickness amongst the slaves, of which many died, thus falling victims to the improvident avarice, as I may call it, of their purchasers. This wretched situation was again aggravated by the galling of the chains, now become insupportable; and the filth of the necessary tubs, into which the children often fell, and were almost suffocated. The shrieks of the women, and the groans of the dying, rendered the whole a scene of horror almost inconceivable. Happily perhaps for myself I was soon reduced so low here that it was thought necessary to keep me almost always on deck; and from my extreme youth I was not put in fetters. In this situation I expected every hour to share the fate of my companions, some of whom were almost daily brought upon deck at the point of death, which I began to hope would soon put an end to my miseries. Often did I think many of the inhabitants of the deep much more happy than myself, I envied them the freedom they enjoyed, and as often wished I could change my condition for theirs. Every circumstance I met with served only to render my state more painful, and heightened my apprehensions and my opinion of the cruelty of the whites. One day they had taken a number of fishes; and when they had killed and satisfied themselves with as many as they thought fit, to our astonishment who were on the deck, rather than give any of them to us to eat, as we expected, they tossed the remaining fish into the sea again, although we begged and prayed for some as well as we could, but in vain; and some of my countrymen, being pressed by hunger, took an opportunity, when they thought no one saw them, of trying to get a little privately; but they were discovered, and the attempt procured them some very severe floggings. One day, when we had a smooth sea and moderate wind, two of my wearied countrymen who were chained together (I was near them at the time), preferring death to such a life of misery, somehow made through the nettings and jumped into the sea: immediately another quite dejected fellow, who on account of his illness, was suffered to be out of irons, also followed their example; and I believe many more would very soon have done the same if they had not been prevented by the ship's crew who were instantly alarmed. Those of us that were the most active were in a moment put down under the deck, and there was such a noise and confusion amongst the people of the ship as I never heard before, to stop her, and get the boat out to go after the slaves. However two of the wretches were drowned, but they got the other, and afterwards flogged him unmercifully for thus attempting to prefer death to slavery. In this manner we continued to undergo more hardships than I can now relate, hardships which are inseparable from this accursed trade. Many a time we were near suffocation from the want of fresh air, which we were often without for whole days together. This, and the stench of the necessary tubs, carried off many. During our passage I first saw flying fishes, which surprised me very much: they used frequently to fly across the ship, and many of them fell on the deck. I also now first saw the use of the quadrant; I had often with astonishment seen the mariners make observations with it, and I could not think what it meant. They at last took notice of my surprise: and one of them, willing to increase it, as well as to gratify my curiosity, made me one day look through it. The clouds appeared to me to be land, which disappeared as they passed along. This heightened my wonder; and I was now more persuaded than ever that I was in another world, and that every thing about me was magic. At last we came in sight of the island of Barbadoes, at which the whites on board gave a great shout, and made many signs of joy to us. We did not know what to think of this; but as the vessel drew nearer, we plainly saw the harbour, and other ships of different kinds and sizes; and we soon anchored amongst them off Bridge-Town. Many merchants and planters now came on board, though it was in the evening. They put us in separate parcels, and examined us attentively. They also made us jump, and pointed to the land, signifying we were to go there. We thought by this we should be eaten by these ugly men, as they appeared to us; and, when soon after we were all put down under the deck again, there was much dread and trembling among us, and nothing but bitter cries to be heard all the night from these apprehensions, insomuch that at last the white people got some old slaves from the land to pacify us. They told us we were not to be eaten, but to work, and were soon to go on land, where we should see many of our country people. This report eased us much; and sure enough, soon after we landed, there came to us Africans of all languages. We were conducted immediately to the merchant's yard, where we were all pent up together like so many sheep in a fold, without regard to sex or age. As every object was new to me, every thing I saw filled me with surprise. What struck me first was that the houses were built with bricks and stories, and in every other respect different from those I had seen in Africa: but I was still more astonished on seeing people on horseback. I did not know what this could mean; and indeed I thought these people were full of nothing but magical arts. While I was in this astonishment one of my fellow prisoners spoke to a countryman of his about the horses, who said they were the same kind they had in their country. I understood them, though they were from a distant part of Africa, and I thought it odd I had not seen any horses there; but afterwards when I came to converse with different Africans, I found they had many horses amongst them, and much larger than those I saw. We were not many days in the merchant's custody before we were sold after their usual manner, which is this: On a signal given, (as the beat of a drum) the buyers rush at once into the yard where the slaves are confined, and make choice of that parcel they like best. The noise and clamour with which this is attended, and the eagerness visible in the countenances of the buyers, serve not a little to increase the apprehension of terrified Africans, who may well be supposed to consider them as the ministers of that destruction to which they think themselves devoted. In this manner, without scruple, are relations and friends separated, most of them never to see each other again. I remember in the vessel in which I was brought over, in the men's apartment, there were several brothers, who, in the sale were sold in different lots; and it was very moving on this occasion to see and hear their cries at parting. O, ye nominal Christians! might not an African ask you, learned you this from your God, who says unto you, Do unto all men as you would men should do unto you? Is it not enough that we are torn from our country and friends, to toil for your luxury and lust of gain? Must every tender feeling be likewise sacrificed to your avarice? Are the dearest friends and relations, now rendered more dear by their separation from their kindred, still to be parted from each other, and thus prevented from cheering the gloom of slavery with the small comfort of being together, and mingling their sufferings and sorrows? Why are parents to lose their children, brothers their sisters, or husbands their wives? Surely this is a new refinement in cruelty, which, while it has no advantage to atone for it, thus aggravates distress, and adds fresh horrors even to the wretchedness of slavery.

Chapter 17

David Walker's Appeal (1829–1830)

Appeal, &c.

Preamble

My dearly beloved Brethren and Fellow Citizens.

Having travelled over a considerable portion of these United States, and having, in the course of my travels, taken the most accurate observations of things as they exist—the result of my observations has warranted the full and unshaken conviction, that we, (coloured people of these United States,) are the most degraded, wretched, and abject set of beings that ever lived since the world began; and I pray God that none like us ever may live again until time shall be no more. They tell us of the Israelites in Egypt, the Helots in Sparta, and of the Roman Slaves, which last were made up from almost every nation under heaven, whose sufferings under those ancient and heathen nations, were, in comparison with ours, under this enlightened and Christian nation, no more than a cypher—or, in other words, those heathen nations of antiquity, had but little more among them than the name and form of slavery; while wretchedness and endless miseries were reserved, apparently in a phial, to be poured out upon our fathers, ourselves and our children, by *Christian* Americans!

These positions I shall endeavour, by the help of the Lord, to demonstrate in the course of this *Appeal*, to the satisfaction of the most incredulous mind—and may God Almighty, who is the Father of our Lord Jesus Christ, open your hearts to understand and believe the truth.

The *causes*, my brethren, which produce our wretchedness and miseries, are so very numerous and aggravating, that I believe the pen only of a Josephus or a Plutarch, can well enumerate and explain them. Upon subjects, then, of such incomprehensible magnitude, so impenetrable, and so notorious, I shall be obliged to omit a large class of, and content myself with giving you an exposition of a few of those, which do indeed rage to such an alarming pitch, that they cannot but be a perpetual source of terror and dismay to every reflecting mind.

I am fully aware, in making this appeal to my much afflicted and suffering brethren, that I shall not only be assailed by those whose greatest earthly desires are, to keep us in abject ignorance and wretchedness, and who are of the firm conviction that Heaven has designed us and our children to be slaves and *beasts of burden* to them and their children. I say, I do not only expect to be held up to the public as an ignorant, impudent and restless disturber of the public peace, by such avaricious creatures, as well as a mover of insubordination—and perhaps put in prison or to death, for giving a superficial exposition of our miseries, and exposing tyrants. But I am persuaded, that many of my brethren, particularly those who are ignorantly in league with slave-holders or tyrants, who acquire their daily bread by the blood and sweat of their more ignorant brethren—and not a few of those too, who are too ignorant to see an inch beyond their noses, will rise up and call me cursed—Yea, the jealous ones among us will perhaps use more abject subtlety, by affirming that this work is not worth perusing, that we are well situated, and there is no use in trying to better our condition, for we cannot. I will ask one question here.—Can our condition be any worse?—Can it be more mean and abject? If there are any changes, will they not be for the better, though they may appear for the worst at first? Can they get us any lower? Where can they get us? They are afraid to treat us worse, for they know well, the day they do it they are gone. But against all accusations which may or can be preferred against me, I appeal to Heaven for my motive in writing—who knows that my object is, if possible, to awaken in the breasts of my afflicted, degraded and slumbering brethren, a spirit of inquiry and investigation respecting our miseries and wretchedness in this *Republican Land of Liberty! ! ! ! ! !*

The sources from which our miseries are derived, and on which I shall comment, I shall not combine in one, but shall put them under distinct heads and expose them in their turn; in doing which, keeping truth on my side, and not departing from the strictest rules of morality, I shall endeavour to penetrate, search out, and lay them open for your inspection. If you cannot or will not profit by them, I shall have done *my* duty to you, my country and my God.

And as the inhuman system of *slavery*, is the *source* from which most of our miseries proceed, I shall begin with that *curse to nations*, which has spread terror and devastation through so many nations of antiquity, and which is raging to such a pitch at the present day in Spain and in Portugal. It had one tug in England, in France, and in the United States of America; yet the inhabitants thereof, do not learn wisdom, and erase it entirely from their dwellings and from all with whom they have to do. The fact is, the labour of slaves comes so cheap to the avaricious usurpers, and is (as they think) of such great utility to the country where it exists, that those who are actuated by sordid avarice only, overlook the evils, which will as sure as the Lord lives, follow after the good. In fact, they are so happy to keep in ignorance and degradation, and to receive the homage and the labour of the slaves, they forget that God rules in the armies of heaven and among the inhabitants of the earth, having his ears continually open to the cries, tears and groans of his oppressed people; and being a just and holy Being will at one day appear fully in behalf of the oppressed, and arrest the progress of the avaricious oppressors; for although the destruction of the oppressors God may not effect by the oppressed, yet the Lord our God will bring other destructions upon them—for not unfrequently will he cause them to rise up one against another, to be split and divided, and to oppress each other, and sometimes to open hostilities with sword in hand. Some may ask, what is the matter with this united and happy people?—Some say it is the cause of political usurpers; tyrants, oppressors, &c. But has not the Lord an oppressed and suffering people among them? Does the Lord condescend to hear their cries and see their tears in consequence of oppression? Will he let the oppressors rest comfortably and happy always? Will he not cause the very children of the oppressors to rise up against them, and oftimes put them to death? "God works in many ways his wonders to perform."

I will not here speak of the destructions which the Lord brought upon Egypt, in consequence of the oppression and consequent groans of the oppressed—of the hundreds and thousands of Egyptians whom God hurled into the Red Sea for afflicting his people in their land—of the Lord's suffering people in Sparta or Lacedemon, the land of the truly famous Lycurgus—nor have I time to comment upon the cause which produced the fierceness with which Sylla usurped the title, and absolutely acted as dictator of the Roman people—the conspiracy of Cataline—the conspiracy against, and murder of Caesar in the Senate house—the spirit with which Marc Antony made himself master of the commonwealth—his associating Octavius and Lipidus with himself in power—their dividing the provinces of Rome among themselves—their attack and defeat, on the plains of Phillippi, of the last defenders of their liberty, (Brutus and Cassius)—the tyranny of Tiberius, and from him to the final overthrow of Constantinople by the Turkish Sultan, Mahomed II. AD 1453. I say, I shall not take up time to speak of the *causes* which produced so much wretchedness and massacre among those heathen nations, for I am aware that you know too well, that God is just, as well as merciful!—I shall call your attention a few moments to that *Christian* nation, the Spaniards—while I shall leave almost unnoticed, that avaricious and cruel people, the Portuguese, among whom all true hearted Christians and lovers of Jesus Christ, must evidently see the judgments of God displayed. To show the judgments of God upon the Spaniards, I shall occupy but a little time, leaving plenty of room for the candid and unprejudiced to reflect.

All persons who are acquainted with history, and particularly the Bible, who are not blinded by the God of this world, and are not actuated solely by avarice—who are able to lay aside prejudice long enough to view candidly and impartially, things as they were, are, and probably will be—who are willing to admit that God made man to serve Him *alone*, and that man should have no other Lord or Lords but Himself—that God Almighty is the *sole proprietor* or *master* of the WHOLE human family, and will not on any consideration admit of a colleague, being unwilling to divide his glory with another—and who can dispense with prejudice long enough to admit that we are *men*, notwithstanding our *improminent noses* and *woolly heads*, and believe that we feel for our fathers, mothers, wives and children, as well as the whites do for theirs.—I say, all who are permitted to see and believe these things, can easily recognize the judgments of God among the Spaniards. Though others may lay the cause of the fierceness with which they cut each other's throats, to some other circumstance, yet they who believe that God is a God of justice, will believe that Slavery *is the principal cause.*

While the Spaniards are running about upon the field of battle cutting each other's throats, has not the Lord an afflicted and suffering people in the midst of them, whose cries and groans in consequence of oppression are continually pouring into the ears of the God of justice? Would they not cease to cut each other's throats, if they could? But how can they? The very support which they draw from government to aid them in perpetrating such enormities, does it not arise in a great degree from the wretched victims of oppression among them? And yet they are calling for *Peace!—Peace!!* Will any peace be given unto them? Their destruction may indeed be procrastinated awhile, but can it continue long, while they are oppressing the Lord's people? Has He not the hearts of all men in His hand? Will he suffer one part of his creatures to go on oppressing another like brutes always, with impunity? And yet, those avaricious wretches are calling for *Peace!!!!* I declare, it does appear to me, as though some nations think God is asleep, or that he made the Africans for nothing else but to dig their mines and work their farms, or they cannot believe history, sacred or profane. I ask every man who has a heart, and is blessed with the privilege of believing—Is not God a God of justice to *all* his creatures? Do you say he is? Then if he gives peace and tranquillity to tyrants, and permits them to keep our fathers, our mothers, ourselves and our children in eternal ignorance and wretchedness, to support them and their families, would he be to us a God of *justice?* I ask, O ye *Christians!!!* who hold us and our children in the most abject ignorance and degradation, that ever a people were afflicted with since the world began— I say, if God gives you peace and tranquillity, and suffers you thus to go on afflicting us, and our children, who have never given you the least provocation—would he be to us *a God of justice?* If you will allow that we are men, who feel for each other, does not the blood of our fathers and of us their children, cry aloud to the Lord of Sabaoth against you, for the cruelties and murders with which you have, and do continue to afflict us. But it is time for me to close my remarks on the suburbs, just to enter more fully into the interior of this system of cruelty and oppression. . . .

. . . I saw a paragraph, a few years since, in a South Carolina paper, which, speaking of the barbarity of the Turks, it said: "The Turks are the most barbarous people in the world—they treat the Greeks more like *brutes* than human beings." And in the same paper was an advertisement, which said: "Eight well built Virginia and Maryland *Negro fellows* and four *wenches* will positively be *sold* this day, *to the highest bidder!*" And what astonished me still more was, to see in this same *humane* paper!! the cuts of three men, with clubs and budgets on their backs, and an advertisement offering a considerable sum of money for their apprehension and delivery. I declare, it is really so amusing to hear the Southerners and Westerners of this country talk about *barbarity*, that it is positively, enough to make a man *smile.*

The sufferings of the Helots among the Spartans, were somewhat severe, it is true, but to say that theirs, were as severe as ours among the Americans, I do most strenuously deny—for instance, can any man show me an article on a page of ancient history which specifies, that, the Spartans chained, and hand-cuffed the Helots, and dragged them from their wives and children, children from their parents, mothers from their suckling babes, wives from their husbands, driving them from one end of the country to the other? Notice the Spartans were heathens, who lived long before our Divine Master made his appearance in the flesh. Can Christian Americans deny these barbarous cruelties? Have you not, Americans, having subjected us under you, added to these miseries, by insulting us in telling us to our face, because we are helpless, that we are not of the human family? I ask you, O! Americans, I ask you in the name of the Lord, can you deny these charges? Some perhaps may deny, by saying, that they never thought or said that we were not men. But do not actions speak louder than words?—have they not made provisions for the Greeks, and Irish? Nations who have never done the least thing for them, while *we*, who have enriched their country with our blood and tears—have dug up gold and silver for them and their children, from generation to generation, and are in more miseries than any other people under heaven, are not seen, but by comparatively, a handful of the American people? There are indeed, more ways to kill a dog, besides choking it to death with butter. Further—The Spartans or Lacedemonians, had some frivolous pretext, for enslaving the Helots, for they (Helots) while being free inhabitants of Sparta, stirred up an intestine commotion, and were, by the Spartans subdued, and made prisoners of war. Consequently they and their children were condemned to perpetual slavery.

I have been for years troubling the pages of historians, to find out what our fathers have done to the *white Christians of America*, to merit such condign punishment as they have inflicted on them, and do continue to inflict on us their children. But I must aver, that my researches have hitherto been to no effect. I have therefore, come to the immoveable conclusion, that they (Americans) have, and do continue to punish us for nothing else, but for enriching them and their country. For I cannot conceive of any thing else. Nor will I ever believe otherwise, until the Lord shall convince me.

The world knows, that slavery as it existed among the Romans, (which was the primary cause of their destruction) was, comparatively speaking, no more than a *cypher*, when compared with ours under the Americans. Indeed I should not have noticed the Roman slaves, had not the very learned and penetrating Mr. Jefferson said, "when a master was murdered, all his slaves in the same house, or within hearing, were condemned to death."—Here let me ask Mr. Jefferson, (but he is gone to answer at the bar of God, for the deeds done in his body while living,) I therefore ask the whole American people, had I not rather die, or be put to death, than to be a slave to any tyrant, who takes not only my own, but my wife and children's lives by the inches? Yea, would I meet death with avidity far! far! ! in preference to such *servile submission* to the murderous hands of tyrants. Mr. Jefferson's very severe remarks on us have been so extensively argued upon by men whose attainments in literature, I shall never be able to reach, that I would not have meddled with it, were it not to solicit each of my brethren, who has the spirit of a man, to buy a copy of Mr. Jefferson's "Notes on Virginia," and put it in the hand of his son. For let no one of us suppose that the refutations which have been written by our white friends are enough—they are *whites*—we are *blacks*. We, and the world wish to see the charges of Mr. Jefferson refuted by the blacks *themselves*, according to their chance; for we must remember that what the whites have written respecting this subject, is other men's labours, and did not emanate from the blacks. I know well, that there are some talents and learning among the coloured people of this country, which we have not a chance to develope, in consequence of oppression; but our oppression ought not to hinder us from acquiring all we can. For we will have a chance to develope them by and by. God will not suffer us, always to be oppressed. Our sufferings will come to an end, in spite of all the Americans this side of *eternity*. Then we will want all the learning and talents among ourselves, and perhaps more, to govern ourselves.—"Every dog must have its day," the American's is coming to an end.

But let us review Mr. Jefferson's remarks respecting us some further. Comparing our miserable fathers, with the learned philosophers of Greece, he says: "Yet notwithstanding these and other discouraging circumstances among the Romans, their slaves were often their rarest artists. They excelled too, in science, insomuch as to be usually employed as tutors to their master's children; Epictetus, Terence and Phaedrus, were slaves,—but they were of the race of whites. It is not their *condition* then, but *nature*, which has produced the distinction." See this, my brethren!! Do you believe that this assertion is swallowed by millions of the whites? Do you know that Mr. Jefferson was one of as great characters as ever lived among the whites? See his writings for the world, and public labours for the United States of America. Do you believe that the assertions of such a man, will pass away into oblivion unobserved by this people and the world? If you do you are much mistaken—See how the American people treat us—have we souls in our bodies? Are we men who have any spirits at all? I know that there are many *swell-bellied* fellows among us, whose greatest object is to fill their stomachs. Such I do not mean—I am after those who know and feel, that we are MEN, as well as other people; to them, I say, that unless we try to refute Mr. Jefferson's arguments respecting us, we will only establish them. . . .

Article II: Our Wretchedness in Consequence of Ignorance

Ignorance, my brethren, is a mist, low down into the very dark and almost impenetrable abyss in which, our fathers for many centuries have been plunged. The Christians, and enlightened of Europe, and some of Asia, seeing the ignorance and consequent degradation of our fathers, instead of trying to enlighten them, by teaching them that religion and light with which God had blessed them, they have plunged them into wretchedness ten thousand times more intolerable, than if they had left them entirely to the Lord, and to add to their miseries, deep down into which they have plunged them tell them, that they are an *inferior* and *distinct race* of beings, which they will be glad enough to recall and swallow by and by. Fortune and misfortune, two inseparable companions, lay rolled up in the wheel of events, which have from the creation of the world, and will continue to take place among men until God shall dash worlds together.

When we take a retrospective view of the arts and sciences—the wise legislators—the Pyramids, and other magnificent buildings—the turning of the channel of the river Nile, by the sons of Africa or of Ham, among whom learning originated, and was carried thence into Greece, where it was improved upon and refined. Thence among the Romans, and all over the then enlightened parts of the world, and it has been enlightening the dark and benighted minds of men from then, down to this day. I say, when I view retrospectively, the renown of that once mighty people, the children of our great progenitor I am indeed cheered. Yea further, when I view that mighty son of Africa, Hannibal, one of the greatest generals of antiquity, who defeated and cut off so many thousands of the white Romans or murderers, and who carried his victorious arms, to the very gate of Rome, and I give it as my candid opinion, that had Carthage been well united and had given him good support, he would have carried that cruel and barbarous city by storm. But they were disunited, as the coloured people are now, in the United States of America, the reason our natural enemies are enabled to keep their feet on our throats.

Beloved brethren—here let me tell you, and believe it, that the Lord our God, as true as he sits on his throne in heaven, and as true as our Saviour died to redeem the world, will give you a Hannibal, and when the Lord shall have raised him up, and given him to you for your possession, O my suffering brethren! remember the divisions and consequent sufferings of *Carthage* and of *Hayti.* Read the history particularly of Hayti, and see how they were butchered by the whites, and do you take warning. The person whom God shall give you, give him your support and let him go his length, and behold in him the salvation of your God. God will indeed, deliver you through him from your deplorable and wretched condition under the Christians of America. I charge you this day before my God to lay no obstacle in his way, but let him go.

The whites want slaves, and want us for their slaves, but some of them will curse the day they ever saw us. As true as the sun ever shone in its meridian splendor, my colour will root some of them out of the very face of the earth. They shall have enough of making slaves of, and butchering, and murdering us in the manner which they have. No doubt some may say that I write with a bad spirit, and that I being a black, wish these things to occur. Whether I write with a bad or a good spirit, I say if these things do not occur in their proper time, it is because the world in which we live does not exist, and we are deceived with regard to its existence.—It is immaterial however to me, who believe, or who refuse—though I should like to see the whites repent peradventure God may have mercy on them, some however, have gone so far that their cup must be filled.

But what need have I to refer to antiquity, when Hayti, the glory of the blacks and terror of tyrants, is enough to convince the most avaricious and stupid of wretches—which is at this time, and I am sorry to say it, plagued with that scourge of nations, the Catholic religion; but I hope and pray God that she may yet rid herself of it, and adopt in its stead the Protestant faith; also, I hope that she may keep peace within her borders and be united, keeping a strict look out for tyrants, for if they get the least chance to injure her, they will avail themselves of it, as true as the Lord lives in heaven. But one thing which gives me joy is, that they are men who would be cut off to a man, before they would yield to the combined forces of the whole world—in fact, if the whole world was combined against them, it could not do any thing with them, unless the Lord delivers them up.

Ignorance and treachery one against the other—a grovelling servile and abject submission to the lash of tyrants, we see plainly, my brethren, are not the natural elements of the blacks, as the Americans try to make us believe; but these are misfortunes which God has suffered our fathers to be enveloped in for many ages, no doubt in consequence of their disobedience to their Maker, and which do, indeed, reign at this time among us, almost to the destruction of all other principles: for I must truly say, that ignorance, the mother of treachery and deceit, gnaws into our very vitals. Ignorance, as it now exits among us, produces a state of things, Oh my Lord! too horrible to present to the world. Any man who is curious to see the full force of ignorance developed among the coloured people of the United States of America, has only to go into the southern and western states of this confederacy, where, if he is not a tyrant, but has the feelings of a human being, who can feel for a fellow creature, he may see enough to make his very heart bleed! He may see there, a son take his mother, who bore almost the pains of death to give him birth, and by the command of a tyrant, strip her as naked as she came into the world, and apply the cow-hide to her, until she falls a victim to death in the road! He may see a husband take his dear wife, not unfrequently in a pregnant state, and perhaps far advanced, and beat her for an unmerciful wretch, until his infant falls a lifeless lump at her feet! Can the Americans escape God Almighty? If they do, can he be to us a God of Justice? God is just, and I know it—for he has convinced me to my satisfaction—I cannot doubt him. My observer may see fathers beating their sons, mothers their daughters, and children their parents, all to pacify the passions of unrelenting tyrants. He may also see them telling news and lies, making mischief one upon another. These are some of the productions of ignorance, which he will see practised among my dear brethren, who are held in unjust slavery and wretchedness, by avaricious and unmerciful tyrants, to whom, and their hellish deeds, I would suffer my life to be taken before I would submit. And when my curious observer comes to take notice of those who are said to be free, (which assertion I deny) and who are making some frivolous pretentions to common sense, he will see that branch of ignorance among the slaves assuming a more cunning and deceitful course of procedure.—He may see some of my brethren in league with tyrants, selling their own brethren into *hell upon earth*, not dissimilar to the exhibitions in Africa, but in a more secret, servile and abject manner. Oh Heaven! I am full!!! I can hardly move my pen!!! and as I expect some will try to put me to death, to strike terror into others, and to obliterate from their minds the notion of freedom, so as to keep my brethren the more secure in wretchedness, where they will be permitted to stay but a short time (whether tyrants believe it or not)—I shall give the world a development of facts, which are already witnessed in the courts of heaven. My observer may see some of those ignorant and treacherous creatures (coloured people) sneaking about in the large cities, endeavouring to find out all strange coloured people, where they work and where they reside, asking them questions, and trying to ascertain whether they are runaways or not, telling them, at the same time, that they always have been, are, and always will be, friends to their brethren; and, perhaps, that they themselves are absconders, and a thousand such treacherous lies to get the better information of the more ignorant!!! There have been and are at this day in Boston, New-York, Philadelphia, and Baltimore, coloured men; who are in league with tyrants, and who receive a great portion of their daily bread, of the moneys which they acquire from the blood and tears of their more miserable brethren, whom they scandalously delivered into the hands of our *natural enemies!!!!!!*

 . . . I say, from the beginning, I do not think that we were natural enemies to each other. But the whites having made us so wretched, by subjecting us to slavery, and having murdered so many millions of us, in order to make us work for them, and out of devilishness—and they taking our wives, whom we love as we do ourselves—our mothers, who bore the pains of death to give us birth—our fathers and dear little children, and ourselves, and strip and beat us one before the other—chain, hand-cuff, and drag us about like rattle-snakes—shoot us down like wild bears, before each other's faces, to make us submissive to, and work to support them and their families. They (the whites) know well, if we are *men*—and there is a secret monitor in their hearts which tells them we are—they know, I say, if we *are* men, and see them treating us in the manner they do, that there can be nothing in our hearts but death alone, for them, notwithstanding we may appear cheerful, when we see them murdering our dear mothers and wives, because we cannot help ourselves. Man, in all ages and all nations of the earth, is the same. Man is a peculiar creature—he is the image of his God, though he may be subjected to the most wretched condition upon earth, yet the spirit and feeling which constitute the creature, man, can never be entirely erased from his breast, because the God who made him after his own image, planted it in his heart; he cannot get rid of it. The whites knowing this, they do not know what to do; they know that they have done us so much injury, they are afraid that we, being men, and not brutes, will retaliate, and woe will be to them; therefore, that dreadful fear, together with an avaricious spirit, and the natural love in them, to be called masters, (which term will yet honour them with to their sorrow) bring them to the resolve that they will keep us in ignorance and wretchedness, as long as they possibly can, and make the best of their time, while it lasts. Consequently they, themselves, (and not us) render themselves our natural enemies, by treating us so cruel. They keep us miserable now, and call us their property, but some of them will have enough of us by and by—their stomachs shall run over with us; they want us for their slaves, and shall have us to their fill. (We are all in the world together!!—I said above, because we cannot help ourselves, (viz. we cannot help the whites murdering our mothers and our wives) but this statement is incorrect—for we can help ourselves; for, if we lay aside abject servility, and be determined to act like men, and not brutes—the murders among the whites would be afraid to show their cruel heads. But O, my God!—in sorrow I must say it, that my colour, all over the world, have a mean, servile spirit. They yield in a moment to the whites, let them be right or wrong—the reason they are able to keep their feet on our throats. Oh! my coloured brethren, all over the world, when shall we arise from this death-like apathy?—And be men!! You will notice, if ever we become men, I mean *respectable* men, such as other people are,) we must exert ourselves to the full. For remember, that it is the greatest desire and object of the greater part of the whites, to keep us ignorant, and make us work to support them and their families.—Here now, in the Southern and Western sections of this country, there are at least three coloured persons for one white, why is it, that those few weak, good-for-nothing whites, are able to keep so many able men, one of whom, can put to flight a dozen whites, in wretchedness and misery? It shows at once, what the blacks are, we are ignorant, abject, servile and mean—and the whites know it—they know that we are too servile to assert our rights as men—they would not fool with us as they do. Would they fool with any other people as they do with us? No, they know too well, that they would get themselves ruined. Why do they not bring the inhabitants of Asia to be body servants to them? They know they would get their bodies rent and torn from head to foot. Why do they not get the Aborigines of this country to be slaves to them and their children, to work their farms and dig their mines? They know well that the Aborigines of this country, or (Indians) would tear them from the earth. The Indians would not rest day or night, they would be up all times of night, cutting their cruel throats. But my colour, (some, not all,) are willing to stand still and be murdered by the cruel whites. In some of the West-India Islands, and over a large part of South America, there are six or eight coloured persons for one white. Why do they not take possession of those places? Who hinders them? It is not the avaricious whites—for they are too busily engaged in laying up money—derived from the blood and tears of the blacks. The fact is, they are too servile, they love to have Masters too well!! Some of our brethren, too, who seeking more after self aggrandisement, than the glory of God, and the welfare of their brethren, join in with our oppressors, to ridicule and say all manner of evils falsely against our Bishop. They think, that they are doing great things, when they can get in company with the whites, to ridicule and make sport of those who are labouring for their good. Poor ignorant creatures, they do not know that the sole aim and object of the whites, are only to make fools and slaves of them, and put the whip to them, and make them work to support them and their families. But I do say, that no man, can well be a despiser of Bishop Allen, for his public labours among us, unless he is a despiser of God and of Righteousness. Thus, we see, my brethren, the two very opposite positions of those great men, who have written respecting this "Colonizing Plan." (Mr. Clay and his slave-holding party,) men who are resolved to keep us in eternal wretchedness, are also bent upon sending us to Liberia. While the Reverend Bishop Allen, and his party, men who have the fear of God, and the wellfare of their brethren at heart. The Bishop, in particular, whose labours for the salvation of his brethren, are well known to a large part of those, who dwell in the United States, are completely opposed to the plan—and advise us to stay where we are. Now we have to determine whose advice we will take respecting this all important matter, whether we will adhere to Mr. Clay and his slave holding party, who have always been our oppressors and murderers, and who are for colonizing us, more through apprehension than humanity, or to this godly man who has done so much for our benefit, together with the advice of all the good and wise among us and the whites. Will any of us leave our homes and go to Africa? I hope not. Let them commence their attack upon us as they did on our brethren in Ohio, driving and beating us from our country, and my soul for theirs, they will have enough of it. Let no man of us budge one step, and let slave-holders come to beat us from our country. America is more our country, than it is the whites—we have enriched it with our *blood and tears*. The greatest riches in all America have arisen from our blood and tears:—and will they drive us from our property and homes, which we have earned with our *blood?* They must look sharp or this very thing will bring swift destruction upon them. The Americans have got so fat on our blood and groans, that they have almost forgotten the God of armies. But let them go on.

ADDITION.—I will give here a very imperfect list of the cruelties inflicted on us by the enlightened Christians of America.—First, no trifling portion of them will beat us nearly to death, if they find us on our knees praying to God,—They hinder us from going to hear the word of God—they keep us sunk in ignorance, and will not let us learn to read the word of God, nor write—If they find us with a book of any description in our hand, they will beat us nearly to death—they are so afraid we will learn to read, and enlighten our dark and benighted minds—They will not suffer us to meet together to worship the God who made us—they brand us with hot iron—they cram bolts of fire down our throats—they cut us as they do horses, bulls, or hogs—they crop our ears and sometimes cut off bits of our tongues—they chain and hand-cuff us, and while in that miserable and wretched condition, beat us with cow-hides and clubs—they keep us half naked and starve us sometimes nearly to death under their infernal whips or lashes (which some of them shall have enough of yet)—They put on us fifty-sixes and chains, and make us work in that cruel situation, and in sickness, under lashes to support them and their families.—They keep us three or four hundred feet under ground working in their mines, night and day to dig up gold and silver to enrich them and their children.—They keep us in the most death-like ignorance by keeping us from all source of information, and call us, who are free men and next to the Angels of God, their property!!!!!! They make us fight and murder each other, many of us being ignorant, not knowing any better,—They take us, (being ignorant,) and put us as drivers one over the other, and make us afflict each other as bad as they themselves afflict us—and to crown the whole of this catalogue of cruelties, they tell us that we the (blacks) are an inferior race of beings! I incapable of self government!!—We would be injurious to society and ourselves, if tyrants should loose their unjust hold on us!!! That if we were free we would not work, but would live on plunder or theft!!!! that we are the meanest and laziest set of beings in the world!!! That they are obliged to keep us in bondage to do us good!!!!!!—That we are satisfied to rest in slavery to them and their children!!!!!!—That we ought not to be set free in America, but ought to be sent away to Africa!!!!!!—That if we were set free in America, we would involve the country in a civil war, which assertion is altogether at variance with our feeling or design, for we ask them for nothing but the rights of man, viz. for them to set us free, and treat us like men, and there will be no danger, for we will love and respect them, and protect our country—but cannot conscientiously do these things until they treat us like men.

How cunning slave-holders think they are!!!—How much like the king of Egypt who, after he saw plainly that God was determined to bring out his people, in spite of him and his, as powerful as they were. He was willing that Moses, Aaron and the Elders of Israel, but not all the people should go and serve the Lord. But God deceived him as he will Christian Americans, unless they are very cautious how they move. What would have become of the United States of America, was it not for those among the whites, who not in words barely, but in truth and in deed, love and fear the Lord?—Our Lord and Master said:— "Who so shall offend one of these little ones which believe in me, it were better for him that a millstone were hanged about his neck, and that he were drowned in the depth of the sea." But the Americans with this very threatening of the Lord's, not only beat his little ones among the Africans, but many of them they put to death or murder. Now the avaricious Americans, think that the Lord Jesus Christ will let them off, because his words are no more than the words of a man!!! In fact, many of them are so avaricious and ignorant, that they do not believe in our Lord and Saviour Jesus Christ. Tyrants may think they are so skillful in State affairs is the reason that the government is preserved. . . .

Chapter 18

The Statement of Nat Turner (1831)

. . . I was thirty-one years of age the second of October last, and born the property of Benjamin Turner, of this county. In my childhood a circumstance occurred which made an indelible impression on my mind, and laid the groundwork of that enthusiasm which has terminated so fatally to many, both white and black, and for which I am about to atone at the gallows. It is here necessary to relate this circumstance. Trifling as it may seem, it was the commencement of that belief which has grown with time; and even now, sir, in his dungeon, helpless and forsaken as I am, I cannot divest myself of. Being at play with other children, when three or four years old, I was telling them something, which my mother, overhearing, said it had happened before I was born. I stuck to my story, however, and related some things which went, in her opinion, to confirm it. Others being called on, were greatly astonished, knowing that these things had happened, and caused them to say, in my hearing, I surely would be a prophet, as the Lord had shown me things that had happened before my birth. And my mother and grandmother strengthened me in this my first impression, saying, in my presence, I was intended for some great purpose, which they had always thought from certain marks on my head and breast. . . .

My grandmother, who was very religious, and to whom I was much attached—my master, who belonged to the church, and other religious persons who visited the house, and whom I often saw at prayers, noticing the singularity of my manners, I suppose, and my uncommon intelligence for a child, remarked I had too much sense to be raised, and, if I was, I would never be of any service to any one as a slave. To a mind like mine, restless, inquisitive, and observant of everything that was passing, it is easy to suppose that religion was the subject to which it would be directed; and, although this subject principally occupied my thoughts, there was nothing that I saw or heard of to which my attention was not directed. The manner in which I learned to read and write, not only had great influence on my own mind, as I acquired it with the most perfect ease,—so much so, that I have no recollection whatever of learning the alphabet; but, to the astonishment of the family, one day, when a book was shown me, to keep me from crying, I began spelling the names of different objects. This was a source of wonder to all in the neighborhood, particularly the blacks—and this learning was constantly improved at all opportunities. When I got large enough to go to work, while employed I was reflecting on many things that would present themselves to my imagination; and whenever an opportunity occurred of looking at a book, when the school-children were getting their lessons, I would find many things that the fertility of my own imagination had depicted to me before. All my time, not devoted to my master's service, was spent either in prayer, or in making experiments in casting different things in moulds made of earth, in attempting to make paper, gunpowder, and many other experiments, that, although I could not perfect, yet convinced me of its practicability if I had the means.

I was not addicted to stealing in my youth, nor have ever been; yet such was the confidence of the Negroes in the neighborhood, even at this early period of my life, in my superior judgment, that they would often carry me with them when they were going on any roguery, to plan for them. Growing up among them with this confidence in my superior judgment, and when this, in their opinions, was perfected by Divine inspiration, from the circumstances already alluded to in my infancy, and which belief was ever afterwards zealously inculcated by the austerity of my life and manners, which became the subject of remark by white and black; having soon discovered to be great, I must appear so, and therefore studiously avoided mixing in society, and wrapped myself in mystery, devoting my time to fasting and prayer.

By this time, having arrived to man's estate, and hearing the Scriptures commented on at meetings, I was struck with that particular passage which says, "Seek ye the kingdom of heaven, and all things shall be added unto you." I reflected much on this passage, and prayed daily for light on this subject. As I was praying one day at my plough, the Spirit spoke to me, saying, "Seek ye the kingdom of heaven, and all things shall be added unto you." *Question.* "What do you mean by the Spirit?" *Answer.* "The Spirit that spoke to the prophets in former days,"—and I was greatly astonished, and for two years prayed continually, whenever my duty would permit; and then again I had the same revelation, which fully confirmed me in the impression that I was ordained for some great purpose in the hands of the Almighty. Several years rolled round, in which many events occurred to strengthen me in this my belief. At this time I reverted in my mind to the remarks made of me in my childhood, and the things that had been shown me; and as it had been said of me in my childhood, by those by whom I had been taught to pray, both white and black, and in whom I had the greatest confidence, that I had too much sense to be raised, and if I was I would never be of any use to anyone as a slave; now, finding I had arrived to man's estate, and was a slave, and these revelations being made known to me, I began to direct my attention to this great object, to fulfill the purpose for which, by this time, I felt assured I was intended. Knowing the influence I had obtained over the minds of my fellow-servants—(not by the means of conjuring and such-like tricks—for to them I always spoke of such things with contempt), but by the communion of the Spirit, whose revelations I often communicated to them, and they believed and said my wisdom came from God,—I now began to prepare them for my purpose, by telling them something was about to happen that would terminate in fulfilling the great promise that had been made to me.

About this time I was placed under an overseer, from whom I ran away, and after remaining in the woods thirty days, I returned, to the astonishment of the Negroes on the plantation, who thought I had made my escape to some other part of the country, as my father had done before. But the reason of my return was, that the Spirit appeared to me and said I had my wishes directed to the things of this world, and not to the kingdom of heaven, and that I should return to the service of my earthly master—"For he who knoweth his Master's will, and doeth it not, shall be beaten with many stripes, and thus have I chastened you." And the Negroes found fault, and murmured against me, saying that if they had my sense they would not serve any master in the world. And about this time I had a vision—and I saw white spirits and black spirits engaged in battle, and the sun was darkened—the thunder rolled in the heavens, and blood flowed in streams—and I heard a voice saying, "Such is your luck, such you are called to see; and let it come rough or smooth, you must surely bear it."

I now withdrew myself as much as my situation would permit from the intercourse of my fellow-servants, for the avowed purpose of serving the Spirit more fully; and it appeared to me, and reminded me of the things it had already shown me, and that it would then reveal to me the knowledge of the elements, the revolution of the planets, the operation of tides, and changes of the seasons. After this revelation in the year 1825, and the knowledge of the elements being made known to me, I sought more than ever to obtain true holiness before the great day of judgment should appear, and then I began to receive the true knowledge of faith. And from the first steps of righteousness until the last, was I made perfect; and the Holy Ghost was with me, and said, "Behold me as I stand in the heavens." And I looked and saw the forms of men in different attitudes; and there were lights in the sky, to which the children of darkness gave other names than what they really were; for they were the lights of the Saviour's hands, stretched forth from east to west, even as they were extended on the cross on Calvary for the redemption of sinners. And I wondered greatly at these miracles, and prayed to be informed of a certainty of the meaning thereof; and shortly afterwards, while laboring in the field, I discovered drops of blood on the corn, as though it were dew from heaven; and I communicated it to many, both white and black, in the neighborhood—and I then found on the leaves in the woods hieroglyphic characters and numbers, with the forms of men in different attitudes, portrayed in blood, and representing the figures I had seen before in the heavens. And now the Holy Ghost had revealed itself to me, and made plain the miracles it had shown me; for as the blood of Christ had been shed on this earth, and had ascended to heaven for the salvation of sinners, and was now returning to earth again in the form of dew, and as the leaves on the trees bore the impression of the figures I had seen in the heavens,—it was plain to me that the Saviour was about to lay down the yoke he had borne for the sins of men, and the great day of judgment was at hand.

About this time I told these things to a white man (Etheldred T. Brantley), on whom it had a wonderful effect; and he ceased from his wickedness, and was attacked immediately with a cutaneous eruption, and blood oozed from the pores of his skin, and after praying and fasting nine days he was healed. And the Spirit appeared to me again, and said, as the Saviour had been baptized, so should we be also; and when the white people would not let us be baptized by the church, we went down into the water together, in the sight of many who reviled us, and were baptized by the Spirit. After this I rejoiced greatly, and gave thanks to God. And on the 12th of May, 1828, I heard a loud noise in the heavens, and the Spirit instantly appeared to me and said the Serpent was loosened, and Christ had laid down the yoke he had borne for the sins of men, and that I should take it on and fight against the Serpent, for the time was fast approaching when the first should be last and the last should be first. *Ques.* "Do you not find yourself mistaken now?"—*Ans.* "Was not Christ crucified?" And by signs in the heavens that it would make known to me when I should commence the great work, and until the first sign appeared I should conceal it from the knowledge of men; and on the appearance of the sign (the eclipse of the sun, last February), I should arise and prepare myself, and slay my enemies with their own weapons. And immediately on the sign appearing in the heavens, the seal was removed from my lips, and I communicated the great work laid out for me to do, to four in whom I had the greatest confidence (Henry, Hark, Nelson, and Sam). It was intended by us to have begun the work of death on the 4th of July last. Many were the plans formed and rejected by us, and it affected my mind to such a degree that I fell sick, and the time passed without our coming to any determination how to commence—still forming new schemes and rejecting them, when the sign appeared again, which determined me not to wait longer.

Since the commencement of 1830 I had been living with Mr. Joseph Travis, who was to me a kind master, and placed the greatest confidence in me; in fact, I had no cause to complain of his treatment to me. On Saturday evening, the 20th of August, it was agreed between Henry, Hark, and myself, to prepare a dinner the next day for the men we expected, and then to concert a plan, as we had not yet determined on any. Hark, on the following morning, brought a pig, and Henry brandy; and being joined by Sam, Nelson, Will, and Jack, they prepared in the woods a dinner, where, about three o'clock, I joined them.

Q. Why were you so backward in joining them?

A. The same reason that had caused me not to mix with them years before,

I saluted them on coming up, and asked Will how came he there. He answered, his life was worth no more than others, and his liberty as dear to him. I asked him if he thought to obtain it. He said he would, or lose his life. This was enough to put him in full confidence. Jack, I knew, was only a tool in the hands of Hark. It was quickly agreed we should commence at home (Mr. J. Travis') on that night; and until we had armed and equipped ourselves, and gathered sufficient force, neither age nor sex was to be spared—which was invariably adhered to. We remained at the feast until about two hours in the night, when we went to the house and found Austin. . . .

I took my station in the rear, and, as it was my object to carry terror and devastation wherever we went, I placed fifteen or twenty of the best armed and most to be relied on in front, who generally approached the houses as fast as their horses could run. This was for two purposes—to prevent their escape, and strike terror to the inhabitants; on this account I never got to the houses, after leaving Mrs. Whitehead's, until the murders were committed, except in one case. I sometimes got in sight in time to see the work of death completed; viewed the mangled bodies as they lay, in silent satisfaction, and immediately started in quest of other victims. Having murdered Mrs. Waller and ten children, we started for Mr. Wm. Williams',—having killed him and two little boys that were there; while engaged in this, Mrs. Williams fled and got some distance from the house, but she was pursued, overtaken, and compelled to get up behind one of the company, who brought her back, and, after showing her the mangled body of her lifeless husband, she was told to get down and lay by his side, where she was shot dead.

The white men pursued and fired on us several times. Hark had his horse shot under him, and I caught another for him as it was running by me; five or six of my men were wounded, but none left on the field. Finding myself defeated here, I instantly determined to go through a private way, and cross the Nottoway River at the Cypress Bridge, three miles below Jerusalem, and attack that place in the rear, as I expected they would look for me on the other road, and I had a great desire to get there to procure arms and ammunition. After going a short distance in this private way, accompanied by about twenty men, I overtook two or three, who told me the others were dispersed in every direction.

On this, I gave up all hope for the present; and on Thursday night, after having supplied myself with provisions from Mr. Travis', I scratched a hole under a pile of fence-rails in a field, where I concealed myself for six weeks, never leaving my hiding-place but for a few minutes in the dead of the night to get water, which was very near. Thinking by this time I could venture out, I began to go about in the night, and eavesdrop the houses in the neighborhood; pursuing this course for about a fortnight, and gathering little or no intelligence, afraid of speaking to any human being, and returning every morning to my cave before the dawn of day. I know not how long I might have led this life, if accident had not betrayed me. A dog in the neighborhood passing by my hiding-place one night while I was out, was attracted by some meat I had in my cave, and crawled in and stole it, and was coming out just as I returned. A few nights after, two Negroes having started to go hunting with the same dog, and passed that way, the dog came again to the place, and having just gone out to walk about, discovered me and barked; on which, thinking myself discovered, I spoke to them to beg concealment. On making myself known, they fled from me. Knowing then they would betray me, I immediately left my hiding-place, and was pursued almost incessantly, until I was taken, a fortnight afterwards, by Mr. Benjamin Phipps, in a little hole I had dug out with my sword, for the purpose of concealment, under the top of a fallen tree.

During the time I was pursued, I had many hair-breadth escapes, which your time will not permit you to relate. I am here loaded with chains, and willing to suffer the fate that awaits me.

Chapter 19

What if I Am a Woman? Maria Stewart (1833)

Mrs. Stewart's Farewell Address to Her Friends in the City of Boston—
Published as Productions of Mrs. Maria W. Stewart
(Boston: William Lloyd Garrison and Knap, 1832)

African rights and liberty is a subject that ought to fire the breast of every free man of color in these United States, and excite in his bosom a lively, deep, decided and heart-felt interest. When I cast my eyes on the long list of illustrious names that are enrolled on the bright annals of fame amongst the whites, I turn my eyes within, and ask my thoughts, "Where are the names of our illustrious ones?" It must certainly have been for the want of energy on the part of the free people of color that they have been long willing to bear the yoke of oppression. It must have been the want of ambition and force that has given the whites occasion to say that our natural abilities are not as good, and our capacities by nature inferior to theirs. They boldly assert that, did we possess a natural independence of soul, and feel a love for liberty within our breasts, some one of our sable race, long before this, would have testified it, notwithstanding the disadvantages under which we labor. We have made ourselves appear altogether unqualified to speak in our own defence, and are therefore looked upon as objects of pity and commiseration. We have been imposed upon, insulted and derided on every side; and now, if we complain, it is considered as the height of impertinence. We have suffered ourselves to be considered as dastards, cowards, mean, faint-hearted wretches; and on this account, (not because of our complexion,) many despise us and would gladly spurn us from their presence.

These things have fired my soul with a holy indignation, and compelled me thus to come forward, and endeavor to turn their attention to knowledge and improvement; for knowledge is power. I would ask, is it blindness of mind, or stupidity of soul, or the want of education, that has caused our men who are 60 or 70 years of age, never to let their voices be heard nor their hands be raised in behalf of their color? Or has it been for the fear of offending the whites? If it has, O ye fearful ones, throw off your fearfulness, and come forth in the name of the Lord, and in the strength of the God of Justice, and make yourselves useful and active members in society; for they admire a noble and patriotic spirit in others—and should they not admire it in us? If you are men, convince them that you possess the spirit of men; and as your day, so shall your strength be. Have the sons of Africa no souls? feel they no ambitious desires? shall the chains of ignorance forever confine them? shall the insipid appellation of "clever negroes," or "good creatures," any longer content them? Where can we find amongst ourselves the man of science, or a philosopher, or an able statesman, or a counsellor at law? Show me our fearless and brave, our noble and gallant ones. Where are our lecturers on natural history, and our critics in useful knowledge? There may be a few such men amongst us, but they are rare. It is true, our fathers bled and died in the revolutionary war, and others fought bravely under the command of Jackson, in defence of liberty. But where is the man that has distinguished himself in these modern days by acting wholly in the defence of African rights and liberty? There was one—although he sleeps, his memory lives.

I am sensible that there are many highly intelligent gentlemen of color in these United States, in the force of whose arguments, doubtless, I should discover my inferiority; but if they are blest with wit and talent, friends and fortune, why have they not made themselves men of eminence, by striving to take all the reproach that is cast upon the people of color, and in endeavoring to alleviate the woes of their brethren in

131

bondage? Talk, without effort, is nothing; you are abundantly capable, gentlemen, of making yourselves men of distinction; and this gross neglect, on your part, causes my blood to boil within me. Here is the grand cause which hinders the rise and progress of the people of color. It is their want of laudable ambition and requisite courage.

Individuals have been distinguished according to their genius and talents, ever since the first formation of man, and will continue to be whilst the world stands. The different grades rise to honor and respectability as their merits may deserve. History informs us that we sprung from one of the most learned nations of the whole earth—from the seat, if not the parent of science; yes, poor, despised Africa was once the resort of sages and legislators of other nations, was esteemed the school for learning, and the most illustrious men in Greece flocked thither for instruction. But it was our gross sins and abominations that provoked the Almighty to frown thus heavily upon us, and give our glory unto others. Sin and prodigality have caused the downfall of nations, kings and emperors; and were it not that God in wrath remembers mercy, we might indeed despair; but a promise is left us; "Ethiopia shall again stretch forth her hands unto God."

But it is of no use for us to boast that we sprung from this learned and enlightened nation, for this day a thick mist of moral gloom hangs over millions of our race. Our condition as a people has been low for hundreds of years, and it will continue to be so, unless, by the true piety and virtue, we strive to regain that which we have lost. White Americans, by their prudence, economy and exertions, have sprung up and become one of the most flourishing nations in the world, distinguished for their knowledge of the arts and sciences, for their polite literature. Whilst our minds are vacant and starving for want of knowledge, theirs are filled to overflowing. Most of our color have been taught to stand in fear of the white man from their earliest infancy, to work as soon as they could walk, and call "master" before they scarce could lisp the name of mother. Continual fear and laborious servitude have in some degree lessened in us that natural force and energy which belong to man; or else, in defiance of opposition, our men before this would have nobly and boldly contended for their rights. But give the man of color an equal opportunity with the white, from the cradle to manhood, and from manhood to the grave, and you would discover the dignified statesman, the man of science, and the philosopher. But there is no such opportunity for the sons of Africa, and I fear that our powerful ones are fully determined that there never shall be. Forbid, ye Powers on High, that it should any longer be said that our men possess no force. O ye sons of Africa, when will your voices be heard in our legislative halls, in defiance of your enemies, contending for equal rights and liberty? How can you, when you reflect from what you have fallen, refrain from crying mightily unto God, to turn away from us the fierceness of his anger, and remember our transgressions against us no more forever. But a God of infinite purity will not regard the prayers of those who hold religion in one hand, and prejudice, sin and pollution in the other; he will not regard the prayers of self-righteousness and hypocrisy. Is it possible, I exclaim, that for the want of knowledge, we have labored for thousands of years to support others, and been content to receive what they chose to give us in return? Cast your eyes about—look as far as you can see—all, all is owned by the lordly white, except here and there a lowly dwelling which the man of color, midst deprivations, fraud and opposition, has been scarce able to procure. Like King Solomon, who put neither nail nor hammer to the temple, yet received the praise; so also have the white Americans gained themselves a name, like the names of the great men who are in the earth, whilst in reality we have been their principal foundation and support. We have pursued the shadow, they have obtained the substance; we have performed the labor, they have received the profits; we have planted the vines, they have eaten the fruits of them.

I would implore our men, and especially our rising youth, to flee from the gambling board and the dance hall; for we are poor, and have no money to throw away. I do not consider dancing as criminal in itself, but it is astonishing to me that our young men are so blind to their own interest and the future welfare of their children, as to spend their hard earnings for this frivolous amusement; for it has been carried on among us to such an unbecoming extent that it has become absolutely disgusting. "Faithful are the wounds of a friend, but the kisses of an enemy are deceitful." Had those men amongst us, who have had an opportunity, turned their attention as assiduously to mental and moral improvement as they have to gambling and dancing, I might have remained quietly at home, and they stood contending in my place. These polite accomplishments will never enroll your names on the bright annals of fame, who admire the belle void of intellectual knowledge, or applaud the dandy that talks largely on politics, without striving to assist his fellow in the revolution, when the nerves and muscles of every other man forced him into the field of action. You have a right to rejoice, and to let your hearts cheer you in the days of your youth; yet remember that for all these things God will bring you into judgment. Then, O ye sons of Africa, turn your mind from these perishable objects, and contend for the cause of God and the rights of man. Form yourselves into temperance societies. There are temperate men amongst you; then why will you any longer neglect to strive, by your example, to suppress vice in all its abhorrent forms? You have been told repeatedly of the glorious results arising from temperance, and can you bear to see the whites arising in honor and respectability, without endeavoring to grasp after that honor and respectability also?

But I forbear. Let our money, instead of being thrown away as heretofore, be appropriated for schools and seminaries of learning for our children and youth. We ought to follow the example of the whites in this respect. Nothing would raise our respectability, add to our peace and happiness and reflect so much honor upon us, as to be ourselves the promoters of temperance, and the supporters, as far as we are able, of useful and scientific knowledge. The rays of light and knowledge have been hid from our view; we have been taught to consider ourselves as scarce superior to the brute creation; and have performed the most laborious part of American drudgery. Had we as people received one half the early advantages the whites have received, I would defy the government of these United States to deprive us any longer of our rights.

I am informed that the agent of the Colonization Society has recently formed an association of young men, for the purpose of influencing those of us to go to Liberia who may feel disposed. The colonizationists are blind to their own interest, for should the nations of the earth make war with America, they would find their forces much weakened by our absence; or should we remain here, can our "brave soldiers" and "fellow citizens," as they were termed in time of calamity, condescend to defend the rights of the whites, and be again deprived of their own, or sent to Liberia in return? O, if the colonizationists are real friends to Africa, let them expend the money which they collect in erecting a college to educate her injured sons in this land of gospel light and liberty; for it would be most thankfully received on our part, and convince us of the truth of their professions, and save time, expense and anxiety. Let them place before us noble objects, worthy of pursuit, and see if we prove ourselves to be those unambitious Negroes they term us. But ah! methinks their hearts are so frozen towards us, they had rather their money should be sunk in the ocean than to administer it to our relief; and I fear, if they dared, like Pharaoh king of Egypt, they would order every male child amongst us to be drowned. But the most high God is still as able to subdue the lofty pride of these white Americans, as He was the heart of that ancient rebel. They say though we are looked upon as things, yet we sprang from a scientific people. Had our men the requisite force and energy, they would soon convince them, by their efforts both in public and private, that they were men, or things in the shape of men. Well may the colonizationists laugh us to scorn for our negligence; well may they cry, "Shame to the sons of Africa." As the burden of the Israelites was too great for Moses to bear, so also is our burden too great for our noble advocate to bear. You must feel interested, my brethren, in what he undertakes, and hold up his hands by your good words, or in spite of himself his soul will become discouraged, and his heart will die within him; for he has, as it were, the strong bulls of Bashan to contend with.

It is of no use for us to wait any longer for a generation of well-educated men to arise. We have slumbered and slept too long already; the day is far spent; the night of death approaches; and you have sound sense and good judgment sufficient to begin with, if you feel disposed to make a right use of it. Let every man of color throughout the United States, who possesses the spirit and principles of a man, sign a petition to Congress to abolish slavery in the District of Columbia, and grant you the rights and privileges of common free citizens; for if you had had faith as a grain of mustard seed, long before this the mountains of prejudice might have been removed. We are all sensible that the Anti-Slavery Society has taken hold of the arm of our whole population, in order to raise them out of the mire. Now all we have to do is, by a spirit of virtuous ambition to strive to raise ourselves; and I am happy to have it in my power thus publicly to say that the colored inhabitants of this city, in some respects, are beginning to improve. Had the free people of color in these United States nobly and boldly contended for their rights, and showed a natural genius and talent, although not so brilliant as some; had they held up, encouraged and patronized each other; nothing could have hindered us from being a thriving and flourishing people. There has been a fault amongst us. The reason why our distinguished men have not made themselves more influential is, because they fear the strong current of opposition through which they must pass, would cause their downfall and prove their overthrow. And what gives rise to this opposition? Envy. And what has it amounted to? Nothing. And who are the cause of it? Our whited sepulchres who want to be great, and don't know how; who love to be called of men "Rabbi, Rabbi," who put on false sanctity, and humble themselves to their brethren, for the sake of acquiring the highest place in the synagogue, and the uppermost seats at the feast. You, dearly beloved, who are the genuine followers of our Lord Jesus Christ, the salt of the earth and the light of the world, are not so culpable. As I told you, in the very first of my writing, I tell you again, I am but as one drop in the bucket—as one particle of the small dust of the earth. God will surely raise up those amongst us who will plead the cause of virtue, and the pure principles of morality, more eloquently than I am able to do.

It appears to me that America has become like the great city of Babylon, for she has boasted in her heart,—"I sit a queen, and am no widow, and shall see no sorrow." She is indeed a seller of slaves and the souls of men; she has made the Africans drunk with the wine of her fornication; she has put them completely beneath her feet, and she means to keep them there; her right hand supports the reins of government, and her left hand the wheel of power, and she is determined not to let go her grasp. But many powerful sons and daughters of Africa will shortly arise, who will put down vice and immorality amongst us, and declare by Him that sitteth upon the throne, that they will have their rights; and if refused, I am afraid they will spread horror and devastation around. I believe that the oppression of injured Africa has come up before the majesty of Heaven; and when our cries shall have reached the ears of the Most High, it will be a tremendous day for the people of this land; for strong is the arm of the Lord God Almighty.

Life has almost lost its charms for me; death has lost its sting and the grave its terrors; and at times I have a strong desire to depart and dwell with Christ, which is far better. Let me entreat my white brethren to awake and save our sons from dissipation, and our daughters from ruin. Lend the hand of assistance to feeble merit, and plead the cause of virtue amongst our sable race; so shall our curses upon you be turned into blessings; and though you shall endeavor to drive us from these shores, still we will cling to you the more firmly; nor will we attempt to rise above you; we will presume to be called equals only.

The unfriendly whites first drove the native American from his much-loved home. Then they stole our fathers from their peaceful and quiet dwellings, and brought them hither and made bond men and bond women of them and their little ones; they have obliged our brethren to labor, kept them in utter ignorance, nourished them in vice and raised them in degradation; and now that we have enriched their soil, and filled their coffers, they say that we are not capable of becoming like white men, and that we never can rise to respectability in this country. They would drive us to a strange land. But before I go, the bayonet shall pierce me through. African rights and liberty is a subject that ought to fire the breast of every free man of color in these United States, and excite in his bosom a lively, deep, decided and heartfelt interest.

Chapter 20

A'n't I a Woman? Sojourner Truth

Excerpt from Anti-Slavery Bugle, June 1851

I want to say a few words about this matter. I am a woman's rights. I have as much muscle as any man, and can do as much work as any man. I have plowed and reaped and husked and chopped and mowed, and can any man do more than that? I have heard much about the sexes being equal. I can carry as much as any man, and can eat as much too, if I can get it. I am as strong as any man that is now. As for intellect, all I can say is, if woman have a pint, and man a quart—why can't she have her little pint full? You need not be afraid to give us our rights for fear we will take too much,—for we can't take more than our pint'll hold. The poor men seem to be all in confusion, and don't know what to do. Why children, if you have woman's rights, give it to her and you will feel better. You will have your own rights, and they won't be so much trouble. I can't read, but I can hear. I have heard the bible and have learned that Eve caused man to sin. Well, if woman upset the world, do give her a chance to set it right side up again. The Lady has spoken about Jesus, how he never spurned woman from him, and she was right. When Lazarus died, Mary and Martha came to him with faith and love and besought him to raise their brother. And Jesus wept and Lazarus came forth. And how came Jesus into the world? Through God who created him and a woman who bore him. Man, where is your part? But the women are coming up blessed be God and a few of the men are coming up with them. But man is in a tight place, the poor slave is on him, woman is coming on him, he is surely between a hawk and a buzzard.

* * *

Wall, chilern, whar dar is so much racket dar must be somethin' out of kilter. I tink dat 'twixt de niggers of de Souf and de womin at de Norf, all talkin' 'bout rights, de white men will be in a fix pretty soon. But what's all dis here talkin' 'bout?

Dat man ober dar say dat womin needs to be helped into carriages and lifted ober ditches, and to hab de best place everywhar. Nobody eber helps me into carriages, or ober mud puddles, or gibs me any best place! And a'n't I a woman? Look at my arm! I have ploughed, and planted, and gathered into barns, and no man could head me! And a'n't I a woman? I could work as much and eat as much as a man—when I could get it—and bear de lash as well! And a'n't I a woman? I have borne thirteen chilren, and seen 'em mos' all sold off to slavery, and when I cried out with my mother's grief, none but Jesus heard me! And a'n't I a woman?

Den dey talks 'bout dis ting in de head: what dis dey call it? ("Intellect," whispered some one near.) Dat's it, honey. What dat got to do wid womin's rights or nigger's rights? If my cup won't hold but a pint, and yourn holds a quart, wouldn't ye be mean not to let me have my little half-measure full?

Den dat little man in black dar, he say women can't have as much rights as men, 'cause Christ wan't a woman! Whar did your Christ come from? Whar did your Christ come from? From God and a woman! Man had nothin' to do wid Him!

If de fust woman God ever made was strong enough to tum de world upside down all alone, dese women togedder (and she glanced her eye over the platform) ought to be able to turn it back, and get it right side up again! And now dey is asking to do it, de men better let 'em.

Chapter 21

The Dred Scott Decision—Judge Roger B. Taney's Opinion

The question is simply this: Can a Negro, whose ancestors were imported into this country, and sold as slaves, become a member of the political community formed and brought into existence by the Constitution of the United States, and as such become entitled to all the rights, and privileges, and immunities, guaranteed by that instrument to the citizen? One of which rights is the privilege of suing in a court of the United States in the cases specified in the Constitution.

It will be observed, that the plea applies to that class of persons only whose ancestors were Negroes of the African race, and imported into this country, and sold and held as slaves. The only matter in issue before the court, therefore, is whether the descendants of such slaves, when they shall be emancipated, or who are born of parents who had become free before their birth, are citizens of a State, in the sense in which the word citizen is used in the Constitution of the United States. . . .

The words "people of the United States" and "citizens" are synonymous terms, and mean the same thing. They both describe the political body who, according to our republican institutions, form the sovereignty, and who hold the power and conduct the government through their representatives. They are what we familiarly call the "sovereign people," and every citizen is one of this people, and a constituent member of this sovereignty. The question before us is, whether the class of persons described in the plea in abatement compose a portion of this people, and are constituent members of this sovereignty? We think they are not, and that they are not included, and were not intended to be included, under the word "citizens" in the Constitution, and can, therefore, claim none of the rights and privileges which that instrument provides for and secures to citizens of the United States. On the contrary, they were at that time considered as a subordinate and inferior class of beings, who had been subjugated by the dominant race, and whether emancipated or not, yet remained subject to their authority, and had no rights or privileges but such as those who held the power and the government might choose to grant them. . . .

It is very clear, therefore, that no State can, by any Act or law of its own, passed since the adoption of the Constitution, introduce a new member into the political community created by the Constitution of the United States. It cannot make him a member of this community by making him a member of its own. And for the same reason it cannot introduce any person, or description of persons, who were not intended to be embraced in this new political family, which the Constitution brought into existence, but were intended to be excluded from it. . . .

In the opinion of the court, the legislation and histories of the times, and the language used in the Declaration of Independence, show, that neither the class of persons who had been imported as slaves, nor their descendants, whether they had become free or not, were then acknowledged as a part of the people, nor intended to be included in the general words used in that memorable instrument.

It is difficult at this day to realize the state of public opinion in relation to that unfortunate race, which prevailed in the civilized and enlightened portions of the world at the time of the Declaration of Independence, and when the Constitution of the United States was framed and adopted. . . .

They had for more than a century before been regarded as beings of an inferior order and altogether unfit to associate with the white race, either in social or political relations; and so far inferior that they had no rights which the white man was bound to respect; and that the Negro might justly and lawfully be reduced to slavery for his benefit. He was bought and sold and treated as an ordinary article of merchandise and traffic whenever a profit could be made by it. This opinion was at that time fixed and universal in the civilized portion of the white race. It was regarded as an axiom in morals as well. . . .

. . . A Negro of the African race was regarded . . . as an article of property and held and bought and sold as such in every one of the thirteen Colonies which united in the Declaration of Independence and afterward formed the Constitution of the United States. The slaves were more or less numerous in the different Colonies, as slave labor was found more or less profitable. But no one seems to have doubted the correctness of the prevailing opinion of the time. . . .

The language of the Declaration of Independence is equally conclusive:

It begins by declaring that "When, in the course of human events, it becomes necessary for one people to dissolve the political bands which have connected them with another, and to assume, among the powers of the earth the separate and equal station to which the laws of nature and nature's God entitle them, a decent respect for the opinions of mankind requires that they should declare the causes which impel them to the separation."

It then proceeds to say: "We hold these truths to be self-evident: that all men are created equal; that they are endowed by their Creator with certain inalienable rights; that among these are life, liberty, and the pursuit of happiness; that to secure these rights, governments are instituted, deriving their just powers from the consent of the governed."

The general words above quoted would seem to embrace the whole human family, and if they were used in a similar instrument at this day would be so understood. But it is too clear for dispute that the enslaved African race were not intended to be included and formed no part of the people who framed and adopted this declaration; for if the language, as understood in that day, would embrace them, the conduct of the distinguished men who framed the Declaration of Independence would have been utterly and flagrantly inconsistent with the principles they asserted; and instead of the sympathy of mankind, to which they so confidently appealed, they would have deserved and received universal rebuke and reprobation.

Yet the men who framed this declaration were great men—high in literary acquirements—high in their sense of honor, and incapable of asserting principles inconsistent with those on which they were acting. They perfectly understood the meaning of the language they used and how it would be understood by others; and they knew that it would not in any part of the civilized world be supposed to embrace the Negro race, which, by common consent, had been excluded from civilized governments and the family of nations and doomed to slavery. They spoke and acted according to the then established doctrine and principles and in the ordinary language of the day, and no one misunderstood them. The unhappy black race were separated from the white by indelible marks, and laws long before established, and were never thought of or spoken of except as property and when the claims of the owner or the profit of the trader were supposed to need protection.

This state of public opinion had undergone no change when the Constitution was adopted, as is equally evident from its provisions and language.

The brief preamble sets forth by whom it was formed, for what purposes, and for whose benefit and protection. It declares that it is formed by the *people* of the United States; that is to say, by those who were members of the different political communities in the several states; and its great object is declared to be to secure the blessing of liberty to themselves and their posterity. It speaks in general terms of the *people* of the United States, and of *citizens* of the several states, when it is providing for the exercise of the powers granted or the privileges secured to the citizen. It does not define what description of persons are intended to be included under these terms, or who shall be regarded as a citizen and one of the people. It uses them as terms so well understood that no further description or definition was necessary. . . .

But there are two clauses in the Constitution which point directly and specifically to the Negro race as a separate class of persons, and show clearly that they were not regarded as a portion of the people or citizens of the Government then formed.

One of these clauses reserves to each of the thirteen States the right to import slaves until the year 1808, if it thinks it proper. And the importation which it thus sanctions was unquestionably of persons of the race of which we are speaking, as the traffic in slaves in the United States had always been confined to them. And by the other provision the States pledge themselves to each other to maintain the right of property of the master, by delivering up to him any slave who may have escaped from his service, and be found within their respective territories. . . . And these two provisions show, conclusively, that neither the description of persons therein referred to, nor their descendants, were embraced in any of the other provisions of the Constitution;

for certainly these two clauses were not intended to confer on them or their posterity the blessings of liberty, or any of the personal rights so carefully provided for the citizen. . . .

Indeed, when we look to the condition of this race in the several States at the time, it is impossible to believe that these rights and privileges were intended to be extended to them. . . .

The legislation of the States therefore shows, in a manner not to be mistaken, the inferior and subject condition of that race at the time the Constitution was adopted, and long afterwards, throughout the thirteen States by which that instrument was framed; and it is hardly consistent with the respect due to these States, to suppose that they regarded at that time, as fellow-citizens and members of the sovereignty, a class of beings whom they had thus stigmatized.

Chapter 22

Plessy v. Ferguson (1896)

BROWN, J. This case turns upon the constitutionality of an act of the general assembly of the state of Louisiana, passed in 1890, providing for separate railway carriages for the white and colored races. . . .

The constitutionality of this act is attacked upon the ground that it conflicts both with the 13th Amendment of the Constitution, abolishing slavery, and the 14th Amendment, which prohibits certain restrictive legislation on the part of the states.

1. That it does not conflict with the 13th Amendment, which abolished slavery and involuntary servitude, except as a punishment for crime, is too clear for argument. . . .

A statute which implies merely a legal distinction between the white and colored races—a distinction which is founded in the color of the two races, and which must always exist so long as white men are distinguished from the other race by color—has no tendency to destroy the legal equality of the two races, or reestablish a state of involuntary servitude. Indeed, we do not understand that the 13th Amendment is strenuously relied upon by the plaintiff in error of this connection. . . .

The object of the amendment was undoubtedly to enforce the absolute equality of the two races before the law, but in the nature of things it could not have been intended to abolish distinctions based upon color, or to enforce social, as distinguished from political, equality, or a commingling of two races upon terms unsatisfactory to either. Laws permitting, and even requiring their separation in places where they are liable to be brought into contact do not necessarily imply the inferiority of either race to the other, and have been generally, if not universally, recognized as within the competency of the state legislatures in the exercise of their police power. The most common instance of this is connected with the establishment of separate schools for white and colored children, which have been held to be a valid exercise of the legislative power even by courts of states where the political rights of the colored race have been longest and most earnestly enforced. . . .

It is claimed by the plaintiff in error that, in any mixed community, the reputation of belonging to the dominant race, in this instance the white race is *property*, in the same sense that a right of action, or of inheritance, is property. Conceding this to be so, for the purposes of this case, we are unable to see how this statute deprives him of, or in any way affects his right to, such property. If he be a white man and assigned to a colored coach, he may have his action for damages against the company for being deprived of his so-called property. Upon the other hand, if he be a colored man and be so assigned, he has been deprived of no property, since he is not lawfully entitled to the reputation of being a white man. . . .

So far, then, as a conflict with the 14th Amendment is concerned, the case reduces itself to the question whether the statute of Louisiana is a reasonable regulation, and with respect to this there must necessarily be a large discretion on the part of the legislature. In determining the question of reasonableness it is at liberty to act with reference to the established usages, customs, and traditions of the people, and with a view to the promotion of their comfort, and the preservation of the public peace and good order. Gauged by this standard, we cannot say that a law which authorizes or even requires the separation of the two races in public conveyances is unreasonable or more obnoxious to the 14th Amendment than the acts of Congress requiring separate schools for colored children in the District of Columbia, the constitutionality of which does not seem to have been questioned, or the corresponding acts of state legislatures.

We consider the underlying fallacy of the plaintiff's argument to consist in the assumption that the enforced separation of the two races stamps the colored race with a badge of inferiority. If this be so, it is not by reason of anything found in the act, but solely because the colored race chooses to put that construction upon it. The argument necessarily assumes that if, as has been more than once the case, and is not unlikely to be so again, the colored race should become the dominant power in the state legislature, and should enact a law in precisely similar terms, it would thereby relegate the white race to an inferior position. We imagine that the white race, at least, would not acquiesce in this assumption. The argument also assumes that social prejudice may be overcome by legislation, and that equal rights cannot be secured to the Negro except by an enforced commingling of the two races. We cannot accept this proposition. If the two races are to meet on terms of social equality, it must be the result of natural affinities, a mutual appreciation of each other's merits and a voluntary consent of individuals. . . . Legislation is powerless to eradicate racial instincts or to abolish distinctions based upon physical differences, and the attempt to do so can only result in accentuating the difficulties of the present situation. If the civil and political right of both races be equal, one cannot be inferior to the other civilly or politically. If one race be inferior to the other socially, the Constitution of the United States cannot put them upon the same plane.

Chapter 23

Plessy v. Ferguson (Justice Harlan's Dissent) (1896)

In respect of civil rights, common to all citizens, the Constitution of the United States does not, I think, permit any public authority to know the race of those entitled to be protected in the enjoyment of such rights. Every true man has pride of race, and under appropriate circumstances, when the rights of others, his equals before the law, are not to be affected, it is his privilege to express such pride and to take such action based upon it as to him seems proper. But I deny that any legislative body or judicial tribunal may have regard to the race of citizens when the civil rights of those citizens are involved. Indeed such legislation as that here in question is inconsistent, not only with that equality of rights which pertains to citizenship, national and state, but with the personal liberty enjoyed by every one within the United States. . . .

In my opinion, the judgment this day rendered will, in time, prove to be quite as pernicious as the decision made by this tribunal in the Dred Scott Case. It was adjudged in that case that the descendants of Africans who were imported into this country and sold as slaves were not included nor intended to be included under the word "citizens" in the Constitution, and could not claim any of the rights and privileges which that instrument provided for and secured to citizens of the United States; that at the time of the adoption of the Constitution they were "considered as a subordinate and inferior class of beings, who had been subjugated by the dominant race, and, whether emancipated or not, yet remained subject to their authority, and had no rights or privileges but such as those who held the power and the government might choose to grant them." The recent amendments of the Constitution, it was supposed, had eradicated these principles from our institutions. But it seems that we have yet, in some of the states, a dominant race, a superior class of citizens, which assumes to regulate the enjoyment of civil rights, common to all citizens, upon the basis of race. The present decision, it may well be apprehended, will not only stimulate aggression, more or less brutal and irritating, upon the admitted rights of colored citizens, but will encourage the belief that it is possible, by means of state enactments, to defeat the beneficent purposes which the people of the United States had in view when they adopted the recent amendments of the Constitution, by one of which the blacks of this country were made citizens of the United States and of the states in which they respectively reside and whose privileges and immunities, as citizens, the states are forbidden to abridge. Sixty millions of whites are in no danger from the presence here of eight millions of blacks. The destinies of the two races in this country are indissolubly linked together, and the interests of both require that the common government of all shall not permit the seeds of race hate to be planted under the sanction of law. What can more certainly arouse race hate, what more certainly create and perpetuate a feeling of distrust between these races, than state enactments which in fact proceed on the ground that colored citizens are so inferior and degraded that they cannot be allowed to sit in public coaches occupied by white citizens? That, as all will admit, is the real meaning of such legislation as was enacted in Louisiana. . . .

If evils will result from the commingling of the two races upon public highways established for the benefit of all, they will be infinitely less than those that will surely come from state legislation regulating the enjoyment of civil rights upon the basis of race. We boast of the freedom enjoyed by our people above all other peoples. But it is difficult to reconcile that boast with a state of the law which, practically, puts the brand of servitude and degradation upon a large class of our fellow citizens, our equals before the law. The thin disguise of "equal" accommodations for passengers in railroad coaches will not mislead anyone, or atone for the wrong this day done. . . .

I am of opinion that the statute of Louisiana is inconsistent with the personal liberty of citizens, white and black, in that state, and hostile to both the spirit and letter of the Constitution of the United States. If laws of like character should be enacted in the several states of the Union, the effect would be in the highest degree mischievous. Slavery as an institution tolerated by law would, it is true, have disappeared from our country, but there would remain a power in the states, by sinister legislation, to interfere with the full enjoyment of the blessings of freedom; to regulate civil rights, common to all citizens, upon the basis of race; and to place in a condition of legal inferiority a large body of American citizens, now constituting a part of the political community, called the people of the United States, for whom and by whom, through representatives, our government is administered. Such a system is inconsistent with the guarantee given by the Constitution to each state of a republican form of government, and may be stricken down by Congressional action, or by the courts in the discharge of their solemn duty to maintain the supreme law of the land, anything in the Constitution or laws of any state to the contrary notwithstanding.

For the reason stated, I am constrained to withhold my assent from the opinion and judgment of the majority.

Section 2—Study Questions

1. In Toni Morrison's *Beloved*, what does Beloved the ghost represent for Sethe, Paul D, and the recently freed slave community?

2. What are the different ways in which Beloved's arrival helps each of the characters, as well as the collective community, in their journeys toward healing?

3. Why has the discussion of Black women's role in the Abolitionist Movement been neglected by mainstream U.S. historians?

4. What were the special hurdles faced by middle-class, lower-class, and formerly enslaved Black women in their struggle to participate in the Abolitionist Movement?

5. What role did Evangelical Christianity play in the formation of Maria Stewart's political thought?

6. How did Maria Stewart support and fight for Black women's education and material upliftment?

7. Briefly describe some of the early attempts to chart the history of Afro-Indian relations. Who were these early historians and what were some of the contributions and drawbacks of their works?

8. Briefly outline the differences between the Black histories, Native histories, and mainstream White American histories of Afro-Indian relations that Jones points out.

9. How does Olaudah Equiano describe the conditions aboard the slave ship?

10. How did the traders punish enslaved Africans who tried to escape imprisonment aboard the slave ships?

11. Identify three key arguments that David Walker uses to make his appeal to "White Christians of America."

12. What differences and similarities between Roman slavery and American slavery does Walker identify?

13. Describe Nat Turner's early education and upbringing.

14. What events led to Nat Turner's decision to lead a slave revolt?

15. In "What if I Am a Woman?" why does Stewart encourage the establishment of "schools and seminaries for the learning of our youth"?

16. What is Stewart's position on the proposals and actions of the Colonization Society?

17. How does Sojourner Truth use her experiences as an enslaved woman to simultaneously question the ideologies of femininity and enslavement?

18. How does Sojourner Truth attack the position of those who claim that "women can't have as much rights as men"?

19. How does Judge Roger B. Taney interpret the Constitution of the United States for the Dred Scott case?

20. How does Judge Taney explain the fundamental contradiction of the Declaration of Independence's proclamation, "that all men are created equal" for the Dred Scott case, and for the condition of American slavery in general?

21. What legal principles are entrenched in the *Plessy vs. Ferguson* decision?

22. How did the *Plessy vs. Ferguson* decision affect African Americans?

23. Outline Justice Harlan's Dissent of 1896.

Section 3

**Freedom, the Resurgence
of White Supremacy,
and Strategies for
Transforming the
Status Quo**

Chapter 24

Freedom, the Resurgence of White Supremacy, and Strategies for Transforming the Status Quo: An Introduction

Gayle T. Tate

The crosscurrents of White resistance to African Americans at the dawn of their emancipation in 1863 was already underfoot and would prove to be enduring. African Americans experienced freedom's bright promise with the 13th Amendment (1865), which guaranteed freedom; the 14th Amendment (1868), which granted them citizenship for the first time since their arrival in 1619; and the 15th Amendment (1870), which granted Black male suffrage. As the Democrats and the combination of Republicans, Blacks, carpet baggers, and scalawags wrestled for control of the South under Radical Reconstruction, it appeared that the political life of African Americans would be short-lived. The Union League of America moved to the South to shore up a Republican (now dubbed the party of Lincoln) political power base, and combined with the Freedmen's Bureau and other agencies began to attract Black members as a substantial Republican voting bloc. In opposition, secret White societies such as Knights of the Ku Klux Klan, Knights of the White Camelia, and the White Brotherhood began to also spread in the South, employing such intimidation methods as arson, bribery, beatings, and lynchings to cow-tow Blacks into submission. With the 1876 presidential election, the Hayes-Tilden Compromise, and the subsequent withdrawal of Northern troops, the White South began the total disfranchisement of Blacks throughout the region.

The rise of Phase I of the Ku Klux Klan (1867–1910) resulted from an initial large following among poor Whites who feared economic competition from Black workers, criminals who wore the convenient disguises to commit their crimes, and ex-Confederate officials who had fought and lost in the Civil War. This illegal organization reinforced the legal methods of disfranchisement that started in Tennessee in 1875 and spread from state to state. The rise of "Jim Crow" and "Jane Crow" segregation, which circumscribed the legal and social rights of African Americans, had a profound effect on their new citizenship status. The erosion of citizenship rights was significant and total. The decision in the legal cases *United States v. Reese & United States v. Cruikshank* eroded Black male suffrage and dovetailed the existing segregated infrastructure that was being put in place. The legal methods of disfranchisement that included literacy tests, the grandfather clause, election laws, manipulation of the vote count, and the poll tax were methods to ensure that Blacks were marginalized as citizens. What may be remarkable in this period is the total complicity of the citizens, political parties, government, and federal courts acting in concert to stymy the progress of African Americans while they simultaneously espoused democracy and patriotism.

One of the ways that African Americans fought their oppression in the South was their investment in education as a vehicle to uplift themselves. Whites in the South also allowed this avenue of Black improvement, undoubtedly seeing it as the way in which Blacks could be educated to become integrated into the marginal jobs in the Southern economy. Segregated education also proved one of the ways that Whites could spend more monies on White students and very little on Black students. Many Blacks saw the possibility of property ownership as a way to be integrated into southern society. Booker T. Washington's gospel of industrial education, with its emphasis on agricultural and industrial education, resonated with many Blacks and Whites in the South. Northern capitalists also saw the cheap labor supply that Blacks would provide with marginal education as a source of compliance and profit. Since Washington did not focus on civil rights and political protest, from the Northern and Southern White perspective, he was supporting a subservient position for Blacks in the economy. William Monroe Trotter, Ida B. Wells-Barnett, W. E. B. Du Bois, and other militants of the age, in direct opposition to Washington's philosophy, saw immediate political equality and protest as critical to securing their rights of first-class citizenship. While Frederick Douglass and Booker T. Washington discouraged Blacks from migrating out of the South, Blacks began to migrate to the North and West in 1879. The founding of all-Black towns certainly shaped some of this movement as Blacks sought freedom from Southern terror and economic crises. Black migration, despite the apprehension of Whites who attempted to seduce Blacks to remain in the South, became a fact of life for those seeking a better life.

Robert Alexander Cole was one of the early Black migrants from Tennessee to Chicago in 1905. In "Robert Alexander Cole: Insurance Company President, Professional Gambler, Community Humanitarian" by Robert E. Weems, Jr., Cole was able to use his gambling prowess, his love and appreciation of his roots as a member of the working class, and his business acumen to launch a stream of successful business enterprises in Chicago. With his friend, Dan Jackson, Cole became a partner of the Metropolitan Funeral System Association (later renamed Chicago Metropolitan Mutual Assurance Company). Cole later expanded his interests to include the emerging Black radio industry, the popular Black magazine, the *Bronzeman*, and the Black baseball team, the Chicago American Giants. Just as Weems, Jr., identified the economic Black nationalism that nurtured the development of Black business enterprises, Gayle T. Tate, in her chapter, "Black Nationalism: An Angle of Vision" frames the discourse on the ideology of Black nationalism in the antebellum era. Tate posits that the ideology grows out of a body of political and social thought that is common to Black people in the diaspora due to their shared oppression. Relevant to Black nationalism are the tenets of religion, racial solidarity, cultural history, and the philosophy of self-determination that not only shaped the movement's dynamism but were components that anchored political protest and the infrastructure of free Black communities. Paul Johnson Edwards, in his essay, "Memories of the Civil War in Popular Song" notes that while many African Americans have viewed the Civil War as part of the journey toward freedom, others, particularly Southerners, saw the Civil War and African Americans somewhat differently and consequently have re-constructed much of their memories of the Civil War and African-Americans out of popular song.

In the next two works by Frederick Douglass and W. E. B. Du Bois, respectively, the thinkers/activists argue for Black male suffrage and the responsibility of slavery in American society. In "What a Black Man Wants," by Frederick Douglass, Douglass argues that the universal enfranchisement of Black men would remove their badge of inferiority. For Douglass, suffrage followed citizenship in America, and the Black man wanted the same rights as everyone else. In this excerpt from *Black Reconstruction*, by W. E. B. Du Bois, Du Bois argues for a factual account of American history that sheds light on the complexities and horrors of the slave experience. This propaganda of history, Du Bois posits, manipulates facts and ideas and new generations are educated with these inaccuracies. Part of the outcome of this process is that America escapes blame and responsibility for slavery and the slave trade and new generations are left with the illusions of slavery and history.

The next three works deal with Booker T. Washington, as well as William Monroe Trotter and W. E. B. Du Bois, two of his critics. In his editorial of December 20, 1902, in the *Boston Guardian*, entitled "Editorial on Booker T. Washington," William Monroe Trotter attacks Washington on his acceptance of the subservient positions of African Americans in the South. Trotter believes that Washington is denying the reality of the material conditions of Southern Blacks and their disfranchisement that is occurring throughout the South. Washington's complacency was deliberately quelling political agitation for Blacks to regain citizenship rights. In 1895, Washington's speech, "The Atlanta Exposition Address," renewed criticism from his detractors. Washington marked his accommodationist position when he argued that Blacks would provide the cheap labor to rebuild the South, "cast down their buckets where they were," and give up the quest for political power and social change. This position found acquiescence with Whites who not only saw Washington's position as non-threatening but as maintaining the status quo of racial hegemony and social segregation.

On the other hand, Washington's position drew fire from his critics in the Black community. One of his critics that took his philosophy to task was Du Bois. Often regarded as the father of modern Pan Africanist thought and practice, W. E. B. Du Bois' life and activism have been central to struggles for Black empowerment in the United States, Africa, and elsewhere in the Black diaspora. In the chapter "The Pan African Ethos of W. E. B. Du Bois, Randall Westbrook explores key elements of Du Bois's activism for Black rights, recognition, and self-determination. In 1903, Du Bois published *The Souls of Black Folk*, where he uses the metaphor of "the Veil" to analyze Black spirituality and culture, and how African Americans exist, albeit separately, within American society. In the excerpt, "Of Our Spiritual Strivings," Du Bois explored the theme of "double consciousness," the struggle of African Americans to deal with their being Black and living primarily in a segregated environment and being American at the same time. The excerpt, "Of Mr. Booker T. Washington and Others," reflects the differences in the philosophies of both men. Du Bois favored the quest for political power and Black political participation, while Washington supported muted emphasis on the quest for civil rights. The two men also differed on some of the inherent notions of capitalism. Washington favored a stronger emphasis on materialism, and Du Bois saw that "greed and avarice" on the part of Blacks would make materialists, not men with strong ideals that would uplift the masses. Even beyond his concept of the Talented Tenth, Du Bois did argue for the social and political advancement of African Americans. For Du Bois, Washington was out of step with the Black leaders of a few decades ago who were more militant in their ideals of progress; Washington believed, however, that he was right on time for what 4 million Blacks needed right out of slavery. The fact that much of what Washington proposed, such as a rising artisan class, was already outmoded did not faze him. But Washington may have responded to his critics somewhat because behind the scenes he did support efforts to stop lynching, encourage boycotts, and other enfranchisement initiatives.

Ida B. Wells-Barnett was one of the leading journalists of the time period, and her work as a political activist involving the economic exploitation of African Americans, women's rights, and civil rights marked her entire life. From her suit against the Chesapeake-Ohio Railway in 1884, to her early publications in the *Evening Star* and the *Living Way* in the late 1880s, to "Booker T. Washington and His Critics" in *World Today* in 1904, to the *Arkansas Race Riot* in 1904, Wells-Barnett's life was integrated in all of the political activism of her time. What has distinguished her commitment to the political equality of African Americans over time was her anti-lynching campaign. This crusade, initiated when friends of hers were lynched in Memphis, Tennessee, because they were becoming prosperous, took her on an international tour to arouse the consciousness of people about the lynching of Black men and women in America. Her crusade and investigative reporting led to the founding of the National Association of Colored Women in 1896 to support her efforts and the attacks against Black women as a result of her activism. This excerpt, "Ida B. Wells and the Anti-Lynching Campaign," identifies the complexities of lynching as a tool of physical intimidation in the lives of Black people.

Wells-Barnett often stood with Marcus Garvey on some of the political issues of the day, and her militancy was a source of controversy. Marcus Garvey was also controversial, and his rapidly growing organization and social movement, the Universal Negro Improvement Association (UNIA) was international in scope. With its emphasis on Black pride, self-reliance, self-determination, and economic nationalism, Garvey and Garveyism captured the masses. By the 1920s, Garvey could boast of over 700 branches in 38 states that did not include his followers in other countries. In 1920, at UNIA's first international conference, *The Declaration of Rights of the Negro Peoples of the World* was ratified. Primarily, the document supported the right to self-determination for all peoples, protested against the racism in the United States and the right of self-defense for Blacks. The document also protested against the hegemony of European powers and the exploitation of Africa. This was a radical doctrine for its time and demonstrated the far-reaching political vision of Marcus Garvey. Equally, his work, *An Appeal to the Conscience of the Black Race to See Itself* in 1925, emphasized his promotion of racial pride and progress. Garvey argues that the racial prejudice against Blacks is partly attributed to their material conditions. An emphasis on progress, self-reliance, and dignity would change the way in which Blacks were regarded as a race of people. Certainly, Garvey argues, if the Black man had his own nation, creating the best environment for the race to survive and flourish, some of the racial prejudice would diminish.

Chapter 25

Robert Alexander Cole:
Insurance Company President, Professional Gambler, Community Humanitarian

Robert E. Weems, Jr.

One of the most intriguing figures in the realm of African American history is Robert A. Cole. His multifaceted activities included: serving as president of a major Black insurance company, being regarded as one of the best blackjack players of his day, and personifying the notion of "Race Man" discussed in Horace Cayton and St. Clair Drake's magisterial 1945 classic, *Black Metropolis*. Although the insurance company he built is no longer in existence, Robert A. Cole Sr.'s story is one worth telling (and knowing).

Robert Alexander Cole, born on October 8, 1882, in Mt. Carmel, Tennessee, was the seventh of Robert and Narcissa Cole's eight children. At the time of Robert's birth, his parents, both of whom were ex-slaves, eked out a tenuous existence as tenant cotton farmers.[1]

Cole's boyhood appears to have been a happy, albeit rigorous, experience. Cotton cultivation was no less labor intensive in the late 19th century than it had been during slavery; therefore, Cole spent more time working on the family farm than in school. He did manage to complete 4 years of formal education. Cole, despite his limited educational background, would later in life refer to the following advice his mother gave him: "If you never learn nothing else, learn how to figure figures."[2]

At the age of 17, Cole decided his future lay outside the drudgery of tenant farming. Armed with a fourth-grade education and a desire to be "somebody," he left home to seek his fortune. The first stop on his journey toward future importance was Paducah, Kentucky, where he found employment in a machine shop. Within a year, he became foreman. Still, despite his rise in occupational status, it became apparent that under the South's racial code he remained a second-class citizen. Cole subsequently left Paducah and spent the next few years as a roustabout. It appears likely that he developed his legendary fondness for gambling during this period.[3]

In 1905, Cole arrived in Chicago seeking the wider opportunities the city reportedly offered Blacks. After working briefly as a busboy, he secured employment as a Pullman porter. He would later assert that the education he received during his 20 years as a Pullman porter compensated for his lack of formal education. While performing his duties, he made a point of talking to business executives and observing their actions. His diligence ultimately resulted in his being promoted to porter-in-charge, the highest position a Black could then reach in the railroad industry.[4]

While Cole worked his way up within the Pullman Company, he established important social ties as well. His friendship with Daniel McKee Jackson, Black Chicago's most prestigious undertaker and the acknowledged czar of South Side gambling activities, appeared especially significant.

Dan Jackson, one of Chicago's most powerful Blacks during the early 20th century, gained this distinction partially through his close association with three-time Republican Mayor William Hale "Big Bill" Thompson.[5] Thompson—who once campaigned in the Black community by stating, "I'll give your people jobs, and any of you who want to shoot craps go ahead and do it"[6]—protected Dan Jackson's various South Side gambling clubs. Jackson, in return, actively campaigned for Thompson among Chicago Blacks. Because

Jackson regularly donated a portion of his gambling profits in the form of money, food, and other provisions to Black Chicago's less fortunate,[7] his endorsement of Thompson carried considerable weight.

This mutually beneficial relationship between Jackson and Thompson ended (temporarily) in 1923 when Democrat William Dever, running on a reform platform, upset Thompson in that year's mayoral election. Significantly, the new Dever administration made closing down Black Chicago's gambling operations a top priority.[8] Thus, Dan Jackson witnessed a dramatic drop in his personal income. This decline of gambling revenue apparently predisposed Jackson to seek a means to compensate for his losses. Therefore, in 1925, when Otto Stevenson, a local Black entrepreneur, approached Jackson about co-establishing a burial insurance association, Jackson agreed to provide funerals if Stevenson coordinated the selling of insurance. Burial insurance associations, a derivative of the mutual-aid and beneficial societies established by African Americans during the late 19th century,[9] provided funerals to persons with limited incomes.

Stevenson's proposal, subsequently named the Metropolitan Funeral System Association (MFSA), quickly gained popularity among Black Chicagoans. In the Windy City, as in other cities across America, the African American population experienced a disproportionately high death rate.[10] Thus, the MFSA, which focused its operations upon serving the Black working poor in Chicago (who were unduly represented in Black Chicago death statistics), had a market eager for such protection. Moreover, the embryonic Metropolitan Funeral System Association enhanced its attractiveness by charging individuals a mere $0.15 weekly premium (regardless of age) and provided the option of being buried in the South.[11]

Despite the MFSA's initial success in securing policyholders, serious financial problems soon beset the company. Because the MFSA failed to fully screen applicants for burial insurance, a number of the company's early policyholders were sick individuals who died shortly after buying their burial policies. Consequently, the premiums they paid did not come close to covering a funeral's cost.[12]

As the young Metropolitan Funeral System Association moved toward impending bankruptcy, Otto Stevenson, a man of apparent limited means, could not use personal resources to counteract the company's growing problems. Significantly, after Stevenson bowed out from his sickly project and returned to obscurity, Daniel Jackson decided to maintain the MFSA. Jackson's decision appears to have been based upon his belief that the company provided a useful and needed service to working-class Black Chicagoans.

In 1926, about the same time that Dan Jackson decided to sustain the MFSA, his friend Robert A. Cole grappled with a serious problem of his own. Cole, despite his status within the Pullman Company, had become deeply dissatisfied with his dead-end position as porter-in-charge. As an ambitious African American male during the early 20th century, Cole felt stifled by the lack of occupational mobility available to him (because of American racism). Moreover, because of his scanty educational background, Cole realized that his options were *especially* limited.

Fortunately for Cole, he possessed one skill that generated significant financial compensation and circumvented American racial barriers. By the mid-1920s, Robert A. Cole had developed a reputation as a skilled blackjack and poker player.[13] In fact, it seems likely that Cole and Jackson's friendship may have been partially based upon their mutual affinity for gambling. Nonetheless, after Cole decided to leave the Pullman Company in 1926, Dan Jackson hired Cole to manage his largest South Side gambling club at 35th and State Street. It appears plausible that the ambitious Cole viewed this position as a step toward eventually owning his own gambling establishment.

The year 1927 proved to be an important turning point in Cole's life. That year featured a mayoral election where "Big Bill" Thompson sought to regain the position he lost in 1923. During Thompson's hiatus from the mayor's office, Dan Jackson's various gambling clubs (including the one Cole managed) had suffered constant harassment.[14] Consequently, Thompson sought and received Dan Jackson's support during the subsequent election. After Thompson's successful reelection campaign, he allowed Dan Jackson's gambling clubs to once again operate with impunity.[15]

Although Dan Jackson appeared understandably jubilant after "Big Bill" Thompson's 1927 reelection, he found himself faced with a dilemma. As his rejuvenated gambling interests took up more of his time, he had less time to oversee the activities of the Metropolitan Funeral System Association. Jackson solved this problem during the summer of 1927 by asking Cole to manage the upstart company.

Shortly after becoming manager of the fledgling company, Robert A. Cole boldly informed Jackson that he desired to own, rather than simply manage, the MFSA. Jackson subsequently allowed Cole to purchase the company for $500.[16] The two men, however, agreed that Dan Jackson would continue to provide funerals for the company.

Although Cole's purchase of the MFSA demonstrated his solid, if not audacious, belief in himself, he remained aware of his limitations. He knew nothing about conducting funerals or selling insurance. Fortunately for Cole, two individuals associated with Dan Jackson and the Metropolitan Funeral System Association, Fred W. Lewing and Ahmad A. Rayner, possessed the skills he needed.

Fred W. Lewing, destined to become Cole's first Agency Director, had operated several businesses before his involvement with Dan Jackson and the MFSA.[17] In 1922, Lewing, then owner of a livery service, secured the right to furnish vehicles for Dan Jackson funerals. Lewing served in this capacity until 1925, when he became one of the Metropolitan Funeral System Association's first agents. Despite the company's tenuous beginning, Lewing distinguished himself as the company's best agent. Ahmad A. Rayner, a graduate of Chicago's Washington School of Mortuary Science, served as Dan Jackson's funeral director when Cole approached him about working for the MFSA full-time.[18]

Once Cole secured the services of Lewing and Rayner, he then sought to reorganize the company's operations, especially the premium payment structure. Otto Stevenson's comprehensive $0.15 weekly premium contributed mightily to the company's early financial problems. Consequently, the Robert A. Cole-led MFSA quickly instituted a differential premium structure based upon age. Moreover, the reorganized burial association required prospective policyholders to complete a detailed application.[19]

After the Cole, Lewing, and Rayner triumvirate paved the way for improved company operations, additional skilled personnel were needed to carry out these plans. Although the reorganized company had a cadre of employees retained from Stevenson's administration, Robert A. Cole sought still more persons willing to take a chance with the fledgling company. The overt discrimination perpetuated against African Americans in the workplace made Cole's search easier.[20]

Although Cole relied heavily upon the expertise of others throughout his presidency of the MFSA, later the Chicago Metropolitan Mutual Assurance Company, he exercised unilateral executive privilege whenever he felt it appropriate. Cole first used this authority concerning the question of claims settlement. Early on, Cole concluded that prompt claims settlements enhanced community trust. Thus, even in instances where there appeared to be fraud on the part of policyholders (those who misrepresented their age or physical condition), the company quickly paid the claim.[21] While such a policy appeared unsound from a business standpoint, Cole gambled that "deadbeats" represented a small minority of the community. This gamble paid off. Within a relatively short period, the company's claim payment policy contributed to a dramatic increase in the number of policyholders.[22]

By 1929, Robert A. Cole's Metropolitan Funeral System Association had grown to the extent that the Illinois-domiciled company began making plans to expand into neighboring states.[23] Yet, two other events that year posed a distinct challenge to the young company. First, in May, Dan Jackson died after a brief illness. This raised the issue of finding new headquarters for the MFSA (the company had been operating out of the basement of Dan Jackson's funeral home at 3400 S. Michigan Avenue). Moreover, Wall Street's October 29, 1929, "crash" potentially threatened the company's very survival.

Of these two problems, the question of finding a new company headquarters proved the easiest to solve. By late 1930, Cole and the MFSA succeeded in making the transition from its earlier dependency upon Dan Jackson. Facilities at 418 E. 47th Street were leased to house the MFSA and the Metropolitan Funeral Parlors.[24] Cole established this latter company to provide funerals for deceased MFSA policyholders (as Dan Jackson had earlier done).

The company's move to 47th Street, besides providing additional office space, gave Cole and the MFSA additional visibility. By 1930, 47th Street, from State Street to Cottage Grove Avenue, began to replace the 35th and State Street district as the center of Black Chicago's commercial activity.[25]

The Great Depression proved to be a far greater challenge to Robert A. Cole. This economic calamity had a profound negative effect upon Chicago's (and the entire nation's) economy. Black Chicago appeared especially hard hit. Not only were numerous Black enterprises forced out of business, but countless working-class Black Chicagoans lost their jobs. Black Chicago workers' growing unemployment posed an especially serious threat to the MFSA, because they represented the company's chief constituency.

Cole's MFSA relied upon three distinct strategies to survive this monumental economic downturn. First, the company, realizing a sizable portion of its policyholders were recently unemployed and on relief, adopted a liberal premium payment policy when appropriate. MFSA agents, in lieu of cash, occasionally accepted such items as butter and government "scrip" for premium payments.[26]

The MFSA also endured the Depression because it expanded operations through a liberal agent hiring policy. The company's Depression-era policy to give all aspirant male agents* a "chance," proved beneficial to both successful agent trainees and the MFSA. During the 1930s, company agents were paid strictly on commission. They received 15% of the weekly premiums of new business generated and 20% commission on collections of previously established accounts.[27] Thus, for an agent to survive, he had to continually sell new policies and collect the weekly premiums on previously sold policies. The pressures from earning a living from commissions prompted many newly-hired MFSA agent trainees to quit after a relatively short period. Yet, those who survived not only helped themselves but the company.

Finally, Robert A. Cole's prowess as a gambler helped the Metropolitan Funeral System Association survive the Great Depression. Cole regularly utilized outside gambling winnings (from poker and blackjack) as a source of additional working capital for the MFSA.[28]

Besides using gambling winnings to keep the MFSA afloat during the Great Depression, Cole also used his unique source of extra capital to subsidize a variety of community improvement activities. Among the projects funded by Cole and the MFSA during the 1930s were building a recording studio for Jack L. Cooper's pioneering "All Negro Radio Hour"; publication of the *Bronzeman* magazine, a precursor of *Ebony* and *Jet*; and the purchase (and revitalization) of the Chicago American Giants, the Windy City's entry in the old Negro Baseball Leagues.[29]

The Metropolitan Funeral System Association's involvement with activities outside the realm of insurance reflected Cole's desire to use the company as a means to undertake a broader "racial mission." As a Pullman porter, he observed, first-hand, the amenities available to the White middle and upper classes in America. One of Cole's chief lieutenants, Fred W. Lewing, shared Cole's intimate knowledge of the superior goods and services available to Whites in early 20th-century America. Lewing, one of the few Blacks to grow up on Chicago's North Side, had once run an exclusive North Side barbershop for Whites.[30]

Cole and Lewing's personal knowledge of racial segregation's inherent inequalities apparently compelled them to attempt to provide Black Chicago residents with a variety of services and facilities comparable to those available to Whites. Subsequent MFSA community projects sought to give Black Chicagoans the same courtesy and consideration that Cole had given White passengers (as a Pullman porter) and Lewing had dispensed to White customers in his exclusive North Side barbershop. Predictably, the MFSA's community improvement projects dramatically improved the company's corporate image.

Robert A. Cole's predilection towards community enhancement, while significant, apparently reflected a common characteristic of historic African American economic development. As Walter B. Weare noted in his examination of the Black-owned North Carolina Mutual Life Insurance Company, Black businesses, historically, can be characterized as economically backward and socially advanced.[31] Although African American enterprises could not compete with most White businesses in terms of economic influence, Black businesses, because they were operated by members of a generally scorned race, often conveyed a special sensitivity to community issues. Thus, the Metropolitan Funeral System Association, similar to North Carolina Mutual and other Black companies, developed into a multifaceted institution that catered to the needs of a people often neglected by governmental agencies and "mainstream" business enterprises.

The Metropolitan Funeral System's first significant community enhancement project, building a recording studio for Jack L. Cooper's "The All Negro Hour," demonstrated Cole's strong sense of community spirit, as well as his business acumen. This radio program, which made its November 3, 1929, debut on Chicago radio station WSBC, marked a milestone in African American history.

Created to counteract "mainstream" radio's stereotypical depictions of Black life, "The All Negro Hour," which included comedy, musical, and religious vignettes, marked the beginning of the Black radio industry.[32] Still, while Cooper had created a format that allowed Blacks to control on-the-air proceedings, White technicians at WSBC continued to direct behind-the-scenes operations. Consequently, Jack L. Cooper felt compelled to secure a Black-staffed recording studio in the Black community, thereby making "The All Negro Hour" an absolute reality.[33]

Cooper sought the support of Black Chicago businessmen to accomplish this goal. Unfortunately, because of the worsening Depression, the years 1929–1930 were not an opportune period to request venture capital from Black Chicago businessmen. When Cooper nearly abandoned his quest for a Black-staffed recording studio, Robert A. Cole agreed to assist him.[34]

---

*Women did not become company agents until the early 1960s.

Cole and the MFSA subsequently granted Cooper virtual freedom in planning, constructing, and equipping the proposed recording studio. The completed facility, located at the Metropolitan Funeral System Association's new headquarters at 418 E. 47th Street, proved beneficial to both Cooper and the MFSA. Because of the company's direct association with an increasingly popular radio program ("The All Negro Hour"), Cole's and the MFSA's stature became enhanced. Moreover, in 1931, the company, under Jack L. Cooper's supervision, sponsored a program entitled "The All Negro Children's Hour." This show, similar to "The All Negro Hour," represented a milestone in radio programming.[35]

While Robert A. Cole and the MFSA were making an important contribution to the embryonic Black radio industry, his company, along with two Black Chicago journalists, Caswell W. Crews and Henry N. Bacon, produced the *Bronzeman* magazine.[36] According to Abby and Ronald Johnson, authors of *Propaganda and Aesthetics: The Literary Politics of Afro-American Magazines in the Twentieth Century*, the *Bronzeman* was one of the most successful Black popular magazines during the Depression.[37] The Johnsons defined a Black popular magazine as one that ". . . tried to entertain rather than instruct or lead the larger Afro-American reading public . . . in pursuit of this aim, Black popular magazines featured light fiction, including true confession stories, success stories, gossip columns, and discussions of fashion, homemaking, and sports."[38] Although the *Bronzeman* generally followed this format, it did attempt to do more than merely entertain its readers.

The *Bronzeman's* "Certificate of Merit" program, inaugurated in May, 1932, reflected the magazine's desire to do more than simply amuse the African American reading public. This award, established to highlight the accomplishments of Black commercial enterprises throughout America, sought to stimulate Black business development by rewarding progressive Black enterprises with favorable publicity. Between May and September, 1932, Mr. R. S. Andrews, the *Bronzeman's* sales representative, traveled to 13 U.S. cities to survey the status of Black business development in those locales and to confer the magazine's "Certificate of Merit" upon deserving enterprises.[39]

Besides such special projects as the "Certificate of Merit" program, the *Bronzeman* included such regular features as a gossip column entitled "A Letter from Hollywood," a children's page entitled "The Junior Bronzeman," and a "Bronze Beauties" (pictorial) section. Moreover, the magazine received favorable reaction from as far away as Liberia, West Africa.[40] Still, after Cole lost a reported $30,000 by 1933 (due to a decline in readership caused by the Depression), he decided the *Bronzeman* should meet an unfortunate, but financially expedient, demise.[41]

Robert A. Cole's association with the Chicago American Giants, similar to his involvement with "The All Negro Hour" and the *Bronzeman*, reflected his desire to enhance the larger Black community. While Cole's critics correctly argued that he used "respectable" enterprises to "launder" illicit gambling winnings, less sanctimonious observers applauded Cole's community investments. His purchase and subsequent rejuvenation of the Chicago American Giants, which literally saved a Black Chicago institution from extinction, appeared especially appreciated.

The team, originally owned by Rube Foster, was the powerhouse of the Negro National League during the early to mid-1920s. Unfortunately, after Foster suffered a 1926 breakdown (that led to his 1930 death), his health, the Chicago American Giants, and the Negro National League (which he founded) rapidly deteriorated.[42] When Cole purchased the team from White florist William E. Trimble in early 1932, the American Giants were a sickly shadow of their former selves.[43]

Cole announced plans for the American Giants' rejuvenation shortly after purchasing the team. During a February 25, 1932, interview with the Chicago *Defender*, Cole asserted that his first priority was renovating Schorling Park, the Giants' home field located at 39th and Wentworth.[44] The American Giants purchased this stadium, the first home of the Chicago White Sox, after Charles Comiskey moved the White Sox to their current 35th and Wentworth location.[45] Schorling Park, named after Rube Foster's White business partner John Schorling, fell into disrepair during Foster's prolonged illness. Besides renovating Schorling Park, subsequently renamed Cole Park, Cole informed the *Defender* that he planned to resuscitate the team itself. He stated his intention to bring such stars as Satchel Paige to Chicago.[46]

Although Cole could not secure Satchel Paige, his team, renamed Cole's American Giants, was an unqualified success. They won the Negro Southern League championship in 1932 and had the best record of the reorganized Negro National League in 1933. Unfortunately, for Cole and his American Giants, Gus Greenlee, President of the new Negro National League and owner of the Pittsburgh Crawfords, inexplicably declared that the Pittsburgh Crawfords were League champions.[47] Cole, embittered by Greenlee's heavy-handedness, subsequently sold his interest in the team to MFSA associate Horace G. Hall.[48]

Perhaps the most important (non-insurance related) services that Cole and the MFSA provided to Black Chicago were the constructions of the Parkway Ballroom in 1940 and the Parkway Dining Room in 1949. These facilities, appendages of the company's home office built at 4455 South Parkway (now King Drive) in 1940, epitomized Cole's quest to provide Black Chicagoans with first-class facilities in their community.

During the mid-20th century in Chicago, Black social and cultural organizations (as well as individuals) were denied equal access to downtown ballroom facilities.[49] In addition, White-owned nightspots in Black Chicago had "Jim Crow" seating policies during the 1930s and 1940s. Whites were seated near the stage while Blacks sat in the rear.[50] The Parkway Ballroom not only provided Black community organizations an elegant setting to hold functions but also provided Black Chicagoans an opportunity to sit anywhere they desired while observing such artists as Duke Ellington and Count Basie.[51]

According to Clarence M. Markham, Jr., who founded *The Negro Traveler and Conventioneer* magazine in 1943, the Parkway Ballroom during the 1940s and 1950s became a favorite of Black visitors to Chicago. At a time when downtown Chicago was "off-limits" to Black travelers and conventioneers, the Parkway Ballroom represented a godsend to Black visitors seeking an elegant place to relax and socialize.[52] Moreover, it has been asserted that, during the 1940s and 1950s, the Parkway Ballroom was the finest ballroom in America (Black or White) that was not affiliated with a hotel.[53]

The Parkway Ballroom's initial success contributed to the construction of the Parkway Dining Room. This restaurant, completed in 1949, provided company personnel and Black Chicago residents a first-class eating facility. Noted for an extensive menu that included filet mignon, the Parkway Dining Room attracted large crowds on Sundays, holidays, and other special occasions.[54]

Another popular aspect of the Parkway Dining Room was its courteous waiter service. Blacks in Chicago, similar to their brethren in other cities, were uncertain as to how they would be treated in restaurants. Black diners in White-owned restaurants frequently experienced slow service or outright verbal abuse. Unfortunately, the majority of Black-owned eating establishments were "chicken shacks" or "rib joints." These facilities, while fine for a snack, were unsuitable for a formal dinner. The Parkway Dining Room, with its exquisitely dressed waiters, provided Black Chicagoans a means to enjoy the amenities associated with formal dining without having to risk insult.[55]

Because of his direct association with a variety of community enhancement activities, Robert A. Cole became recognized as one of Black America's most community-minded businessmen. Moreover, it was not coincidental that most of the projects he sponsored were related to entertainment. Cole, who stood 6 foot 3 inches and weighed 270 pounds, appeared to be the consummate "free spirit." Besides his unabashed love for gambling, Cole also enjoyed good food and drink. In addition, he possessed a keen sense of humor and a hearty laugh legendary for its volume.[56] Since genteel behavior has historically been expected of Black professionals and businessmen,[57] Cole's flamboyant demeanor, his lack of formal education, as well as his fondness for gambling predictably elicited the ire of some "respectable" Black Chicagoans. Still, among Chicago's Black working classes, the people who owned MFSA burial insurance policies, "King Cole" had become a beloved figure appreciated for both his down-to-earth demeanor and his numerous community investments.

Significantly, Cole's sense of community service extended beyond the boundaries of Chicago's South Side. During World War II, the Metropolitan Funeral System Association purchased $1,021,000.00 worth of United States War Bonds. Moreover, the company's 175 employees averaged 10.3% of their salaries in bond purchases. This figure represented a higher employee bond purchase ratio than many corporations holding war contracts.[58]

The MFSA's conscientious support of the war effort, early on, attracted the attention of the U.S. Treasury Department's War Savings Section. The U.S. government subsequently asked Cole, who spearheaded the MFSA's bond purchase program, to publicly promote the War Bond drive to Black and White audiences. In 1942, Cole spoke to a gathering of over 6,000 employers in Chicago. During this address, he forcefully urged greater business participation in support of the war effort.[59]

Significantly, Cole's active promotion of the War Bond drive appeared to have been based upon more than patriotism. His efforts in this regard marked the beginning of a conscious attempt to downplay how gambling contributed to his business success. Moreover, local Black media assisted Cole's quest to rehabilitate his image. For example, the December 12, 1942, Chicago *Defender* featured a profile of Cole entitled "From Cabin to Riches," which failed to mention the central role of gambling in Cole's background.[60]

By the mid-1940s, Robert A. Cole and his company were highly regarded in both local and national circles. Moreover, the Metropolitan Funeral System Association's numerous community service activities enhanced the company's principal mission of providing economical burial insurance. For instance, between 1940 and 1945, the MFSA's net premium income increased from $623,744.28 to $1,328,961.34, and the number of policyholders grew from 56,317 to 124,289. Moreover, the company's surplus expanded from $538,894.83 to $1,747,790.12 during the same period.[61] This dramatic growth contributed to the company's 1946 decision to issue life insurance policies in addition to burial coverage. In October 1946, the company assumed a new name, the Metropolitan Mutual Assurance Company of Chicago, to coincide with its new status as a legal reserve insurance company. Moreover, it changed from a proprietary company owned by Cole to a mutual company owned by policyholders. Besides being compensated for his previous financial stake in the company, Cole retained the presidency along with proprietary ownership of the Metropolitan Funeral Parlors.[62]

While a company's commitment to community service can be measured by its contributions to the larger society, one can also gauge a commercial enterprise's sense of fairness by the way it treats its employees. During the years immediately following the company's reorganization, Robert A. Cole sought to make his employees the best-treated workers in Chicago. By the late 1940s, Metropolitan Mutual Assurance Company of Chicago personnel had access to such on-site perquisites as bowling alleys, a recreation room equipped with pool and billiard tables, a sauna, and a masseur. Moreover, when the Parkway Dining Room opened in 1949, a liberal meal ticket program allowed employees to purchase $10.00 worth of food (tickets) for $5.00. Employees lucky (or astute) enough to be in the Parkway Dining Room when Robert A. Cole appeared for a meal were generally able to eat for free (at Cole's request).[63]

Robert A. Cole's generous nature also extended to company policyholders. He furnished the cashier's section of the home office with plush couches for policyholders comfort while they transacted business. Moreover, in a skillful melding of courtesy with business acumen, if more than four policyholders were waiting in a line to pay their premiums, Cole would often direct company clerical workers to serve as temporary cashiers.[64]

The early 1950s represented a period of high visibility for Cole and his company. Not only did Metropolitan Mutual establish offices in cities throughout Illinois and neighboring states, but the company also fought a well-publicized 1951 lawsuit filed by the giant Metropolitan Life Insurance Company over Metropolitan Mutual's use of the generic term *Metropolitan*. Metropolitan Life claimed that Metropolitan Mutual's "deceptive" use of the term *Metropolitan* created confusion among Black consumers. Specifically, Met Life asserted that, because of the similarity of the names of the two companies, Blacks who thought they were buying Metropolitan Life policies, were misled into buying Metropolitan Mutual policies.[65]

Metropolitan Mutual, in response, declared that Metropolitan Life's claims were ludicrous because Metropolitan Life did not employ Black agents to sell to Black consumers.[66] As one Metropolitan Mutual policyholder succinctly described the situation:[67]

> *How foolish! How dumb do they think Negroes are? We know that Negroes cannot sell Metropolitan Life; we know that Metropolitan Life only gives us a second-rate policy. We know that when a Negro agent offers us a first-rate policy under any name, it is a Negro company, and that is what hurts Metropolitan Life.*

The subsequent trial basically upheld Metropolitan Mutual's defense. Still, it did substantiate Metropolitan Life's assertions that Blacks often referred to Metropolitan Mutual simply as "Metropolitan." A November 7, 1952, consent decree ultimately settled the conflict over the use of "Metropolitan." This document ordered the Metropolitan Mutual Assurance Company of Chicago to change its name to Chicago Metropolitan Mutual Assurance Company within a year. However, the court also directed Metropolitan Life to pay the Black Chicago company $6,000 to cover the legal cost of this move.[68]

Robert A. Cole and company employees and policyholders hailed the consent decree as a victory.[69] Not only did it deny damages to Metropolitan Life, but Metropolitan Mutual maintained the legal right to continue using "Metropolitan" in its company name. Moreover, by essentially winning what the Chicago *Defender* aptly described as a "David and Goliath legal battle,"[70] the company (and its President) attracted more positive media attention.

The January 1953 issue of *Ebony* magazine included a laudatory feature story on Metropolitan Mutual and Robert A. Cole. Besides praising Cole and his company for 25 years of service to the Black community, *Ebony* saluted Cole for succeeding despite a limited educational background.[71]

Cole's stature among African Americans received further enhancement when his semi-autobiographical essay entitled "How I Made a Million" appeared in *Ebony's* September 1954 issue. Ostensibly written to inspire achievement among Black youth, Cole asserted that if someone with his background could achieve success, any Black could.[72]

Along with the Black media's favorable depiction of Robert A. Cole, White publications were also impressed with him. On July 9, 1955, the Chicago *Tribune* published an extensive article entitled "200,000 Trust Robert A. Cole with Their Savings." The following excerpt illustrated the tone of this piece:[73]

> *The modern building at 4455 South Parkway, which houses this business (Chicago Metropolitan) stands as testimony to a man who demonstrated vision and daring in the best rags-to-riches tradition. More important, Cole operates one of the largest aggregations of private capital ever assembled in a single Chicago enterprise directed by a Negro.*

The July 1955 *Chicago Tribune* article appeared to represent yet another important milestone in Robert A. Cole's career. While Black Chicagoans had long been aware of Cole and his company's activities, this *Tribune* article introduced thousands of White Chicagoans to him and the Chicago Metropolitan Mutual Assurance Company. Unfortunately, the warm breezes of adulation and praise soon gave way to the cold winds of scandal.

On December 2, 1955, Chicago police arrested Mrs. Mary F. Cole, Robert A. Cole's wife, for her alleged participation in an extortion ring. Mrs. Cole, along with two accomplices, reportedly extorted (at gunpoint) over $20,000 from Chicago Metropolitan officials Horace G. Hall and James D. Grantham.[74] According to a knowledgeable informant, Hall and Grantham apparently elicited Mrs. Cole's ire because they opposed her bid for Chicago Metropolitan board membership.

Mary F. Cole, before her arrest, appeared prestigious in her own right. Mrs. Cole, a licensed mortician, was the first Black to serve on the faculty of Chicago's Worsham College of Mortuary Science. Besides her teaching duties, Mary Cole served as an assistant manager of her husband's Metropolitan Funeral Parlors.[75]

Mary Cole's arrest appeared to have been the culmination of events that had disturbed Robert A. Cole for some time. Evidence suggests that while his public stature reached a zenith of recognition and admiration, his home life plummeted at an equal pace. Chief among Cole's concerns was his wife's growing extravagance and her growing attachment to her chauffeur, Robert (Kelly) Rose.[76] Still Mary Cole's purported attempt to extort funds from company officials moved Cole's marital problems into the realm of public scrutiny. Ironically, Robert A. Cole's enhanced visibility transformed his wife's arrest into a scandal of major proportions.

Fortunately for Chicago Metropolitan, the Mary Cole debacle did not have an adverse effect upon the company's prestige and profitability. For instance, during the period of 1955–1956, Chicago Metropolitan witnessed an increase in its total admitted assets, weekly premium income, and number of policyholders.[77] Nevertheless, for Robert A. Cole, public disclosure of his marital problems proved to be enormously embarrassing. The robust "King Cole" of Chicago, a man noted for his jovial good nature and genuine love for people, soon became a sickly recluse. Until his death on July 27, 1956, Cole avoided such important functions as the January 16, 1956, Annual Meeting and all 1956 Board of Directors meetings.[78]

Robert A. Cole's passing, while predictably mourned by Chicago Metropolitan personnel and policyholders, generated considerable sadness among other Black Chicagoans. Unlike many business executives, he remained in touch with the "man on the street." Despite his stature as a successful entrepreneur, Cole, because of his limited educational background, apparently felt a special affinity with Chicago Metropolitan's overwhelmingly working-class constituency. Thus, even later in life, when universally lauded for his accomplishments, it was not uncommon to observe "King Cole" strolling though the streets of Black Chicago exchanging greetings with old friends and passersby.[79]

Robert A. Cole's life and career, while significant in its own right, illuminated an important characteristic of historic and contemporary Black business. It is common knowledge that Black entrepreneurs have had, and continue to have, problems in gaining access to capital for business start-up and expansion. This problem was especially acute during the early 20th century. Thus, denied access to "respectable" sources of business funding, some pioneer Black entrepreneurs felt compelled to raise capital through such creative means as gambling.

Although gambling, in many instances, represents a negative activity, some Black entrepreneurs, like Robert A. Cole, used their expertise in this area to make a positive contribution to the community. Moreover, when one reflects upon how various states currently use lotteries to finance a variety of worthwhile projects, the activities of Robert A. Cole appear far from dishonorable. In fact, it appears that all entrepreneurs, considering the risks involved with business enterprise, are gamblers at heart. (Not to mention all the "respectable" people who "play" the stock market.)

Endnotes

1. *Chicago Tribune*, July 9, 1955, 8; Chicago *Defender*, December 12, 1942, 15.
2. Ibid.
3. Ibid.
4. Ibid.
5. Gosnell, Harold F. (1935). *Negro Politicians: The Rise of Negro Politics in Chicago*. Chicago: University of Chicago Press, 130–33; Chicago *Defender*, May 18, 1929, 1.
6. Spear, Allan H. (1967). *Black Chicago: The Making of a Negro Ghetto*. Chicago, 187.
7. Gosnell, Harold. (1935). *Negro Politicians*, 131.
8. Ibid., 132.
9. Trent, William J. (1932). "Development of Negro Life Insurance Companies," M.A. thesis, University of Pennsylvania, 44–49; Weare, Walter B. (1973). *Black Business in the New South: A Social History of the North Carolina Mutual Life Insurance Company*. Urbana: University of Illinois Press, 5–16; Benson Henderson, Alexa. (1990). *Atlanta Life Insurance Company: Guardian of Black Economic Dignity*. Tuscaloosa: University of Alabama Press, 3–11.
10. Harris, Jr., Harrison L. (1927). "Negro Mortality Rates in Chicago," *Social Service Review* 1 (March): 64.
11. Interview, Lee L. Bailey, May 16, 1986. Mr. Bailey joined the MFSA as an agent in 1928. Before the company's ultimate demise in 1996, Bailey was viewed as the company "griot."
12. Ibid.
13. Interviews, Dorothy Harper, December 4, 1985; Robert A. Cole, Jr. March 4, 1986; Lee L. Bailey, May 16, 1986. These individuals personally knew Mr. Cole and his fondness for (and skill in) gambling. In fact, Robert A. Cole, Jr., the son of Robert A. Cole, appeared proud of his father's stature as a master card player.
14. Gosnell, Harold. (1935). *Negro Politicians*, 132.
15. Ibid.
16. Lee L. Bailey, May 16, 1986.
17. Chicago *Defender*, May 26, 1945, 3.
18. Ibid.; Interview, Ann Childs, August 4, 1986. Mrs. Childs was Ahmad A. Rayner's daughter.
19. Minutes, Organizational Meeting, Metropolitan Funeral System Association, December 19, 1927.
20. Cayton, Horace R. and Drake, St. Clair. (1945). *Black Metropolis: A Study of Negro Life in a Northern City*. (New York, 1945), 223.
21. Interview, Jesse L. Moman, March 6, 1986. Mr. Moman coordinated the writing of a brief company history in 1977 (commemorating the 50th Anniversary of Robert A. Cole's taking control of the company); Illinois Department of Insurance Examination of the Metropolitan Funeral System Association, November 24, 1931, 4.
22. Ibid., 15.
23. Minutes, Executive Committee Meeting, MFSA, September 9, 1929.
24. *A Place in the Sun: A Pictorial and Graphic Review of the Rise of the Metropolitan Funeral System Association*. Chicago, 1930, no pagination.
25. "Black Metropolis Historic District," proposal submitted to the Commission on Chicago Historical and Architectural Landmarks, March 7, 1984, 5.
26. Lee L. Bailey, May 16, 1986.

27. Illinois Department of Insurance Examination of the MFSA, November 24, 1931, 4.

28. Robert A. Cole, Jr., March 4, 1986; Jesse L. Moman, March 6, 1986; Lee L. Bailey, May 16, 1986.

29. *Bronzeman*, April 1932, 24; June 1931, 7, 8; Johnson, Abby Arthur, and Johnson, Ronald Maberry. (1979). *Propaganda Aesthetics: The Literary Politics of Afro-American Magazines in the Twentieth Century.* Amherst, 109; Chicago *Defender*, February 27, 1932, 8; October 9, 1932, 10.

30. Chicago *Defender*, May 26, 1945, 3.

31. Weare, Walter B. (1973). *Black Business in the New South*, 100–1.

32. Newman, Mark. (1983). "On the Air with Jack L. Cooper; the Beginnings of Black Appeal Radio," *Chicago History* 12 (Summer): 51, 54–56.

33. *Bronzeman*, April 1932, 24.

34. Ibid.

35. Ibid.

36. *Bronzeman*, June 1931, 7, 38.

37. Johnson and Johnson. (1979). *Propaganda and Aesthetics*, 109.

38. Ibid.

39. *Bronzeman*, May 1932, 6; June 1932, 23; July 1932, 30; August 1932, 22; September 1932, 29. The cities Andrews visited were Indianapolis, St. Louis, Kansas City (Kansas), Oklahoma City, Tulsa, New Orleans, Dallas, Houston, Birmingham, Memphis, Nashville, Louisville, and Cincinnati.

40. *Bronzeman*, July 1931, 6; August 1931, 6; September 1931, 5.

41. Cole, Robert A. (1954). "How I Made a Million," *Ebony* 9 (September), 50.

42. Peterson, Robert. (1984; first published in 1970). *Only the Ball was White*. New York: Prentice Hall, 114–15.

43. Ibid., 114.

44. Chicago *Defender*, February 27, 1932, 8.

45. Illinois Writers Project, Negro in Illinois Series, MSS IWP 132, Folder 1, Memorandum dated December 20, 1941, Vivian Harsh Collection, Carter G. Woodson Regional Library, Chicago, Illinois.

46. Chicago *Defender*, February 27, 1932, 8.

47. Chicago *Defender*, October 9, 1932, 10; Peterson, Robert. (1984). *Only the Ball Was White*, 93.

48. Chicago *Defender*, November 2, 1935, 13. Horace G. Hall would go on to play a central role in the formation of the Negro American League in 1937 (see Peterson, *Only the Ball was White*, 93).

49. Travis, Dempsey J. (1983). *An Autobiography of Black Jazz*. Chicago, 86.

50. Ibid., 43.

51. Jesse L. Moman, September 24, 1985.

52. Interview, Clarence M. Markham, Jr., February 19, 1986.

53. Interview, Etta Moten-Barnett, December 8, 1985. Mrs. Moten-Barnett, the widow of Claude A. Barnett (the founder of the Associated Negro Press), was prestigious in her own right. She gained fame as a concert singer and actress. In 1942, she sang the lead in the Broadway production of *Porgy and Bess*. During her professional career, Mrs. Moten-Barnett had the opportunity to travel extensively. Consequently, her assertion that the Parkway Ballroom was the finest ballroom in America not associated with a hotel must be taken seriously.

54. "Insurance Anniversary: Metropolitan Mutual of Chicago Marks 25th Year," *Ebony* 8 (January 1953), 81; Jesse L. Moman, September 24, 1985; Clarence M. Markham, Jr., February 19, 1986.

55. Interview, Edward A. Trammell, October 9, 1985. Mr. Trammell was a long-time employee with the company.

56. Interview, Earl B. Dickerson, November 26, 1986. Mr. Dickerson was a noted Black Chicago lawyer and past president of Supreme Life, another important Black insurance company based in Chicago.

57. Cayton, Horace R., and Drake, S. *Black Metropolis*, 526–63.

58. Minutes, General Meeting, MFSA, January 21, 1946; Chicago *Defender*, December 12, 1942, 1; 4.

59. Ibid.

60. Ibid.

61. Illinois Department of Insurance Examination of the Metropolitan Funeral System Association, July 30, 1941, 24; October 1, 1943, 20; September 11, 1944, 20; June 24, 1947, 11; Minutes, MFSA Annual Meetings, January 15, 1945; January 21, 1946.

62. MFSA to Illinois Department of Insurance, September 30, 1946.

63. Company pamphlet, "Metropolitan Mutual Assurance Company," 1950, no pagination; Jesse L. Moman, September 24, 1985.

64. Interview, Louise Wood, April 22, 1986. Mrs. Wood was a long-time company employee.

65. Complaint against the Metropolitan Mutual Assurance Company of Chicago filed by the Metropolitan Life Insurance Company, Case #51C-66, United States District Court for the Northern District of Illinois/Eastern Division, U.S. National Archives, Chicago, Illinois, 3–4.

66. Metropolitan Mutual Assurance Company of Chicago's response to the January 12, 1951, complaint filed by the Metropolitan Life Insurance Company, Case #51 C-66, United States District Court for the Northern District of Illinois/Eastern Division, U.S. National Archives.

67. "Metropolitan Mutual: A Monument to Integrity," Chicago Courier, July 7, 1951, 5.

68. Consent Decree, November 7, 1952, Case #51 C-66, *Metropolitan Life vs. Metropolitan Mutual*, U.S. National Archives, Chicago, Illinois.

69. Minutes, Annual Meeting, Metropolitan Mutual Assurance Company of Chicago, January 19, 1953.

70. Chicago *Defender*, January 20, 1951, 1.

71. "Insurance Anniversary: Metropolitan Mutual of Chicago Marks 25th Year," *Ebony* 8 (January 1953), 79–82.

72. Cole, Robert A. (1954). "How I Made a Million," *Ebony* 9 (September), 43–52.

73. Chicago *Tribune*, July 9, 1955, 8. The article failed to mention the important role that gambling played in Cole's rise to prominence and prestige.

74. Chicago *Sun Times*, December 3, 1955, 1; Chicago *American*, December 4, 1955, 1, 6; Associated Negro Press, News Releases, December 12, 1955, December 14, 1955, Claude A. Barnett Papers, Chicago Historical Society.

75. Chicago *Defender*, March 8, 1941, 6; September 27, 1941, 19; October 27, 1945, 3.

76. Chicago *American*, December 4, 1955, 6; Associated Negro Press, News Releases, December 12, 1955, December 14, 1955, Claude A. Barnett Papers, Chicago Historical Society.

77. Minutes, Annual Meeting, Chicago Metropolitan Mutual Assurance Company, January 21, 1957. Mary Cole was subsequently acquitted because evidence secured through a wire tap could not be used as evidence. See Associated Negro Press News Release, August 1, 1956, Claude A. Barnett Papers, Chicago Historical Society.

78. Minutes, Annual Meeting, CMMAC, January 16, 1956; Board Meetings, January 16, 1956, February 6, 1956, March 19, 1956, April 16, 1956, April 30, 1956, June 18, 1956.

79. Interview, Baker Cole, February 26, 1986. Mr. Cole, a former Chicago Metropolitan employee, was the nephew of Robert A. Cole.

Chapter 26

Black Nationalism: An Angle of Vision

Gayle T. Tate

Introduction

Since the fiery speech by Henry Highland Garnet in 1843, "Address to the Slaves," Black nationalism has generated a great deal of interest. The interest, however, did not fully address the fact that Garnet's speech was a connection to earlier nationalist thought. This direct linkage can be traced to David Walker, whose pamphlet in 1829, "Appeal to the Coloured Citizens of the World" shaped the beginnings of Black nationalism. Originally, the nationalist direction of Walker's pamphlet was submerged under its impassioned rhetoric of radical agitation. The bond between the two works was more discernable, however, when Garnet published a compendium including his speech and Walker's pamphlet in 1843. By doing this, Garnet also established himself in the tradition of Black nationalism. For it was Walker, along with Robert Alexander Young, Maria W. Stewart, and Reverend Lewis W. Woodson, that gave Black nationalism its definitive form. They defined and clarified, under the rubric of collective elevation, the themes of freedom, justice, the role of women in conflict, and the universality of the Black liberation struggle. Additionally, they established Black nationalism's four primary ideological constants of religion, racial unity, cultural history, and the philosophy of self-determination. This article will discuss the early Black nationalist themes as well as those fundamental ideological properties that nurtured its evolution.

Black nationalism of the 1830s embraced the political realities, aspirations, and destiny of Black Americans. Thus, the vision of Black people as a self-determined nation was always juxtaposed to the realities of their political plight in America. Black nationalism was no small feat for the intensity of these political realities—racism and segregation—were largely dependent upon, although not always, the concentration of Black Americans within a specified geographic location. Against this backdrop, Black nationalism clarified, defined, and analyzed the political struggle and suggested a specific course of action. As an ideology, Black nationalism also mirrored the pithy disillusionment of the Black experience in America. That experience, one of suffering and resistance, was embedded into the Black consciousness. Black nationalism, then, sought to capture the essence of pathos and hope that spoke to the sojourn of Blacks in America.

Many factors contributed to the development of Black nationalism as an ideology. First, kinship ties of common African descent bound Blacks to each other in the new alien land. Second, the institution of slavery and the racial discrimination of free Blacks made all Blacks suffer under the common yoke of oppression. While slaves were physically and economically tied to their masters, free Blacks endured legal constraints and racial prejudice daily.[1] Still another ingredient that fostered their unity was their yearning for freedom. All Blacks, whether slave or free, were linked in a common struggle for liberation. More importantly, however, Blacks wanted the opportunity to determine their own destiny. Reverend Lewis Woodson, who some have dubbed, "the father of Black nationalism" urged Blacks to "settle themselves in communities in the country, and establish society, churches, and schools of their own."[2]

In the early 1800s, Black Americans were victimized by both Northern racism and Southern slavery. Southern slavery was totally dependent upon Black servile labor. Without this economic base, the system would have collapsed. The master-slave relationships that were built upon the economic system of slavery were maintained by absolute authority. The psychological component of reducing slaves, in white minds, to stereotypical images of inferiority also served to buttress the system. Thus, the economic foundation tied Blacks to the land for the surplus value they produced; and the psychological element served as justification for the continuous exploitation.[3] On the other hand, Northern racism had greater subtleties and was infinitely more complex. While Blacks looked to the North for its promises of freedom, Northern racial discrimination severely confined their freedom and opportunities. These Northern restrictions included employment opportunities, housing, suffrage, civil and legal rights, admission to public facilities, and the use of public conveyances.[4] Northern segregation and Southern slavery created two social structures, one black and one white. In the South, the overall oppression was clearly definitive and the oppressor had a face. Northern racism, however, was much more depersonalized and hid behind the ambiguities of federal, state, and local institutions and customs. These harsh political and social realities contributed to the nationalist cause.

Black Nationalist Thought

Collective elevation was the crux of Black nationalist thought. Viewed also as moral upliftment, it was the commitment of Black Americans to spiritually improve themselves.[5] But the concept held a deeper meaning. Collective elevation was also seen as the spiritual regeneration of the race and the first step toward full equality in American society. Moreover, moral improvement was only possible as one developed a sense of Black consciousness. This heightened sense of political and spiritual awareness nurtured community ambition and engendered development through education. The challenge to oppression followed this enlightened process. The idea of freedom transcended the psychological and emotional boundaries to become a call for action.

Collective elevation was both an individual and group moral task. Black Americans essentially saw their uplift as group members. While individual accomplishments validated Black claim to full citizenship, by themselves, however, they did not serve to move the group forward. It was rather the collective strivings of the entire group that would make full equality possible for the individual. Woodson believed this transmutation of the Black psyche was necessary for freedom and equality:

> To produce a moral revolution, such as is needed in our case, has ever been found a work of the greatest difficulty, even when every facility for its accomplishment was afforded. But how much more difficult must it be with us, when a thousand obstacles are thrown in the way.[6]

While collective elevation was the thrust of nationalist thought, freedom and liberation emerged as its overriding themes. The freedom concept held the idea of emancipation because Black Americans wanted to be free from both Southern bondage and Northern oppression. Nationalists, such as Maria W. Stewart, saw little difference between the condition of slaves and free Blacks, believing that free Black "conditions but little better than that."[7] The idea of liberation for Black Americans, however, contained the same sentiments of liberty and equality that inspired the American revolutionaries: " . . . our souls are fired with the same love of liberty and independence with which your souls are fired."[8] Black nationalism was an acknowledgement of Black Americans as an oppressed people and liberation was their desire to be free from that oppression. Inspired by other struggles, "all the nations of the earth are crying out for Liberty and Equality,"[9] liberation was the inherent belief of a wronged people waging a righteous struggle.

Although the primary focus of Black nationalism was on freedom and liberation, it was the realities of slavery and oppression that provided its internal dynamism. The stimuli of Southern slavery and Northern racism consistently gave Black nationalism its passion. Moreover, this same stimuli forged the bond of racial unity for a suffering people in a hostile environment. Racial unity provided the strength to surpass the oppression and collectively protest the political plight of Black Americans. Nationalism encouraged this challenge against oppression by diminishing the power of the slaveholding class and, at the same time, mythologizing the collective powers of the slaves. The slaves' power, ever present, was merely lying dormant waiting for their collective consciousness to be awakened. Shoring up their strength was the coming of the Messiah. Still, the faith of the believers held fast to the idea that the Messiah would one day appear. This Messiah, "the man we proclaim ordained by God, to call together the black people as a nation in themselves,"[10] would arouse the slaves to battle and guide Blacks in their liberation struggle to victory.

The tenets of justice and wisdom turned on both a religious and worldly realm in Black nationalism. Containing intertwining sacred and secular chords, justice and wisdom were derived both from human reason and God's law. Justice was the moral principle guiding human conduct, imbuing them with the knowledge of right and wrong. Entering the sacred realm, justice was the understanding and wisdom that God gave humankind. For nationalists, their sense of justice was their connection to the Deity. It was that special quality that placed the human species on a higher plateau than other forms of animal life. All actions, then, both virtuous and political, must follow principles of morality and conform ultimately with God's law. Slavery not only violated human reason but destroyed the spiritual union of Blacks with God. Young proclaimed slavery to be "contrary to the knowledge of justice, as hath been implanted of God in the souls of man. . . ."[11] Thus, any war waged against this system would be in keeping with God's law. The abolition of slavery was not only a political cause, but a moral right as well.

Morality was also central to the material world-view of antebellum Black women and was at the core of their political activism. Black women viewed their morality, aspirations, and political commitment all through a religious prism. It was their spiritual consciousness that defined the parameters of their political action. For them piety and the freedom cause were one. With their religious beliefs serving as the spring board for their spiritual rebirth, Black women saw moral regeneration paving the way to economic and political opportunities. With the recognition of limited material opportunities, Black women developed a keen sense of political realities. Thus, Black women with economic and political aspirations confronted the social conditions of Blacks fired with new energy to "plead the cause of his(her) brethren." The religious reverence of Black women was essential in directing the path of the struggle. Their sanctity was further buttressed by their unity as sisters. Maria Stewart constantly admonished Black women that not "till we become united as one, and cultivate among ourselves the pure principles of piety, morality and virtue,"[12] would they be morally victorious.

To play a decisive role in the freedom cause, Black women were urged to go beyond the traditional roles of antebellum women. "How long shall the fair daughters of Africa be compelled to bury their minds and talents beneath a load of iron pots and kettles?"[13] The mushrooming of Black female benevolent and literary associations, for mutual aid, moral improvement, and political development, in the early 1800s testified to Black women's commitment for community improvement. In this early period, there were societies founded by working-class women as well as women with means, all mirroring the participation of Black women in varied phases of Black struggle. As early as 1793, the Female Benevolent Society was founded by a group of Black women for the expressed purpose of mutual relief.[14] While early female benevolent societies reflected and imitated white female societies of the period, the emphasis on racial consciousness, self-improvement, and social responsibility were paramount in Black female associations.[15] This focus was in keeping with the central theme of collective elevation in the Black community. It was the growth of these female societies in the 1800s, followed by antislavery societies founded by Black women in the 1830s, that reflected the continuous commitment of Black women to social reform in general and the Black liberation struggle in particular.

Black women were not only charged with the moral responsibility of developing their human potential, but the additional task of training all of the descendants. Thus, education which has always been germane to the Black experience proved also to be important in Black nationalism. For Black women, it was crucial because the employment opportunities were limited to field work, domestic service, seamstress, and elementary education. The realities of life for the Black woman placed her in triple jeopardy due to her race, gender, and economic circumstances. Stewart, one of the first females of any color to speak from the public platform, was acutely aware of the racism and sexism peculiar to Black women in American society. She charged Black women with the moral responsibility of distinguishing their talents so that the world could assess and measure their accomplishments. The recognition for their accomplishments would also restore their dignity which had been stripped away under slavery and racism. But their talents and gifts could then be passed on to their descendents providing intellectual continuity. These inter-generational achievements would earn the respect of nations. Stewart implored Black women to "O, ye daughters of Africa, awake! awake! arise! no longer sleep nor slumber, but distinguish yourselves. Show forth to the world that ye are endowed with noble and exalted faculties."[16]

Stewart saw a connection between America's domestic policy of racism, sexism, and slavery and its emerging foreign policy toward the new republic of Haiti. In her eyes, America's failure to recognize the birth of Haiti, which culminated a fierce revolutionary struggle, and at the same time, support other revolutionary causes world-wide, was hypocritical. Undoubtedly, America's failure to recognize this new Black government added zeal to Black nationalism. Moreover, because early nationalism had a profound recognition for the universality of the Black liberation struggle, this failure on America's part denoted racism to the nationalists. Stewart, in her lecture at the Franklin Hall in Boston in 1832, was highly critical of America's foreign policy:

> *We know that you are raising contributions to aid the gallant Poles; we know that you have befriended Greece and Ireland; and you have rejoiced with France, for her heroic deeds of valor. You have acknowledged all of the nations of the earth, except Hayti.*[17]

The Haitian Revolution of 1804 sparked Black nationalism in America. The slave uprising that eventually culminated in Haitian independence did much to encourage Black Americans in their own liberation struggle. Although Haiti became the first Black government in the Western Hemisphere, its vision of becoming the center of pan-Africanism never materialized. Still, the raw courage of the slaves and the mere existence of the Black government was enough for Black Americans to celebrate. At the same time, it restored their faith in their own capabilities of self-government while nourishing their embryonic pan-Africanism. "But what need have I to refer to antiquity, when Hayti, the glory of the blacks and terror of tyrants, is enough to convince the most avaricious and stupid of wretches. . . ."[18] Black Americans also saw some similarities between the two struggles. Haitians were Black descendants from Africa; were brought to the Western Hemisphere as slaves; and had liberated themselves from oppression. Black Americans were also brought to the West as African slaves and were fighting for self-emancipation. For Stewart, the battle lines were clearly drawn: "Many will suffer for pleading the cause of oppressed Africa, and I shall glory in being one of her martyrs. . . . "[19]

Black Americans, glorifying in the victory of the African descendants against their oppressors, received much encouragement from the new Haitian government. This support in addition to the Haitian emigrant plans of Black Americans served to infuse pan-Africanist thought in Black nationalism. Henri Christophe, the enlightened ruler of Haiti, 1811–1820, noted for his famous laws and decrees, agreed to a resettlement plan with Prince Saunders. Saunders, an early Haitian emigrant from America, had formerly worked under Christophe in the Haitian ministry of education.[20] Under the plan Black Americans would settle in Haiti with the Haitian government underwriting their relocation. The assassination of Christophe, in 1820, put a temporary stop to all emigration efforts. Immediately thereafter, however, Prince Saunders entered into negotiations with Christophe's successor, Alexandre Petion, who also favored Black American emigration. To demonstrate his commitment to the plan, Petion emphasized employment for Black emigrants. In Haiti, Black Americans saw a Black sanctuary as well as an opportunity for economic prosperity. Support for Haitian emigration was drawn principally from New York City and Philadelphia. Roughly 13,000 free Blacks emigrated to Haiti between 1824–28.[21] Despite the enthusiasm, this emigration plan was largely unsuccessful in that many Black emigrants suffered innumerable hardships in Haiti, employment did not materialize for many, low-wage employment for many others, and some returned wearily to America. Emigration fever would not die, however, nor did Black Americans relinquish their ties to Haiti. In the 1850s, a turbulent time in racist America, emigration was again rekindled.

Emigrationism contained the hope, longing, and acute disillusionment of the political plight of Black Americans. It was one of the most volatile issues in Black nationalism and has always been resurrected in times of despair. Even for those Black Americans formerly opposed to emigration plans, Haiti was a symbol of freedom. David Walker vehemently opposed all colonization efforts, and perceived them as, "a plan to get those of the coloured people, who are said to be free, away from among those of our brethren whom they unjustly held in bondage. . . ."[22] Yet, with a profound recognition of a weary warrior, Walker responded to hopeful emigrants with sensitivity. For those who wanted a new life in freedom, Walker implored, ". . . go to our brethren, the Haytians, who, according to their word, are bound to protect and comfort us."[23] Seeking solace and freedom, when the tides of racism peaked and Black Americans suffered despair, they looked beyond America's shores for their dignity.

Emigrationism, the resettlement of Blacks beyond American borders, was one of the ways in which Black Americans sought to uplift themselves. It co-existed with those themes of freedom, justice, and the role of Black women in struggle, in determining the political direction of Black Americans. These themes did not always co-exist harmoniously, but were determined by the political fluidity of the times. Black Americans consistently refortified their struggle with shifting priorities and directions to meet the contemporary political currents. Due to the urgency of the time, there was a noted strident militancy inherent in Black nationalism and there were reasons why this was so. The early Black nationalists, such as Young, Walker, Stewart, and Woodson were young men and women that represented a new generation in the free Black community that openly acknowledged violence as a necessary part of struggle. Just as importantly, they also believed that Blacks must direct their liberation cause themselves. If others were allowed to plead their cause, they would also determine its political direction. The militancy, then, inherent in Black nationalism reflected the need for a collective Black agenda. But nationalists who were articulate, charismatic, and forceful, were impatient with others who lacked political clarity on the conditions of Black Americans. Black nationalists, never exclusively Black in their world-view, recognized self-determination as connoting responsibility, commitment, and political action. By drawing on their bi-cultural history of Africa and America, they fashioned ideological components that became the vehicles for shoring up the dignity of Black Americans as well as the impetus for social change. The genesis for the ideological components evolved from the freedom struggle of Black Americans.

Ideological Components

Religion

Black religion, with its transcendental and temporal functions, was found in the slave community. With dual purpose, Black religion addressed the psychological needs for survival in the material world as well as freedom in the after life. Religion was not peculiar to the Black slaves' presence in America. For Africans had had prior exposure to Christianity, Islam, and traditional African religious systems. In all of them, religion was the foci of life. It was this ethos, this historical memory, that traversed the seas with the Africans in the Middle Passage and, undoubtedly, aided their survival in the new world. Black religion is a union of several qualities. It is the merging of the traditional African belief systems, the spiritual life of the slave community shaped by slavery, and white Christianity, all providing a holistic balm for the Blacks' total existence. This religious experience was shaped, too, by the physical distance of many of the slave communities on the larger plantations from the domiciles of the planters. This separation gave the slaves space to retain their African spirituality. At the same time, the temporal function of religion, which is the criticism of societal norms, was being expressed in the form of resistance. Varied forms of resistance included work stoppage, destroying equipment, "hush harbor meetings," conspiring with fugitives, and escaping as ways of protest.[24] Resistance, the highest stage of societal criticism, was rooted in the slaves' spiritual commitment to freedom. Resistance in the form of Black rebellions was also the fusion of religion and the desire for liberation. The slaves' sense of spirituality, then, was strengthened the more they faced White oppression.[25] The retention of this spirituality, of understanding the very essence of life through religion, was carried into freedom, the Black Church, and Black protest.

Black religion has always served a dual function within the Black community. And the Black Church, due to its autonomous position in the Black community, has maintained that duality. Although recognized for its Africanization of Christianity, the early Black church consistently sounded the clarion call of protest of the political plight of Black Americans. Providing a sanctuary for the weary and challenging political repression has been its primary functions and the two factors are inseparable. The need for sanctuary and freedom is carried forward by the "prophetic tradition" of the Black Church. With the Black minister as spiritual messenger, "The Black Church maintains a clear prophetic tradition . . . This tradition brings into judgment not only the institutions of society (such as political structures), but the institutional church as well."[26]

The religious world-view of the slave became an ideological component of Black nationalism. This spirituality of life that endures oppression and, yet, contests it in all forms, was the sustaining force of Black nationalism. Early Black theologians supported the political and religious direction of nationalists by merging nationalism with theology. God, a benevolent Deity, was one who provided both justice and equality for all people. By executing good Christian deeds, one could hope to achieve divine grace. These deeds regenerated individual spirituality that led first to the rebirth of the individual and then ultimately the race itself.[27] It was the collective elevation of the Black race that would initially be achieved through moral regeneration. The spirituality of this process provided the needed incentive and commitment in the Black community. Political protest and challenges to the evil system of slavery were synonymous with the achievements of justice, virtue, and divine grace. Decidedly guiding this righteous course, God would avenge His people and set them free.

Even though Black nationalism moved into the secular community in the 1830s, and began to be spearheaded by secular leaders, early nationalists were fundamentally pious. In their angle of vision there remained a connection between religious and political struggle: "The Lord has a suffering people, whose moans and groans at his feet for deliverance from oppression and wretchedness, pierce the very throne of Heaven, and call loudly on the God of Justice, to be revenged."[28]

Racial Unity

Racial unity, the cornerstone of Black nationalism, was the belief and feeling that Blacks must align themselves against common oppression. The crux of racial unity was to unite Blacks regardless of social class, geographic location, and disparate political positions found within the Black community. Focusing on the shared experiences of traditions, history, and suffering, Blacks were defined as a people. Inherent in racial unity was also the concept that all Blacks had a common racial destiny. The belief, implicitly, was that the past and present had largely been determined by racism, but Blacks themselves could shape their future.

Early evidences of racial consciousness was manifest in the slave community both in the shared culture as well as the collective resistance to bondage. The mixtures of languages, institutions, and religions of the African slave didn't alter their common world-view of life itself. It was this outlook of being one with nature that forged a common bond. The contact with Euro-American culture, sharpened by the realities of the slave experiences, enhanced their sense of racial consciousness. Slaves quickly learned that their survival depended upon the extent to which they supported each other. The cohesiveness of the slave community was more clearly seen in the emerging slave culture with its religious worship, extended non-familial bonding, music, folktales, and child-rearing practices. It was in this way the community was able to objectify its oppression and enhance the individual's psychological self-worth despite harsh circumstances. Members of the slave community also secretly aided fugitives and escapees from the plantations. The closeness of the slave community members can be readily observed in the fugitives' flight patterns. In many cases, fugitives merged with the maroon settlements in the mountainous or swampy regions near plantations, particularly if family members were still in bondage. Others mingled with the free Black population of the South that had settled near plantations hoping to set family members free. Still others that escaped North and to Canada returned to aid the escapes of family members and friends. These flight patterns not only demonstrate strong kinship ties but also a common bond based on the commonality of oppression as well as racial identity.

Racial solidarity became an effective political instrument in the antebellum Black community. There were several pragmatic realities that sustained the concept of racial unity as a political force for Blacks. For one, free Blacks, never constituting more than 14 percent of the total Black population, and were dispersed over the entire nation. Carrying the early protest efforts mainly by themselves, Blacks needed a unifying force. There was none more compelling than uniting under the umbrella of racial solidarity. The experience of witnessing racial oppression daily heightened the self-awareness of free Blacks. Secondly, racial cohesiveness was an effective way of dealing with the diverse social classes that were starting to emerge in the Black community. The 1830s brought with it a small Black elite, who, while economically experiencing some success, were still the victims of racial discrimination and limited social opportunities. The indignities they suffered also propelled the ideal of racial unity forward. Racial unity also served to unite free and enslaved Blacks, so that the struggle of free Blacks was always dependent upon the resistance of the slaves. Equally important was that slave resistance fueled Black protest forward. At all stages of development, racial unity provided the rationale for struggle and remained the underpinnings of Black protest.

Nationalists sought racial unity as the key to freedom. Blacks, in combining their efforts, would challenge American racism. Yet, racial unity was seen through different prisms. Young saw it providing a renewal of spirit that would unite Blacks as a people worldwide. Walker saw racial unity as necessary for the abolition of slavery. The primary focus of Stewart was upon unity as the foundation for all moral and intellectual achievements. "I am of a strong opinion, that the day on which we unite, heart and soul, and turn our attention to knowledge and improvement, that day the hissing and reproach among the nations of the earth against us will cease."[29] On the other hand, Woodson's concern was for the dispersed Black population. He saw the need for a general convention to bring together the collective wisdom of Black Americans. Undoubtedly, modeling his convention after the National Negro Convention Movement which had fallen into disarray by 1838, Woodson believed that was the type of forum best to encourage and sustain racial unity. All nationalists, however, yielded that the crux of racial unity was for Black Americans to determine their own political struggle.

The element of racial solidarity spearheaded the development of the Black Church and other separatist organizations in the Black community. In one way, they were responding to the acute segregation in America that circumscribed their lives; in another, they responded to their own needs for self-government and the freedom to define their own potential. For those nationalists who did not yield to the temptation to emigrate to countries governed by Black leaders, segregated, autonomous institutions fulfilled those nationalist sentiments. It was with the latter sense of purpose that Blacks built their organizations that were expressions of their nationalism. Black leadership did emerge from these organizations which provided much of the sustenance to the early Black community. With nationalist leaders Blacks began to determine their political direction.

Cultural History and the Philosophy of Self-Determination

One of the most prodigious efforts of Black nationalism was the restoration of the dignity of Afro-Americans through the retrieval of African history. This recovery was important to both the psychological and political consciousness of Afro-Americans. Nationalists held a cyclical view of history asserting that just as Blacks ruled the ancient world, so they would once again. They argued that Africans, having long excelled in the arts and sciences, provided the foundation for western civilization. It was the African genius, in fact, that nurtured the foundation of Greek civilization. Nationalists further contended that African history proved the capabilities of Afro-Americans in self-determination. They pointed to the great African empires of Mali, Songhay, and Ghana that not only substantiated African legislative ability but also validated the African capacity for self-government. Nationalists further contended that the greatness of African history had been suppressed in order to continually exploit her descendants around the world.

> When we take a retrospective view of the arts and sciences—the wise legislators—the Pyramids, and other magnificent buildings—the turning of the channel of the river Nile, by the sons of Africa or of Ham, among whom learning originated, and was carried thence into Greece, where it was improved upon and refined.[31]

The center of the African ontological system was the belief that the natural and supernatural worlds represented a continuity to the purpose of life. The material world and the spiritual world "were all united in one comprehensive, invisible system that has its own laws which sustain the visible world and ordinary life for the good of all."[32] This world-view, this harmonious view of the natural order, was brought into conflict with the European political and economic expansionism of the 16th and 17th centuries. In the clash of technology, which culminated in the repeated raping of Africa's resources, was also the colliding of world-views. African people conquered, displaced, and scattered throughout the world is evidence of two worlds still grappling with competing ideologies.

By bringing their world-view in harmony once again with the universe, Afro-Americans will redeem themselves by once again restoring Africa's place in the sun. To nationalists, redemption was possible because Black enslavement was mutable. Once freed, Afro-Americans would regain their former stature. The enslavement of Afro-Americans had a redemptive value offering spiritual redemption, even a spiritual platform, by which Blacks would challenge their oppression. Psychological benefits provided the healing whereby Blacks could reclaim their history and rescue their dignity. This mutability of their circumstances formed the core of their philosophy of self-determination.

The philosophy of self-determination was the driving force behind Black nationalism. Moreover, it was the pragmatic outgrowth of nationalist expression of Black Americans. For Afro-Americans it meant that they could challenge, protest, and change the political conditions affecting their lives. And they were determined to do so. This expression took shape in the organizations that Afro-Americans founded in the early 1800s. Paramount to the focus on improving the Black community were these organizations' commitment to political protest. Most organizations of this time period served as ancillaries of the Black Church due to the Church's sphere of influence in the Black community. Still, the secular movement extended nationalism to the state and national levels. As state and national organizations developed, such as the National Negro Convention Movement (1830) and the State Convention Movement (1835), the spirituality of protest remained central to the fundamental concerns of Black Americans.

Although the decisive force was still the Black Church carrying the movement forward, Black organizations added a broader national focus to the political struggle. With national and state level organizations, the emergence of secular leadership was noticeable. Sacred and secular leadership provided continuity to the nationalist movement and enhanced its viability as a method of political protest. On the national level, the most prominent organization was the National Negro Convention Movement. Although founded specifically to deal with the cause of emigration, the movement dealt with the common concerns of emancipation, education, moral reform, and employment plaguing Black Americans.[33] With this focus, the movement hoped to achieve its goal of moral upliftment for all Black Americans. Although the movement had its stops and starts in the 1830s and 1840s, racial uplift was always the primary goal.

Nationalist expression was also evident on the state and local levels as well. The State Convention Movement, initiated in 1835, was an attempt by Black Americans to deal with their political and civil rights on state levels.[34] The practices of racism and the legal proscriptions surrounding the lives of Black Americans varied from state to state. State organizations challenged the legal apparatus of particular states. On the community level, there were a myriad of organizations reflecting a nationalist stance. There were mutual benefit societies, moral improvement societies, antislavery societies, and literary and self-improvement associations. These societies and associations, despite their cultural tone, dealt with those real issues in the Black community such as education, self-improvement, morality, financial needs for widows, and abolitionism.[35] It was their commitment to racial upliftment and self-determination that reflected their nationalism.

Conclusions and Summary

Black nationalism evolved from the oppression suffered by Afro-Americans in the early 1800s. At its core, nationalist thought challenged the political and social realities of Black life. For it was the daily confrontation of racism that shaped and defined the nationalist struggle. But Black nationalist thought and expression of that time also emanated from the needs of the Afro-Americans to define themselves as a people. Unquestionably, nationalism was a nurturing philosophy that empowered Blacks to contest injustice and criticize the hypocrisies in American democracy. However, nationalism was also the essence of who they were—their history, culture, and spirituality—as a people.

The ideological beginnings of Black nationalism reflected the assessment of Black Americans of their political plight. The overall theme of collective elevation (i.e., moral upliftment) embodied all of the nationalist strivings of Black Americans. It is with this definitive purpose that Black Americans struggled for their freedom. And the opposing forces were arduous, for racism and slavery were life-threatening to the Black community. Although racial discrimination varied from region to region, and as a result was frustratingly unpredictable, racism was clearly circumscribed oppression. Thus, early ideological beginnings was the clarion call of the nationalists in the Black community for freedom from racist oppression. Nationalists emphasized those themes of justice and liberation to counterpoise those forces of racism and oppression.

Inherent in Black nationalism were the ideological elements that provided its foundation. Religion and spirituality were the sources for its perpetual dynamism. Racial unity formed the underpinnings of nationalist thought and served as positive forces in the Black community uniting all Blacks despite disparate circumstances. Cultural history was the psychological and political reinforcement for a beleaguered people. Shoring up their dignity, it was the belief that the future of Afro-Americans was rooted in their past history of greatness. The pragmatic philosophy of self-determination was the backbone of the movement ensuring its organizational focus of Black Americans defining their struggle for themselves. At the heart of that struggle was Black nationalism giving meaning to the place of Black Americans in the universe.

Endnotes

1. Litwack, Leon F. (1961). *North of Slavery,* Chicago: The University of Chicago Press, 64; Foner, Philip S. (1983). *History of Black Americans,* vol. II, Westport: Greenwood Press, 191–3.

2. Augustine, *The Colored American,* Schomburg Center for Research in Black Culture, 28 July 1838 (Note: Augustine is Lewis Woodson who used the name as a pseudonym).

3. Genovese, Eugene D. *The World the Slaveholders Made,* New York: Vintage Books, 3–10.

4. Litwack, 153.

5. Augustine, *The Colored American,* 10 February 1838; and Tate, Gayle T., (1984). *Tangled Vines: Ideological Interpretations of Afro-Americans in the Nineteenth Century,* PhD dissertation, City University of New York, 121–3.

6. Augustine, ibid.

7. Stewart, Maria W. (1832). *Productions of Mrs. Maria W. Stewart*, Boston, 1835, Lecture delivered at Franklin Hall, Boston, 51–2.

8. Ibid., 19. The pamphlet entitled "Religion and the Pure Principles of Morality, the Sure Foundation on Which We Must Build," 1831, has been included in the larger, more comprehensive *Productions*.

9. Ibid., 9.

10. Young, Robert Alexander. The Ethiopian Manifesto, found in Sterling Stuckey's *The Ideological Origins of Black Nationalism*, Boston: Beacon Press, 1972, 37.

11. Ibid., 34.

12. Stewart, 6.

13. Ibid., 16.

14. Sterling, 105–8.

15. Sterling, Dorothy (ed.). *We Are Your Sisters: Black Women in the Nineteenth Century*, New York: W. W. Norton & Company, 105; Giddings, Paula. (1984). *When and Where I Enter: The Impact of Black Women on Race and Sex in America*, New York: Bantam Books, 49–50; and Porter, Dorothy. (1936). "The Organized Educational Activities of Negro Literary Societies, 1828–1846" *Journal of Negro Education*, 5 (October) 279, 281, 283, 287.

16. Stewart, 6.

17. Ibid., 19.

18. Walker, 21.

19. Stewart, 5.

20. Carlisle, Robert. (1975). *The Roots of Black Nationalism*, New York: Kennikat Press Corp., 50–4; Foner, 302–3; Harding, Vincent. *There Is A River*, New York: Random House. 58–9, 192–3, 214; and Lynch, Hollis R. (1968). "Pan-Negro Nationalism in the New World, Before 1862," in August Meier and Elliott Rudwick, (eds.), *The Making of Black America*, vol. 1, New York: Atheneum, 44–5.

21. Carlisle, ibid.

22. Walker, 47.

23. Ibid., 56.

24. Foner, vol. II, chapter 7, "Slave Resistance in the Antebellum South"; Harding, 103–8; and Davis, Angela. "Reflections in the Black Woman's Role in the Community of Slaves" in *The Black Scholar*, 12, 12 (November/December): 2–15.

25. Wilmore, Gayraud S. (1983). *Black Religion and Black Radicalism*, New York: Orbis Books, 2nd ed. 51–2.

26. McClain, William B. (1974). "Free Style and A Closer Relationship to Life," in *The Black Experience in Religion*, C. Eric Lincoln, (ed.), New York: Anchor Press, 5.

27. Fordham, Monroe. (1975). *Major Themes in Northern Black Religious Thought, 1800–1860*, New York: Exposition Press, 37–41.

28. Walker, 48–9.

29. Stewart, 15.

30. Augustine, *The Colored American*, 15 December 1837.

31. Walker, 19.

32. Wilmore, 19.

33. Bell, Howard. (ed.). Minutes of the Proceedings of the National Negro Conventions, 1830–1864; 1830, 1831, 1834, 1836 conventions; and Harding, 138–9.

34. Foner, 322–3.

35. Foner, 239–249; Sterling, 104–119; and Porter, 288.

Chapter 27

Memories of the Civil War in Popular Song

Paul Johnson Edwards

Introduction

Music compositions, arrangements, and lyrics mirror the complex individual and institutional sentiments, problems, politics, and socio-economic conditions and shifts of the time period in which it is created. Music reveals the temperament of the era and becomes integral to historical interpretations of a time period. Popular song, the music of the masses, is highly responsive to the changing moods of the times and, as such, reveals an important critique and perception of the era, but one that could differ, perhaps significantly, from those offered by elites and their cultural products. However, it is this popular perception that influences how Americans remember the Civil War. As James Davis states in the anthology *Music and History*:

> Much Civil War music was used to bind the people, either through political propaganda or by means of declaring one's loyalties . . . Singing patriotic songs at rallies and at home was a way for citizens to participate in the war, to be intimately involved in something that was connected to the war movement without being on the front lines.[1]

In this article, I examine the specific issues of trauma, memory, and cultural shifts as they appear in music. Specifically, I analyze the popular song of the Civil War era as well as contemporary popular songs that continue the narrative themes and traditions of the war. By comparing the past and present structure and function of this music, I reveal how music works to contain, expand, and control our understanding of the Civil War.

The Civil War decimated the South, took over 600,000 American lives, and altered the social, political, and cultural landscape of the United States. The high death toll challenged the way Americans previously conceived of mortality, the South struggled with its identity and the purpose of secession, and women took up a new position within American culture that had denied them any formal status and participation in male spheres of influence. This article analyzes how music helped shape these subjects, not only during the Civil War era, but also in contemporary popular music.

As the United States experienced massive loss of life and the burgeoning nature of the military industry, the one major industry that continued to prosper was music publishing. Both the North and South published a treasure trove of music. As John Tasker Howard wrote in his study of American music history, the Civil War era produced so many songs that they "could be arranged in proper sequence to form an actual history of the conflict; its events, its principal characters, and the ideals and principles of the opposing sides."[2] This collection of music expressed a shared community during the Civil War so powerfully that contemporary music has retained concepts and ideals of the Civil War into the present.

During the Civil War music was produced for a variety of purposes, from patriotic marches, to songs of secessionism to songs for victorious returns. Drew Gilpin Faust notes that the limited literacy of the Southern population led to a culture that relied heavily on spoken accounts as a way of disseminating information. In understanding the history of the Confederacy, music became the most important example of "southern orality." As music was the most produced publication in the South during the war, it became the main mode through which soldiers and those at home could share in an "imagined community." Even when sheet music was unavailable, the nature of music (including meter, rhythm, and rhyme) allowed for the oral tradition to carry on when songs in print were unavailable.[3]

As Reconstruction turned into Jim Crow racial terrorism and segregation, the nation's political and economic power structures turned their focus away from America's black population. Instead, the nation turned to century spanning stereotypes of black inferiority and a national fear of black freedom and empowerment. As these shifts toward Jim Crow segregation and discrimination occurred and became fixed in the national consciousness and culture, the nation re-shaped the Civil War and black freedom as national tragedies. Therefore, it should not surprise scholars of American and African American cultural history that the music and the musical memories of the Civil War have constructed African Americans out of the story of the war. Thus, this article does not seek to reclaim the African American construction of the Civil War in music.

Instead of examining the music of the Civil War as expressed within the African American experience, this article demonstrates the central role that African Americans have played in shaping the broad landscape of American culture. While many of the songs analyzed in this article do not explicitly mention slavery, slaves, or the freedom that black people proclaimed as soon as Union troops drew near, this article demonstrates that the presence of black people defined America, its Civil War, and its music. The issues I address in this article—the Good Death, the Lost Cause, and Gender—all resonate within the realities and constructions of African American slavery and freedom.

While African Americans claimed the Civil War as their battle for freedom other people understood the war as a conflict over national sovereignty versus states' rights or a war between hostile economic interests. The Civil War was also a struggle over social and cultural difference, where two differing value systems clashed to assert which one was morally superior. Slavery as a positive good or slavery as an ideological and spiritual abomination stood at the center of the moral argument. For example, the image of the Confederate Battle Flag still elicits contentious meanings: where one might see a symbol of slavery, others see the memory of rebellion against a tyrannical federal government.[4] Similarly, a song such as "Dixie" poses questions of intent and content. Is it a racist song, an important cultural marker that epitomizes the social structure of the South, or is it both? Analyzing songs such as "Dixie," this article connects the Civil War era's markers: mortality, regionalism, and gender as they relate to contemporary music. It reveals how twentieth and twenty-first century songs continue to focus on the Civil War and also use the same themes which concerned songwriters a century earlier.

The Good Death in the Civil War Song

In Drew Faust's book *This Republic of Suffering*, she posits that the Civil War marks a turning point in how white Americans understood death. For Americans, "loss became commonplace; death was no longer encountered individually; death's threat, its proximity, and its actuality became the most widely shared of the war's experience."[5] Music offered the nation a medium to express the meaning of death.

From 1861–1865 2.1 million northerners and 880,000 southerners fought in the Civil War. By war's end over 600,000 people had lost their lives fighting in the conflict. Entering into warfare, drafted soldiers had to contemplate what it meant to fight and what it meant to die. In this aspect men joined in the tradition of *ars moriendi*. Using Jeremy Taylor's *The Rule and Exercise of Holy Dying*, Faust explains "how to give one's soul 'gladlye and willfully [sic].'"[6] The Good Death became an important concept for those at home and those in battle. When young men fought and died far from home and without family, fellow soldiers, nurses, chaplains, and doctors had to carry on the tasks that would have been family responsibilities. Those who were dying spoke of their religious faith as well as their willing and honorable sacrifice for their country. In their capacity as a soldier's family, those who witnessed the death took it upon themselves to pass on the word to the family. For those in the heat of battle, the best that they could do was to keep paper on hand in order to pen a letter as they prepared for death. Others penned letters before going into battle. With so many in the field experiencing death around them, it is not surprising that the subject of "letters home" permeated Civil War songs and in many ways became their own genre.[7]

Faust comments that "Death transformed the American nation as well as the hundreds of thousands of individuals directly affected by loss."[8] It is this transformation that created the language that persists in American music's reconstruction of the Civil War narrative. Songs of the era were unafraid of tackling the issue of death. Although the music from the era ranged from minstrel music ("Dixie" and "Kingdom Come,

Year of the Jubiloh"), to marches ("Tramp, Tramp, Tramp"), room was made for songs of the Good Death ("Just Before the Battle, Mother" and "Dead on the Battle Field"). The songs of the Good Death did not stray from gruesome detail despite the fact that the soldiers singing the song around a campfire one night could be fighting and dying the next morning. These fictional songs quote and recall those who have passed. Each song recalls their service and their willingness to fight and those who weep are those outside the battle who recognize the important of the soldier's sacrifice. "Dead on the Battle Field" lauds the soldier who is

> Dead upon the battlefield
> The bravest of the brave
> In the foremost ranks he nobly fought
> And found a soldier's grave.
> His country mourns his loss
> A nation o'er him weeps.
> But glory guilds the honored name
> Our fond remembrance keeps.[9]

The song is written as a eulogy to one of the thousands of dead soldiers. The ubiquitous experience of death during the 1860s made this song and others like it a way for soldiers to retain faith in their cause as well as a way to remember those who had died. The song not only honors the correct sociological responses of the soldier and the nation, but it also infers that the soldier has attained immortality through his service and his death.

Faust's concept of the "imagined community" may be the best way to understand how contemporary songs are able to portray the concepts that come from a previous era.[10] Music has the ability not only to carry a message or a narrative, but also to personify the times in which we live. Journalists and music critics have commented on how often songs rely on the tropes of love as a way of exploring a larger world, but through even more specific songs—even songs of war and death—we can discover America's cultural history.

Contemporary popular songs continue to construct the same narrative around the concept of the Good Death. One of the best examples of this is a song that the folklorist A. P. Carter found called "When the Roses Bloom Again."[11] Carter's lyrics were modified by Woody Guthrie and proliferated by the band Wilco as a b-side from the Woody Guthrie archive project *Mermaid Avenue* in the late 1990s.[12] The song tells the story of an officer who leaves a loved one behind and dies in the midst of battle. The ending of the song exemplifies a Good Death; the officer dies with full mental and spiritual faculties and without fear.

For the living, the death of a soldier added to the work at the end of the battle. For the first time in United States history the nation had to deal with such an overwhelming loss of life. Faust makes it clear that although the noble death of a soldier was important, so was respect for the deceased body. To Americans during the Civil War era, the body was sacred. Officials also made an effort to dispose of dead bodies to protect public health. Whenever they were able to do so, both sides took time to bury the dead after battle and even placed the bodies into coffins. However as the war worsened, there was neither labor nor resources to ensure proper burials. Up to the end of the war, figuring out how to handle the burial of soldiers was a constant concern.[13]

The concept of "Burying" from the Civil War era has been reclaimed in modern song. "Yankee Bayonet (I Will Be Home Then),"[14] written in 2006 by the band the Decemberists, relies on a similar rhetoric of leaving bodies to decompose. This Confederate soldier's life ends like that of 300,000 others who remained without proper burial due to the war reality of too meager resources. Where the soldier sings lines such as "Look for me when the sun-bright swallow/Sings upon the birch bow high," his wife responds with "But you are in the ground with the wolves and the weevils/All a-chew on your bones so dry."[15] What makes this song so peculiar is the placement of the narrative. This story is not told from the point of view of a dying soldier or of a soldier about to go off to battle. The unburied body of the dead soldier tells the story. The lyrics reveal a real fear and reality that bodies would not be properly handled after death.

Regionalism, Confederate Nationalism, and the Lost Cause

The songs of the Civil War not only retold stories of battles and the different ideals for which each side fought, but they also outlined the prevalent social and political movements that dictated the lives of Southerners after the Civil War. Whereas some songs written during the war focused specifically on recapturing events, the exaltation of military and political leaders, or boosting morale, others focused on the Lost Cause.

James McPherson describes the Lost Cause as the Confederacy's understanding that the loss of the war was due not only to external forces but also to forces within. McPherson explains that the internal defeat or the "loss of the will to fight" came through after the Fall of 1863 with Northern victories at Gettysburg, Vicksburg, and Chattanooga and expanded with the capture of Atlanta and Sheridan's defeat of Early's army in the Shenandoah Valley. However, what McPherson ultimately argues is that each issue of the Lost Cause movement is a fallacy. At the outset of the war it was the North that was first seized by a feeling of defeatism for the first few years of the war.

In Gary Gallagher and Alan Nolan's compendium of essays, *The Myth of the Lost Cause and Civil War History*, Nolan finds that the Lost Cause narrative began shortly after the war ended. The term, according to Gallagher, was coined by Edward A. Pollard and first appeared in his 1867 publication, *The Lost Cause: The Standard Southern History of the War of the Confederates*. The entire point of Nolan's argument is that the Lost Cause is a myth that has overridden and erased the history of the cause of the Civil War and that the victims of the myth have primarily been the civilian, the common soldier and, I would add, African Americans. Nolan explains that by rewriting the history, it is no longer the narrative of 300,000 deaths of those who fought for the preservation or dissolution of the Union. Retained in this myth is the character of Southerners as intrinsically and racially different, having come from superior and nobler Norman stock than the Anglo-Saxon Northerners.[16] Music helped to create and perpetuate the idea of the Lost Cause. Confederate nationalism and the Lost Cause myth have created a musical dialogue in which music has become harbored in the memory of the short-lived nation-state. The ideas first created during the 1860s in the South have, for better or worse, become part of the American historical narrative; the ideas of the Lost Cause have become part of popular history and culture.

The Lost Cause has been referred to as the "Southern myth," "myth of the Lost Cause," and "the Lost Cause myth." However, the beliefs of the Lost Cause vary according to motives for the start of the war and reasons for the loss of the war. One of the most explored tenets of the Lost Cause is the belief that slavery was not an issue of secession. In spite of the historical evidence that the South sought to expand slavery rather than end it, this argument asserted that slavery was a benign institution in which masters were paternal figures to the slaves and that slave states would, and perhaps should, gradually abolish slavery.[17] However, another part of the Lost Cause myth does paint the fight as a poor man's fight for a rich man's war, specifically arguing that non-slaveholders were fighting for the aristocratic slave owners. Another important aspect of the Lost Cause is the belief in Southern nobility in military campaigns and the hagiography of Stonewall Jackson and Robert E. Lee as opposed to the brutality of Sherman, Sheridan, and Grant, especially Grant's total war policies. Romanticizing not only generals and officers, but also the ordinary soldier, played a major role in constructing the Civil War as a cause with the highest and noblest purpose. Unable to compete with the Northern military cultural and economic juggernaut, the South feared the Northern threat to its way of life and imagined itself to be the North's moral and cultural superior.[18]

The Confederacy is rarely viewed as its own nation-state. Drew Gilpin Faust has proved in her studies that the Confederacy had begun to establish not only its own brand of republican democracy, but it had also worked on creating national identity by the end of 1860. One of the most compelling and subversive points in creating rhetoric of nationhood for the Confederacy was through music. "I Wish I Was in Dixie," a Northern minstrel song that became the anthem of the Southern nation; "I'm A Good Old Rebel," a Reconstruction-era song; and Hank Williams Jr.'s twentieth-century song, "If the South Woulda Won," are all songs that return to the issue of Southern nationhood. These songs show that beyond the political and economic repercussions of forming a new government, the South made an earnest attempt to create, culturally as well as politically, a new nation.

One of America's biggest myths has permeated and pervaded popular music and has become one of the firmly held beliefs in American popular history. As mentioned Mark LaSalle's review of the Civil War movie *Cold Mountain*,

> The South lost the Civil War, but they've won the literature ever since. They even won Ken Burns' "Civil War" documentary . . . The lost cause of the South has become enshrined as noble, a last gasp of romance and gentility soon to be swept under by an ungainly tide of urbanization, industrialization and immigration.[19]

This myth lies at the center of the absence of Civil War motifs within African American music and the absence of African Americans in white America's Civil War music. LaSalle illuminates the ways in which popular history has become the de facto Civil War history. As the conflict was between sections of the United States, romanticizing the event has become a way for white Americans to deal with the harsher truth of Civil War and American history: slavery. Romantic views of the Civil War have influenced musicians' understanding of the events of the war and how that subverted view has fed into the broader pathos about the war, the antebellum era, and slavery itself.

"Dixie" and the Birth of a Southern Nation

"I Wish I Was in Dixie" was written during the antebellum era in New York City by Daniel Decatur Emmett. "Dixie" traveled from the Northern minstrel stage to the South where it became the anthem of Southern secession. The song helped establish the word "Dixie" as a reference to the South. The song became so pervasive within the Lost Cause myth that the song was still sung at my mother's predominantly white high school in Columbus, Georgia, in the 1970s until African American football players threatened to leave the team if the song and the Confederate flag remained at pep rallies. The song and flag were quickly banned from the school.

The popularity of the song arose from Northern minstrel shows performed first in New York by Bryant's Minstrels.[20] Its continued popularity during the antebellum period points to several elements that would come to define the myth of the Lost Cause. Whereas the first verse portrays a wistful yearning to return to the South, the remaining lyrics focus on the story of a woman who has her heart broken. The narrator focuses on the character of a picturesque South, and, indeed creates a pastoral image of southern culture into the American imagination.

The song was popular first in the North, but it became a useful song for the South as a militant call during the Civil War. For example, a version was titled "Dixie War Song":

> Hear ye not the sounds of battle,
> Sabres clash and muskets rattle?
> To arms! To arms! To arms in Dixie!
> Hostile footsteps on our border,
> Hostile columns treat in order
> To arms! To arms! To arms in Dixie![21]

Another version, called "The Bayou City Guards' Dixie" specifically targeted Abraham Lincoln:

> You've heard of Abe, the gay deceiver,
> Who went to Sumter to relieve her;
> Look away! Look away! Look away! Dixie land.
> But Beauregard said, "Save your bacon
> Sumter's ours and must be taken!"
> Look away! Look away! Look away! Dixie land.[22]

The North used the song with new lyrics that reflected the changing mood as slavery became a focus of the war. "Dixie Unionized" mentions slavery explicitly. "O! I'm glad I live in a land of freedom / Where we have no slave nor do we need them."[23] Although the original song reflects the myth of slavery as benign and paternalistic, and slaves as happy servants, its tune and words move effortlessly from the Northern minstrel show to become the unofficial anthem of the Confederate States of America. "Dixie" represents one of the few Northern antebellum minstrel songs that Southerners trusted. Prior to adopting "Dixie" as a national or regional anthem, Southerners considered minstrel shows politically suspect. During the first decade of minstrel shows (1843–1853), performances went beyond romanticizing the plantation and its paternal nature. These shows showed slaves tricking and sabotaging their masters' plans and plantations. It was not uncommon to see Gabriel Prosser or Nat Turner used in several skits.[24]

Understanding this transformation of Northern minstrelsy into Southern anthem lies within the nature and history of minstrel shows. Believed to have started in 1843, the Virginia Minstrels put on the first burnt cork performance in New York City's Bowery Amphitheater. The show claimed to be an evening of "Ethiopian entertainment" and soon thousands of ensembles were performing this stylized entertainment genre. The shows revealed how race relations were perceived by the white imagination of the time. The Englishman Charles Matthews is most noted for creating the caricatures of black culture from his studies of slaves in 1822 which became the basis of the character Jim Crow and the Zip Coon. Perhaps what is most notable about the song "The Zip Coon" is how the character is portrayed as a "larned skolar [sic]" who goes on to become President of the United States.[25] However, during the Civil War, minstrel music stuck rather closely to the racist caricatures of Blacks even as Northern minstrel composers like Stephen Foster wrote songs for Colored Regiments.

The nature of a war between the North and South turned minstrelsy from a Northern showcase into a Southern dominated performance.[26] As minstrel shows usually glorified the life of Southerners, it no longer became appropriate for Northerners to depict the enemy in such a way. What "Dixie" reveals is in the nature of what it does not reveal. The characters who sang this song were not concerned with the political or socio-logical world in which they lived. Instead Emmett's song created a false cultural identity for Blacks in the South. The song rationalized and solidified the South's political and social position, which Faust analyzes at length, as integral to forming the Confederacy. Minstrelsy reconfirmed the place of slaves in the nation as well as formed the basis of how the Lost Cause myth became such an integral part of the post-War South. In its lyrics, the song wishes for a return to the old ways. It is this romantic belief that makes the song have such a strong emotional pull as the Confederate national anthem. Unlike the "Battle Hymn of the Republic," "Dixie" invokes memories of home and the overall song is easy enough for soldiers or civilian groups to sing without practice, unlike the more elaborate orchestration of the "Battle Hymn." Instead, this song with its "land of cotton" reminds the listener and singer of the origins of the song. "Dixie" created the picturesque language that became the trademark of songs and other media interpretations of Southern living.

The most significant change to "Dixie" is how the song became less reliant on the vernacular and was replaced with standard American English. The original lyrics were sung as:

> I wish I was in de land ob cotton
> Old times dar am not forgotten
> Look away! Look away! Look away! Dixie land
> In Dixie land whar I was born in
> Early on one frosty mornin'
> Look away! Look away! Look away! Dixie land[27]

The change was due, as Faust notes, to the Confederacy's efforts to establish a national identity. Part of their attempt to create national consciousness was to get rid of "Yankee degeneracies [sic]" and caricatured "Africanisms."[28]

Dixon, "Dixie," and *The Clansmen*

"Dixie" mirrored the world of Southern cultural reclamation with the same lens that defined the post-war South. Almost half a century after the rise of "Dixie," Thomas Dixon, Jr., a North Carolina politician, lawyer, minister, playwright, and author, wrote *The Clansmen* in 1905. Dixon's book relied on the Southern myths that rationalized slavery and perverted history to turn heroes into villains and villains into heroes. *The Clansmen* rewrote Reconstruction history into an era in which black men robbed white men of their political power. When Dixon turned the book into the film, *Birth of a Nation* directed by D.W. Griffith, he sought approval and endorsements from governors and other politicians, including his former classmate, Woodrow Wilson.

"Dixie" became pertinent to Dixon's attempts to reconfigure Southern ideas of the war and his active attempt to recreate an innocent South where the land of cotton was noble and chivalrous. More to the point, the song has become a relic of the antebellum South and worked within the framework of the Lost Cause simply by playing within the lyrical world that was cohabitated by Dixon's book *The Clansmen*. As "Dixie" first created the imagined perfect South, Dixon's work refashioned history to trump reality with fiction. What the South really wanted was white paternity, not Dixon's picture of black tyranny enforced by the federal government. Yet black tyranny made the South embrace a memory of slavery reconfigured as white paternity and "darkies" in their proper, subordinate place.

Oh, I'm a Good Old Rebel

A Confederate officer, Major Innes Randolph, wrote "Good Old Rebel" shortly after the end of the Civil War. The song typifies many of the tenets of the Lost Cause movement specifically through the narrator's lack of apology or need for reconciliation. The narrator simply points to the new problems created by the Northern invasion of the South. This song reveals the supposed plight of the common Southern man and perverts the history of the war by focusing on perceived Northern aggression. The narrator holds contempt for the Freedman's Bureau, the primary symbol federal protection of black rights, but mentions how the North has stolen his freedom. Nolan asserts that part of the myth of the Lost Cause was the idealization of the Confederate soldier. That the confederate soldier "was invariably heroic, indefatigable, gallant and law-abiding,"[29] became the perception of the fighting force of the Confederacy. However, in Innes Randolph's song we have a narrator that finds grievance with the North. These sentiments fit within the Lost Cause myth, not only in their contempt for the North, but specifically in the absence of slavery as a central or even peripheral theme.

Hank Williams Jr.'s South

Hank Williams Jr.'s 1988 song, "If the South Woulda Won," provides an interesting case study considering the song was written a century after "I'm a Good Ol' Rebel." The song is steeped in two conflicting eras. One era wishes to return to a simpler time without, what Mark LaSalle sees as, the issues of "immigration, industrialization and urbanization."[30] The other is the modern era of Southern iconography. The musical form follows this conflict as it travels from playing "Dixie," to Southern rock, to fiddle, to slide guitar, and finally to a New Orleans horn section.

Perhaps one of the most noticeable qualities of Hank Williams, Jr.'s song is that it only implicitly mentions the Civil War, without the clear bitterness expressed in "Good Old Rebel." Williams follows the narrative of the Lost Cause straight to its twentieth-century conclusion. He works against the North's cultural and political defeat of the South. Within the lyrics, Williams explicates how the South has been unable to express itself within a cultural framework. He admits that even though Hank Williams, Sr. isn't on the hundred dollar bill, two Virginians and a Carolinian do grace American currency (i.e., Washington, Jefferson, and Jackson, respectively). However, Williams resides in the current era where he regrets that the cultural significance of the South remains in the past. The recollection is a culturally nostalgic one, referring to 1950s era Southern culture, Patsy Cline, Elvis Presley, and Hank Williams, Sr.

As Williams's music expresses various cultural backgrounds of the South from Appalachian fiddles to Lynyrd Skynyrd guitar riffs, the vocal delivery is oddly un-Southern. Williams travelled around the South, yet he chose a more midwestern accent for "If the South Woulda Won." Williams's vocal delivery aimed for greater appeal beyond a stylized Southern drawl. He chose a voice that would be widely accepted, not only in the South, but also in the North. Williams needed to create this song with a universal appeal by creating a narrative voice with a muted Southern accent, yet he did so in a pro-Confederate song. Williams's effort to take a pro-Confederate song to a national audience reveals how much the national consciousness and imagination could embrace Southern antebellum culture—slavery, Lost Cause, and the myths created around each of these.

A Return to *Cold Mountain* and Southern Hospitality

The medium of film provides valuable insights into how Americans view their own history. A plethora of films address the Civil War within several different perspectives, from *Glory*'s depiction of a black infantry unit to *Gods and Generals* that focuses on the beginning of the Civil War. *Cold Mountain*, directed by Anthony Minghella, fits the specific criteria for this study: the film's music claims to reflect authentic Civil War era life and the film represents recent historical interpretations of the Civil War.[31] It is this point that makes the film an appropriate topic for an analysis of the historicity of the Lost Cause, a topic which film critics rarely mentioned. Instead critics compared the film to *Gone with the Wind*, specifically highlighting both film's involved love story and the setting of the failing Confederacy. However, *New York Times* critic A. O. Scott briefly touches the issue of authenticity, although from an academic perspective, he may have missed the point:

> *"Cold Mountain," which stars Jude Law and Nicole Kidman as would-be lovers separated by the cruelty and privation of the American Civil War, distinguishes itself from such middlebrow conversation-stoppers. Its sober good taste is enlivened by large doses of intelligence and humor, and even a touch of authentic cinematic grandeur.*[32]

Scott briefly mentions an issue important to the academic study of a historical narrative: authenticity. Scott points out the tension between the film's narrative and its historical accuracy. Even more problematic for academics is the implication that narrative should have precedence over authenticity.

In his pursuit of the most compelling narrative, Minghella created a movie that embraces the Lost Cause myth at the expense of authenticity and historical accuracy. *Cold Mountain* presents itself specifically as a Southern tale, taking place primarily in Virginia and North Carolina. The story is a dual narrative, focusing on the character Ada, a woman of privilege who struggles to sustain her land on Cold Mountain after the death of her father. The other half of the narrative follows W. P. Inman, a native of Cold Mountain who volunteers for the Confederacy. The majority of the story follows Inman's desertion as he tries to return to Cold Mountain and Ada. Throughout the film, Inman confronts numerous characters that become personifications of the authentic and the inauthentic South.

The movie begins with Union soldiers placing dynamite underground, below Southern lines at the Siege of Petersburg in 1864. As the men place the explosives, the camera slowly pans up through the dirt to the Southern line waiting in trenches. In this opening shot, the film immediately portrays Union troops as deceitful and unfair as they decide to use a cowardly tactic, deception, rather than bravery. The film also leaves out the story of black soldiers who had been trained to run around the crater created by the blast; the lead general sent in the white soldiers instead. After the explosives detonate, these untrained troops rush into the crater, unwittingly trapping themselves as the Confederates have a "turkey shoot." What this scene and others portray of Union soldiers is that they are villainous and do not have the moral fiber and character common among Southern men. As the film continues, the audience gets flashbacks to Inman first meeting Ada at Cold Mountain. Nicole Kidman narrates this section, explaining that Ada and her father moved to Cold Mountain to leave behind "slaves, corsets and cotton." This immediately adds sympathy to Ada's character as she characterizes herself as someone opposed to racism and also sexism. However, Ada's family does own slaves and she does wear corsets.

As Inman recovers from the explosion from the battle, he recalls singing with Ada in church. Appropriate for the battle that Inman fights and for the scene of the Battle of the Crater, "Idumea" is a song of death that resembles the opening barrage of violence in the film, *Saving Private Ryan*.

However, the film presents Jude Law's character with various Homeric challenges on his return home. Each one of these vignettes portrays the cowardice of those who did not fight: from Giovanni Ribisi's character who traps deserters to Philip Seymour Hoffman's character who tries to drown a slave girl he impregnated. As Inman's character encounters these men and more, he faces the tragedy of what has become of the South when the "good men" have all gone off to fight the war. As Inman makes his way home, Ada is continually confronted by a member of the Home Guard named Teague. His only aspirations are to own Cold Mountain and to win over Ada. However, his methods of dealing with deserters and their families are too cruel for Ada to love Teague as she would love Inman. At the climax of the film Inman and Teague square off, and Inman successfully kills Teague but is mortally wounded in the process. He dies in Ada's arms. At the close of the film we see Ada with a child that was conceived from Inman and Ada's one night together.

What Inman's odyssey teaches the viewer is that while noble Southern men were off fighting for their country, less noble creatures infiltrated the South and corrupted the land of Dixie. And although men like Inman were deserters, they returned home to correct the wrongs of those who had polluted the tranquility of Southern life. The film asserts that although men act like Inman by deserting the military in order take care of the "home," these men sacrificed the noble parts of themselves to protect the South.

Truth and Romance

Songs such as "Dixie" helped infuse a generation of Southerners with specific ideas and views of what it meant to be Southern. The literature and films of the Lost Cause only furthered the ideas that were first created in such forms as published music. By creating a specific cultural history that rivals "real history," musicians and other artists have embraced the authenticity within the South's "imagined community" and within the Civil War's multivalent narratives. Instead of having to confront past generations' involvement with the Civil War or even with twentieth-century civil rights, musicians can portray a history that is unashamed of or unconcerned with the morally ambiguous.

Gendering War

During the Civil War period, the dynamics of gender roles changed with American views on regional identity and the concept of life and death. The war especially disrupted gender conventions in the South where little had changed to redefine public and private spheres or masculine and feminine. As Drew Faust writes in *Mothers of Invention*:

> The North . . . had inaugurated its reexamination of gender assumptions more than a generation earlier, as women's rights advocates began to destabilize traditional understandings of men's and women's roles. In the south, by contrast, emergent nineteenth-century feminism had by 1861 exerted almost no impact, and understandings of womanhood had remained rigidly biological and therefore seemingly natural and immutable. In the eyes of many of the South's defenders, this contrast was in itself evidence of the superiority of southern civilization and of the dangerous tendencies inherent in the northern way of life.[33]

In her book *Manifest Manhood and the Antebellum American Empire*, Amy Greenberg investigates the meaning of manifest destiny for American men and women in the years between the U.S.–Mexico and Civil Wars. To Greenberg, restrained manhood

> was practiced by men in the North and South who grounded their identities in their families, in the evangelical practice of their Protestant faith, and in success in the business world. Their masculine practices valued expertise. Restrained men were strong proponents of domesticity or 'true womanhood.' The belief that the domestic household was the moral center of the world, and the wife and mother its moral compass . . . They were generally repulsed by the violent blood sports that captivated many urban working men.[34]

In contrast to that, there is martial manhood where men

> rejected the moral standards that guided restrained men; they often drank to excess with pride, and they reveled in their physical strength and ability to dominate both men and women . . . they were not, in general, supporters of the moral superiority of women and the values of domesticity. Martial men believed that the masculine qualities of strength, aggression, and even violence, better defined true man than did the firm and upright manliness of restrained men.[35]

While Civil War songs defined men in martial terms of bravery and death, they also underscored men's desire to return to the domesticity of their home lives. These men longed for home: returning to a wife who had waited and managed the home and returning to his tasks as husband.[36] These songs reflected a desire for antebellum gender ideals, especially since women also confronted their own hardships and shifting roles during the war. As Confederate soldiers moved from state to state, displaced women took inverse trips around the South moving farther away from home as the battlefield continually encroached upon her domestic sphere. Elite women could afford to move from city to city as the war began to engulf the South. These trips created a new social dynamic as elite women interacted with working class, landless, and poor Whites. Rather than using the urgency of war as a means of creating a sense of Southern gender solidarity, elite women clung even more tenaciously to their social status and lower class women saw the fleeing Southern belles as cowards. To people of the low country, elites were "refugees," women unwilling to take a stand at their home. Making class distinctions even more complicated, elite women had no choice but to accept hospitality offered by poorer households who could not afford to flee. Such hospitality proved especially costly as the price of home goods rose uncontrollably.[37]

Womanhood: Go fight for us, we'll pray for you. Our mothers did so before us.

Prior to the Civil War, American society expected middle class and elite white women to refrain from activities outside the domestic sphere, with the exception of institutions, like the church, that blurred public and private boundaries and where society expected women to be charitable, moral caretakers of the public good. However, the mobilization of men during the war required that women take on larger roles in the public sphere. In spite of women's expanding roles, or perhaps because of it, men's narration in Southern songs sought to idealize antebellum ideas of Southern women's roles in the domestic sphere.

As expounded in Faust's book, *Mothers of Invention*, the elite women in the South during the Civil War took a larger role in political and social spheres. She writes: "War necessitated significant alterations—even perversions—of this ideology of behavior and identity."[38] In Philadelphia, women worked not only for churches, but also operated their own societies to address issues of slavery, alcoholism, immigration, and slavery.[39] Whereas women of the North had been working in charitable benefit societies since the founding of the nation, the Southern caste system did not present a similar range and depth of opportunities for Southern women to work in urban aid institutions. The abolition of slavery was certainly not among the list of issues discussed in Southern elite white women's circles. However, as the war continued and the number of men dwindled, Southern white women took the place of men in voluntary associations.

As most Civil War songs were written by men, although not necessarily men on the field of battle, these songs dealt not only with fighting the enemy, but also with hopes of returning to an unchanged home front. The songs that idealized the home constructed women's readiness to fulfill their traditional antebellum duties, but the war had pushed women into the public sphere as much as it had men. In doing so, the war changed women and their roles.

Even more importantly, the analysis of white Southern elite gender roles ignores the centrality of slave labor that defined the Southern micro and macro economy, i.e., the domestic and public spheres. The absence of white males in the South during the war created an absence of white male authority and control over slaves, many of whom fled to the closest Union lines in a bid for freedom. They presumed, like Frederick Douglass, that black freedom lay at the heart of the Union cause.[40] What the South bemoaned and resented was not only the change in gender roles, but the stark reality of the region's utter dependence on black labor.

For Duty Calls Your Sweetheart's Name Again: Honor, Manhood, and Antebellum America

As the battles pushed the Confederacy farther and farther toward economic and military defeat and disaster, women fought secession battles on the home front. Expressing their struggles in songs and poetry, women asked the Confederacy to recall their men and to send them home. In their desire for the return of their fighting men, white Southern women used several Civil War songs in their fight for the return of domesticity and in so doing, masked the reality that such domesticity also required the return of slavery.

The Civil War was the last war the nation fought exclusively on American soil. The war provided an interesting social dynamic between those on the home front and those on the frontlines. It was possible and common for those at home to share letters with soldiers who were stationed in close proximity to home. Faust finds that in their separation, men and women developed a new understanding of gendered spheres. Distanced for long periods of time from daughters, wives, and lovers, men longed for the old order. In their letters home, men from elite households directed the women they left behind to maintain order in the household, i.e., to maintain authority and control over slaves. Women worked to keep the household the way their husbands remembered it. But as the war eroded the Southern economy and infrastructure, it also undermined the elite lifestyle of the planter class. In the absence of patriarchal order elite white Southern women grew accustomed to roles that they had never occupied. Southern elite women also took on responsibilities previously deemed to have been the work of men and "Yankee women." For many women this shift in responsibility was so distressing that they wrote to their husbands on the front to ask advice on what to do. In response to these letters, many men made an attempt to defer having women engage in such work; many men wanted their wives and daughters to keep within the limits of the domestic sphere even in their absence.

Still the songs of this time period rarely focused on the plight women experienced at home without the presence of men, nor did the songs affirm the inextricable link between shifting gender roles and shifting race and labor relations as slaves fled the plantation. One reason for the lack of songs is the domination of song-writing and performance as a male vocation. While several songs did take on the female persona, these songs did not give voice to the concerns actually felt by elite white women on the home front. In modern popular songs the narratives remained in the male sphere. Where women had to show their own courage in keeping up homes without male support, songs show the much desired and unchanged face of domesticity.

In the Decembrist contemporary song, "Yankee Bayonet,"[41] the female protagonist describes the allure of home for the soldier against the backdrop of brutality of home for the woman who remains there. While her man fights amongst the "bones," she sits on the "bile" of the Carolina coast. Furthermore, in the narrative of the song, she sits at home pregnant and lacks the male figure that would be necessary to raise a child. In the song's representations of manhood and womanhood, men represent the ideas of independent living and being able to forge one's own destiny, while women represent dependency and the tragedy of war as the absence of men in the lives of women.

The contributions women did make in the domestic sphere were turned into songs, such as "The Homespun Dress":

> Three cheers for the homespun dress
> The Southern ladies wear.
> Now Northern goods are out of date,
> And since old Abe's blockade
> We Southern girls can be content
> With goods that's southern made
> We scorn to wear a bit of silk
> A bit of Northern lace,
> But make our homespun dresses up
> And wear them with a grace.[42]

The song focuses on the tasks of using fabrics available at home instead of relying on Northern imports that the Union naval blockade obstructed. This song specifically calls on women to not only make a sacrifice of the luxuries they were used to, but also to perform tasks that called on them to act independently. These roles show women taking on common domestic roles in support of the Confederate cause. Southern elites preferred women to be involved in the war as standard bearers of virtue and a virtuous war launched against an enemy who, according to Southern sensibilities, sought to change societal and gender norms. By getting involved in the war through their own available sphere, women were able to contribute moral support to the Confederacy and possibly garner men's support for their contributions.

Experiencing Manhood

The song "Aura Lee, the Maid with the Golden Hair"[43] was central to the novel *Cold Mountain*, as it reminds Inman of the woman he left behind. Songs such as "Aura Lee" were commonly sung by soldiers during the Civil War. Songs such as these provided a sense of nostalgia for men at the front. For some, the song served as a reminder of their purpose and goal, but for the majority of soldiers, it became a reminder of what was awaiting them: a desirable woman and a chance to escape the pain, death, and horror of the battlefront. In the song, the narrator experiences birds, flowers, and other parts of nature singing to him about Aura Lee. The song starts with a bird singing of Aura Lee; then the rose reminds the narrator of her blush, followed by the willows' long branches representing her hair. In the song the stars are her eyes and sunshine is her face. For the narrator, the very land/nation he walks upon reminds him of the woman. Beyond the personification of nature, the soldier/narrator can see the longing not only for the woman he loves but also for the land that he fights to save.

Men craved a sense of what was awaiting them at home. Men used songs to take their minds off of fighting. A song commonly sung before battle, "Rock Me to Sleep, Mother," pleads for an escape from war and a return to childhood and a mother's protecting arms:

Backward turn backward, oh! Time in your flight
Make me a child again, just for tonight:
Mother, come back from the echoless shore
Take me again to your heart, as of yore.[44]

This is the kind of song that illuminates the ways modern songs depict the Civil War. It is no mere coincidence that the Band, the Decemberists, Wilco's cover, and Justin Townes Earl all recorded and released their songs during a time of national conflict. The narrators in these songs speak of valor and honor as they reflect an important concept during times of war: the idea of male bravery. Although these songs are far from critiques of war, they offer no flag-waving celebration of war bravery.

In Justin Townes Earl's song "Lone Pine Hill," the narrator has lost his bravery and wishes to return to his lover. The narrator has been fighting since 1861 and is waiting for "Sheridan to bring us to our knees."[45] Out of fear of death and wanting to return home, he begs for God's forgiveness as he runs away to return home. He reasons that since he had never owned a slave, the Civil War is not his fight. This demonstrates a change from the reason he gives earlier for why he enlisted: to fight for his homeland. For Earl's narrator, the valor of war is gone since, from his point of view, the battles have become senseless slaughters. He recounts the battles he has fought in, and after fighting for four years, hope is lost since Richmond is under siege. He is stationed at Five Forks, the "Waterloo of the Confederacy." Why should the narrator continue to fight when there is nothing left of the Confederacy? His narration reveals how powerful forces control his fate and his ability to return to the home he remembers. When his valor becomes meaningless, the soldier no longer needs to prove his bravery as a sign of his masculinity. Disillusionment in the cause displaces the importance of bravery.

In his autobiography on the Band, Levon Helm said:

> We did a few press conferences, which got a little embarrassing in Sweden because we were apolitical . . . the Stockholm press is peppering us with questions . . . and what could we say except that we hated war as much as anyone . . . none of us ever thought to write a song about . . . war, revolution, civil war, turmoil. Our songs were trying to take you someplace else.[46]

Although the Band wrote a song explicitly about the Civil War, it was a personal narrative that was not aiming for a grandiose statement about the times, either the 1860s or the 1960s. However, it expressed sympathy for the South. Like most songs by the Band, the songs are about an escape to the past and away from the present and the future.[47]

The Importance of Male Sacrifice

The importance and pervasiveness of the male narrative in the concept of the Good Death became routed in the psyche of white Northerners and Southerners. It also formed the racial and gendered basis of Northern rejection of black soldiers who Whites, neither in the North nor South, constructed as their male/masculine equals. Although black soldiers' valor disproved such racist notions, Civil War and Reconstruction myths, like those depicted in The Clansmen and *Birth of a Nation*, displaced and denied the bravery and Good Death of black soldiers. As such, only white men were "soldiers," the ones to give the ultimate sacrifice to their nation. The importance of that sacrifice overshadowed valorous black men and women and the responsibilities and life of white women and children on the home front.

Motherhood

While white women were kept out of the discourse of song narratives, they nevertheless played an important part in crafting the idea of the Confederate nation, specifically, by educating the youth and guiding the growth of the Southern national identity. By the end of the Civil War, over half of all teachers were women in the South, when previously they accounted for less than eight percent. The ascendency of women's dominance as teachers corresponds to the idea of Republican Motherhood when, at the beginning of the American democracy at the turn of the nineteenth century, women passed on the idea and virtues of citizenship to their children. The South expected mid-century Southern women to pass on to their sons the values that would be essential for citizens of the new Southern nation.

In "Yankee Bayonet," the woman is left to fend for the unborn child on her own. In an environment that looked to mothers as a source of education, it fell on the unnamed mother to bring up the child in the ideals of Southern society and culture. At the end of the song the dead soldier and his wife sing a duet. The soldier explains that he will return to her "on the breath of the wind." He will return to her as a memory and through her unborn child.

During the Civil War, women were in search of a way to be of use in an event that called almost exclusively for violent action from men. In a confrontation that was decided through military victory on the battlefield, women felt excluded from active roles, although the reality of warfare on the doorsteps meant that they were intricately involved in, for example, fund-raising, making clothes, and nursing. The construction of gender in the South caused Southern men to look unfavorably on involving women in the difficulties of war and so men actively tried to keep the woman's sphere separate. And yet women's opportunity for involvement in the public sphere grew. With men away from home, these elite white women had a chance to explore a new realm of possible independence.

In a novel called *Maccaria; or, Altars of Sacrifice* written by Augusta Jane Evans during the Civil War and published in 1864, the protagonist of the novel, Irene, may choose a life that is scripted for her or she may make a choice that allows her to lead her own life. "Sacrifice" refers to Irene's duty to sacrifice her own desires for those around her.[48] However, as she must "sacrifice," Irene, a young Southern heiress, lets her true love go off to battle while she stays behind to marry someone her father had chosen for her. Yet before the war, Irene doesn't allow a slave to carry her books for her and instead takes it upon herself to be as independent as she can be as an elite white woman in a slave household.

According to Faust, the quest that the male protagonist goes on in search of self-identification typifies a novel of the period. In most nineteenth-century novels, white women seek an idyllic romantic fulfillment. Evans's novel breaks away from this model by presenting Irene the opportunity and chance to explore her place in the world. The absence of her true love who goes off to war and her husband who dies allows Irene to explore several of the necessary tasks of women in the Confederacy: she starts a school and an orphanage. In her roles, Irene undertakes several of the goals established first in the Northern United States in the antebellum period. Women in places such as Philadelphia and New York had been involved with benefit societies for the poor and homeless long before the war. As a result of male absence Southern women for the first time became public figures. Prior to the war, people of the South believed that a woman doing certain kinds of labor was a "Northerner" with "Yankee" attributes, but with the sudden absence of men in the South, women's labor achieved higher value. It became a necessity.

In contemporary song women are still portrayed as if they were not major figures in the Civil War. However, by the end of the war women both north and south of the Mason-Dixon line were experiencing a high level of interest and access to public life. In modern songs such as "Yankee Bayonet" and "The Night They Drove Old Dixie Down," the role of women is only the observational role of a mother in charge of the home. Although both songs do not explicitly take on the point of view of the elite South, they preserve gender hierarchy that is stressed by men of the 1860s. Perhaps strong women are neglected in the Civil War song narrative because their roles are condemned as having less relevance than the role of men. For example, in contemporary American society, we no longer view household chores as solely women's work. Perhaps, as men share increasingly in these necessary tasks, household duties have taken on greater significance as essential to daily living and the quality of social and economic life. For some people, these gender shifts have become normative. However, for a band like the Band, known for their wildman-in-the-woods appearance, the old standards that they appear to typify may have leaked into their song that tries to establish the Southern way of life in Civil War songs.[49]

Conclusion: Connecting with the Present

Music is both deeply rooted and transient. It dissolves into space while simultaneously settling into individual and collective memory. Yesterday's songs trigger today's tears. Music harbors the habitual, but also acts as a herald of change. It helps to orchestrate personal, local, regional, ethnic, religious, linguistic, and national identity. Stable yet constantly in flux, music offers both striking metaphors and tangible data for understanding societies at moments of transition.[50]

Mark Slobin's opening introduction to the book of essays, *Retuning Culture*, is exactly why studying the historical trends of music provides a critical lens through which historians can analyze American life and culture. Although specific note selection, motifs, and sequences can be important to a song's meaning, there is a wide variance as to how the creator, performer, and audience perceives and responds to a piece of music.

Music can be a troublesome way of exploring history. A song can begin with clear intentions and in a few years it may become an anthem for the opposing cause. "Dixie" has proved to be a most troublesome song in American history. Soon after the capture of Ft. Sumter, Southerners sang "Dixie" as a sign of support for secession.[51] And yet, by the end of the war Abraham Lincoln, a fan of the song, requested to hear "Dixie" at a shipboard party. He reportedly stated "that tune is now Federal property."[52] Although what Lincoln did was only a symbolic act of unifying the country, it was also an admission that the song had become part of the construction of the Confederate nation and, like the South, had to be reclaimed.

Music can magnify the beliefs of a people as it reveals how people relate to one another and to their society. For 150 years, a series of events in American history has had far-reaching consequences in how Americans experience the trauma of war as well as how they remember the historical event. Music has been a way of remembering history since the birth of the ballad form. Popular musicians have never backed away from songs about history or myths. But the times when modern songs have chosen to look back into history have often been periods of upheaval. People yearn to imagine a different era as a place of higher ideals that have not been muddied by the complexities of modern life. "The Night They Drove Old Dixie Down" came out during the Vietnam War and "If The South Woulda Won" came out after the Iran-Contra affair and the beginning of War on Drugs. Despite war being a topic that can bring sorrow, these songs look at the romantic past and look not only at the need for sacrifice, but also at the possibilities of a better tomorrow.

The Civil War precipitated major social and cultural changes that were transmitted in songs. The changes and the way people understood them transcended the war period and became artifacts of modern songs. Contemporary songwriters have been able to take historical fact and use fictional narrative to turn the Civil War into a source of multiple meanings in the American songbook. Where the Civil War had been a specific event in American history with reasons for the upheaval and its resolution, songwriters have built upon the events to create a reinterpreted war which reinvented personal, regional, and national history.

Endnotes

1. James A. Davis. (2005). "Hearing History: Music in the History Classroom." *Music and History*. Jackson: University Press of Mississippi, 203–204.
2. John Tasker Howard. (1946). *Our American Music: Three Hundred Years of It*. New York: Thomas Y. Crowell Company, 254.
3. Drew Gilpin Faust. (1988). *The Creation of Confederate Nationalism*. Baton Rouge: Louisiana State University Press, 17–18.
4. Michael Cooper, "Confederate Flag Takes Central Stage Again." *New York Times*, January 18, 2008.
5. Drew Gilpin Faust. (2008). *This Republic of Suffering*. New York: Alfred A. Knopf, xiii.
6. Faust, 6.
7. Ibid., 12–19.
8. Ibid., xiii.
9. M. L. Hofford. (1862). "Dead of the Battlefield."
10. Faust. (1988). *The Creation of Confederate Nationalism*. Baton Rouge: Louisiana State University Press, 17–18.
11. Ibid.
12. Robert Christigau, "What if Woody Guthrie Led a Rock Band?" *New York Times*, June 28, 1998.
13. Faust. *This Republic of Suffering*, 61–65.
14. The Decemberists. (2006). *The Crane Wife*. CD. Capitol.
15. Ibid.

16. Gallagher, W. Gallagher and Alan T. Nolan (Eds.). (2000). *The Myth of the Lost Cause and Civil War History.* Bloomington and Indianapolis: Indiana University Press, 16–23.

17. Ibid.

18. James McPherson. (1988). *Battle Cry for Freedom: The Civil War Era.* Oxford: Oxford University Press, 854–855.

19. Mark LaSalle. "War is Hell in the grueling, thrilling 'Cold Mountain,' and only his fierce longing for the woman he loves keeps Jude Law, as a Confederate deserter, alive and on the run." *San Francisco Chronicle.* December 25, 2003.

20. Steven Cornelius. (2004). *Music of the Civil War Era.* Connecticut: Greenwood Press, 33.

21. Ibid., 34.

22. Ibid., 35.

23. Ibid.

24. Faust, *The Creation of Confederate Nationalism,* 67.

25. Cornelius, 139.

26. Faust, *The Creation of Confederate Nationalism,* 65–67.

27. Cornelius, 31.

28. Faust, *The Creation of Confederate Nationalism,* 11.

29. Gallagher and Nolan, 17–18, 24–25.

30. LaSalle.

31. Andrew Sarris. "Cold Mountain's Aching Love Story-Literary, Well-Acted, Meandering." *The New York Observer,* July 11, 2004.

32. A. O. Scott. "Lovers Striving for a Reunion, With a War in the Way." *New York Times,* December 25, 2003.

33. Faust. *Mothers of Invention,* 5.

34. Amy Greenberg. (2005). *Manifest Manhood and the Antebellum American Empire.* Cambridge: Cambridge University Press, 11.

35. Ibid.

36. Drew Gilpin Faust. (1996). *Mothers of Invention.* Chapel Hill: University of North Carolina Press, 5.

37. Ibid., 32.

38. Ibid., 17.

39. Bruce Dorsey. (2002). *Reforming Men and Women.* Ithaca, New York: Cornell University Press.

40. David Blight. (1991). *Frederick Douglass's Civil War: Keeping Faith in Jubilee.* Baton Rouge: Louisiana State University Press.

41. The Decemberists. (2006). "Yankee Bayonet," *The Crane Wife,* CD, Capitol Records.

42. Arthur Palmer Hudson. (1936). *Folksongs of Mississippi and their Background.* Chapel Hill: University of North Carolina Press.

43. W. W. Fosdick. (1861). "Aura Lee."

44. Lyrics are by Florence Percy and the music is by John Hill Hewitt.

45. Justin Townes Earl. (2008). *The Good Life.* CD, Bloodshot Records.

46. Levon Helm. (2000). *This Wheel's On Fire.* Chicago: Chicago Review Press, 165.

47. Barney Hoskyns. (2006). *Across The Great Divide: The Band and America.* New York: Hal Leonard, 194.

48. August Jane Evans. (1864). *Macaria; or Altars of Sacrifice.* Richmond: West & Johnston.

49. Jay Cocks. "Mellow Harvest." *Time Magazine,* August 31, 1970.

50. Mark Slobin. (1996). *Retuning Culture.* Durham: Duke University Press, 1.

51. Kenneth A. Bernard. (1966). *Lincoln and the Music of the Civil War.* Caldwell, Idaho: Caxton Printers, LTD., 12–13.

52. James A. Davis. (2005). "Hearing History: Music in the History Classroom." In Jeffrey H. Jackson and Stanley C. Pelkey (Eds.) *Music and History: Bridging the Disciplines,* Jackson: University Press of Mississippi, 214.

Chapter 28

What the Black Man Wants—Frederick Douglass (1865)

(Excerpt of Speech delivered in 1865)

I came here, as I come always to the meetings in New England, as a listener, and not as a speaker; and one of the reasons why I have not been more frequently to the meetings of this society, has been because of the disposition on the part of some of my friends to call me out upon the platform, even when they knew that there was some difference of opinion and of feeling between those who rightfully belong to this platform and myself; and for fear of being misconstrued, as desiring to interrupt or disturb the proceedings of these meetings, I have usually kept away, and have thus been deprived of that educating influence, which I am always free to confess is of the highest order, descending from this platform. I have felt, since I have lived out West, that in going there I parted from a great deal that was valuable; and I feel, every time I come to these meetings, that I have lost a great deal by making my home west of Boston, west of Massachusetts; for, if anywhere in the country there is to be found the highest sense of justice, or the truest demands for my race, I look for it in the East, I look for it here. The ablest discussions of the whole question of our rights occur here, and to be deprived of the privilege of listening to those discussions is a great deprivation.

I do not know, from what has been said, that there is any difference of opinion as to the duty of abolitionists, at the present moment. How can we get up any difference at this point, or any point, where we are so united, so agreed? I went especially, however, with that word of Mr. Phillips, which is the criticism of Gen. Banks and Gen. Banks' policy. I hold that that policy is our chief danger at the present moment; that it practically enslaves the Negro, and makes the Proclamation of 1863 a mockery and delusion. What is freedom? It is the right to choose one's own employment. Certainly it means that, if it means anything; and when any individual or combination of individuals undertakes to decide for any man when he shall work, where he shall work, at what he shall work, and for what he shall work, he or they practically reduce him to slavery. He is a slave. That I understand Gen. Banks to do—to determine for the so-called freedman, when, and where, and at what, and for how much he shall work, when he shall be punished, and by whom punished. It is absolute slavery. It defeats the beneficent intention of the Government, if it has beneficent intentions, in regards to the freedom of our people.

I have had but one idea for the last three years to present to the American people, and the phraseology in which I clothe it is the old abolition phraseology. I am for the "immediate, unconditional, and universal" enfranchisement of the black man, in every State in the Union. Without this, his liberty is a mockery; without this, you might as well almost retain the old name of slavery for his condition; for in fact, if he is not the slave of the individual master, he is the slave of society, and holds his liberty as a privilege, not as a right. He is at the mercy of the mob, and has no means of protecting himself.

It may be objected, however, that this pressing of the Negro's right to suffrage is premature. Let us have slavery abolished, it may be said, let us have labor organized, and then, in the natural course of events, the right of suffrage will be extended to the Negro. I do not agree with this. The constitution of the human mind is such, that if it once disregards the conviction forced upon it by a revelation of truth, it requires the exercise of a higher power to produce the same conviction afterwards. The American people are now in tears. The Shenandoah has run blood—the best blood of the North. All around Richmond, the blood of New England and of the North has been shed—of your sons, your brothers and your fathers. We all feel, in the existence of this Rebellion, that judgments terrible, wide-spread, far-reaching, overwhelming, are abroad in the land; and we feel, in view of these judgments, just now, a disposition to learn righteousness. This is the hour. Our streets are in mourning, tears are falling at every fireside, and under the chastisement of this Rebellion we have almost come up to the point of conceding this great, this all-important right of suffrage. I fear that if we fail to do it now, if abolitionists fail to press it now, we may not see, for centuries to come, the same disposition that exists at this moment. Hence, I say, now is the time to press this right.

It may be asked, "Why do you want it? Some men have got along very well without it. Women have not this right." Shall we justify one wrong by another? This is a sufficient answer. Shall we at this moment justify the deprivation of the Negro of the right to vote, because some one else is deprived of that privilege? I hold that women, as well as men, have the right to vote, and my heart and my voice go with the movement to extend suffrage to woman; but that question rests upon another basis than that on which our right rests. We may be asked, I say, why we want it. I will tell you why we want it. We want it because it is our *right*, first of all. No class of men can, without insulting their own nature, be content with any deprivation of their rights. We want it again, as a means for educating our race. Men are so constituted that they derive their conviction of their own possibilities largely from the estimate formed of them by others. If nothing is expected of a people, that people will find it difficult to contradict that expectation. By depriving us of suffrage, you affirm our incapacity to form an intelligent judgment respecting public men and public measures; you declare before the world that we are unfit to exercise the elective franchise, and by this means lead us to undervalue ourselves, to put a low estimate upon ourselves, and to feel that we have no possibilities like other men. Again, I want the elective franchise, for one, as a colored man, because ours is a peculiar government, based upon a peculiar idea, and that idea is universal suffrage. If I were in a monarchial government, or an autocratic or aristocratic government, where the few bore rule and the many were subject, there would be no special stigma resting upon me, because I did not exercise the elective franchise. It would do me no great violence. Mingling with the mass I should partake of the strength of the mass; I should be supported by the mass, and I should have the same incentives to endeavor with the mass of my fellow-men; it would be no particular burden, no particular deprivation; but here where universal suffrage is the rule, where that is the fundamental idea of the Government, to rule us out is to make us an exception, to brand us with the stigma of inferiority, and to invite to our heads the missiles of those about us; therefore, I want the franchise for the black man.

There are, however, other reasons, not derived from any consideration merely of our rights, but arising out of the conditions of the South, and of the country—considerations which have already been referred to by Mr. Phillips—considerations which must arrest the attention of statesmen. I believe that when the tall heads of this Rebellion shall have been swept down, as they will be swept down, when the Davises and Toombses and Stephenses, and others who are leading this Rebellion shall have been blotted out, there will be this rank undergrowth of treason, to which reference has been made, growing up there, and interfering with, and thwarting the quiet operation of the Federal Government in those States. You will see those traitors, handing down, from sire to son, the same malignant spirit which they have manifested, and which they are now exhibiting, with malicious hearts, broad blades, and bloody hands in the field, against our sons and brothers. That spirit will still remain; and whoever sees the Federal Government extended over those Southern States will see that Government in a strange land, and not only in a strange land, but in an enemy's land. A post-master of the United States in the South will find himself surrounded by a hostile spirit; a collector in a Southern port will find himself surrounded by a hostile spirit; a United States marshal or United States judge will be surrounded there by a hostile element. That enmity will not die out in a year, will not die out in an age. The Federal Government will be looked upon in those States precisely as the Governments of Austria and France are looked upon in Italy at the present moment. They will endeavor to circumvent, they will endeavor to destroy, the peaceful operation of this Government. Now, where will you find the strength to counterbalance this spirit, if you do not find it in the Negroes of the South? They are your friends, and have always been your friends. They were your friends even when the Government did not regard them as such. They comprehended the genius of this war before you did. It is a significant fact, it is a marvellous fact, it seems almost to imply a direct interposition of Providence, that this war, which began in the interest of slavery on both sides, bids fair to end in the interest of liberty on both sides. It was begun, I say, in the interest of slavery on both sides. The South was fighting to take slavery out of the Union, and the North fighting to keep it in the Union; the South fighting to get it beyond the limits of the United States Constitution, and the North fighting to retain it within those limits; the South fighting for new guarantees, and the North fighting for the old guarantees;—both despising the Negro, both insulting the Negro. Yet, the Negro, apparently endowed with wisdom from on high, saw more clearly the end from the beginning than we did. When Seward said the status of no man in the country would be changed by the war, the Negro did not believe him. When our generals sent their underlings in shoulder-straps to hunt the flying Negro back from our lines into the jaws of slavery, from which he had escaped, the Negroes thought that a mistake had been made, and that the intentions of the Government had not been rightly understood by our officers in shoulder-straps, and they continued to come into our lines, threading their way through bogs and fens, over briers and thorns, fording streams, swimming rivers, bringing us tidings as to the safe path to march, and pointing out the dangers that threatened us. They are our only friends in the South, and we should be true to them in this their trial hour, and see to it that they have the elective franchise.

I know that we are inferior to you in some things—virtually inferior. We walk about among you like dwarfs among giants. Our heads are scarcely seen above the great sea of humanity. The Germans are superior to us; the Irish are superior to us; the Yankees are superior to us; they can do what we cannot, that is, what we have not hitherto been allowed to do. But while I make this admission, I utterly deny, that we are originally, or naturally, or practically, or in any way, or in any important sense, inferior to anybody on this globe. This charge of inferiority is an old dodge. It has been made available for oppression on many occasions. It is only about six centuries since the blue-eyed and fair-haired Anglo-Saxons were considered inferior by the haughty Normans, who once trampled upon them. If you read the history of the Norman Conquest, you will find that this proud Anglo-Saxon was once looked upon as of coarser clay than his Norman master, and might be found in the highways and byways of old England laboring with a brass collar on his neck, and the name of his master marked upon it. *You* were down then. You are up now. I am glad you are up, and I want you to be glad to help us up also.

The story of our inferiority is an old dodge, as I have said; for wherever men oppress their fellows, wherever they enslave them, they will endeavor to find the needed apology for such enslavement and oppression in the character of the people oppressed and enslaved. When we wanted, a few years ago, a slice of Mexico, it was hinted that the Mexicans were an inferior race, that the old Castilian blood had become so weak that it would scarcely run down hill, and that Mexico needed the long, strong and beneficent arm of the Anglo-Saxon care extended over it. We said that it was necessary to its salvation, and a part of the "manifest destiny" of this Republic, to extend our arm over that dilapidated government. So, too, when Russia wanted to take possession of a part of the Ottoman Empire, the Turks were "an inferior race." So, too, when England wants to set the heel of her power more firmly in the quivering heart of old Ireland, the Celts are an "inferior race." So, too, the Negro, when he is to be robbed of any right which is justly his, is an "inferior man." It is said that we are ignorant; I admit it. But if we know enough to be hung, we know enough to vote. If the Negro knows enough to pay taxes to support the government, he knows enough to vote; taxation and representation should go together. If he knows enough to shoulder a musket and fight for the flag, fight for the government, he knows enough to vote. If he knows as much when he is sober as an Irishman knows when drunk, he knows enough to vote, on good American principles.

But I was saying that you needed a counterpoise in the persons of the slaves to the enmity that would exist at the South after the Rebellion is put down. I hold that the American people are bound, not only in self-defence, to extend this right to the freedmen of the South, but they are bound by their love of country, and by all their regard for the future safety of those Southern States, to do this—to do it as a measure essential to the preservation of peace there. But I will not dwell upon this. I put it to the American sense of honor. The honor of a nation is an important thing. It is said in the Scriptures, "What doth it profit a man if he gain the whole world, and lose his own soul?" It may be said, also, What doth it profit a nation if it gain the whole world, but lose its honor? I hold that the American government has taken upon itself a solemn obligation of honor, to see that this war—let it be long or let it be short, let it cost much or let it cost little—that this war shall not cease until every freedman at the South has the right to vote. It has bound itself to it. What have you asked the black men of the South, the black men of the whole country, to do? Why, you have asked them to incur the deadly enmity of their masters, in order to befriend you and to befriend this Government. You have asked us to call down, not only upon ourselves, but upon our children's children, the deadly hate of the entire Southern people. You have called upon us to turn our backs upon our masters, to abandon their cause and espouse yours; to turn against the South and in favor of the North; to shoot down the Confederacy and uphold the flag—the American flag. You have called upon us to expose ourselves to all the subtle machinations of their malignity for all time. And now, what do you propose to do when you come to make peace? To reward your enemies, and trample in the dust your friends? Do you intend to sacrifice the very men who have come to the rescue of your banner in the South, and incurred the lasting displeasure of their masters thereby? Do you intend to sacrifice them and reward your enemies? Do you mean to give your enemies the right to vote, and take it away from your friends? Is that wise policy? Is that honorable? Could American honor with-stand such a blow? I do not believe you will do it. I think you will see to it that we have the right to vote. There is something too mean in looking upon the Negro, when you are in trouble, as a citizen, and when you are free from trouble, as an alien. When this nation was in trouble, in its early struggles, it looked upon the Negro as a citizen. In 1776 he was a citizen. At the time of the formation of the Constitution the Negro had the right to vote in eleven States out of the old thirteen. In your trouble you have made us citizens. In 1812 Gen. Jackson addressed us as citizens—"fellow-citizens." He wanted us to fight. We were citizens then! And now, when you come to frame a conscription bill, the Negro is a citizen again. He has been a citizen just three times in the history of this government, and it has always been in time of trouble. In time of trouble we are citizens. Shall we be citizens in war, and aliens in peace? Would that be just?

I ask my friends who are apologizing for not insisting upon this right, where can the black man look, in this country, for the assertion of his right, if he may not look to the Massachusetts Anti-Slavery Society? Where under the whole heavens can he look for sympathy, in asserting this right, if he may not look to this platform? Have you lifted us up to a certain height to see that we are men, and then are any disposed to leave us there, without seeing that we are put in possession of all our rights? We look naturally to this platform for the assertion of all our rights, and for this one especially. I understand the anti-slavery societies of this coun-try to be based on two principles,—first, the freedom of the blacks of this country; and, second, the elevation of them. Let me not be misunderstood here. I am not asking for sympathy at the hands of abolitionists, sym-pathy at the hands of any. I think the American people are disposed often to be generous rather than just. I look over this country at the present time, and I see Educational Societies, Sanitary Commissions, Freedmen's Associations, and the like,—all very good: but in regard to the colored people there is always more that is benevolent, I perceive, than just, manifested towards us. What I ask for the Negro is not benevolence, not pity, not sympathy, but simply *justice*. The American people have always been anxious to know what they shall do with us. Gen. Banks was distressed with solicitude as to what he should do with the Negro. Everybody has asked the question, and they learned to ask it early of the abolitionists, "What shall we do with the Negro?" I have had but one answer from the beginning. Do nothing with us! Your doing with us has already played the mischief with us. Do nothing with us! If the apples will not remain on the tree of their own strength, if they are wormeaten at the core, if they are early ripe and disposed to fall, let them fall! I am not for tying or fastening them on the tree in any way, except by nature's plan, and if they will not stay there, let them fall. And if the Negro cannot stand on his own legs, let him fall also. All I ask is, give him a chance to stand on his own legs! Let him alone! If you see him on his way to school, let him alone, don't disturb him! If you see him going to the dinner-table at a hotel, let him go! If you see him going to the ballot-box, let him alone, don't disturb him! If you see him going into a work-shop, just let him alone,—your interference is doing him a positive injury. Gen. Banks' "preparation" is of a piece with this attempt to prop up the Negro. Let him fall if he cannot stand alone! If the Negro cannot live by the line of eternal justice, so beautifully pictured to you in the illustration used by Mr. Phillips, the fault will not be yours, it will be his who made the Negro, and established that line for his government. Let him live or die by that. If you will only untie his hands, and give him a chance, I think he will live. He will work as readily for himself as the white man. A great many delu-sions have been swept away by this war. One was, that the Negro would not work; he has proved his ability to work. Another was, that the Negro would not fight; that he possessed only the most sheepish attributes of humanity; was a perfect lamb, or an "Uncle Tom"; disposed to take off his coat whenever required, fold his hands, and be whipped by anybody who wanted to whip him. But the war has proved that there is a great deal of human nature in the Negro, and that "he will fight," as Mr. Quincy, our President, said, in earlier days than these, "when there is a reasonable probability of his whipping anybody."

Chapter 29

Editorial on Booker T. Washington—
William Monroe Trotter
The Boston Guardian, December 20, 1902 (Excerpt)

Under the caption, "Principal Washington Defines His Position," the *Tuskegee Student*, the official organ of Tuskegee, prints the institute letter in which Mr. Washington said: "We cannot elevate and make useful a race of people unless there is held out to them the hope of reward for right living. Every revised constitution throughout the southern states has put a premium upon intelligence, ownership of property, thrift and character." This little sheet begins by saying that the letter "appeared in all of the important papers of the country on Nov. 28. It has been unstintingly praised from one section of the country to the other for its clarity and forcefulness of statement, and for its ringing note of sincerity." Although such words are to be expected from the employees of the school they are for the most part only too true. It is true that, although the letter was sent to the *Age Herald* of Birmingham, Alabama, it appeared simultaneously "in all the important papers of the country." Then its effect must be admitted to have been greater than if any other Negro had written it, for admittedly no other Negro's letter could have obtained such wide publicity. If it had in it aught that was injurious to the Negro's welfare or to his manhood rights, therefore, such worked far more damage than if any other Negro or any other man, save the president himself, had written the words.

What man is there among us, whether friend or foe of the author of the letter, who was not astounded at the reference to the disfranchising constitutions quoted above. "Every revised constitution throughout the southern states has put a premium upon intelligence, ownership of property, thrift and character," and all the more so because Mr. Washington had not been accused by even the southerners of opposing these disfranchising constitutions. . . . If the statement is false, if it is misleading, if it is injurious to the Negro, all the more blamable and guilty is the author because the statement was gratuitous on his part.

Is it the truth? Do these constitutions encourage Negroes to be thrifty, to be better and more intelligent? For this sort of argument is the most effective in favor of them. . . . Where is the Negro who says the law was or is ever intended to be fairly applied? . . . If so, then every reputable Negro orator and writer, from Hon. A. H. Grimke on, have been mistaken. If so, every Negro clergyman of standing, who has spoken on the subject . . . have been misinformed. We happen to know of an undertaker who has an enormous establishment in Virginia, who now can't vote. Is that encouraging thrift? Two letter carriers, who have passed the civil service examinations, are now sueing because disfranchised. Is that encouraging intelligence? . . . Even a Republican candidate for governor in Virginia recently said Negro domination was to be feared if 10 Negroes could vote because they could have the balance of power. Mr. Washington's statement is shamefully false and deliberately so.

But even were it true, what man is a worse enemy to a race than a leader who looks with equanimity on the disfranchisement of his race in a country where other races have universal suffrage by constitutions that make one rule for his race and another for the dominant race, by constitutions made by conventions to which his race is not allowed to send its representatives, by constitutions that his race although endowed with the franchise by law are not allowed to vote upon, and are, therefore, doubly illegal, by constitutions in violation to the national constitution, because, forsooth, he thinks such disfranchising laws will benefit the moral character of his people. Let our spiritual advisers condemn this idea of reducing a people to serfdom to make them good.

But what was the effect of Mr. Washington's letter on the northern white people? . . .

No thinking Negro can fail to see that, with the influence Mr. Washington yields [wields] in the North and the confidence reposed in him by the white people on account of his school, a fatal blow has been given to the Negro's political rights and liberty by his statement. The benevolence idea makes it all the more deadly in its effect. It comes very opportunely for the Negro, too, just when Roosevelt declares the Negro shall hold office, . . . when Congress is being asked to enforce the Negro's constitutional rights, when these laws are being carried to the Supreme Court. And here Mr. Washington, having gained sufficient influence through his doctrines, his school and his elevation by the President, makes all these efforts sure of failure by killing public sentiment against the disfranchising constitutions.

And Mr. Washington's word is the more effective for, discreditable as it may seem, not five Negro papers even mention a statement that belies all their editorials and that would have set aflame the entire Negro press of the country, if a less wealthy and less powerful Negro had made it. Nor will Negro orators nor Negro preachers dare now to pick up the gauntlet thrown down by the great "educator." Instead of being universally repudiated by the Negro race his statement will be practically universally endorsed by its silence because Washington said it, though it sounds the death-knell of our liberty. The lips of our leading politicians are sealed, because, before he said it, Mr. Washington, through the President, put them under obligation to himself. Nor is there that heroic quality now in our race that would lead men to throw off the shackles of fear, of obligation, of policy and denounce a traitor though he be a friend, or even a brother. It occurs to none that silence is tantamount to being virtually an accomplice in the treasonable act of this Benedict Arnold of the Negro race.

O, for a black Patrick Henry to save his people from this stigma of cowardice; to rouse them from their lethargy to a sense of danger; to score the tyrant and to inspire his people with the spirit of those immortal words: "Give Me Liberty or Give Me Death."

Chapter 30

The Atlanta Exposition Address—
Booker T. Washington (1895)

Delivered Atlanta, Georgia, September 18, 1895

One-third of the population of the South is of the Negro race. No enterprise seeking the material, civil, or moral welfare of this section can disregard this element of our population and reach the highest success. I but convey to you, Mr. President and Directors, the sentiment of the masses of my race when I say that in no way have the value and manhood of the American Negro been more fittingly and generously recognized than by the managers of this magnificent exposition at every stage of its progress. It is a recognition that will do more to cement the friendship of the two races than any occurrence since the dawn of our freedom.

Not only this, but the opportunity here afforded will awaken among us a new era of industrial progress. Ignorant and inexperienced, it is not strange that in the first years of our new life we began at the top instead of at the bottom; that a seat in Congress or the State Legislature was more sought than real estate or industrial skill; that the political convention or stump-speaking had more attraction than starting a dairy farm or truck garden.

A ship lost at sea for many days suddenly sighted a friendly vessel. From the mast of the unfortunate vessel was seen a signal: "Water, water; we die of thirst!" The answer from the friendly vessel at once came back: "Cast down your bucket where you are." A second time the signal, "Water, water; send us water!" ran up from the distressed vessel, and was answered: "Cast down your bucket where you are." And a third and fourth signal for water was answered, "Cast down your bucket where you are." The captain of the distressed vessel, at last heeding the injunction, cast down his bucket, and it came up full of fresh, sparkling water from the mouth of the Amazon River. To those of my race who depend upon bettering their condition in a foreign land, or who underestimate the importance of cultivating friendly relations with the Southern white man who is their next-door neighbor, I would say: "Cast down your bucket where you are"—cast it down in making friends, in every manly way, of the people of all races by whom we are surrounded.

Cast it down in agriculture, mechanics, in commerce, in domestic service, and in the professions. And in this connection it is well to bear in mind that whatever other sins the South may be called to bear, when it comes to business, pure and simple, it is in the South that the Negro is given a man's chance in the commercial world, and in nothing is this Exposition more eloquent than in emphasizing this chance. Our greatest danger is that in the great leap from slavery to freedom we may overlook the fact that the masses of us are to live by the productions of our hands, and fail to keep in mind that we shall prosper in proportion as we learn to dignify and glorify common labor, and put brains and skill into the common occupations of life; shall prosper in proportion as we learn to draw the line between the superficial and the substantial, the ornamental gewgaws of life and the useful. No race can prosper till it learns that there is as much dignity in tilling a field as in writing a poem. It is at the bottom of life we must begin, and not at the top. Nor should we permit our grievances to overshadow our opportunities.

To those of the white race who look to the incoming of those of foreign birth and strange tongue and habits for the prosperity of the South, were I permitted, I would repeat what I say to my own race, "Cast down your bucket where you are." Cast it down among the eight million Negroes whose habits you know, whose fidelity and love you have tested in days when to have proved treacherous meant the ruin of your firesides. Cast down your bucket among these people who have without strikes and labor wars tilled your fields, cleared your forests, builded your railroads and cities, brought forth treasures from the bowels of the earth, and helped make possible this magnificent representation of the progress of the South. Casting down your bucket among my people, helping and encouraging them as you are doing on these grounds, and, with education of head, hand, and heart, you will find that they will buy your surplus land, make blossom the waste places in your fields, and run your factories. While doing this, you can be sure in the future, as in the past, that you and your families will be surrounded by the most patient, faithful, law-abiding, and unresentful people that the world has seen. As we have proved our loyalty to you in the past, in nursing your children, watching by the sick bed of your mothers and fathers, and often following them with tear-dimmed eyes to their graves, so in the future, in our humble way, we shall stand by you with a devotion that no foreigner can approach, ready to lay down our lives, if need be, in defense of yours, interlacing our industrial, commercial, civil, and religious life with yours in a way that shall make the interests of both races one. In all things that are purely social we can be as separate as the fingers, yet one as the hand in all things essential to mutual progress.

There is no defense or security for any of us except in the highest intelligence and development of all. If anywhere there are efforts tending to curtail the fullest growth of the Negro, let these efforts be turned into stimulating, encouraging, and making him the most useful and intelligent citizen. Effort or means so invested will pay a thousand per cent interest. These efforts will be twice blessed—"Blessing him that gives and him that takes."

There is no escape through law of man or God from the inevitable:

> The laws of changeless justice bind
>   Oppressor with oppressed;
> And close as sin and suffering joined
>   We march to fare abreast.

Nearly sixteen million hands will aid you in pulling the load upward, or they will pull, against you, the load downward. We shall constitute one-third and more of the ignorance and crime of the South, or one-third its intelligence and progress; we shall contribute one-third to the business and industrial prosperity of the South, or we shall prove a veritable body of death, stagnating, depressing, retarding every effort to advance the body politic.

Gentlemen of the Exposition, as we present to you our humble effort at an exhibition of our progress, you must not expect overmuch. Starting thirty years ago with ownership here and there in a few quilts and pumpkins and chickens (gathered from miscellaneous sources), remember, the path that has led from these to the inventions and production of agricultural implements, buggies, steam engines, newspapers, books, statuary carving, paintings, the management of drugstores and banks, has not been trodden without contact with thorns and thistles. While we take pride in what we exhibit as a result of our independent efforts, we do not for a moment forget that our part in this exhibition would fall far short of your expectations but for the constant help that has come to our educational life, not only from the Southern states, but especially from Northern philanthropists, who have made their gifts a constant stream of blessing and encouragement.

The wisest among my race understand that the agitation of questions of social equality is the extremest folly, and that progress in the enjoyment of all the privileges that will come to us must be the result of severe and constant struggle rather than of artificial forcing. No race that has anything to contribute to the markets of the world is long, in any degree, ostracized. It is important and right that all privileges of the law be ours, but it is vastly more important that we be prepared for the exercise of those privileges. The opportunity to earn a dollar in a factory just now is worth infinitely more than the opportunity to spend a dollar in an opera house.

In conclusion, may I repeat that nothing in thirty years has given us more hope and encouragement, and drawn us so near to you of the white race, as this opportunity offered by the Exposition; and here bending, as it were, over the altar that represents the results of the struggles of your race and mine, both starting practically empty-handed three decades ago, I pledge that, in your effort to work out the great and intricate problem which God has laid at the doors of the South, you shall have at all times the patient, sympathetic help of my race; only let this be constantly in mind, that while, from representations in these buildings of the product of field, of forest, of mine, of factory, letters, and art, much good will come, yet far above and beyond material benefits will be that higher good, that, let us pray God, will come in a blotting out of sectional differences and racial animosities and suspicions, in a determination to administer absolute justice, in a willing obedience among all classes to the mandates of law. This, coupled with our material prosperity, will bring into our beloved South a new heaven and a new earth.

Chapter 31

The Pan African Ethos of W. E. B. Du Bois

Randall O. Westbrook

W. E. B. Du Bois is the embodiment of the Africana thinker. In a career that spanned more than three-quarters of a century, his work defined the manner in which African Americans were viewed, and viewed themselves. His public intellectualism included pioneering academic achievement, groundbreaking research on the human condition, and iconic literary efforts. His social and political presence was central to the formation of several civil rights organizations; his embrace of African American artistic endeavor both for its aesthetic and socio-political value encouraged a protracted, if celebrated and unprecedented, period of appreciation of that art which remains a paragon for the African American artist. In short, his ability to identify and articulate the social, educational, and political essence of the African American experience provided a set of guiding principles and a vocabulary of relevance and self-determination for African Americans in the twentieth century.

Born in Great Barrington, Massachusetts, in 1868, Du Bois boasted ancestral participation in freedom movements from the Revolutionary War to Haiti to the Civil War. This appeared to have imbued him with a sense of credibility as a clear voice in the struggle for African American political relevance, as well as an inherited sense of responsibility for "race" leadership. Such attributes were evidenced early, as Du Bois began finding his voice as a 14-year-old, writing for two newspapers, one regional, another with limited national exposure for primarily African American readership. Despite his youth and the limited scope and exposure to his work, Du Bois often called upon his readers to consider broader implications:

> There is on foot a movement looking toward holding of a county convention of the colored Republicans of this county, which is meeting with great favor and regarded as a move in the right direction. There also seems to be a general regret that among all the people that there are no business men among us, and desire to remedy this evil is becoming more and more manifest. (cited from Aptheker 1985:83)

After being the sole African American graduate of his class at Great Barrington High School, and following a yearlong hiatus due to the ill health and death of his mother, Du Bois enrolled at Fisk University in Nashville, Tennessee. His three years at the predominantly black college accorded him his first experiences with African Americans who aspired to intellectual leadership. When Du Bois arrived on the campus of Fisk University in the fall of 1885, despite his experience in discussing matters of importance in the African American community, he was unaware of the subtleties and nuances of racial dynamics in the south. He was equally naïve about the nature of everyday life for African Americans, and what role education played in those lives. In the summer of 1886, and again in the following summer of 1887, Du Bois ventured about 60 miles east from the Fisk campus to Alexandria, Tennessee. What he found was a town scarcely removed from the ravages of slavery. He set up the school and worked his way deftly around the farming schedules of the families whose children attended the school. While he slept in the schoolhouse during the week, on the weekends Du Bois stayed in the homes of the various families of his students. In addition to bearing direct witness to the meager nature of the accommodations, these visits provided for Du Bois the most intimate sense of the manner in which the families lived. In all, his experiences over those two summers would last but four months, however, they would have a lasting impact on his life, work, and perspective.

Following his graduation from Fisk in 1888, Du Bois enrolled at Harvard University. As social mores restricted his social interaction with other students, he found intellectual camaraderie with faculty members such as William James, founder of Pragmatism. James was key in encouraging Du Bois to pursue graduate study in history, as the best means to articulate race leadership.

In October of 1890, Du Bois composed a short essay entitled "Something About Me," for a graduate writing course. He wrote: "In early youth a great bitterness entered my life and kindled a great ambition. I wanted to go to college because others did. I came and graduated and am now in search of a Ph.D. and bread. I believe, foolishly perhaps but sincerely, that I have something to say to the world and I have taken English twelve in order to help me say it" (Du Bois, 1985:16–17). This brief sample of Du Bois's writing showed that although secure about his ability to speak to his sense of mission for racial uplift, he was aware of the link between literacy and leadership and sought to improve his abilities to that end. It also showed that he was beginning to develop the better understanding of the role of education in his efforts toward Negro uplift. In much of his work of the period of the study, Du Bois continued to speak of education as a means to achieve and sustain relevant citizenship.

As he neared completion of his master's degree, toward the end of 1890, accounts of a speech at Johns Hopkins University was brought to Du Bois's attention that altered the way he thought about himself and his role as a burgeoning African American public intellectual. Former president of the United States, Rutherford B. Hayes, in his capacity as administrator of the John F. Slater Fund (a trust fund established for Negro colleges and their students) discussed progress made by Negro students striving to gain the skills necessary to ensure academic success at the collegiate level (Hogeboom, 1995:518). He also expressed skepticism about the ability of Negro college students to pursue graduate study at European universities:

> We are willing to give him money for the education to Europe or to give him an advanced education, but hitherto their chief and almost only gift has been that of oratory . . . but I do not despair of the other negroes (sic.), but am rather hopeful of their being uplifted in the future (Hayes, 1959:159).

Reactions were swift in the days immediately following Hayes's comments. He received letters of inquiry from several African American students seeking funding for study in Europe; one such request came from Du Bois, the day after the speech was recounted in the pages of *The Boston Herald*. Du Bois's letter was different from the others, primarily in that the quality of his educational experiences far exceeded other applications. Further, he provided a rather high-powered list of references, including three college presidents and eight professors, most of whom were from Fisk and Harvard (Hayes, 1959:281).

In the ensuing exchange between Hayes and Du Bois, the aspiring scholar came just short of calling the ex-president a liar. Du Bois criticized Hayes for his disparaging comments about the African American intellectual acuity, labeling the Slater Fund as hypocritical; seemingly more concerned with producing men and women of questionable character (and even more questionable intellect) than it was in engaging in the encouragement of scholarship for the purpose of Negro uplift:

> You went before a number of keenly observant men who looked upon you as an authority in the matter, and told them in substance that the Negroes of the United States either couldn't or wouldn't embrace a more liberal opportunity for advancement . . . the offer is suddenly withdrawn while the impression remains (Du Bois, 1985:13–14).

It is unclear whether Du Bois was cognizant of the concern that a scholarship offer made to an African American with his credentials (a two baccalaureate degrees, and a master's degree from Harvard) might result in recrimination against the scholarship fund. Based purely on his accomplishments, his application would surely have been the most worthy of the applicants, thereby making any other candidate's acceptance suspicious. His circle of friends included others with enviable academic credentials, all with an eye toward uplift. Therefore, a rebuff held implications far beyond a fellowship for study. To Du Bois, it signaled that the interest in and support for the training of African Americans to lead themselves into the next phase of enlightened citizenship would have to increasingly come from African Americans themselves.

The ensuing responses from Hayes were polite, but non-committal about Du Bois's prospects for earning the fellowship. For his part, Du Bois continued to correspond, sending supplemental information about future plans and his socioeconomic and ethnic background. Despite the quality of his application, on May 2, 1891, he received word of the Slater Fund's decision to not finance his plan to study in Europe. In his response, Du Bois, in resigning hopes, stated bitterly his belief that the outcome while disappointing was not unexpected. He continued, questioning the veracity of the offer of the scholarship, as well as the motives of Hayes and other members of the board. He concluded his letter by demanding an apology—not to himself, but to "the Negro people" (Du Bois, 1985). Finally, in April of 1892, eighteen months after his initial inquiry, he was awarded a package of grants and loans, which he used for study at the University of Berlin.

For Du Bois, the two years in Berlin were intellectually and culturally enlightening; he took all of his courses in German and experienced a different level of interaction between student and teacher—one much more formal, and seemingly, more to his liking than his studies at Fisk or Harvard. Socially, for the first time since his childhood days in Great Barrington, Du Bois also found himself as a part of a White sub-culture for which the sting of racism was more muted than he'd experienced in America: "I had a very, very interesting time. I began to realize that white people were human," he recounted of his experiences (Du Bois, 1960:76).

In late February of 1893, four months after arriving on the campus of the University of Berlin, Du Bois celebrated his birthday solemnly, and alone, in his boarding house room. As he did with most of his comings and goings of this period, Du Bois recorded the "festivities" in his journal. Entered as a "Program for the Celebration of My Twenty-Fifth Birthday," it included music (singing dirges and Negro spirituals), refreshment (sliced oranges and wine), and concluded with a prayer for his parents. Filled with emotion, Du Bois offered a vow to a renewed direction for his life: "I go to bed after one of the happiest days of my life," he effused, "I am glad I am living. I rejoice as a strong man to run a race, and I am strong—is it egotism—is it assurance—or is it the silent call of the world spirit that makes me feel that I am royal and that beneath my scepter the kings of the world bow" (Du Bois, 1985:27–28).

As he concluded, Du Bois reminded himself (in a manner as if he was aware that the world was watching, of his aim to work toward the ends of racial uplift, through the means of his extraordinary intellectual gifts:

> I therefore take the work that the Unknown lay in my hands and work for the rise of the Negro people, taking for granted that their best development means the best development of the world . . . these are my plans: to make a name in science, to make a name in literature and thus to raise my race. Or perhaps to make a visible empire in Africa thro' England, France or Germany. I wonder what will be the outcome? Who knows? (Du Bois, 1985:29)

Du Bois fell short of his goal of completing his doctoral studies in Berlin, having been informed that his fellowship would not be renewed. And so, he returned home, having realized the significance of his superior academic accomplishment on the landscape of progressive African American leadership. He was invited to complete his studies at Harvard, becoming the first African American to complete a Harvard PhD. In doing so, given his other work at Fisk, Harvard, and Berlin Du Bois emerged as one of the most educated men in the United States. Despite his accomplishments, he still realized that opportunities for consideration and advancement would be limited by the strictures of race.

Paradoxically, Du Bois often girded himself against such rebuffs by cloaking himself in what biographers and contemporaries (both supporters and opponents) considered "racial fluidity." That is, at times, he used phrases that seemed to suggest that he had options in the way of the manner in which he identified himself racially, as if he was Black "by choice." Throughout his life, Du Bois spoke of his embrace of race leadership as a noble endeavor, even one that he felt necessary, yet one that appeared to simultaneously give him a sense of moral superiority over anyone—White or Black—who challenged the validity of his work. This theme would be repeated—occasionally with perplexing results throughout his career and life.

Du Bois spent nearly two years in Germany, taking all courses in German, and was only months away from having earned a PhD from one of the most prestigious universities in the world. Had he been able to complete it, by any measurable standard, Du Bois would have returned to America as one of the country's most intellectually credentialed men. However, the Slater Fund rejected his appeal for an extension, and encouraged him to return home, and to Harvard University to complete his doctorate. Shortly after his return, Du Bois was offered and accepted a teaching position at Wilberforce University. While there, he completed his dissertation on Atlantic slave trade during this time. At the end of the school year, Du Bois married, and also accepted an offer to become the lead researcher on a project to study living conditions of "Negroes in Philadelphia," at the University of Pennsylvania.

In 1897, Du Bois was called upon to lead a study about living conditions among the African American population in Philadelphia. For his groundbreaking study, *The Philadelphia Negro*, he personally conducted interviews of more than 2,000 families in Philadelphia's South Ward. Largely ignored by the sponsoring institution, the University of Pennsylvania, Du Bois concluded his work and accepted a position at Ohio's Wilberforce University for one year.

Also during the time that Du Bois embarked on research for **The Philadelphia Negro**, he was invited to join with a group of Negro intellectuals in the development of The American Negro Academy. Despite sporadic attendance and participation, Du Bois contributed immediately, writing the organization's first position paper, "The Conservation of the Races." In addition to identifying goals and objectives of the Academy, he encouraged self-determination and development of political and cultural development among African Americans to ensure their survival:

As such, it is our duty to conserve our physical powers, our intellectual endowments, our spiritual ideals; as a race we must strive by race organization, by race solidarity, by race unity to the realization of that broader humanity which freely recognizes differences in men, but sternly deprecates inequality in their opportunities of development.

For accomplishment of these ends we need race organizations: Negro colleges, Negro newspapers, Negro business organizations, a Negro school of literature and art, and an intellectual clearing house for all these products of the Negro mind, which we may call a Negro Academy. Not only is all this necessary for positive advance, it is absolutely imperative for negative defense (Du Bois, 1897:12).

The goal of this group of accomplished Negro intellectuals who made up the American Negro Academy was to use their intellectual gifts to develop strategies to elevate African–Americans' socio-economic status. Some of them were more effective in bringing these issues to the attention of non-Blacks in position to join them in developing and effecting solutions. But ultimately, it was through this work, that Du Bois grew in intellectual stature and political prominence, emerging as a voice for more progressive change in the social and political status for African Americans.

Although the original stated purpose of the American Negro Academy was development of an African American think tank, in a short time, given the political climate of the country at that time, the philosophical direction of the ANA crystallized around a growing distrust of and concern over policies and practices of Booker T. Washington. Du Bois led the organization, but he was by no means the sole dissenting voice—contrary to the distress of Washington. As a result of his misinterpretation, and misinformation from his minions, Washington and Du Bois continued to trade barbs for 20 years. What was briefly a precarious, but polite association became increasingly personal and acrimonious, until the rivalry, and the stridency and divergence of political philosophy of adherents of their respective ideologies would threaten to distract the progress of African American political progress for decades.

The struggle with Washington marked the first significant pushback against Du Bois in his burgeoning career as a Race Leader. He was often criticized about what was believed to be the loftiness of his ideas, and disaffection for the black underclass. Du Bois was able to turn aside much of the criticism, but only occasionally, and while the names of his detractors may have changed, while the stiffness of the opposition ebbed and flowed, for most of his long career Du Bois was nevertheless forced to dodge such criticism.

In 1898, Du Bois accepted a position at Atlanta University, in which in addition to teaching courses in sociology (something he had been prohibited from doing at Wilberforce), he was to lead an ambitious research program. On the heels of the critically received **Philadelphia Negro**, Du Bois was asked to direct long-term research about the lives of African Americans in the mold of his own research efforts and similarly focused studies conducted at Tuskegee Institute. Despite his growing reputation as the pre-eminent scholar of the African American experience, Du Bois struggled with gaining interest and credibility for what would become known as the **Atlanta University Studies**:

I was very much disappointed at the results of my studies. They had become important, they were known all over the world; in Germany, in England, France they had been noticed and referred to, and in the United States all college libraries had sets of them. But it didn't have much effect upon what the people were doing and thinking in the South. And I began to realize that I had overworked a theory—that the cause of the problems was the ignorance of the people; that the cure wasn't simply telling people the truth, it was inducing them to act on the truth. . . . It wasn't enough, in other words simply to study the Negro problem and put the truth before people. You've got to begin with propaganda and tell the people; when you know something is wrong, you've got to do something about it (Du Bois, 1960:146–147).

Although recognized early, this "revelation" of sorts energized Du Bois's future research and provided him with clearer themes around which his work could be based. Going forward, he would endeavor to use his research to encourage self-reliance among African Americans and inform white readers of his work of the richness of the African American experience.

At the bridge between the nineteenth and twentieth centuries, Du Bois re-doubled his efforts to connect to an African consciousness. He continued his research on African American life, through his "Atlanta University Studies," as well as his somewhat detached stewardship of the American Negro Academy. In 1899, he began work on the development of the "American Negro Exhibit" for the 1900 World's Fair in Paris. His work on this effort earned him honors as a presenter, as well as acclaim from his broadest audience to date. Weeks later, as one of the delegates to the London Pan African Congress, Du Bois made remarks that he would later prophetically echo in *The Souls of Black Folk*, when he declared that "the problem of the twentieth century is the problem of the colour line . . ." These remarks punctuated the first period in which Du Bois articulated the global significance of the richness of the African experience to the world (Du Bois, 1969:10).

In 1903, the increasingly contentious relationship between Du Bois and Booker T. Washington played out on the pages of several widely read books about the African American experience. *The Negro Problem: A Series of Articles by Representative American Negroes of Today*, was an anthology featuring works from a number of prominent African American political thinkers, including Du Bois, Washington, Charles W. Chesnutt, and Paul Laurence Dunbar. Washington's essay, "Industrial Education" extolled the virtues of the industrial education, and seemed to suggest dismissal of intellectual training as "the pushing of mere abstract knowledge" (Washington, 1903 and others:16). Du Bois's essay, "The Talented Tenth," rebutted many of Washington's points, calling for, among other things, the development of a leadership elite from the small but swelling ranks of college-educated African Americans. He also suggested a certain hypocrisy in Washington's public aversion to intellectuals, betrayed in his preference for the hiring of scholars at Tuskegee Institute, the college Washington founded in 1881:

> *Thus, again, in the manning of trade schools and manual training schools we are thrown back upon the higher training as its source and chief support. There was a time when any aged and worn out carpenter could teach in a trade school. But not so to-day. Indeed the demand for college-bred men by a school like Tuskegee, ought to make Mr. Booker T. Washington the firmest friend of higher training. Here he has as helpers the son of a Negro senator, trained in Greek and the humanities, and graduated at Harvard; the son of a Negro congressman and lawyer, trained in Latin and mathematics, and graduated at Oberlin; he has as his wife, a woman who read Virgil and Homer in the same class room with me; he has as college chaplain, a classical graduate of Atlanta University; as teacher of science, a graduate of Fisk; as teacher of history, a graduate of Smith, indeed some thirty of his chief teachers are college graduates, and instead of studying French grammars in the midst of weeds, or buying pianos for dirty cabins, they are at Mr. Washington's right hand helping him in a noble work. And yet one of the effects of Mr. Washington's propaganda has been to throw doubt upon the expediency of such training for Negroes, as these persons have had. (Du Bois, 1969:73-74)*

Shortly after the publication of *The Negro Problem*, Du Bois's own anthology of essays *The Souls of Black Folk* was published. The fifteen essays, which ranged from the personal to the political, fiction, as well as fact-based, gave Du Bois another opportunity to discuss his developing his uniquely Africana ideology. It also allowed him to continue to address mounting concerns about claims Booker T. Washington made that seemed to diminish the importance of traditional, academic education for African Americans. The book, which was a critical and popular success, marked the low point of the contentious relationship between the two titans of African American political leadership in the early part of the twentieth century.

In 1909, Du Bois was central to the founding of the National Association for the Advancement of Colored People (NAACP). He served as Director of Research as well as editor-in-chief for *The Crisis*, the periodical of the organization. While the research he conducted and supervised provided the organization a sense of direction, validating their work in the struggle against race-based oppression, it was his vision of the presentation of words and images in the pages of *The Crisis* that resonated and attracted the first loyal members. Notably, *The Crisis* showed readers first glimpses of the works of many of the famed artists from the "Harlem Renaissance" period.

During the 1920s, Du Bois experienced a curious reversal of fortune, when his primacy on the landscape of African American political leadership occasioned a challenge by the new generation of political leaders who considered him too conservative to bring substantive progress for African Americans. Young firebrands such as A. Philip Randolph and Marcus Garvey represented the first test to Du Bois's leadership since Booker T. Washington. However, unlike the earlier conflict between Du Bois and Washington—in which the two principals largely limited their public struggles to philosophical direction—the enmity between Du Bois and Garvey descended into more openly public personal attacks and character assassination. Although both individuals claimed that the root of their conflict was political and ideological, often, it was neither. The contentious nature of their differences seemed to be based upon a fundamental, personal dislike, accelerated with a focus on social class, regional points of origin and skin color gradation. Garvey questioned Du Bois's legitimacy as a Race Leader based on Du Bois's Eurocentric formal education and his comparatively light skin color; Du Bois spoke of Garvey's dark complexion, other physical characteristics, and the pomposity present in Garvey's public dealings. Garvey's arrest and virtual exile was met with indifference by Du Bois, to the point where even some of Du Bois's most ardent supporters wondered aloud if he had gone too far in his attacks, and to what extent such attacks contributed to Garvey's arrest.

For Du Bois, the 1920s represented more than a period of fending off the advances of pretenders to his primacy as a race leader in the decade following the death of Booker T. Washington. Du bois continued his role as scholar-provocateur, convening a series of conferences that revolved around Pan African concerns. These iterations of Pan African Conferences, brought together intellectuals from the United States and the Caribbean; European émigrés of African descent and aspiring leaders from emerging African nations. These meetings, in which Du Bois was invariably found at or near the epicenter of the calls for self-reliance for peoples of African descent, left little doubt as to the degree to esteem in which he was held outside the United States. And while an honorific from the United States, as an emissary in Liberia, seemed to suggest that he was gaining recognition and approval as a race leader on a broader scale, his furtive support of African American students at historically black colleges resulted in unprecedented recognition and acclaim, and yielded unexpected results among African Americans. It was during this period that Fisk and Howard, under the weight of student demonstrations and searing editorials in *The Crisis* appointed their first African American presidents.

Du Bois's unique perspective about the importance of all aspects of the African experience in America and elsewhere allowed him to vociferously support efforts of the artisans who comprised the talent of the Harlem Renaissance. However, Du Bois went well beyond trumpeting their exploits; his uncompromising insistence on the inherent politicization of all products emerging from the African experience—particularly those bursting forth from the "New Negro," in America—led him to exhort artists to view their work as powerfully transformative, and provocative tools of self-reliance:

> I stand in utter shamelessness and say that what art I have for writing has been used always for propaganda for gaining the right of black folk to love and enjoy. I do not care a damn for any art that is not used for propaganda. But I do care when propaganda is confined to one side while the other is stripped and silent . . . (Du Bois, 1995:514).

Du Bois's espousal of this race-rich ethos rankled many of the younger artists of the period, but the rising tide of resistance that questioned his fidelity to the cause of African American self-reliance was momentarily stilled.

In the 1930s and 1940s, Du Bois grew increasingly disillusioned with the pace of progress of African Americans. The stridency of his views, in which he moved further and inexorably away from integrationism to separatism, alienated him from most "mainstream" organizations interested in African American uplift. In 1934, constant calls for him to moderate his views prompted him to resign from the editor's chair of *The Crisis*. For the next decade and a half, Du Bois moved between Atlanta University and the offices of the NAACP, teaching, continuing his research at the former, and engaging in increasingly frustrating conflicts with the latter. Finally, after nearly 40 years with the organization he helped found, Du Bois and the NAACP bitterly parted ways in 1948.

While revered abroad, the late 1940s and early 1950s presented the effective end to Du Bois's political relevance in the United States. His growing disaffection for African American social elite was represented by his expulsion from the NAACP, and removal from Atlanta University. As much as his increasingly public enmity—which threatened fund-raising efforts and invited unwanted, undue scrutiny for both organizations, it was Du Bois's political shift that many found troubling. He continued to embrace causes believed to have their roots in socialism and communism. For his part, Du Bois maintained that the interests of such groups as the Council for African Affairs, and the Progressive Party, was speaking to the needs of the African American masses in a way the NAACP and the emerging black middle class had long since abdicated. When, in 1951, he was indicted for his affiliation with leftist groups in the United States and Europe, voices of those groups who once held him up as a standard bearer fell strangely silent. And although ultimately acquitted, the trial proved embarrassing for a man once considered to be among the most influential African Americans leaders since Reconstruction. This lack of support from African American leadership exacerbated his disaffection, not only with his country, but especially with other African Americans (particularly those whose ascent to positions of prominence was largely owed to Du Bois's activism), whose reluctance to fully engage politically. Du Bois believed that this disengagement was harmful to African American advancement. He publicly vented his frustration during this period, most notably in a 1948 speech dubbed "The Talented Tenth Memorial Address." In this speech, he expressed disappointment in that segment of African American leadership, and proposed a "reorientation" of his original iteration:

> Willingness to work and make personal sacrifice for solving these problems was of course, the first prerequisite and sine qua non, I did not stress this, I assumed it. In my youth and idealism, I did not realize that selfishness is even more natural than sacrifice. I made the assumption of its wide availability because of the spirit of sacrifice learned in my mission school training [at Fisk] . . .

> My [new] Talented Tenth must be more than talented, and work not simply as individuals. Its passport to leadership was not alone learning but expert knowledge of modern economics as it affected American Negroes; and in addition to this and fundamental, would be its willingness to sacrifice and plan . . . as would make the rise of our group possible (Du Bois, 1948:350).

In his final years, despite views many considered too far left to allow full participation in the evolving dialogue, Du Bois began to slowly regain his political stature as a venerated elder statesman in the African American community. After regaining his visa, Du Bois was allowed to travel outside the United States, to such places as the Soviet Union and to China, where he was lauded as a hero. In 1961, following endorsement of the Ghanaian parliament, Du Bois was invited to Ghana to initiate work on an encyclopedia of African peoples around the world. Kwame Nkrumah, president of Ghana, and a Du Bois devotee, asked him to remain in the country to complete the work and to serve as an advisor. Ultimately, the Encyclopedia was not completed, as Du Bois died at the age of 95 on August 27, 1963, on the eve of the historic "March on Washington."

Conclusion

In a 1915 essay "the African Roots of war," W. E. B. Du Bois in discussing the potential of political and cultural primacy in Africa, presciently warned: "These nations and races, composing as they do a vast majority of humanity, are going to endure this treatment just as long as they must and not a moment longer. Then they are going to fight and the War of the color Line will outdo in savage inhumanity any war this world has yet seen…" Eight years before his first trip to Africa, and nearly a half century prior to his decision to emigrate to Ghana, where he lived out the rest of his remarkable 95 years, Du Bois presented what could be called a Pan African manifesto. This was not the first time Du Bois effectively sent a shot across the bow of those who would seek to limit the progress or the aspirations of peoples of African descent—nor would it be the last.

Du Bois began writing for public consumption in 1882, as an adolescent, and continued writing until days before his death in the summer of 1963. During that time, he saved nearly everything he wrote, and was written to him, including correspondence and even personal notes and memos to himself. This provides students of his life and work invaluable opportunities to extract fuller contextual understanding of him relative to Africana thought.

There were several milestone moments in his life that marked significant points of interest in his political development and his contributions to Pan-African thought. His early years, prior to his arrival at Fisk offered an impressive foreshadowing of his interest in public intellectualism; an opportunity to use intellect as a means of empowering African Americans in an era when such notions were met with strident opposition. His years at Fisk University providing him with the first glimpse of what he envisioned as "The Talented Tenth." During this time, his work as a rural school teacher energized him in his belief in the transformative power of education for African Americans in the generation following Emancipation.

Du Bois's life at Harvard, the University of Berlin and back to Harvard, provided students of his work with the fire within, as Du Bois began to find his calling and his voice. During this time, he came to grips with a truer understanding of himself and his role as an emerging leader of the African American intelligentsia. As he strived toward being the first African American to earn a Harvard PhD, he continued on to other groundbreaking work, notably *The Philadelphia Negro*. Whether through his correspondence surrounding his 18 months in Berlin, or the completion of his monumental dissertation, or his sociological works, Du Bois made America aware of the potency of the African American mind and spirit.

The turn of the century brought new leadership challenges, as Du Bois began to exert himself beyond the boundaries of the "Negro" world, and beyond the borders of the United States. His editorial leadership on the *Atlanta University Studies*, work at the World's Fair of 1900, and the succeeding Pan African conferences, rendered him for the first time, a citizen of the world to be reckoned with. And although the first instances of his troubling "racial fluidity," began to appear, Du Bois could still often be found as the clearest, most salient voice speaking on behalf of peoples of African descent. Any doubts to this effect would have been definitively put to rest with the publication of "The Talented Tenth," and *The Souls of Black Folk.*

Although there were times where Du Bois appeared to suggest that his "blackness" was somehow a choice, or circumstance—and thereby occasionally calling into question his commitment to the cause of Black Liberation—Du Bois remained a central player in the development of Black leadership, not only politically, through his work with the NAACP, and national Urban League, but through his many publications, and his editorship of *The Crisis*, but through his support of the artistic explosion called the Harlem Renaissance. Again during this time, Du Bois found himself in the middle of a "turf war" with the likes of A. Philip Randolph, Marcus Garvey, and others, who questioned whether Du Bois' methods and philosophy was in step with the rest of African Americans.

The 1930s and 1940s allowed Du Bois to continue to write research and exercise his political muscle. However, constant pushback by his colleagues at the NAACP, among others, sought not only a reduced role but a reduction in volume, rhetoric, and tone on Du Bois's part. His effectual ousting from the NAACP represented a period of decline in Du Bois's political relevance. The near-end came in the late 1940s and 1950s when people formerly loyal to Du Bois—or at least his ideals—no longer embraced him for fear of political reprisal. The denouement of this episode may have come as he essentially declared his once vaunted "Talented Tenth" nearly dead as a conversation. And while he was able to rebuild some of his political relevance before his death, Du Bois can be said to have never fully been able to bask in the glory of the lives of African Americans for whom he waged a more than 80-year battle.

W. E. B. Du Bois's name evokes pride, fidelity to a sense of commitment to uplift for peoples of African descent the world over, as much as it inspires excellence, and the clarion cries for freedom, self-determination and strong intelligent leadership. And although his most famous works—still quoted as if being penned now—were written in the early hours of the twentieth century, they reverberate into the twenty-first century with the same searing impact and relevance. Ultimately, whatever shame the nation and the world may feel at the righteous indignation occasioned by the slow pace of progress, it can be said with pride that a titan in the person of Du Bois gave voice to the voiceless whose cries still need to be heard.

References

Andrews, William L. (Ed.). (1985). Critical Essays on W. E. B. Du Bois. Boston: G.K. Hall and Company.

Aptheker, Herbert (Ed.). (1973). *The Education of Black People: Ten Critiques, 1906–1960 by W. E. B. Du Bois*. New York: The Monthly Review Press.

_____. (1973). *The Correspondence of W. E. B. Du Bois, Volume I*. Amherst, Massachusetts: University of Massachusetts Press.

_____. (1976). *The Correspondence of W. E. B. Du Bois, Volume II*. Amherst, Massachusetts: University of Massachusetts Press.

_____. (1978). *The Correspondence of W. E. B. Du Bois, Volume III*. Amherst, Massachusetts: University of Massachusetts Press.

_____. (1982). *Writings by W. E. B. Du Bois in Periodicals Edited By Others: Volume 1, 1891–1909*. Millwood, NY: Kraus-Thomson Organization Limited.

_____. (1985). *Against Racism: Unpublished Essays, Papers, Addresses, 1887–1961 by W. E. B. Du Bois*. Amherst, Massachusetts: The University of Massachusetts Press.

_____. (1989). *The Literary Legacy of W. E. B. Du Bois*. White Plains, New York: Kraus International Publications.

The Atlanta University Publications, Nos. 1, 2, 4, 8, 9, 11, 13, 14, 15, 16, 17, 18. (1968). New York: Arno Press.

The Atlanta University Publications, Nos. 3, 5, 6, 7, 10, 12, 19, 20. (1969). New York: Arno Press.

Broderick, Francis L. (1959). *W. E. B. Du Bois: Negro Leader in a Time of Crisis*. Stanford: Stanford University Press.

Du Bois, Shirley Graham. (1971). *His Day is Marching On: A Memoir of W. E. B. Du Bois*. Philadelphia: J. B. Lippincott and Company.

Du Bois, W. E. B. (1897). The American Negro Academy Occasional Papers, New York: Arno Press.

_____. (1935). *Black Reconstruction in America*. Antheneum. New York.

_____. (1960). Oral History Interview, Columbia University Oral History Project, New York: Columbia University.

_____. (1967). *The Philadelphia Negro*. New York: Schocken Books.

_____. (1968). *Autobiography of W. E. B. Du Bois*. International Publishers. USA.

_____. (1968). *Dusk of Dawn*. New York: Schocken Books.

_____. (1969). *The Souls of Black Folk*. New York: Signet Classic.

_____. (1969). *The Suppression of the African Slave Trade*. Baton Rouge: Louisiana State University Press.

_____. (1970). *The Gift of Black Folk: The Negro in the Making of America*. New York: Washington Square Press.

_____. (1975). *Darkwater: Voices from Within the Veil*. Millwood, New York: Kraus-Thomson Organization Limited.

_____. (1976). *In the Battle for Peace*. Millwood, New York: Kraus-Thompson Organization Limited.

_____. (1995). "Criteria of Negro Art," in David Levering Lewis (ed.), W. E. B. Du Bois: A Reader, New York: Henry Holt and Co.

Franklin, John Hope and Moss, Alfred A. (1994). *From Slavery to Freedom: A History of African Americans*. New York: Alfred A. Knopf.

Frantz, Nevin R. Jr. (1997). "The Contributions of Booker T. Washington and W. E. B. Du Bois in the Development of Vocational Education." Journal of Industrial Teacher Education. Summer 1997.

Green, Dan and Driver, Edwin D. (Eds.). (1978). *W. E. B. Du Bois on Sociology and the Black Community*. Chicago: The University of Chicago Press.

Harlan, Louis R. (1972). *Booker T. Washington: The Making of a Black Leader; 1856–1901*. New York: Oxford University Press.

_____. (1983). *Booker T. Washington: The Wizard of Tuskegee; 1901–1915*. New York: Oxford University Press.

Harris, Thomas E. (1993). *Analysis of the Clash over Issues between Booker T. Washington and W. E. B. Du Bois*. New York: Garland Publishing.

Hayes, Rutherford B. (1959). Teach the Freeman: The Corrrespondence of Rutherford B. Hayes and the Slater Fund for Education, 1881–1893. Edited by Louis D. Rubin, Baton: Rouge: Louisiana State University Press.

Hogeboom, Ari. (1995). *Rutherford B. Hayes Warrior and President*. Lawrence, Kansas: University of Kansas Press.

Horne, Gerald. (1986). *Black and Red: W. E. B. Du Bois and the Afro-American Response to the Cold War, 1944–1963*. Albany, New York: State University of New York Press.

Juguo, Zhang. (2001). *W. E. B. Du Bois: The Quest for the Abolition of the Color Line*. New York: Routledge Press.

Katz, Michael B. and Sugrue, Thomas J. (Eds.) (1998). *W. E. B. Du Bois, Race and the City: The Philadelphia Negro and Its Legacy*. Philadelphia: University of Pennsylvania Press.

Lewis, David Levering. (1979). "Dr. Johnson's Friends." The Massachusetts Review. August 1979.

_____. (1979). *When Harlem Was in Vogue*. New York: Oxford University Press.

_____. (1993). *W. E. B. Du Bois: Biography of a Race, 1868–1919*. New York: Henry Holt and Company.

_____. (1995). *W. E. B. Du Bois: W. E. B. Du Bois: A Reader*. New York: Henry Holt and Company.

_____. (2000). *W. E. B. Du Bois: The Fight for Equality and the American Century, 1919–1963*. New York: Henry Holt and Company.

Locke, Alain. (Ed.). (1968). *The New Negro: An Interpretation*. New York: Arno Press.

Logan, Rayford. (Ed.). (1971). *W. E. B. Du Bois: A Profile*. New York: Hill and Wang.

Marable, Manning. (1986). *W. E. B. Du Bois: Black Radical Democrat*. G.K. Hall and Company.

Martin, Tony. (1976). *Race First*. Dover, Massachusetts: The Majority Press.

Moon, Henry Lee. (Ed.) (1972). *The Emerging Thought of W. E. B. Du Bois*. New York: Simon and Schuster.

Moss, Alfred A. (1981). *American Negro Academy: Voice of the Talented Tenth*. Baton Rouge: Louisiana State University Press.

Myrdal, Gunnar. (1962). *An American Dilemma*. New York: Harper and Row, Publishers.

Ovington, Mary White. (1947). *Walls Came Tumbling Down*. New York: Harcourt, Brace and Company.

Proceedings of the National Negro Conference 1909. (1969). New York: Arno Press.

Provenzo, Eugene F. Jr. (Ed.) (2002). *Du Bois on Education*. Walnut Creek, California: Alta Mira Press.

Rampersad, Arnold. (1990). *The Art and Imagination of W. E. B. Du Bois*. New York: Schocken Books.

Reed, Adolph L. Jr. (1997). *W. E. B. Du Bois and American Political Thought; Fabianism and the Color Line*. New York: Oxford University Press.

Rubin, Louis D. (Ed.). (1959). *Teach the Freeman; The Correspondence of Rutherford B. Hayes and Slater Fund for Education, 1881–1893*. Baton Rouge: Louisiana State University Press. Reprint 1969. New York: Kraus Publishing.

Rudwick, Elliot M. (1972). *W. E. B. Du Bois: Propagandist of the Negro Protest*. New York: Antheneum.

Washington, Booker T. (1963). *Up From Slavery*. Garden City, New York: Doubleday and Company.

_____. (1969). *The Story of My Life and Work*. New York: Negro University Press.

_____. (1969). *Working With Hands*. New York: Negro University Press.

Washington, Booker T. and others. (1903). *The Negro Problem*. New York: James Pott and Company.

Woodson, Carter G. (2000). *The Miseducation of the Negro*. New York: African American Images.

Zamir, Shamoon. (1995). *Dark Voices: W. E. B. Du Bois and American Thought, 1888–1903*. Chicago: The University of Chicago Press.

Zuckerman, Phil. (2000). *Du Bois on Religion*. Walnut Creek, California: Alta Mira Press.

Chapter 32

The Souls of Black Folk, W. E. B. Du Bois, Selected Chapters (1903)

The Forethought

Herein lie buried many things which if read with patience may show the strange meaning of being black here at the dawning of the Twentieth Century. This meaning is not without interest to you, Gentle Reader; for the problem of the Twentieth Century is the problem of the color line. I pray you, then, receive my little book in all charity, studying my words with me, forgiving mistake and foible for sake of the faith and passion that is in me, and seeking the grain of truth hidden there.

I have sought here to sketch, in vague, uncertain outline, the spiritual world in which ten thousand thousand Americans live and strive. First, in two chapters I have tried to show what Emancipation meant to them, and what was its aftermath. In a third chapter I have pointed out the slow rise of personal leadership, and criticized candidly the leader who bears the chief burden of his race to-day. Then, in two other chapters I have sketched in swift outline the two worlds within and without the Veil, and thus have come to the central problem of training men for life. Venturing now into deeper detail, I have in two chapters studied the struggles of the massed millions of the black peasantry, and in another have sought to make clear the present relations of the sons of master and man. Leaving, then, the white world, I have stepped within the Veil, raising it that you may view faintly its deeper recesses,—the meaning of its religion, the passion of its human sorrow, and the struggle of its greater souls. All this I have ended with a tale twice told but seldom written, and a chapter of song.

Some of these thoughts of mine have seen the light before in other guise. For kindly consenting to their republication here, in altered and extended form, I must thank the publishers of the *Atlantic Monthly, The World's Work,* the *Dial, The New World,* and the *Annals of the American Academy of Political and Social Science.* Before each chapter, as now printed, stands a bar of the Sorrow Songs,—some echo of haunting melody from the only American music which welled up from black souls in the dark past. And, finally, need I add that I who speak here am bone of the bone and flesh of the flesh of them that live within the Veil?

W. E. B. Du Bois
Atlanta, Ga., Feb 1, 1903

Of Our Spiritual Strivings

O water, voice of my heart, crying in the sand,
　All night long crying with a mournful cry,
As I lie and listen, and cannot understand
　The voice of my heart in my side or the voice of the sea,
　O water, crying for rest, is it I, is it I?
　All night long the water is crying to me.

Unresting water, there shall never be rest
  Till the last moon droop and the last tide fail,
And the fire of the end begin to burn in the west;
    And the heart shall be weary and wonder and cry like the sea,
  All life long crying without avail,
    As the water all night long is crying to me.

ARTHUR SYMONS

Between me and the other world there is ever an unasked question: unasked by some through feelings of delicacy; by others through the difficulty of rightly framing it. All, nevertheless, flutter round it. They approach me in a half-hesitant sort of way, eye me curiously or compassionately, and then, instead of saying directly, How does it feel to be a problem? they say, I know an excellent colored man in my town; or, I fought at Mechanicsville; or, Do not these Southern outrages make your blood boil? At these I smile, or am interested, or reduce the boiling to a simmer, as the occasion may require. To the real question, How does it feel to be a problem? I answer seldom a word.

And yet, being a problem is a strange experience,—peculiar even for one who has never been anything else, save perhaps in babyhood and in Europe. It is in the early days of rollicking boyhood that the revelation first bursts upon one, all in a day, as it were. I remember well when the shadow swept across me. I was a little thing, away up in the hills of New England, where the dark Housatonic winds between Hoosac and Taghkanic to the sea. In a wee wooden schoolhouse, something put it into the boys' and girls' heads to buy gorgeous visiting-cards—ten cents a package—and exchange. The exchange was merry, till one girl, a tall newcomer, refused my card,—refused it peremptorily, with a glance. Then it dawned upon me with a certain suddenness that I was different from the others; or like, mayhap, in heart and life and longing, but shut out from their world by a vast veil. I had thereafter no desire to tear down that veil, to creep through; I held all beyond it in common contempt, and lived above it in a region of blue sky and great wandering shadows. That sky was bluest when I could beat my mates at examination-time, or beat them at a foot-race, or even beat their stringy heads. Alas, with the years all this fine contempt began to fade; for the words I longed for, and all their dazzling opportunities, were theirs, not mine. But they should not keep these prizes, I said; some, all, I would wrest from them. Just how I would do it I could never decide: by reading law, by healing the sick, by telling the wonderful tales that swam in my head,—some way. With other black boys the strife was not so fiercely sunny: their youth shrunk into tasteless sycophancy, or into silent hatred of the pale world about them and mocking distrust of everything white; or wasted itself in a bitter cry, Why did God make me an outcast and a stranger in mine own house? The shades of the prison-house closed round about us all: walls strait and stubborn to the whitest, but relentlessly narrow, tall, and unscalable to sons of night who must plod darkly on in resignation, or beat unavailing palms against the stone, or steadily, half hopelessly, watch the streak of blue above.

After the Egyptian and Indian, the Greek and Roman, the Teuton and Mongolian, the Negro is a sort of seventh son, born with a veil, and gifted with second-sight in this American world,—a world which yields him no true self-consciousness, but only lets him see himself through the revelation of the other world. It is a peculiar sensation, this double-consciousness, this sense of always looking at one's self through the eyes of others, of measuring one's soul by the tape of a world that looks on in amused contempt and pity. One ever feels his twoness,—an American, a Negro; two souls, two thoughts, two unreconciled strivings; two warring ideals in one dark body, whose dogged strength alone keeps it from being torn asunder.

The history of the American Negro is the history of this strife,—this longing to attain self-conscious manhood, to merge his double self into a better and truer self. In this merging he wishes neither of the older selves to be lost. He would not Africanize America, for America has too much to teach the world and Africa.

He would not bleach his Negro soul in a flood of white Americanism, for he knows that Negro blood has a message for the world. He simply wishes to make it possible for a man to be both a Negro and an American, without being cursed and spit upon by his fellows, without having the doors of Opportunity closed roughly in his face.

This, then, is the end of his striving: to be a co-worker in the kingdom of culture, to escape both death and isolation, to husband and use his best powers and his latent genius. These powers of body and mind have in the past been strangely wasted, dispersed, or forgotten. The shadow of a mighty Negro past flits through the tale of Ethiopia the Shadowy and of Egypt the Sphinx. Through history, the powers of single black men flash here and there like falling stars, and die sometimes before the world has rightly gauged their brightness. Here in America, in the few days since Emancipation, the black man's turning hither and thither in hesitant and doubtful striving has often made his very strength to lose effectiveness, to seem like absence of power, like weakness. And yet it is not weakness,—it is the contradiction of double aims. The double-aimed struggle of the black artisan—on the one hand to escape white contempt for a nation of mere hewers of wood and drawers of water, and on the other hand to plough and nail and dig for a poverty-stricken horde—could only result in making him a poor craftsman, for he had but half a heart in either cause. By the poverty and ignorance of his people, the Negro minister or doctor was tempted toward quackery and demagogy; and by the criticism of the other world, toward ideals that made him ashamed of his lowly tasks. The would-be black *savant* was confronted by the paradox that the knowledge his people needed was a twice-told tale to his white neighbors, while the knowledge which would teach the white world was Greek to his own flesh and blood. The innate love of harmony and beauty that set the ruder souls of his people a-dancing and a-singing raised but confusion and doubt in the soul of the black artist; for the beauty revealed to him was the soul-beauty of a race which his larger audience despised, and he could not articulate the message of another people. This waste of double aims, this seeking to satisfy two unreconciled ideals, has wrought sad havoc with the courage and faith and deeds of ten thousand thousand people,—has sent them often wooing false gods and invoking false means of salvation, and at times has even seemed about to make them ashamed of themselves.

Away back in the days of bondage they thought to see in one divine event the end of all doubt and disappointment; few men ever worshipped Freedom with half such unquestioning faith as did the American Negro for two centuries. To him, so far as he thought and dreamed, slavery was indeed the sum of all villainies, the cause of all sorrow, the root of all prejudice; Emancipation was the key to a promised land of sweeter beauty than ever stretched before the eyes of wearied Israelites. In song and exhortation swelled one refrain—Liberty; in his tears and curses the God he implored had Freedom in his right hand. At last it came,—suddenly, fearfully, like a dream. With one wild carnival of blood and passion came the message in his own plaintive cadences:—

"Shout, O children!
Shout, you're free!
For God has bought your liberty!"

Years have passed away since then,—ten, twenty, forty; forty years of national life, forty years of renewal and development, and yet the swarthy spectre sits in its accustomed seat at the Nation's feast. In vain do we cry to this our vastest social problem:—

"Take any shape but that, and my firm nerves
Shall never tremble!"

The Nation has not yet found peace from its sins; the freedman has not yet found in freedom his promised land. Whatever of good may have come in these years of change, the shadow of a deep disappointment rests upon the Negro people,—a disappointment all the more bitter because the unattained ideal was unbounded save by the simple ignorance of a lowly people.

The first decade was merely a prolongation of the vain search for freedom, the boon that seemed ever barely to elude their grasp,—like a tantalizing will-o'-the-wisp, maddening and misleading the headless host. The holocaust of war, the terrors of the Ku-Klux Klan, the lies of carpet-baggers, the disorganization of industry, and the contradictory advice of friends and foes, left the bewildered serf with no new watchword beyond the old cry for freedom. As the time flew, however, he began to grasp a new idea. The ideal of liberty demanded for its attainment powerful means, and these the Fifteenth Amendment gave him. The ballot, which before he had looked upon as a visible sign of freedom, he now regarded as the chief means of gaining and perfecting the liberty with which war had partially endowed him. And why not? Had not votes made war and emancipated millions? Had not votes enfranchised the freedmen? Was anything impossible to a power that had done all this? A million black men started with renewed zeal to vote themselves into the kingdom. So the decade flew away, the revolution of 1876 came and left the half-free serf weary, wondering, but still inspired. Slowly but steadily, in the following years, a new vision began gradually to replace the dream of political power,—a powerful movement, the rise of another ideal to guide the unguided, another pillar of fire by night after a clouded day. It was the ideal of "book-learning"; the curiosity, born of compulsory ignorance, to know and test the power of the cabalistic letters of the white man, the longing to know. Here at last seemed to have been discovered the mountain path to Canaan; longer than the highway of Emancipation and law, steep and rugged, but straight, leading to heights high enough to overlook life.

Up the new path the advance guard toiled, slowly, heavily, doggedly; only those who have watched and guided the faltering feet, the misty minds, the dull understandings, of the dark pupils of these schools know how faithfully, how piteously, this people strove to learn. It was weary work. The cold statistician wrote down the inches of progress here and there, noted also where here and there a foot had slipped or some one had fallen. To the tired climbers, the horizon was ever dark, the mists were often cold, the Canaan was always dim and far away. If, however, the vistas disclosed as yet no goal, no resting-place, little but flattery and criticism, the journey at least gave leisure for reflection and self-examination; it changed the child of Emancipation to the youth with dawning self-consciousness, self-realization, self-respect. In those sombre forests of his striving his own soul rose before him, and he saw himself,—darkly as through a veil; and yet he saw in himself some faint revelation of his power, of his mission. He began to have a dim feeling that, to attain his place in the world, he must be himself, and not another. For the first time he sought to analyze the burden he bore upon his back, that dead-weight of social degradation partially masked behind a half-named Negro problem. He felt his poverty, without a cent, without a home, without land, tools, or savings, he had entered into competition with rich, landed, skilled neighbors. To be a poor man is hard, but to be a poor race in a land of dollars is the very bottom of hardships. He felt the weight of his ignorance,—not simply of letters, but of life, of business, of the humanities; the accumulated sloth and shirking and awkwardness of decades and centuries shackled his hands and feet. Nor was his burden all poverty and ignorance. The red stain of bastardy, which two centuries of systematic legal defilement of Negro women had stamped upon his race, meant not only the loss of ancient African chastity, but also the hereditary weight of a mass of corruption from white adulterers, threatening almost the obliteration of the Negro home.

A people thus handicapped ought not to be asked to race with the world, but rather allowed to give all its time and thought to its own social problems. But alas! while sociologists gleefully count his bastards and his prostitutes, the very soul of the toiling, sweating black man is darkened by the shadow of a vast despair. Men call the shadow prejudice, and learnedly explain it as the natural defence of culture against barbarism, learning against ignorance, purity against crime, the "higher" against the "lower" races. To which the Negro cries Amen! and swears that to so much of this strange prejudice as is founded on just homage to civilization, culture, righteousness, and progress, he humbly bows and meekly does obeisance. But before that nameless prejudice that leaps beyond all this he stands helpless, dismayed, and well-nigh speechless; before that personal disrespect and mockery, the ridicule and systematic humiliation, the distortion of fact and wanton license of fancy, the cynical ignoring of the better and the boisterous welcoming of the worse, the all-pervading desire to inculcate disdain for everything black, from Toussaint to the devil,—before this there rises a sickening despair that would disarm and discourage any nation save that black host to whom "discouragement" is an unwritten word.

But the facing of so vast a prejudice could not but bring the inevitable self-questioning, self-disparagement, and lowering of ideals which ever accompany repression and breed in an atmosphere of contempt and hate. Whisperings and portents came borne upon the four winds: Lo! we are diseased and dying, cried the dark hosts; we cannot write, our voting is vain; what need of education, since we must always cook and serve? And the Nation echoed and enforced this self-criticism, saying: Be content to be servants, and nothing more; what need of higher culture for half-men? Away with the black man's ballot, by force or fraud,—and behold the suicide of a race! Nevertheless, out of the evil came something of good,—the more careful adjustment of education to real life, the clearer perception of the Negroes' social responsibilities, and the sobering realization of the meaning of progress.

So dawned the time of *Sturm und Drang:* storm and stress to-day rocks our little boat on the mad waters of the world-sea; there is within and without the sound of conflict, the burning of body and rending of soul;

inspiration strives with doubt, and faith with vain questionings. The bright ideals of the past,—physical freedom, political power, the training of brains and the training of hands,—all these in turn have waxed and waned, until even the last grows dim and overcast. Are they all wrong,—all false? No, not that, but each alone was over-simple and incomplete,—the dreams of a credulous race-childhood, or the fond imaginings of the other world which does not know and does not want to know our power. To be really true, all these ideals must be melted and welded into one. The training of the schools we need to-day more than ever,—the training of deft hands, quick eyes and ears, and above all the broader, deeper, higher culture of gifted minds and pure hearts. The power of the ballot we need in sheer self-defence,—else what shall save us from a second slavery? Freedom, too, the long-sought, we still seek,—the freedom of life and limb, the freedom to work and think, the freedom to love and aspire. Work, culture, liberty,—all these we need, not singly but together, not successively but together, each growing and aiding each, and all striving toward that vaster ideal that swims before the Negro people, the ideal of human brotherhood, gained through the unifying ideal of Race; the ideal of fostering and developing the traits and talents of the Negro, not in opposition to or contempt for other races, but rather in large conformity to the greater ideals of the American Republic, in order that some day on American soil two world-races may give each to each those characteristics both so sadly lack. We the darker ones come even now not altogether empty-handed: there are to-day no truer exponents of the pure human spirit of the Declaration of Independence than the American Negroes; there is no true American music but the wild sweet melodies of the Negro slave; the American fairy tales and folklore are Indian and African; and, all in all, we black men seem the sole oasis of simple faith and reverence in a dusty, desert of dollars and smartness. Will America be poorer if she replace her brutal dyspeptic blundering with light-hearted but determined Negro humility? or her coarse and cruel wit with loving jovial good-humor? or her vulgar music with the soul of the Sorrow Songs?

Merely a concrete test of the underlying principles of the great republic is the Negro Problem, and the spiritual striving of the freedmen's sons is the travail of souls whose burden is almost beyond the measure of their strength, but who bear it in the name of an historic race, in the name of this the land of their fathers' fathers, and in the name of human opportunity.

And now what I have briefly sketched in large outline let me on coming pages tell again in many ways, with loving emphasis and deeper detail, that men may listen to the striving in the souls of black folk.

Of Mr. Booker T. Washington and Others

From birth till death enslaved; in word, in deed, unmanned!

*   *   *   *   *   *   *   *

Hereditary bondsmen! Know ye not
Who would be free themselves must strike the blow?

BYRON

Easily the most striking thing in the history of the American Negro since 1876 is the ascendancy of Mr. Booker T. Washington. It began at the time when war memories and ideals were rapidly passing; a day of astonishing commercial development was dawning; a sense of doubt and hesitation overtook the freedmen's sons,—

then it was that his leading began. Mr. Washington came, with a simple definite programme, at the psychological moment when the nation was a little ashamed of having bestowed so much sentiment on Negroes, and was concentrating its energies on Dollars. His programme of industrial education, conciliation of the South, and submission and silence as to civil and political rights, was not wholly original; the Free Negroes from 1830 up to war-time had striven to build industrial schools, and the American Missionary Association had from the first taught various trades; and Price and others had sought a way of honorable alliance with the best of the Southerners. But Mr. Washington first indissolubly linked these things; he put enthusiasm, unlimited energy, and perfect faith into his programme, and changed it from a by-path into a veritable Way of Life. And the tale of the methods by which he did this is a fascinating study of human life.

It startled the nation to hear a Negro advocating such a programme after many decades of bitter complaint; it startled and won the applause of the South, it interested and won the admiration of the North; and after a confused murmur of protest, it silenced if it did not convert the Negroes themselves.

To gain the sympathy and coöperation of the various elements comprising the white South was Mr. Washington's first task; and this, at the time Tuskegee was founded, seemed, for a black man, well-nigh impossible. And yet ten years later it was done in the word spoken at Atlanta: "In all things purely social we can be as separate as the five fingers, and yet one as the hand in all things essential to mutual progress." This "Atlanta Compromise" is by all odds the most notable thing in Mr. Washington's career. The South interpreted it in different ways: the radicals received it as a complete surrender of the demand for civil and political equality; the conservatives, as a generously conceived working basis for mutual understanding. So both approved it, and to-day its author is certainly the most distinguished Southerner since Jefferson Davis, and the one with the largest personal following.

Next to this achievement comes Mr. Washington's work in gaining place and consideration in the North. Others less shrewd and tactful had formerly essayed to sit on these two stools and had fallen between them; but as Mr. Washington knew the heart of the South from birth and training, so by singular insight he intuitively grasped the spirit of the age which was dominating the North. And so thoroughly did he learn the speech and thought of triumphant commercialism, and the ideals of material prosperity, that the picture of a lone black boy poring over a French grammar amid the weeds and dirt of a neglected home soon seemed to him the acme of absurdities. One wonders what Socrates and St. Francis of Assisi would say to this.

And yet this very singleness of vision and thorough oneness with his age is a mark of the successful man. It is as though Nature must needs make men narrow in order to give them force. So Mr. Washington's cult has gained unquestioning followers, his work has wonderfully prospered, his friends are legion, and his enemies are confounded. To-day he stands as the one recognized spokesman of his ten million fellows, and one of the most notable figures in a nation of seventy millions. One hesitates, therefore, to criticise a life which, beginning with so little, has done so much. And yet the time is come when one may speak in all sincerity and utter courtesy of the mistakes and shortcomings of Mr. Washington's career, as well as of his triumphs, without being thought captious or envious, and without forgetting that it is easier to do ill than well in the world.

The criticism that has hitherto met Mr. Washington has not always been of this broad character. In the South especially has he had to walk warily to avoid the harshest judgments,—and naturally so, for he is dealing with the one subject of deepest sensitiveness to that section. Twice—once when at the Chicago celebration of the Spanish-American War he alluded to the color-prejudice that is "eating away the vitals of the South," and once when he dined with President Roosevelt—has the resulting Southern criticism been violent enough to threaten seriously his popularity. In the North the feeling has several times forced itself into words, that Mr. Washington's counsels of submission overlooked certain elements of true manhood, and that his educational programme was unnecessarily narrow. Usually, however, such criticism has not found open expression, although, too, the spiritual sons of the Abolitionists have not been prepared to acknowledge that the schools founded before Tuskegee, by men of broad ideals and self-sacrificing spirit, were wholly failures or worthy of ridicule. While, then, criticism has not failed to follow Mr. Washington, yet the prevailing public opinion of the land has been but too willing to deliver the solution of a wearisome problem into his hands, and say, "If that is all you and your race ask, take it."

Among his own people, however, Mr. Washington has encountered the strongest and most lasting opposition, amounting at times to bitterness, and even today continuing strong and insistent even though largely silenced in outward expression by the public opinion of the nation. Some of this opposition is, of course, mere envy; the disappointment of displaced demagogues and the spite of narrow minds. But aside from this, there is among educated and thoughtful colored men in all parts of the land a feeling of deep regret, sorrow, and apprehension at the wide currency and ascendancy which some of Mr. Washington's theories have gained. These same men admire his sincerity of purpose, and are willing to forgive much to honest endeavor which is doing something worth the doing. They coöperate with Mr. Washington as far as they conscientiously can; and, indeed, it is no ordinary tribute to this man's tact and power that, steering as he must between so many diverse interests and opinions, he so largely retains the respect of all.

But the hushing of the criticism of honest opponents is a dangerous thing. It leads some of the best of the critics to unfortunate silence and paralysis of effort, and others to burst into speech so passionately and intemperately as to lose listeners. Honest and earnest criticism from those whose interests are most nearly touched,—criticism of writers by readers, of government by those governed, of leaders by those led,—this is the soul of democracy and the safeguard of modern society. If the best of the American Negroes receive by outer pressure a leader whom they had not recognized before, manifestly there is here a certain palpable gain. Yet there is also irreparable loss,—a loss of that peculiarly valuable education which a group receives when by search and criticism it finds and commissions its own leaders. The way in which this is done is at once the most elementary and the nicest problem of social growth. History is but the record of such group-leadership; and yet how infinitely changeful is its type and character! And of all types and kinds, what can be more instructive than the leadership of a group within a group?—that curious double movement where real progress may be negative and actual advance be relative retrogression. All this is the social student's inspiration and despair.

Now in the past the American Negro has had instructive experience in the choosing of group leaders, founding thus a peculiar dynasty which in the light of present conditions is worth while studying. When sticks and stones and beasts form the sole environment of a people, their attitude is largely one of determined opposition to and conquest of natural forces. But when to earth and brute is added an environment or men and ideas, then the attitude of the imprisoned group may take three main forms,—a feeling of revolt and revenge; an attempt to adjust all thought and action to the will of the greater group; or, finally, a determined effort at self-realization and self-development despite environing opinion. The influence of all of these attitudes at various times can be traced in the history of the American Negro, and in the evolution of his successive leaders.

Before 1750, while the fire of African freedom still burned in the veins of the slaves, there was in all leadership or attempted leadership but the one motive of revolt and revenge,—typified in the terrible Maroons, the Danish blacks, and Cato of Stono, and veiling all the Americas in fear of insurrection. The liberalizing tendencies of the latter half of the eighteenth century brought, along with kindlier relations between black and white, thoughts of ultimate adjustment and assimilation. Such aspiration was especially voiced in the earnest songs of Phyllis, in the martyrdom of Attucks, the fighting of Salem and Poor, the intellectual accomplishments of Banneker and Derham, and the political demands of the Cuffes.

Stern financial and social stress after the war cooled much of the previous humanitarian ardor. The disappointment and impatience of the Negroes at the persistence of slavery and serfdom voiced itself in two movements. The slaves in the South, aroused undoubtedly by vague rumors of the Haytian revolt, made three fierce attempts at insurrection,—in 1800 under Gabriel in Virginia, in 1822 under Vesey in Carolina, and in 1831 again in Virginia under the terrible Nat Turner. In the Free States, on the other hand, a new and curious attempt at self-development was made. In Philadelphia and New York color-prescription led to a withdrawal of Negro communicants from white churches and the formation of a peculiar socio-religious institution among the Negroes known as the African Church,—an organization still living and controlling in its various branches over a million of men.

Walker's wild appeal against the trend of the times showed how the world was changing after the coming of the cotton-gin. By 1830 slavery seemed hopelessly fastened on the South, and the slaves thoroughly cowed into submission. The free Negroes of the North, inspired by the mulatto immigrants from the West Indies, began to change the basis of their demands; they recognized the slavery of slaves, but insisted that they themselves were freemen, and sought assimilation and amalgamation with the nation on the same terms with other men. Thus, Forten and Purvis of Philadelphia, Shad of Wilmington, Du Bois of New Haven, Barbadoes of Boston, and others, strove singly and together as men, they said, not as slaves; as "people of color," not as "Negroes." The trend of the times, however, refused them recognition save in individual and exceptional cases, considered them as one with all the despised blacks, and they soon found themselves striving to keep even the rights they formerly had of voting and working and moving as freemen. Schemes of migration and colonization arose among them; but these they refused to entertain, and they eventually turned to the Abolition movement as a final refuge.

Here, led by Remond, Nell, Wells-Brown, and Douglass, a new period of self-assertion and self-development dawned. To be sure, ultimate freedom and assimilation was the ideal before the leaders, but the assertion of the manhood rights of the Negro by himself was the main reliance, and John Brown's raid was the extreme of its logic. After the war and emancipation, the great form of Frederick Douglass, the greatest of American Negro leaders, still led the host. Self-assertion, especially in political lines, was the main programme, and behind Douglass came Elliot, Bruce, and Langston, and the Reconstruction politicians, and, less conspicuous but of greater social significance, Alexander Crummell and Bishop Daniel Payne.

Then came the Revolution of 1876, the suppression of the Negro votes, the changing and shifting of ideals, and the seeking of new lights in the great night. Douglass, in his old age, still bravely stood for the ideals of his early manhood,—ultimate assimilation *through* self-assertion, and on no other terms. For a time Price arose as a new leader, destined, it seemed, not to give up, but to re-state the old ideals in a form less repugnant to the white South. But he passed away in his prime. Then came the new leader. Nearly all the former ones had become leaders by the silent suffrage of their fellows, had sought to lead their own people alone, and were usually, save Douglass, little known outside their race. But Booker T. Washington arose as essentially the leader not of one race but of two,—a compromiser between the South, the North, and the Negro. Naturally the Negroes resented, at first bitterly, signs of compromise which surrendered their civil and political rights, even though this was to be exchanged for larger chances of economic development. The rich and dominating North, however, was not only weary of the race problem, but was investing largely in Southern enterprises, and welcomed any method of peaceful cooperation. Thus, by national opinion, the Negroes began to recognize Mr. Washington's leadership; and the voice of criticism was hushed.

Mr. Washington represents in Negro thought the old attitude of adjustment and submission; but adjustment at such a peculiar time as to make his programme unique. This is an age of unusual economic development, and Mr. Washington's programme naturally takes an economic cast, becoming a gospel of Work and Money to such an extent as apparently almost completely to overshadow the higher aims of life. Moreover, this is an age when the more advanced races are coming in closer contact with the less developed races, and the race-feeling is therefore intensified; and Mr. Washington's programme practically accepts the alleged inferiority of the Negro races. Again, in our own land, the reaction from the sentiment of war time has given impetus to race-prejudice against Negroes, and Mr. Washington withdraws many of the high demands of Negroes as men and American citizens. In other periods of intensified prejudice all the Negro's tendency to self-assertion has been called forth; at this period a policy of submission is advocated. In the history of nearly all other races and peoples the doctrine preached at such crises has been that manly self-respect is worth more than lands and houses, and that a people who voluntarily surrender such respect, or cease striving for it, are not worth civilizing.

In answer to this, it has been claimed that the Negro can survive only through submission. Mr. Washington distinctly asks that black people give up, at least for the present, three things,—

First, political power,

Second, insistence on civil rights,

Third, higher education of Negro youth,—

and concentrate all their energies on industrial education, and accumulation of wealth, and the conciliation of the South. This policy has been courageously and insistently advocated for over fifteen years, and has been triumphant for perhaps ten years. As a result of this tender of the palm-branch, what been the return? In these years there have occurred:

1. The disfranchisement of the Negro.
2. The legal creation of a distinct status of civil inferiority for the Negro.
3. The steady withdrawal of aid from institutions for the higher training of the Negro.

These movements are not, to be sure, direct results of Mr. Washington's teachings; but his propaganda has, without a shadow of doubt, helped their speedier accomplishment. The question then comes: Is it possible, and probable, that nine millions of men can make effective progress in economic lines if they are deprived of political rights, made a servile caste, and allowed only the most meagre chance for developing their exceptional men? If history and reason give any distinct answer to these questions, it is an emphatic *No*. And Mr. Washington thus faces the triple paradox of his career:

1. He is striving nobly to make Negro artisans business men and property-owners; but it is utterly impossible, under modern competitive methods, for workingmen and property-owners to defend their rights and exist without the right of suffrage.

2. He insists on thrift and self-respect, but at the same time counsels a silent submission to civic inferiority such as is bound to sap the manhood of any race in the long run.
3. He advocates common-school and industrial training, and depreciates institutions of higher learning; but neither the Negro common-schools, nor Tuskegee itself, could remain open a day were it not for teachers trained in Negro colleges, or trained by their graduates.

This triple paradox in Mr. Washington's position is the object of criticism by two classes of colored Americans. One class is spiritually descended from Toussaint the Savior, through Gabriel, Vesey, and Turner, and they represent the attitude of revolt and revenge; they hate the white South blindly and distrust the white race generally, and so far as they agree on definite action, think that the Negro's only hope lies in emigration beyond the borders of the United States. And yet, by the irony of fate, nothing has more effectually made this programme seem hopeless than the recent course of the United States toward weaker and darker peoples in the West Indies, Hawaii, and the Philippines,—for where in the world may we go and be safe from lying and brute force?

The other class of Negroes who cannot agree with Mr. Washington has hitherto said little aloud. They deprecate the sight of scattered counsels, of internal disagreement; and especially they dislike making their just criticism of a useful and earnest man an excuse for a general discharge of venom from small-minded opponents. Nevertheless, the questions involved are so fundamental and serious that it is difficult to see how men like the Grimkes, Kelly Miller, J. W. E. Bowen, and other representatives of this group, can much longer be silent. Such men feel in conscience bound to ask of this nation three things:

1. The right to vote.
2. Civic equality.
3. The education of youth according to ability.

They acknowledge Mr. Washington's invaluable service in counselling patience and courtesy in such demands; they do not ask that ignorant black men vote when ignorant whites are debarred, or that any reasonable restrictions in the suffrage should not be applied; they know that the low social level of the mass of the race is responsible for much discrimination against it, but they also know, and the nation knows, that relentless color-prejudice is more often a cause than a result of the Negro's degradation; they seek the abatement of this relic of barbarism, and not its systematic encouragement and pampering by all agencies of social power from the Associated Press to the Church of Christ. They advocate, with Mr. Washington, a broad system of Negro common schools supplemented by thorough industrial training; but they are surprised that a man of Mr. Washington's insight cannot see that no such educational system ever has rested or can rest on any other basis than that of the well-equipped college and university, and they insist that there is a demand for a few such institutions throughout the South to train the best of the Negro youth as teachers, professional men, and leaders.

This group of men honor Mr. Washington for his attitude of conciliation toward the white South; they accept the "Atlanta Compromise" in its broadest interpretation; they recognize, with him, many signs of promise, many men of high purpose and fair judgment, in this section; they know that no easy task has been laid upon a region already tottering under heavy burdens. But, nevertheless, they insist that the way to truth and right lies in straightforward honesty, not in indiscriminate flattery; in praising those of the South who do well and criticising uncompromisingly those who do ill; in taking advantage of the opportunities at hand and urging their fellows to do the same, but at the same time in remembering that only a firm adherence to their higher ideals and aspirations will ever keep those ideals within the realm of possibility. They do not expect that the free right to vote, to enjoy civic rights, and to be educated, will come in a moment; they do not expect to see the bias and prejudices of years disappear at the blast of a trumpet; but they are absolutely certain that the way for a people to gain their reasonable rights is not by voluntarily throwing them away and insisting that they do not want them; that the way for a people to gain respect is not by continually belittling and ridiculing themselves; that, on the contrary, Negroes must insist continually, in season and out of season, that voting is necessary to modern manhood, that color discrimination is barbarism, and that black boys need education as well as white boys.

In failing thus to state plainly and unequivocally the legitimate demands of their people, even at the cost of opposing an honored leader, the thinking classes of American Negroes would shirk a heavy responsibility,—a responsibility to themselves, a responsibility to the struggling masses, a responsibility to the darker races of men whose future depends so largely on this American experiment, but especially a responsibility to this nation,—this common Fatherland. It is wrong to encourage a man or a people in evil-doing; it is wrong to aid and abet a national crime simply because it is unpopular not to do so. The growing spirit of kindliness and reconciliation between the North and South after the frightful difference of a generation ago ought to be a source of deep congratulation to all, and especially to those whose mistreatment caused the war; but if that reconciliation is to be marked by the industrial slavery and civic death of those same black men, with permanent legislation into a position of inferiority, then those black men, if they are really men, are called upon by every consideration of patriotism and loyalty to oppose such a course by all civilized methods, even though such opposition involves disagreement with Mr. Booker T. Washington. We have no right to sit silently by while the inevitable seeds are sown for a harvest of disaster to our children, black and white.

First, it is the duty of black men to judge the South discriminatingly. The present generation of Southerners are not responsible for the past, and they should not be blindly hated or blamed for it. Furthermore, to no class is the indiscriminate endorsement of the recent course of the South toward Negroes more nauseating than to the best thought of the South. The South is not "solid"; it is a land in the ferment of social change, wherein forces of all kinds are fighting for supremacy; and to praise the ill the South is today perpetrating is just as wrong as to condemn the good. Discriminating and broad-minded criticism is what the South needs,—needs it for the sake of her own white sons and daughters, and for the insurance of robust, healthy mental and moral development.

Today even the attitude of the Southern whites toward the blacks is not, as so many assume, in all cases the same; the ignorant Southerner hates the Negro, the workingmen fear his competition, the money-makers wish to use him as a laborer, some of the educated see a menace in his upward development, while others—usually the sons of the masters—wish to help him to rise. National opinion has enabled this last class to maintain the Negro common schools, and to protect the Negro partially in property, life, and limb. Through the pressure of the money-makers, the Negro is in danger of being reduced to semi-slavery, especially in the country districts; the workingmen, and those of the educated who fear the Negro, have united to disfranchise him, and some have urged his deportation; while the passions of the ignorant are easily aroused to lynch and abuse any black man. To praise this intricate whirl of thought and prejudice is nonsense; to inveigh indiscriminately against "the South" is unjust; but to use the same breath in praising Governor Aycock, exposing Senator Morgan, arguing with Mr. Thomas Nelson Page, and denouncing Senator Ben Tillman, is not only sane, but the imperative duty of thinking black men.

It would be unjust to Mr. Washington not to acknowledge that in several instances he has opposed movements in the South which were unjust to the Negro; he sent memorials to the Louisiana and Alabama constitutional conventions, he has spoken against lynching, and in other ways has openly or silently set his influence against sinister schemes and unfortunate happenings. Notwithstanding this, it is equally true to assert that, on the whole the distinct impression left by Mr. Washington's propaganda is, first, that the South is justified in its present attitude toward the Negro because of the Negro's degradation; secondly, that the prime cause of the Negro's failure to rise more quickly is his wrong education in the past; and, thirdly, that his future rise depends primarily on his own efforts. Each of these propositions is a dangerous half-truth. The supplementary truths must never be lost sight of: first, slavery and race-prejudice are potent if not sufficient causes of the Negro's position; second, industrial and common-school training were necessarily slow in planting because they had to await the black teachers trained by higher institutions,—it being extremely doubtful if any essentially different development was possible, and certainly a Tuskegee was unthinkable before 1880; and, third, while it is a great truth to say that the Negro must strive and strive mightily to help himself, it is equally true that unless his striving be not simply seconded, but rather aroused and encouraged, by the initiative of the richer and wiser environing group, he cannot hope for great success.

In his failure to realize and impress this last point, Mr. Washington is especially to be criticised. His doctrine has tended to make the whites, North and South, shift the burden of the Negro problem to the Negro's shoulders and stand aside as critical and rather pessimistic spectators; when in fact the burden belongs to the nation, and the hands of none of us are clean if we bend not our energies to righting these great wrongs.

The South ought to be led, by candid and honest criticism, to assert her better self and do her full duty to the race she has cruelly wronged and is still wronging. The North—her co-partner in guilt—cannot salve her conscience by plastering it with gold. We cannot settle this problem by diplomacy and suaveness, by "policy" alone. If worse come to worst, can the moral fibre of this country survive the slow throttling and murder of nine millions of men?

The black men of America have a duty to perform, a duty stern and delicate,—a forward movement to oppose a part of the work of their greatest leader. So far as Mr. Washington preaches Thrift, Patience, and Industrial Training for the masses, we must hold up his hands and strive with him, rejoicing in his honors and glorying in the strength of this Joshua called of God and of man to lead the headless host. But so far as Mr. Washington apologizes for injustice, North or South, does not rightly value the privilege and duty of voting, belittles the emasculating effects of caste distinctions, and opposes the higher training and ambition of our brighter minds,—so far as he, the South, or the Nation, does this,—we must unceasingly and firmly oppose them. By every civilized and peaceful method we must strive for the rights which the world accords to men, clinging unwaveringly to those great words which the sons of the Fathers would fain forget: "We hold these truths to be self-evident: That all men are created equal; that they are endowed by their Creator with certain unalienable rights; that among these are life, liberty, and the pursuit of happiness."

Of the Coming of John

What bring they 'neath the midnight,
    Beside the River-sea?
They bring the human heart wherein
    No nightly calm can be;
That droppeth never with the wind,
    Nor drieth with the dew;
O calm it, God; thy calm is broad
    To cover spirits too.
        The river floweth on.
            MRS. BROWNING.

Carlisle Street runs westward from the centre of Johnstown, across a great black bridge, down a hill and up again, by little shops and meat-markets, past single-storied homes, until suddenly it stops against a wide green lawn. It is a broad, restful place, with two large buildings outlined against the west. When at evening the winds come swelling from the east, and the great pall of the city's smoke hangs wearily above the valley, then the red west glows like a dreamland down Carlisle Street, and, at the tolling of the supper-bell, throws the passing forms of students in dark silhouette against the sky. Tall and black, they move slowly by, and seem in the sinister light to flit before the city like dim warning ghosts. Perhaps they are; for this is Wells Institute, and these black students have few dealings with the white city below.

And if you will notice, night after night, there is one dark form that ever hurries last and late toward the twinkling lights of Swain Hall,—for Jones is never on time. A long, straggling fellow he is, brown and hard-haired, who seems to be growing straight out of his clothes, and walks with a half-apologetic roll. He used perpetually to set the quiet dining room into waves of merriment, as he stole to his place after the bell had tapped for prayers; he seemed so perfectly awkward. And yet one glance at his face made one forgive him much,—that broad, good-natured smile in which lay no bit of art or artifice, but seemed just bubbling good-nature and genuine satisfaction with the world.

He came to us from Altamaha, away down there beneath the gnarled oaks of Southeastern Georgia, where the sea croons to the sands and the sands listen till they sink half drowned beneath the waters, rising only here and there in long, low islands. The white folk of Altamaha voted John a good boy,—fine plough-hand, good in the rice-fields, handy everywhere, and always good-natured and respectful. But they shook their heads when his mother wanted to send him off to school. "It'll spoil him,—ruin him," they said; and they talked as though they knew. But full half the black folk followed him proudly to the station, and carried his queer little trunk and many bundles. And there they shook and shook hands, and the girls kissed him shyly and the boys clapped him on the back. So the train came, and he pinched his little sister lovingly, and put his great arms about his mother's neck, and then was away with a puff and a roar into the great yellow world that flamed and flared about the doubtful pilgrim. Up the coast they hurried, past the squares and pal-mettos of Savannah, through the cotton-fields and through the weary night, to Millville, and came with the morning to the noise and bustle of Johnstown.

And they that stood behind, that morning in Altamaha, and watched the train as it noisily bore play-mate and brother and son away to the world, had thereafter one ever-recurring word,—"When John comes." Then what parties were to be, and what speakings in the churches; what new furniture in the front room,—perhaps even a new front room; and there would be a new schoolhouse, with John as teacher; and then per-haps a big wedding; all this and more—when John comes. But the white people shook their heads.

At first he was coming at Christmas-time,—but the vacation proved too short; and then, the next sum-mer,—but times were hard and schooling costly, and so, instead, he worked in Johnstown. And so it drifted to the next summer, and the next,—till playmates scattered, and mother grew gray, and sister went up to the Judge's kitchen to work. And still the legend lingered,—"When John comes."

Up at the Judge's they rather liked this refrain; for they too had a John—a fair-haired, smooth-faced boy, who had played many a long summer's day to its close with his darker namesake. "Yes, sir! John is at Princeton, sir," said the broad-shouldered gray-haired Judge every morning as he marched down to the post-office. "Showing the Yankees what a Southern gentleman can do," he added; and strode home again with his letters and papers. Up at the great pillared house they lingered long over the Princeton letter,—the Judge and his frail wife, his sister and growing daughters. "It'll make a man of him," said the Judge, "college is the place." And then he asked the shy little waitress, "Well, Jennie, how's your John?" and added reflectively, "Too bad, too bad your mother sent him off,—it will spoil him." And the waitress wondered.

Thus in the far-away Southern village the world lay waiting, half consciously, the coming of two young men, and dreamed in an inarticulate way of new things that would be done and new thoughts that all would think. And yet it was singular that few thought of two Johns,—for the black folk thought of one John, and he was black; and the white folk thought of another John, and he was white. And neither world thought the other world's thought, save with a vague unrest.

Up in Johnstown, at the Institute, we were long puzzled at the case of John Jones. For a long time the clay seemed unfit for any sort of moulding. He was loud and boisterous, always laughing and singing, and never able to work consecutively at anything. He did not know how to study; he had no idea of thorough-ness; and with his tardiness, carelessness, and appalling good-humor, we were sore perplexed. One night we sat in faculty-meeting, worried and serious; for Jones was in trouble again. This last escapade was too much, and so we solemnly voted "that Jones, on account of repeated disorder and inattention to work, be suspended for the rest of the term. "

It seemed to us that the first time life ever struck Jones as a really serious thing was when the Dean told him he must leave school. He stared at the gray-haired man blankly, with great eyes. "Why,—why," he fal-tered, "but—I haven't graduated!" Then the Dean slowly and clearly explained, reminding him of the tardi-ness and the carelessness, of the poor lessons and neglected work, of the noise and disorder, until the fellow hung his head in confusion. Then he said quickly, "But you won't tell mammy and sister,—you won't write mammy, now will you? For if you won't I'll go out into the city and work, and come back next term and show you something." So the Dean promised faithfully, and John shouldered his little trunk, giving neither word nor look to the giggling boys, and walked down Carlisle Street to the great city, with sober eyes and a set and serious face.

Perhaps we imagined it, but someway it seemed to us that the serious look that crept over his boyish face that afternoon never left it again. When he came back to us he went to work with all his rugged strength. It was a hard struggle, for things did not come easily to him,—few crowding memories of early life and teaching came to help him on his new way; but all the world toward which he strove was of his own building, and he builded slow and hard. As the light dawned lingeringly on his new creations, he sat rapt and silent before the vision, or wandered alone over the green campus peering through and beyond the world of men into a world of thought. And the thoughts at times puzzled him sorely; he could not see just why the circle was not square, and carried it out fifty-six decimal places one midnight,—would have gone further, indeed, had not the matron rapped for lights out. He caught terrible colds lying on his back in the meadows of nights, trying to think out the solar system; he had grave doubts as to the ethics of the Fall of Rome, and strongly suspected the Germans of being thieves and rascals, despite his textbooks; he pondered long over every new Greek word, and wondered why this meant that and why it couldn't mean something else, and how it must have felt to think all things in Greek. So he thought and puzzled along for himself,—pausing perplexed where others skipped merrily, and walking steadily through the difficulties where the rest stopped and surrendered.

Thus he grew in body and soul, and with him his clothes seemed to grow and arrange themselves; coat sleeves got longer, cuffs appeared, and collars got less soiled. Now and then his boots shone, and a new dignity crept into his walk. And we who saw daily a new thoughtfulness growing in his eyes began to expect something of this plodding boy. Thus he passed out of the preparatory school into college, and we who watched him felt four more years of change, which almost transformed the tall, grave man who bowed to us commencement morning. He had left his queer thought-world and come back to a world of motion and of men. He looked now for the first time sharply about him, and wondered he had seen so little before. He grew slowly to feel almost for the first time the Veil that lay between him and the white world; he first noticed now the oppression that had not seemed oppression before, differences that erstwhile seemed natural, restraints and slights that in boyhood days had gone unnoticed or been greeted with a laugh. He felt angry now when men did not call him "Mister," he clenched his hands at the "Jim Crow" cars, and chafed at the color-line that hemmed in him and his. A tinge of sarcasm crept into his speech, and a vague bitterness into his life; and he sat long hours wondering and planning a way around these crooked things. Daily he found himself shrinking from the choked and narrow life of his native town. And yet he always planned to go back to Altamaha,—always planned to work there. Still, more and more as the day approached he hesitated with a nameless dread; and even the day after graduation he seized with eagerness the offer of the Dean to send him North with the quartette during the summer vacation, to sing for the Institute. A breath of air before the plunge, he said to himself in half apology.

It was a bright September afternoon, and the streets of New York were brilliant with moving men. They reminded John of the sea, as he sat in the square and watched them, so changelessly changing, so bright and dark, so grave and gay. He scanned their rich and faultless clothes, the way they carried their hands, the shape of their hats; he peered into the hurrying carriages. Then, leaning back with a sigh, he said, "This is the World." The notion suddenly seized him to see where the world was going; since many of the richer and brighter seemed hurrying all one way. So when a tall, light-haired young man and a little talkative lady came by, he rose half hesitatingly and followed them. Up the street they went, past stores and gay shops, across a broad square, until with a hundred others they entered the high portal of a great building.

He was pushed toward the ticket-office with the others, and felt in his pocket for the new five-dollar bill he had hoarded. There seemed really no time for hesitation, so he drew it bravely out, passed it to the busy clerk, and received simply a ticket but no change. When at last he realized that he had paid five dollars to enter he knew not what, he stood stockstill amazed. "Be careful," said a low voice behind him; "you must not lynch the colored gentleman simply because he's in your way," and a girl looked up roguishly into the eyes of her fair-haired escort. A shade of annoyance passed over the escort's face. "You *will* not understand us at the South," he said half impatiently, as if continuing an argument. "With all your professions, one never sees in the North so cordial and intimate relations between white and black as are everyday occurrences with us. Why, I remember my closest playfellow in boyhood was a little Negro named after me, and surely no two,—*well!*" The man stopped short and flushed to the roots of his hair, for there directly beside his reserved orchestra chairs sat the Negro he had stumbled over in the hallway. He hesitated and grew pale with anger, called the usher and gave him his card, with a few peremptory words, and slowly sat down. The lady deftly changed the subject.

All this John did not see, for he sat in a half-daze minding the scene about him; the delicate beauty of the hall, the faint perfume, the moving myriad of men, the rich clothing and low hum of talking seemed all a part of a world so different from his, so strangely more beautiful than anything he had known, that he sat in dreamland, and started when, after a hush, rose high and clear the music of Lohengrin's swan. The infinite beauty of the wail lingered and swept through every muscle of his frame, and put it all a-tune. He closed his eyes and grasped the elbows of the chair, touching unwittingly the lady's arm. And the lady drew away. A deep longing swelled in all his heart to rise with that clear music out of the dirt and dust of that low life that held him prisoned and befouled. If he could only live up in the free air where birds sang and setting suns had no touch of blood! Who had called him to be the slave and butt of all? And if he had called, what right had he to call when a world like this lay open before men?

Then the movement changed, and fuller, mightier harmony swelled away. He looked thoughtfully across the hall, and wondered why the beautiful gray-haired woman looked so listless, and what the little man could be whispering about. He would not like to be listless and idle, he thought, for he felt with the music the movement of power within him. If he but had some master-work, some life-service, hard,—aye, bitter hard, but without the cringing and sickening servility, without the cruel hurt that hardened his heart and soul. When at last a soft sorrow crept across the violins, there came to him the vision of a far-off home, the great eyes of his sister, and the dark drawn face of his mother. And his heart sank below the waters, even as the sea-sand sinks by the shores of Altamaha, only to be lifted aloft again with that last ethereal wail of the swan that quivered and faded away into the sky.

It left John sitting so silent and rapt that he did not for some time notice the usher tapping him lightly on the shoulder and saying politely, "Will you step this way, please, sir?" A little surprised, he arose quickly at the last tap, and, turning to leave his seat, looked full into the face of the fair-haired young man. For the first time the young man recognized his dark boyhood playmate, and John knew that it was the Judge's son. The White John started, lifted his hand, and then froze into his chair; the black John smiled lightly, then grimly, and followed the usher down the aisle. The manager was sorry, very, very sorry,—but he explained that some mistake had been made in selling the gentleman a seat already disposed of; he would refund the money, of course,—and indeed felt the matter keenly, and so forth, and—before he had finished John was gone, walking hurriedly across the square and down the broad streets, and as he passed the park he buttoned his coat and said, "John Jones, you're a natural-born fool." Then he went to his lodgings and wrote a letter, and tore it up; he wrote another, and threw it in the fire. Then he seized a scrap of paper and wrote: "Dear Mother and Sister—I am coming—John."

"Perhaps," said John, as he settled himself on the train, "perhaps I am to blame myself in struggling against my manifest destiny simply because it looks hard and unpleasant. Here is my duty to Altamaha plain before me; perhaps they'll let me help settle the Negro problems there,—perhaps they won't. 'I will go in to the King, which is not according to the law; and if I perish, I perish.'" And then he mused and dreamed, and planned a life-work; and the train flew south.

Down in Altamaha, after seven long years, all the world knew John was coming. The homes were scrubbed and scoured,—above all, one; the gardens and yards had an unwonted trimness, and Jennie bought a new gingham. With some finesse and negotiation, all the dark Methodists and Presbyterians were induced to join in a monster welcome at the Baptist Church; and as the day drew near, warm discussions arose on every corner as to the exact extent and nature of John's accomplishments. It was noontide on a gray and cloudy day when he came. The black town flocked to the depot, with a little of the white at the edges,—a happy throng, with "Good-mawnings" and "Howdys" and laughing and joking and jostling. Mother sat yonder in the window watching; but sister Jennie stood on the platform, nervously fingering her dress, tall and lithe, with soft brown skin and loving eyes peering from out a tangled wilderness of hair. John rose gloomily as the train stopped, for he was thinking of the "Jim Crow" car; he stepped to the platform, and paused: a little dingy station, a black crowd gaudy and dirty, a half-mile of dilapidated shanties along a straggling ditch of mud. An overwhelming sense of the sordidness and narrowness of it all seized him; he looked in vain for his mother, kissed coldly the tall, strange girl who called him brother, spoke a short, dry word here and there; then, lingering neither for hand-shaking nor gossip, started silently up the street, raising his hat merely to the last eager old aunty, to her open-mouthed astonishment. The people were distinctly bewildered. This silent, cold man,—was this John? Where was his smile and hearty hand-grasp? "'Peared kind o' down in the mouf," said the Methodist preacher thoughtfully. "Seemed monstus stuck up," complained a Baptist sister. But the white postmaster from the edge of the crowd expressed the opinion of his folks plainly. "That damn Nigger," said he, as he shouldered the mail and arranged his tobacco, "has gone North and got plum full o' fool notions; but they won't work in Altamaha." And the crowd melted away.

The meeting of welcome at the Baptist Church was a failure. Rain spoiled the barbecue, and thunder turned the milk in the ice-cream. When the speaking came at night, the house was crowded to overflowing. The three preachers had especially prepared themselves, but somehow John's manner seemed to throw a blanket over everything,—he seemed so cold and preoccupied, and had so strange an air of restraint that the Methodist brother could not warm up to his theme and elicited not a single "Amen"; the Presbyterian prayer was but feebly responded to, and even the Baptist preacher, though he wakened faint enthusiasm, got so mixed up in his favorite sentence that he had to close it by stopping fully fifteen minutes sooner than he meant. The people moved uneasily in their seats as John rose to reply. He spoke slowly and methodically. The age, he said, demanded new ideas; we were far different from those men of the seventeenth and eighteenth centuries,—with broader ideas of human brotherhood and destiny. Then he spoke of the rise of charity and popular education, and particularly of the spread of wealth and work. The question was, then, he added reflectively, looking at the low discolored ceiling, what part the Negroes of this land would take in the striving of the new century. He sketched in vague outline the new Industrial School that might rise among these pines, he spoke in detail of the charitable and philanthropic work that might be organized, of money that might be saved for banks and business. Finally he urged unity, and deprecated especially religious and denominational bickering. "To-day," he said, with a smile, "the world cares little whether a man be Baptist or Methodist, or indeed a churchman at all, so long as he is good and true. What difference does it make whether a man be baptized in river or washbowl, or not at all? Let's leave all that littleness, and look higher." Then, thinking of nothing else, he slowly sat down. A painful hush seized that crowded mass. Little had they understood of what he said, for he spoke an unknown tongue, save the last word about baptism; that they knew, and they sat very still while the clock ticked. Then at last a low suppressed snarl came from the Amen comer, and an old bent man arose, walked over the seats, and climbed straight up into the pulpit. He was wrinkled and black, with scant gray and tufted hair; his voice and hands shook as with palsy; but on his face lay the intense rapt look of the religious fanatic. He seized the Bible with his rough, huge hands; twice he raised it inarticulate, and then fairly burst into words, with rude and awful eloquence. He quivered, swayed, and bent; then rose aloft in perfect majesty, till the people moaned and wept, wailed and shouted, and a wild shrieking arose from the corners where all the pent-up feeling of the hour gathered itself and rushed into the air. John never knew clearly what the old man said; he only felt himself held up to scorn and scathing denunciation for trampling on the true Religion, and he realized with amazement that all unknowingly he had put rough, rude hands on something this little world held sacred. He arose silently, and passed out into the night. Down toward the sea he went, in the fitful starlight, half conscious of the girl who followed timidly after him. When at last he stood upon the bluff, he turned to his little sister and looked upon her sorrowfully, remembering with sudden pain how little thought he had given her. He put his arm about her and let her passion of tears spend itself on his shoulder.

Long they stood together, peering over the gray unresting water.

"John," she said, "does it make every one—unhappy when they study and learn lots of things?"

He paused and smiled. "I am afraid it does," he said.

"And, John, are you glad you studied?"

"Yes," came the answer, slowly but positively.

She watched the flickering lights upon the sea, and said thoughtfully, "I wish I was unhappy,—and—and," putting both arms about his neck, "I think I am, a little, John."

It was several days later that John walked up to the Judge's house to ask for the privilege of teaching the Negro school. The Judge himself met him at the front door, stared a little hard at him, and said brusquely, "Go 'round to the kitchen door, John, and wait." Sitting on the kitchen steps, John stared at the corn, thoroughly perplexed. What on earth had come over him? Every step he made offended some one. He had come to save his people, and before he left the depot he had hurt them. He sought to teach them at the church, and had outraged their deepest feelings. He had schooled himself to be respectful to the Judge, and then blundered into his front door. And all the time he had meant right,—and yet, and yet, somehow he found it so hard and strange to fit his old surroundings again, to find his place in the world about him. He could not remember that he used to have any difficulty in the past, when life was glad and gay. The world seemed smooth and easy then. Perhaps,—but his sister came to the kitchen door just then and said the Judge awaited him.

The Judge sat in the dining-room amid his morning's mail, and he did not ask John to sit down. He plunged squarely into the business. "You've come for the school, I suppose. Well, John, I want to speak to you plainly. You know I'm a friend to your people. I've helped you and your family, and would have done more if you hadn't got the notion of going off. Now I like the colored people, and sympathize with all their reasonable aspirations; but you and I both know, John, that in this country the Negro must remain subordinate, and can never expect to be the equal of white men. In their place, your people can be honest and respectful; and God knows, I'll do what I can to help them. But when they want to reverse nature, and rule white men, and marry white women, and sit in my parlor, then, by God! we'll hold them under if we have to lynch every Nigger in the land. Now, John, the questions is, are you, with your education and Northern notions, going to accept the situation and teach the darkies to be faithful servants and laborers as your fathers were,—I knew your father, John, he belonged to my brother, and he was a good Nigger. Well—well, are you going to be like him, or are you going to try to put fool ideas of rising and equality into these folks' heads, and make them discontented and unhappy?"

"I am going to accept the situation, Judge Henderson," answered John, with a brevity that did not escape the keen old man. He hesitated a moment, and then said shortly, "Very well,—we'll try you awhile. Good-morning."

It was a full month after the opening of the Negro school that the other John came home, tall, gay, and headstrong. The mother wept, the sisters sang. The whole white town was glad. A proud man was the Judge, and it was a goodly sight to see the two swinging down Main Street together. And yet all did not go smoothly between them, for the younger man could not and did not veil his contempt for the little town, and plainly had his heart set on New York. Now the one cherished ambition of the Judge was to see his son mayor of Altamaha, representative to the legislature, and—who could say?—governor of Georgia. So the argument often waxed hot between them. "Good heavens, father," the younger man would say after dinner, as he lighted a cigar and stood by the fireplace, "you surely don't expect a young fellow like me to settle down permanently in this—this God-forgotten town with nothing but mud and Negroes?" "I did," the Judge would answer laconically; and on this particular day it seemed from the gathering scowl that he was about to add something more emphatic, but neighbors had already begun to drop in to admire his son, and the conversation drifted.

"Heah that John is livenin' things up at the darky school," volunteered the postmaster, after a pause.

"What now?" asked the Judge, sharply.

"Oh, nothin' in particulah,—just his almighty air and uppish ways. B'lieve I did heah somethin' about his givin' talks on the French Revolution, equality, and such like. He's what I call a dangerous Nigger."

"Have you heard him say anything out of the way?"

"Why, no,—but Sally, our girl, told my wife a lot of rot. Then, too, I don't need to heah: a Nigger what won't say 'sir' to a white man, or—"

"Who is this John?" interrupted the son.

"Why, it's little black John, Peggy's son,—your old playfellow. "

The young man's face flushed angrily, and then he laughed.

"Oh," said he, "it's the darky that tried to force himself into a seat beside the lady I was escorting—"

But Judge Henderson waited to hear no more. He had been nettled all day, and now at this he rose with a half-smothered oath, took his hat and cane, and walked straight to the schoolhouse.

For John, it had been a long, hard pull to get things started in the rickety old shanty that sheltered his school. The Negroes were rent into factions for and against him, the parents were careless, the children irregular and dirty, and books, pencils, and slates largely missing. Nevertheless, he struggled hopefully on, and seemed to see at last some glimmering of dawn. The attendance was larger and the children were a shade cleaner this week. Even the booby class in reading showed a little comforting progress. So John settled himself with renewed patience this afternoon.

"Now, Mandy," he said cheerfully, "that's better; but you mustn't chop your words up so: 'If—the—man—goes.' Why, your little brother even wouldn't tell a story that way, now would he?"

"Naw, suh, he cain't talk."

"All right; now let's try again: 'If the man—'"

"John!"

The whole school started in surprise, and the teacher half arose, as the red, angry face of the Judge appeared in the open doorway.

"John, this school is closed. You children can go home and get to work. The white people of Altamaha are not spending their money on black folks to have their heads crammed with impudence and lies. Clear out! I'll lock the door myself. "

Up at the great pillared house the tall young son wandered aimlessly about after his father's abrupt departure. In the house there was little to interest him; the books were old and stale, the local newspaper flat, and the women had retired with headaches and sewing. He tried a nap, but it was too warm. So he sauntered out into the fields, complaining disconsolately, "Good Lord! how long will this imprisonment last!" He was not a bad fellow,—just a little spoiled and self-indulgent, and as headstrong as his proud father. He seemed a young man pleasant to look upon, as he sat on the great black stump at the edge of the pines idly swinging his legs and smoking. "Why, there isn't even a girl worth getting up a respectable flirtation with," he growled. Just then his eye caught a tall, willowy figure hurrying toward him on the narrow path. He looked with interest at first, and then burst into a laugh as he said, "Well, I declare, if it isn't Jennie, the little brown kitchen-maid! Why, I never noticed before what a trim little body she is. Hello, Jennie! Why, you haven't kissed me since I came home," he said gaily. The young girl stared at him in surprise and confusion,—faltered something inarticulate, and attempted to pass. But a wilful mood had seized the young idler, and he caught at her arm. Frightened, she slipped by; and half mischievously he turned and ran after her through the tall pines.

Yonder, toward the sea, at the end of the path, came John slowly, with his head down. He had turned wearily homeward from the schoolhouse; then, thinking to shield his mother from the blow, started to meet his sister as she came from work and break the news of his dismissal to her. "I'll go away," he said slowly; "I'll go away and find work, and send for them. I cannot live here longer." And then the fierce, buried anger surged up into his throat. He waved his arms and hurried wildly up the path.

The great brown sea lay silent. The air scarce breathed. The dying day bathed the twisted oaks and mighty pines in black and gold. There came from the wind no warning, not a whisper from the cloudless sky. There was only a black man hurrying on with an ache in his heart, seeing neither sun nor sea, but starting as from a dream at the frightened cry that woke the pines, to see his dark sister struggling in the arms of a tall and fair-haired man.

He said not a word, but, seizing a fallen limb, struck him with all the pent-up hatred of his great black arm, and the body lay white and still beneath the pines, all bathed in sunshine and in blood. John looked at it dreamily, then walked back to the house briskly, and said in a soft voice, "Mammy, I'm going away—I'm going to be free."

She gazed at him dimly and faltered, "No'th, honey, is yo' gwine No'th agin?"

He looked out where the North Star glistened pale above the waters, and said, "Yes, mammy, I'm going—North."

Then, without another word, he went out into the narrow lane, up by the straight pines, to the same winding path, and seated himself on the great black stump, looking at the blood where the body had lain. Yonder in the gray past he had played with that dead boy, romping together under the solemn trees. The night deepened; he thought of the boys at Johnstown. He wondered how Brown had turned out, and Carey? And Jones,—Jones? Why, *he* was Jones, and he wondered what they would all say when they knew, when they knew, in that great long dining-room with its hundreds of merry eyes. Then as the sheen of the starlight stole over him, he thought of the gilded ceiling of that vast concert hall, heard stealing toward him the faint sweet music of the swan. Hark! was it music, or the hurry and shouting of men? Yes, surely! Clear and high the faint sweet melody rose and fluttered like a living thing, so that the very earth trembled as with the tramp of horses and murmur of angry men.

He leaned back and smiled toward the sea, whence rose the strange melody, away from the dark shadows where lay the noise of horses galloping, galloping on. With an effort he roused himself, bent forward, and looked steadily down the pathway, softly humming the "Song of the Bride,"—

"Freudig geführt, ziehet dahin."

Amid the trees in the dim morning twilight he watched their shadows dancing and heard their horses thundering toward him, until at last they came sweeping like a storm, and he saw in front that haggard white-haired man, whose eyes flashed red with fury. Oh, how he pitied him,—pitied, him,—and wondered if he had the coiling twisted rope. Then, as the storm burst round him, he rose slowly to his feet and turned his closed eyes toward the Sea.

And the world whistled in his ears.

Of the Sorrow Songs

I walk through the churchyard
　　To lay this body down;
I know moon-rise, I know star-rise;
I walk in the moonlight, I walk in the starlight;
I'll lie in the grave and stretch out my arms,
I'll go to judgment in the evening of the day,
And my soul and thy soul shall meet that day,
　　When I lay this body down.

NEGRO SONG.

They that walked in darkness sang songs in the olden days—Sorrow Songs—for they were weary at heart. And so before each thought that I have written in this book I have set a phrase, a haunting echo of these weird old songs in which the soul of the black slave spoke to men. Ever since I was a child these songs have stirred me strangely. They came out of the South unknown to me, one by one, and yet at once I knew them as of me and of mine. Then in after years when I came to Nashville I saw the great temple builded of these songs towering over the pale city. To me Jubilee Hall seemed ever made of the songs themselves, and its bricks were red with the blood and dust of toil. Out of them rose for me morning, noon, and night, bursts of wonderful melody, full of the voices of my brothers and sisters, full of the voices of the past.

Little of beauty has America given the world save the rude grandeur God himself stamped on her bosom; the human spirit in this new world has expressed itself in vigor and ingenuity rather than in beauty. And so by fateful chance the Negro folk-song—the rhythmic cry of the slave—stands to-day not simply as the sole American music, but as the most beautiful expression of human experience born this side the seas. It has been neglected, it has been, and is, half despised, and above all it has been persistently mistaken and mis-understood; but notwithstanding, it still remains as the singular spiritual heritage of the nation and the greatest gift of the Negro people.

Away back in the thirties the melody of these slave songs stirred the nation, but the songs were soon half forgotten. Some, like "Near the lake where drooped the willow," passed into current airs and their source was forgotten; others were caricatured on the "minstrel" stage and their memory died away. Then in war-time came the singular Port Royal experiment after the capture of Hilton Head, and perhaps for the first time the North met the Southern slave face to face and heart to heart with no third witness. The Sea Islands of the Carolinas, where they met, were filled with a black folk of primitive type, touched and moulded less by the world about them than any others outside the Black Belt. Their appearance was uncouth, their language funny, but their hearts were human and their singing stirred men with a mighty power. Thomas Wentworth Higginson hastened to tell of these songs, and Miss McKim and others urged upon the world their rare beauty. But the world listened only half credulously until the Fisk Jubilee Singers sang the slave songs so deeply into the world's heart that it can never wholly forget them again.

There was once a blacksmith's son born at Cadiz, New York, who in the changes of time taught school in Ohio and helped defend Cincinnati from Kirby Smith. Then he fought at Chancellorsville and Gettysburg and finally served in the Freedmen's Bureau at Nashville. Here he formed a Sunday-school class of black children in 1866, and sang with them and taught them to sing. And then they taught him to sing, and when once the glory of the Jubilee songs passed into the soul of George L. White, he knew his life-work was to let those Negroes sing to the world as they had sung to him. So in 1871 the pilgrimage of the Fisk Jubilee Singers began. North to Cincinnati they rode,—four half-clothed black boys and five girl-women,—led by a man with a cause and a purpose. They stopped at Wilberforce, the oldest of Negro schools, where a black bishop blessed them. Then they went, fighting cold and starvation, shut out of hotels, and cheerfully sneered at, ever northward; and ever the magic of their song kept thrilling hearts, until a burst of applause in the Congregational Council at Oberlin revealed them to the world. They came to New York and Henry Ward Beecher dared to welcome them, even though the metropolitan dailies sneered at his "Nigger Minstrels." So their songs conquered till they sang across the land and across the sea, before Queen and Kaiser, in Scotland and Ireland, Holland and Switzerland. Seven years they sang, and brought back a hundred and fifty thousand dollars to found Fisk University.

Since their day they have been imitated—sometimes well, by the singers of Hampton and Atlanta, sometimes ill, by straggling quartettes. Caricature has sought again to spoil the quaint beauty of the music, and has filled the air with many debased melodies which vulgar ears scarce know from the real. But the true Negro folk-song still lives in the hearts of those who have heard them truly sung and in the hearts of the Negro people.

What are these songs, and what do they mean? I know little of music and can say nothing in technical phrase, but I know something of men, and knowing them, I know that these songs are the articulate message of the slave to the world. They tell us in these eager days that life was joyous to the black slave, careless and happy. I can easily believe this of some, of many. But not all the past South, though it rose from the dead, can gainsay the heart-touching witness of these songs. They are the music of an unhappy people, of the children of disappointment; they tell of death and suffering and unvoiced longing toward a truer world, of misty wanderings and hidden ways.

The songs are indeed the siftings of centuries; the music is far more ancient than the words, and in it we can trace here and there signs of development. My grandfather's grandmother was seized by an evil Dutch trader two centuries ago; and coming to the valleys of the Hudson and Housatonic, black, little, and lithe, she shivered and shrank in the harsh north winds, looked longingly at the hills, and often crooned, a heathen melody to the child between her knees, thus:

The child sang it to his children and they to their children's children, and so two hundred years it has travelled down to us and we sing it to our children, knowing as little as our fathers what its words may mean, but knowing well the meaning of its music.

This was primitive African music; it may be seen in larger form in the strange chant which heralds "The Coming of John":

> "You may bury me in the East,
> You may bury me in the West,
> But I'll hear the trumpet sound in that morning,"

—the voice of exile.

Ten master songs, more or less, one may pluck from the forest of melody—songs of undoubted Negro origin and wide popular currency, and songs peculiarly characteristic of the slave. One of these I have just mentioned. Another whose strains begin this book is "Nobody knows the trouble I've seen." When, struck with a sudden poverty, the United States refused to fulfill its promises of land to the freedmen, a brigadier-general went down to the Sea Islands to carry the news. An old woman on the outskirts of the throng began singing this song; all the mass joined with her, swaying. And the soldier wept.

The third song is the cradle-song of death which all men know,—"Swing low, sweet chariot,"—whose bars begin the life story of "Alexander Crummell." Then there is the song of many waters, "Roll, Jordan, roll," a mighty chorus with minor cadences. There were many songs of the fugitive like that which opens "The Wings of Atalanta"; and the more familiar "Been a-listening." The seventh is the song of the End and the Beginning—"My Lord, what a mourning! when the stars begin to fall"; a strain of this is placed before "The Dawn of Freedom." The song of groping—"My way's cloudy"—begins "The Meaning of Progress"; the ninth is the song of this chapter—"Wrestlin' Jacob, the day is a-breaking,"—a pæan of hopeful strife. The last master song is the song of songs—"Steal away,"—sprung from "The Faith of the Fathers."

There are many others of the Negro folk-songs as striking and characteristic as these, as, for instance, the three strains in the third, eighth, and ninth chapters; and others I am sure could easily make a selection on more scientific principles. There are, too, songs that seem to be a step removed from the more primitive types: there is the maze-like medley, "Bright sparkles," one phrase of which heads "The Black Belt"; the Easter carol, "Dust, dust and ashes"; the dirge, "My mother's took her flight and gone home"; and that burst of melody hovering over "The Passing of the First-Born"—"I hope my mother will be there in that beautiful world on high."

These represent a third step in the development of the slave song, of which "You may bury me in the East" is the first, and songs like "March on" (chapter six) and "Steal away" are the second. The first is African music, the second Afro American, while the third is a blending of Negro music with the music heard in the foster land. The result is still distinctively Negro and the method of blending original, but the elements are both Negro and Caucasian. One might go further and find a fourth step in this development, where the songs of white America have been distinctively influenced by the slave songs or have incorporated whole phrases of Negro melody, as "Swanee River" and "Old Black Joe." Side by side, too, with the growth has gone the debasements and imitations—the Negro "minstrel" songs, many of the "gospel" hymns, and some of the contemporary "coon" songs,—a mass of music in which the novice may easily lose himself and never find the real Negro melodies.

In these songs, I have said, the slave spoke to the world. Such a message is naturally veiled and half articulate. Words and music have lost each other and new and cant phrases of a dimly understood theology have displaced the older sentiment. Once in a while we catch a strange word of an unknown tongue, as the "Mighty Myo," which figures as a river of death; more often slight words or mere doggerel are joined to music of singular sweetness. Purely secular songs are few in number, partly because many of them were turned into hymns by a change of words, partly because the frolics were seldom heard by the stranger, and the music less often caught. Of nearly all the songs, however, the music is distinctly sorrowful. The ten master songs I have mentioned tell in word and music of trouble and exile, of strife and hiding; they grope toward some unseen power and sigh for rest in the End.

The words that are left to us are not without interest, and, cleared of evident dross, they conceal much of real poetry and meaning beneath conventional theology and unmeaning rhapsody. Like all primitive folk, the slave stood near to Nature's heart. Life was a "rough and rolling sea" like the brown Atlantic of the Sea Islands; the "Wilderness" was the home of God, and the "lonesome valley" led to the way of life. "Winter'll soon be over," was the picture of life and death to a tropical imagination. The sudden wild thunderstorms of the South awed and impressed the Negroes,—at times the rumbling seemed to them "mournful," at times imperious:

> "My Lord calls me,
>   He calls me by the thunder,
>   The trumpet sounds it in my soul."

The monotonous toil and exposure is painted in many words, One sees the ploughmen in the hot, moist furrow, singing:

> "Dere's no rain to wet you.
>   Dere's no sun to bum you,
>   Oh, push along, believer,
>   I want to go home."

The bowed and bent old man cries, with thrice-repeated wail:

> *"O Lord, keep me from sinking down,"*

and he rebukes the devil of doubt who can whisper:

> *"Jesus is dead and God's gone away."*

My   soul wants something, that's new, that's new,

Yet the soul-hunger is there, the restlessness of the savage; the wail of the wanderer, and the plaint is put in one little phrase:

Over the inner thoughts of the slaves and their relations one with another the shadow of fear ever hung, so that we get but glimpses here and there, and also with them, eloquent omissions and silences. Mother and child are sung, but seldom father; fugitive and weary wanderer call for pity and affection, but there is little of wooing and wedding: the rocks and the mountains are well known, but home is unknown. Strange blending of love and helplessness sings through the refrain:

> "Yonder's my ole mudder,
>   Been waggin' at de hill so long;
>   'Bout time she cross over.
>   Git home bime-by."

Elsewhere comes the cry of the "motherless" and the "Farewell, farewell, my only child."

Love-songs are scarce and fall into two categories—the frivolous and light, and the sad. Of deep successful love there is ominous silence, and in one of the oldest of these songs there is a depth of history and meaning:

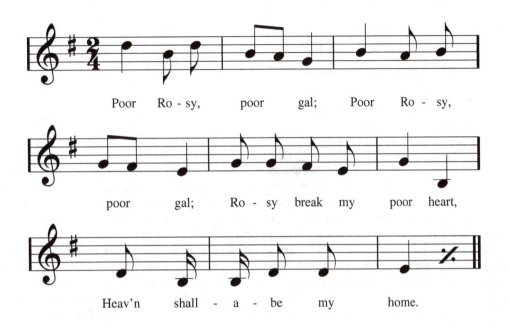

Poor Ro - sy, poor gal; Poor Ro - sy,

poor gal; Ro - sy break my poor heart,

Heav'n shall - a - be my home.

A black woman said of the song, "It can't be sung without a full heart and a troubled sperrit." The same voice sings here that sings the German folk-song:

"Jetz Geh i' an's brunele, trink' aber net."

Of death the Negro showed little fear, but talked of it familiarly and even fondly as simply a crossing of the waters, perhaps—who knows?—back to his ancient forests again. Later days transfigured his fatalism, and amid the dust and dirt the toiler sang:

"Dust, dust and ashes, fly over my grave,
But the Lord shall bear my spirit home."

The things evidently borrowed from the surrounding world undergo characteristic change when they enter the mouth of the slave. Especially is this true of Bible phrases. "Weep, O captive daughter of Zion," is quaintly turned into "Zion, weep-a-low," and the wheels of Ezekiel are turned every way in the mystic dreaming of the slave, till he says:

"There's a little wheel a-turnin' in-a-my heart."

As in olden time, the words of these hymns were improvised by some leading minstrel of the religious band. The circumstances of the gathering, however, the rhythm of the songs, and the limitations of allowable thought, confined the poetry for the most part to single or double lines, and they seldom were expanded to quatrains or longer tales, although there are some few examples of sustained efforts, chiefly paraphrases of the Bible. Three short series of verses have always attracted me,—the one that heads this chapter, of one line of which Thomas Wentworth Higginson has fittingly said, "Never, it seems to me, since man first lived and suffered was his infinite longing for peace uttered more plaintively." The second and third are descriptions of the Last Judgment,—the one a late improvisation, with some traces of outside influence:

"Oh, the stars in the elements are falling,
And the moon drips away into blood,
And the ransomed of the Lord are returning unto God,
Blessed be the name of the Lord."

And the other earlier and homelier picture from the low coast lands:

> "Michael, haul the boat ashore,
> Then you'll hear the horn they blow,
>
> Then you'll hear the trumpet sound.
> Trumpet sound the world around,
> Trumpet sound for rich and poor,
> Trumpet sound the Jubilee,
> Trumpet sound for you and me."

Through all the sorrow of the Sorrow Songs there breathes a hope—a faith in the ultimate justice of things. The minor cadences of despair change often to triumph and calm confidence. Sometimes it is faith in life, sometimes a faith in death, sometimes assurance of boundless justice in some fair world beyond. But whichever it is, the meaning is always clear: that sometime, somewhere, men will judge men by their souls and not by their skins. Is such a hope justified? Do the Sorrow Songs sing true?

The silently growing assumption of this age is that the probation of races is past, and that the backward races of to-day are of proven inefficiency and not worth the saving. Such an assumption is the arrogance of peoples irreverent toward Time and ignorant of the deeds of men. A thousand years ago such an assumption, easily possible, would have made it difficult for the Teuton to prove his right to life. Two thousand years ago such dogmatism, readily welcome, would have scouted the idea of blond races ever leading civilization. So wofully unorganized is sociological knowledge that the meaning of progress, the meaning of "swift" and "slow" in human doing, and the limits of human perfectability, are veiled, unanswered sphinxes on the shores of science. Why should Æschylus have sung two thousand years before Shakespeare was born? Why has civilization flourished in Europe, and flickered, flamed, and died in Africa? So long as the world stands meekly dumb before such questions, shall this nation proclaim its ignorance and unhallowed prejudices by denying freedom of opportunity to those who brought the Sorrow Songs to the Seats of the Mighty?

Your country? How came it yours? Before the Pilgrims landed we were here. Here we have brought our three gifts and mingled them with yours: a gift of story and song—soft, stirring melody in an ill-harmonized and unmelodious land; the gift of sweat and brawn to beat back the wilderness, conquer the soil, and lay the foundations of this vast economic empire two hundred years earlier than your weak hands could have done it; the third, a gift of the Spirit. Around us the history of the land has centred for thrice a hundred years; out of the nation's heart we have called all that was best to throttle and subdue all that was worst; fire and blood, prayer and sacrifice, have billowed over this people, and they have found peace only in the altars of the God of Right. Nor has our gift of the Spirit been merely passive. Actively we have woven ourselves with the very warp and woof of this nation,—we fought their battles, shared their sorrow, mingled our blood with theirs, and generation after generation have pleaded with a headstrong, careless people to despise not Justice, Mercy, and Truth, lest the nation be smitten with a curse. Our song, our toil, our cheer, and warning have been given to this nation in blood-brotherhood. Are not these gifts worth the giving? Is not this work and striving? Would America have been America without her Negro people?

Even so is the hope that sang in the songs of my fathers well sung. If somewhere in this whirl and chaos of things there dwells Eternal Good, pitiful yet masterful, then anon in His good time America shall rend the Veil and the prisoned shall go free. Free, free as the sunshine trickling down the morning into these high windows of mine, free as yonder fresh young voices welling up to me from the caverns of brick and mortar below—swelling with song, instinct with life, tremulous treble and darkening bass. My children, my little children, are singing to the sunshine, and thus they sing:

And the traveller girds himself, and sets his face toward the Morning, and goes his way.

Chapter 33

Ida B. Wells and the Anti-Lynching Campaign

Excerpts from Speech delivered at the National Negro Conference, 1909

The lynching record for a quarter of a century merits the thoughtful study of the American people. It presents three salient facts:

First: Lynching is color-line murder.

Second: Crimes against women is the excuse, not the cause.

Third: It is a national crime and requires a national remedy.

Proof that lynching follows the color line is to be found in the statistics which have been kept for the past twenty-five years. During the few years preceding this period and while frontier lynch law existed, the executions showed a majority of white victims. Later, however, as law courts and authorized judiciary extended into the far West, lynch law rapidly abated, and its white victims became few and far between.

Just as the lynch-law regime came to a close in the West, a new mob movement started in the South. This was wholly political, its purpose being to suppress the colored vote by intimidation and murder. Thousands of assassins banded together under the name of Ku Klux Klans, "Midnight Raiders," "Knights of the Golden Circle," et cetera, et cetera, spread a reign of terror, by beating, shooting and killing colored people by the thousands. In a few years, the purpose was accomplished, and the black vote was suppressed. But mob murder continued.

From 1882, in which year fifty-two were lynched, down to the present, lynching has been along the color line. Mob murder increased yearly until in 1892 more than two hundred victims were lynched and statistics show that 3,284 men, women and children have been put to death in this quarter of a century. During the last ten years from 1899 to 1908 inclusive the number lynched was 959. Of this number 102 were white, while the colored victims numbered 857. No other nation, civilized or savage, burns its criminals: only under the Stars and Stripes is the human holocaust possible. Twenty-eight human beings burned at the stake, one of them a woman and two of them children, is the awful indictment against American civilization—the gruesome tribute which the nation pays to the color line.

Why is mob murder permitted by a Christian nation? What is the cause of this awful slaughter? This question is answered almost daily—always the same shameless falsehood that "Negroes are lynched to protect womanhood." Standing before a Chautauqua assemblage, John Temple Graves, at once champion of lynching and apologist for lynchers, said: "The mob stands today as the most potent bulwark between the women of the South and such a carnival of crime as would infuriate the world and precipitate the annihilation of the Negro race. This is the never-varying answer of lynchers and their apologists. All know that it is untrue. The cowardly lyncher revels in murder, then seeks to shield himself from public execration by claiming devotion to woman. But truth is mighty and the lynching record discloses the hypocrisy of the lyncher as well as his crime.

The Springfield, Illinois, mob rioted for two days, the militia of the entire state was called out, two men were lynched, hundreds of people driven from their homes, all because a white woman said a Negro assaulted her. A mad mob went to the jail, tried to lynch the victim of her charge and, not being able to find him, proceeded to pillage and burn the town and to lynch two innocent men. Later, after the police had found that the woman's charge was false, she published a retraction, the indictment was dismissed and the intended victim discharged. But the lynched victims were dead. Hundreds were homeless and Illinois was disgraced.

As a final and complete refutation of the charge that lynching is occasioned by crimes against women, a partial record of lynchings is cited; 285 persons were lynched for causes as follows:

Unknown cause, 92; no cause, 10; race prejudice, 49; miscegenation, 7; informing, 12; making threats, 11; keeping saloon, 3; practicing fraud, 5; practicing voodooism, 2; bad reputation, 8; unpopularity, 3; mistaken identity, 5; using improper language, 3; violation of contract, 1; writing insulting letter, 2; eloping, 2; poisoning horse, 1; poisoning well, 2; by white caps, 9; vigilantes, 14; Indians, 1; moonshining, 1; refusing evidence, 2; political causes, 5; disputing, 1; disobeying quarantine regulations, 2; slapping a child, 1; turning state's evidence, 3; protecting a Negro, 1; to prevent giving evidence, 1; knowledge of larceny, 1; writing letter to white woman, 1; asking white woman to marry, 1; jilting girl, 1; having smallpox, 1; concealing criminal, 2; threatening political exposure, 1; self-defense, 6; cruelty, 1; insulting language to woman, 5; quarreling with white man, 2; colonizing Negroes, 1; throwing stones, 1; quarreling, 1; gambling, 1.

Is there a remedy, or will the nation confess that it cannot protect its protectors at home as well as abroad? Various remedies have been suggested to abolish the lynching infamy, but year after year, the butchery of men, women and children continues in spite of plea and protest. Education is suggested as a preventive, but it is as grave a crime to murder an ignorant man as it is a scholar. True, few educated men have been lynched, but the hue and cry once started stops at no bounds, as was clearly shown by the lynchings in Atlanta, and in Springfield, Illinois.

Agitation, though helpful, will not alone stop the crime. Year after year statistics are published, meetings are held, resolutions are adopted and yet lynchings go on. Public sentiment does measurably decrease the sway of mob law, but the irresponsible bloodthirsty criminals who swept through the streets of Springfield, beating an inoffensive law-abiding citizen to death in one part of the town, and in another torturing and shooting to death a man who for threescore years had made a reputation for honesty, integrity and sobriety, had raised a family and had accumulated property, were not deterred from their heinous crimes by either education or agitation.

The only certain remedy is an appeal to law. Lawbreakers must be made to know that human life is sacred and that every citizen of this country is first a citizen of the United States and secondly a citizen of the state in which he belongs. This nation must assert itself and defend its federal citizenship at home as well as abroad. The strong arm of the government must reach across state lines whenever unbridled lawlessness defies state laws and must give to the individual citizen under the Stars and Stripes the same measure of protection which it gives to him when he travels in foreign lands.

Federal protection of American citizenship is the remedy for lynching. Foreigners are rarely lynched in America. If, by mistake, one is lynched, the national government quickly pays the damages. The recent agitation in California against the Japanese compelled this nation to recognize that federal power must yet assert itself to protect the nation from the treason of sovereign states. Thousands of American citizens have been put to death and no President has yet raised his hand in effective protest, but a simple insult to a native of Japan was quite sufficient to stir the government at Washington to prevent the threatened wrong. If the government has power to protect a foreigner from insult, certainly it has power to save a citizen's life.

The practical remedy has been more than once suggested in Congress. Senator Gallinger, of New Hampshire, in a resolution introduced in Congress called for an investigation "with the view of ascertaining whether there is a remedy for lynching which Congress may apply." The Senate Committee has under consideration a bill drawn by A. E. Pillsbury, formerly Attorney General of Massachusetts, providing for federal prosecution of lynchers in cases where the state fails to protect citizens or foreigners. Both of these resolutions indicate that the attention of the nation has been called to this phase of the lynching question.

As a final word, it would be a beginning in the right direction if this conference can see its way clear to establish a bureau for the investigation and publication of the details of every lynching, so that the public could know that an influential body of citizens has made it a duty to give the widest publicity to the facts in each case; that it will make an effort to secure expressions of opinion all over the country against lynching for the sake of the country's fair name; and lastly, but by no means least, to try to influence the daily papers of the country to refuse to become accessory to mobs either before or after the fact. Several of the greatest riots and most brutal burnt offerings of the mobs have been suggested and incited by the daily papers of the offending community. If the newspaper which suggests lynching in its accounts of an alleged crime, could be held legally as well as morally responsible for reporting that "threats of lynching were heard"; or, "it is feared that if the guilty one is caught, he will be lynched"; or, "there were cries of 'lynch him,' and the only reason the threat was not carried out was because no leader appeared," a long step toward a remedy will have been taken.

In a multitude of counsel there is wisdom. Upon the grave question presented by the slaughter of innocent men, women and children there should be an honest, courageous conference of patriotic, law-abiding citizens anxious to punish crime promptly, impartially and by due process of law, also to make life, liberty and property secure against mob rule.

Time was when lynching appeared to be sectional, but now it is national—a blight upon our nation, mocking our laws and disgracing our Christianity. "With malice toward none but with charity for all" let us undertake the work of making the "law of the land" effective and supreme upon every foot of American soil—a shield to the innocent; and to the guilty, punishment swift and sure.

Section 3—Study Questions

1. How did the Great Depression affect Robert A. Cole's entrepreneurial activities?

2. How did Robert A. Cole utilize his knowledge of racial segregation's inequalities to meet the needs of Chicago's Black residents?

3. According to Tate, why was nationalism central to Black empowerment in the United States?

4. List and explain the core ideological principles of Black nationalism.

5. In your personal music collection, are there examples of music that give an account of history? Are they popular perceptions or historical ones?

6. Do you think the "Good Death" still resonates as a concept not only for soldiers but for everyday people?

7. Is the Hank Williams' Jr. song offensive/regressive? Why or why not?

8. What parts of the contemporary songs seem like "history lessons" or simply a well-constructed story or narrative? What makes them captivating?

9. What are some ways that these songs reveal either race, class, or gender issues?

10. What reasons does Frederick Douglass provide for the importance of Black enfranchisement?

11. Why does Douglass demand that "if the Negro cannot stand on his own legs, let him fall also. All I ask is, give him a chance to stand on his own legs! Let him alone!"

12. Why does William Monroe Trotter argue that Booker T. Washington has delivered a "fatal blow . . . to the Negro's political rights and identity by his enslavement"?

13. Why does Trotter call Washington the "Benedict Arnold of the Negro Race"?

14. Briefly outline Booker T. Washington's educational philosophy for the recently freed African Americans.

15. What is Washington's position on African American "agitation for social equality"?

16. What was Du Bois's concept of "The Talented Tenth".

17. What was the conflict between Du Bois and Marcus Garvey?

18. Explain the metaphor of the veil in the "Forethought" of W. E. B. Du Bois's *The Souls of Black Folk.*

19. Why did Du Bois consider Booker T. Washington's strategies tantamount to legitimizing White oppression against Blacks?

20. How does Du Bois's fictional account of the two Johns connect to the themes in "Chapter 1: Our Spiritual Strivings"?

21. Why were the Sorrow Songs integral to Black existential empowerment in the United States?

22. What does Ida B. Wells identify as the remedy for lynching?

23. What are some of the causes that Wells identifies for the "awful slaughter" of lynching?

Section 4

The Civil Rights and Black Power Movements

Chapter 34

The Civil Rights and Black Power Movements:
An Introduction

Gayle T. Tate

The modern Civil Rights Movement grew out of the long struggle for freedom of African Americans in American society. The 20th century momentum gained currency with the founding of organizations at the beginning of the century that built the infrastructure for social change. So that a movement could be created and flourished, African Americans employed different organizational strategies to fight racial discrimination and social segregation. These included the NAACP (National Association for the Advancement of Colored People), which attacked racial discrimination through political protest and an assault on the legal system to remove the barriers of social segregation; NUL (National Urban League), to assist Southern Blacks in their adjustment to Northern industrial cities; UNIA (Universal Negro Improvement Association), which restored racial pride and economic Black nationalism to Blacks; and CORE (Congress of Racial Equality), committed to nonviolent direct action in the spirit of Mahatma Gandhi. Other short-lived organizations also had an impact upon Blacks and helped create the political environment of protest, intellectual debate, and analysis. They included the ABB (the African Blood Brotherhood), which advocated suffrage for Black Southerners and armed resistance to lynching; NERL (the National Equal Rights League), under William Monroe Trotter who advocated political protest and immediate political and social equality; and SNYC (Southern Negro Youth Congress) with a focus on civil rights. These secular organizations were buttressed by the growth of the urban church in the South and the expansion of the Black church in the North, which served during the modern Civil Rights Movement as a cross-fertilization of ideas, information, and resources. Together, all of these organizations and institutions created the infrastructure and foundation for social change.

Undoubtedly, *Brown v. Board of Education of Topeka, Kansas I & II (1954–55)* was the political spark that gave rise to the modern Civil Rights Movement. In response to the White resistance on the heels of *Brown*, and the creation of White organizations like the National Association of White People, White Brotherhood, and the White Citizens' Council, Blacks began boycotts against segregation. The Baton Rouge Boycott was the first boycott, and by using direct action as a strategy of mass resistance, moved the movement into its next phase. The Montgomery Bus Boycott gained its momentum when Rosa Parks, a seasoned civil rights activist, refused to give up her seat in the "no man's land" section on segregated buses. Parks, who had trained at the Highlander Folk School in Monteagle, Tennessee, on desegregation, and was an NAACP Youth Advisor, had a history of resistance. The organizational backing of the Women's Political Council, led by Jo Ann Robinson, was instrumental in mobilizing the Black community to respond to a one-day boycott in support of Parks' action. The boycott campaign turned into 381 days of mass protest and culminated with the integration of the buses. This boycott was followed by others in other Southern cities, and the mass movement, along with its dramatic coverage worldwide, turned the lens on the Southern struggle. As the movement grew and catapulted the plight of African Americans to the national political stage, the increasing numbers of Black and White activists—as well as the leadership of Martin Luther King, Jr., Ella Baker, E. D. Nixon, and others—began to dislodge southern complacency with segregation.

The "movement within the movement" began in 1960 when college students became a force to be reckoned with inside the movement with older leadership while they simultaneously broadened the political base of the movement where several strategies could be employed. Student participation brought a new vitality to the movement, and the sit-ins, jail-ins, freedom rides, boycotts, marches, forums, intergenerational bonding, and voter registration drives were institutionalized, creating a new phase of the movement. The massive student activism kept the national attention on the struggle for social justice and illuminated, for the world, entrenched White resistance. The mass demonstrations in Albany, Georgia, and Birmingham, Alabama, in 1961, 1962, and 1963; the March on Washington in 1963; the Voter Registration Drive initiated by SNCC workers in 1964; and the Freedom Summer of 1964, which brought young White college students to Mississippi to help in the voter registration drive all met White resistance. The death of three young civil rights workers early in the students' efforts highlighted for the nation not only the dangerous work that these students were doing but also the ugly face of White racism.

The creation of the Mississippi Freedom Democratic Party, using approximately 60,000 newly registered Black voters to unseat the state Democratic Party's delegation, was unsuccessful. However, the poignant and eloquent testimony of Fannie Lou Hamer regarding segregation in Mississippi aroused the political awareness of a national audience. The provisional compromise that the next convention, in 1968, would refuse to seat a delegate who practiced racial discrimination was hallow at best. In contrast, many political activists, who had witnessed the lives lost of fallen comrades, the increased White violence against the activists—the manipulation of state officials and laws to enforce segregation, daily harassment by police officers, and now the obvious political manipulation of the democratic process—became disillusioned and sought other alternatives such as the rising interest in Black power.

The rise of the Black Power Movement was located in the North and the South as Blacks were confronting two faces of racial oppression. Although the movement was initiated on a civil rights march between Memphis, Tennessee, and Jackson, Mississippi, its impetus would embrace northern industrial cities as well. On one hand, the seasoned civil rights workers in the South had witnessed the political compromises that leaders made that yielded few tangible benefits and recognized that the dismantling of Jim Crow segregation would not achieve political equality. On the other hand, Northern Blacks felt the same powerlessness confronting daily racial discrimination, high unemployment, segregated housing, poor education, poverty, and police brutality. The urban uprisings that shaped so much of the 1960s from 1964 forward shed a great deal of light on the frustration and powerlessness, alongside the police brutality, that Blacks endured as a part of their daily experience. Over 300 cities, including Philadelphia, Jersey City, Newark, Chicago, Washington, D.C., Hartford, Providence, and San Francisco, became powder kegs as Blacks fought against their deprivation, racial discrimination, and the lack of opportunity in the inner cities. These uprisings resulted in loss of life, property damage, and the police retaliation that turned these inner-city communities into occupied territories.

While there are several definitions on what Black Power meant, the intellectual debate and activism surrounding the Black Power Movement went on well into the 1970s and 1980s. Some political and social scholars began to look at the "internal colonial thesis" as a model, that the Black community had the same relationship to the United States that colonies had with their mother country. Others saw a class analysis, that Blacks were impoverished not because of their race but because they were members of a class of poor people in society. Some others saw it strictly through a capitalist lens, as a matter of providing access to capitalist power and resources and upward class mobility. Still others believed that the Black Power Movement spoke to the political, economic, and social development of Black communities and Black autonomy as a critical necessity.

Malcolm X emerged as the ideological leader of the Black Power Movement. His message embracing Black nationalism and its emphasis on autonomous organizational leadership, economic development, pride in African ancestry, and political power resonated with urban youth. The influence of Marcus Garvey, Noble Drew Ali, and Elijah Muhammad were integral to Malcolm X's thinking, particularly when he called for Black self-determination and self-reliance, community control, and racial pride and dignity. The Black Power Movement was pervasive and Malcolm X's influence dominated the movement long after his death. Black organizations that emerged in this period took on the militant rhetoric of Black Power as well as some of the concerns for the community that Malcolm X espoused. The Black Panther Party for Self-Defense, founded in 1966, which had Marxist-Nationalist leanings, sought revolutionary changes in the society and community initiatives that included a school, a breakfast program, and a day-care center. Other groups, like the Revolutionary Action Movement, who argued that armed self-defense was integral to Black liberation struggle, and the Dodge Revolutionary Union Movement, which sought better conditions in the workplace, were founded during this period. The Black Arts Movement, which was "the esthetic and spiritual sister of the Black Power concept" was founded shortly after the assassination of Malcolm X. All aspects of the rise in Black consciousness in the 1970s and 1980s—which included the development of Black studies in predominantly White colleges and universities, the donning of African garb and hairstyles, the international political and social awareness of African Americans, the growing systematic study of the diaspora, and the celebration of Kwanzaa—have roots in the Black Power Movement.

Edward Ramsamy, in his work, "Conceptualizing the Civil Rights Movement" argues that we must widen our lens if we are going to understand that the modern phase of the Civil Rights Movement is integral to the larger struggle that has existed since African Americans came to these shores. This political context of struggle broadens our understanding of American democracy, its promise to all of its citizens, the political rhetoric of each epoch, and its performance, particularly as it deviates from basic notions of egalitarianism in regards to Blacks. In large part, Donna Auston's "Color Me Invisible: The Hidden Legacy of African American Muslims" notes that African American Muslims have been invisible in the body politic and generally left out of the African American historical narrative. Yet their presence has not only shaped much of black culture, particularly the elements of religion, music, and resistance, but continuously defines the larger global dimensions of the diaspora. African Americans, in seeking social justice, utilize the Constitution of the United States as a barometer for their quest of political equality. In Louis Ray's chapter, "'He baked no bread of his own': Charles H. Thompson and the Struggle for Civil Rights," Ray critically examines Charles H. Thompson's significant role in the Civil Rights Movement. Thompson, the editor of the *Journal of Negro Education*, was instrumental in shaping the public policy debates around the educational inequities and citizenship rights for African Americans and other minorities. Using his editorials in the *Journal of Negro Education* as an integral component of the growing debate on education, he provided debate and discourse as well as direction and leadership for the coming battles on school segregation. Alongside being used as an expert witness for the National Association for the Advancement of Colored People for those landmark cases leading up to *Brown v. Board of Education*, Thompson strategically created an environment for the cross-fertilization of ideas on social justice to gain credence.

There were others shaping the discourse and direct action of the movement as well. Gayle T. Tate, in her chapter, "The Wellspring of Resistance: Black Women's Collective Action" views Black female activists at the epicenter of the movement. Black female activists, grounded in collective action, were instrumental in building the infrastructure of the movement, providing its interior psychological and social dimensions, and connecting participants to the leadership cadre in terms of ideas, policies, and course of action, as well as forging alliances. These activists also paved the way for future suffrage, playing a major role in the establishment of citizenship schools. This collective action was a thread that was initiated in slave communities, became an important organizational factor of free Black women in the antebellum era, and was later used during the Civil Rights Movement to sustain the dynamism of the quest for political and social equality. One of the women was civil rights activist, Ruby Hurley. In Allison A. McGevna's chapter, "The Unsung Heroism of Ruby Hurley," she chronicles the civil rights activism of Hurley, first as an NAACP organizer in the late 1930s, and then the national youth secretary in the 1940s. That job was to take Hurley into the South to investigate the murders of Reverend George W. Lee, who had encouraged his parishioners to register to vote, and Emmett Till, who "had talked fresh" to a White woman. Working alongside Medgar Evers and Amzie Moore in a charged and dangerous atmosphere, Hurley found witnesses to the murder of Till. Hurley continued to work in the South and provided support for Autherine Lucy when, challenged by White resistance, she attempted to gain admittance to the University of Alabama.

While the Black church has been an integral part of the struggle for Civil Rights, it has also functioned under the cloud of sexism and homophobia. Cheryl Clarke examines this contradiction in the Black church in her article "Ecstatic Fallacies: The Politics of the Black Store Front". In the article titled, "College Football Drives Desegregation of Schools in the Southeastern Conference" Donald Heilman examines the important, but often neglected, theme of how football played a role in the desegregation of all-white Southern universities.

Regina Jennings examines how Malcolm X used his influence in the Black Power Movement to reconnect African Americans with their African heritage. In her work, "Malcolm X: A Nationalist Internationalist," Jennings chronicles how the transformation of Malcolm X to a minister of the Islamic faith correspondingly created a change in the names of Black people in America from Negro to African American. With Malcolm's guidance of reinterpreting ancient African history, as well as illuminating for his audiences the inherent contradictions in American history, he raised the political awareness and consciousness of his audience to reconnect to their African past with knowledge, pride, and dignity. Malcolm X, then, helped shape the intellectual inquiry of Black people on the authentic truths of African history and, in so doing, internationalized the struggle for freedom.

The long legal battle of the NAACP shepherded initially by Charles Hamilton Houston and subsequently by Thurgood Marshall produced the milestone decision in *Brown v. Board of Education of Topeka, Kansas I (1954)*. While there were four cases from Kansas, South Carolina, Virginia, and Delaware that were consolidated into *Brown v. Board of Education*, the central question in all of the cases was whether Black children could attend public schools on an integrated basis. In prior challenges to segregated education, despite some victories of individual graduate school cases, the Supreme Court did not overturn *Plessy v. Ferguson (1896)*, which maintained separate but equal facilities for Blacks and Whites. In *Brown I*, however, the Supreme Court overturned *Plessy v. Ferguson*, ruling that segregated education deprived Black children of equal educational opportunities as well as equal protection of the law. *Brown II (1955)*, where the Supreme Court relegated compliance "with all deliberate speed" to local communities, encountered stiff White resistance. The Civil Rights Act of 1964 enacted by Congress came a full decade after the rise of White resistance on the heels of *Brown I & II (1954 & 1955)* and continued political protest against segregation. The massive demonstrations, the sit-ins by college students, and White retaliation had captured the world's attention and, just as importantly, had caused the disruption of business in local communities where sustained protest occurred. The Civil Rights Act of 1964 banned racial discrimination on public conveyances and in public accommodations, in employment, voting, education, and other federally assisted agencies and programs. The Act established a federal Community Relations Service to assist communities in addressing civil rights issues and authorized the United States Office of Education to assist communities in the efforts toward school desegregation, which was moving at a snail's pace.

Despite the "White backlash" that contributed to the long, hot summer of 1964, it became increasingly clear that the recent civil rights legislation was not sufficient to remedy past racial discrimination, and suffrage was the key to Black inclusion in the body politic. Before the Voting Rights Act of 1965 (Government Document), suffrage for African Americans had been tentative at best. Prior to the Civil War, some Northern states had restrictive suffrage for Black males. Although Black male suffrage was granted in 1870 with the ratification of the Fifteenth Amendment, and approximately 1 million freed men began to vote, and some were able to hold elective office, their suffrage was short-lived. Following a short period of less than a decade, the encroaching disfranchisement to depress Black voter turnout in some states and to eliminate it altogether in other states moved rapidly across the South. Redemption, the gerrymandering of districts to dilute Black voting strength in elections, and legal methods of disfranchisement including poll tax, the grandfather clause, understanding clause, literacy tests, and vouchers of "good character" were all ways of undermining Black suffrage. Black women did not get the vote until the passage of the Nineteenth Amendment in 1920 and despite their valiant efforts, much of their political participation was also eroded. The Supreme Court, largely through the legal battles of the NAACP, began to reluctantly invalidate some of these disfranchisement methods and "laws." Turning-point cases included: *Guinn v. United States (1915)*, which declared the grandfather clause unconstitutional; *Smith v. Allwright (1944)*, which ruled that barring Blacks from Democratic primaries was a violation of the Fifteenth Amendment; and *Gomillion v. Lightfoot (1960)*, which ruled that the gerrymandering of city districts to eliminate Black voters was a violation of the Fifteenth Amendment. Despite these victories, voting discrimination remains widespread.

The Selma-to-Montgomery March on March 7, 1965, known as Bloody Sunday, had the nation riveted as people watched Alabama state troopers attacked and beat the marchers at the Edmund Pettus Bridge. This action galvanized support for the passage of the Voting Rights Act of 1965. In the aftermath of the Selma-Montgomery March, President Lyndon B. Johnson's Voting Rights Address was a poignant plea and, simultaneously, a political and legal critique of the deprivations that African Americans had suffered. President Johnson linked the citizenship of Blacks with their right to suffrage. He urged the passage of the Voting Rights Act and an elimination of racial discrimination. The Voting Rights Act of 1965 granted Blacks the right to vote and, critically, utilize federal officials in lieu of local White registrars to assist Blacks registering to vote. The Voting Rights Act of 1965 was amended in 1982 and will be once again up for extension in 2007. With recent elections, particularly the presidential elections, allegations of voter fraud, voter manipulation, and the failure to count ballots, and thereby deny representation, voting rights takes on increased significance. The Fair Housing Act and Presidential Executive Orders on Discrimination barred racial discrimination in the buying, selling, or renting of housing or in receiving financial assistance in securing homes. While this law has received less importance than some of the other laws of the civil rights era, it is important to realize that segregated housing leads to many of the problems that African Americans are confronting today.

Chapter 35

Traditions of Resistance and Phases of the Civil Rights Movement: A Conceptual Overview

Edward Ramsamy

Freedom is central to America's national identity. The belief that "America is the land of the free and the home of the brave" is deeply embedded in the popular psyche. However, freedom is an evolving and contested idea. The freedoms that Americans enjoy and celebrate "is the fruit of struggle, tragic failures, tears, sacrifices and sorrow" (Samuel Du Bois Cook, cf: Foner, 1998: p. xxi). While freedom is central to America's constitutional framework, African Americans have experienced some of its benefits, such as full legal citizenship rights, for only the last 41 years of the 230-year history of the United States as a republic. Thus, one of the key themes of American history is the struggle of marginalized groups to contest the exclusive enjoyment of freedom by some at the expense of many. America is a "freer nation" today because of the heroic struggles of African Americans and other oppressed groups to expand the definition of freedom and demand inclusion in American democracy (Foner, 1998).

One of the most significant efforts in this regard was the Civil Rights Movement (CRM) of the 1950s and 1960s. On December 1, 1955, the burgeoning movement gained national visibility when Rosa Parks was arrested in Montgomery, Alabama, for refusing to give up her seat to a White patron on a public bus. Her courageous act of defiance ignited a year-long boycott of segregated public transportation and launched the civil rights struggle into national prominence. This chapter offers an overview of the political traditions that informed the strategy of the Civil Rights Movement and examines the evolving concerns of the CRM, with a focus on Martin Luther King, Jr.

The Civil Rights Movement and Traditions of Resistance

The CRM ought to be situated in the context of Black struggle for human dignity and democratic rights in the United States. The movement drew inspiration from various traditions of resistance against racial oppression. Pulitzer Prize-winning historian David Levering Lewis (1978, 86–88) postulates that the CRM represents a "creative syncretism" among "four contradistinctive ideologies" of African American resistance:

> **The Denmark Vesey/Nat Turner Tradition:** This tradition held that elitist bands of armed militants can rally the Black masses to assault White power through armed insurrection. The fear of armed revolt was expected to compel White authorities to enforce drastic social change.

> **Booker T. Washington's Tradition:** Washington argued for a delineation of economic and social matters. He accepted social separation as long as Blacks were afforded the opportunity to advance economically because, in his view, Blacks could overcome the restrictions of segregation through prosperity. Also, for this reason, he believed that Blacks ought to accommodate the realities of White power.

> **Delany-Garvey Tradition:** This tradition was deeply pessimistic toward the possibility of Blacks and Whites finding a common political space in American society. It called for Black

migration to Africa or, alternatively, the formation of a separate Black state in the United States.

Frederick Douglass/W. E. B Du Bois Tradition: Both Douglass and Du Bois advocated political activism to challenge segregation and racism. Du Bois initially believed that a cadre of intellectuals, "the Talented Tenth," will "lead the race forward" but later embraced socialism as the means of Black empowerment and racial justice.

I would add a fifth ideological strand to the four advanced by Lewis. The Civil Rights Movement was deeply influenced by Black Christian traditions that argued that religion ought not be concerned solely with other-worldly matters. As one of the first institutions that African Americans controlled independently of Whites, the Black church, in addition to its religious function, frequently served as a gathering place and staging ground for political activism (Foner, 1988). Many civil rights leaders and activists were intimately associated with the Black church. West (1988: 5) points out that:

> *The major focus of the prophetic Black Christian World view was neither an escapist pie-in-the sky heaven nor a political paradise on earth. Rather the stress was on marshalling and garnering resources from fellowship, community, and personal strength (meditation and prayer) to cope with overwhelmingly limited options dictated by institutional and personal evil. In short, this Black Christian perspective indeed affirmed a sustaining eschatology (that is, a heaven orientation) and a moral critique of pervasive White racism—but its emphasis was on survival and struggle in the face of an alternative of absurdity and insanity.*

Each of the aforementioned traditions informed the CRM. For example, The Reverend Martin Luther King, Jr., a leading force in the movement, often praised the legacy of Booker T. Washington. In fact, the early CRM combined street activism with accommodationist politics. While the CRM disavowed the violence of Nat Turner and the separatism of Delany and Garvey, it gave expression to Black anger in the form of militant yet nonviolent street protest. Like Garvey's nationalism, the CRM appealed to the Black masses and not just the elite. While King admired the early Du Bois, he felt "in the very nature of Du Bois's outlook there was no room for the whole people. It was a tactic for an aristocratic elite who would themselves be benefited while leaving behind the untalented 90 percent" (cf: Lewis, 1978: 88). However, King eventually changed his mind and during the mid- to late-1960s, the CRM came to appreciate Du Bois's later concerns with social justice.

Finally, I would add that the movement was also shaped by forces beyond the geographic borders of the United States. In addition to Black resistance traditions in the United States, anti-colonial struggles and events in South Africa during the late 1800s and early 1900s, especially the activism of Mahatma Gandhi, deeply influenced the strategies of the movement, King in particular.

The fact that Gandhi's strategy of nonviolent socio-political transformation had a profound influence on King and the Civil Rights Movement in general is often overlooked in most accounts. For King, "Christ furnished the spirit and motivation, while Gandhi furnished the method" of the movement (King, 1993). Lewis (1978: 86) observes that "For Martin and his associates . . . non-violent passive resistance was a *Weltansicht*, not merely a technique but the sole authentic approach to the problem of social injustice." South Africa was the birthplace of *satyagraha*, Mahatma Gandhi's political philosophy. It was in South Africa, while fighting for the rights of Indian indentured workers, that Gandhi shed the arrogance of his youth and began to develop a method of compassionate resistance. Reflecting on Gandhi's life and legacy, South African liberation leader Nelson Mandela (*Time*, December 31, 1999) stated that:

> *India is Gandhi's country of birth; South Africa his country of adoption. He was both an Indian and South African citizen. Both countries contributed to his intellectual and moral genius, and he shaped the liberatory movements in both colonial theaters.*

It is difficult to trace exactly when and how King developed an intellectual interest in Gandhi's activism. Baldwin (1995) postulates that it grew out of King's family background. For example, King's father corresponded with the leadership of the African National Congress (ANC) of South Africa. In 1948, ANC leader and future Nobel Peace Laureate Albert Luthuli visited Atlanta, where he met a number of African American leaders, including King's father. King and his father frequently discussed Black struggles in a global context and, in all likelihood, discussed Luthuli's visit, and hence Gandhi, who was Luthuli's political mentor.

At Crozer Theological Seminary, King developed a strong interest in the role of Christianity in the struggle for social justice. In *Stride Toward Freedom*, King wrote that "Not until I entered Crozer Theological Seminary in 1948, . . . did I begin a serious intellectual quest for a method to eliminate social ills" (cf: Lewis, 1978: 34). At Crozer, King enrolled for a course taught by Professor George W. Davis on the psychology of religion, where Gandhi's philosophy of nonviolence was analyzed in detail. Davis himself saw God "as a deity intimately and intricately involved in human history—a working, toiling God who labors through human beings to realize the ultimate end and aim of history" (West, 1988: 8). For King, Davis's idea resonated with Gandhi's conception of religion as a vehicle in the struggle for social justice and transformation.

King's interest in Gandhi's activism was further stimulated by the addresses of Crozer President Benjamin E. Mays, who frequently discussed South African issues during the compulsory chapel services (Baldwin, 1995). A lecture by the prominent theologian and President of Howard University, Mordecai Johnson, on his travels in India also left a strong impression on King, who recalls that "his message was so profound and electrifying that I left the meeting and bought a half-dozen books on Gandhi's life and works" (King, 1998: 23).

King traveled to Ghana's independence celebrations in March 1957, where he met a delegation of South African clergy associated with the passive resistance and defiance campaigns there that were originally set in motion by Gandhi. The campaigns protested South African laws that restricted the rights of Indians to own or occupy land. Over 15,000 people had pledged to defy the law on June 13, 1946; protestors even pitched tents and squatted in defiance. The authorities had taken no action when White vigilante groups attacked the Indian protestors. Racist violence toward the protestors had deeply troubled one Reverend Michael Scott, an English Anglican priest and member of the delegation, especially when an Indian woman activist was attacked and left bleeding. Reverend Scott recalled to King that as the woman lay dying, she had told him, "it is not their fault—they don't know what they are doing." Deeply moved by her empathy, Reverend Scott shared with King that "her religion has taught her more than the attackers had found in the story of the crucifixion" (www.anc.co.za). More than 2000 nonviolent protestors also had been arrested in that campaign. News of the ensuing Defiance Campaign, a joint effort by African and Indian movements to confront the unjust laws of the apartheid regime in South Africa, further aroused King. During this conversation, King expressed deep admiration for the bus boycott outside of Johannesburg, in which thousands of ordinary people chose to walk, in the tradition of Gandhi, 10 to 15 miles a day in protest of segregated transportation, unjust fares, and poor service. King became thoroughly convinced of Gandhi's reasoning that "the willingness to suffer will eventually make the oppressor ashamed of his method" (cf: Baldwin, 1995: 10). Thus, in addition to existing African American traditions of resistance, a confluence of international political events and ideological trends informed the Civil Rights Movement in the United States, and King's thinking in particular.

In 1959, King finally visited India. Upon his arrival at New Delhi airport, he told newspaper reporters:

> *To other countries I may go as a tourist, but to India I come as a pilgrim. This is because India means to me Mahatma Gandhi, a truly great man of the age. (cf: Momin, 2001)*

In India, King had an audience with Prime Minister Jawaharlal Nehru, with whom he discussed racial and caste injustices. Nehru informed King that caste discrimination was illegal and punishable under the Indian constitution, and that India's affirmative action programs gave preferential treatment to the untouchable castes in university admissions and public sector employment. A member of King's delegation inquired as to whether this amounted to discrimination in reverse, to which Nehru replied, "Well it may be, but this is our way of atoning for centuries of injustices we have inflicted upon these people" (cf: Lewis, 1978: 100). The encounter with Prime Minister Nehru left a profound impression on King, and "undoubtedly quickened his formulation of a program of governmentally promoted compensatory treatment for African-Americans" (Lewis, 1978: 100). King focused on this issue during the later years of the Civil Rights Movement.

Phases of the Civil Rights Movement

The CRM passed through two phases that emphasized different priorities. The first phase may be seen as beginning with the Montgomery bus boycott and ending with the Selma-Montgomery march of 1965. After the march, the movement's second phase lasted through King's assassination in April 1968. The first phase concentrated on securing voting rights, legal protections, and the desegregation of public facilities. During this period, important changes were ignited in American society through a combination of activism and skillful negotiations. The *Brown vs Board of Education* decision of 1954, the Civil Rights Acts of 1964, and the Voting Rights Act of 1965 were legislative landmarks that allowed Blacks to exercise their democratic rights for the first time in the history of the nation. The overt symbols of racism in hotels, rest rooms, water fountains, and other facilities were brought down. As institutions of higher education were desegregated, newly admitted students of color began to organize on campuses across the country for more inclusive curricula. Soon, Blacks Studies departments grew out of this mobilization. In the decade between the Montgomery bus boycott and the Selma-Montgomery march, African Americans made monumental strides in tearing down the walls of *de jure* segregation and realizing the promises of the 13th, 14th, and 15th Amendments to the Constitution, more than a 100 years after their codification.

However, it is often forgotten that the CRM went on to demand greater social change, given the fact that structural inequalities such as unequal employment and segregated housing remained. The memory and legacy of King and the struggle is frequently limited to the legislative achievements of the movement. During Black History Month, for example, all national media are saturated with King's historic "I Have a Dream" speech in which he postulates a future beyond the color line. Seldom is the second phase of the movement recalled, in which King and others repeatedly stressed that economic inequalities, in addition to civil rights, will have to be addressed in order to build the "Beloved Community." By the mid-1960s, King and his associates realized that civil rights, although important, did little to address the serious economic disparity between Blacks and Whites. For instance, King once commented, "what good is it to vote when you don't have a job or an income?" (cf: *Eyes on the Prize*, PBS Documentary, 1995). At the time, Black unemployment was two and a half times that of Whites. The average Black family's income was half that of their White counterparts. In order to "make freedom real and substantive," the movement realized that economic inequality needed to be addressed on a national scale. In 1964, King called for a "Bill of Rights for the Disadvantaged," and urged the country "to mobilize the nation's resources to abolish the scourge of economic deprivation" (Foner, 1998: 282). Stressing that racism is a national, rather than a regional issue of the South, King and other leaders tried to test their strategies in the urban centers of the North. They launched the Chicago Freedom Movement (CFM) in 1966, which demanded better employment opportunities for Blacks, equal treatment in mortgage lending, and the construction of new low-income housing. They ambitiously sought to dismantle the city's Black ghetto and transform it into a democratic urban space. As part of their effort to highlight the structural features of racism in Chicago, the CFM organized a march through predominantly White neighborhoods, thinking that the tactics used to gain voting rights in the South would succeed in impressing upon White Chicago that segregation was immoral (Kelly and Lewis, 2000). To their chagrin, the movement encountered intense resistance from Mayor Richard Daley, a Democrat who had supported the CRM in the South, and ferocious opposition from Chicago's all-White suburbs. A disappointed King (1998: 304–305) wrote:

> After the riot in Chicago that summer, I was greatly discouraged. . . . Bottles and bricks were thrown at us; we were often beaten. . . . Swastikas bloomed in Chicago parks like misbegotten weeds. Our marches were met with a hailstorm of bricks, bottles and firecrackers. "White power" became the racist catcall, punctuated by the vilest of obscenities—most frequently directed at Catholic priests and nuns among the marches. I've been to many demonstrations in the South, but I can say that I have never seen, even in Mississippi, mobs as hostile and as hate-filled as in Chicago.

Despite White resistance in Chicago, the CRM spawned the interracial, class-based *Poor People's Campaign*, which highlighted the need for radical economic reforms to address persistent and widespread poverty in the United States. Trade union leader A. Philip Randolph and civil rights leader Bayard Rustin proposed a "Freedom Budget" in 1966, calling for a 10-year, $100 billion federal program to address urban poverty. The Southern Christian Leadership Conference (SCLC) planned a massive interracial march on Washington in the summer of 1968 to demand that the federal government address socioeconomic inequality.

This phase of the CRM increasingly emphasized the systemic nature of racism and began to "articulate a democratic socialist vision for American society," as noted by Marable (1991: 103). King saw the need for a fundamental restructuring of American society and called for federal programs to address poverty and unemployment immediately. In explaining the rationale for the Poor Peoples' Campaign at an SCLC meeting King (cf: Gates, 1998) said:

At the very same time that America refused to give the Negro any land, through an act of Congress our government was giving away millions of acres of land in the West and the Midwest, which meant that it was willing to undergird its White peasants from Europe with an economic floor.

But not only did they give the land, they built land grant colleges with government money to teach them how to farm. Not only that, they provided county agents to further their expertise in farming. Not only that, they provided low interest rates in order that they could mechanize their farms.

Not only that, today many of these people are receiving millions of dollars in federal subsidies not to farm, and they are the very people telling the Black man that he ought to lift himself by his own boot-straps. And this is what we are faced with, and this is the reality. Now, when we come to Washington in this campaign, we are coming to get our check.

During this period, King also began to link poverty in the United States and the Vietnam War. In his historic address *Beyond Vietnam: A Time to Break the Silence* King (1967) noted that:

It seemed as if there was a real promise of hope for the poor—both Black and White—through the poverty program. There were experiments, hopes and new beginnings. Then came the buildup in Vietnam, and I watched this program broken and eviscerated, as if it were some idle political plaything of society gone mad on war, and I knew that America would never invest the necessary funds or energies in rehabilitation of its poor so long as adventures like Vietnam continue to draw men and skills and money like some demonic destructive suction tube. So, I was increasingly compelled to see the war as an enemy of the poor and to attack it as such.

For a time, the CRM succeeded in placing economic justice on the national agenda. The "War on Poverty," a part of Lyndon Johnson's Great Society program, was in part a response to the second phase of the CRM. While the "War on Poverty" did succeed in addressing poverty on a small scale, such as establishing Medicare and Medicaid, the escalating costs of the Vietnam War and a rising conservative tide in the nation stymied the initiative and left many racial issues unresolved. It was estimated that the United States spent about $500,000 to kill a single enemy soldier but only $35 a year to assist one of its own poor (Kelly and Lewis, 2000). King (1998: 336) wryly remarked, "The great tragedy was that our government declared a war against poverty, and yet it only financed a skirmish against poverty."

The Poor Peoples' Campaign, protests against the Vietnam War, and a sanitation workers' strike in Memphis consumed King's energies during the last years of his life. On April 15, 1967, 11 days after his historic address against the war at New York City's Riverside Church, King led 125,000 people in a march to protest American involvement in Vietnam because his conscience left him "no other choice," but his stance fractured the civil rights coalition. Prominent Black leaders like Ralph Bunche, Edward Brooke, Jackie Robinson, Bayard Rustin, Roy Wilkins, and Whitney Young denounced King for his condemnation of the War, arguing that he was jeopardizing Blacks' hard-won gains, but King held steadfast to his course. While on that radical path, King spoke at a celebration commemorating the 100th anniversary of Du Bois's birth on February 28, 1968. Although Du Bois laid much of the intellectual and political foundations of the CRM, the movement had steered away from him because of his socialist leanings, fearing the loss of White support and government retribution. In his speech, King (*Freedom Ways*, Spring 1968) went against the political grain to embrace Du Bois's legacy:

We cannot talk about Du Bois without recognizing that he was a radical. Some people would like to ignore that fact that he was a Communist in his later years. It is worth noting that Abraham Lincoln warmly welcomed the support of Karl Marx during the Civil War and corresponded with him freely. . . . It is time to cease muting the fact that Du Bois was a genius and chose to be a communist. Our obsessive anti-communism has led us into too many quagmires.

Thus, King's concerns toward the end of his life were very different from the goals of the Montgomery bus boycott. Still, it is important to see his activism as part of an intellectual continuum. For example, he never wavered in his deep commitment to nonviolence, but he realized that abstract political freedoms must be accompanied by tangible material gains. The last 3 years of his life were dedicated to building a multiracial coalition to fight poverty and inequality. In February 1968, sanitation workers in Memphis sought the support of the SCLC in their struggle for union recognition. Black garbage collectors took to the streets when some Black workers were sent home without pay because of inclement weather while White workers were given a full day's pay. In March 1968, King repeatedly traveled to Memphis to support the sanitation workers in their struggle against the local municipality. In an electrifying speech on April 3, 1968, King predicted the sanitation workers' victory over the Memphis authorities, but midway through his speech, he suddenly changed focus and talked about his own mortality:

> *I don't know what will happen now. But it really doesn't matter to me now. Because I have been to the mountain top. I won't mind. Like anybody, I would like to live a long life. Longevity has its place. But I am not concerned about that now. I just want to do God's will. And He's allowed me to go up to the mountain. And I've looked over, and I have seen the promised land. . . . I may not get there with you but I want you to know tonight that we as a people will get to the promised land. So I am happy tonight. I am not worried about anything. I am not fearing any man. Mine eyes have seen the glory of the coming of the Lord.*

The next day, April 4, 1968, Martin Luther King, Jr. was assassinated by James Earl Ray. His death was a grievous loss to the struggle for racial equality and social justice. Cornel West (1993: 59) aptly characterized King as a "race-transcending prophetic leader" who was deeply rooted in the Black resistance tradition but also, nevertheless, rallied people from various racial identities to join the struggle for human dignity. In his *Letters from a Birmingham Jail* (1963) he wrote that "injustice anywhere is a threat to justice everywhere. We are caught in an inescapable network of mutuality, tied in a single garment of history. Whatever affects one directly affects us all indirectly." In the contradictory period of deepening globalization that we live in, narrow nationalisms and parochialism are gaining political favor. King's vision of the "Beloved Community" is more relevant today than ever.

References

Baldwin, Lewis L. (1995). *Toward the Beloved Community: Martin Luther King and South Africa.* Cleveland: The Pilgrim Press.

Foner, Eric. (1988). *Reconstruction: America's Unfinished Revolution.* New York: Harper and Row, Publishers.

Foner, Eric. (1998). *The Story of American Freedom.* New York: W. W. Norton & Company.

Gates, Henry Louis. (1998). *The Two Nations of Black America.* PBS Documentary, Aired on February 10, 1998.

Kelly, Robin D. G., & Lewis, Earl. (2000). *To Make Our World New: A History of African Americans.* New York: Oxford University Press.

King, Martin Luther. (1963). "Letters from a Birmingham Jail" in James M. Washington (ed.). *I Have a Dream: Writings and Speeches that Changed the World.* San Francisco: Harper Collins.

King, Martin Luther. (1967). *Beyond Vietnam: A Time to Break the Silence.* Address at Riverside Church, New York City, April 4, 1967.

King, Coretta Scott. (1993). *The Martin Luther King Companion.* New York: St. Martin's Press.

King, Martin Luther. (1998). *The Autobiography of Martin Luther King Jr.* New York: Warner Books.

Lewis, David L. (1978). *King: A Biography.* Urbana, IL: University of Illinois Press.

Mandela, Nelson. (1999). "The Sacred Warrior," *Time,* December 31, pp. 124–5.

Momin, Syed Mehdi. (2001). Martin Luther King, Jr. and Mahatma Gandhi, available at *http://www.independent-bangladesh.com/news/jan/20/2001 2006mg.htm#A8*

West, Cornel. (1988). *Prophetic Fragments.* Grand Rapids: William B. Eerdmans B. Publishing Company.

West, Cornel. (1993). *Race Matters.* Boston: Beacon Press.

Chapter 36

Color Me Invisible:
The Hidden Legacy of African American Muslims

Donna A. Auston

I am an invisible man. No, I am not a spook like those who haunted Edgar Allen Poe; nor am I one of your Hollywood-movie ectoplasms. I am a man of substance, of flesh and bone, fiber and liquids—and I might even be said to possess a mind. I am invisible, understand, simply because people refuse to see me.

—Ralph Ellison

The world had prepared no place for you, and if the world had its way, no place for you would ever exist.

—James Baldwin

"Where are you from?" A neutral question, perhaps. One that I am asked with enough frequency to make me doubt at times the presumption that there is nothing to the inquiry other than an attempt to make small talk. Since I am a woman who wears a *hijab*[1], the question, more often than not, comes with the assumption that the answer is some faraway place on the other side of the world. This generally becomes evident when the reply is met with a look of surprise and follow-up questions intended to really get to the bottom of things: *"Where are you originally from?," "What country are you from?," "Where are your parents from?,"* or the most euphemistic of them all: *"What language do you speak?"*

I am, in fact, American. African American, to be more precise. What is more, I am a Muslim. (And a woman!) Some of my component identities supposedly do not mix well with some of the others; this perhaps is enough to explain why perplexed looks and requests for clarification meet me when I answer the aforementioned inquiry. There is no exotic Eastern place of origin in my ancestry for at least the six preceding generations of my family tree that I have been able to trace, at least not as far as I can tell.

My people are *originally* from Virginia, at least since the beginning of the nineteenth century. I am one of the many thousands of African Americans who have discovered and embraced the Muslim faith over the years. The reasons and circumstances behind the faith transformations and journeys of the individuals who make up this community are unique, varied, and deeply personal. At the same time, there are enough people whose stories share threads common to my own that we have become a phenomenon worthy of study for those interested in the richness and diversity of the African Diaspora. And yet, in many cases the tendency has been and continues to be to overlook (not always purposely, perhaps) the presence of African American Muslims and the impact that we have had on the experiences and history of African Americans, the broader American Muslim *ummah,*[2] and the general American historical and religious experience. In a sense, like Ralph Ellison's protagonist quoted at the opening of this essay, African American Muslims have been rendered invisible by the refusal or inability of some to see us.

From the perspective of the African American community, there is often a tendency to forge a single overarching narrative of black people in this country, perhaps in response to the fact that we have been singularly targeted as objects of racism and discrimination without regard to any internal variation we may have.

In some ways, this is a necessary survival tactic intended to combat the cultural obliteration that has been inflicted on African Americans by the architects of the slave system and its offspring that still plague us today. But we do ourselves a disservice by not embracing the fullness of that narrative, in all of its diversity. Black people in the United States do in fact share a common set of experiences *vis a vis* the larger society, yet at the same time, our community is not entirely monolithic. Black culture in New Orleans, for example, is distinctive in many ways from its counterpart in Los Angeles; black culture in New York is different from both of these. We have regional, religious, linguistic, and class differences, for starters—but there is often a tendency to reduce all of our collective diversity into a single, monotone portrait. This being the case, it is perhaps not particularly surprising that the contributions of a religious group which stands outside of the dominant narrative of the black Church are not always recognized.

With regard to greater American society, much of the traditional European antagonism with Islam has been imported to these shores, and the portrayal of Islam as the exotic and foreign "Other" is a popular refrain. This has been particularly true post-9/11; much of the inflammatory rhetoric circulated in the aftermath of the events of that day regarding the "clash of civilizations" is a good illustration of this point. Islam and Muslims are from *"over there"*; *"they"* hate *"us"* and *"our way of life."* While this simplistic (and erroneous) explanation may comfort some individuals seeking to make sense of a terrible and tragic event, or provide rationale for questionable foreign policy decisions, once again it overlooks the fact that a large number of "them" are in fact African Americans indigenous to this land. This blindness is also evident in the proclamations of many prominent media outlets. For example, the *New York Times* declared confidently that there is "a growing demand for the rare American Imam,"[3] in spite of the fact that the majority of the Imams in predominantly African American mosques are in fact African American—and that this has been the case for several decades, at least. It is hard to tell which set of blinders are responsible for such oversights. Is it the general ignorance of the nuances of the American Muslim community, or are we as a society still struggling with the notion that Blacks are really Americans?

In any case, there is a good chance that you have encountered "them" before. After all, second to Christianity, Islam is the largest religious group in the black community. Maybe one of those Muslims is your sister, cousin, neighbor, or co-worker. Their narratives are among those of the millions who fell victim to the slave trade. You may have glimpsed some of them as you walked down a crowded Brooklyn sidewalk. Perchance you grooved as they tapped out jazz rhythms with Dizzy Gillespie or as they rocked the mic with their Native Tongues. If you listen, you can hear them among the voices of Black Power—in Malcolm X, H. Rap Brown, and the Last Poets. You can see them working hard to restore hope to many inner city neighborhoods, establishing food pantries and negotiating gang truces. You may have seen them in the boardroom, in the classroom, or on Capitol Hill. In short, "they" are everywhere.

African Americans comprise the largest racial group in the American Muslim *ummah*, generally believed to be around 35 percent of the total number.[4] Besides sheer numbers, the impact that they have had on opening up public space for Islam and Muslims in the U.S. has been substantial. Young Cassius Clay stunned the world when he announced his name change and conversion to Islam. Other prominent athletes have followed in his footsteps, such as basketball greats Kareem Abdul-Jabbar and Mahmoud Abdul Rauf. Zakia Mahasa became the first Muslim woman to serve as a judge in the United States. North Carolina state senator, Larry Shaw, was the first Muslim in the nation elected to a state legislature. The first, and only, to date, Muslims to serve in Congress are both African Americans, Keith Ellison of Minnesota and Andre Carson of Indiana. African American inmates have struggled in institutions across the country to have their religious rights as Muslims respected and accommodated by the prison system. Muslim police officers in Newark, New Jersey, took the fight to wear their religiously mandated beards—which were generally not allowed by the police department—all the way to the Supreme Court, and won. And one of the most inspiring examples of all is that of the 2006 Lady Caliphs basketball team from W.D. Mohammed high school in Atlanta. The girls covered their bodies in accordance with Islamic requirements for modesty, wearing sweatpants and headscarves on the court. They also played games, winning many of them, while observing the Islamic fast of Ramadan, a rite that requires believers to abstain from food and drink entirely during the daylight hours. In spite of often being taunted by intolerant crowds, these girls finished their season at 21–1. Their inspiring story was featured on ESPN. Notwithstanding the difficulties of being a double minority, African American Muslims have left their mark in many arenas.

This essay is primarily an attempt to highlight some of the history and contributions of African American Muslims to the mosaic that is the Diaspora. To that end, what follows will be a) a brief historical overview of the development of Islam among African Americans, from the pre-Columbian era through the birth and evolution of some of the significant early indigenous African American Islamic organizations; and b) a discussion of how the particular historical circumstances of Blacks in the U.S. served to both attract them in significant numbers to Islam and to shape the manner in which adherents to the faith have expressed their belief and commitment to its ideals.

Nomenclature

It is probably useful here to clarify some terminology before proceeding. Within the context of the African American Islamic experience, there are many distinct groups which have historically used Islamic nomenclature.[5] Many times the term "Muslim" is applied interchangeably to members of all of these various denominations, but the reality of the situation is that each of these sects has theology and practice which varies quite a bit from that of the others. The Moorish Science Temple of America (MSTA) founded by Noble Drew Ali, the Nation of Islam (NOI), which has become synonymous with the historic figures of Malcolm X and Elijah Muhammad, the Five Percent Nation (an offshoot of the NOI), and Sunni Islam have generally been the most prominent modes of Islamic expression in the black community.[6] However, while they are all distinct in many important ways, and there certainly have been tensions at times between the various sects, the individual narratives of each of these groups overlap and connect in many places. There have been, over the years, many transitions by individuals and whole communities from one or more of these groups to another. Some of the more notable transitions include that of Muhammad Ezzaldeen, African American Sunni Muslim pioneer and founder of one of the seminal movements in African American Sunni Islam, who initially was a follower of Noble Drew Ali; Nation of Islam founder Master Fard Muhammad and Elijah Muhammad are both reported to have once been affiliated with the MSTA.[7]

Malcolm X began his career in the NOI but eventually left the movement and converted to Sunni Islam, taking many of the faithful with him; he was later followed in this regard by both Muhammad Ali and Warith Deen (né Wallace) Muhammad, son of Elijah Muhammad. Imam Muhammad, as he was later known, was appointed leader of the NOI after his father's passing in 1975. He disbanded that organization and spearheaded the integration of thousands of its former members into the worldwide community of Sunni Muslims. Prominent Imam Siraj Wahhaj, of Brooklyn, one of the most widely recognized figures in the worldwide English-speaking Sunni community, was previously a minister in the NOI.[8] This is to say nothing of the common believers; one routinely meets members of one group who have transitioned there from one or more of the others. From a historical and sociological point of view, then, in spite of the significant variations in their respective ideologies, it is helpful to view the divergent movements as individual pieces of a larger puzzle. The focus of this work will primarily be Sunni Islam, for although the majority of African American Muslims are in fact Sunni, it has generally received the least amount of attention in the literature. However, the above-mentioned cross-pollination between the various manifestations of African American Islam should be born in mind throughout this discussion.

Historical Overview

Several scholars have contended that the presence of Islam in the New World began in the pre-Columbian era. Perhaps the most well-known proponent of this position is the late Ivan Van Sertima, who argued that there is tangible evidence across various disciplines, both in the New World and in Africa, that Africans reached the New World centuries before the first known European contact. His works catalogue the various types of documentation: primary sources such as the diaries of Christopher Columbus and other explorers, artifacts found in the New World later proven to be of African origin, and other types of supporting evidence belonging to over a dozen different categories.[9] Van Sertima further contends that there were at least two distinct periods of African contact with the New World: explorers from ancient Egypt, and later sailors from the empire of Mali. In spite of the amount of evidence he presented, his thesis has not been universally accepted, which is not surprising given that it challenges many of the foundational premises of the generally accepted history of the Americas. In any case, this is certainly a question which deserves further research, to shine light on the many open questions which exist.

While there may still be room for debate on the presence of African Muslims in the Americas prior to Columbus, there is no longer any doubt that Muslims were among the millions of Africans of various faiths who were kidnapped and transported to the New World as part of the trans-Atlantic slave trade. Sylviane Diouf, one of the foremost researchers in this field, notes many of the difficulties in arriving at an accurate estimate given the nature of the events in question. Based on her extensive research, she offers a figure of around 15 to 20 percent of the total slave population throughout North and South America and the Caribbean Islands.[10] It has also been well-documented that these Muslims struggled to maintain their faith and practice in spite of the harsh conditions of their bondage, and resisted in ways that are both surprising and inspirational. Among the many acts of Islamic observance recorded, there are accounts of Muslim slaves risking punishment in order to observe the five daily prayers which are a pillar of the faith; writing parts of the Qur'an in Arabic; observing, at least partially, religious dietary prohibitions regarding pork and/or meat not slaughtered according to Islamic law; and giving Arabic names to their children.[11]

In spite of the fact that African Muslims were brought to the Americas in significant numbers, and that many were able to maintain, to varying degrees, the practice of their own faith in a particularly hostile environment, there does not seem to be any indication that as a whole Islam was able to survive the assault of the slave system to such an extent that would enable it to be passed down in a systematic manner from generation to generation of African Americans. The subsequent emergence of Islam as a prominent mode of religious expression in the black community begs the question—if Islam was not passed down by the slaves who adhered to it, then where did it come from? The phenomenon is even more curious given the fact that one of the recurring themes present in African American Islamic movements, both orthodox and otherwise, historically, has been the idea that Islam is somehow connected intrinsically with black people, a more natural state of being for African Americans. In short, Islam came to represent a return to a heritage taken away from those caught up in the unfortunate reality of slavery. Without direct transmission from African Muslim slaves, as far as is evident, in some way or another, Islam became fundamentally connected with a pre-slavery cultural and civilizational history of African Americans.

It seems to be the case that the rebirth of Islam in the African American community was the result of several processes operating separately, yet more or less simultaneously; some natural and organic, others more organized and deliberate. Arab immigrants, Christian and Muslim alike, began to arrive in the United States from the Ottoman Empire in the period following the Civil War, settling along the eastern seaboard and in the Midwest.[12] Muslims from other parts of the world, including British India, Central Asia, and Southern Europe immigrated to the U.S. as well beginning in the late nineteenth century. Though some of these groups began to establish mosques in their communities, there does not seem to be evidence of organized missionary work undertaken by most of these early immigrant Muslim populations.

Some researchers have noted that while organized missionary institutions were not generally established by immigrants from the Muslim world prior to World War I, many of these newcomers did interact with Americans of various backgrounds via their participation in large numbers as traveling peddlers in the cities where they settled. In this regard it is significant to note that according to NOI sources, W. D. Fard (the founder of that movement) and his teachings are said to have first made their appearance among African Americans in Detroit, while he was selling wares in black neighborhoods of that city.[13] In addition, as has often been the case with settlers in new lands, it is noted that some of these Muslim immigrants, unable to return home to start their families, married women living here, including African American women. Shaykh Daud Faisal, founder of the pioneering State Street Mosque in Brooklyn, and his wife Khadijah, are both reported to have been the product of such unions.[14]

In terms of organized outreach, many writers tracing the origins of modern African American Islamic movements have pinpointed the appearance of Indian missionaries from the Ahmadiyyah Movement in some black communities as another source of influence for the subsequent flowering of Islam there.[15] In 1920, Mufti Muhammad Sadiq, an Ahmadi preacher, traveled to America from India for the purpose of conducting missionary work on behalf of that organization. He established headquarters for his mission in New York, and began the work of spreading the message. The Ahmadis did not exclusively target African Americans for their missionary activities, but they did focus a good deal of their efforts in black communities. This strategy paid off for the movement, for clearly the majority of their American converts were black, at least in the early days. This sect, however, is no longer a major point of entry to Islam for African Americans.

There seem to have been other individuals and groups besides the Ahmadiyyah conducting deliberate missionary activities, however, though perhaps not on the same scale. Prior to the turn of the twentieth century there was the American Islamic Propaganda, an organization established by Muhammad Alexander Russell Webb, an American diplomat to the Philippines and an early white American convert to Islam. Webb gave public lectures on Islam and published a newspaper in the 1890s. Although he was committed to spreading the message of Islam in America, Webb did not specifically target African Americans as potential converts. He expressed many of the racial views that were common during his day, and thus direct outreach to Blacks on his part seems unlikely.[16] This does not, however, necessarily rule out an indirect flow of information.

Another such individual, a young Sudanese by the name of Satti Majid, reportedly arrived in the United States in 1904, and, dismayed by the presence of misinformation being disseminated in the press about Islam and by native groups teaching unorthodox versions of the faith, established several Islamic organizations in at least three cities (New York, Pittsburgh, and Detroit) during the course of his short career in the U.S. These associations existed both to promote Islamic teachings and to serve the needs of Muslims living in the area. According to sources, he established the African Muslim Welfare Society in Pittsburgh in 1927 or 1928.[17] This organization apparently functioned as a mosque with Majid initially serving as Imam and director, remaining in existence until the early years of World War II.[18] It seems that while this mosque served the population of mostly Arab Muslims living in Pittsburgh, there were also some African American converts who were a part of this community. While in America, Majid encountered the teachings of Noble Drew Ali and the MSTA, and, as an orthodox Muslim, was apparently outraged at the theological claims made by the latter. He left America for the prestigious Al Azhar University in Cairo, seeking a *fatwa*[19] from the religious authorities there regarding the teachings of the MSTA. The edict was written, but it is not clear whether it was ever shared with followers of Majid in America. He was never able to return to the States himself, and he died in Sudan, as far as sources tell.

Given the activities of Satti Majid in Pittsburgh, it may not be a coincidence that one of the earliest African American Sunni Muslim communities was established there in 1932. There are, however, gaps in the available sources on his life and activities, so at this point it is difficult to know for sure if there is a direct connection between his missionary work and the subsequent establishment of the community in that city. In any case, First Muslim Mosque of Pittsburgh, as it was named, by existing accounts, evolved out of a series of transformations and splits, which were reflective of growth through exposure to new sources of information on Islam. The MSTA was active in this city and had won converts; the first schism in the community occurred when the Ahmadiyyah eventually entered the picture and certain individuals from that movement, most notably an Indian Muslim named Dr. Yusuf Khan began to influence believers from the congregation. Later, a second split occurred when members of the community could not agree on whether to align with the Ahmadiyyah or the Sunni tradition. Ultimately, when the mosque was incorporated, those inclined toward Sunni Islam had become the prevailing voices, and it was established as an institution of that tradition. A highly dedicated group of believers formed the core of the community, local Muslim historians note that when the mosque was moved across town from its original location just outside of the city in Braddock, Pennsylvania, many of the faithful still living in the vicinity of the old location regularly walked to the new building in Pittsburgh's Hill District, a distance of some eight miles in each direction.[20] Several sources point to the fact that there was a close connection between the Pittsburgh Muslim community and that of Cleveland, Ohio; in fact the First Muslim Mosque of Cleveland was incorporated two years after Pittsburgh. First Muslim Mosque in Pittsburgh is still in existence today, and is one of the oldest continuously operating mosques in the country.

From here, there are several pioneering African American movements in the Sunni Islamic tradition in various American cities that are noteworthy as major contributors to the phenomenon of African American Islam, but a detailed history of each of them would be too lengthy to chronicle here. Among the most significant was Addeynu Allahe Universal Arabic Association (AAUAA). This organization grew out of the efforts of former MSTA member and convert to Sunni Islam, Muhammad Ezzaldeen. After leaving the Moorish movement, Ezzaldeen spent several years in Egypt studying Arabic and orthodox Islam. He returned to the United States in the late 1930s, and his efforts led eventually to the establishment of affiliated communities in various places, including Newark, New Jersey; Rochester, New York; Philadelphia; Jacksonville, Florida; and Detroit.[21] There was also, as previously mentioned in this essay, the Islamic Mission of America (commonly known as the State Street Mosque) headed by Caribbean born Shaykh Daud Faisal. Shaykh Daud immigrated to the United States to pursue a career as a musician, converted to Islam, and subsequently went on to be the leader of one of the most notable African American Sunni communities. It is interesting to note that at least one researcher, Michael Gomez, posits a possible connection between the missionary activities of Satti Majid and the establishment of the State Street Mosque.[22] This movement remained influential for decades to come, with its leader, Shaykh Daud passing away in 1980. Also significant is the establishment of the Dar al Islam movement (commonly known as the Dar), founded in NYC in 1962. Among other things, this group was very active in prison outreach and advocacy for accommodation of Muslim religious practices for inmates in the state prison in Green Haven, New York. This list is not exhaustive, by a long shot, there are many other organizations and leaders that were operating in various American cities whose stories are important pieces of the overall puzzle.

Independent of the development of these African American Sunni communities, of course, is the Nation of Islam. A detailed history of the NOI can be found in many places, thus there is no need to repeat it here. Where the trajectories of the two communities intersect in a pivotal way—after the death of Elijah Muhammad—ushers in a new era in the history of African American Islam. Warith Deen Muhammad's decision to lead the membership of thousands into Sunni Islam is a watershed moment in the American Islamic narrative. Referred to often in African American Muslim circles as "The Transition," or "The Change," it is probably the largest mass conversion in American religious history. After assuming the mantle of leadership of the NOI, Imam Muhammad dismantled the organization, denounced many of the previous beliefs and practices, and gradually introduced creed and rituals that were in line with those of Muslims around the world.[23] The Imam himself would go on to become a prominent religious leader—among his many achievements was becoming the first Muslim to give the invocation to the U.S. Senate in 1992. He was very active in interfaith activities around the world, and frequently met with heads of state and dignitaries from various countries, including the late Pope John Paul II and several U.S. Presidents. Imam Muhammad passed away in September 2008.

Finally, there is the phenomenon among African Americans of exposure to Islam outside of organized movements and efforts to proselytize. More than a decade ago, I had the pleasure of being introduced to an African American family from Philadelphia who was, at that time, able to claim five generations of Sunni Muslims, none of whom had spent any time with the Ahmadiyyah, the MSTA or the NOI. Their saga started with a young man from the family who entered the merchant marine, and through his journeys to the Muslim world he came to embrace Islam. After his conversion, he was able to convince his mother and the woman he ultimately married to follow in his footsteps. His daughters spent a good deal of time entertaining those of us gathered with stories of being Muslim in the 1950s—with strange names and habits—before Islam had become a fixture on any large scale in American cities. The numbers of such individuals, those who embraced Islam in a similar fashion, are likely extremely small; however, they apparently do exist. As with many other questions relating to the development of African American Islam, this phenomenon merits further study.

Marcus Garvey's UNIA and the Development of African American Islam

The Universal Negro Improvement Association of Jamaican-born Marcus Mosiah Garvey was a movement that managed to unite people of African descent from around the world on a scale never seen before or, arguably, since. The group's publication, *The Negro World*, was translated into several languages, and in spite of the eventual downfall of Garvey and his movement, his ideas certainly have had a lasting impact on those struggling for the freedom and equality throughout the Diaspora. Perhaps as an attempt to create a "big tent," where Black people of various stripes would find a place where they could feel at home, the gatherings of the UNIA often featured presentations on various religions. Muhammad Sadiq of the Ahmadiyyah movement is known to have been a regular speaker at UNIA functions, and is said to have had some success in converting members. It is not surprising, then, that this movement proved to be an incubator for the eventual rebirth of Islam among black Americans. Perhaps even more significant than the efforts of Sadiq in UNIA circles, Duse Mohammad Ali, an orthodox Muslim and Pan Africanist thinker, was a mentor to Garvey himself. It is not unlikely that other Muslims were involved in the UNIA as well, and even if they did not proselytize in any formal way, their presence would have provided an awareness among other Garveyites of Islam. Once again, interestingly enough, the name of Satti Majid surfaces here. A documentary produced detailing the history of Islam in the city of Pittsburgh states that Majid was active with the

UNIA locally and was involved in establishing a branch in nearby Wilkinsburg.[24] Whether or not this is accurate is unclear, however other sources note that "It seems possible to deduce from his letters that he was seen by his American followers in an increasingly Garveyist mode."[25] In short, it is clear that Garvey's movement became one of the avenues by which African Americans became exposed to Islam—and it is not far-fetched to surmise that the *leitmotif* of Islam as the "natural religion of black people" throughout the divergent black Islamic movements is at least partially attributable to the fact that for some, at least, initial exposure came via the Garvey movement or other Pan Africanist circles.

Looking for Self

One of my most significant encounters with Islam in the years before I embraced the faith was through Alex Haley's discovery of his own Islamic heritage. When *Roots* aired on ABC in the late seventies I was a young girl, and I cannot say that I remember Islam much from what I saw then. But what I do remember is the fact that everyone in my family and community planted themselves squarely in front of the television set each night for the next installment; and discussed the most poignant scenes to no end everywhere we gathered. In particular, we were all deeply impressed by Alex Haley's ancestor adamantly insisting, in spite of the overseer and his whip, that his name was *not* Toby. My mother kept a copy of *Roots* in our book cupboard for as long as I can remember. Years later as a teenager, searching for my own identity and still impressed with the images in my mind acquired all those years ago, I took the book from the shelf and began to read. The early chapters of the work, of course, are an attempted re-creation of Kunta Kinte's life before he was kidnapped and sold; a life in which Islam was a central theme. I was deeply impressed by many things, mainly, by the portrayal of a slave as someone with a story of his own, a story that was not always defined by his subjugated status, a powerful reminder that all of our captured ancestors were people, rather than chattel. These notions are fairly obvious, or at least they should be; but rarely is African American history recounted from this vantage point. And though I had known, previous to this, that many West Africans were traditionally Muslim, this is the first time I can recall recognizing that this fact had any connection with me as a descendant of Africans. I never forgot this "Aha!" moment; and though I did not think of becoming Muslim myself at the time, this was a very influential moment in my own journey. From this point on, I viewed Islam as a component of my lost cultural heritage.

While, of course, each person's journey is unique, it cannot be denied that this notion of "a religion of our own" has struck a chord, very deeply, with African American Muslims in particular. As stated earlier, it is a notion which has been articulated, to some degree or another, in the majority of black American Islamic movements across the board. Sherman Jackson asserts that the success of Islam among African Americans is partially attributable to the ability of "Islamizers" on the scene in black America to appropriate Islam into something that they owned. He further argues that the phenomenon of Islam in black America falls under the larger umbrella of what he terms "Black Religion":

> ". . . the central and most enduring feature of Black Religion is its sustained and radical opposition to racial oppression. At bottom, Black Religion is an instrument of holy protest against white supremacy and its material and psychological effects. While it is an inextricably religious orientation, it refuses to separate the quest for otherworldy salvation from the struggle for temporal liberation and a dignified existence."[26]

Black Religion as he defines it, is neither exclusively Christian, Muslim, or otherwise, rather it springs from the particular circumstances of slavery and continued oppression experienced by black people in the U.S. This is critical, I believe, because the presence of these inclinations as a driving force in African American Islamic movements across the board, combined with Islam's fundamental teachings regarding the equality of humankind and the importance of social justice, has enabled these groups as a collective to contribute significantly to the discourse of African American liberation in both overt and subtle ways. In every arena where African American Muslims have participated, from political discourse and community activism to cultural productions such as poetry and music, this aesthetic has been a consistent theme. Acts as seemingly divergent as the fiery, eloquent rhetoric of Malcolm and the syncopated rhythms produced by Muslim jazz musicians all share a common thread.

When the undercurrent of Black Religion, which African American converts to the faith were perhaps predisposed were due to their social and cultural reality in America, became linked with Islam, the two systems combined in a synergistic way to create a dynamic expression of religious belief that was very much at home in black America. Islam has, at its core, a very firm message regarding the essential equality of all human beings before God. The very story of the origins of the Prophet of Islam, peace be upon him, and the movement which he led, pits the early Muslim community in Mecca on the one hand, weak and few in number, against the powerful Quraysh tribe, who were at that time the rulers of the city. Members of that early community were persecuted relentlessly, though eventually, after enduring years of ridicule, grew numerous and triumphed over their former oppressors. In addition, the early community of Muslims, while primarily Arab, included prominent figures from other backgrounds, not least of which is the well-known former Abyssinian slave Bilal.[27] Thus the possibility of a truly multiracial spiritual environment, something that had been elusive in America, was introduced to the descendants of former slaves. The Arabian tribal system, while different in many important respects from the American classification based strictly on color, shared many of the latter's disadvantages. Status in society was based largely on accident of birth; in this case lineage and clan affiliation rather than race. The Prophet Muhammad, peace be upon him, attacked many of the existing social taboos that protected the well-connected and made others vulnerable, including slaves, those who had no clan, and women. It is not difficult to see how African Americans, as perpetual second class citizens, would find inspiration in such a narrative.

This powerful combination of ideas not only proved attractive to many African American seekers, thereby becoming a magnet which drew many into the faith, but also served as a catalyst in the development of an aesthetic of determined self-definition that has permeated black American Muslim movements, both orthodox and more unconventional ones. Sunni movements have, in some ways expressed this undercurrent in different ways than the less traditional groups; however, the tendency still has been strong. Groups such as the MSTA, NOI, and later, the Five Percenters, have generally taken the existing framework of Islamic doctrine and radically reinterpreted it, producing mythologies and/or scriptures that were reflective of the African American narrative and experience. Black American Sunni movements have shied away from this approach, preferring instead to remain religiously aligned with global Islamic community, and at the same time, using the religion as a framework to create and assert an independent cultural identity, and interpreting its teachings as a means to address the realities of their own situation in America, at least in the earliest days. For both camps, then, there has historically been a pronounced and shared yearning for an identity that originated from within, rather than having been bestowed by white America. It is well-known how deeply affected black Americans have been by slavery and subsequent oppression; combating the effects of the continuous assault on the culture and identity of the African American population is a subject that many of our sages have grappled with. Frederick Douglass, W. E. B. Du Bois, Marcus Garvey, and Malcolm X, just to name a few, have very eloquently put forth on the problem and its possible solutions. In keeping with that tradition, and in seeking to construct a remedy to these issues of identity and self-determination, most of the earliest African American Islamic proselytizers adopted (and adapted) Islam both for the spiritual considerations and because of its usefulness in confronting the dilemma of a people without an independent sense of self. Imam Muhammad discussed this question in a 1976 essay which explains in detail the methodology employed by Master Fard Muhammad in bringing Islam to African Americans, and the reasons why it was, in his estimation, necessary:

> *"You can go to poor people on any continent and you can teach them civilization if they do not have it, you can teach them science and industry if they do not have it, you can teach them religion if they do not have it, but you do not need to teach them everything because they have not lost everything . . . But over here it was different with us. We had nothing at all but the false picture of ourselves that was given to us by a people who were intent upon keeping us empty-headed slaves for all of our lives."*[28]

Although the leaders of the early black Sunni movements were more inclined to work within the framework of pre-existing Islamic theology, they were no less a product of their environment than were their less orthodox contemporaries, and the rhetoric of these groups reflected this. Professor Ezzaldeen of the AAUAA constructed an alternate identity for his followers, declaring that they were in fact Hametic Arabs, i.e., descended from Ham.[29] In the view of Ezzaldeen, the true Arabs were black. Historically, in American circles, "the curse of Ham" was one of the most consistently repeated religious justifications for the enslavement of

Blacks, in spite of the fact that the Bible never connects this "curse" with a specific racial group. According to the story in the book of Genesis, Noah's son Ham was cursed by his father for looking upon the latter's nakedness while he was drunk, and thus he and his descendants would be destined to be "a slave of slaves to his brothers." It is interesting to note here that the very mythology and terminology by which the denigration and enslavement of African Americans had been justified was appropriated and turned into something positive. This is a tactic that has been used repeatedly by various liberation movements; for example, the move by some feminists to transform derogatory terms used for women or parts of their anatomy into expressions of empowerment.[30]

In addition to overt attempts at constructing an alternate identity, the very acts associated with practicing Islam can, and I believe, have historically been viewed by many African American adherents as a means of solidifying their independence via allegiance to a set of norms that run counter to those established by the mainstream society. While, in fact, Islam and Christianity have a great deal in common in terms of religious narrative and essential values, the particulars of practice vary quite a bit. Entering Islam and observing its norms generally requires, for example, that one not consume particular foods common to other Americans, that one observe a dress code that differs somewhat from the society at large; it also means that cultural customs such as religious holidays and marriage rites differ as well. In addition to the strictly required changes, it is fairly common, though not mandatory, that converts adopt "Islamic" names. Most often, these names are Arabic.[31] In any case, for many African Americans entering the faith, this ability to replace given names, which historically have been associated with the cultural annihilation of those subject to the slave system, with those of one's own choosing and somehow associated with one's "true culture/religion," is a powerful statement and revolutionary act. It is also worth noting that these names have migrated outward from the Muslims and have become common among African Americans of all religious backgrounds. Names such as Hasan, Karim, Rahim, Jamal, Omar, Latifah, and Aisha have become widespread in the non-Muslim black community. Rapper, singer, and actress Queen Latifah (née Dana Owens), who is not a Muslim, talked about the latent power contained in the act of choosing an alternate name for herself:

> "For me, Latifah was freedom. I loved the name my parents gave me . . . But I knew that something as simple as picking a new name for myself would be the first act of defining who I was—for myself and for the world . . . Becoming Latifah would give me the autonomy to be what I chose to be—without being influenced by anyone else's expectations of what a young girl from Newark is supposed to be. Or what she is supposed to do. Or what she is supposed to want."[32]

The observations made by Queen Latifah also shed light on another dimension of the quest for self definition on the part of black American Muslims, and the assertion of the right to color one's own canvas, so to speak. In many of the religious practices and restrictions found in Islam, for example, abstention from pork and alcohol, or the emphasis on chastity and the maintaining of strong family units, one finds the opposite of many of the negative stereotypes of black people. It has been the case, and still is at times, that African Americans are depicted as immoral, irresponsible, hyper-sexual, and lazy. Adopting a way of life which takes a very firm stance against many of these behaviors that black people are "supposed to" engage in is yet another means by which African American Muslims have rejected the negative self-images given by mainstream society and asserted their right to self-definition.

It is important to stress that although these questions of identity and conscientious dissent to a system of injustice have been recurring themes in many African American manifestations of Islam, Dr. Jackson points out, as with Black Religion in general, it is important to note that ". . . it refuses to separate the quest for otherworldy salvation from the struggle for temporal liberation and a dignified existence." Many writers mistakenly characterize the phenomenon of Islam among black Americans as a strictly political statement; underestimating or dismissing altogether the co-existing spiritual motivations that have always been an essential part of the equation. There are various reasons for this, including unfamiliarity with Islam's spiritual teachings and persistent stereotypes both of black people and of Islam. Specifically, the image of the "angry" black person is unfortunately more readily comprehensible to much of the mainstream society than is the spiritual. In addition, most Western public discourse regarding Islam occurs in the context of political events, and therefore an appreciation of its sacred concerns is typically absent from the conversation. Even when devotional beliefs or practices are discussed, usually it is within the context of political events, for example controversies surrounding Muslim women's headscarves or Islamic belief in the afterlife as it pertains to suicide bombers. In any case, the spiritual considerations are, and have always been inseparable from the quest for social justice on the part of African American Muslims. To suggest otherwise is to fall into the trap of painting an unflattering and one-dimensional caricature of a deeply religious community. This distortion is simply another means by which black American Muslims are rendered invisible.

The Song of Rebellion

A popular depiction of Islam in general by Western media is that of a puritanical culture where cultural expressions such as art, poetry, and music are forbidden, and therefore nonexistent. This view is often promulgated by sensational headlines about strict regimes in parts of the Muslim world closing movie theaters or similar stories. In fact, there are unresolved debates among scholars of Islamic law with regard to the permissibility of music, particularly as it relates to certain instruments. Nevertheless Muslim cultures from around the world have produced music, many times as sacred exercise. It is outside of the scope of this work to address such arguments, here I am more interested in highlighting the fact that African American Muslims have, in fact, contributed in significant numbers to the cultural productions of black America. The genres of jazz and hip-hop have been the areas where Muslim contributions have been felt the most. The fact that, as far as American music goes, the African American Muslim presence has been heaviest in these two areas, is, in my estimation, not an accident. Rather, I believe it is a reflection of the presence of aesthetic of conscientious dissent in the community of American Muslims of African descent.

American Studies researcher John D. Baskerville notes the importance of musical analysis taking into consideration the social and cultural milieu in which it was created. With regard to African American music, this is especially important.

> *"The study of musicians, music, and its production has traditionally been the domain of musicologists who primarily study music from a 'score-centered orbit,' concentrating on the notes or formal relations. Such formal analysis has been less than exhaustive, especially the study of African American musical expression. African American music, and other forms of expression, cannot be thoroughly understood if social, cultural, and economic contexts are not considered."[33]*

While jazz and hip-hop are undoubtedly very distinct genres, they share quite a bit in common, especially in terms of their origins as marginalized art forms and their subsequent gradual migration into broader acceptance by mainstream society. Both of these genres also have benefited greatly from the contributions of Muslims. One notable example is that of jazz legend Dizzy Gillespie. His band included several converts, Talib Dawud (Alphonso Rainey), Yusuf Lateef (Bill Evans), Hajj Rashid (Lyn Hope), Liaqat Ali Salaam (Kenny Clarke), and Mustafa Dalil (Oliver Mesheux).[34] Hip-hop has also benefited from the presence and participation of a significant number of performers claiming allegiance to some form of Islam and/or using Islamic phrases or terminology in their music, including DJ Ali Shaheed Muhammad and rapper Q-Tip from A Tribe Called Quest, Big Daddy Kane, Rakim, Public Enemy, Mos Def, Lupe Fiasco, and the Roots.

Significantly, what has also historically been common to these two genres, particularly in their earlier years, is how well they both managed to express the aspirations of a marginalized and oppressed community. The resistance to established norms regarding what music should be and should sound like is in and of itself a powerful act of dissent and self-assertion. Jazz also came to be influenced heavily by the Diaspora, as many of the musicians involved in this art form looked outside of the realm of the Western musical cannon, to Africa and the Caribbean, for sources of inspiration. In the case of hip-hop, in the early days, the fact that it did not rely on instruments or singing at all, led many to debate whether or not it could even properly be called music. Muslim participation in these genres in significant numbers, especially as compared with their collective presence in other types of music, I believe, is at least partially attributable to the fact that both genres originated outside of the hegemony of what was considered "popular" or "normal" musically, and offered a creative means by which strong statements could be made in resistance to those very norms. Muslims did not create this atmosphere, obviously, but it influenced them (in some cases being the means by which they accepted the religion in the first place), and they in turn have had a collective impact on the music as a whole. In the case of hip-hop, it is also worth noting that many Muslim artists have been strongly associated with "conscious" rap—though not all of their material is or was exclusively political.

Conclusion

As time has progressed, and African American Muslim communities have grown and evolved, the discourse surrounding the question of identity has changed as well. Though the "natural religion of the black man" theme has not completely disappeared from the landscape, it is not nearly as prominent as it once was. African Americans entering Islam beginning in the 1980s, and certainly by the 1990s, by and large were less influenced by racial politics than their predecessors. This, I believe, is due to both the internal evolution of the community and its continuing development, along with the overall shift in circumstances for black Americans as a whole. Internally, for starters, there are now large numbers of black Americans born into Islam. While this fact does not preclude a political stance, there is a difference in the mindset of someone who deliberately chooses to step outside of predominant cultural norms as a way of combating oppression and someone who inherits that resulting way of life from birth. This in no way impugns the dedication and seriousness of subsequent generations of African American Muslims, it simply draws attention to the fact that their experiences and those of their parents and grandparents are different. Equally significant is the fact that as the community itself has grown and developed, various philosophies have emerged in relation to the question of communal identity. Should we be aligned with African Americans of other faiths, should we be aligned with the worldwide ummah, or is there an appropriate middle ground between the two? What should our relationship with the immigrant Muslim community in America be? And where does our American identity fit into all of this? These debates are by no means settled definitively; we continue to grapple with these existential questions. And as with any community, we are still experiencing our share of growing pains.

The racial environment in the country as a whole has changed dramatically, and the effects have not bypassed the Muslims. At the time that many of these early communities were developing, for example, black people in many parts of America were still being forcibly denied the right to vote; today, the President of the United States is a black man (with an "Islamic" name, no less). While we have not eradicated racism by a long shot, it is undeniable that the ground under us has shifted a great deal.

What can no longer be overlooked is the fact that Muslims have become a significant presence in the African American community. The history and struggle of this community within a community is inseparable from the greater narrative of the Diaspora; it simultaneously has shaped and has been shaped by the fact that these Muslims are also people of African descent living in America. By the same token, the stories of Islam and Muslims are intricately woven into the fabric of this country, in large part due to the efforts of African American adherents to the faith to carve out a unique space in the landscape where they would be able to exercise a degree of autonomy over their mode of religious expression, their identity, and indeed, their very destiny. And it is in the telling of this particular story, of all of our particular stories, that we begin to perhaps correct the condition in which we have existed as black Americans—as Invisible Men.

Endnotes

1. Hijab is an Arabic word meaning "screen." It is commonly used to refer to the practice of Muslim women to cover their bodies, hair, and sometimes faces in accordance with Islamic law. The word is also commonly used to refer to the headscarf itself.

2. Ummah is Arabic for "community" or "nation."

3. Neil MacFarquhar. "A Growing Demand for the Rare American Imam." *New York Times.* (1 June 2007). Available at http://www.nytimes.com/2007/06/01/us/01imam.html. Accessed 1 August 2009. The Arabic word Imam means "leader"; in Islamic contexts an Imam generally leads the congregational prayers, and usually also gives sermons and/or functions as a religious teacher.

4. *See Muslim Americans: A National Portrait. Gallup Center for Muslim Studies. 2009.* http://www.abudhabigallupcenter.com/144332/Muslim-Americans-National-Portrait.aspx (accessed June 15, 2009). This is believed to be the first nationally representative, randomly selected sample poll of the American Muslim population. Many earlier estimates of numbers have been unreliable; some studies relied on culling "Muslim names" from a phone book or other questionable methodologies. Obtaining accurate demographic figures for the American Muslim population is also complicated by the fact that it is a population which has tended to change relatively rapidly due to conversion and immigration, thus figures often become obsolete fairly quickly.

5. The number of distinct groups of African American Muslims is constantly in flux, as old organizations die out, evolve, merge, or split. In her book, Dr. Aminah McCloud identified, at the time the work was published, ". . . seventeen distinct communities of Islamic expression." See Aminah Beverly McCloud. (1995). *African American Islam.* New York: Routledge, 52. Not all of the groups that she identified are/were exclusively, or even mostly African American, and her identification includes both orthodox and unorthodox movements. In any case, more recently, there has been less of a tendency for black American Muslim organizations to operate on the model of a "movement," with centralized branches in various cities across the country.

6. Many comprehensive works on the histories and doctrines of these various sects are available. See Malcolm X and Alex Haley. (1999). *The Autobiography of Malcolm X (As Told to Alex Haley).* New York: Ballantine Books, and Richard Brent Turner, (1997), *Islam and the African American Experience,* Indianapolis: Indiana University Press.

7. Karl Evanzz. (1999). The Messenger: The Rise and Fall of Elijah Muhammad. New York: Pantheon Books, 62. Whether or not Elijah Muhammad was ever a member of the Moorish movement is contested. The Nation of Islam has denied his involvement, Evanzz bases his assertion upon reports from members of the MSTA and information in Elijah Muhammad's FBI file. Master Fard Muhammad's involvement in the MSTA is attested to by several sources.

8. The mosque where Imam Siraj Wahhaj currently serves as imam, *Masjid at Taqwa*, has been best known for its success in ridding the neighborhood where it is located of crack dealers in the 1980s. Over the last few decades, he has been one of the most prolific speakers in the English-speaking Muslim world, traveling to Muslim communities worldwide. For more information, see Jessica Du Long, "The Imam of Bedford-Stuyvesant." *Saudi Aramco World*, 56(3).

9. Ivan Van Sertima. (1976). *They Came Before Columbus.* New York: Random House.

10. Sylviane Diouf. (1998). *Servants of Allah: African Muslims Enslaved in the Americas.* New York: New York University Press, 48.

11. Diouf, 63.

12. Sulayman S. Nyang. (1999). *Islam in the United States of America.* Chicago: ABC International/Kazi.

13. Dennis Walker. (2005). *Islam and the Search for African American Nationhood: Elijah Muhammad, Louis Farrakhan and the Nation of Islam.* Atlanta: Clarity Press, 257.

14. Nyang, 49.

15. This movement was founded in the late nineteenth century India by Mirza Ghulam Ahmad. The beliefs of this sect are similar in some ways to those of mainstream Islam, but is generally considered heretical by most Muslims. This assertion is due to, among other teachings, the declaration that the movement's founder was a prophet, whereas traditional Islam holds that there are no prophets after the prophet Muhammad, peace be upon him. The Ahmadiyyah eventually split into two factions, the Lahore and Qadiani branches.

16. Umar F. Abd-Allah. (2006). *A Muslim in Victorian America: The Life of Muhammad Alexander Russell Webb.* Oxford: Oxford University Press, 135–136.

17. A. I. Abou Shouk, John O. Hunwick, & R. S. O'Fahey, "A Sudanese Missionary to the United States: Satti Majid, 'Shaykh al Islam in North America,' and His Encounter with Noble Drew Ali, Prophet of the Moorish Science Temple Movement," 145. This source sets the founding of this organization in 1928, while Dr. Sulayman Nyang sets the date at 1927. See next note.

18. Sulayman Nyang. *Saudi Gazette.* 19 October 1983.

19. A fatwa is a declaration, a formal religious ruling issued by Islamic religious authorities.

20. *An Oral History of Islam in Pittsburgh.* (2006). online video, researched and produced by Haroon al Qahtani. Pittsburgh, PA: Haroon al Qahtani. Available from IslaminPittsburgh.com at http://video.google.com/videoplay?docid=-7363431744141688988 (accessed April 4, 2009).

21. Robert Dannin. (2002). *Black Pilgrimage to Islam.* New York: Oxford University Press, 33.

22. Michael Gomez. (2005). Black Crescent: The Experience and Legacy of African Muslims in the Americas. Cambridge: Cambridge University Press, 254.

23. The current leader of the NOI, Louis Farrakhan, initially followed Imam Mohammed in the many doctrinal and organizational changes that the former made to the group. Eventually, however, he parted ways with Mohammed and established the original teachings and infrastructure of the NOI in a separate organization.
24. Al Qahtani.
25. Abou Shouk, Hunwick, & O'Fahey.
26. Sherman Jackson. (2005). *Islam and the Blackamerican: Looking Towards the Third Resurrection*. Oxford: Oxford University Press, 31.
27. As a slave, Bilal was brutally tortured by his master for his declaration of faith in Islam. After his very public punishment, he was purchased and immediately freed by Abu Bakr a wealthy Muslim who eventually assumed leadership of the Muslim community upon the death of the Prophet. Bilal is well-known in Islamic history for his many outstanding deeds, but is most recognized for his role as the first muezzin; the person who gave the call to prayer five times daily from the mosque in Madina. See Tariq Ramadan. (2007). *In the Footsteps of the Prophet: Lessons from the Life of Muhammad*. Oxford: Oxford University Press.
28. W. D. Mohammed. (1985). "Self Government in the New World." *Afro-American Religious History: A Documentary Witness*. Milton C. Sernett (Ed.). Durham: Duke University Press, 417.
29. Michael Nash. (2008). Islam among Urban Blacks: Muslims in Newark, New Jersey: A Social History. New York: University Press of America, 44.
30. Helene A. Shugart. (1997). "Counterhegemonic Acts: Appropriation as a Feminist Rhetorical Strategy." *Quarterly Journal of Speech*, 83(2), 210–229.
31. It is not religiously required for a person to change their name upon conversion, but it is a common practice, taken up by many converts to signal a new beginning of sorts. Nor is there a requirement that the chosen name be Arabic, though most often this is the practice. The instances where it becomes strongly recommended religiously to change a given name is where the person's original name has a meaning that is unbecoming to Islamic principles. In any case, in spite of common practice to the contrary, it is frowned upon to change one's family name, as Islam places a great deal of emphasis on knowing and preserving one's lineage. For African American Muslims, this remains an unresolved debate, as the issue of "slave names," bestowed by slave masters to their human property, are often argued not to be reflective of one's true lineage, and thus are able to be discarded.
32. Queen Latifah (with Karen Hunter). (2003). *Ladies First: Revelations of a Strong Woman*, (New York: William Morrow, 1999), quoted in Leola A. Johnson, "The Queen in Hip-Hop Culture," in *Noise and Spirit: The Religious and Spiritual Sensibilities of Rap Music*. Anthony B. Pinn (Ed.). New York: New York University Press, 164.
33. John D. Baskerville. (2003). *The Impact of Black Nationalist Ideology on American Jazz Music of the 1960s and 1970s*. Lewiston: The Edwin Mellen Press, 1.
34. Dannin, 58.

References

Abd-Allah, Umar, F. (2006). *A Muslim in Victorian America: The Life of Alexander Russell Webb*. Oxford: Oxford University Press.

Abd-Allah, Umar F. (2009). "Islam and the Cultural Imperative." Nawawi Foundation. Available at: http://nawawi.org/downloads/article3.pdf (accessed March 3, 2009).

Abou Shouk, A. I., Hunwick, J., & O'Fahey, R. S. (1997). "A Sudanese Missionary to the United States: Satti Majid, Shaykh al-Islam in North America, and His Encounter with Noble Drew Ali, Prophet of the Moorish Science Temple Movement." *Sudanic Africa: A Journal of Historical Sources*. 8, 137–192.

An Oral History of Islam in Pittsburgh, Online Video. (2006). Researched and produced by Haroon Al-Qahtani. Pittsburgh, PA: Haroon Al-Qahtani. Available at http://video.google.com/videoplay?docid=7363431744141688988 (accessed April 4, 2009).

Baldwin, James. (1961). "The Black Boy Looks at the White Boy." *Nobody Knows My Name: More Notes of a Native Son*. New York: Dial Press.

Baskerville, John D. (2003). *The Impact of Black Nationalist Ideology on American Jazz Music of the 1960s and 1970s*. Lewiston, New York: The Edwin Mellen Press.

Conyers, James L., Jr. (Ed.). (2001). *African American Jazz and Rap: Social and Philosophical Examination of Black Expressive Behavior*. London: McFarland & Co.

Conyers, James L, Jr. (2007). "The Nation of Islam: An Historiography of Pan-Africanist Thought and Intellectualism." *Engines of the Black Power Movement: Essays on the Influence of Civil Rights Actions, Arts, and Islam*. James L. Conyers, Jr. (Ed). London: McFarland & Co.

Curtis, Edward E. (2005). "African American Islamization Reconsidered: Black History Narrative and Muslim Identity." *Journal of the American Academy of Religion*, (September 2005) 73(3), 559–684.

Dannin, Robert. (2002). *Black Pilgrimage to Islam*. Oxford: Oxford University Press.

Diouf, Sylviane. (1998). *Servants of Allah: African Muslims Enslaved in the Americas*. New York: New York University Press.

Ellison, Ralph. (1989). *Invisible Man*. New York: Vintage Books.

Evanzz, Karl. (1999). *The Messenger: The Rise and Fall of Elijah Muhammad*. New York: Pantheon Book.

Floyd-Thomas, Juan M. (2003). "A Jihad of Words: The Evolution of African American Islam and Contemporary Hip-Hop." *Noise and Spirit: The Religious and Spiritual Sensibilities of Rap Music*. Anthony B. Pinn (Ed.). New York: NYU Press.

Gomez, Michael A. (2005). *Black Crescent: The Experience and Legacy of African Muslims in the Americas*. Cambridge: Cambridge University Press.

Hakim, Jameela A. (1979). *History of the First Muslim Mosque of Pittsburgh, Pennsylvania*. Cedar Rapids: Igram Press.

Jackson, Sherman A. (2005). *Islam and the Blackamerican: Looking Toward the Third Resurrection*. Oxford, Oxford University Press.

Johnson, Leola A. (2003). "The Queen in Hip-Hop Culture." *Noise and Spirit: The Religious and Spiritual Sensibilities of Rap Music*. Anthony B. Pinn (Ed.). New York: NYU Press.

Karim, Jamillah A. (2006). "To Be Black, Female, and Muslim: A Candid Conversation about Race in the American *Ummah*." *Journal of Muslim Minority Affairs*. August 2006, 26(2), 225–233.

MacFarquar, Neil. (2009). "A Growing Demand for the Rare American Imam." *New York Times* (June 1, 2007): New York Times. Available at http://www.nytimes.com/2007/06/01/us/01imam.html?page wanted=1&_r=2 (accessed July 15, 2009).

McAlister, Melani. (2002). "Nation Time: Black Islam and African American Cultural Politics." *Faith in the Market: Religion and the Rise of Urban Commercial Culture*. John M. Giggie and Diane Winston (Eds.). New Brunswick, New Jersey: Rutgers University Press.

McCloud, Aminah Beverly. (1995). *African American Islam*. New York: Routledge.

Muhammad, Wallace D. (1985). "Self-Government in the New World." *Afro-American Religious History: A Documentary Witness*. Milton C. Sernett (Ed.). Durham: Duke University Press.

Muslim Americans: A National Portrait. 2009. Gallup Center for Muslim Studies. Available at http://www.abudhabigallupcenter.com/144332/Muslim-Americans-National-Portrait.aspx (accessed June 15, 2009).

Nash, Michael. (2008). *Islam Among Urban Blacks: Muslims in Newark, New Jersey: A Social History*. New York: University Press of America.

Nimer, Mohamed. (2002). "Muslims in American Public Life." *Muslims in the West: From Sojourners to Citizens*. Yvonne Yazbeck Haddad (Ed.). Oxford: Oxford University Press.

Nyang, Sulayman. (1983). "Growing of Islam in America." *Saudi Gazette*. October 19, 1983. Islam In Pittsburgh. Available at http//www.islaminpittsburgh.com (accessed April 14, 2009).

Nyang, Sulayman S. (1999). *Islam in the United States of America*. Chicago: ABC International/Kazi.

Pharr, Pauline C. (1993). "Onomastic Divergence: A Study of Given-Name Trends among African Americans." *American Speech* (Winter 1993), 68(4), 400–409.

Pinn, Anthony B. (2006). *The African American Religious Experience in America*. Westport, CT: Greenwood Press.

Ramadan, Tariq. (2007). *In the Footsteps of the Prophet: Lessons from the Life of the Muhammad*. Oxford: Oxford University Press.

Reeves, Marcus. (2008). *Somebody Scream: Rap Music's Rise to Prominence in the Aftershock of Black Power.* New York: Faber & Faber.

Shakir, Zaid. (2005). "Islam, the Prophet Muhammad, and Blackness." *Seasons: Semiannual Journal of Zaytuna Institute* (Spring/Summer 2005), 2(2), 69–79.

Shugart, Helene A. (1997). "Counterhegemonic Acts: Appropriation as a Feminist Rhetorical Strategy." *Quarterly Journal of Speech,* 83(2), 210–229.

Simawe, Saadi A. "Islam in the Civil Rights Movement." *Engines of the Black Power Movement: Essays on the Influence of Civil Rights Actions, Arts, and Islam.* James L. Conyers, Jr. (Ed). London: McFarland & Co, 2007.

Singleton, Brent D. (2006). "Minarets in Dixie: Proposals to Introduce Islam in the American South." *Journal of Muslim Minority Affairs* (August 2006), 26(2), 433–444.

Turner, Richard Brent. (1997). *Islam in the African American Experience.* Indianapolis: Indiana University Press.

Van Sertima, Ivan. (1976). *They Came Before Columbus.* New York: Random House.

Walker, Dennis. (2005). *Islam and the Search for African-American Nationhood: Elijah Muhammad, Louis Farrakhan, and the Nation of Islam.* Atlanta: Clarity Press.

Wyche, Karen Fraser. (2004). "African American Muslim Women, an Invisible Group." *Sex Roles* 51. No. 5/6, 319–328.

X, Malcolm and Alex Haley. (1999). *The Autobiography of Malcolm X.* New York: Ballantine Books.

Chapter 37

"He baked no bread of his own":
Charles H. Thompson and the Struggle for Civil Rights

Louis Ray

Introduction

In *The Souls of Black Folk*, Du Bois described the African American experience in terms of isolation and invisibility. He wrote of African Americans as a people compelled to live behind a physical and psychological "veil" designed for obscuring if not erasing their humanity from view. In his autobiographies, Du Bois charted his personal mission for leading African Americans from the mudsill of American life to the mountain top of freedom and self-realization. Journeying to the Deep South for the first time to attend Fisk University located in Nashville, Tennessee, in 1885, Du Bois has portrayed this journey as a catalyst solidifying his identity and linking his fortune irrevocably with that of African Americans. His years at Fisk University, he informed us, also were crucial to forging his ideals of leadership and his identity as an African American leader.

To survive and grow it is axiomatic that an organization, group, or "race" must have what Du Bois described as "far-seeing" leaders.[1] A voluminous literature exists on the requirements of leadership. Moreover, there is an ongoing debate among a swelling chorus of sages vying over which leadership style works best in general, during specific situations, or over the long haul. Undoubtedly, the education, acculturation, and development of leaders are important social functions.

The question remains, after emancipation how did African Americans sustain a 10-decade challenge to racism and segregation? How did they develop the organization and discipline to keep "their eyes on the prize" of equal citizenship rights and freedom? How did they manage daily tasks and activities such as earning a livelihood or raising a family while channeling time, thought, and attention into social activism? This essay will examine the editorial thought of Charles H. Thompson, an important, but little-known African American intellectual. The essay will argue Thompson drew from the best of the legacy of Booker T. Washington and W. E. B. Du Bois, synthesizing or weaving their ideas into his educational and social philosophy. Moreover, the essay will contend Thompson's work is important for developing a fuller understanding of Du Bois's scholarly project. At the end of his long, productive life Du Bois would leave the *Encyclopedia of the Negro* unfinished. This project the historian Henry Louis Gates and philosopher K. Anthony Appiah would bring to fruition in 1999 by publishing it as computer software and as a hardcover book entitled *Encarta Africana* and *Africana: The Encyclopedia of the African and African American Experience*, respectively.

In part, Thompson's brilliance stems from the fact that he had the courage to submerge his ego devoting himself to the cause he described as "the good for Negro education as a whole."[2] Instead, he read widely and critically, building on the best thought of his age and that of his intellectual forebears. Thompson would be better known today had he left an intellectual legacy in the form of books and monographs reflecting his ideas and perspectives. Historians then could look at those artifacts and marvel at his audacity and brilliance. Instead, he chose to develop and promote the work of other researchers in order to build within the span of his lifetime a solid literature related to African American education.

Analysis and synthesis were among his favorite intellectual tools. By bringing together the best ideas on a subject, Thompson hoped to make significant intellectual breakthroughs possible. He used analysis and synthesis for making plain the contributions as well as the faults of previous studies. Thompson was, as the historian Rayford W. Logan referred to African American scholars of Logan's generation, a genuine "disciple of Du Bois."[3] The model upon which Thompson designed the *Journal of Negro Education*, particularly its annual yearbooks, is largely based upon the model of Du Bois's Atlanta University Conference series published between 1898 and 1914.[4] Thompson also modeled the *Journal of Negro Education* after the *Journal of Negro History* and the brilliant example of historian Carter G. Woodson.

As editor of the *Journal of Negro Education*, Charles H. Thompson spent 31 years fulfilling in part the 100-year publishing cycle Du Bois had planned for the Atlanta University Conference series. Yet, Thompson's work is not significant because of his role in fulfilling Du Bois's agenda, but for his role in undermining racial segregation as public policy in the United States. Thompson's thought is of continuing interest today because his method, clarity of vision, forcibleness of expression, and most important, his insights, example, courage, and integrity, remain relevant. In Thompson's editorial thought we have the views of an important strategist, activist, and observer of the Civil Rights Movement in the United States. As reflections upon the national and international implications of segregation and the changing terrain of African American education, his work allows us to better grasp the size and complexity of the problem facing those seeking to keep educational discrimination and racial segregation from sapping all life and purpose from a people. In time, if unchecked, the logic of state-sponsored racism, educational discrimination, and racial segregation would have reduced the value of African Americans' human capital to less than zero.

It is often said that those who do not understand history are doomed to repeat it. It may also be said that those who do not fully comprehend the shaping of historical events inevitably repeat the mistakes of the past without ascending the palace of the intellect and from its upper rooms gaining better insight into the present as well as the future. Thompson argued that subordinate groups' social status reflected the social space the opinion of dominant groups had carved out of them. In Thompson's view, individual accomplishments notwithstanding, an individual's status equaled the respect the dominant community accorded the group to which that person was linked.

The Howard University philosopher Alain Locke summed up the social philosophy of "thinking Negroes" of Thompson's generation when describing the New Negro Movement.[5] The intellectual currents of the New Negro Movement resonated through much of Thompson's life and work. According to Locke, New Negroes shared a belief in "the efficacy of collective efforts in race cooperation." Moreover, Locke contended, New Negroes valued self-respect and treasured self-reliance. They renounced dependency and double standards, insisting that the same standards applied to the dominant group also be applied to the subordinate group. Instead of calculating how much the world owed them for living, the focus of the New Negro was on fulfilling their social responsibilities and being of service to the nation by making the social contributions required of citizens in a democracy.

Locke noted the New Negro refused to use discrimination as an excuse for personal or group failings. They were propelled to action by the "ideals of American institutions and democracy" on the one hand and the urgency of "repair[ing] a damaged group psychology and reshap[ing] a warped [group] social perspective" on the other. New Negroes welcomed "objective and scientific appraisal" of the African American experience, Locke asserted. It is possible to infer from Locke's writing the idea that New Negroes would approve of social engineering based on valid research.

Based upon a conversation with one of Thompson's former students, the historian Michael R. Winston learned of how inspiring Thompson's lectures on research methods were for students interested in combating educational discrimination.[6] According to Winston, Thompson counseled students to "get the facts, get the facts" and to let the findings take care of themselves. For Thompson, properly defining the problem under investigation was a major step in conducting valid educational research. Thompson insisted upon analyzing policymakers' assumptions because he believed the policies they pursued flowed directly from those assumptions as well as the biases and preconceptions they brought to an issue.

According to an October 1932 *Journal* editorial by Thompson, as early as 1927 critics ranging from newspaper columnists, contributors to professional journals, and speakers at various educational assemblies contended that African American colleges produced more teachers than the market could absorb.[7] They called for a significant reduction in the teacher training activities of the African American colleges. In the editorial, Thompson highlighted two studies, including the July 1932 *Journal* yearbook entitled "A Critical Survey of the Negro Elementary School," to refute the contention that the supply of African American teachers exceeded the demand.

The *Journal* yearbook authors assumed the supply of teachers and their educational levels should be approximately equal for the White and African American elementary schools of a community. For example, if the pupil-to-teacher ratio of the White public schools in a given community was 35 pupils to 1 teacher, the pupil-to-teacher ratio of the African American public schools in that community should be the same. If the education of the average White teacher was 2 years beyond high school, the education of the average African American teacher should be the same, Thompson wrote. Their assumptions and criterion were legally sound, he averred, because these assumptions reflected the separate but equal doctrine that was the legal basis of racial segregation in the United States.

Among the important findings reported in the 1932 yearbook was the need for 17,190 additional teachers to make the supply of African American teachers proportionately equal to the teaching staff employed by the White schools. Assuming that the school enrollment of African American children equaled that of White children, Thompson estimated that it would require another 10,000 teachers in addition to the 64,230 African American teachers required for providing numerically proportional teaching staffs for the dual school systems. Approximately 13,184 of the 46,047 African American teachers employed in 1931 required retraining or replacement to bring their educational level up to that of the average White teacher, he noted.

Thus, very different assumptions may lead to very different conclusions and very different conclusions may lead to very different consequences socially. For Thompson, asking good questions and developing tentative hypotheses based upon the investigation of those problems was crucial for developing a literature useful to scholars and policymakers alike. In his mind, the thought and energy expended in developing sound questions and hypotheses were central to the creative intellectual act. We enter a world shaped by others and struggle to define ourselves largely by rummaging through the cultural catalogs or peering into the mirrors lining the walls, floors, and ceilings of the production floors and warehouses of culture. Discovering ideas, and roles we wish to adapt, we clothe ourselves in those roles and ideas, cherishing them as if they were our own. Understanding ideas in their historical context was a requirement for effective problem solving, Thompson opined. Before embarking upon a journey of any length, he advised, one must not only be reasonably certain that the path taken leads to the desired destination but that the trip was worth taking in the first place.

Changes in the U.S. Racial Landscape: 1910 to 1934

Anti-Negro prejudice escalated in the United States between 1880 and 1910 as the practice of racial segregation spread East, West, North, and South. Anti-Negro prejudice increased so much after the economic recession following World War I, Marguerite Wills Meadows (1984) argued, that by 1917, the national popular magazines such as *The Saturday Evening Post, McClures,* and *Collier's* had helped to create a national consensus in support of disfranchisement and segregation.[8]

Yet, during the years between 1910 and 1930, important developments had occurred within American society and the African American community. The complexity of the modern era compelled many American policymakers and citizens to accept the need for social engineering and the leadership of experts. According to participants and observers such as commentator Walter Lippmann, between 1910 and the 1930s, the professional authority of experts in the United States increased significantly. By 1930, conditions much more favorable to using scholarship as an instrument of social reform were in existence in the United States. Moreover, resurgence of the abolitionist tradition in the United States also occurred, as was evident by the founding of the NAACP in 1909.

According to historian John Hope Franklin, during the 1920s a new assertiveness and an "awakened consciousness" developed among African Americans that would be associated with the New Negro Movement.[9] Educational historians Michael Fultz and Ann Horton argued that the period between 1906 and 1935 also reflected a significant growth in African American professional and civic organizations and the African American middle class.[10] According to Horton, members of the emerging African American middle class poured their energy into organizations and associations, including the NAACP (1909) and the Association of Colleges for Negro Youth (1913). They founded the Association of Deans of Women and Advisers to Girls in Negro Colleges (1929) and the National Council of Negro Women (1935). The National

Association of Teachers in Colored Schools (1906) and the Association for the Study of Negro Life and History (1916) are two organizations of the period deserving special mention.

Established in 1916 by Carter G. Woodson, the founder of African American history, the membership of the Association for the Study of Negro Life and History (ASNLH) consisted largely of teachers who valued education, history, self-reliance, and racial pride. The National Association of Teachers in Colored Schools (NATCS) was noted for its size and activist orientation. While representing at its peak approximately 6,000 members, the NATCS was the largest national organization directed by African Americans during the 1930s and 1940s.[11] Several important administrators and activists were members of the NATCS, including John Hope, the president of Atlanta Baptist College (later Morehouse College) and Atlanta University, and Mary McCleod Bethune, the president of Bethune-Cookman College. Harper Council Trentholm, the president of Alabama State University and Mordecai W. Johnson, the president of Howard University, were members.[12] So, too, was the historian John Hope Franklin who served as a consultant to Thurgood Marshall and the NAACP legal team litigating *Brown v. Board of Education* (1954).[13]

The proliferation of protest literature by the writers of the Harlem Renaissance also documented this important attitudinal shift among African Americans, John Hope Franklin observed (499–501).[14] So, too, did the migration of African Americans from the rural South to the cities of the South and to the improved economic, political, and educational opportunities of the North.[15]

According to historian John Dittmer and sociologists Horace Cayton and St. Clair Drake, in African American communities of the period, education was an important indicator of social status for the Negro bourgeoisie.[16] Race relations work also was a respected activity and a requirement of leadership. The sociologist E. Franklin Frazier argued that what differentiated the emerging African American leaders from their older counterparts were the younger leaders' superior university training and their practical approach to racial issues. Frazier argued that these scholars whom he referred to as "functional leaders" sought to remove emotion from racial problems as they applied the scientific method to their resolution.[16]

In terms of their social philosophy, the younger leaders were closely aligned with the New Negro Movement. They were mostly "forced radicals" who, according to Locke, were only radical on the race question and moderate to conservative generally on other social issues.[17] Concurring with Alain Locke, the historian Michael R. Winston argued that with the exception of segregation, the young African American scholars of the 1930s accepted most of the premises of American society as well as the methods of American scholarship.[18]

The rise of Howard University as the only university in the universe of African American education has been aptly discussed by Winston. According to Winston, President Franklin D. Roosevelt decided there was more political reward than risk in transforming Howard University into "a vital symbol of 'Negro progress.'"[19] Roosevelt's decision substantially increased the federal financial commitment to the university, especially for its building program, Winston observed. For many years, Winston continued, "the science facilities at Howard University were the best available to Negro scientists in universities."[20]

During the 1930s, several leading architects of the NAACP litigation strategy to eradicate racial segregation served on the faculty of the recently accredited Law School of Howard University. According to Logan (1969) and Winston (1971) these architects included Charles Hamilton Houston, William H. Hastie, James M. Nabrit, Jr., Leon A. Ransom, and George E. C. Haynes.[21] Houston, Hastie, Nabrit, Ransom, and Haynes were among the most successful practitioners of public policy law in the United States from the 1930s to 1954, Winston argued. Moreover, Thompson, Houston, Nabrit, Ransom, and E. Franklin Frazier formed what Winston has referred to as the "public policy nucleus" at Howard during the 1930s, 1940s, and 1950s.[22]

The significance of the "public policy nucleus" at Howard was in assembling part of the expertise required for prosecuting an important phase of the Civil Rights Struggle. It is reasonable to argue similar "public policy nuclei" existed within African American professional associations such as the National Association of Teachers in Colored Schools (NATCS). Thompson's *Journal* editorials were significant because his editorials informed and provided guidance and coherence of tactics and strategy for African American activists and their allies much as did Du Bois's editorials in *The Crisis*.

Thompson: A Scholar and Activist within the University Setting

In a personal interview, Dr. Rachel Weddington, an emeritus administrator at Howard University and former student of Thompson, described him as a racial diplomat second in influence only to Charles S. Johnson.[23]

Thompson was born in Jackson, Mississippi in 1896, the year that the U.S. Supreme Court upheld racial seg-regation as constitutional as long as the state provided benefits to its residents on a separate but equal basis. He knew the unvarnished South as did few of his contemporaries at Howard University. His *Journal* editori-als revealed his understanding of the deep-seated prejudices maintaining racial segregation in law and prac-tice and the positive role public opinion could play in expanding human rights.

In the terminology of the period, Thompson was a pioneer or a true innovator. In 1925, he graduated magna cum laude from the University of Chicago as the first African American to earn a Ph.D. in education.[24] The following year, he began a 40-year career at Howard University, rapidly earning professional recognition. Beginning as an associate professor of education in 1926, Thompson's promotion to professor took place 3 years later in 1929. In addition to teaching, Thompson held a succession of important administrative posi-tions at Howard University. From 1932 to 1933, he served as acting dean of the College of Education. From 1938 to 1943, he served as dean of the College of Liberal Arts dean and was Graduate School dean from 1944 to 1961.[25]

Thompson was an insider who excelled in professional arenas outside Howard University. He was a fel-low of the American Association for the Advancement of Science and a member of the National Society for the Study of Education. In 1922 and again in 1940 the yearbooks of the National Society for the Study of Education featured debates over evidence regarding African Americans' alleged mental inferiority.[26]

Thompson also served as an editorial consultant to *Nation's Schools* and the *World Book Encyclopedia*. Consistent with his efforts to fulfill the unfinished research agenda of Du Bois, he was a member of the *Encyclopedia of the Negro* Board of Directors. From 1946 to 1949, he served on the United States National Commission for UNESCO. Thompson was a member of the Committee on Discrimination in College Admission, American Council of Education from 1948 to 1957.[27]

In terms of this essay, Thompson's most important affiliation was his membership on the national board of the National Association for the Advancement of Colored People (NAACP) Legal Defense Fund. He served as a Board member during the years when the NAACP Legal Defense Fund lawyers fought school segregation in the courts.[28] Moreover, Thompson also was an expert witness in several landmark court cases about the edu-cational inequities resulting from racial segregation. He was an expert witness for the NAACP Legal Defense Fund in *Sipuel v. Board of Regents of the University of Oklahoma*, 1948, *Sweatt v. Painter*, 1950, and *McLaurin v. Oklahoma State Regents*, 1950.[29]

As the *Journal* editor from 1932 to 1963, the research studies Thompson published were often the first comprehensive, scientific studies of various aspects of African American education. As such, this research often provided the baseline data by which to measure the effectiveness of school policy initiatives and the claims that separate, equal educational opportunities existed in the southern states. Richard Bardolph (1961), the author of *The Negro Vanguard*, asserted that the *Journal* during Thompson's editorship earned its reputa-tion as one of the finest publications of its kind.[30] In 1947, the distinguished historian John Hope Franklin discussed the July yearbook issues of the *Journal* that Thompson edited. For Franklin, the *Journal* yearbooks were "one of the most important sources of information on the historical, sociological and educational aspects of Negro life."[31]

In *Simple Justice*, Richard Kluger underscored the importance of Thompson's contribution to the history of African American education. Kluger wrote that Thompson launched the *Journal* with only enough funds to pay for printing and postage. On this slim budget, Thompson created a national, scholarly forum for docu-menting the inequitable condition of African American education and exploring the implications of segre-gation. After Du Bois resigned as *The Crisis* editor in 1934, Kluger contended that Thompson's *Journal* became the major intellectual forum of the struggle against segregation. According to Kluger, through skillful editing and a deft sense of timing, Thompson transformed a scholarly journal into an organ that not only informed but also aroused and inspired people to engage in social action.[32]

From the outset, Thompson styled the *Journal* as a forum "for continuous, critical appraisal and discus-sion of the present and proposed practices relating to the education of Negroes."[33] In fact, by July 1933, he regarded critical evaluation as the primary function that the *Journal* fulfilled. In April 1932, Thompson argued the discussion about African American education conducted in other fora consisted mostly of inspirational talks. Before April 1932, there was no forum in African American education for the "critical appraisal of the assumptions underlying certain basic procedures and proposals," he observed. Thompson filled this gap by providing skillful editing and a "ready and sympathetic outlet for publication" through the *Journal*. He encouraged more African American educators to research "the problems incident to the education of Negroes."[34] According to Dr. Carroll L. Miller, the dean emeritus of the Howard University Graduate School and a *Journal* assistant editor in April 1932, Thompson was constantly seeking to discover new talent and new material.[35] He used an interracial network of educators and activists as a means of discovering new voices and pertinent data. Moreover, for a period of 31 years, the *Journal* was his forum for identifying and suggesting areas in need of systematic study.

It is possible to argue that Thompson considered the thoughtfulness and discipline required for conducting scientific research and the willingness to act upon valid findings as attributes of educational leadership. He believed the development and distribution of a valid and relevant literature had important public policy implications in a modern democracy such as the United States.

Winston recalled Thompson had a gift for aphorisms. One of his aphorisms was: "If you keep sawing wood long enough, the tree will fall,"[36] meaning persistence and fortitude are essential for those committed to redressing entrenched social problems or opening the doors of freedom to those who have been locked out. In fact, during his years as an undergraduate at Virginia Union if not before, Thompson began to saw wood. As the *Journal* editor, he envisioned a role for scientific research in realizing the principle of equal opportunity for underprivileged people and minority groups in the United States and throughout the world.

The application of critical analysis, synthesis, and the scientific method were the metaphorical saws Thompson applied persistently to the looming tree of racial segregation, injustice, and African Americans' second-class citizenship status. Thompson appeared to have viewed the connection between valid research and social action as inevitable and immutable. In his view, the serious scholar investigated problems not merely for personal understanding and edification but as the first among a series of acts of public service aimed at improving the life chances and social conditions of the populace. Remarkably, Thompson maintained an optimistic outlook, while acknowledging the irrationality and intractability of segregation and racial prejudice.

In fact, in *The Secret City*, Green argued that Thompson thought the U.S. Supreme Court ruling in *Brown v. Board of Education* (1954) would result in greater and more rapid equalization of the dual school systems.[37] The 1954 U.S. Supreme Court ruling to reverse *Plessy v. Ferguson* (1896) was surprising for Thompson. Yet, Winston argued Thompson was among the few of his contemporaries at Howard who correctly anticipated the extent of the resistance following the desegregation decree.[38]

Throughout his long, professional career, Thompson maintained a positive belief in the efficacy of education and envisioned a significant social function for African American education beyond segregation. Many social problems, especially those stemming from prejudice, were fundamentally educational problems, he reasoned. Yet, he acknowledged the influence of education upon remedying problems such as race relations or social justice was as indirect and imperceptible as sand generated by rain falling upon a mountain. Thompson believed that persistence, timing, and valid data were tools for guiding and hastening the reform process.

Any successful social movement requires sufficient consensus, coherence of thought, and unity of action of its membership. The communication of ideas is important to the survival of any social movement. Situated between world wars, Thompson painstakingly shaped a distinctive view in the *Journal of Negro Education*. He not only drew upon the talents of the university faculty. Thompson drew upon the educational authority and prestige of the university to persuade distinguished White scholars, nationally and internationally, to contribute articles and reviews to the *Journal*.

Thompson designed the *Journal* as an international, interracial forum of public policy research centered on the problem of gaining equal educational opportunities and equal citizenship rights for minority groups, particularly African Americans. Moreover, he designed his *Journal* editorials to provide direction and leadership in the policy debates regarding African American education during the period 1932 to 1963 and beyond. The fact that the *Journal* has published continuously for more than 64 years from 1932 to 2004 is testimony to the soundness of his design and the acuity of his vision.

Selected Examples of Thompson's *Journal* Editorial Thought

Thompson's editorials, his selection of *Journal* topics and issues and his efforts to develop a national audience, and by implication his efforts to sustain a national movement, are important for understanding the evolution of the civil rights struggle in the inter-war period. Winston (1971) has argued that Thompson's editorials represented shrewd public policy assessments and assessments of developments within African American education.[39] His editorials provided a national perspective and context by which historians may better gauge local developments during the 1930s, 1940s, 1950s, and early 1960s. In Thompson, we have a sustained editorial voice during major periods of U.S. history and African American history, including the Great Depression, World War II, the Civil Rights Movement, and the De-Colonial or Independence Movement. The major theme of Thompson's thought was his unswerving opposition to social injustice, racial segregation, and racial discrimination. Thompson believed strongly in the expansion of participatory democracy on the African American college campuses and throughout the United States and the world. Self-determination and the responsibility of oppressed people to engage in critical study and analysis, to organize and to work diligently toward the improvement of their social condition were important emphases for Thompson.

Thompson sought to encourage the wider exercise of African American leadership. Yet, he did not see African American leadership as a panacea. For he argued mediocre, condescending, and authoritarian African American chief executives were just as bad as mediocre, condescending, and authoritarian White American chief executives. He argued that thoughtful, direct, individual, and collective action were the means by which African Americans and other oppressed people and their allies could achieve equal educational opportunity and equal citizenship rights. He believed only critical thought would allow a movement to stay on course while making the innumerable adjustments required for reaching its goals in a timely manner.

For Thompson, the growth of an increasingly technological society with vast concentrations of wealth held serious implications for the poor and the uneducated. Charles S. Johnson's *The Shadow of the Plantation* discussed the rise of agribusiness in the South and the displacement of African American sharecroppers fueled by racism, economic depression, and mechanization. A quality education and effective vocational or career guidance were important concerns for Thompson because he anticipated, as did Du Bois, the bumpy transition of unskilled workers from a reserve labor force to obsolescence in knowledge-driven, capital intensive economies. In Thompson's editorials, we see not only the complexity of segregation as a social institution, but also the problems posed for people, especially uneducated, unskilled people in a world in which education reproduces class and knowledge is a major factor in economic growth.

Much as did Du Bois, Thompson planned to re-investigate educational and social problems at 10-year intervals. Therefore, the first decade of his editorial thought represented the initial presentation, or "roll out," of the major topics he selected for critical evaluation. Thompson wrote 41 *Journal* editorials during the first 10 years of his editorship, from 1932 to 1941. The editorial "Why a Class B Negro College?" penned in October 1933 was selected for its brilliant resonance of the New Negro social philosophy in its opposition to double standards. Thompson opposed lesser standards because double or lesser standards implied an acceptance of the premises and rationale underlying racial segregation. African Americans' support of voluntary segregation to obtain limited benefits or perks such as teaching positions in segregated schools, he argued, was a growing obstacle to the achievement of greater economic and social opportunities, and equal citizenship rights. Moreover, Thompson viewed double standards as retarding the development of the first-class educational institutions that were required for developing the leadership and expertise for challenging and defeating racism and segregation.

Anticipating the rise of independent nation states in Asia and Africa, the second editorial is a cogent statement of the common need for self-government or self-determination by minority groups and colonial peoples throughout the world. In "The Education of Subject and Underprivileged Peoples" written in January 1934, Thompson endorsed the de-colonial or national liberation movements. He admonished African Americans for wasting energy in escapism, fatalism, and psychological depression. Instead, he encouraged them to struggle against racism at home as a means of providing leadership and support for the worldwide struggle against colonialism and imperialism.

The third editorial reflects, as do the first and second, Thompson's debt to the intellectual legacy of Du Bois and the New Negro Movement. "Investing in Negro Brains," composed in April 1935, reflected Thompson's concern that African Americans assume greater responsibility for the identification, selection, education, and support (through national merit scholarships) of the most intellectually talented African American students. Thompson argued African Americans could not afford to waste even one of the 25,000 college seats available during the period. How, he asked, could African Americans deny, in essence, the benefits of higher education to more than 8,000 academically talented African American students by allowing "sub-collegiate" students to take their places? "Thinking Negroes" were a resource many African American communities lacked because the supply was severely limited. "Thinking Negroes" were a civic resource providing services and leadership while serving as conduits of culture. African American communities had a desperate need for better-trained teachers, ministers, lawyers, doctors, social workers, and other professionals,

Thompson argued. Yet, he opined, its colleges barred entry to many intellectually gifted African American students because of family status and income.

"Why a Class "B" Negro College?" (October 1933)

By 1930, accreditation was synonymous with the value of an education a school or college provided. As late as 1930 the Southern Association of Colleges and Secondary Schools refused to evaluate any African American schools and colleges in the South. The onus of this decision was borne not only by the African American schools and colleges in the region but was borne especially by African American high school and college graduates seeking admission to advanced study. Thompson described the predicament typically faced by African American college graduates seeking admission to graduate or professional school. If they were admitted at all, it was with the condition that they repeat a significant percentage of their undergraduate courses before pursuing a graduate or professional degree.

Placing the issue in its historical context, Thompson traced the developments leading to the Southern Association's decision to evaluate the dual schools and colleges in its region. First, pressure taking the form of "much discussion and agitation" from liberal White and Black southerners "induced" the Association to change its longstanding policy. A "special committee" was appointed to study the issue and make recommendations. As a first step, the special committee decided to broaden its membership by adding "several Negroes and interested white men."

According to Thompson, two issues absorbed the special committee's time and attention. Approval by the Association implied membership and the right to attend association meetings, Thompson wrote. Because most of the association membership found "objectionable" equal social relations between the races, the committee decided to recommend limiting the Association's role to evaluation only. Approval would not confer membership upon an African American school or college, nor would its personnel be permitted to attend Association meetings.

The second major issue absorbing the special committee's attention was evaluation standards. Should the committee recommend applying *"exactly* the same rigid standards" as were applied to White colleges or adopt easier standards for African American colleges? This issue split the committee. One group consisting entirely of Whites supported easier or double standards in recognition of the economic and educational hurdles African American colleges and schools had to overcome. To the contrary, the second group comprised of the African American members of the committee joined by several Whites argued for applying the same rating standards as were applied to the White colleges. Their reasoning was that no other major accrediting agency had adopted the procedure. More importantly, double standards would not facilitate the unconditional admission of African American students to graduate programs. The view of the second group prevailed.

Nonetheless, the Southern Association chose to employ different standards when rating African American schools and colleges as opposed to the White colleges of the region. The class "A" rating indicated that an African American college met the same standards as applied to the White colleges of the region. The class "B" rating indicated that while aspects of its program were commendable, the African American college failed to meet one or more of the standards applied to the White colleges of the region. What Thompson found especially troubling was that the association class "B" rating was allegedly the equivalent of its class "A" rating. Theoretically, either rating qualified a graduate for unconditional admission to graduate study. After 18 months of research into the practice, Thompson found that graduate schools only admitted without condition the graduates of the three African Americans colleges that had achieved the association class "A" rating.

He argued that the class "B" rating was "confusing, misleading and unnecessary," and recommended its elimination. Differentiated standards were a disincentive to engaging in the study, sacrifice, and effort necessary for meeting more exacting performance standards. In practice, differentiated standards were deceptive; graduates of class "B" colleges did not gain unconditional admission to graduate programs. Moreover, the association did not apply the class "B" rating to either the African American or White secondary schools. While applying differentiated standards to the African American junior colleges, the association applied one uniform standard to the White junior colleges in the region. For Thompson, racially differentiated standards stemmed from the same premises as those that sought to justify racial segregation.

In Thompson's view, differentiated ratings not only retarded the development of the African American colleges; they eroded the standards and authority of the Southern Association of Colleges and Secondary

Schools. Why did the association refuse to endorse "nonmember White colleges" for their failure to meet one or more standard, Thompson asked. Yet, its class "B" rating implied an endorsement of African American colleges for their failure to meet one or more rating standard. According to Thompson, the North Central Association and Middle States Association applied uniform accreditation standards to all colleges and universities in their regions without detriment to the African American colleges. By eliminating the class "B" rating, the Southern Association of Colleges and Secondary Schools would render an even "greater service to Negro education," he argued.

"The Education of Subject and Underprivileged Peoples" (January 1934)

A major theme of history was the conquest, domination, and exploitation of weaker people by those that were politically, economically, or technologically stronger, Thompson wrote. Because of the imperialism of England, Europe, the United States, and Japan, economically or politically subordinated people comprised approximately one-half of the world's population. Despite the progress represented by the reduction of slavery, Thompson argued that social Darwinism encouraged and stimulated "the policy and practice of exploitation"(p. 2). Social Darwinism provided the rationale for either neglecting the education of underprivileged or subject people or providing an education designed for expediting their exploitation.

"Agitation [by] humanitarians" and "the principle of self-determination," which Woodrow Wilson championed at the conclusion of World War I, created a "more humane definition of the relationship between exploiter and the exploited," in Thompson's view. He argued that implicit in the "principle of trusteeship" was the recognition of the right of colonial peoples to self-determination. Moreover, for "the principle of trusteeship" to become operative it was necessary for the function of education to be that of preparing colonial peoples for self-government. Thompson noted a wide gulf existed between agreement in principle and actual practice. He agreed that the policy of fostering division and dependence was better suited to the imperialists' ambitions and interest in the continued confiscation of others' wealth, land, and labor.

Thompson argued that the basic problem confronting African Americans and subject peoples throughout the world was fundamentally the same. Neither could practice freely the rights and responsibilities that were theoretically available to them. According to Thompson, an alert and enlightened world opinion among the oppressed as well as their allies was the only safeguard for preventing their continued oppression and "the violation of the contract implicit in the principle of trusteeship" (p. 3). Yet, he viewed many African Americans as ignorant of or oblivious to the exploitation of other oppressed peoples. Moreover, many subject and oppressed people were as unenlightened to their common self-interest by being ignorant of or indifferent to African Americans' oppression. This shared ignorance and indifference was a barrier to the development of alliances for gaining leverage through "concerted protest or action" (p. 3). Their mutual indifference to the oppression they shared hindered the development of "an alert and enlightened world opinion" in Thompson's view (p. 3). A world opinion that allowed the continued exploitation of any particular oppressed group encouraged the exploitation of all oppressed people, he asserted. The world was dynamic and increasingly interdependent in his view.

Thompson criticized many African Americans' unbridled individualism and materialism and their surrender to what he characterized as "the philosophy of escape" (p. 3). In his view, in American society the improvement of group status was the most reliable means for improving individual status. Thompson argued "If [African Americans] are to improve their status as an oppressed group, they must be interested in and work for the improvement of oppressed peoples the world over" (p. 4).

Three reasons compelled Thompson to design the January 1934 *Journal* quarterly for a comprehensive discussion of the education of underprivileged and subject people. Although the problem of oppression was at different stages of solution throughout the world, it was fundamentally the same the world over, he contended. The realization that they were part of a worldwide struggle might encourage African Americans to renew their courage and their opposition to injustice, discrimination, and segregation. Thompson believed African Americans might find inspirational the courage and example of resistance of other people who continued to struggle despite experiencing even more brutal forms of oppression, control, and exploitation. The discussion might inspire African Americans to engage in the "persistent and insistent fight to be allowed to participate in and contribute to the culture of the country on equal terms with any other American citizen," he wrote (p. 4). That was the only goal a self-respecting people would deign to pursue, he contended.

"Investing in Negro Brains" (April 1935)

In December 1934, Professor Paul A. Witty and Martin D. Jenkins, a graduate student of Witty and protégé of Thompson, discovered an African American girl in Chicago with an I.Q. of 200. For Thompson, the significance of Witty and Jenkins's discovery was that it provided concrete evidence that the "range of intelligence" among African Americans was as high as the "[range of intelligence] among other racial groups" (p. 153). Moreover, Witty and Jenkins's discovery provided evidence refuting the contentions of some psychologists that African Americans were mentally inferior to Whites because there was no known case of an African American who had tested in "the highest I.Q. range," Thompson wrote (p. 153).

It was very significant that the young African American girl lived and attended school in Chicago all her life, Thompson argued. The above-average environment and school facilities of Chicago were conducive to the development of superior intelligence, he contended. He estimated the chances statistically of a person having an "I.Q. of 200 or higher [were] 1:1,000,000" (p. 153).

According to Thompson, researchers had made only a "few, sporadic efforts to discover gifted [African American] children" (p. 153). He knew of only four studies on the subject; of the four studies, only two received wider distribution through publication. Witty and Jenkins's work established the range of intelligence of African Americans was as high as other racial groups. Therefore, in Thompson's opinion, it was not essential to expend energy and resources searching for African Americans with an I.Q. of 200 or higher. Instead, African American researchers and educators should focus upon identifying and training the "very superior" African American children who possessed an I.Q. of 125 or higher. In Thompson's estimation, only 3% of the U.S. population would be categorized as having an I.Q. of 125 or higher. Nationwide, at least 1 million school children would meet or exceed this criterion according to conservative estimates. Of these 1 million school children, approximately 50,000 to 75,000 school children would be African Americans, Thompson asserted.

Thompson declared a major limitation hindering African American progress and development was African Americans' most talented potential leaders remained "buried, undeveloped and unused" (p. 154). Too few ministers, lawyers, physicians, and teachers from whom African Americans selected leaders were "very superior" in terms of intelligence, he noted. In fact, Thompson claimed a major obstacle hindering the development of the African American community was that African American leaders had "more than their *necessary* share of incompetence" (p. 154).

While there were more than enough gifted African American youth to fill every seat at every African American college and professional school in the United States, less than one-quarter of the 25,000 African American undergraduates and graduate students in 1935 had an I.Q. of 125 or higher, Thompson argued. He wondered, had African Americans made the best use of their educational facilities? Moreover, he questioned whether racial and national progress was imperiled by training average students when students of superior intelligence were available.

According to Thompson, identifying and educating gifted children would prove a boon to the African American community and the United States as it had for Japan. He suggested that African Americans undertake two steps immediately to remedy the problem. First, they should develop comprehensive "machinery" or methods for identifying all African American students who possessed an I.Q. of 125 or higher. Canvassing and testing African American high school seniors before graduation was one means for accomplishing this objective, he suggested. Second, African Americans and the administrators and trustees at the African American colleges should raise the money necessary to ensure that every gifted African American student could attend college regardless of family income. Every year African Americans should make a significant investment in Negro talent. Because there was no substitute for superior intelligence, the significant and systematic investment in African American youth of superior intelligence was an important means for improving African Americans' socioeconomic and political status, he asserted.

Endnotes

1. Du Bois, W. E. B. (1903/1990). *The Souls of Black Folk.* New York: Vintage Books.
2. Thompson, Charles. H. (1940). "The Educational and Administrative Re-organization of Hampton Institute," *Journal of Negro Education* 9 (April): 139.
3. Logan, Rayford W. (1969). *Howard University: The First Hundred Years, 1867–1967.* New York: New York University Press.
4. Du Bois, W. E. B. *The Souls of Black Folk.* See, especially, "Chronology," 193–217.
5. Locke, Alain. (1925/2004). "Enter the New Negro," *Survey Graphic Harlem Number.* Available online at *http://etext.virginia.edu/harlemlLocEnteF.html* (22 October 2004).
6. Dr. Michael R. Winston, personal interview, Silver Spring, Maryland, 17 April 1996.
7. Thompson, Charles H. (1932). "Is There an Oversupply of Negro Teachers?" *Journal of Negro Education* 1 (October): 343–6.
8. Meadows, Doris M. W. (1984). "Creed of Caste: Journalism and the Race Question during the Progressive Era, 1900–1914." PhD dissertation, New York University.
9. Franklin, John Hope. (1947/1967). *From Slavery to Freedom, A History of Negro Americans.* (3rd ed.). New York: Alfred A. Knopf.
10. Fultz, G. Michael. (1987). "'Agitate then, Brother': Education in the Black monthly periodical press, 1900–1939," Ed. D. dissertation, Harvard University; Horton, Ann. (1991). "History of the 'Quarterly Review of Higher Education Among Negroes,' 1933–1969," PhD dissertation, Loyola University of Chicago; Urban, Wayne. (1992). *Black Scholar: Horace Mann Bond, 1904–1972.* Athens, GA: University of Georgia Press.
11. Thompson, Charles H. (1935). "Coordination of National Organizations." *Journal of Negro Education* 4 (April): 155–8.
12. "Black History Month spotlight—American Teachers Association: The story of the ATA and NEA." Available online at *http://www.nea.org/events/ATA.html#history* (22 October 2004).
13. Franklin, Dr. John Hope, personal interview by telephone, 21 June 1996.
14. Franklin, John Hope. *From Slavery to Freedom, A History of Negro Americans.*
15. Anderson, James D. (1988). *The Education of Blacks in the South, 1860–1935.* Chapel Hill: University of North Carolina Press, 186,202–3,260–1; Bond, Horace Mann. (1934/1966). *Education of the Negro in the American Social Order.* New York: Octagon Books, Inc. 201–2.
16. Frazier, E. Franklin. (1997). *The Black Bourgeoisie.* New York: Simon and Schuster.
17. Locke, Alain. (1925/2004). "Enter the New Negro," *Survey Graphic Harlem Number.* Available online at *http://etext.virginia.edu/harlem/LocEnteF.html* (22 October 2004).
18. Winston, Michael R. (1971). "Through the Back Door: Academic Racism and the Negro Scholar in Historical Perspective," *Daedalus: the Journal of the American Academy of Arts and Sciences,* (Summer): 678–719.
19. Winston, Michael R. (1971). "Through the Back Door."
20. Ibid.
21. Ibid.; Logan, Rayford W. (1969). *Howard University: The First Hundred Years, 1867–1967.*
22. Dr. Rachel Weddington, personal interview, New York City, 12 August 1996.
23. Wright, Stephen J., Thompson, Charles H. (1979). "Founder and Seminal Editor-in-Chief of the Journal of Negro Education," *Journal of Negro Education,* 48 (Fall): 447–8; "Dr. C. H. Thompson, Dies, Dean Emeritus at Howard." *The Washington Post,* 23 January 1980. p. C4.
24. Who's Who in American Education questionnaire dated 26 December 1957, Howard University Moorland–Spingarn Research Center, School of Education, Box 1894, Folder: Journal of Negro Education, Thompson, Charles H., Biographical Material.

25. Who's Who in American Education questionnaire dated 26 December 1957, Howard University Moorland–Spingarn Research Center, School of Education, Box 1894, Folder: Journal of Negro Education, Thompson, Charles H., Biographical Material.

26. Newby, James E. (1974). "Equality of Educational Opportunity: Content Analysis of Six Selected Negro Authors, 1960–1970," EdD dissertation, University of Southern California; Jones, Faustine C. (1980). "In Memoriam: Dean Charles H. Thompson (1896–1980)," *Journal of Negro Education Forty-Nine*, (Spring): 113–4. "Dr. C. H. Thompson, Dies, Dean Emeritus at Howard," *Washington Post*, 23 January 1980: p. C4.

27. Newby, James E. (1974). "Equality of Educational Opportunity: Content Analysis of Six Selected Negro Authors, 1960–1970." Jones, Faustine C. (1980). "In Memoriam: Dean Charles H. Thompson (1896–1980)."

28. Logan, Rayford W. (1969). *Howard University: The First Hundred Years, 1867–1967.*

29. Bardolph, Richard. (1959). *The Negro Vanguard.* New York: Rinehart.

30. Franklin, John Hope. (1947/1967). *From Slavery to Freedom, A History of Negro Americans.*

31. Kluger, Richard. (1977). *Simple Justice: The History of* Brown v. Board of Education *and Black America's Struggle for Equality.* New York: Knopf.

32. Thompson, Charles H. (1932). "Why a Journal of Negro Education?" *Journal of Negro Education* 1 (April): 1–4.

33. Ibid.

34. Dr. Carroll L. Miller, personal interviews, Washington, D.C., 23 January 1996.

35. Dr. Michael R. Winston, personal interview, Silver Spring, Maryland, 17 April 1996.

36. Green, Constance McL. (1967). *The Secret City: A History of Race Relations in the Nation's Capital.* Princeton: Princeton University Press.

37. Dr. Michael R. Winston, personal interview, Silver Spring, Maryland, 17 April 1996.

38. Dr. Michael R. Winston, personal interview, Silver Spring, Maryland, 17 April 1996.

39. Thompson, Charles H. (1932). "The Problem of Negro Higher Education," *Journal of Negro Education* 1 October: 419–34.

Chapter 38

The Wellspring of Resistance:
Black Women's Collective Activism

Gayle T. Tate

Much of the contemporary Civil Rights Movement located Black women's political participation at the epicenter of that movement. In varied ways of direct action, Black female Civil Rights activists sustained that movement and simultaneously transformed it into a movement for social change. While, indeed, the role that Black female political activists played in the Civil Rights Movement emerged as a central core of collective action, their activism was built upon centuries of struggle originating in slave communities in the New World. As part of an aggrieved population in their continuous struggle for liberation and civil equality, African American women activists understood the role of collective action and unity as well as the critical need of political allies in projected struggle. Not only have African American movements matured over centuries with political goals that utilize collective action as its galvanizing force, they have also shaped much of the tactics and strategies of political protest in contemporary society. Dennis Chong, in his book, *Collective Action and the Civil Rights Movement*, notes this influence:

> The modern civil rights movement is probably the quintessential example of public-spirited collective action in our time. Not only did it spark radical changes in American society, it also served in subsequent years as the inspiration and model for a host of new public concerns. The student movement, the peace movement, the women's movement, the homosexual rights movement, and other social movements are all to a significant extent riding on the coattails of the civil rights movement.[1]

The epicenter of Black women's political struggle in slave communities was their collective action—that is, their planned activities thwarting oppression and undermining the slave system.[2] Collective action became most noticeable in female labor units under plantation slavery. This common praxis emerged both as vehicles in their labor units as well as their common struggles and strategies for freedom. In part, collective action served as a training ground in intergenerational cohesion between slave women and slave girls, where teens became conscious of struggles that impact the lives of slave women. Collective action could also be the strategies that were planned as slave women rearranged labor assignments to protect lactating women from punishment. Episodic rebellions, truancy, and escapes also involved collective action for support, participation, and empowerment. "Many people, when they are suffering and they see their people suffering, they want direct participation. They want to be able to say, what I'm doing here gives me power and is going to help us change this business. . . . "[3] Black women's collective action was reinforced by the African-centeredness of slave communities as well as the limited plantation mobility that circumscribed their lives.

Despite the vicissitudes of slavery, the material realities of the system fostered the development of Black women's political consciousness and activism in the form of protest, challenges, and retaliation to the system. As the institutionalization of slavery gained broad currency in the efforts to promote cash crop commodity production, simultaneously a counter force of resistance also formed among slave women. These women engaged in all types of resistance. Survival as a framework for resistance suggested a protracted struggle of word and action as well as the tedious creation of political space where struggle can flourish. "In a system such as slavery, survival for the oppressed group was the greatest form of resistance."[4] While some slaves saw their freedom struggle tied to their immediate liberation from slavery, others saw their freedom quest commemorating their African past. "I had always heard it talked among the slaves, that we ought not to be held as slaves; that our forefathers and mothers were stolen from Africa, where they were free men and free women."[5]

Patricia Hill-Collins, notes in *Black Feminist Thought: Knowledge, Consciousness, and the Politics of Empowerment*, that Black slave women created a "culture of resistance" that permeated life in slave communities.[6] Resistance was one of the ways that slaves reaffirmed their human dignity, clarified their role in the struggle, and spearheaded collective action. Frequently intertwined in slave women's labor activity, resistance was either in their involuntary labor as agriculturalists or their voluntary labor as caretakers, caring for family members or other members of the slave community. It was in these activities that slave women could claim agency over their labor and their lives and reinforce the discovery of their own being on a daily basis. Slave women also employed their role as cultural transmitters planting seeds of resistance in their children. This critical part of the socialization of their children was also a reflection of the love that slave women had for their children. Historian Wilma King comments that slave mothers utilized varied methods in protecting their children against slavery. One slave, Lucy Delany, recalls the early teachings of her mother to her and her sister about escaping to freedom. "By the time Lucy was twelve years old, she planned to run away and was forever on the alert for a chance to escape."[7] This idea of defiance against oppression was planted early in slave children and many sought opportunities to escape to freedom.

Insurgency, a form of dramatic rebellion, created both renewed courage in the slave quarters as well as new waves of brutal reprisals on the part of planters; these upheavals, as well as social and labor disruptions were critical to the development of a freedom ethos in slave communities. Slaves took pride in passing down stories of collective resistance. A former Georgia slave, Leah Garret, recalled that a slave couple with three children survived for 7 years in a nearby cave because "diffunt folks helped keep 'em in food."[8] Female slave networks, fostering the environment of survival and resistance in slave communities, were formed along intergenerational lines where girls and women of all ages shared common labor assignments. But these female collectives were also opportunities to transmit survival stories and slave women's experiences to prepare slave girls to cope with their approaching maturity, to protect and nurture lactating women, to plan and implement tactics and strategies of work stoppage, sabotage of agricultural production, destruction of farm equipment, truancy, to carry vital news of the selling of slaves, and to prepare and implement escape plans. These female units engendered female solidarity and labor distribution and, sometimes, redistribution to meet the exigencies of a labor detail.[9] One of its other functions was to serve as centers for an evolving political consciousness to take shape.[10] For these oppressed slave women, most of their activism centered on their varied roles in female collectives, which legitimized their right to challenge their enslavement. Overall, the freedom ethos nurtured the members of the slave quarters to transcend the material forces of oppression, contour a protracted struggle of survival, shape strategies and endless plans for freedom, and hope ultimately that one prevailed.

In freedom, these female collectives will be transformed into mutually benevolent societies, community associations, and church groups, which were the heart and soul of community activism, the abolitionist struggle, as Black female activists became an organizing force in Black communities.

Free Black Women, Vision and Abolitionism

As free Blacks migrated to Northern and Southern cities, they developed communities that afforded them the opportunities to develop as a free people. But their freedom in antebellum America afforded them quasi-free status at best. Freedom, for Blacks, was deeply mired in the murkiness of a quasi-free status of second-class citizenship. Blacks were encumbered with legal restrictions, racial customs, social proscriptions, and laws that became increasingly more fluid in relegating African Americans to a permanent subordinate position in society. Such factors as Southern slavery or the gradual abolition of slavery in Northern states, the brisk volume of kidnapping of free Blacks for reenslavement, which was a perennial problem for free Blacks, and the illicit slave trade in the North and South made free Blacks vulnerable on a daily basis. This persistent climate of antipathy reinforced White supremacy and, in contrast, a pervasive Black inferiority. This caste system where White were accorded first-class citizenship and Blacks second-class citizenship would remain an integral component of American democracy, providing a sharp contrast to the egalitarian ethos permeating the rapidly developing new nation. Coupled with this social degradation of Blacks was the lessening of economic anxiety for Whites who saw in Southern slavery and Northern industrial capitalism economic protection against fair competition and access to prosperity.

Within Black communities, free Black women, particularly in Northern industrial "freedom cities" Boston, Philadelphia, and New York, comprised the majority of the free Black population. These Black women had all sorts of prior legal status, which made them particularly vulnerable in cities where bounty hunters made a living capturing Blacks for reenslavement. Some Black women were born free, while others were recently manumitted. While some former slave women had bought their freedom and some escaped from bondage, both used the cities as a subterfuge and sanctuary. Regardless of their former or present legal status, the common thread that bound all of these women together was slavery, the threat of reenslavement, the daily taunts of hoodlums in the streets, and daily forms of racial discrimination that were all too commonplace living in urban centers. Class and gender cleavages were also emerging in the industrial centers, stagnating Black women's economic development. In the North, as White women who had recently got factory jobs shunned Black women, they were relegated to domestic work. Ironically, in Southern industrial cities, like Richmond, Virginia, for example, Black women were not only domestic laborers but worked in tobacco factories and iron and flour mills, just as they had done during slavery. But the stark reality of their labor remained. Despite the labor expansion for Whites under nascent capitalism, Black female laborers were relegated to the bottommost tier of the economic ladder where they remained throughout much of the next century. In a sense, nascent capitalism and slavery limited Black women's labor development.

Even though their wages were meager, Black women's earnings were integral to Black community life, and their wages and activism gave most communities their vibrancy. By the antebellum era, Blacks in Richmond, Virginia, began to purchase their own churches, pooling monies that urban slaves and free Blacks earned in "overtime work" from their factory jobs.[11] The Black church was at the helm of Black community life, and although the Black male hierarchy dominated the ecclesiastical leadership, Black women provided critical leadership in church societies, fund-raisers, and prayers groups, and at times challenged the Black male ministerial leadership. Evangelists like Jarena Lee, Elizabeth, and Zilpha Elaw, believing that they had a divine right to preach, began to challenge ecclesiastical sexism in the early 1800s. Organizing under the umbrella of collective action, Northern free Black women organized a plethora of mutual benefit societies, associations, and ad hoc community committees, which in some instances were ancillaries to Black churches, and led to the spearheading of community social and economic improvement. Black women were conscious as they formed community groups, which had overlapping purposes and memberships, to submerge the fact that they espoused a political commitment to abolitionism. While in the South, Black men and women had organized illegal "secret societies," Northern societies functioned in the open but maintained a dual purpose that was indicative of their quasi-free status. For example, the Ladies Literary Society of New York embraced a dual mission. On one hand, they demonstrate a commitment to self-improvement on the surface, while on the other hand, they continued their subterranean commitment to political change.

Women in this society demonstrated their political commitment by furnishing monies to sustain the Black newspaper the Colored American, *an institutional voice for Black communities. The society also consistently channeled funds to support David Ruggles for harboring fugitives and supplying them with food, clothing, shelter, safe passage, and, when necessary, temporary employment.[12]*

Free Black women kept faith with enslaved Blacks by centering their political commitment on militant abolitionism. Militant abolitionism, the immediate emancipation of the slaves, was at the heart of the political struggle in Black communities. With their community activism, Black activists were able to create the infrastructure of the abolitionist movement. The two-prong approach of abolitionism of eradicating slavery and simultaneously uplifting the Black community was the galvanizing force of the movement to emancipate the slaves, and both issues, as far as Black abolitionists were concerned, were kept at the center of the protest movement.[13] Although Black female abolitionists belonged to predominantly Black antislavery societies, like the active Manhattan Anti-Slavery Society, they also joined biracial antislavery organizations. In the predominantly Black antislavery societies, Black female activists could focus on both themes of abolitionism, where the emphasis on community improvement was muted in the biracial antislavery societies. However, Black female abolitionists frequently used their collective strategies on managerial boards to alter the perspectives and agenda of biracial societies by raising Black community concerns. Maria W. Stewart, Hetty Reckless, Hetty Burr, Sarah Forten, Margaretta Forten, Harriet Forten, Sarah Mapps Douglass, Susan Paul, Frances Ellen Watkins

Harper, Julia A. J. Foote, and Nancy Prince all belonged to biracial antislavery organizations where, in some instances, most particularly as members of the Philadelphia Female Anti-Slavery Society, operated as a collective voting body to get operating funds for Black community activities.[14]

Black female abolitionists largely saw a two-prong complementary praxis of abolitionist struggle. On one hand, they participated in biracial antislavery organizations where they promoted lectures, petitions to end slavery, fund-raisers to sustain the organization, and became national and international spokespersons for the cause. Sarah Parker Remond and Frances Ellen Watkins Harper were well-known abolitionists on the lecture circuit. On the other hand, female abolitionists engaged in subversive activities that directly undermine the slave institution and functioned as an illegal operation.

> *This dual approach to abolitionism in black women's organizations created a vehicle for the covert direction of black female activists. This covert direction was the illegal participation of black female activists in dramatic slave rescues, vigilance committees, protests, raising monies, and the multifarious operations on the Underground Railroad.*[15]

The question of liberty for African Americans was mired in contradictions. As the nation proclaimed liberty and equality for all people, they, as well as other people of color and women, were left out of this political process. And Black Americans occupied a dubious legal status at best. If they were enslaved, they were chattel property and dehumanized as human beings and forced to create wealth and prosperity for the planter class. If they were free, their legal status was tenuous and they were, in reality, segregated from the larger society. Looking beyond the republican ideals of liberty, which came with its own inherent contradictions particularly when it concerned the freedom and franchise for African Americans, Black female abolitionists, alongside of Black male abolitionists, believed that the liberation of their people from oppression constituted the first act of liberty.

In many ways, the abolitionist movement had been the proving ground for the women's movement, and the political consciousness of Black female activists was refined during that era. Empowered during the antebellum era, Black female activists participated in both the abolitionist movement and suffrage campaign, just as White female activists did, and continued to struggle for the ballot until the passage of the 19th Amendment in 1920. For Black women, both movements were intertwined and proved to be a journey of self-discovery. And Black female abolitionists, like Maria W. Stewart, were really in the forefront of that struggle. Indeed, Stewart distinguished herself by arguing for women's equality, as well as identifying the organic relationship between slavery, racism, and sexism in the early 1830s before the women's movement was founded in Seneca Falls, New York, in 1848.

Mary Ann Shadd Cary, Sarah Parker Remond, Sojourner Truth, and Frances Ellen Watkins Harper were all abolitionists as well as early Black suffragists and understood that the ballot was intrinsic to their overall struggle for freedom and the advancement of African Americans. Although many White suffragists like Susan B. Anthony came to believe that the vote would be a panacea for all societal maladies, Black male and female suffragists, taking stock of their experiences in American society, believed that the ballot for Black women could transform the legal status of African Americans by bringing about political equality for all African Americans. But the vote for Black women was a force to be reckoned with, and efforts to curtail their suffrage by White suffragists and White male politicians were pervasive. "It soon became evident to White politicians that African American women would resist any attempt to disfranchise Blacks. As a result, White Democratic Party southerners in particular feared the political clout that Republican Party African American females could develop not only for themselves and for their race as a whole, but against the southern Democrats."[16] Thus, the struggle for Black male suffrage in the post-emancipation era and the Black women's struggle for the ballot over several decades were viewed as components of a shared Black struggle and the African American quest for freedom.

As the suffrage campaign picked up steam, it was clear to Black female suffragists that the growing conservative postures of the National American Women Suffrage Association were racist and sexist strategies to exclude Black women from the vote.[17] As the Black women's club movement spearheaded its broad-based initiatives (National Association of Colored Women)—largely through such leaders as Ida B. Wells-Barnett, Mary Church Terrell, Adella Hunt Logan, Josephine St. Pierre Ruffin, and Fannie Barrier Williams—a clear political and social program emerged as they championed the ballot. Black women organized petition drives, block canvassing, fund-raisers, and voting education seminars to educate the Black public around citizenship and to politicize the importance of Black female suffrage in Black communities. Alongside Black men, Black women worked toward the passage of the Anthony Amendment, which would guarantee all women the right to vote; it had become clear to them that if they were not vigilant and continued to keep the issue of Black female suffrage before the public and lobby the Congressional legislature around the issue, that Black women would be excluded from the federal amendment. Both Mary Church Terrell, then-president of the National Association of Colored Women, and Walter White, president of the NAACP, were of one mind that White suffragists would "exclude Black women from the franchise if possible." Mary Church Terrell reported to the NAACP that White suffragists in Florida "discriminated against Black women in their attempts to recruit support for the campaign."[18] Despite the contentious battles between the two camps—White suffragists and White male politicians and Black men and women—Black women were enfranchised in 1920. "After the passage of the Nineteenth Amendment in 1920, Black women formed and participated in voter education leagues throughout the country and especially in the South, where opposition to African American women voters was greatest."[19] The opposition to Black female suffrage was coupled with the opposition to Black male suffrage, and it became a lighting rod on one hand for segregationists to deny Blacks their civil rights and, on the other, for African Americans to champion the cause of social justice. The erosion of civil rights for African Americans became commonplace by the 1930s. By the 1950s, the struggle for the ballot had entered a new phase and a new generation had to once more take up the gauntlet, in spite of the 15th and the 19th Amendments, for the disfranchised.

Black Women and Social Justice

The political consciousness that was so much a part of Black women's activism flowed into the Civil Rights Movement, where Blacks played pivotal roles. Civil rights activist, Ella Baker, believed that the role of Black women in the Civil Rights Movement was tied to their roles in the Black church. Baker observed that "the movement of the fifties and sixties were carried largely by women, since it came largely out of church groups. It was sort of second nature to women to play a supportive role. How many made a conscious decision on the basis of the larger goals, how many on the basis of habit pattern, I don't know. But it's true that the number of women who carried the movement is much larger than that of men."[20] As these Black female activists transformed themselves into agents of social change, they also transformed the dynamics of the Civil Rights Movement because Black women knew firsthand the realities of White southern resistance, violence, and economic reprisals. Believing that Black suffrage was tied to their socioeconomic conditions, Black female activists mobilized, covertly and overtly, local communities around voter registration and their legitimate right to social justice. Black female civil rights activists, as indeed all movement activists, claimed both the national and international stage in placing the grievances of African Americans in the political arena.

Black women functioned as "bridge leaders," mobilizing the disparate people of the community together for collective protest and political participation.[21] Forming this cohesive unit of an aggrieved population was very much in keeping with their role in slave communities, where networking proved essential for subversive activities. Contemporary female civil rights activists came to the movement with varied political and social experiences and talents. Some had long protest histories, like Rosa Parks, who had been secretary for the NAACP and its youth advisor for over a decade when she was arrested in 1955.[22] Others, like Ethel T. Overby, had more than three decades as a social activist. Becoming an educator and ultimately the first Black female principal of a public school in Richmond, Virginia, Overby used her role as educator in the cause of civil rights by incorporating voter education for Black children and adults as a part of the curriculum.[23] This, she asserted, was the responsibility of citizenship. "Overby carried out her program of citizenship education by staging mock elections and educating Blacks about the poll tax, and by stressing the importance of Blacks voting in large numbers. She was convinced that if Blacks voted in large numbers, they could alter their unbearable conditions."[24] Still others were like Fannie Lou Hamer from Rulesville, Mississippi, who reflected the "soul" of the movement, and Annie Raines of Lee County, Georgia, and Unita Blackwell of Mayersville, Mississippi, who were all indigenous "bridge leaders" linking the local community to the larger movement around the citizenship issue of voter registration and mobilization.[25] In doing so, these leaders not only transformed themselves but changed the interior dynamics of the mass movement.

Disfranchisement of Blacks was not only the legal barrier to the exercise of their civil rights but embraced the inherent inferiority of the race as well. For them, citizenship schools, voter registration classes, and voting was essential to the larger political context of civil equality for African Americans. Thus, disfranchisement was viewed as one of the last vestiges of legal segregation and to dismantle it was the first step toward full citizenship. For African Americans, circumscribed by social segregation, voting proved far more complicated than it was for White citizens. Former President Lyndon B. Johnson, who signed the Civil Rights Act of 1964 and the Voting Rights Act of 1965, spoke on the entrenched White supremacy that denied Blacks their citizenship rights:

> *Every device of which human ingenuity is capable has been used to deny this right. The Negro citizen may go to register only to be told that the day is wrong, or the hour is late, or the official in charge is absent. And if he persists and if he manages to present himself to the registrar, he may be disqualified because he did not spell out his middle name or because he abbreviated a word on the application. And if he manages to fill out an application he is given a test. The registrar is the sole judge of whether he passes this test. He may be asked to recite the entire Constitution, or explain the most complex provisions of state laws. And even a college degree cannot be used to prove that he can read and write.[26]*

And there were more violent reprisals for Blacks who attempted to vote. For one thing, Blacks faced threats, humiliation, beatings, continuous harassment, and death as well as loss of job, future employment, and home for attempting to register to vote. For another, the mechanics of exclusion were everpresent, such as the literacy test, the daunting examination of reading, writing, and interpreting the federal and state constitutions, all designed to bar Blacks from political participation. Failing to enforce the mechanism of voting registration, violent reprisals that followed were threats of intimidation. When an individual attempted to register, the violent reprisals usually put the entire family at risk.

To facilitate the process of citizenship and enable African Americans to actively participate in the American body politic, educational centers were established. Major civil rights organizations like SNCC (Student Nonviolent Coordinating Committee), and alternately SCLC (Southern Christian Leadership Conference) and movement centers like Highlander Folk School established citizenship schools. These workshops or citizenship schools had a four-step process that included the development of literacy, voter registration, voting and active political participation in the body politic, and the development of indigenous Black leadership.[27] Septima Poinsette Clark, who established the citizenship school at Highlander Folk School in Monteagle, Tennessee, and under the aegis of SCLC, others throughout the Southeastern states, was particularly responsible for their pervasive influence in the movement.

But citizenship schools were houses of resistance and intrinsically more than what they appeared on the face. In a sense, these community participants were being trained in the tactics, strategies, and techniques of protest and resistance. These educational centers were designed to galvanize and mobilize an aggrieved population to fight the White political power structure for a redistribution of resources and force a shared power arrangement in the body politic. The right to petition and the right of peaceful assembly on the part of Blacks, for example, were both viewed as lighting rods in the South to the White citizens fearful that Blacks were violating the social etiquette of segregation and disenfranchisement indicative of the region. Whereas education was the framework for citizenship instruction, these citizenship schools were also the first steps to Black political and social empowerment.

The political maturity of Black female civil rights activists was honed by the collective action that spearheaded and contoured the movement's development and momentum. While Black women primarily functioned as "bridge leaders" and thus constituted a critical part of the movement's leadership, they also provided the organizational infrastructure as well. "Certain women operated as network centers, mobilizing existing social networks around the organizing goals, mediating conflicts, conveying information, coordinating activity. . . ."[28] This new generation of Black female civil rights activists provided much of the rank and file in maintaining the protest lines to desegregate stores and leading and sustaining protests in cities and towns until conflict resolution was obtained. For example, the boycott of Thalhimer's Department Store in 1960 in Richmond, Virginia, was maintained by Black women and college students from Virginia Union University. "Therefore, women walking the picket lines in Richmond seems to be consistent with the notion of gendered roles in the civil rights movement. Older men were frequently absent from the picket lines because they had to work. However, those women who were professionals also had to work."[29]

The transformation of Black women's political consciousness via struggle is noted in the Civil Rights Movement. Some of these female activists had peered beyond the Civil Rights Movement as a national struggle and instead viewed it as an integral aspect of the international human rights struggle of all oppressed people throughout the diaspora. By the early 1970s, Fannie Lou Hamer had embraced the idea of universal suffrage and the broader democratic ideals of freedom, justice, and equality. In 1971, when Fannie Lou Hamer cast her hat in the ring to run for state senator of Mississippi, she noted the breadth and depth of her philosophy and political consciousness. At this stage, Hamer declared that she was fighting "for the liberation of all people, because nobody's free until everybody's free. . . . I've passed equal rights; I'm fighting for human rights."[30] Similar to Fannie Lou Hamer's broadness of social and political vision, Unita Blackwell also embraced a larger philosophical vision of Blacks in the diaspora. Blackwell, a civil rights activist who became the first Black female mayor in Mayersville, Mississippi, where she had previously been denied the right to vote, argued that Blacks had "a sense of destiny with the vast majority of colored people all over the world [and] were becoming conscious of their power and the role they must play in the world."[31]

The strident criticism of the 1950s and 1960s by the movement's detractors, the need to live with daily violence and attend funerals of those that had fought and died in the movement, and contending with an entrenched power structure in the South that would not yield were factors in honing the political development of Black female activists. In sharp contrast to their detractors who believed that there was no need for a Civil Rights Movement or that the movement itself was initiated and sustained by outside agitators or communist influence, these Black women confronted the internal contradictions that were inherent in American democracy on a daily basis. For many of these women, the material realities as well as the ongoing exchanges with an intellectual cadre of activists that consistently challenged racial exclusion in American society also shaped their consciousness. Ruby Doris Smith Robinson, one of the more powerful leaders and administrators in SNCC during the early- to mid-1960s, looked beyond racism in identifying Black oppression. In her biography of Robinson, *Soon We Will Not Cry*, Cynthia Briggs Fleming asserts that Robinson also looked beyond race in identifying oppression of African Americans. "On the contrary, she reasoned, racism spawned economic oppression, which, in turn, reinforced African American powerlessness."[32]

Certainly, the political vision of Ella Baker was grounded in the working-class struggles that were taking place all over the world. Baker, whose activism spanned more than five decades, brought a wealth of social and political experience to the movement. A seasoned activist, Baker's philosophical worldview of universal humanism rested not only upon the Christian teachings of her youth but the radical intellectual and political thought of the 1930 and 1940s that were so pervasive in New York City where she lived as a young adult. Baker's sense of political mission undoubtedly led her to become one of the co-founders of the organization, In Friendship, in New York City in 1956, a group that concentrated their efforts on providing monies for the Southern Civil Rights Movement. By the late 1950s and early 1960s, her mission had taken her to the South, where she played a founding role in SCLC and SNCC. In the former organization, Baker coordinated the Crusade for Citizenship, using her vast networking system of Black southerners that she had established throughout the South when she worked for the NAACP in the 1940s. "Following the February 12 meetings the SCLC began implementing the Crusade for Citizenship program. Its basic approach was to organize the movement by mobilizing the masses through preexisting political organizations and churches, coordinated by the SCLC."[33] Working with the latter organization, SNCC activists reflected the grassroots organizing, voter registration drives, and group-centered leadership that typified Baker's radical politics. Her pragmatic approach to grassroots politics shaped a new generation of civil rights activists. Her biographer, Barbara Ransby, in her work, *Ella Baker & the Black Freedom Movement: A Radical Democratic Vision*, comments:

> The patchwork quilt reminds me of how Baker served the movement: identifying the value in people who were raggedy, worn, and a little bit tattered—people who were seen by some as the scraps, the remnants, the discarded ones. In each one, as in each strip of fabric, Ella Baker saw enormous beauty and potential. And, like the quilting tradition itself, her life's work was collective work."[34]

Concluding Note

Much of the African American women's struggle for social justice and equality in American society has been circumscribed by White political and economic domination. These antagonistic struggles have been a part of American life for several centuries and, indeed, elitism, racism, and sexism rest upon the struggle over political and economic power and the profound inability for Americans to redistribute wealth and equality in the society. Thus, the African American women's struggle for social change must be viewed in the context of an aggressive environment that shapes its contentious battles, the terrain of its discourse, and collective activism. Black female political activism, where Black women fought alongside of Black men, was never in a vacuum but drew, in part, on the larger national reform efforts in American society as well as the international struggles for equality and access to political and social resources in the diaspora. In both the 19th and 20th centuries, bridges forged by the struggle for civil rights between the 19th and 20th centuries had been sustained by Black female political activism.

Black female political activism, whether it was during the enslavement period being fought out against the vagaries of cash crop commodity production, during the turbulent early emancipation period that was shaping the nation-state anew, or the chaotic contemporary civil rights period, grew out of a resistance that was honed over centuries of political struggle. In each period, Black women utilized collective action as a primary vehicle of slave or free resistance. Collective action became one of the major ways that Black women organized themselves around their grievances and waged a battle against injustice. This foundation of resistance and subsequent collective action heightened the political awareness and consciousness of Black women in particular and Black communities in general. At all times, this struggle for freedom was a dialectical one, pitting Black protest against White hegemonic power.

Universal suffrage is viewed by African Americans as the bridge to equality, and its future may still be somewhat nebulous. Black female activists who campaign for women's suffrage and their Black male counterparts believe it would expand the boundaries of freedom, justice, and equality for all African Americans. But despite a protracted struggle and measured victories—evinced in the Civil Rights Act of 1957, the Civil Rights Act of 1964, and the Voting Rights Act of 1965 and its renewal in 1982 (albeit supported by President Ronald Reagan with some reluctance)—Black Americans still must wage protest over their voting rights. Once again, in 2007, African Americans will need the Voting Rights Act of 1965 to be renewed in order to continue their suffrage, a basic right of all American citizens. These haunting specters of second-class citizenship still serve to circumscribe the freedom of all Blacks.

Suffrage continues to be a daunting task for African Americans, and their voices have been muted in the American body politic. Hazel N. Norris, a Brooklyn activist, noted: "We were disenfranchised in the 2000 presidential election, and our votes were not counted in 2004."[35] The 2000 presidential elections appeared to be rife with inconsistencies and irregularities. With allegations of voter intimidation, voter fraud, manipulation, and other irregularities circumscribing Black suffrage, African Americans need suffrage protection in Florida and other Southern states as well. Although Florida received national attention and the spotlight, other states demonstrated similar problems. Jonah H. Goldman notes in *Crisis*:

> This is not a problem peculiar to Florida. In fact, according to a study by CalTech and MIT, 4 million to 6 million votes were lost across the nation in 2000. Illinois, South Carolina and Georgia all had higher rates of spoiled and uncounted ballots than Florida did four years ago.[36]

Despite the efforts of activists in the presidential election of November 2004, there were wide discrepancies in the ballot counting in this election as well. Civil rights activists are once again mobilizing nationally to protect the rights of Black voters in the mid-term elections of 2006 so that they can participate in the democratic process. Overwhelmingly, those that were disfranchised in the 2000 election were from minority neighborhoods (and many Black activists believe in the 2004 elections as well) and those that consistently have been underrepresented voting blocs in the electorate. At the heart of Black suffrage, particularly for American society, despite the professed ideals of American democracy, is that Black voters in varied regions throughout the country can determine the local, state, and national electoral outcomes that clearly translate into sustainable political power. The dawning of the new century leaves African Americans with vestiges from the same struggles of citizenship and, concomitantly, Black female activists are a critical necessity.

Endnotes

1. Chong, Dennis. (1991). *Collective Action and the Civil Rights Movement*. Chicago: The University of Chicago Press, 1.
2. Ibid., 1–4.
3. Morris, Aldon D. (1984). *The Origins of the Civil Rights Movement: Black Communities Organizing for Change*. New York: The Free Press, 124.
4. Lerner, Gerda (ed.). (1973). *Black Women in White America: A Documentary History*. New York: Vintage Books, 27.

5. Blassingame, John W. (ed.). (1977). "Narrative of James Curry," in *Slave Testimony: Two Centuries of Letters, Speeches, Interviews, and Autobiographies*. Baton Rouge: Louisiana State University Press, 131.

6. Hill-Collins, Patricia. (1991). *Black Feminist Thought: Knowledge, Consciousness, and the Politics of Empowerment*. New York: Routledge, 10.

7. King, Wilma. (1995). *Stolen Childhood: Slave Youth in Nineteenth Century in America*. Bloomington: Indiana University Press, 120.

8. Rawick, George P. (1978). "Leah Garret, Ex-Slave," in *The American Slave: A Composite Autobiography*. Westport, Conn.: Greenwood Pub. Co., Supplement Series I, Georgia Narratives, Part 2, col. 4, 14–5.

9. White, Deborah Gray. (1985). *Ar'n't I a Woman? Female Slaves in the Plantation South*. New York: W. W. Norton, 119–141.

10. Ibid.; and Wright, Michelle D. (1991). "African American Sisterhood: The Impact of the Female Slave Population on American Political Movements," in *Western Journal of Black Studies* (Spring): 35.

11. Randolph, Lewis A. & Tate, Gayle T. (2003). *Rights for a Season: The Politics of Race, Class, and Gender in Richmond, Virginia*. Knoxville, TN: The University of Tennessee Press, 64–9.

12. Tate, Gayle T. (2003). *Unknown Tongues: Black Women's Political Activism in the Antebellum Era, 1830–1860*. East Lansing, MI: Michigan State University Press, 155; Porter, Dorothy (1936). "The Organized Educational Activities of Negro Literary Societies, 1828–1846," *Journal of Negro Education* 5 (October); and Porter, Dorothy. (1943). "David Ruggles, an Apostle of Human Rights," *Journal of Negro History* 28, no. 1 (January): 23–50.

13. Quarles, Benjamin. (1969). *Black Abolitionists*. New York: Oxford University Press, 49.

14. Sumler-Lewis, Janice. "The Forten-Purvis Women of Philadelphia and the American Anti-Slavery Crusade," *Journal of Negro History* 66, no. 4, 283.

15. Tate, Gayle T. (2003). *Unknown Tongues: Black Women's Political Activism in the Antebellum Era, 1830–1860*, 189.

16. Terborg-Penn, Rosalyn. (1998). *African American Women in the Struggle for the Vote, 1850–1920*. Bloomington, IN: Indiana University Press, 108.

17. Ibid., 56.

18. Ibid., 130.

19. Ibid., 163.

20. Baker, Ella. (1972). "Developing Community Leadership," in *Black Women in White America: A Documentary History*, Gerda Lerner, (ed.). New York: Vintage Books.

21. Robnett, Belinda. (1997). *How Long? How Long?: African-American Women in the Struggle for Civil Rights*. New York: Oxford University Press, 7, 17–32.

22. Morris, Aldon D. (1984). *The Origins of the Civil Rights Movement: Black Communities Organizing for Change*. New York: The Free Press, 51.

23. Randolph, Lewis A. & Tate, Gayle T. (2003). *Rights for a Season: The Politics of Race, Class, and Gender in Richmond, Virginia*. Knoxville, TN: The University of Tennessee Press, 155, 173–4.

24. *Rights for a Season*, 174; and note Ethel Thompson Overby's autobiography, *It's Better to Light a Candle than to Curse the Darkness: The Autobiographical Notes of Ethel Thompson Overby*, Richmond: Ethel Thompson Overby, 1975, 11.

25. Robnett, Belinda. (1997). *How Long? How Long? African American Women in the Struggle for Civil Rights*. New York: Oxford University Press, 146–7.

26. Johnson, Lyndon B. (1965). "The Voting Rights Act Should Be Passed," *Congressional Record*. 89th Congress, 1st session, vol. 3, no. 47 (March 15).

27. McFadden, Grace Jordan. (1993). "Septima P. Clark and the Struggle for Human Rights," in *Women in the Civil Rights Movement: Trailblazers & Torchbearers, 1941–1965*. Vicki Crawford, Jacqueline Rouse, and Barbara Woods (eds.). Bloomington, IN: Indiana University Press, 90–3.

28. Payne, Charles. (1990). "Men Led, but Women Organized: Movement Participation of Women in the Mississippi Delta," in *Women in the Civil Rights Movement: Trailblazers & Torchbearers, 1941–1965*, Vicki L. Crawford, Jacqueline Anne Rouse, and Barbara Woods (eds.). Bloomington, IN: Indiana University Press, 8.

29. Randolph, Lewis A. and Tate, Gayle T. (2003). *Rights for a Season: The Politics of Race, Class, and Gender in Richmond, Virginia.* Knoxville: The University of Tennessee Press, 190–1.

30. Shanahan, Eileen. "Women Organize for Political Power," *New York Times,* 11 July 1971.

31. Carson, Clayborne. (1981). *In Struggle: SNCC and the Black Awakening of the 1960s.* Cambridge, MA: Harvard University Press, 151; and Morrison, Minion K. C. (1987). *Black Political Mobilization: Leadership, Power and Mass Behavior.* New York: State University of New York Press, chapter 4, 95–122.

32. Fleming, Cynthia Briggs. (1998). *Soon We Will Not Cry: The Liberation of Ruby Doris Smith Robinson.* Lanham, Maryland: Rowman & Littlefield Publishers, Inc., 166.

33. Morris, Aldon. (1984). *The Origins of the Civil Rights Movement,* 109.

34. Ransby, Barbara. (2003). *Ella Baker & the Black Freedom Movement: A Radical Democratic Vision.* Chapel Hill, NC: The University of North Carolina Press, 373–4.

35. "Marching to Vote," *New York Amsterdam News,* August 11–August 17, 2005, vol. 96, no. 33, p. 37.

36. Goldman, Jonah H. (2004). "Voters Beware: Efforts to Disenfranchise Democracy Are Alive and Well," *Crisis,* vol. 111/5 (September/October): 14.

Chapter 39

The Unsung Heroism of Ruby Hurley

Allison A. McGevna

The Civil Rights Movement is perhaps the most important social movement in 20th-century America. Indeed, many of its greatest heroes, Martin Luther King, Jr., Medgar Evers, and A. Philip Randolph are a mere handful of names among the men who dedicated themselves to the struggle for equality in the United States. Yet, a great number of dedicated women fought alongside those men, often finding themselves overlooked in history books. The list includes Ella Baker, Fannie Lou Hamer, Daisy Bates, and Ruby Hurley. In particular, Ruby Hurley, who worked as an administrator with the National Association for the Advancement of Colored People (NAACP) from the 1940s through the 1970s was one of the great unsung heroines of the Civil Rights Movement.

There has been a significant lack of coverage on women in the Civil Rights Movement. Names that should find themselves on the lips of elementary and high school teachers everywhere are completely absent. The young student knows few, if any, female activist names aside from Rosa Parks. Parks' contribution to the movement was undeniable, of course. But it leads one to wonder about the women who served on the front lines every day for years. There were female bosses, such as Ruby Hurley as Southeast Regional Director, to whom some of the bravest and noblest men answered. Where are these women? The college scholar who studies African American history may know some of the stories of other women who have recently come to light.

Yet over the past decade, historians have begun to produce new information on the role of women in the movement. Included in these observations are women ranging from administrators, such as Ella Baker, to local women who became heroes, such as Fannie Lou Hamer. Some historians, including Paula Giddings and Deborah Gray White, have traced the relationship between Black women and racial advancement much earlier than the movement is traditionally thought to have begun.[1] Indeed, it has been shown that women such as Ida B. Wells were integral in the establishment of the NAACP. Furthermore, historian Belinda Robnett explains the role of women in relation to men in the movement in her book, *How Long? How Long? African-American Women in the Struggle for Civil Rights*. She reveals that in many cases, men were the leaders while women were the organizers. Calling women, "bridge leaders," or women who fostered the ties between the social movement and the community, she describes the glass ceiling that women faced.[2] In all likelihood, the major reason that heroines such as Ruby Hurley are unknown is because of sexism. As Steven Lawson writes, "whether they were ministers or secular leaders of civil rights organizations, men commanded the bulk of the publicity devoted to coverage of the freedom struggle."[3] In his autobiography, Vernon Jordan Jr., a former field staff member of Hurley's, elaborates on this phenomenon:

> *There is no doubt in my mind that if she had been a man,*
> *Ms. Hurley would have been a natural to ascend to the top*
> *spot in the NAACP. But she was a woman, and therefore,*
> *ineligible to be considered a viable head of that organization,*
> *or of any other major civil rights group. It was a paradox, a*
> *movement designed to bring about human rights for all*
> *citizens was as much hobbled by sexism as society at*
> *large. Even though she worked hard, and was greatly*
> *respected, Ruby Hurley never got her due.[4]*

When one reads the autobiographies and profiles of the countless male civil rights activists, it becomes increasingly clear that sexism was the dirty little secret of the Civil Rights Movement. Female presence was most certainly there, but recognition is not. Look at any photograph of a protest, you will see women. Look at any petition for rights from the era, you will see female signatures, but look at most history books and you will undoubtedly not see women in the pages.

Black women were integral to the movement, not only for their participation, but for their recruitment of friends, husbands, and children to the cause. Their voluntary work kept the churches working during the week and filled on Sundays. In addition, "their social clubs and interactions extended the lines of communication throughout the community to bring Black people of different classes and social standing together in times of crisis."[5]

In this way, Belinda Robnett is correct in her assessment of many women in the movement as bridge leaders. They served as intermediaries between local communities where they wielded great power and regional and national civil rights organizations. Ruby Hurley was indeed one of the bridge leaders in the movement. Although an administrator, she served as the intermediary between her local staff and her superiors Gloster Current and Roy Wilkins in the national office. When Current or Wilkins was dissatisfied with the performance of a field secretary or branch president, it was she to whom they turned. This was true in relation to Medgar Evers, whom Hurley often reprimanded for his cooperation with other, more militant organizations. While Hurley may not have been central to any one Civil Rights Movement event in particular, it was her ability as a professional bridge leader to lead and communicate that kept the Southeast Regional activity alive.

None can deny the importance of Hurley as a female administrator in the Jim Crow South. Furthermore, at the NAACP's height during the 1950s, it was Hurley's work in her region that contributed greatly to its success. Roy Wilkins, Executive Secretary of the NAACP, was one of the most important figures of the movement. But his offices were hundreds of miles away in New York City. Hurley was no armchair warrior, she was living the movement; she had her life threatened daily and watched old friends and colleagues die or become shadows of their former selves in fear of the violence that accompanied White supremacy. She was the NAACP investigator of such brutal murders as Emmett Till, George W. Lee, and Lamar Smith. She was the woman next to Autherine Lucy as she registered for classes at the University of Alabama. She was the one who infamous Birmingham police chief "Bull" Connor knew by name, making her a vulnerable target.

In attempts to bring the work of females in the struggle to light, there is often a desire to romanticize them. Yet, women were complex, multi-dimensional figures. Danger and personal sacrifice were all too familiar to women in the movement. As Lawson points out, "many women saw their marriages and personal relationships buckle under the pressure of participating in a stressful and time consuming political and social revolution."[6] Indeed, perhaps the disappearance of Hurley's husband from public records is a result of this as well. In early years, William Hurley's name is present in Ruby Hurley's correspondences. When she was working in New York, she often requested to have room and board to accommodate both of them. But in 1951, when she relocated to the Southeast Region, those letters, as well as William Hurley's name disappeared. Having a job such as hers, which required constant dedication and thousands of miles of travel every year, would undeniably cause any marriage to suffer.

Yet, while Hurley was similar in her sacrifice to other female leaders in the movement, she was quite unlike them in her leadership style. Her most well-known colleague, Miss Ella Baker, once worked for the NAACP as Director of Branches. Yet Baker left the NAACP because she felt stifled by its highly structured and bureaucratic style of operation. Many historians have concluded that, as a result, the NAACP was an organization that prevented female administrators from advancement. "[Baker] recognized that top-down leadership . . . in hierarchical secular groups, like the NAACP, marginalized the efforts of women and relegated them mainly to secretarial and clerical positions."[7]

While a glass ceiling may have indeed existed, there were women, such as Hurley or Constance Baker Motley, whose careers departed from the norm. Hurley rose rapidly through the ranks of the NAACP, beginning her career as a general member and finishing as an administrator of the most powerful region in the country. Thus, the career of Hurley suggests that the NAACP was a place where professional bridge leaders could flourish. Indeed, in the NAACP's highly structured bureaucratic system, where communication had to go through officials at different levels, bridge leaders were a necessity. Furthermore, as Belinda Robnett suggests, sexism was not unique to the NAACP, and therefore one can conclude that a main reason women, such as Ella Baker, left the association was because of ideological conflicts rather than solely an issue of sexism.

Even in her day, Ruby Hurley was a name not well known outside of the Southeast Region. She was indeed a private person. Yet it seems baffling that in a region so frequently in the headlines, one of its leader's names was virtually unknown. In the 1950s, as a public relations move, an NAACP spokeswoman tried to get *McCall's Magazine* and *Pageant Magazine* to do a profile of Hurley. Both magazines turned down the offers, however, citing Hurley's relative anonymity as their reason for rejection.

Yet, this is not to argue that Hurley was completely unknown in her own circles. Her field secretaries had nothing but respect for her as a boss and as a woman as well. Vernon Jordan continues today to describe her as, "a marvelous, marvelous woman for whom I worked. We learned a lot from her and she was very smart, very loyal to the establishment. . . ."[8] Robert Saunders, the director of NAACP chapters in Florida, described his "tremendous respect and admiration" for her.[9] Hurley demanded to be treated as an equal to the men in the NAACP. Medgar Evers, the NAACP field director in Mississippi, a naturally outspoken man with a considerable ego, knew that Hurley was the boss and that he was not to question her decisions. She gave her field secretaries room to grow and run their states as they saw fit, but ultimately, she had the final say. It is clear that Hurley was no ordinary woman of her day.

This respect that Hurley commanded was not exclusive to the NAACP, and it often benefitted her region greatly. Her Southeastern Regional Conferences and assemblies attracted many celebrities interested in civil rights. The list included former Yankee catcher Elston Howard, fighter Archie Moore, comedian Dick Gregory, and singer Lena Horne. Jackie Robinson, the Major League Baseball legend, lavished great praise on Hurley and was a regular at her events as well. In one of their many correspondences, he told her, "I wish we had a thousand more like you. If we did, the Association would reach its goal much faster. I know of no person more deserving of the Association's thanks than you."[10] Even Martin Luther King possessed a great deal of respect for her. Despite the competition between his Southern Christian Leadership Conference (SCLC) and the NAACP, she was by his side as a comrade many times, including the Albany Movement in Georgia in 1961.

Still, as the years progressed, that very competition would prove to be one of Hurley's greatest difficulties. To profile Hurley's career is to profile the challenges to the NAACP for power within the Civil Rights Movement. Prior to the 1950s, for all intents and purposes, the NAACP was the sole organization for civil rights. At the height of its power, during Hurley's first 10 years as Southeast Regional Director (1951–1961), no other organization came close in terms of money, public authority, or membership numbers. Naturally, this made the organization enemy number one in racist America. Before they could be hired, teachers were forced to swear that they were not members of the NAACP. Known members were subject to losing jobs and being denied bank loans and other forms of community assistance. In the McCarthy era, the NAACP was constantly called an extremist and/or Communist organization. In response, Hurley once told a *Look* magazine reporter that, "If we're Communists, then Jesus Christ was a Communist, because he preached what we teach—one God and the brotherhood of man under one God!"[11]

But these attacks reflected the pressure of a powerful organization. *The Brown v Board of Education* decision in 1954 pierced through the heart of Jim Crow policy, that of separate but equal facilities. An NAACP achievement, it was arguably the most important moment in the movement because it set a precedent for further civil rights legislation. Because of the success of the *Brown* decision, officials like Hurley believed intensely that working through the United States courts was essential. However, working through the courts was slow; too slow for many Black Americans. Inevitably, while the NAACP paved the way for other civil rights organizations, newer, nonviolent-but-direct-action tactics would take over. Nonviolent direct action, best exemplified by the SCLC, created in 1957, and the Student Non-Violent Coordinating Committee (SNCC), formed in 1960, in reaction to the Woolworth counter sit-ins in Greensboro, North Carolina, got national attention in a way that the NAACP did not. Direct action captured the hearts of young protesters everywhere, and a newer, more militant generation of civil rights advocates was born. At first, Hurley, like so many other civil rights workers, praised the results that direct action protest achieved through sit-ins, jail-ins, and boycotts. Vernon Jordan described how "healthy competition with the other civil rights organizations pushed the NAACP into directions we would not have gone but for the rivalry."[12] And while Hurley's NAACP would organize numerous boycotts and sit-ins, ultimately its fundamental belief in legal change became outdated to many.

As the 1960s progressed, so did the intensity of the action. SNCC protesters' desire for direct action became insatiable, ultimately ending in its affiliation with the militant Black Panther Party in the late 1960s. By then, young Black militants no longer wanted to align themselves with moderate White America. Stokely

Carmichael's "Black Power" became the slogan of a generation disillusioned by the so-called "liberal White politician." As a result, groups like SNCC would publicly denounce the NAACP, while affiliating themselves with the Black Panther Party. As this trend intensified, national attention for the NAACP all but disappeared. NAACP officials like Hurley found themselves facing a complete reversal of fortune; whereas once their work had been put in danger because of their notoriety, now their work was in danger because of their relative anonymity.

A number of explanations were offered for the reason the NAACP fell out of fashion with youth in the 1960s and 1970s. Perhaps it was in relation to the fact that most of the NAACP officials were significantly older than the young protesters who gained power in the movement. Another explanation was that the slow pace of working through the courts made SNCC and other groups impatient. This is best summed up in a letter from a young man to Roy Wilkins in 1966. He wrote:

> You, Dr. ML King . . . and a great many others have done a marvelous and outstanding feat and I sincerely and wholeheartedly thank you for it, but there is a biblical connotation that I believe has pertinence to our revolution, that is, God replaced Moses when he couldn't communicate with his followers in the wilderness. He replaced him with Joshua, a young militant warrior, who led the children of Israel to the promised land . . . God Almighty knew he was a man, and indeed so was Malcolm X and most certainly is Stokely Carmichael.[13]

Yet, ultimately the contribution of Hurley and the national NAACP officers was arguably more tangible than Carmichaels'. While he would contribute highly to the movement with the creation of the notion of Black Power, it was the work of the NAACP that put laws into practice. Furthermore, long after the SNCC and the SCLC fell apart, the NAACP remains in existence. This is true for a number of reasons. First, the NAACP maintained close ties with the federal government and remained well-respected by many Whites and Blacks despite the fact that their tactics lost popularity among younger Blacks. Furthermore, those who remained loyal to the association were a largely middle-class crowd who continued to supply it with funds for activity. Therefore, while the NAACP lost media and national attention, it remained a functioning organization.

Thus, it is clear that Ruby Hurley's contribution to the Civil Rights Movement and American history is undeniable. Yet, to date, there has previously been no book-length monograph written about her. In NAACP papers, files, and books, her name is found in sporadic patterns. Without her, however, the group's greatest years in the most difficult of regions would not have been the same. Above all else, Hurley believed in her work with an unprecedented passion. This work begins to put scattered facts together into a biography. However, there still remain numerous holes in the story. The fate of many of Hurley's loved ones remains a mystery, including her parents and her husband. Most of the friends and colleagues who knew her are either dead or out of the public eye. The generation that knew and admired her as a civil rights veteran from afar knows very little about her personal life. In order to tell her full story, it will take years more of in-depth research beyond books and correspondences. For this reason, this essay is a political rather than a personal biography. Nevertheless, despite the missing links in her story, it is an undisputed fact that Ruby Hurley was one of the great American unsung heroines.

Ruby Hurley was born on November 7, 1909, to Alice and Edward Ruffin of Virginia. Her parents' fate remains a mystery, and census records of 1920 have Hurley listed as a "roomer" with Emma and Percy Ray, two teachers based out of Washington, D.C. She attended public schools and, in 1926, graduated from Dunbar High School. In later years, she attended Miner Teachers College and Terrell Law School at night. Yet, she did not go on to become a lawyer. Instead, she worked for the Industrial Bank of Washington, a Black institution, as well as working for a United States Government Agency. She married Lt. William L. Hurley of the U.S. Army Corps of Engineers. They had no children.[14]

Hurley first found herself interested in civil rights in the late 1930s, serving on a committee that successfully fought to get renowned Black singer Marian Anderson space to perform her concert that was banned from segregated Constitution Hall in Washington, D.C. Her next endeavor brought her to the organization that would become her life's work. Over the next four years, she worked diligently to reorganize the Washington, D.C. branch of the National Association for the Advancement of Colored People (NAACP). Her colleagues would credit her as having been largely responsible for the conversion of the Marian Anderson Citizens' Committee and another organization, the New Negro Alliance, into a new branch of the NAACP. She worked with the Washington Branch first as a charter member, then as a member of the Executive

Committee, and finally as an organizer and sponsor of the Youth Council. In a few short years, she more than tripled the youth membership. Her work with the D.C. Youth Councils gained her positive attention from the NAACP national office. In late June of 1943, she was asked to take over for Madison Jones, Jr. as the National Youth Work Secretary of the NAACP. She accepted, and was officially appointed to the job on July 1, 1943. The job would relocate her to the NAACP headquarters in New York City.[15]

Hurley came to the national office of the NAACP at a time when its power was greatly increasing. The "Association," as it was often called by its members, had begun in 1908 in response to a race riot in Springfield, Illinois. An interracial, though predominantly White group of people came together, appalled at the violent treatment of Blacks. Membership increased rapidly throughout the country, and the Association became involved in its quest to attain fair treatment for Blacks. In its earlier years, it focused mainly on anti-lynching campaigns, as lynching had been plaguing Blacks for years.

The NAACP ran itself in a highly structured, bureaucratic manner. Based out of New York City, it insisted on maintaining control of its programs from a top-down leadership style. It had its own legal defense team, and recruited talented lawyers, including Thurgood Marshall, to take on discrimination cases.[16] Furthermore, it had strict rules for its operations and avoided working in conjunction with other organizations. NAACP veterans insisted on complete self-containment.[17] Moreover, its officials were under strict instruction to remain non-partisan in political activity.[18]

As Youth Work Secretary, Hurley would add to the swelling membership numbers that the NAACP would see. Her job description included the organization of various committees, including membership, finance, press, and publicity. As early as 1945, she had completely changed the Youth division. That year, groups increased from 82 Youth Councils and 17 chapters to 190 and 27, respectively, with a membership totaling more than 15,000. By 1951, Council numbers were more than 280 and membership had almost doubled to 25,000. Indeed, the NAACP saw her leadership as necessary in a more significantly dangerous area. In 1951, following the commencement of the NAACP's attacks on school segregation, she was asked by the national office to relocate from New York City to Birmingham, Alabama, the city Martin Luther King would call, "the most segregated city in America."[19] Hurley found the adjustment a difficult one.

> *I had a tremendous personal job to do in getting over moving from New York to the South. Although born up South in Washington, I had not had the experience of living in a city completely segregated by law. I point out always that when I moved to Birmingham in April of 1951. I found that on the statute of books were city ordinances which included one that said Negroes and Whites could not play checkers together.*[20]

Still, she realized the task at hand and persisted. She was asked to oversee membership drives in Alabama, Florida, Georgia, Mississippi, and Tennessee. Subsequently, North and South Carolina were added to the list, and the area became collectively known as the Southeast Region (Region V). In 1952, Hurley was named Southeast Regional Director and a temporary assignment became a full-time commitment. In addition to the difficult level of regional adjustment, Hurley was also the first full-time staff member of the NAACP in the South.[21]

She became Regional Director just as the pace of the Civil Rights Movement was drastically changing. On Monday, May 17, 1954, the Supreme Court came to a decision in the *Brown v Board of Education* case, reversing the *Plessy v Ferguson* decision that had ruled the South for nearly 60 years. The *Plessy v Ferguson* decision had rules in 1896 that "separate but equal" facilities on the basis of race were acceptable by law on intrastate railroads.[22] However, the South would use *Plessy* to justify separate White and Black facilities in all areas of life. The 1954 *Brown* decision, however, ruled unanimously that separate educational facilities were inherently unequal. Therefore, they were a violation of the 14th Amendment to the United States Constitution, which guaranteed all citizens "equal protection of the law." The Supreme Court, however, put the implementation of the *Brown* decision in the hands of the southern federal courts. They were instructed to move ahead with "all deliberate speed." As Steven Lawson observed, "whatever the phrase signified, it did not mean soon 'soon'."[23] Nevertheless, the *Brown* decision was a colossal victory for the NAACP. It solidified the power of the group, which had steadily been increasing since the *Smith v Allwright* decision in 1944 that declared all-White primary elections unconstitutional. A second great legal victory in less than 10 years indicated that the NAACP's legal tactics were a valid and successful option in combating discrimination.

Yet, with an increase in popularity and success, the NAACP and its members saw an increase in the backlash from its White supremacist counterparts. In addition to desegregation attempts, the NAACP focused on increasing the number of Black registered voters. This was done primarily on the local level, with NAACP chapter presidents doing a great deal of recruitment under the supervision of Field and Regional Secretaries such as Ruby Hurley. The year 1955 was a profoundly violent and difficult year for staff members in the South. In what came to be termed the Mississippi "Reign of Terror," many Blacks were tortured.

However, certain hate crimes went beyond torture. On May 7, 1955, in Belzoni, Mississippi, the Reverend George W. Lee was shot and killed while driving home. Lee, a pastor of two or three churches in Humphries County had been responsible for the voter registration of over 30 Blacks in Belzoni. He had been telephoned by Whites in opposition and warned to "get the niggers to take their names off the book."[24] Lee refused to back down. Returning by car from the tailor shop with his suit ready for Sunday service, he was shot in the jaw. Hurley was the only professional civil rights worker in Mississippi to investigate the story.[25] She spoke with numerous witnesses who told her bits and pieces of a story that she compiled into a report for the national office. She described the situation to Howell Raines:

> When I went in to investigate that case and saw the place where he had been killed, it was just cold blooded murder. And then when I saw his body in the casket—I will not be able to forget how the whole lower half of his face had been shot away.[26]

Hurley found the police report to be full of holes, so she took it upon herself, with the help of Medgar Evers, to find out the truth. Together, they searched for witnesses, examined the crime scene, and inquired with locals about the facts of the murder. In addition, she personally interviewed the coroner extensively to find out details that she felt the authorities hid from her.[27] According to Hurley's report, the only woman reported to have seen the murder, a Black woman, "moved suddenly from her home during the night following the murder and has not been heard from since."[28] Witnesses who heard the crash of his automobile and saw the aftermath said that at or around midnight on May 7, shots were heard, followed by an automobile crash. Another automobile, a car carrying several Whites and possibly one Black man, was seen speeding away from the scene. Lee was pulled from his car after it crashed into the front of a small cottage. He had been fatally injured by a shot to his jaw and neck and died in the backseat of a taxicab on the way to the hospital. The coroner described to Hurley that his jaw was shattered into multiple pieces. The soft tissue was reported to have the appearance of "having gone through a hamburger grinder."[29] Six pieces of lead found in the tissue and crime scene evidence indicated that Lee was shot with buckshot.

However, most officials involved attempted to cover up the crime. The coroner, Dr. A. H. McCoy, president of the Mississippi State Conference, reported to Hurley that some explanations offered were that he "could have been punched in the jaw by a scantling (or angry person) when he crashed into the house," or that he "could have died from shock." Yet, the most startling explanation was that the lead found in his mouth could have been "dental filling from his teeth."[30] However, McCoy concluded that "it was clearly evident to me that Reverend Lee's death was caused by blasts from a shotgun. Lead is not used for filling teeth."[31] Hurley found herself disappointed in the law enforcement's lackadaisical attitudes toward the situation. She felt that there was no indication that they made any attempts to gather witnesses or to apprehend a murder suspect. Under the firm grip of the Citizen's Council as well as other White supremacist groups, Black voter registration numbers in Belzoni declined from 400 to 91.[32] Despite the fact that certain men, including a man named Rainey, were identified in numerous reports as having been associated with the murder, no one was charged.

Less than a few weeks later, Hurley found herself again faced with the job of investigating a brutal hate crime. On Saturday, August 13, 1955, 63-year-old Lamar Smith was shot and killed on the courthouse lawn in Brookhaven, Mississippi, for urging Black citizens to vote. She recalled that "anybody who knows any Southern town on a Saturday afternoon knows that somebody would see something around a courthouse square. Nobody saw anything surrounding the murder of Lamar Smith, who had been active in registration and voting in that community."[33] Brookhaven sheriff Ike Shelton saw a White man leaving the scene with "blood all over him," but still no one admitted to being a witness.[34]

Hurley found herself again disheartened by the officials' lack of interest in the murder of Black citizens. Another Mississippi sheriff, when asked about the case, declared to local newspapers that there was "nothing special" about the case of Smith being shot. Three suspects, Noah and Mack Smith and Chas Falvey, were arrested and released on bail. Due to a lack of witnesses willing to come forward, Smith's killers were never tried.[35]

Unfortunately, the violence against Black Mississippians did not cease. Two weeks after Smith's murder, Emmett Till was brutally murdered, and Hurley found herself again drawn into the investigation. The incident took place in Money, Mississippi, deep inside the Delta. It began in a local grocery store owned by 24-year-old Roy Bryant and his wife, 21-year-old Carolyn Bryant on the evening of August 24, 1955. Carolyn was inside working the counter with her sister-in-law Juanita Milam. Bryant was out of the state working part time as a truck driver. Juanita's husband was "Big" J. W. Milam, a 36-year-old World War II veteran. A man who ran a farm that was once a slave plantation, he was known to the townspeople as the man "who could handle Negroes better than anybody in the country." He was six-feet-two and 235 pounds.

"Bobo" Till and his friends sat outside of the store on the evening of August 24, laughing and talking. Till had just turned 14 one month earlier, but he walked with the swagger and confidence of a man. He was five-feet-four and stocky.[36] Born and raised in Chicago, he was in Money visiting his uncle, Moses "Preacher" Wright, for 2 weeks. He was bold and spoke with what Carolyn Bryant would call a "Northern brogue."[37] When he was a child, he had suffered from infantile paralysis. As a result, he had a speech impediment that caused him to whistle when he attempted to annunciate.[38]

As the youths got to talking, Till began to brag of a White girlfriend he had back home. Several of the boys accused him of being a liar. They dared him to prove it by going inside and talking to the White woman at the counter. Till accepted. What happened next is still to this day unclear. Carolyn Bryant testified at the trial that a young Negro man, whom she did not identify, entered the store and asked for 2 cents worth of bubble gum. She handed it to him and he asked for a date.[39] Then, as he left the store, he allegedly wolf-whistled at her. Till's defenders thought that Bryant had mistaken the speech impediment for a proposition.[40]

Till's cousins would later tell Hurley that they knew immediately that he was in great danger. They left Bryant's store immediately. Carolyn Bryant told *Look* magazine reporter William Bradford Huie that she told only Jaunita Milam what had happened. She said they were determined to keep the story from their "menfolks."[41] Yet, Money was a small town, and within a few days, Roy Bryant heard rumors of the story. He asked Carolyn what happened, and she told him. Once Bryant knew, he felt that he had to do something. He went to his half brother, J.W. Milam to talk about revenge. Milam contended that their intentions were "just to whip him . . . and scare some sense into him."[42] Shortly after midnight on August 28, they traveled in Milam's pickup to Mose Wright's home, some 3 miles outside of Money. Pounding on the door with a gun and a flashlight in his hands, Milam demanded to be led to Till. Mose took them to the back room. Milam asked Till if he was the "nigger who did the talking?" and Till answered "yeah." Mose Wright and his wife pleaded with Milam to spare their nephew, stating that the boy "has no sense" and did not know what he was doing. Milam responded by instructing, "you niggers go back to sleep."[43] They forced Till into the back of the pickup and drove off. First, they pistol whipped Till with the back of a .45 automatic pistol. But that did not satisfy their desires. Milam felt that Till did not show enough fear. He told Huie:

> Well, what else could we do? He was hopeless. I'm no bully: I never hurt a nigger in my life. I like niggers—in their place—I know how to work 'em. But I just decided it was time a few people got put on notice. As long as I live and can do anything about it, niggers are gonna stay in their place. Niggers ain't gonna go to school with my kids. And when a nigger gets close to mentioning sex with a White woman, he's tired o' livin'. I'm likely to kill him.[44]

He decided he was going to act. Searching for a weight, he recalled seeing two men lifting a discarded fan used in cotton ginning. They put him back in the truck and headed west to a steep river bank to retrieve it. He recalled, "When we got that gin, it was daylight, and I was worried for the first time. Somebody might see us and accuse us of stealing the fan."[45]

Tired out from the experience, they made the wounded Till load the fan. When they reached the river bank, they ordered him to get out, carry the fan to the edge and strip naked. Milam asked him one last time, "you still had White women?" Till responded once again with, "yeah." Milam then shot Till in the right ear, destroying half of his face. They barb-wired the gin to his neck and rolled him into 20 feet of water in the Tallahatchie River.[46]

Three days later, Till's body was found partially submerged in the river by a White youth who was fishing. There was a great deal of evidence pointing to both Milam and Bryant. However, the NAACP knew that before there was even a possibility of a conviction, there would have to be a thorough investigation. They called upon Ruby Hurley to do it. As expected, Black people in Money were afraid to come forward as witnesses. Hurley and her staff attempted to keep it quiet that she was the NAACP investigator. Risking her life, she began her search for the truth.

> I got the information on who saw that. . . . Those persons heard by way of the grapevine that I was investigating the case, and they passed the word back to me that they wouldn't talk to anybody but me. So I had to put on some cotton pickin' clothes, literal cotton-pickin clothes for those days, and make my way on the plantation.[47]

Hurley was forced to go through four families in four different places in that case to find people willing to talk to her. She recalled, "You never went directly to a place . . . [there was] never an exact phraseology being used, never the clear language, always in some form that you have to sorta try to figure out what people meant."[48] The Till case proves the best example of Hurley as a bridge leader. In order to secure a formal report for both the national office and subsequently, federal authorities, Hurley went to her community. The fact that witnesses would only speak with her demonstrates the integral role Hurley played in the movement. Without her work, the NAACP would not have had details on the Till case. Furthermore, Hurley played a huge role in acquiring witnesses for the trial itself.

Three weeks later, the trial of Milam and Bryant took place in Sumner, Mississippi. Upon advice and promised compensation from Hurley and the NAACP, Mose Wright testified in court against the defendants. Another young man, 18-year-old Willie Reid, testified that he had seen Till on the back of a pickup truck with Milam and Bryant and that he had later heard beatings. After the trial, both Black men were never able to return to their homes in Mississippi. Reid suffered a nervous breakdown and was hospitalized some weeks later.[49]

The trial itself was described by Hurley as, "just like a circus. The defendants were sitting up there eating ice cream cones and playing with their children in court just like they were out at a picnic."[50] In the segregated courtroom, the defense team urged the all-White jury that their "forefathers would turn over in their graves," should they convict Milam and Bryant. After 1 hour and 7 minutes, the jury acquitted the two men. One juror argued that it would have been "much sooner, except we took a soda-pop break, to make it look good."[51] The two men kissed their wives, lit up cigars, and grinned for photographers and the many well-wishers who congratulated them on their victory.[52]

At the heart of the defense's argument was an attack on the NAACP. They alleged that the bloated and mutilated body was not Till's, but a body that had been planted by the NAACP. This allegation came in spite of the fact that his mother had identified the body and that it bore his ring on his finger. Sheriff H. C. Strider, in charge of the investigation, agreed with this accusation. John C. Whitten, a member of the defense counsel, urged that the NAACP was not above an action such as this should it aid in their quest to "destroy the customs of the Southern people."[53]

During the trial, the NAACP had invited reporters from around the country to Mississippi to cover the case. Moreover, it urged the Federal Government to participate as well. It called upon the Justice Department to, "delay no longer in calling a halt to the jungle fury unloosed in Mississippi."[54] These pleas generally fell on deaf ears, and Hurley found herself greatly outnumbered in her investigation and attempts to combat the Mississippi "reign of terror." Many White Mississippians found themselves uncomfortable with the amount of attention their state was receiving. Local law enforcement had attempted to keep the media out of the trial. Sheriff Strider had attempted to have Till's body buried immediately in Money. The *Jackson Daily News* later reported that "it is best for all concerned that the Bryant-Milam case be forgotten as quickly as possible." But Till's mother, Mamie, fought to have his body brought back to Chicago. Partly due to media attention energized by the NAACP, Mamie Till was successful. At his funeral, she insisted on an open casket for her son. Furthermore, she had allowed the body to be photographed for *Jet* magazine. Nearly 50,000 people attended the funeral. Thousands across the world protested the verdict in the case. Letters of sympathy and outrage flooded NAACP offices and the home of Mamie Till. Nevertheless, in 1955, the only thorough investigation available to the nation was Ruby Hurley's.[55] Although she was forced to travel alone, so as not to attract suspicion, she later learned that, "there were [black] men around with shotguns standing in various spots to be sure that I got where I was going and got back. . . . "[56]

Hurley found it difficult to forget the violent summer of 1955. Many Black Mississippians were crippled with fear of the Citizen's Councils and the "Reign of Terror." Yet, the Till case would inspire many to join the movement. Indeed, many famous activists that would later join NAACP youth councils and other civil rights organization were from Emmett Till's generation.

Yet, Hurley's work on the front lines was far from over in 1955. The following year, she served as an advisor to Autherine Lucy Foster, the first Black student to be admitted to the University of Alabama. During the Lucy Case, Hurley's office in Birmingham was flooded with reporters from around the world, including England, France, Sweden, Russia, and India. Hurley described the period during and after the case as the time when "[the NAACP] was threatened and harassed more than at anytime in the five years the office had been in Birmingham." Hurley was served with a subpoena on arrival at the airport to be a witness for the state in the Lucy Case. Furthermore, the office was served with papers for a 4 million dollar damage suit, also an outgrowth of the case.[57]

In addition, both she and the lawyers in the case faced constant threatening telephone calls to their unlisted phone numbers. Hurley, who lived alone in Birmingham, found this quite unnerving.

> *Each night, the phone would ring, and when I picked it up, the person on the other end would hang up. Sometimes there would be threats to kill me. This went on all night at regular half-hours intervals.*[58]

Another common occurrence in Hurley's life was that she could "be riding down the street and white men would drive by and say 'We gon' get you'. Bombs were thrown at [her] house. . . . "[59] It was only later that Hurley learned Black taxi drivers circled her house from dusk until dawn to protect her during that time. In this way, Hurley indirectly gave Black men a way to demonstrate their masculinity. Despite the fact that she was a strong and independent woman, her unspoken need of protection forged an unbreakable tie between Hurley and the Black men of her community.

Over the course of the next few years, the pace of the Civil Rights Movement would change dramatically. Black discontent in the 1950s had radically altered American society. Indeed, the *Brown v Board of Education* decision and the 1957 Voting Act had been monumental successes. White supremacists in the South had found, in the NAACP and other civil rights organizations at the forefront of the battle, a formidable enemy. Yet, the actions of the 1950s has not reversed the Jim Crow system entirely. These final and necessary changes would come in the 1960s, with the rise of a newer, more militant generation of youth, mostly as members of the Student Nonviolent Coordinating Committee (SNCC) and the Congress of Racial Equality (CORE). These new groups would turn to a direct form of nonviolent protest best exemplified by sit-ins of various Jim Crow institutions. SNCC sought to replace the NAACP's tactics of legal negotiation with the nonviolent power of "a people no longer the victim of racial evil who can act in a disciplined manner to implement the Constitution."[60] While Martin Luther King's organization, the Southern Christian Leadership Conference (SCLC) did not necessarily align itself with SNCC, they were united in their belief that the NAACP tactics would no longer suffice. At an SCLC meeting in Raleigh, North Carolina, King publicly announced his approval that the sit-in demonstrators were moving away from "tactics which are suitable merely for gradual and long-term change."[61] It was no secret that these statements were a direct criticism of the NAACP. Naturally, Hurley and the NAACP vehemently rejected such criticism. Indeed, for her, by 1960, the Movement had already been long and cost a high price. She recalled:

> *I listen to young folks nowadays talking about old folks "taking it." They don't know how we didn't take it. There were those who died rather than take it. . . . I had gotten down in weight. I couldn't eat, and days I'd go without food because I just could not eat in Jim Crow places. . . . So if I ran out of Hershey Bars, then I didn't eat until I got some place where I could be fed. . . . This was segregation.*[62]

However, none could deny that the new phase of direct action in the movement was taking over. Hurley, her field staff, and the national office would find themselves in constant battle to resist being overshadowed by the younger generation of protesters.

The 1960s was a decade that would shape the lives of all Americans, both Black and White alike. Ruby Hurley continued to serve as the highest official in her region during these years. Furthermore, she served as an NAACP official representative at such monumental events as the Albany Movement in 1961, the March on Washington in 1963, and the marches in Selma in 1965. It was a decade that saw many great victories, including the passage of the 1964 Civil Rights Act, outlawing discrimination in all public places, and the 1965 Voting Rights Act.

With those victories came a great price; for the 1960s was also a decade of great and profound American loss. Such civil rights heroes as Martin Luther King, Malcolm X, Robert Kennedy, and President John F. Kennedy were all assassinated for their belief and promotion of equality among the races. Perhaps most painful to Ruby Hurley was the loss of her friend and colleague Medgar Evers in 1963. Indeed, her pain must have been indescribable, watching a friend she'd shared many years with shot in cold blood. It was she who convinced his wife, Myrlie Evers, to have him buried as a true American hero in Arlington National Cemetery. Yet, throughout the course of the decade, she persisted in her quest for equality, even as media attention began to fade. While the struggle to end racism undoubtedly continues even today, the Civil Rights Movement, as a headline, became a thing of the past.

In the decade of the 1970s, Ruby Hurley continued her work as Southeast Regional Director. Discrimination was still very much a part of the southern way of life, and she continued to bring to light cases documenting it. Information regarding her work in the 1970s becomes more and more sparse, as the NAACP turned a great deal of its focus northward, focusing on such issues as desegregation in Boston, Massachusetts, schools and later affirmative action. Yet, it is clear that her work did not stop after the 1960s. She remained well respected in her region. In 1973, the South made headlines once again as Maynard Jackson was elected the first African American mayor of Atlanta, Georgia. He achieved a number of great things including the implementation of affirmative action into the city, building the international airport with the participation of Black workers. He also hired a number of Black females to city political positions. One of these women was Ruby Hurley. In 1977, she was appointed to the Atlanta City License Review Board. After thirty-five years with the NAACP, Ruby Hurley retired on March 31, 1978.[63]

An active Christian throughout her life, in her later years she served as president of the United Methodist Women. She also continued to work with youth, volunteering for the YWCA. Additional work included membership in the interracial Southern Regional Council. On August 9, 1980, Ruby Hurley died at the age of 71.

Hurley's contribution to the Civil Rights Movement is unmatched by most people, especially female administrators. Few other women worked so highly in the ranks of any of the civil rights organizations, especially in the NAACP. Whereas her contemporary and friend, Ella Baker left the NAACP because of the NAACP's structured bureaucratic system, Ruby Hurley remained and became the most successful female administrator in the Southeast Region to date. During her years as Regional Director, she saw the movement at its earliest stages and remained until its last formal years. She never forgot the brutal years of the 1950s Jim Crow South, when the NAACP found itself alone and outnumbered by White supremacists. She dealt with the enormous pressure in ways that most could not, even remaining relatively lighthearted about it. In 1956, when angry Whites left small Black dolls with red paint across their necks as a warning to Hurley outside one of her speaking engagements, she picked up one of the dolls and kept it in her office for the remainder of her years. In contrast to many of her Black colleagues, she never came to hate the White race. When Ernest Dunbar asked her in 1957 why she did not, she replied, ". . . because I'm a Christian and because I know there are many whites who are Christians also—or at least who want to be Christians. I know they are having terrible struggles with their consciences over this thing. But I have faith that they will eventually see the truth."[64]

The life and work of Ruby Hurley is a valuable tool for studying the role of Black women in the movement. The NAACP was dominated by strong male leaders, yet Hurley rose through the ranks rather quickly. Indeed after less than 10 years, she was named the official of the most dangerous and active region in the country. She remained the undisputed head of NAACP operations in the Southeast for more than two decades. Sexism was an issue most women faced continuously in their institutions, but her bold and outspoken personality helped her persevere through it. Moreover, in her correspondences and interviews, she did not complain about sexism. As was the case with many of her female colleagues, Hurley saw the sole purpose of her work with the NAACP to achieve racial equality.

When one examines Ruby Hurley's work as a female in the NAACP along with her other female colleagues, including Constance Baker Motley and Marian Wright Edelman, it becomes apparent that the NAACP was an organization that attracted strong women. Sexism was not unique to the NAACP, as it existed in all of the other organizations. While the SCLC had female workers, its officials were almost exclusively men. Historian Belinda Robnett argues that there were indeed female officials in SNCC, but that they also faced sexism. For example, if they wanted to have high status in the organization, their working record in civil rights would have to be twice that of their male counterparts.[65] Since it was an issue in all of the organizations, it indicates that what led women to leave the NAACP were more ideological than sexism issues. The NAACP had maintained its system since its establishment. Hurley agreed with the organization's tactics, strategy, and approach and vigorously implemented them. In this way, she was what Robnett calls a "professional bridge-leader." Bridge leaders were the stepping stones for possible constituents and adherents to cross formidable barriers between their personal lives and the political life of civil rights organizations.[66] As a bridge leader, Hurley was able to cross boundaries between the public life of an organization and the personal life of a participant. In this way, she was able to form relationships with both the inner circle and the local people that most other people could not.

Furthermore, she constantly enforced the rules of the national office to her local staff. When Wilkins or Current had issues with Medgar Evers, Robert Saunders, Vernon Jordan, or other field directors, they rarely contacted them directly. Instead, they contacted Hurley and asked her to reprimand them. Similarly, across her region, Hurley maintained close relationships with Black ministers, activists, and leaders. Indeed, without her, the national office in New York could have faced numerous internal problems; especially in the case of Medgar and Charles Evers, with whom Roy Wilkins had tensions. Furthermore, Hurley maintained a relationship with her staff that enabled her to be their friend, while still commanding respect from them. She was also an important bridge leader because of her ability to organize effectively, inspire her staff, and provide valuable advice on her experiences concerning dangerous situations that the movement inevitably spawned. Many of the NAACP-driven boycotts in the South were planned by her. Her field staff valued her as an advisor when they needed to know how to organize a boycott or prepare a letter of protest to a politician. Yet, perhaps Hurley was most valuable because of her speaking capabilities. In an average year, she traveled thousands of miles to fulfill hundreds of speaking engagements. Her speeches were informative, and the language she used was inspiring for those who heard it. Despite all of these commitments and traveling, Hurley still personally responded to almost all of her letters. In 1957, she impressed *Look* magazine reporter Ernest Dunbar when she stayed as a guest in six different homes. "Ruby also ate six successive fried-chicken dinners. Tactfully, she praised them all."[67] While she may not have been a person who served as a central figure in one big event, she was irreplaceable to the movement for her unmatched passion, inspiration, and dedication as a bridge leader.

In light of Hurley's success, one is tempted to argue that sexism was not a serious issue for her. However, her anonymity has lasted for decades, while her male counterparts have had numerous monographs published on their work. As a woman, although she was extremely important and involved, she has not received the recognition that men with much less power than she have received. Applying Robnett's theory, the issue becomes one undeniably based on gender. "Several women who were professional [bridge leaders] were not privy to the formal leaders' inner circle, as were men of their status. Rather because of their gender, they could obtain power and high status only as bridge leaders, which were usually the highest position attainable for women."[68] While Hurley was close with Roy Wilkins and Gloster Current, she did not have the same contacts with influential government officials as they did. As a woman, she was never consulted for advice by politicians or even Wilkins on civil rights legislation, though as head of the Jim Crow region, she was undeniably the most experienced. Furthermore, it is clear by examining NAACP papers that Wilkins often cited her reports as his own in public speeches. Yet, her name appears on exactly two pages of his 343-page autobiography. While she associated with the inner circle, she was not formally a part of it.

Nevertheless, Hurley dedicated her life to work in which she believed with all of her heart. It was the only life she knew as an adult, beginning her work at the young age of 20. Few others had seen the South as she had, having been there through the brutal Jim Crow years to the election of a Black mayor in control of one of its biggest cities. Despite racism, competition, false accusations, and sexism, she defied the odds for her cause. Her brave work and dedication remain traits that all Americans can admire. She spent 35 years risking her life in a dedication to her people that few could match. In an excerpt from one of her hundreds of speeches, she described her reason for her fervent belief in her work. She remarked, in rather gender-biased language:

> . . . *The Negro in the South has been hurting for a long time. He has known a number of Emmett Tills. . . . He has sat on death row. . . . He is not unaccustomed to pain and death. But, he still wants his freedom. He wants life and liberty like other Americans. And he plans to catch with happiness, not just pursue it, but enjoy it.*[69]

Indeed, he could not have gotten there without Ruby Hurley.

Endnotes

1. Lawson, Steven. (2002). "Civil Rights and Black Liberation." *A Companion to American Women's History.* Nancy Hewitt (ed.). Malder: Blackwell Publishing, 399.
2. Robnett, Belinda. (1997). *How Long? How Long? African-American Women in the Struggle for Civil Rights.* New York: Oxford University Press, 20.
3. Lawson, Steven F. (2002.) *Civil Rights and Black Liberation.*
4. Vernon, Jordan E. (2001). *Vernon Can Read! A Memoir.* New York: Public Affairs.
5. Lawson, Steven. (2002). *Civil Rights and Black Liberation,* 398.
6. Ibid., 408.
7. Ibid., 398.
8. Jordan, Vernon. available online at *http://www.virginia.edu/uvanewsmakers/newsmakers/jordan.html.* Accessed 08/23/04.
9. Saunders, Robert. (2000). *Bridging the Gap: Continuing the Florida Legacy of Harry T. Moore, 1952–1966.* Tampa, FL: University of Tampa Press, 66.
10. Jackie Robinson letter to Ruby Hurley, 1962. NAACP Papers.
11. Dunbar, Ernest. (1957). "Inside the NAACP," *Look,* 21 (Aug. 6), 64.
12. Jordan, Vernon. *Vernon Can Read,* 147.
13. Wilkins, Roy and Matthews, Tom. (1982). *Standing Fast: An Autobiography of Roy Wilkins.* New York: The Viking Press, 314.
14. Lawson, Steven. (2005). "Ruby Hurley." In *Notable American Women.* Susan Ware, (ed.). Cambridge: Harvard University Press, 318–320.
15. Memo from National Office, June, 1943. NAACP Papers, Library of Congress, Washington, D.C.
16. Kellog, Charles. (1967). *The NAACP: A History of the National Association for the Advancement of Colored People,* vol. 1 1909–1920. Baltimore: Johns Hopkins Press, 146.
17. Ibid., 146.
18. Letter to Ruby Hurley from National Office, 1966, NAACP Papers, Washington, D.C.
19. Alabama Moments. Available online at *www.alabamamoments.state.al.us/sec62.htm.* Accessed 09/24/04.
20. Raines, Howell. (1977). *My Soul Is Rested: Movement Days in the Deep South Remembered.* New York: GP Putnam and Sons, 131.
21. Lawson, Steven. (2005). *Ruby Hurley,* 318–320.
22. Lawson, Steven. (1997). *Running for Freedom: Civil Rights and Black Politics in America Since 1941.* 2nd ed. New York: McGraw Hill, 45.
23. Ibid.
24. Ibid.
25. Dittmer, John. (1994). *Local People: The Struggle for Civil Rights in Mississippi.* Urbana: University of Illinois Press, 54.
26. Raines, Howell. (1977). *My Soul Is Rested.* New York: GP Putnam and Sons, 132.
27. Dittmer. *Local People,* 51.
28. Ibid.
29. Ruby Hurley, Report to Roy Wilkins, 1955. NAACP Papers.
30. Ruby Hurley, Memorandum to Region Staff, May 13, 1955. NAACP Papers.
31. Ruby Hurley, Report to Roy Wilkins, 1955. NAACP Papers.
32. Ruby Hurley, Memorandum to Region Staff, May 13, 1955. NAACP Papers.
33. Raines, Howell. (1977). *My Soul Is Rested,* 132.
34. Ibid.
35. Dittmer, *Local People,* 52.
36. Whitfield, Steven. (1991). *A Death in a Delta: The Story of Emmett Till.* Baltimore: Johns Hopkins University Press.
37. Dittmer. *Local People,* 55.
38. Ibid.
39. Raines, Howell. (1977). *My Soul Is Rested,* 133.
40. Dittmer. *Local People,* 55.
41. Raines, Howell. (1977). *My Soul Is Rested,* 133.
42. *Look* Magazine. Available online at *www.pbs.org/wgbh/amex/till/filmmore/index.htm.* Accessed 12/28/05.

43. Ibid.
44. Ibid.
45. Ibid.
46. Ibid.
47. Raines, Howell. (1977). *My Soul Is Rested*, 133.
48. Ibid.
49. Whitfield, Steven. (1991). *A Death in a Delta*, 100–3.
50. Raines, Howell. (1977). *My Soul Is Rested*, 133.
51. Dittmer. *Local People*, 57.
52. Ibid.
53. Ibid.
54. Memo from Roy Wilkins to NAACP, 1955. NAACP Papers.
55. *www.cbsnews.com/stories/2004/10/21/60minutes/main650652.html* Accessed 01/05/05. *Protected legally from double jeopardy, Milam and Bryant sold their story to journalist William Bradford Huie for $4,000 cash. Though in 2004 both Milam and Bryant were dead, the United States Justice Department reopened the case. Some 14 people are under suspicion in connection with the murder. At the top of the list is Carolyn Bryant, who remarried in 1979, and today goes by the name Carolyn Donham. It is believed by some that she was in the truck at the time of Till's abduction.
56. Raines, Howell. (1977). *My Soul Is Rested*, 133–4.
57. Annual Southeast Region Report, Ruby Hurley, 1956. NAACP Papers.
58. Raines, Howell. (1977). *My Soul Is Rested*, 134.
59. Ibid.
60. Lawson, Steven. (1997). *Running for Freedom: Civil Rights and Black Politics in America Since 1941*. 2nd ed. New York: McGraw Hill, 71.
61. Wilkins, Roy, and Matthews, Tom. (1982). *Standing Fast: The Autobiography of Roy Wilkins*. New York: The Viking Press, 269.
62. Raines, Howell. (1977). *My Soul Is Rested*, 135–6.
63. Lawson, Steven. (2005). *Ruby Hurley*, 318–320.
64. Dunbar, Ernest. (1957). "Inside Ruby Hurley's South," *Look*, vol. 21, August, 58–64.
65. Robnett, Belinda. (1997). *How Long? How Long?*, 103.
66. Ibid., 19.
67. Dunbar. *Inside the NAACP's South*, 58–64.
68. Robnett, Belinda. (1997). *How Long? How Long?*, 20.
69. Ruby Hurley, NAIRO Conference Paper, Nov. 10, 1961. NAACP Papers.

Chapter 40

Ecstatic Fallacies:
The Politics of the Black Storefront

Cheryl Clarke

"you think i accept this Pentecostal church in exchange for the lands you stole"

(Jayne Cortez, "Do You Think," 1978)

Crucified Jesus. Stolen, enslaved, and forced Black Bodies: a stunning "imitation" of the suffering Son of God. I resisted the ecstasy of the black church; its unconditional love of my slave body. Though the stripes on my breasts, back, and buttocks attest to my worthiness, I took no consolation from the vision of that old rugged cross nor found any balm (only boredom) in the somber Latin-said masses of my faked childhood meditation on that distant Lord, his bloody sweat, crown of thorns, studded palms pulped into that Eldora do gold crucifix up there on its silk covered marble slab.

But I do so love a good gospel choir.

Ecstatic. Charismatic. Vatic. Don't let go that far back. The demand on the soul (which I do believe in, like the Big O singing "I been loving you too long to stop now") is too perilous. One gets tired of a prophet. All my life, from the time of my post-Reconstruction North Carolinian maternal grandmother's fixation on the white proto-"televangelist" Oral Roberts of Tulsa, Oklahoma, I've laughed at Bible-beating proselytizers, or, in my young, bourgeois Roman Catholic days, thought them ignorant of the Canon, trashy, and country with all that sweating and shouting and spitting. Now, they are running the country. And I'm back on the dock of the bay.

But why does Bishop Harry R. Jackson, Jr. (Note: they're often "Jr.'s": so we'll assume their mothers were *married* to their fathers?) author of the "Black Contract With America on Moral Values" and pastor of Hope Christian Church, a so-called "megachurch" of 2,000, in College Park, Maryland, think by offering up gays and lesbians on the altar of "marriage protection" (aka: anti-gay marriage; or in the lesbian feminist terms Adrienne Rich, "compulsory heterosexuality"), he's got a place at the table—a metaphor all the pundits on "both sides of the aisle" recite regularly (*Sunday Times*, March 6, 2005, p. 23; *Free Republic*, 4/25/2005, *www.freerepublic.com/focus/f-news/1391049/posts*; "Black Contract with America on Moral Values," HIMPACT/ High Impact Leadership Coalition," *www.thehopeconnection.org/contract.htm* last accessed June 2009; Blumenthal, "Justice Sunday Preachers," *The Nation, www.thenation.com/doc.mhtml/blumenthal* (last accessed June 2009). All this, because seven percent more black people voted for Bush in 2004 than in 2000? Bishop Jackson's a little taken with his ecstatic fallacy. He was said to be collecting a million signatures endorsing his "Contract" to present to President Bush on February 1 of 2006. He was among the Judas black preachers Bush invited to the White House in January and the only black preacher at Justice Sunday—a campaign holiday for Bill Frist. Meanwhile, the United States has kept not one of its own contracts (e.g., viz., the Constitution and its assorted amendments) with its black citizens. Why would it honor one drawn up by a coalition of black preachers, conservative though they be? Blacks in the funky U.S. can't use a contract of "moral values." Given our history here, we have a surfeit of moral values and no dearth of contracts with America. I hope Bishop Jackson is not mistaken for an intruder as he proceeds toward the White House, briefcase brimming with those million signatures: rather like Ellison's Invisible Man, carrying *The New York Times* and a briefcase with the message, "Keep this nigger running," hidden inside.

There's dissension in the King family. Rev. Bernice King—a preacher, too, and youngest daughter of Martin Luther King, Jr.—led a cynical march with the Bishop Eddie Long, homophobic pastor of the New Birth Missionary Baptist Church, a mega megachurch of 25,000 (!), through Atlanta in December of 2004 to support a Constitutional ban on same-sex marriage: "I know deep down in my sanctified soul that he [Dr. King] did not take a bullet for same-sex unions," said the young Reverend. Well, in a way, Dr. King did die so that gay people could be free. Liberations stand in for one another. (Queer liberation is Black liberation.) Joseph Lowery and John Lewis, two of King's close associates, both said Dr. King would never have marched for a constitutional ban on gay marriage. I believe King—whatever his sexual preferences and proclivities—would have preferred a world in which he could receive all the counsel he needed from Bayard Rustin, a black gay man and mentor to the Civil Rights Movement, without censure and blackmail. And I believe both the young Rev. King and Bishop Long doth protest too much.

Nine months before her daughter's ecstatic fallacy last December, Coretta Scott King stood up for the right of gays and lesbians to marriage equality: "Gay and lesbian people have families and their families should have legal protection, whether by marriage or civil union. A constitutional amendment banning same-sex marriages is a form of gay bashing and it would do nothing at all to protect traditional marriage" (*GayPASG.org.*, "Split in Martin Luther King's family reflects gay marriage debate," Jan. 16, 2005).

> I learned to love the gospel music
> swelling up past garbage cans in the summer
> backyards of my childhood Armageddon.

("About Religion," Audre Lorde, 1978)

But who could have predicted this black turn to what Martin Kilson identifies as "Christian fundamentalist atavism," reaching back to Old Testament values to justify hatred of queers and women and to wedge their way onto the Republican agenda. Easier to do that than for "the black storefront" to face other realities black people are living with: in almost forty years the seven-year disparity in life expectancy between Whites and Blacks in this country only decreased six-tenths of a percent; the foundering underfunded urban public school systems (yeah, who does love the children Jesus suffered to come unto him, especially the poor ones) are wasting the minds of another generation of students of color; the crisis of AIDS, which along with heart disease, cancer, cirrhosis, diabetes, murder, and car accidents account for more than eighty percent of all "excess deaths" in African American communities. The gross disparity of incomes. So many people making so little money. And a real dire need for all of us to do something for our queer children of color. Wherever we find them, as Audre Lorde says, the children are *our* children too. Yet, the "black storefront" keeps throwing up "The Family" in our faces as the answer. The Family is not sufficient, efficient, or safe for children.

Keith Boykin, gay activist and former Clinton aide, speaks on homophobic black preachers, in a pithy piece of writing, "Gay Rights, Civil Rights":

"[A] black minister in Chicago told *The New York Times*, 'If the KKK opposes gay marriage, I would ride with them.' Dozens of other black ministers have gone on national television and radio programs to condemn homosexuality. . . . If that's not enough to spark black LGBT activism, I'm not sure what is" (Wharton and Philips, eds., *I Do/I Don't: Queers on Marriage*, 2005). I remember reading that amnesiac, ecstatic preacher's statement and thinking, *This is a crazy enemy. His blackness notwithstanding.* And yes, I ask myself the same question Mr. Boykin begs: *Where is black LGBT activism?* But that isn't enough either.

Some Black Christians, like Mrs. King, Rep. Lewis, Rev. Lowery, have refused the "Black Contract with America on Moral Values" and the buffoonery of other black preachers promoting homophobia in the black community? They know, for example, that the new white right is the old Invisible Empire? Suits and Gucci pumps instead of capes and hoods. (Alabama native and lesbian writer, Minnie Bruce Pratt whispers to me, "You could always tell a klansman by his shoes."). They've been summoned inside the Beltway from the dark ghosts wailing in the Delta to press the flesh of the "white corporate oligarchs" (Kilson 2005). Homophobia stands in for and "structures" racism, xenophobia, and anti-Arab and anti-Muslim profiling and surveillance. Traditional Values Coalition is the White Citizens Council.

But can Black Christians (many of whom are queer) take back the church, that has been your shelter when you had none, your sanctuary from the snare of enemies, your nation within a hostile nation, your courage in the face of attack dogs, fire hoses, tear gas, beating, jail, and horrific death? Or, like *Beloved*'s Baby Suggs, start a new one.

Chapter 41

College Football Drives Desegregation of Schools in the Southeastern Conference

Donald C. Heilman

"Sam Cunningham did more to integrate Alabama in 60 minutes than Martin Luther King had accomplished in 20 years."

—Jerry Claiborne

This essay will deal with the surprising (and ongoing) role that college football played in the racial desegregation of the highly resistant former all-white universities of the Deep South. In the years following World War II, Americans became increasingly aware of their own institutionalized and legally protected practices of racism. In a war where Americans fought to liberate peoples around the world from oppressive governments like Nazi Germany and militaristic Japan, whose leaders espoused theories of superior and inferior races, the United States was increasingly recognized for its hypocritical stance in regard to Blacks and other minorities at home (Patterson, 2001, p. xiv). What became known as the Civil Rights Movement moved forward in fits and starts of gains and setbacks for Blacks and others seeking political redress from racial discrimination. American society reacted in a wide range of responses, one of which is examined here, and how it played out on American colleges and universities. In the South particularly—or the former Confederate States—the reaction was almost always earmarked by resistance, and often by violence. But in some instances the breakthrough came as the result of college football.

The major universities of the South, most of them in an athletic conference known as the Southeastern Conference (SEC), remained defiantly all-white, or virtually all-white through the mid-1970s despite the ruling in landmark United States Supreme Court cases like Brown versus the Board of Education of Topeka, Kansas 1954 (347 U.S. 483); The Civil Rights Act of 1964; and President Lyndon Johnson's Executive Order 11246 in 1964. These measures attacked the de jure establishment or support of "separate but equal" public institutions of education, long a reality for Blacks in America, who attended "separate but equal" schools for black and white children. The Supreme Court case *Plessy v. Ferguson* (163 U.S. 537) decided in 1896, confirmed the racist two-system approach to almost everything in the South—a system popularly called "Jim Crow." (Patterson, 2001, pp. xvi–xvii, xx, 90–91).

Despite the language and intent of the court in *Brown*, the Civil Rights Act of 1964, and Executive Order 11246, the SEC continued to openly defy integration (Cremin, 1988, pp. 203–204), and the large publicly-funded universities of the South remained closed to Blacks with no hope of change in sight (Thelin, 2004, pp. 301–304). In 1965, Mississippi State University, for example, needed the assistance of the National Guard to integrate the Mississippi State student body (Longman, Glier, 2003). Regardless of the by-then already-acknowledged prowess of black athletes in professional sports, and college athletics elsewhere in the country, SEC teams refused to allow a black to play for them.

But in 1970, the violence, the hatred, the anger, and the stubborn resistance of racial prejudice in the South ran head-on into the powerful allure of college football. The University of Alabama was still without a black football player on its squad in 1971—17 years after *Brown* and 16 years after Alabama had admitted its first black student, Autherine Lucy. Many Southern schools had a state-enforced policy prohibiting their state colleges and universities from playing against other teams with black players on them. (See for example Lapchick, 2008; Reese 1999; Smith, 2007, p. 4.)

But on September 12, 1970, things changed in the SEC forever. Southern California's fullback was a black man named Sam Cunningham, who ran the ball and dominated the University of Alabama and legendary coach Paul "Bear" Bryant's Crimson Tide for 135 yards and 2 touchdowns in a display of speed, power, and determination. Later, the *Los Angeles Times,* quoting former Bryant assistant Jerry Claiborne—who went on to become the head coach at Virginia Tech, Maryland, and Kentucky—as saying "Sam Cunningham did more to integrate Alabama in 60 minutes than Martin Luther King had accomplished in 20 years." (JBHE, Autumn 1998, p. 65; Zinser, 2004).

What soon followed was a significant influx of black athletes attending traditionally all-white universities, opening the door for non-athlete students of color. Apparently, nothing bothers alumni and trustees more than losing a big football game, and so, Southern institutions of higher learning that had traditionally excluded Blacks from athletic teams—specifically football teams—were forced to change that policy.

Background and Timeline

The *Brown* case was hailed, appropriately, as a landmark decision when it was handed down in 1954. In that decision, the court unanimously ruled that separate schools for Blacks and Whites were inherently unequal. This reasoning was soon applied to other areas of society that were governed by the "Jim Crow" laws that grew out of the *Plessy* decision which allowed states to provide "separate but equal" opportunities for Blacks and Whites. That decision paved the way for not only separate schools, but separate hotels, restaurants, train cars, bus seats, hospital floors, and professional sports teams.

In the South, large state universities refused acceptance to Blacks, no matter how qualified, and their sports teams reflected this "Whites only" policy. The South was not alone in this department. Racism, bias, and prejudice were the norm in other regions. Ignorance regarding race prevailed throughout American society and upheaval—in retrospect—was overdue.

With the passage of the Civil Rights Act of 1964, state and federal courts now had the legislative teeth to enforce *Brown,* allowing no institution with significant public contacts to deny equal access to that institution, or its goods and services, on the basis of race. The legal attack in the South came against institutions that supported de jure discrimination—that is discrimination based on legislative product, case law, or administrative action (Patterson, 2001, p. xx). In the SEC, as elsewhere in the South, resistance to the 1964 legislation was swift, often violent, and entrenched. The state of Virginia, for example, "seized, closed and locked the doors" on its public schools (Thelin, 2004, p. 349). It is true that attempts to desegregate by the Department of Health, Education and Welfare (HEW) occurred at every level, but nowhere more so than in the public schools K–12, which HEW and courts alike targeted as the place where desegregation was to start (Patterson, 2001, pp. 138–140).

Higher education, however, was not subjected to those same forces of change that public elementary and secondary schools faced from local politicians, school boards, parent's groups, and state and national bureaucracies. And so, these large state universities remained essentially all-white, despite the fact that many were in states with significant black populations. The inequity was obvious on its face, but remedies seemed non-existent. The Supreme Court may have ruled in *Brown* 17 years before the Alabama–USC game that "separate was inherently unequal," but separate is how the SEC adamantly remained. Resistance to integration often took the form of institutionalized racism stemming from the highest levels of state power.

For example, writing for ESPN.com in Black History Month, Richard Lapchick (Lapchick, 2008) noted, that with its deep Southern roots, the SEC was the last major conference in America to be integrated. Some member schools, he wrote, not only fought to keep Blacks off their own teams, but also refused to compete against other teams that included them on their rosters.

According to Lapchick, in 1956, the state of Louisiana passed a law banning interracial sports competition, which was overturned by the U.S. Supreme Court in 1959. In Mississippi, legislators threatened to stop funding schools that competed against integrated teams. For that reason, Mississippi State skipped the NCAA basketball tournament in 1959, 1961, and 1962. It took Kentucky another 12 years after Brown, to put Nat Northington and Greg Page, two Blacks, on its football team in 1966. They were the first black student-athletes in the football-dominated SEC. But resistance remained high in the SEC, and it was not until 1972 that every SEC school had at least one black student-athlete (Lapchick, 2008). University of Mississippi coach

John Howard Vaught's stock answer to the question of when Old Miss would start recruiting black football players was "never." (*Atlanta Journal Constitution*, 2006) He was asked to retire in 1970.

An early example of how the South resisted the process of integration that universities elsewhere had adopted came in December of 1955. In a Sugar Bowl match-up between Georgia Tech and Pittsburgh, the segregationist Governor of Georgia at the time, Marvin Griffin, asked Georgia Tech to reject their bowl bid because Pittsburgh had a black player (Hinton, Reese, Davidson, 1986, pp. C1–C12). Writing for the *Michigan Historical Review*, John Matthew Smith (Smith, 2007, pp. 6–9) observed that all-white Southern colleges and universities did everything they could to block Blacks from attending their schools. When Lucy enrolled at the University of Alabama in February 1956, she was met by a mob of Confederate flag-wavers who threw rotten eggs at her while they shouted "kill her, kill her." She soon withdrew from school. The next month, writes Smith, 101 members of Congress signed the "Southern Manifesto," which denounced the *Brown* decision, claiming it would destroy "amicable relations between the White and Negro races." As a result, observes Smith, for at least a decade after *Brown*, white politicians and university administrators prevented Blacks from sharing classrooms and locker rooms with Whites in the South (Smith, 2007, pp. 6–7).

Before the USC game in 1970, Bryant had vowed not to integrate football at Alabama. Alabama as a state had already experienced racial upheaval, including the bombing of the 16th Street Baptist Church in Birmingham, which killed four young girls; Governor George Wallace's attempt to block the university's first two black students from entering their classrooms; and, the Selma marches, where 600 Civil Rights protestors were attacked by state and local police with tear gas and clubs (Walsh, 2008). What all this added up to was a violent, deep-rooted hatred of Blacks and an almost total resistance to integration at the large SEC universities.

Professional sports had been virtually the same in their "Whites only" sensibility before and in the early years after World War II, with notable exceptions in boxing and track and field (Reese, 1999). Major league baseball remained without a black player until Jackie Robinson, an All-American football player and track star from UCLA, broke the color barrier in 1947. Robinson's endurance of racial hatred and his courage have been well-documented. Other professional teams soon followed suit, but wholesale acceptance of black athletes was slow—the New York Yankees, for example, had only one black on their regular roster for the 1964 season. In the universities that formed the Southeastern Conference, acceptance was non-existent. Twenty-four years after Robinson broke into major league baseball, 17 years after *Brown* and seven years after the Civil Rights Act of 1964, the University of Alabama had yet to play a single black football player in a varsity game and had none on scholarship.

All of the universities in the SEC are in former slaveholding states and/or Jim Crow states. Presently, the conference is composed of the University of Kentucky, The University of Alabama, Auburn University, the University of South Carolina, the University of Georgia, Florida State University, Mississippi State University, the University of Southern Mississippi, the University of Tennessee, Louisiana State University, Vanderbilt University, and the University of Arkansas. For many residents of these states, the American Civil War did not end in 1865 (Hinton, Reese & Davidson, 1986).

Football Forces Reform

Is college football that powerful of a social force for change? The answer is yes, and it's not for the first time. In the chapter entitled "The Rise of Football," historian Frederick Rudolph (1962, 1990) writes in his standard-setting text, *The American College and University: A History*, about the rapid spread of the sport in the late nineteenth century. "Few movements so captured the colleges and universities," he writes. "Indeed the game became so widely adopted that for the first time since the founding of Harvard College in 1636, colleges began to recognize the existence of intercollegiate relations." (Rudolph, 1962, 1990, p. 374). Schools, Rudolph points out, now found it desirable to consult each other on matters like curriculum and athletic regulations. Midwestern colleges, by the middle of the 1880s had already gotten together to resolve such matters as to how many faculty and how many professionals each team could field! (Rudolph, 1962, 1990, p. 374).

Once the game had been accepted by the colleges, Rudolph observes, they had to be won. There was, he says, no stopping its growth. It appealed to too many people in too many ways. It represented too many of the collegiate ideals extant during its formularizing years: regionalism; martial spirit; competition in the marketplace; egalitarianism; teamwork; social Darwinism, American Industrial Imperialism; you name it, and the American-psyche flavor of the month found its personification in football (Paul, McGhee & Fant, 1984, pp. 284–287). Football was recognized from its earliest days for its democratizing affect on the student body—players came from every walk of life and every socio-economic station (Rudolph, 1962, 1990, p. 378).

Even the rise of women's rights found football to be an engine for social change, notes Rudolph. Before the rise of college football women had often been forbidden to attend sporting events, but by 1885, 35 years before they acquired the national right to vote, women were apparently flocking to the Yale–Princeton game in New Haven, Connecticut. The game was now officially established on the social calendar of the Eastern Establishment (proving it could be a social force for change in its own right). College football's ability to draw large numbers of money-paying customers has eventually evolved into huge television and merchandising revenues, championships, bowl games, rivalries, and bragging rights (Rudolph, 1962, 1990, pp. 373–393).

And so, like women before them, Blacks found that college football could be an impetus for social change. And once it was changed there was no going back. The list of reasons for the final acceptance of black football players, and eventually black students at previously all-white, segregated universities and colleges has two very powerful ones: (1) Apparently, even the most dyed-in-the-wool segregationists finally had to admit that they hated losing a football game to their fiercest rivals more than anything, even at the price of desegregation, and (2) Losing football programs make bad economic sense.

Some Severe Limitations and Other Ways of Seeing

The admission of Blacks to play football and other sports in the SEC was revolutionary, but its advent produced some severe limitations on any claim to total victory. Acceptance of Blacks on the football fields of American colleges did not lead immediately to acceptance of Blacks in the classroom. In fact, there was actually a "Double Jim Crow," what Lewis calls "racial stacking" aspect of desegregation in southern colleges and universities—Blacks were allowed on the field and in the gym, but elsewhere on campus it was separate as usual; race mattered at the fraternities; in the cafeteria; and, in the library. Indeed, at many Southern schools, Blacks represented such a small percentage of the student population that a white student could go his or her entire school career and never see a black student in class (Lewis, 1995, pp. 431–445). As a result, several unfortunate stereotypes arose almost immediately in the early 1970s:

1. The only Blacks in school were athletes and they were treated as mercenaries.
2. Blacks were perceived as not capable of college level work, but were tolerated because of their athletic prowess.
3. Athletes (white and black) at large "football factories" were often kept in separate housing—dining apart from the student body and giving up so much of their daily time to practice, that the rest of the student body never interacted with any athlete, reinforcing the mistaken impression that the black athletes were separate entities from the rest of the student population (Lewis, 1995, pp. 431–441).

This state of affairs was further aggravated by the common misperception repeatedly voiced by coaches nationwide, that the Blacks were not smart enough to play those positions believed to require higher intelligence and leadership skills such as quarterback (Lewis, 1995, pp. 435–437). In fact, there were no black head coaches in the SEC until after the 2003 season (Longman & Glier, 2003). As a result, Blacks were subjected to a sort of "double Jim Crow" standard that persisted for decades (See, for example, Lewis, 1995, pp. 432–434).

In their article "Brown at 50: King's Dream or Plessy's Nightmare" (Orfield & Lee, 2004) authors Gary Orfield and Chungmei Lee examine the rate and amount of integration that took place at Southern public schools following the Brown decision in 1954. Their data, obtained from Southern Educational Reporting Service and NCES Common Core of Data, shows, for example, that between 1954 and 1966 less than 5% of Southern blacks went to majority-white schools (K–12). However, by 1976, after the advent of forced busing and other affirmative measures, that number rose dramatically to 35%—and was already at 25% by 1969. Southern colleges and universities experienced no similar growth. They were not forced to bus; HEW did not force the issue of affirmative action upon universities with the same drive and passion that they compelled elementary and secondary schools to integrate. Entrance exams and standards alone, as well as Southern white hostility, could serve as an effective barrier to integration (Orfield & Lee, 2004, pp. 13–19).

But, another way of looking at the situation can be based on data provided by Orfield & Lee (2004, pp. 13–19). In the South, over the course of the data used in their study (1954–2003), black student population K–12 has been consistently in the 26–27% range; after 15 years of resistance, court-enforced integration began to produce results and as a consequence, several of the formerly most segregated states stand today as the most integrated states in the K–12 public-school arena—Kentucky ranks number one as the most integrated state for public schooling; Delaware is number five, North Carolina is number 10, and South Carolina is number 12. Integration at higher education can, therefore, be explained in similar fashion, as institutionalized resistance wore down, and as a more integrated cohort progressed through the K–12 ranks to arrive at college. Clearly, the threat of withholding federal funding to higher education was another important stick used against the Southern universities (Thelin, 2004, 338–339).

Further, the courts continued to put pressure on higher education. Maybe just as effective and occurring at the same time was the economically directed case of *Adams v. Richardson* (351 F.Supp. 363, 1972), which ruled that the United States government could cut off federal funds for higher education in ten states where it felt that sufficient progress had not been made to desegregate higher education (Brubacher & Rudy, 1976, pp. 78–79).

However, it has been argued that nothing changed significantly in the SEC between the enactment of the 1964 Civil Rights bill and the late 1970s that would account for the sudden influx of black students at previously resistant public universities: black test scores did not go up; black high school graduation rates hardly went up; white institutions of higher learning were not suddenly seeing the error of their ways. The only difference was that Blacks were now allowed to play football at these schools and they couldn't win without them. Integration at the college level, at the very least, made certain, undeniable economic sense, and this in the end may have proved to be the most effective engine for change. College athletics in general and football in particular have become a multi-billion dollar industry (Smith, 2007, pp. 7–9).

Show Me the Money

In the 1960s college football was governed—for the most part—by the NCAA (National Collegiate Athletic Association), an administrative organization that took over the task of organizing rules, playoff systems, season start and finish times, etc. It was then on its way to becoming an enormous, money-generating entity in its own right. But even at the start of the 1970s, the NCAA—in an almost refreshing breath of idealism—would only allow television the weekly rights to broadcast four games—one nationally, and three regionally—on Saturdays. In 1970, there were only 11 major college bowl games at the end of the season. Conferences like the Big Ten and the PAC Eight (Pacific Athletic Conference Eight), would only allow its conference winner to go to a bowl game. Between the three seasons 1972–1974, the University of Michigan (for example) went 30-2-1, but because it didn't win the Big Ten Conference outright, it never went to a bowl game (University of Michigan Athletics History Website). By the end of the decade of the 1980s, college football had undergone a revolution that included a proliferation of bowl games—from 11 to 19 (currently there are 34; Van Avery, 2008) and a change in NCAA policy allowing multiple college football games to be shown nationally five nights a week. Black athletes were front and center of this economic explosion, selling university merchandise and tickets, and drumming up unprecedented alumni financial support every time they took the field—especially when the game was televised on national TV. There is no doubt that SEC integration can be said to have occurred just in time to reap the financial benefits of this economic bonanza, but it can be equally accurate to state that the obvious economic advantages helped fuel and sustain the desegregation movement in the SEC. The money was just too powerful of an incentive to allow any president or board of governors to permit their university to be on the outside looking in.

Success or Tokenism

It should also be noted that institutional racism was by no means limited to these SEC schools, with a similar prejudice against black athletes and black college students being existent in Texas, Virginia, Maryland, North Carolina, and Delaware, to name other bastions of Jim Crow. There had not been a black football player named to the Walter Camp All American Team since Paul Robeson of Rutgers in 1918 until 1937 (Pennington, 2008). Black football players, like black students in general, went to the traditional all-black colleges if they wanted to play and study in the South. As a result, small black colleges like Morgan State in Maryland and Grambling in Louisiana generated a disproportionate number of professional football players.

Another limitation to claims of success can be viewed in statistics concerning how many black non-athletes actually attend the large public institutions in the South. Integration in Southern colleges and universities were reflected in statistics compiled for an article in *The Journal for Blacks in Higher Education* by JBHE for the Winter 2003/2004 (pp. 28–30) edition that show the wide range of integration success/failure in the former Confederacy. Wake Forest in North Carolina, which plays in the Atlantic Coast Conference, contained the highest percentage of black football players among its total black student population (considered a negative statistic, or representative of tokenism). At Wake Forest at the time of the study, the total black male population was 290 and 55 of them were football players, meaning 19% of all black males at Wake Forest were football players. In the SEC, the school with the highest proportion of black athletes compared to total black student population is Vanderbilt in Tennessee, which had 35 black football players out of a black student population of 352 for 9.9%, or almost half the proportion of Wake Forest. Wake Forest is an example of the high end of the spectrum, and proves that integration of Southern universities remains a work in progress as far as integration goes. Mississippi State University (SEC) boasts a black student population of 15% (899 black males) of which 10% are black football players. For comparison, college football originator Rutgers, which is in the Big East Conference and the state university of New Jersey, had 849 black males constituting 7% of the male student population at the time of the study, and 89 black football players comprising 11% of the total black male population.

According to Richard Lewis, Jr. (Lewis 1995, pp. 438–441) black player totals in professional football increased significantly between 1960 and 1972. In 1960 they comprised 12% of all professional football players. By 1972 blacks represented nearly 40%. During that same period of time, black representation at SEC universities remained essentially zero, for football and non-football players alike. So, while Wake Forest has a high percentage, it is still a vast improvement from the time in the late 1960s when black student population was less than 1% and black football players often represented virtually all of the black students on campus in former all-white institutions of higher learning in the SEC.

This data can also support, however, the conclusion that in the SEC, comparatively significant gains have been made in overall black student integration since the initial integration of their respective football teams in the late 1960s and through the 1970s at a time when television and college sports were discovering their mutual benefit. Smith (2007, pp. 7–8) says that there is no coincidence that all three elements combined to drive desegregation efforts in higher education.

Conclusion

At a time in American history when the Civil Rights Movement and desegregation were major social issues of change and reform across a large portion of the spectrum of American society, those changes received impetus from, perhaps, unexpected sources. In this case the co-occurring explosion of college football, televised sports entertainment, and the growth of the American university after World War II, coalesced in the late 1960s to early 1970s to successfully drive desegregation efforts among previously all-white institutions of higher learning in the Deep South, in a manner, and to ends, that had until that point successfully withstood every other effort to integrate. Football, particularly big time football on the national scale, turns out to have made a critical difference.

References

Atlanta Journal Constitution, Obituary, *In from the Cold, John Howard Vaught RIP.* Posted On-line Feb. 6, 2006.

Brubacher, J. & Rudy, W. (1976). *Higher Education in Transition*, 3rd ed. New York: Harper & Row.

Cremin, L. (1988). *American Education: The Metropolitan Experience 1876–1980.* New York: Harper & Row.

Hinton, E., Reese, E., & Davidson, D. (1986). "Run for Respect: A Study of Black Football Players and the South," *Atlanta Journal Constitution.* Series September 7–14.

JBHE (Autumn 1998). Recalling the Death of Racial Segregation in Southern College Football. *The Journal of Blacks in Higher Education*, No. 21. 64–65.

JBHE (Winter 2002–2003). A Strong Football Effort May Distort JBHE's Black Enrollment Count at Academically Selective Institutions. *Journal of Blacks in Higher Education*, No. 38, 28–30.

Lapchick, R. (Feb. 2008). Breaking the College Color Barrier: Studies in Courage. *ESPN.com Black History Month*.

Lewis, R. (March 1995). Racial Position segregation: A Case Study of Southwest Conference Football, 1978 and 1989. *Journal of Black Studies*, 25(4), 431–446.

Lederman, D. (Jan. 11, 2008). Diversifying Through Football. *Inside Higher Education*. Posted on *insidehighered.com*.

Longman, J. & Glier, R. (2003). College Football; S.E.C. has a Black Football Coach. *The New York Times* April 19, 2003. Posted on *nytimes.com*.

Orfield, G. & Lee, C. (2004). Brown at 50: King's Dream or Plessey's Nightmare? *The Civil Rights Project*. Harvard University, Cambridge, MA.

Patterson, J. (2001). *Brown v. Board of Education: A Civil Rights Milestone and Its Troubled Legacy*. New York: Oxford University Press.

Paul, J. & McGhee, R.V., and Fant, H. (1984). The Arrival and Ascendancy of Black Athletes in the Southeastern Conference 1966–1980. *Phylon*, Clark Atlanta University. XLV(4).

Pennington, R. (Jan. 6, 2008). Racial Integration of College Football in Texas (from Invisible Texans). *Richard Pennington.Com*

Reese, R. (Spring 1999). Cal Poly Pomona. The Socio-Political Context of the Integration of Sports in America. *Journal of African American Men* 4(3).

Rudolph, F. (1962, 1990). *The American College and University: A History*. The University of Georgia Press, Athens, 373–394.

Smith, J. M. (Fall 2007). "Breaking the Plane": Integration and Black Protest in Michigan State University Football during the 1960s. *Michigan Historical Review*, 33(2).

Southern Educational Reporting Service in Reed Sarratt, The Ordeal of Desegregation. (1966). HEW Press Release, May 27, 1968; OCR data tapes; 1992–93, 1994–95, 1996–97, 1998–99, 2000–01, 2001–02 NCES Common Core of Data. New York: Harper & Row.

Thelin, J. (2004). *A History of American Higher Education*. Baltimore: The Johns Hopkins University Press.

University of Michigan Athletic History. Bentley Historical Library. *MGOBLUE.com*. *http://bentley.umich.edu/athdept/football/football.htm*

Van Avery, D. (2008). A Brief History of College Bowl Games: From the Rose Bowl to the BCS Championship. Suite 101.com (December 13). *http://college-football.suite101.com/article.cfm/history_of_college_bowl_games*

Walsh, C. (Feb. 22, 2008). Influence of UA's first black athlete endures. *Tuscaloosa.News.com*.

Zinser, L. (July 18, 2004). College Football; Crimson Tide Pioneer is Often Overlooked. *The New York Times*. Retrieved from *nytimes.com*.

Chapter 42

Malcolm X: A Nationalist Internationalist

Regina Jennings

Malcolm X (1925–1965), an extraordinary intellectual/activist of the 1960s, disrupted the protest methodology of the Civil Rights Movement with his forceful personality and rhetoric that defined a transformation of the "so-called n/Negro" into an African American. To ignite this psychological and semantic shift, Malcolm X spoke oratory that deconstructed the history of the United States and forthrightly charged White America with injustices against Black people. Unlike other major leaders of the Civil Rights Movement, Malcolm X did not push for integration within the apartheid social system in America. Instead, he argued for separation from the dominant culture's ideology, religion, and aesthetics. In the early part of his public career, he also argued for a geographic separation, a back-to-Africa idea similar to Marcus Garvey's vision during the Harlem Renaissance (1920–1935). He also spoke of the 19th century doctor, explorer, and author Martin Delany who devised an emigration scheme for Blacks to settle in South America. Additionally, Malcolm promoted an international perspective for analyzing and confronting American injustices, internationalizing the Negro. In this context and characterization he reinvigorates ideology and activism that W. E. B. Du Bois, Langston Hughes, and Paul Robeson started in literature, poetry, oratory, and song. Malcolm X, with insightful originality, pointed out problems within the Negro aggregate that debilitated the group. Challenging every possible obstacle that confronted the n/Negro, Malcolm X created a new people in America. His image countenanced an intelligently angry Black male (and female) persona that influenced activists and artists in the 1960s. This article examines components of Malcolm X's nationalism and internationalism that created a new American people. This creation happened with the semantic and psychological transformation of the Negro into the African-American, starting with the rejection of the race name "negro."

The Problems with n/Negro

Discarding the name "negro" from the lexicon of English was a tenet that Elijah Muhammad, head of the Nation of Islam, (NOI) taught Malcolm X and other members of the NOI. Most of Malcolm X's sharp political Black Nationalism sprung from Elijah Muhammad. X is not the sole architect of his reformation, from hustler to international leader. Elijah Muhammad is the man responsible for the prototypical patterns of thought that built Malcolm X into a world leader.

Elijah Muhammad was born October 7, 1897, to sharecroppers Wali and Marie Poole. He grew up in poverty along with 12 brothers and sisters in Bold Springs, near Sandersville, Georgia. Witnessing a brutal lynching when he returned home from school, young Elijah, early in life, was indelibly and negatively affected by White tyranny against Black people. The lynched man had been a member of his father's church. This killing compounded with poverty, inequality, segregation, and discrimination followed him into his adult life, where he steadfastly searched for answers to eradicate White horrific behavior and to build Black independence from White America. White men (and women) who lynched Black males were never prosecuted. Therefore, the possibility of maiming or death by mob violence lived in the mentality of Black Americans, particularly males.

After marrying Clara Evans in 1917, Elijah Muhammad became a Pullman porter until racism, an attack by a White male, caused him (and his family) to leave for Detroit where he met a northern version of "racism, discrimination, hunger, and despair."[1] On his search to understand, challenge, and eradicate White supremacy and to develop Black autonomy, Elijah Muhammad joined Marcus Garvey's Universal Negro Improvement Association. Garvey's Black Nationalist organization developed businesses, an army, and an ideology of self (race) empowerment for American Blacks. Additionally, Garvey had a plan and a mission to send Blacks to Africa to rebuild the motherland and to initiate trade between Africans on the continent and those in his organization. However, hounded and harassed by federal officials, the police, and integration-minded Blacks, Garvey was exiled from America in 1929. Yet, the absence of Garvey never deterred Elijah from his mission to find answers to reduce the effect of or to eradicate White supremacy and to create Black autonomy. He found his answer the following year.

In 1930, Elijah joined a religious group in the Paradise Valley section of Detroit where he met Wallace Fard Muhammad, "a mystic who taught a radical religion named Islam. Fard Muhammad's religion taught that blacks are mutually good and that whites are devils."[2] In *Inside the Nation of Islam* (2001), Vibert White explains the monumental importance of Wallace Fard Muhammad's impression on Black people. He writes that:

> Fard, as he was often called, not only cleaned people's homes in exchange for a captive audience but he occasionally paid people twenty-five cents to come to Nation of Islam Sunday meetings to hear his lectures. According to many of the first followers, this was the only way to get blacks to hear Fard's fiery and antiwhite rhetoric. To an oppressed people hearing someone call them great, wonderful, and gods, while referring to white store owners, landlords, and racist police as swine, devils, and the great Satan, allowed them to redeem a little of the self-worth that white America had taken from them.[3]

Casting the Whites as "devils" appealed directly to how Elijah Muhammad living in America had realized the behavior of White Americans. This Manichean view of the races seemed to fit his search for meaning and for reasons why Whites murdered Blacks with impunity. At the same time, the authorities were alerted about Fard's seminars with oppressed people, and in later years scholars documented his possible criminal activities and deceptions.[4] They also in reductive measure lessened his significance in the promotion of Manichean thought by pointing to what some call the "bizarre" religious narrative of the Nation of Islam's theology. This narrative presents how Whites were created and according to this view they emerged or were grafted from the Blacks. However, despite the denouncement of this religious narrative, and its messenger, it assisted in motivating the adherents to attempt self-reliance as opposed to dependency on White America. Similarly, Elijah Muhammad is often dismissed as a religious faker, adulterer, dictator, and racist. He has been compared to Hitler and Mussolini[5] and presented as a hypocritical criminal for taking money from White supremacist organizations. Yet, whatever his contradictions, Elijah Muhammad created from almost nothing an empire on which Blacks and Malcolm X in particular could fly. The Nation of Islam, once Fard Muhammad "disappeared" and Elijah Muhammad headed the organization, became the most powerful and independent economic enterprise for American Blacks. It practiced a separatist ideology that forced the members to think and to act in terms that related solely to one another, not to a government or a society where daily they faced humiliating injustices.

Such nationalism was not new in America, first emerging in the 19th century when Blacks were in bondage. During that epoch, free Blacks often aided those escaping from chattel slavery. As well, those still in bondage helped whenever possible the ones escaping towards a nominal freedom in a different geographic area. Nineteenth-century narratives by Frederick Douglass, Linda Brent/Harriet Jacobs, and others depict this race-on-race assistance and in contemporary, historical fiction Toni Morrison in *Beloved* (1987) portrays the race love inspired liaisons among Blacks, along with the disruptions. Thus, the collective history and experiences of the n/Negro people in America caused a perpetual bonding that, despite variations in political thought, has never dissipated.

Elijah Muhammad created a new God for the Blacks, Allah, a new code of conduct, and most significantly the confidence to believe in self and race, a monolithic roadblock to racial self-hatred. The racial inferiority of the period and the psychological distortions are evident in literature and in media images from the 1940s to the 1960s. Consider *Native Son* (1940), *Invisible Man* (1952), *Go Tell it on the Mountain* (1953), the 1950s television programs "The Little Rascals," and "Amos n' Andy," and the movie *Imitation of Life*. In the literature, the authors highlight the psychological trauma that afflicted (afflicts) Black people; the television programs show race specific characters that are simply silly. The film *Imitation of Life* portrays a biracial character's enormous desire for total Whiteness as well as the negation of the Black identity.

In contrast, in the Nation of Islam, the Black identity was examined through African-centered history, the Bible, and the Koran. Culturally, both genders were taught proper etiquette and for the males, the responsibility of being husbands and fathers, and for the women, the importance of domesticity, child rearing, and teaching. All studied history, politics, and psychology that elucidated the devastation of the Africans' forced importation to and existence in America. Because of the enslavement of Africans and the transformation of the African into the n/Negro, Muhammad believed that the history of Negroes in the United States was a history of losses.[6]

* * *

During the incarceration of Malcolm X (1946–1952), to offset such losses, he reeducated himself under the guidance of the Honorable Elijah Muhammad, head of the Nation of Islam (NOI). Once released from prison, Malcolm never ceased his stewardship to learning from Muhammad along with studying scholarship and journalism outside of the NOI. Readying himself for teaching the masses of Blacks (and Whites), X searched for material relative to his people normally omitted from schools, colleges, and universities. What he found was astounding, and he immediately constructed lectures on African-centered history that linked the American African to the ancient civilization of Kemet. Kemet is sometimes spelled Kemit, and the sacred symbol itself transliterates into Kmt. This important association provided his audience with an ancient, classical history that destroyed the notion of the savage African replicated in American texts and rhetoric. Like the 19th century White scholars who linked their history to the Greeks, X highlighted Kemet as the classical civilization of the Blacks, laying the foundation for a reemergence of a new people. The Kemetic interrelationship was simply a beginning.

Along with this Kemetic conjoining, X addressed the memory lost or dormancy in what Muhammad and the Muslims coined, the "so-called negro."[7] This issue forwards the (re)naming[8] subject, which Malcolm urged in his lectures with religious zeal. In the rhetorical process of persuading his audience to (re)name, X placed "so-called" before the word "negro," to immediately disturb the term's authenticity and value. Such devaluing encouraged the people so named to desire something else. In his oratory, X disapproved of the race name n/Negro, and he addressed the collective memory loss of the people so named. Once he introduced the vacuum of no authentic race name and an excluded or falsified history, X configured the space with an extraordinary African identity. About internationalism and African identity, X sums up its importance in remarks about "so-called negro" history week:

> *Negro History Week . . . doesn't remind us of past achievements. It reminds us only of the achievements we made in the Western Hemisphere under the tutelage of the white man. So that whatever achievement that was made in the Western Hemisphere that the spotlight is put upon, this is the white man's shrewd way of taking credit for whatever we have accomplished.*[9]

According to X's thought, prior to this African association, the celebration of "Negro History week" was a masquerade, a dressed up domestic form of subservience to White America. It showcased the "up from slavery" mentality that the descendants of enslavers or recipients of White privilege could boast as an American accomplishment. In the same excerpt X further says that:

> *But he never lets us know of an accomplishment that we made prior to being born here. This is another trick. The worst trick of all is when he names us Negro and calls us Negro.*

This omission of knowledge that preceded the n/Negro's arrival in America is important to address because it contributes to the total memory loss that debilitated the psychology of the n/Negro. Prior to the addressing of this omission, most n/Negros only sought to imitate and emulate Whites, knowing nothing else. Early Black literature exposes this obvious and understandable trend. Take the poetry of Phillis Wheatley, the first Black to publish poetry in a volume in 1773. In her poetics she naturally glorifies the ideology and aesthetics of enslavers. A century later, Frederick Douglass in his narrative fights against bondage and welcomes the culture and mores of the dominant society. This is the reason that he and Martin Delany fought over issues of Black Nationalism.[10] Similarly, a glorification of White aesthetics and ideals appears in 19th and 20th century Black poetry specifically in the artistry of Frances Ellen Watkins Harper and later Countee Cullen.[11] Understandably, the transformed African into the n/Negro the perpetual slave of American society caused a deliberate eradication of useful history of the continent. To make a slave, those in authority denied people in bondage the right to literacy, and the enslavers denied Africa's contribution to world civilization.

Acknowledging this absence clarifies why Malcolm X inspired and encouraged the Black Studies demand during the 1960s. He sought to fill the horrifying absence of civilization and history that beset the "negro," the (re)naming that X called "the worst trick of all." A kind of nihilism existed prior to X's revolutionary pronouncements during the 1960s that resembles the one that Cornel West addresses in *Race Matters* (1994). That nihilism involves contemporary youth (and older people) of the late 20th and early 21st century detached from one another, mostly because of corporate manufactured culture. Black people live lacking hope or meaning. Interestingly enough, West's antidote is to provide the "best of black nationalist movements"[12] to this illness, particularly among the young. This is exactly what Malcolm X put into practice. X's pre-1960s nihilism among Blacks concerned a lack of racial knowledge outside of bondage. Elijah Muhammad taught Malcolm X that the series of historical and racial omissions that distinguish Western history and literature composed an ideology that Muhammad called "tricknology." To change a group of Africans into a collection of n/Negroes, synonyms for slaves, required the metaphorical sleight of hand of enslavers.

Malcolm, deducing trickery and separation in the (re)naming of the African, insists that:

We're not Negroes, and have never been until we were brought here and made into that. We were scientifically produced by the white man. . . .

Humans are not "scientifically produced." Objects are. X's scientific reconstruction accents the commodity status of the (once) African stripped to nonhuman chattel, purchased and sold for centuries. The racial appellation "negro" refers to that shift into debasement, commodity status, and degradation. Basing his argument on the problematic nature and essence of the term "negro," X encourages a semantic erasure, to re(re)name.[13]

His use of history to fortify his argument is a literary resistance technique that David Walker started in his *Appeal* (1829). This text provides foundational points for the ideology of Elijah Muhammad's Islam. For example, Walker describes Whites as "devils" and as the Blacks' "natural enemies," referring to appearance and behavior. Elijah Muhammad dusted off this 19th century terminology, which was activated during enslavement, but may have had ritual and spiritual roots in Africa. For example, when Olaudah Equiano, an African, first saw White enslavers, he thought they were ghosts, their color ghastly.[14] In Yoruba culture, the color w/White has multiple connotations of death and of honor.[15]

The distance between the African and the Negro was a malcolmian leitmotif later implemented in poetry by Haki Madhubuti and other Black Arts authors of the 1960s. Malcolm X was a major impulse for the Black Arts Movement, a group of writers who made art out of rage, resistance, and intelligence. The (re)naming of the African to n/Negro and the sale of negroes for three centuries throughout America and other parts of the globe turned a people into a commodity.

The Changing Same n/Negro

The idea and reality of (re)naming is vital to understanding the depth of negative change that beset the (re)named African. In the 15th century, Portuguese explorers raiding the territory south of the Senegal River captured Africans for Prince Henry, "the Infante." Normally referring to Africans above the Senegal river as Moors or Azenegues, once enslaving started, the latter was shortened to negro and used as a noun, not as an adjective for color.[16]

The significance of X attacking the term Negro encourages his listeners to internationalize American history, reconsider history, and review language and its relationship to social conditions. Once the Negro realized the enormous deficiency in being (re)named, Malcolm then provided a new vision of and about Africa. The necessity of providing new information about Africa is based on the previous perspective of the Continent consistent with the debilitation of the slave and the continuance of enslavement. White American statesmen since the 17th century discount and discredit African culture and civilization. A sample of what

Henry Louis Gates writes about and quotes from the 18th century statesman David Hume centers on the enormity of the challenge to redefine the "so-called Negro:" "Hume posited with all of the authority of philosophy the fundamental identity of [negro] complexion, character, and intellectual capacity:"

> *I am apt to suspect the negroes and in general all the other species of men (for there are four or five different kinds) to be naturally inferior to the whites. There never was a civilized nation of any complexion than white, nor even any individual eminent either in action or speculation. No ingenious manufacturers amongst them, no arts, no sciences.*[17]

Such ideology adversely affects the Negro from then until now, and this explains why Malcolm X fought so valiantly for the "so-called negroes'" physical and mental inversion from Western ideology. The physical change induces a separation from "the White man," the dominant culture's aesthetics, education, religion, and social structure. The mental change involves connecting to an Africa that inverts Hume's more familiar racist version. Malcolm's history lessons about ancient civilizations such as Sumer, Meroe, Ghana, Mali, and most importantly, Egypt (Kemet) prepared his people to desire an international *and* an African link.

Malcolm's history lessons exceeded what Elijah Muhammad taught in his education classes. Malcolm's precise comprehension of ancient African civilizations were directions that gave birth to scholarship by Ivan Van Sertima and his series *They Came Before Columbus* (1976); Runoko Rashidi, *African Presence in Early Asia* (1985); Molefi Asante, *The Afrocentric Idea* (1987); Edward Bruce Bynum, *The African Unconscious* (1999); Tsenay Serequeberehan, *African Philosophy* (1991). Additionally, Malcolm's internationalism influenced or reintroduced the research and writing of other scholars such as Cheikh Anta Diop, Drusilla Dunjee Houston, and Theophile Obenga. Opening up the corridors of 19th century nationalism, X reinvigorated this body of thought with Pan-Africanism that offered a Nile Valley recollection. About the Nile Valley, he says the following:

> *Now the black civilization that shook the white man up the most was the Egyptian civilization, and it was a black civilization.*[18]

Malcolm preached this intercontinental relationship during the 1960s and this liaison has been one that even some contemporary scholars attempt to refute. The image of Africa is more comfortably accepted from the vision of Hume. A subservient and colonized Africa fits the vision of European expansionism. Moreover, if Egypt is considered more White than Black, the Whites can claim its ancient unfathomable greatness. Thus, an independent Africa causes cognitive dissonance, the jarring that Malcolm gave to his multiracial audiences. In the following, X locates and describes how Egypt is attached to the African world.

> *It was along the banks of the Nile which runs through the heart of Africa. . . . This tricky white man was able to take the Egyptian civilization, write books about it, put pictures in those books, make movies for television and the theatre—so skillfully that he has even convinced other white people that the ancient Egyptians were white people themselves. They were African, they were as much African as you and I.*[19]

When Malcolm made this speech in 1964, no such thing as an "African American" existed. There were Africans on the continent and in America there were Negroes. The relationship between these two groups was rather obscure and not normally emphasized. In those same books that Malcolm discussed previously, Eurocentric scholars described Africa in a manner that caused enormous shame and distance from the continent among American Negroes. Hence, in Malcolm's previous speech, he creates a new people, himself included, "you and I." In his oratory, he separates the American Negroes from American society, binding them to Africa as he has bound himself. This is a distinction that Malcolm X had from his spiritual guide, the Honorable Elijah Muhammad. And this attention to Africa also caused later riffs in X's final two groups, the Muslim Mosque Inc. and the Organization of Afro-American Unity.[20] Malcolm's internationalism sometimes negatively affected his disciples.

The fundamental and colossal significance of linking Egypt/Kemet to Africa carries an intellectual and cultural magnitude that the Senegalese physicist Cheikh Anta Diop says "dazzles" even today. How, why, and when the pyramids and the sphinx were built are still in question. Some have argued that they are archaeological wonders of the world built by geniuses who could not possibly be related to other Africans enslaved for centuries. The intellectual separation of Egypt from the rest of the African continent is largely grounded on such racist ideology.

The explorer Graham Hancock explains the difficulty the ancients underwent in order to square the base of the Great Pyramid. He concludes with: "All that we can say for sure is that the base *is* square and that the monument *is* locked into the cardinal axes of our planet with great care and precision."[21] Yet, this is still the question: How could the ancients meticulously transfer, handle, and carve rock and stone weighing hundreds of tons? No one knows the answer. If the ancients were stargazers, as some Egyptologists claim, then how could Pythagoras, the touted father of mathematics, be the inventor of pi? John Anthony West interrogates this same point:

> *Arguments had long ranged over whether the proportions of the Great Pyramid were deliberate or purely fortuitous. The pyramid's height stands in a precise pi relationship to the perimeter of the base. Pi (3.1416 . . .) is the transcendental that defines the ratio between the diameter of a circle and its circumference. At the same time, pi is related to another, more interesting, irrational, phi, the so-called Golden Section. It had been observed—and ignored by Egyptologists—that not only the Great Pyramid but the other pyramids as well made use of different phi relations in their construction.*[22]

The various uses of phi and pi may still be in debate, yet all scholars on Egypt agree that the pyramids were constructed thousands of years prior to the Greek mathematician Pythagoras (sixth century B.C.). However, it is him that Western education salutes as the inventor of pi. Paradoxically, the ancient Greek masterminds admit to the extraordinary teachings and teachers of Kemet. About their own personal limitations they say this:

> *We Greeks are in reality children compared with the people with traditions ten times older. And as nothing of precious remembrance of the past would long survive in our country, Egypt has recorded and kept eternally the wisdom of the old times. The walls of its temples are covered with inscriptions and the priests have always under their own eyes that divine heritage. . . . The generations continue to transmit to successive generations these sacred things unchanged: songs, dances, rhythms, rituals, music, paintings, all coming from time immemorial when gods governed the earth in the dawn of civilization.* [23]

Malcolm X connected the American Negro debased in history to those who were "gods" governing "the earth." In telling the "lost/found black man" (and woman) that they were the original people and the builders of such civilizations, he linked his listeners to a boundless expansiveness and success. Muhammad had taught Malcolm about the "devil White man's" stripping of the Asiatic Black man from his position of power millennia ago. Fard taught Muhammad that message. X gave this narrative a historical foundation that he physically visited in order to view the teachings firsthand. This general dichotomy between the races is also examined in Cheikh Anta Diop's two-cradle theory where climate factors into creating racial personalities. Diop writes:

> *The history of humanity will remain confused as long as we fail to distinguish between the two cradles in which Nature fashioned the instincts, temperament, habits and ethical concepts of the [Blacks and Whites] before they met each other after a long separation dating back to prehistoric times. . . . The abundance of vital resources, its sedentary, agricultural character, the specific conditions of the [Nile] valley will engender in man, that is, in the Negro, a gentle, idealistic, peaceful nature endowed with a spirit of justice and gaiety. . . . By contrast, the ferocity of nature in Eurasian steppes, the barrenness of those regions, the overall circumstances of material conditions, were to create instincts necessary for survival in such an environment. . . . Man in those regions long remained a nomad. . . . He was cruel. . . . All the peoples of the area whether white or yellow, were instinctively to love conquest, because of a desire to escape from those hostile surroundings.*[24]

In putting forward theories for racially distinctive behaviors, Diop, Muhammad, and X alerted the Negro to examine his former owners instead of himself as a problem. The psychological damage of generational chattel slavery, discrimination, segregation, lynching had burdened the Negro, and Malcolm through semantics inverted that mental monolith.

In the 20th century, this mode of intellectualism is in the tradition of Marcus Garvey, activating group independence and self-reliance. The might of Malcolm's message, his tone, wit, and humor engaged and entertained his audience with ideas normally not publicized. In the following excerpt, we sample his masterful rhetorical style that inspired his listeners. At Abyssinian Baptist Church, Adam Clayton Powell questions Malcolm about the contradiction in practicing Islam and barring Whites from membership in the Nation of Islam. When Powell asks Malcolm if he hates the White man, X signifies:

> *We don't even think about him. How can anybody ask us do we hate the man who kidnapped us 400 years ago, brought us here and stripped us of our history, stripped us of our culture, stripped us of our language, stripped us of everything that you could use today to prove that you were ever part of the human family, brought you down to the level of an animal, sold you from plantation to plantation like a sack of wheat, sold you like a sack of potatoes, sold you like a horse and a cow, and then hung you up from one end of the country to the other, and then you ask me do I hate him?*[25]

Malcolm's verbal fluency and scathing attack on the historical treatment suffered under White authority is a rhetorical method similar to X's destruction of "Negro." To remove the term from American language, he surrounded it with the "logically unexpected" "so-called." This "circumlocution" upheld the race name for a fresh examination. Circumlocution, "indirection" and the "logically unexpected" are aspects of signifying.[26] In his successful mission to erase the term Negro, he often employed word substitutions. According to Benjamin (2X) Goodman, a protegee of Malcolm's, the minister normally spoke two hours long. To determine how often he repeated his persuasive argument to re(re)name, I conducted a quantitative analysis of four of X's speeches. The speeches are "Black Man's History" (1962); "The Old Negro and the New Negro"(1963); "God's Judgement of White America: The Chickens Are Coming Home to Roost" (1963); and a speech-interview with A. B. Spellman in 1964. This is what I found: In "Black Man's History," Malcolm says "so-called Negroes" 14 times. In "The Old Negro and the New Negro," he repeats it 14 times, with a questioner saying it back to him, demonstrating speaker/audience acceptance. In the speech-interview, X uttered "so-called Negroes" 10 times. The median number is 12.6, suggesting the magnetic power of repetition occurring whenever Malcolm speaks. In "God's Judgement of White America: The Chickens Are Coming Home to Roost" he abandons "so-called Negroes," substituting "so-called Negroes" with "lost sheep," "lost tribe," "lost people of God," and coupling "Negro" with "exslaves" seven times.

Before Malcolm reached national and international fame, he lectured three times a week at Temple #7, located on Lenox Avenue and 116th Street in Harlem. He lectured twice during the week and once on Sunday subtly urging re(re)naming, and when he traveled he spread his message even more. The scholar Katherine Bankole explains why Malcolm verbally fought to remove the race name "negro." She writes that:

> *Regardless of the 'Black Firsts'—achievements and contributions by certain African Americans—the masses of Black people were burdensome to society at best ("The Negro Problem"). The Negro could not get beyond the negative origins of the term. The "Negro" would always be less than his/her individual contributions to American society. The Negro, deemed as inherently inferior, ugly, and subhuman, had low identity-self esteem. Most of all the Negro had no history. . . . Even now the "Negro" is a contemptuous being—the parent of the damnable "Nigger."*[27]

With the formation of the negro taking shape during the enslavement of Africans, the renamed people became a collection of war-time captives who repressed defeat. This repression and condition spawned patterns of behavior that accentuated the superiority of Whites, fostering White supremacy. This is a problem even during the Civil Rights struggle, when Negroes fought to have the same opportunities and access to the same facilities as Whites. On the surface that attainment reflects the hypocrisy of the American ideal of freedom. Yet, beneath the surface, this reach for opportunity reinforces White superiority. Although it bravely and creatively challenged White hegemony, it also upheld White privilege as the concluding prize. To put it succinctly, Negroes had to reach up to gain White privilege. In this spatial reach, Malcolm's dichotomous racial language shifted the "Negro struggle" from desiring White privilege to determining one's own destiny. Racial name change begins that process.

Malcolm as an internationalist always included in his oratory the 700 million Muslims worldwide, the people in Latin America, Asia, Africa, and of course Blacks throughout the Diaspora. Malcolm was a man of the world, a humanist who also discussed his enemies in terms of globalization. In one of his final speeches, "A Worldwide Revolution," he says:

> There're a worldwide revolution going on. And it's in two phases. Number one, what is it revolting against? The power structure. The American power structure? No. The French power structure? No. The English power structure? No. Then what power structure? An international Western power structure. An international power structure consisting of American interest, French interest, English interests, Belgian interests, European interests. Those countries that formerly colonized the dark man formed into a giant international combine.

This international combine exposed itself when Malcolm was assassinated, with mourners sending condolences read by Ruby Dee from Africa, Pakistan, London, Ghana, South Africa, and Switzerland. In Indonesia people plastered anti-American signs all over the United States ambassador's house, blaming the American government for X's murder.[28] Yet, of course, nowhere was he mourned more deeply than in America among the Negroes, transforming, becoming something else because of X—that new people he uttered into being in the 1960s, that new people he presciently called in the "Ballot or the Bullet":

> Right now, in this country, [we are] 22 million African-Americans—that's what we are. . . .[29] (my emphasis)

No one said the term "African American" before him and over 25 years later, in 1988, X's people demanded this race name and discarded n/Negro forever. Negro is a pejorative in the Black lexicon. Thus, Malcolm X is the creator of a new American people, up from bondage, a people who re(re)named themselves in preparation for determining a new agency and identity.

Endnotes

1. White, Vibert L. (2001). *Inside the Nation of Islam: A Historical and Personal Testimony by a Black Muslim.* Gainsville: University of Florida Press, 23.
2. Ibid., 25.
3. Ibid., 25.
4. Ibid., 30–1 and Clegg III, Claude Andrew. (1997). *An Original Man: The Life & Times of Elijah Muhammad.* New York: St. Martins Press, 20–30.
5. Lewy, Ernst. (1979). "Historical Charismatic Leaders and Mythical Heroes." *Journal of Psychohistory,* 6.
6. Karim, Benjamin, Gallen, David and Skutches, Peter. (1992). *Remembering Malcolm.* New York: Ballantine, 90.
7. I deliberately lowercase the "n" in Negro to emphasize its presentation from American enslavement of the African to the 20th century when Marcus Garvey, W. E. B. Du Bois and others demanded the capitalization of the "n."
8. The parenthesis around the "re" in (re)naming represents the instability of being renamed, and it signifies on the racist assertion to (re)name a people, a disrespect to the people's original appellation.
9. Clarke, John Henrik. (1969). *Malcolm X: The Man and His Times* Canada: The Macmillan Company, 322–3.
10. For a detailed comparative analysis between Douglass and Delany, see Levine, Robert S. (1997). *Martin Delany Frederick Douglass: and the Politics of Representative Identity.* Chapel Hill, The University of North Carolina Press.

11. For an in-depth study of this omission, read Jennings, Regina. (2003). "From nigger to negro: Dysfunctional Beginnings of Identity for New World Africans" in *African-Centered Psychology: Culture-Focusing for Multicultural Competence*, Daudi Ajani ya Azibo. (ed.). Durham: Carolina Academic Press.

12. West, Cornel. (1994). *Race Matters*. New York: Random House, 30.

13. To re(re)name is a term I coined to state the affirming act of the n/Negro becoming African American. This is more fully rendered in the text: *Malcolm X: The Music in Madhubuti's Horn*. (2003). Forthcoming, McFarland Press.

14. Edwards, Paul. (ed.). (1977). *Equiano's Travels*. London: Heinemann, 25–8.

15. Thompson, Robert Farris. (1983). *Flash of the Spirit: African and Afro-American Art and Philosophy*. New York: Random House, 134–8.

16. Moore, Richard. (1991). *The Name Negro its Origin and Evil Use*. Baltimore: Black Classic Press, 36–40.

17. Gates, Henry Louis. (1987). *Figures in Black: Words, Signs, and the Racial Self*. New York: Oxford University Press, 18.

18. Breitman, George. (ed.). (1982). *Malcolm X on Afro-American History*. New York: Pathfinder Press, 20.

19. Ibid., 20.

20. Sale, William. *From Civil Rights to Black Liberation: Malcolm X and the Organization of Afro-American Unity*. Boston: South End Press.

21. Hancock, Graham and Bauval, Robert. (1996). *The Message of the Sphinx: A Quest for the Hidden Legacy of Mankind*. New York: Three Rivers Press, 198.

22. West, John Anthony. (1993). *Sterpent in the Sky: The High Wisdom of Ancient Egypt*. Wheaton, IL: Quest Books, 21.

23. Quoted in Hancock, Graham, and Bauval, Robert. (1996). *The Message of the Sphinx*. New York: Three Rivers, 198.

24. Diop, 1974, 111–3.

25. Goodman, 79–80.

26. Smitherman, Geneva. (1977). *Talking and Testifying: The Language of Black America*. Detroit: Wayne University Press, 121.

27. Bankole, Katherine O. (2001). *You Left Your Mind in Africa: Journal Observations and Essays on African American Self-Hatred*. Dellsslow, West Virginia: Nation House Foundation, 17.

28. Grant, Earl. (1990). "The Last Days of Malcolm X" in *Malcolm X: The Man and His Times*. John Henrik Clarke, (ed.). Trenton: African World Press, 101–3.

29. Breitman, George (ed.). (1989). *Malcolm X Speaks: Selected Speeches and Statements*. New York: Pathfinder Press, 36.

Chapter 43

Brown v. Board of Education of Topeka, Kansas, 1954

The plaintiffs contend that segregated public schools are not "equal" and cannot be made "equal," and that hence they are deprived of the equal protection of the laws. Because of the obvious importance of the question presented, the Court took jurisdiction. Argument was heard in the 1952 Term, and reargument was heard this Term on certain questions propounded by the Court.

Reargument was largely devoted to the circumstances surrounding the adoption of the Fourteenth Amendment in 1868. It covered exhaustively consideration of the Amendment in Congress, ratification by the states, then existing practices in racial segregation, and the views of proponents and opponents of the Amendment. This discussion and our own investigation convince us that, although these sources cast some light, it is not enough to resolve the problem with which we are faced. At best, they are inconclusive. The most avid proponents of the post-War Amendments undoubtedly intended them to remove all legal distinctions among "all persons born or naturalized in the United States." Their opponents, just as certainly, were antagonistic to both the letter and the spirit of the Amendments and wished them to have the most limited effect. What others in Congress and the state legislatures had in mind cannot be determined with any degree of certainty.

An additional reason for the inconclusive nature of the Amendment's history, with respect to segregated schools, is the status of public education at that time. In the South, the movement toward free common schools, supported by general taxation, had not yet taken hold. Education of white children was largely in the hands of private groups. Education of Negroes was almost nonexistent, and practically all of the race were illiterate. In fact, any education of Negroes was forbidden by law in some states. Today, in contrast, many Negroes have achieved outstanding success in the arts and sciences as well as in the business and professional world. It is true that public school education at the time of the Amendment had advanced further in the North, but the effect of the Amendment on Northern States was generally ignored in the congressional debates. Even in the North, the conditions of public education did not approximate those existing today. The curriculum was usually rudimentary; ungraded schools were common in rural areas; the school term was but three months a year in many states; and compulsory school attendance was virtually unknown. As a consequence, it is not surprising that there should be so little in the history of the Fourteenth Amendment relating to its intended effect on public education.

In the first cases in this Court construing the Fourteenth Amendment, decided shortly after its adoption, the Court interpreted it as proscribing all state-imposed discriminations against the Negro race. The doctrine of "separate but equal" did not make its appearance in this Court until 1896 in the case of *Plessy v. Ferguson* involving not education but transportation. American courts have since labored with the doctrine for over half a century. In this Court, there have been six cases involving the "separate but equal" doctrine in the field of public education. In more recent cases, all on the graduate school level, inequality was found in that specific benefits enjoyed by white students were denied to Negro students of the same educational qualifications. In none of these cases was it necessary to re-examine the doctrine to grant relief to the Negro plaintiff.

In approaching this problem, we cannot turn the clock back to 1868 when the Amendment was adopted, or even to 1896 when *Plessy v. Ferguson* was written. We must consider public education in the light of its full development and its present place in American life throughout the Nation. Only in this way can it be determined if segregation in public schools deprives these plaintiffs of the equal protection of the laws.

Today, education is perhaps the most important function of state and local governments. Compulsory school attendance laws and the great expenditures for education both demonstrate our recognition of the importance of education to our democratic society. It is required in the performance of our most basic public responsibilities, even service in the armed forces. It is the very foundation of good citizenship. Today it is a principal instrument in awakening the child to cultural values, in preparing him for later professional training, and in helping him to adjust normally to his environment. In these days, it is doubtful that any child may reasonably be expected to succeed in life if he is denied the opportunity of an education. Such an opportunity, where the state has undertaken to provide it, is a right which might be made available to all on equal terms.

We come then to the question presented: Does segregation of children in public schools solely on the basis of race, even though the physical facilities and other "tangible" factors may be equal, deprive the children of the minority group of equal educational opportunities? We believe that it does.

In *Sweatt v. Painter* in finding that a segregated law school for Negroes could not provide them equal educational opportunities, this Court relied in large part on "those qualities which are incapable of objective measurement but which make for greatness in a law school." In *McLaurin v. Oklahoma State Regents* the Court, in requiring that a Negro admitted to a white graduate school be treated like all other students, again resorted to intangible considerations: ". . . his ability to study, to engage in discussions and exchange views with other students, and, in general, to learn his profession." Such considerations apply with added force to children in grade and high schools. To separate them from others of similar age and qualifications solely because of their race generates a feeling of inferiority as to their status in the community that may affect their hearts and minds in a way unlikely ever to be undone. The effect of this separation on their educational opportunities was well stated by a finding in the Kansas case by a court which nevertheless felt compelled to rule against the Negro plaintiffs:

> "Segregation of white and colored children in public schools has a detrimental effect upon the colored children. The impact is greater when it has the sanction of the law; for the policy of separating the races is usually interpreted as denoting the inferiority of the negro group. A sense of inferiority affects the motivation of a child to learn. Segregation with the sanction of law, therefore, has a tendency to [retard] the educational and mental development of negro children and to deprive them of some of the benefits they would receive in a racial(ly) integrated school system."

What ever may have been the extent of psychological knowledge at the time of *Plessy v. Ferguson*, this finding is amply supported by modern authority. Any language in *Plessy v. Ferguson* contrary to this finding is rejected.

We conclude that in the field of public education the doctrine of "separate but equal" has no place. Separate educational facilities are inherently unequal. Therefore, we hold that the plaintiffs and others similarly situated for whom the actions have been brought are, by reason of the segregation complained of, deprived of the equal protection of the laws guaranteed by the Fourteenth Amendment.

Chapter 44

The Civil Rights Act, 1964

Title I—Voting

Prohibits registrars from applying different standards to white and Negro voting applicants and from dis-qualifying applicants because of inconsequential errors on their forms. Requires that literacy tests be in writing, except under special arrangements for blind persons, and that any applicant desiring one be given a copy of the questions and his answers. Make a sixth-grade education a rebuttable presumption of literacy. Allows the Attorney General or defendant state officials in any voting suit to request trial by a three-judge Federal Court.

Title II—Public Accommodations

Prohibits discrimination or refusal of service on account of race in hotels, motel, restaurants, gasoline stations and places of amusement if their operations affect interstate commerce or if their discrimination "is supported by state action." Permits the Attorney General to enforce the title by suit in the Federal courts if he believes that any person or group is engaging in a "pattern or practice of resistance" to the rights declared by the title. The latter language was added in the Senate, which also authorized three-judge courts for suits under this title.

Title III—Public Facilities

Requires that Negroes have equal access to, and treatment in, publicly owned or operated facilities such as parks, stadiums, and swimming pools. Authorizes the Attorney General to sue for enforcement of these rights if private citizens are unable to sue effectively.

Title IV—Public Schools

Empowers the Attorney General to bring school desegregation suits under the same conditions as in Title III. Authorizes technical and financial aid to school districts to assist in desegregation. The Senate strengthened a provision in the House bill saying that the title does not cover busing of pupils or other steps to end "racial imbalance."

Title V—Civil Rights Commission

Extends the life of the Civil Rights Commission until January 31, 1968.

Title VI—Federal Aid

Provides that no person shall be subjected to racial discrimination in any program receiving Federal aid. Direct Federal agencies to take steps against discrimination, including—as a last resort, and after hearings— withholding of Federal funds from state or local agencies that discriminate.

Title VII—Employment

Bans discrimination by employers or unions with 100 or more employees or members the first year the act is effective, reducing over four years to 25 or more. Establishes a commission to investigate alleged discrimination and use persuasion to end it. Authorizes the Attorney General to sue if he believes any person or group is engaged in a "pattern or practice" of resistance to the title, and to ask for trial by a three-judge court. The Senate added the "pattern-or-practice" condition and shifted the power to sue from the commission to the Attorney General.

Title VIII—Statistics

Directs the Census Bureau to compile statistics of registration and voting by race in areas of the country designated by the Civil Rights Commission. This might be used to enforce the long-forgotten provision of the 14th Amendment that states that [to] discriminate in voting shall lose seats in the House of Representatives.

Title IX—Courts

.Permits appellate review of decisions by Federal District judges to send back to the state courts criminal defendants who have attempted to remove their cases on the ground that their civil rights would be denied in state trials. Permits the Attorney General to intervene in suits filed by private persons complaining that they have been denied the equal protection of the laws.

Title X—Conciliation

Establishes a Community Relations Service in the Commerce Department to help conciliate racial disputes. The Senate removed a House ceiling of seven employees.

Title XI—Miscellaneous

Guarantees jury trials for criminal contempt under any part of the act but Title I—a provision added in the Senate. Provides that the statue shall not invalidate state laws with consistent purposes, and that it shall not impair any existing powers of Federal officials.

Chapter 45

Before the Voting Rights Act of 1965

United States Department of Justice

Reconstruction and the Civil War Amendments

Before the Civil War the United States Constitution did not provide specific protections for voting. Qualifications for voting were matters which neither the Constitution nor federal laws governed. At that time, although a few northern states permitted a small number of free black men to register and vote, slavery and restrictive state laws and practices led the franchise to be exercised almost exclusively by white males.

Shortly after the end of the Civil War Congress enacted the Military Reconstruction Act of 1867, which allowed former Confederate States to be readmitted to the Union if they adopted new state constitutions that permitted universal male suffrage. The 14th Amendment, which conferred citizenship to all persons born or naturalized in the United States, was ratified in 1868.

In 1870 the 15th Amendment was ratified, which provided specifically that the right to vote shall not be denied or abridged on the basis of race, color, or previous condition of servitude. This superseded state laws that had directly prohibited black voting. Congress then enacted the Enforcement Act of 1870, which contained criminal penalties for interference with the right to vote, and the Force Act of 1871, which provided for federal election oversight.

As a result, in the former Confederate States, where new black citizens in some cases comprised outright or near majorities of the eligible voting population, hundreds of thousands—perhaps one million—recently-freed slaves registered to vote. Black candidates began for the first time to be elected to state, local, and federal offices and to play a meaningful role in their governments.

Disfranchisement

The extension of the franchise to black citizens was strongly resisted. Among others, the Ku Klux Klan, the Knights of the White Camellia, and other terrorist organizations attempted to prevent the 15th Amendment from being enforced by violence and intimidation. Two decisions in 1876 by the Supreme Court narrowed the scope of enforcement under the Enforcement Act and the Force Act, and, together with the end of Reconstruction marked by the removal of federal troops after the Hayes-Tilden Compromise of 1877, resulted in a climate in which violence could be used to depress black voter turnout and fraud could be used to undo the effect of lawfully cast votes.

Once whites regained control of the state legislatures using these tactics, a process known as "Redemption," they used gerrymandering of election districts to further reduce black voting strength and minimize the number of black elected officials. In the 1890s, these states began to amend their constitutions and to enact a series of laws intended to re-establish and entrench white political supremacy.

Such disfranchising laws included poll taxes, literacy tests, vouchers of "good character," and disqualification for "crimes of moral turpitude." These laws were "color-blind" on their face, but were designed to exclude black citizens disproportionately by allowing white election officials to apply the procedures selectively. Other laws and practices, such as the "white primary," attempted to evade the 15th Amendment by allowing "private" political parties to conduct elections and establish qualifications for their members.

As a result of these efforts, in the former Confederate states nearly all black citizens were disenfranchised and removed from voting by 1910. The process of restoring the rights stolen by these tactics would take many decades.

Attacks on Disfranchisement Before the Voting Rights Act

In *Guinn v. United States*, 238 U.S. 347 (1915), the Supreme Court held that voter registration requirements containing "grandfather clauses," which made voter registration in part dependent upon whether the applicant was descended from men enfranchised before enactment of the 15th Amendment violated that amendment. The Supreme Court found the Oklahoma law was adopted in order to give whites, who might otherwise have been disfranchised by the state's literacy test, a way of qualifying to vote that was not available to blacks. In 1944, the Supreme Court held that the Texas "white primary" violated the 15th Amendment. *Smith v. Allwright*, 321 U.S. 649 (1944). The Southern states experimented with numerous additional restrictions to limit black participation in politics, many of which were struck down by federal courts over the next decade.

Congress passed legislation in 1957, 1960, and 1964 that contained voting-related provisions. The 1957 Act created the Civil Rights Division within the Department of Justice and the Commission on Civil Rights; the Attorney General was given authority to intervene in and institute lawsuits seeking injunctive relief against violations of the 15th Amendment. The 1960 Act permitted federal courts to appoint voting referees to conduct voter registration following a judicial finding of voting discrimination. The 1964 Act also contained several relatively minor voting-related provisions. Although court decisions and these laws made it more difficult, at least in theory, for states to keep all of their black citizens disenfranchised, the strategy of litigation on a case-by-case basis proved to be of very limited success in the jurisdictions that were sued and it did not prompt voluntary compliance among jurisdictions that had not been sued. Literacy tests, poll taxes, and other formal and informal practices combined to keep black registration rates minimal in Alabama, Louisiana, and Mississippi, and well below white registration rates in the others.

Faced with the prospect that black voter registration could not be suppressed forever, however, some states began to change political boundaries and election structures so as to minimize the impact of black re-enfranchisement. In 1960, the Supreme Court struck down one such effort, in which the state legislature had gerrymandered the city boundaries of Tuskegee, Alabama, so as to remove all but a handful of the city's black registered voters. The Supreme Court ruled that by doing so Alabama had violated the 15th Amendment. *Gomillion v. Lightfoot*, 364 U.S. 339 (1960).

The "Reapportionment Revolution"

In the early 1960s, the Supreme Court also overcame its reluctance to apply the Constitution to unfair redistricting practices. Prior to 1962, the United States Supreme Court had declined to decide constitutional challenges to legislative apportionment schemes, on the grounds that such "political questions" were not within the federal courts' jurisdiction. In *Baker v. Carr*, 369 U.S. 186 (1962), however, the Supreme Court recognized that grossly malapportioned state legislative districts could seriously undervalue—or dilute—the voting strength of the residents of overpopulated districts while overvaluing the voting strength of residents of underpopulated districts. The Supreme Court found that such malapportionment could be challenged in federal court under the Equal Protection Clause of the 14th Amendment.

In later cases including *Reynolds v. Sims*, 377 U.S. 533 (1964), and *Wesberry v. Sanders*, 376 U.S. 1 (1964), the Supreme Court established the one-person, one-vote principle. Because in many states malapportioned legislative districts had resulted in sparsely-populated rural counties having a much greater share of their state's political power than their state's population, correcting this imbalance led to dramatic realignments of political power in several states. In *Fortson v. Dorsey*, 379 U.S. 433 (1965), the Supreme Court suggested, but did not hold, that certain types of apportionment might unconstitutionally dilute the voting strength of racial minorities.

Chapter 46

President Lyndon Johnson's
Voting Rights Address, 1965

March 15, 1965

Mr. Speaker, Mr. President, Members of the Congress:

I speak tonight for the dignity of man and the destiny of democracy.

I urge every member of both parties, Americans of all religions and of all colors, from every section of this country, to join me in that cause.

At times history and fate meet at a single time in a single place to shape a turning point in man's unending search for freedom. So it was at Lexington and Concord. So it was a century ago at Appomattox. So it was last week in Selma, Alabama.

There, long-suffering men and women peacefully protested the denial of their rights as Americans. Many were brutally assaulted. One good man, a man of God, was killed.

There is no cause for pride in what has happened in Selma. There is no cause for self-satisfaction in the long denial of equal rights of millions of Americans. But there is cause for hope and for faith in our democracy in what is happening here tonight.

For the cries of pain and the hymns and protests of oppressed people have summoned into convocation all the majesty of this great Government—the Government of the greatest Nation on earth.

Our mission is at once the oldest and the most basic of this country: to right wrong, to do justice, to serve man.

In our time we have come to live with moments of great crisis. Our lives have been marked with debate about great issues; issues of war and peace, issues of prosperity and depression. But rarely in any time does an issue lay bare the secret heart of America itself. Rarely are we met with a challenge, not to our growth or abundance, our welfare or our security, but rather to the values and the purposes and the meaning of our beloved Nation.

The issue of equal rights for American Negroes is such an issue. And should we defeat every enemy, should we double our wealth and conquer the stars, and still be unequal to this issue, then we will have failed as a people and as a nation.

For with a country as with a person, "What is a man profited, if he shall gain the whole world, and lose his own soul?"

There is no Negro problem. There is no Southern problem. There is no Northern problem. There is only an American problem. And we are met here tonight as Americans—not as Democrats or Republicans—we are met here as Americans to solve that problem.

This was the first nation in the history of the world to be founded with a purpose. The great phrases of that purpose still sound in every American heart, North and South: "All men are created equal"—"government by consent of the governed"—"give me liberty or give me death." Well, those are not just clever words, or those are not just empty theories. In their name Americans have fought and died for two centuries, and tonight around the world they stand there as guardians of our liberty, risking their lives.

Those words are a promise to every citizen that he shall share in the dignity of man. This dignity cannot be found in a man's possessions; it cannot be found in his power, or in his position. It really rests on his right to be treated as a man equal in opportunity to all others. It says that he shall share in freedom, he shall choose his leaders, educate his children, and provide for his family according to his ability and his merits as a human being.

To apply any other test—to deny a man his hopes because of his color or race, his religion or the place of his birth—is not only to do injustice, it is to deny America and to dishonor the dead who gave their lives for American freedom.

The Right to Vote

Our fathers believed that if this noble view of the rights of man was to flourish, it must be rooted in democracy. The most basic right of all was the right to choose your own leaders. The history of this country, in large measure, is the history of the expansion of that right to all of our people.

Many of the issues of civil rights are very complex and most difficult. But about this there can and should be no argument. Every American citizen must have an equal right to vote. There is no reason which can excuse the denial of that right. There is no duty which weighs more heavily on us than the duty we have to ensure that right.

Yet the harsh fact is that in many places in this country men and women are kept from voting simply because they are Negroes.

Every device of which human ingenuity is capable has been used to deny this right. The Negro citizen may go to register only to be told that the day is wrong, or the hour is late, or the official in charge is absent. And if he persists, and if he manages to present himself to the registrar, he may be disqualified because he did not spell out his middle name or because he abbreviated a word on the application.

And if he manages to fill out an application he is given a test. The registrar is the sole judge of whether he passes this test. He may be asked to recite the entire Constitution, or explain the most complex provisions of State law. And even a college degree cannot be used to prove that he can read and write.

For the fact is that the only way to pass these barriers is to show a white skin.

Experience has clearly shown that the existing process of law cannot overcome systematic and ingenious discrimination. No law that we now have on the books—and I have helped to put three of them there—can ensure the right to vote when local officials are determined to deny it.

In such a case our duty must be clear to all of us. The Constitution says that no person shall be kept from voting because of his race or his color. We have all sworn an oath before God to support and to defend that Constitution. We must now act in obedience to that oath.

Guaranteeing the Right to Vote

Wednesday I will send to Congress a law designed to eliminate illegal barriers to the right to vote.

The broad principles of that bill will be in the hands of the Democratic and Republican leaders tomorrow. After they have reviewed it, it will come here formally as a bill. I am grateful for this opportunity to come here tonight at the invitation of the leadership to reason with my friends, to give them my views, and to visit with my former colleagues.

I have had prepared a more comprehensive analysis of the legislation which I had intended to transmit to the clerk tomorrow but which I will submit to the clerks tonight. But I want to really discuss with you now briefly the main proposals of this legislation.

This bill will strike down restrictions to voting in all elections—Federal, State, and local—which have been used to deny Negroes the right to vote.

This bill will establish a simple, uniform standard which cannot be used, however ingenious the effort, to flout our Constitution.

It will provide for citizens to be registered by officials of the United States Government if the State officials refuse to register them.

It will eliminate tedious, unnecessary lawsuits which delay the right to vote.

Finally, this legislation will ensure that properly registered individuals are not prohibited from voting.

I will welcome the suggestions from all of the Members of Congress—I have no doubt that I will get some—on ways and means to strengthen this law and to make it effective. But experience has plainly shown that this is the only path to carry out the command of the Constitution.

To those who seek to avoid action by their National Government in their own communities; who want to and who seek to maintain purely local control over elections, the answer is simple:

Open your polling places to all your people.

Allow men and women to register and vote whatever the color of their skin.

Extend the rights of citizenship to every citizen of this land.

The Need for Action

There is no constitutional issue here. The command of the Constitution is plain.

There is no moral issue. It is wrong—deadly wrong—to deny any of your fellow Americans the right to vote in this country.

There is no issue of States rights or national rights. There is only the struggle for human rights.

I have not the slightest doubt what will be your answer.

The last time a President sent a civil rights bill to the Congress it contained a provision to protect voting rights in Federal elections. That civil rights bill was passed after 8 long months of debate. And when that bill came to my desk from the Congress for my signature, the heart of the voting provision had been eliminated.

This time, on this issue, there must be no delay, no hesitation and no compromise with our purpose.

We cannot, we must not, refuse to protect the right of every American to vote in every election that he may desire to participate in. And we ought not and we cannot and we must not wait another 8 months before we get a bill. We have already waited a hundred years and more, and the time for waiting is gone.

So I ask you to join me in working long hours—nights and weekends, if necessary—to pass this bill. And I don't make that request lightly. For from the window where I sit with the problems of our country I recognize that outside this chamber is the outraged conscience of a nation, the grave concern of many nations, and the harsh judgment of history on our acts.

We Shall Overcome

But even if we pass this bill, the battle will not be over. What happened in Selma is part of a far larger movement which reaches into every section and State of America. It is the effort of American Negroes to secure for themselves the full blessings of American life.

Their cause must be our cause too. Because it is not just Negroes, but really it is all of us, who must overcome the crippling legacy of bigotry and injustice.

And we shall overcome.

As a man whose roots go deeply into Southern soil I know how agonizing racial feelings are. I know how difficult it is to reshape the attitudes and the structure of our society.

But a century has passed, more than a hundred years, since the Negro was freed. And he is not fully free tonight.

It was more than a hundred years ago that Abraham Lincoln, a great President of another party, signed the Emancipation Proclamation, but emancipation is a proclamation and not a fact.

A century has passed, more than a hundred years, since equality was promised. And yet the Negro is not equal.

A century has passed since the day of promise. And the promise is unkept.

The time of justice has now come. I tell you that I believe sincerely that no force can hold it back. It is right in the eyes of man and God that it should come. And when it does, I think that day will brighten the lives of every American.

For Negroes are not the only victims. How many white children have gone uneducated, how many white families have lived in stark poverty, how many white lives have been scarred by fear, because we have wasted our energy and our substance to maintain the barriers of hatred and terror?

So I say to all of you here, and to all in the Nation tonight, that those who appeal to you to hold on to the past do so at the cost of denying you your future.

This great, rich, restless country can offer opportunity and education and hope to all: black and white, North and South, sharecropper and city dweller. These are the enemies: poverty, ignorance, disease. They are the enemies and not our fellow man, not our neighbor. And these enemies too, poverty, disease and ignorance, we shall overcome.

An American Problem

Now let none of us in any sections look with prideful righteousness on the troubles in another section, or on the problems of our neighbors. There is really no part of America where the promise of equality has been fully kept. In Buffalo as well as in Birmingham, in Philadelphia as well as in Selma, Americans are struggling for the fruits of freedom.

This is one Nation. What happens in Selma or in Cincinnati is a matter of legitimate concern to every American. But let each of us look within our own hearts and our own communities, and let each of us put our shoulder to the wheel to root out injustice wherever it exists.

As we meet here in this peaceful, historic chamber tonight, men from the South, some of whom were at Iwo Jima, men from the North who have carried Old Glory to far corners of the world and brought it back without a stain on it, men from the East and from the West, are all fighting together without regard to religion, or color, or region, in Vietnam. Men from every region fought for us across the world 20 years ago.

And in these common dangers and these common sacrifices the South made its contribution of honor and gallantry no less than any other region of the great Republic—and in some instances, a great many of them, more.

And I have not the slightest doubt that good men from everywhere in this country, from the Great Lakes to the Gulf of Mexico, from the Golden Gate to the harbors along the Atlantic, will rally together now in this cause to vindicate the freedom of all Americans. For all of us owe this duty; and I believe that all of us will respond to it.

Your President makes that request of every American.

Progress Through the Democratic Process

The real hero of this struggle is the American Negro. His actions and protests, his courage to risk safety and even to risk his life, have awakened the conscience of this Nation. His demonstrations have been designed to call attention to injustice, designed to provoke change, designed to stir reform.

He has called upon us to make good the promise of America. And who among us can say that we would have made the same progress were it not for his persistent bravery, and his faith in American democracy.

For at the real heart of battle for equality is a deep-seated belief in the democratic process. Equality depends not on the force of arms or tear gas but upon the force of moral right; not on recourse to violence but on respect for law and order.

There have been many pressures upon your President and there will be others as the days come and go. But I pledge you tonight that we intend to fight this battle where it should be fought: in the courts, and in the Congress, and in the hearts of men.

We must preserve the right of free speech and the right of free assembly. But the right of free speech does not carry with it, as has been said, the right to holler fire in a crowded theater. We must preserve the right to free assembly, but free assembly does not carry with it the right to block public thoroughfares to traffic.

We do have a right to protest, and a right to march under conditions that do not infringe the constitutional rights of our neighbors. And I intend to protect all those rights as long as I am permitted to serve in this office.

We will guard against violence, knowing it strikes from our hands the very weapons which we seek—progress, obedience to law, and belief in American values.

In Selma as elsewhere we seek and pray for peace. We seek order. We seek unity. But we will not accept the peace of stifled rights, or the order imposed by fear, or the unity that stifles protest. For peace cannot be purchased at the cost of liberty.

In Selma tonight, as in every—and we had a good day there—as in every city, we are working for just and peaceful settlement. We must all remember that after this speech I am making tonight, after the police and the FBI and the Marshals have all gone, and after you have promptly passed this bill, the people of Selma and the other cities of the Nation must still live and work together. And when the attention of the Nation has gone elsewhere they must try to heal the wounds and to build a new community.

This cannot be easily done on a battleground of violence, as the history of the South itself shows. It is in recognition of this that men of both races have shown such an outstandingly impressive responsibility in recent days—last Tuesday and again today.

Rights Must Be Opportunities

The bill that I am presenting to you will be known as a civil rights bill. But, in a larger sense, most of the program I am recommending is a civil rights program. Its object is to open the city of hope to all people of all races.

Because all Americans just must have the right to vote. And we are going to give them that right.

All Americans must have the privileges of citizenship regardless of race. And they are going to have those privileges of citizenship regardless of race.

But I would like to caution you and remind you that to exercise these privileges takes much more than just legal right. It requires a trained mind and a healthy body. It requires a decent home, and the chance to find a job, and the opportunity to escape from the clutches of poverty.

Of course, people cannot contribute to the Nation if they are never taught to read or write, if their bodies are stunted from hunger, if their sickness goes untended, if their life is spent in hopeless poverty just drawing a welfare check.

So we want to open the gates to opportunity. But we are also going to give all our people, black and white, the help that they need to walk through those gates.

The Purpose of the Government

My first job after college was as a teacher in Cotulla, Tex., in a small Mexican-American school. Few of them could speak English, and I couldn't speak much Spanish. My students were poor and they often came to class without breakfast, hungry. They knew even in their youth the pain of prejudice. They never seemed to know why people disliked them. But they knew it was so, because I saw it in their eyes. I often walked home late in the afternoon, after the classes were finished, wishing there was more that I could do. But all I knew was to teach them the little that I knew, hoping that it might help them against the hardships that lay ahead.

Somehow you never forget what poverty and hatred can do when you see its scars on the hopeful face of a young child.

I never thought then, in 1928, that I would be standing here in 1965. It never even occurred to me in my fondest dreams that I might have the chance to help the sons and daughters of those students and to help people like them all over this country.

But now I do have that chance—and I'll let you in on a secret—I mean to use it. And I hope that you will use it with me.

This is the richest and most powerful country which ever occupied the globe. The might of past empires is little compared to ours. But I do not want to be the President who built empires, or sought grandeur, or extended dominion.

I want to be the President who educated young children to the wonders of their world. I want to be the President who helped to feed the hungry and to prepare them to be taxpayers instead of taxeaters.

I want to be the President who helped the poor to find their own way and who protected the right of every citizen to vote in every election.

I want to be the President who helped to end hatred among his fellow men and who promoted love among the people of all races and all regions and all parties.

I want to be the President who helped to end war among the brothers of this earth.

And so at the request of your beloved Speaker and the Senator from Montana; the majority leader, the Senator from Illinois; the minority leader, Mr. McCulloch, and other members of both parties, I came here tonight—not as President Roosevelt came down one time in person to veto a bonus bill, not as President Truman came down one time to urge the passage of a railroad bill—but I came down here to ask you to share this task with me and to share it with the people that we both work for. I want this to be the Congress, Republicans and Democrats alike, which did all these things for all these people.

Beyond this great chamber, out yonder in 50 States, are the people that we serve. Who can tell what deep and unspoken hopes are in their hearts tonight as they sit there and listen. We all can guess, from our own lives, how difficult they often find their own pursuit of happiness, how many problems each little family has. They look most of all to themselves for their futures. But I think that they also look to each of us.

Above the pyramid on the great seal of the United States it says—in Latin—"God has favored our undertaking."

God will not favor everything that we do. It is rather our duty to divine His will. But I cannot help believing that He truly understands and that He really favors the undertaking that we begin here tonight.

Chapter 47

The Voting Rights Act of 1965

United States Department of Justice

The 1965 Enactment

By 1965 concerted efforts to break the grip of state disfranchisement had been under way for some time, but had achieved only modest success overall and in some areas had proved almost entirely ineffectual. The murder of voting-rights activists in Philadelphia, Mississippi, gained national attention, along with numerous other acts of violence and terrorism. Finally, the unprovoked attack on March 7, 1965, by state troopers on peaceful marchers crossing the Edmund Pettus Bridge in Selma, Alabama, en route to the state capitol in Montgomery, persuaded the President and Congress to overcome Southern legislators' resistance to effective voting rights legislation. President Johnson issued a call for a strong voting rights law and hearings began soon thereafter on the bill that would become the Voting Rights Act.

Congress determined that the existing federal anti-discrimination laws were not sufficient to overcome the resistance by state officials to enforcement of the 15th Amendment. The legislative hearings showed that the Department of Justice's efforts to eliminate discriminatory election practices by litigation on a case-by-case basis had been unsuccessful in opening up the registration process; as soon as one discriminatory practice or procedure was proven to be unconstitutional and enjoined, a new one would be substituted in its place and litigation would have to commence anew.

President Johnson signed the resulting legislation into law on August 6, 1965. Section 2 of the Act, which closely followed the language of the 15th Amendment, applied a nationwide prohibition against the denial or abridgment of the right to vote on the literacy tests on a nationwide basis. Among its other provisions, the Act contained special enforcement provisions targeted at those areas of the country where Congress believed the potential for discrimination to be the greatest. Under Section 5, jurisdictions covered by these special provisions could not implement any change affecting voting until the Attorney General or the United States District Court for the District of Columbia determined that the change did not have a discriminatory purpose and would not have a discriminatory effect. In addition, the Attorney General could designate a county covered by these special provisions for the appointment of a federal examiner to review the qualifications of persons who wanted to register to vote. Further, in those counties where a federal examiner was serving, the Attorney General could request that federal observers monitor activities within the county's polling place.

The Voting Rights Act had not included a provision prohibiting poll taxes, but had directed the Attorney General to challenge its use. In *Harper v. Virginia State Board of Elections*, 383 U.S. 663 (1966), the Supreme Court held Virginia's poll tax to be unconstitutional under the 14th Amendment. Between 1965 and 1969 the Supreme Court also issued several key decisions upholding the constitutionality of Section 5 and affirming the broad range of voting practices that required Section 5 review. As the Supreme Court put it in its 1966 decision upholding the constitutionality of the Act:

> *Congress had found that case-by-case litigation was inadequate to combat wide-spread and persistent discrimination in voting, because of the inordinate amount of time and energy required to overcome the obstructionist tactics invariably encountered in these lawsuits. After enduring nearly a century of sys-*

tematic resistance to the Fifteenth Amendment, Congress might well decide to shift the advantage of time and inertia from the perpetrators of the evil to its victims.

South Carolina v. Katzenbach, 383 U.S. 301, 327–28 (1966).

The 1970 and 1975 Amendments

Congress extended Section 5 for five years in 1970 and for seven years in 1975. With these extensions Congress validated the Supreme Court's broad interpretation of the scope of Section 5. During the hearings on these extensions Congress heard extensive testimony concerning the ways in which voting electorates were manipulated through gerrymandering, annexations, adoption of at-large elections, and other structural changes to prevent newly-registered black voters from effectively using the ballot. Congress also heard extensive testimony about voting discrimination that had been suffered by Hispanic, Asian, and Native American citizens, and the 1975 amendments added protections from voting discrimination for language minority citizens.

In 1973, the Supreme Court held certain legislative multi-member districts unconstitutional under the 14th Amendment on the ground that they systematically diluted the voting strength of minority citizens in Bexar County, Texas. This decision in *White v. Regester,* 412 U.S. 755 (1973), strongly shaped litigation through the 1970s against at-large systems and gerrymandered redistricting plans. In *Mobile v. Bolden,* 446 U.S. 55 (1980), however, the Supreme Court required that any constitutional claim of minority vote dilution must include proof of a racially discriminatory purpose, a requirement that was widely seen as making such claims far more difficult to prove.

The 1982 Amendments

Congress renewed in 1982 the special provisions of the Act, triggered by coverage under Section 4 for twenty-five years. Congress also adopted a new standard, which went into effect in 1985, providing how jurisdictions could terminate (or "bailout" from) coverage under the provisions of Section 4. Furthermore, after extensive hearings, Congress amended Section 2 to provide that a plaintiff could establish a violation of the Section without having to prove discriminatory purpose.

Chapter 48

Fair Housing Laws and Presidential Executive Orders on Discrimination, 1968

The Fair Housing Laws

Fair Housing Act

Title VIII of the Civil Rights Act of 1968 (Fair Housing Act), as amended, prohibits discrimination in the sale, rental, and financing of dwellings, and in other housing-related transactions, based on race, color, national origin, religion, sex, familial status (including children under the age of 18 living with parents of legal custodians, pregnant women, and people securing custody of children under the age of 18), and handicap (disability). More on the Fair Housing Act.

Title VI of the Civil Rights Act of 1964

Title VI prohibits discrimination on the basis of race, color, or national origin in programs and activities receiving federal financial assistance.

Section 504 of the Rehabilitation Act of 1973

Section 504 prohibits discrimination based on disability in any program or activity receiving federal financial assistance.

Section 109 of Title I of the Housing and Community Development Act of 1974

Section 109 prohibits discrimination on the basis of race, color, national origin, sex, or religion in programs and activities receiving financial assistance from HUD's Community Development and Block Grant Program.

Title II of the Americans with Disabilities Act of 1990

Title II prohibits discrimination based on disability in programs, services, and activities provided or made available by public entities. HUD enforces Title II when it relates to state and local public housing, housing assistance, and housing referrals.

Architectural Barriers Act of 1968

The Architectural Barriers Act requires that buildings and facilities designed, constructed, altered, or leased with certain federal funds after September 1969 must be accessible to and useable by handicapped persons.

Age Discrimination Act of 1975

The Age Discrimination Act prohibits discrimination on the basis of age in programs or activities receiving federal financial assistance.

Title IX of the Education Amendments Act of 1972

Title IX prohibits discrimination on the basis of sex in education programs or activities that receive federal financial assistance.

Fair Housing-Related Presidential Executive Orders

Executive Order 11063

Executive Order 11063 prohibits discrimination in the sale, leasing, rental, or other disposition of properties and facilities owned or operated by the federal government or provided with federal funds.

Executive Order 11246

Executive Order 11246, as amended, bars discrimination in federal employment because of race, color, religion, sex, or national origin.

Executive Order 12892

Executive Order 12892, as amended, requires federal agencies to affirmatively further fair housing in their programs and activities, and provides that the Secretary of HUD will be responsible for coordinating the effort. The Order also establishes the President's Fair Housing Council, which will be chaired by the Secretary of HUD.

Executive Order 12898

Executive Order 12898 requires that each federal agency conduct its program, policies, and activities that substantially affect human health or the environment in a manner that does not exclude persons based on race, color, or national origin.

Executive Order 13166

Executive Order 13166 eliminates, to the extent possible, limited English proficiency as a barrier to full and meaningful participation by beneficiaries in all federally-assisted and federally conducted programs and activities.

Executive Order 13217

Executive Order 13217 requires federal agencies to evaluate their policies and programs to determine if any can be revised or modified to improve the availability of community-based living arrangements for persons with disabilities.

Section 4—Study Questions

1. Why did Donna Auston feel that she was invisible?

2. What cultural roles do African American Muslims play in American society or African American black communities?

3. Briefly outline five major components of Charles H. Thompson's social philosophy.

4. List five ways in which the *Journal of Negro Education,* under Thompson's editorial leadership, transformed African American social consciousness.

5. How did enslaved women's collectives create a "culture of resistance"?

6. Describe how the National American Women's Suffrage Association sought to exclude Black women from their struggle for enfranchisement.

7. Why have histories of the Civil Rights struggle frequently neglected the role played by women in the movement?

8. What were some of Ruby Hurley's accomplishments as NAACP investigator, and what challenges did she face in this position?

9. What are some of Cheryl Clarke's criticisms of the Black church with respect to its attitude toward and treatment of gays and lesbians?

10. What is "Christian fundamentalist atavism" according to Cheryl Clarke?

11. How did college football force social change at southern colleges and universities?

12. How did money and sports mitigate the impact of racism at southern colleges and universities?

13. What role did Elijah Muhammad play in the formation of Malcolm X's political and social philosophy?

14. Describe how Malcolm X's speeches and writings establish a relationship between Americans of African ancestry and continental Africans.

15. Which Supreme Court decision did *Brown v. Board of Education* reverse?

16. Outline the basic components of the *Brown v. Board of Education* decision.

17. Explain how Black democratic rights were thwarted prior to the passing of the voting rights of 1965.

18. Cite specific examples of how Lyndon B. Johnson embraced the rhetoric of the Civil Rights Movement in his historic Voting Rights Address of 1965.

19. What specific legal measures did Lyndon B. Johnson call for to address Black disenfranchisement in his voting rights speech?

20. Outline the core legal principles entrenched in the Voting Rights Act of 1965. How did this help overcome the barriers to Black voting in the South?

Section 5

Identity, Globalization, and Contemporary Struggles

Chapter 49

Identity, Globalization, and Contemporary Struggles: An Introduction

Edward Ramsamy

The Civil Rights Movement (CRM) of the 1950s and 1960s opened up a number of spaces that were previously closed to African Americans. Within a decade, mass non-cooperation overturned the foundations of *de jure* segregation and won voting rights for Black citizens of the South. The number of Black elected officials has increased dramatically since the 1960s. For example, there were just five Black members in Congress and no African American mayors during the era of Jim Crow segregation. However, at present, there are about 50 Blacks in Congress, as well as more than 40 African Americans mayors. Stone Mountain, Georgia, the birthplace of the Klu Klux Klan, elected an African American mayor in 1997, and Illinois elected a Black senator, Barack Obama, by a wide margin in the 2004 election. In education, Blacks gained access to institutions from which they were previously excluded. Finally, Black median incomes also increased. Barack Obama's election as the first Black president of the United States was an event of enormous historical significance. Forty-three years after passage of the Voting Rights Act of 1965, there were many who, although they had participated and struggled in the modern Civil Rights Movement, did not believe that they would ever live to see a person of African ancestry elected to the highest office in America. Yet that is, in fact, exactly what had happened when Barack Obama made history with his victory in the November 2008 presidential election.

Most notably, these historical gains led to the establishment of a stable Black middle class, a segment of which has enjoyed great success in both the private and public sectors. In January 2002, *Newsweek Magazine's* cover featured three Black CEOs of Fortune 500 companies, representing what the magazine termed "The New Black Power." The fact that these men head American Express, AOL-Time Warner, and Merrill Lynch would have been unimaginable before the CRM. The December issue of that year featured Condoleezza Rice, who is dubbed "the most powerful woman in Washington." As National Security Advisor, Rice joined Secretary of State Colin Powell in holding one of the most important positions in George W. Bush's administration during his first presidential term. Rice, regarded by many as the most influential National Security Advisor since Henry Kissinger, followed in Kissinger's career path and became Secretary of State in Bush's second term. She is also the first African American woman to occupy this position. In the field of medicine, one of the country's leading pediatric neurosurgeons, Ben Carson, is an African American. In the increasingly popular world of reality television, Randal Pinkett, Rutgers University undergraduate, Rhodes Scholar, and M.I.T. PhD, triumphed on Donald Trump's *The Apprentice*. These success stories are frequently viewed as proof of the triumph of the Civil Rights Movement and evidence that the nation has moved beyond Du Bois's ominous proclamation in *The Souls of Black Folk* that "the problem of the 20th century is the problem of the color line." Media coverage of Black achievement seems to suggest that the "color line" is no longer an issue in the 21st century.

Images of Black attainment obscure other realities of Black life in contemporary America. In March 1999, three different, equally distinguished Black men appeared on the front page of the *New York Times*, but in handcuffs. Charles Rangel, David Dinkins, and Al Sharpton were being arrested in front of NYPD headquarters for protesting the shooting of African immigrant Amadou Diallo by NYPD officers. Rangel, a congressman from Harlem, is the ranking Democrat on the House Ways and Means Committee, one of the most powerful committees in Congress. Dinkins was the first African American mayor of New York City. Reverend Sharpton has been an outspoken voice against racism and injustice for several decades. Yet these figures, who have gained access to the corridors of power regionally and nationally, had to resort to the tactics of the Civil Rights Movement in order to protest police brutality in New York City. The fact that these powerful men had no other recourse but civil disobedience is revealing. Their arrest is symbolic of the pervasive sense of powerlessness that many Black Americans feel in spite of the much touted gains of the CRM. More recently, Hurricane Katrina and its aftermath serve as stark reminders of the existence of racial inequality; anyone living under the illusion that the color line had evaporated need only consider the fact that the hurricane's victims were predominantly Black and poor.

The Black experience in America after 1960 has to be conceptualized in terms of the contrasting images mentioned previously. There have been important and impressive gains since the 1960s. While gains ought to be celebrated, it is premature to dismiss Du Bois's assertion that race is the defining variable in American society. In fact, William Faulkner's observation that "The past is not dead, it isn't even past" could very well apply to the state of race relations in the United States. While some progress has been made, contemporary America is still a deeply divided society—two nations, as it were. As West notes, "Oprah the billionaire, and the Black judges and chief executives and movie stars do not mean equality, or even equality of opportunity yet" (*The Guardian*, September 11, 2005). The reality is that the rate of African American unemployment is more than twice that of White unemployment, 11% and 5%, respectively. While the national poverty rate is 12%, the rate for African Americans is 23%. From 1979 to 1989, the poverty rate for Black America rose to and remained unchanged at around 30%. During the "roaring 1990s" the Black poverty rate dropped to 22%, the lowest since the government began measuring poverty in 1959, but it is still twice the national average. Some of the gains of the 1990s are eroding as the economy is slowing down and national efforts to address racial inequality increasingly are being abandoned. For instance, 50 years after the historic *Brown v. Board of Education* decision, segregation and "educational apartheid" remain realities of American society. There is still a high correlation between predominantly Black school districts, poverty, and lower educational achievement (Kozol, 2005).

African Americans may be well represented in government structures, especially in urban areas, but greater representation has not translated into increased power. For example, Harold Washington's hard-won electoral battle to become the first Black mayor of Chicago led to other struggles that proved futile. During his campaign, Washington promised to transform the culture of city governance in Chicago and address the socioeconomic disparities between the Black and White populations. He supported the unionization of city employees and an increase in the number of women and African Americans in city government. However, upon taking office, he encountered an entrenched city bureaucracy that was resistant to change and confronted economic forces that were beyond his control. This reality is also illustrated in the case of Atlanta, Georgia, where Blacks hold all the key elected positions in city government. The mayor, congressmen, and majority of the city council are all African Americans. Yet, while Atlanta's economy has boomed under Black stewardship, a disproportionate share of the economic development agenda was devoted to the city's affluent White suburbs. This has contributed to a sense of frustration and disillusionment among the Black urban poor.

One of the major issues affecting contemporary American race relations is the conservative ideological shift in policy. In the aftermath of the urban unrest that swept the nation during the mid-1960s, President Lyndon Johnson had appointed a commission to investigate its causes. The Kerner Commission, as it was known, had asked three basic questions with respect to the urban unrest: "What happened? Why did it happen?" and "What can be done to prevent it from happening again?" (Chapter 12). The Kerner Report had found that the United States "is moving toward two societies, one black, one white—separate and unequal." The Commission went on to conclude that "What white Americans have never fully understood—but what the Negro can never forget—is that white society is deeply implicated in the ghetto. White institutions created it, white institutions maintain it, and white society condones it."

In contrast to the mainstream perspective that saw the urban unrest as an outcome of pathological, aberrant behavior by Black youth, the Kerner Report had argued that the riots were a form of social protest and blamed "white racism" for instigating them. In spite of its shortcomings, the report was a significant document in that "never before had the nation gone so far toward accepting the collective responsibility for the terrible repercussions of white racism" (Steinberg, 1995: 79). The concluding sections of the report had made a series of policy recommendations that included improving access to education, employment, housing, and welfare. However, the recommendations of the report proved to be short-lived as conservative, behaviorist perspectives eclipsed structural arguments once again. Richard Nixon's election in 1968 signaled the end of any attempt by the government to see racism as a systemic feature of American society. In fact, Nixon claimed that the report divided the nation and that the absence of "law and order" was the central problem in urban America. This rightward shift in attitude and policy toward racial inequality is clearly evident in the federal government's responses to subsequent urban crises.

The two major urban uprisings since the 1960s were both ignited by incidents of police brutality. In December 1979, Arthur McDuffie was beaten to death by police officers in Dade County, Florida, for allegedly driving recklessly and resisting arrest. The poor and predominantly Black sections of Miami erupted in protest when an all-White jury returned a "not-guilty" verdict and acquitted the officers responsible for McDuffie's death. Three days of rioting in the Overtown and Liberty City Sections of Miami caused more than $250 million in damages to property and 1200 arrests. However, President Jimmy Carter, who himself enjoyed strong Black support, chose to treat the riot as a local problem and refused to offer federal funds to rebuild the shattered neighborhoods. He maintained that the local authorities needed to take the initiative and that the federal government would only play a small, complementary role to their efforts. Toward the end of his life, Martin Luther King, Jr. had emphasized the fact that racism was a national problem that required national solutions. The recommendations of the Kerner Commission also had offered a roadmap for addressing the systemic problems confronting urban poor. Yet, even President Carter, who was generally sympathetic to the plight of the urban poor, embraced the conservative language of local solutions.

In 1992, Los Angeles burst into flames when four White policemen were acquitted after beating Rodney King. While frustrations over the unfair verdicts ignited both the Miami and Los Angeles riots, the underlying cause had to do with an increasing sense of powerlessness that marginalized urban communities felt as a consequence of structural changes in the urban political economy. These economic changes were accompanied by the dismantling of federal support structures for the poor. By the 1980s, the criminal justice system emerged as the primary means for addressing inner-city problems. Furthermore, the influx of new immigrants brought Blacks into competition with other groups in a declining economic environment. In such a climate, civil unrest was almost inevitable. Ignoring these material realities, however, Vice President Dan Quayle (*New York Times*, May 20, 1992) claimed that:

> *I believe that lawless social anarchy which we saw is directly related to the breakdown of family structure, personal responsibility and social order in too many areas of our society. . . . It doesn't help matters when prime-time TV has Murphy Brown—a character who supposedly epitomizes today's intelligent, highly paid professional women—mocking the importance of fathers, by bearing a child alone, and calling it another life choice.*

In contrast to the language of the Kerner Commission, Quayle's statements indicate how far to the right the pendulum of public opinion had swung by the 1990s. Behavior and culture were once again seen as the primary impediments to Black progress. The 1980s and 1990s saw a proliferation of literature that lent intellectual credence to this argument. Some popular examples are *Race and Culture*, *The Content of our Character*, and *Losing Ground*. A particularly egregious work was *The Bell Curve*, by Harvard psychologist Richard Herrnstein and Charles Murray of the American Enterprise Institute, which argued that Blacks were genetically less intelligent than Whites and Asians, as measured by performance on IQ tests. These conservative views present a narrow choice of genes or culture as explanations for racial inequality, leaving no room for the public policy interventions called for by the Kerner commission. One of the world's leading evolutionary biologists, Stephen Jay Gould (1995: 4), surmised that the success of such ideas "in winning our attention must reflect the depressing temper of our times—a historical moment of unprecedented ungenerosity, when a mood for slashing social programs can be powerfully abetted by an argument that beneficiaries cannot be helped, owing to inborn cognitive limits expressed as low IQ scores."

A key point of struggle during the CRM was the right to vote. However, the specter of disenfranchisement has risen again with the increasing number of African Americans entangled in the criminal justice system. Forty-eight states have some form of felony disfranchisement, while 11 of those states disfranchise felons indefinitely. Most of these laws originated during the Reconstruction era in order to circumvent the 13th, 14th, and 15th Amendments to the Constitution. As a consequence, one-quarter of the Black male population in many Southern states is permanently disfranchised today. If these trends are not reversed, one-third of the nation's Black men will have lost the vote by 2010 (Mallaby, 2001).

The articles in this section of the book examine the preceding themes in greater detail. In her interview with Edward Ramsamy, Susan Fainstein reflects on the underlying reasons for sociocultural conflict in major metropolitan areas in the United States and identifies race as an increasingly divisive factor in the urban crisis of poverty. This crisis, Fainstein argues, has worsened over the years as the result of these factors: decreased funding from government programs to help the urban poor; the tendency of both the Republican and Democratic parties to utilize the racial divide as a point of tension between urban Blacks and working-class Whites; and a restructuring of the American economy that has increased the standard of living for only the wealthiest Americans, at the expense of all others. In her essay, "Black-Asian Relations in the United States: Negotiating Globalization and Racialization," Kavitha Ramachandran offers a rejoinder to themes raised in the first section of this book in her discussion of the relationship between "race," "racism," and "racialization." She proceeds to develop a conceptual framework for race relations between Blacks and Asians as urban populations in light of globalization and resultant trends in immigration and employment. Ramachandran situates the Los Angeles riots of 1992, the most commonly cited "example" of Black-Asian relations, in the context of a rapidly deteriorating economic environment resulting from deindustrialization and the loss of manufacturing jobs, on one hand, and economic restructuring, on the other hand, that created an influx of immigrants into American cities to work in the burgeoning service sector. Blacks and Asians, she argues, must develop a grammar of coexistence in order to jointly resist the assault of corporate power, racism, and patriarchy.

Same-sex marriage has emerged in recent decades as a pivotal Civil Rights issue. In her essay, "The Prong of Permanency: a Rant" Cheryl Clark critically examines the politics of same-sex marriages. The urban sphere is also the focus of Robert E. Weems, Jr.'s essay, "Racial Desegregation and the Decline of Black Urban Landmarks," which discusses physical spaces of historical significance for African Americans. Weems's essay describes the impressive buildings erected by African American entrepreneurs in urban Black America during the early part of the 20th century, which have been abandoned since the era of racial desegregation. According to Weems, these buildings housed Black-owned institutions that played a critical role in providing African Americans with quality insurance, banking, hotel, and restaurant services at a time when White companies denied them access to these necessities. In his essay, "Ameriflora Comes to 'Bronzeville': A Political Battle Over an Urban Landmark in Columbus, Ohio," Lewis A. Randolph discusses the history of Franklin Park, an urban landmark of great cultural and emotional significance for Columbus, Ohio's Black residents. He traces the Black presence in this area from the days of the abolition movement and describes the tensions generated when Ameriflora, an international floral show and Disney theme park event, chose Franklin Park as its site of exposition.

The importance of the political, social, and historical studies that the essays in this section have undertaken is underscored by the crucial role of Africana Studies scholarship in the continuing struggle for civil rights. In her essay, "Africana Studies, the Politics of Knowledge and New Media Technologies," Gloria Harper Dickinson discusses the impact of new media technologies such as the Internet, CD-ROMs, and other electronic resources on the field of Africana Studies, and the new challenges and opportunities that these technologies present for scholars and students. In his interview with Edward Ramsamy, Haki Madhubuti stresses the need for scholars in Africana Studies, as well as leaders from Black churches and Black professional and political organizations, to work through, from, and with the Black community to invest their skills, knowledge, and leadership in Black civic life. According to Madhubuti, the need for such community-based struggle is especially urgent during these conservative times in which governmental programs established during the 1960s to assist Blacks and the poor are being dismantled.

Perhaps the best recent example of the American government's neglect of the Black poor is its response to Hurricane Katrina. In his essay, "Hurricane Katrina: Winds of Change?" Ben Wisner argues that numerous lessons can be learned from the Katrina disaster about the severity of racial and class-based poverty in America. For Wisner, the government's numerous failures in protecting and assisting the people of the New Orleans region are a clear demonstration of its hypocrisy and flawed priorities. According to Wisner, the extent of Katrina's devastation could have been curtailed had numerous warnings been heeded and the programs for protecting the area from such natural hazards been funded. Wisner describes how the needs of the impoverished African American families living in the area were neglected in favor of anti-union chemical industries which, through their operation in the coastal wetland region, weakened any natural protection that the wetlands could have provided for those people. Indeed, the many losses of the Katrina disaster exposes yet another type of racism—environmental racism.

The section concludes with "The President's Initiative on Race: One America in the 21st Century." This document discusses the experiences and impact of racial discrimination, as well as discrimination based on other aspects of identity, in contemporary America. It describes the challenges that lie ahead for the nation if the promises of our chartering documents—equal opportunity, equal protection—are to be realized and honored for all Americans.

In the concluding chapter of the book, "Black Blame, Barack Obama, and the Future of Black Politics," Melanye Price focuses on this landmark event in American history. Price, however, goes on to take a closer look at the Obama presidency, focusing particularly on frequent references by President Obama about Black cultural and behavioral disfunctionalities as a way of explaining away the social and economic problems encountered by the Black poor. According to Price, "Obama's deployment of Black blame coupled with his deracialized campaign style . . . presents real problems for Black politics."

References

Gould, Stephen Jay. (1995). "Mismeasure by Any Measure," in *The Bell Curve Debate*. Russell Jacoby and Naomi Glauberman (eds.). New York: Random House.

Kozol, Jonathan. (2005). "Still Separate, Still Unequal: America's Educational Apartheid," *Harper's Magazine*, September: 41–54.

Mallaby, Sebastian. (2001). "Two Million Behind Bars," in *The World in 2001*. London: The Economist Group.

Steinberg, Stephen. (1995). *Turning Back: The Retreat from Racial Justice in American Thought and Policy.* Boston: Beacon Press.

Chapter 50

Report of the National Advisory Commission on Civil Disorders

The summer of 1967 again brought racial disorders to American cities, and with them shock, fear, and bewilderment to the nation.

The worst came during a two-week period in July, first in Newark and then in Detroit. Each set off a chain reaction in neighboring communities.

On July 28, 1967, the President of the United States established this Commission and directed us to answer three basic questions:

> What happened?
> Why did it happen?
> What can be done to prevent it from happening again?

To respond to these questions, we have undertaken a broad range of studies and investigations. We have visited the riot cities; we have heard many witnesses; we have sought the counsel of experts across the country.

This is our basic conclusion: Our nation is moving toward two societies, one black, one white—separate and unequal.

Reaction to last summer's disorders has quickened the movement and deepened the division. Discrimination and segregation have long permeated much of American life; they now threaten the future of every American.

This deepening racial division is not inevitable. The movement apart can be reversed. Choice is still possible. Our principal task is to define that choice and to press for a national resolution.

To pursue our present course will involve the continuing polarization of the American community and, ultimately, the destruction of basic democratic values.

The alternative is not blind repression or capitulation to lawlessness. It is the realization of common opportunities for all within a single society.

This alternative will require a commitment to national action—compassionate, massive, and sustained, backed by the resources of the most powerful and the richest nation on this earth. From every American it will require new attitudes, new understanding, and, above all, new will.

The vital needs of the nation must be met; hard choices must be made, and, if necessary, new taxes enacted.

Violence cannot build a better society. Disruption and disorder nourish repression, not justice. They strike at the freedom of every citizen. The community cannot—it will not—tolerate coercion and mob rule.

Violence and destruction must be ended—in the streets of the ghetto and in the lives of people.

Segregation and poverty have created in the racial ghetto a destructive environment totally unknown to most white Americans.

What white Americans have never fully understood—but what the Negro can never forget—is that white society is deeply implicated in the ghetto. White institutions created it, white institutions maintain it, and white society condones it.

It is time now to turn with all the purpose at our command to the major unfinished business of this nation. It is time to adopt strategies for action that will produce quick and visible progress. It is time to make good the promises of American democracy to all citizens—urban and rural, white and black, Spanish-surname, American Indian, and every minority group.

Our recommendations embrace three basic principles:

- To mount programs on a scale equal to the dimension of the problems;
- To aim these programs for high impact in the immediate future in order to close the gap between promise and performance;
- To undertake new initiatives and experiments that can change the system of failure and frustration that now dominates the ghetto and weakens our society.

These programs will require unprecedented levels of funding and performance, but they neither probe deeper nor demand more than the problems which called them forth. There can be no higher priority for national action and no higher claim on the nation's conscience.

We issue this Report now, five months before the date called for by the President. Much remains that can be learned. Continued study is essential.

As Commissioners we have worked together with a sense of the greatest urgency and have sought to compose whatever differences exist among us. Some differences remain. But the gravity of the problem and the pressing need for action are too clear to allow further delay in the issuance of this Report.

Chapter 51

Tensions in U.S. Cities:
The Perspectives of Susan Fainstein

Edward Ramsamy

The 1992 riots in Los Angeles highlighted the socioeconomic and political crises facing many major cities in the United States and violently revived national interest in urban crises. The potential for escalating sociocultural conflict in major metropolitan areas still remains high as resources dwindle and the majority of new immigrants settle in cities. In the following interview, Professor Susan S. Fainstein of Columbia University shares her views on the problems facing American cities today.

Ramsamy: What are some of the underlying reasons for the present political and fiscal crisis facing U.S. cities?

Fainstein: If we look back at the 1960s, we can identify a trend in American government toward addressing urban issues. At first there was, in part, a response to the Civil Rights and Black Power Movements, as well as an attempt by a liberal government in Washington to develop a constituency among the new groups in the cities, namely Blacks who migrated from the South during the previous two decades. At the time, Blacks were displacing the old urban blue-collar ethnics who had formed the basis of the Democratic Party until then. The manner in which the Vietnam War siphoned resources away from domestic programs and the social divisions caused by the urban riots at the time led quite directly to the Nixon election in 1968. The Republicans, for many years, used race as a method of dividing the American public and gaining support from working class people who probably would vote Democratic otherwise. Thus, race became an increasingly divisive factor. It was frequently argued that welfare programs caused the fiscal crisis, creating the perception that the government was taxing the middle class in order to give money to people on welfare. By-and-large, the public does not realize how little money goes to welfare programs, that much more of their tax dollars goes to support agricultural subsidy programs, veterans programs, and all kinds of other programs they don't think about. Instead, they see a liberal government as one that taxes the middle class and spends on the poor. These views, when reinforced by politicians, lead to a generally hostile attitude towards the aspirations of low-income people. Since low-income people predominantly live within central cities, the crisis of poverty in America is an urban crisis. Therefore, the crisis has worsened as a result of this increasingly hostile government policy. However, government is not the only reason for the crisis. Much of it relates to the restructuring of the American economy, which has meant that nobody, except the very wealthy, saw an improvement in their standard of living. Therefore, people are much less willing to be generous with a pie that does not grow larger. The ability of each person to do better than s/he had done in the past depends on getting more from somebody else. It is a zero sum game where any kind of redistribution is painful because it means giving up what one has instead of giving up from some future increment.

Ramsamy: In 1968 the Kerner Commission, appointed by President Johnson to investigate the urban riots of the 1960s, concluded that "our nation is moving toward two societies: one Black, one White, separate and unequal." The report seemed to attribute racial tensions to the political and economic makeup of this country. Why are behavioral explanations for poverty becoming popular today?

Fainstein: I don't think the focus on behavior is anything new. From the 19th century onward there has always been a distinction between the so-called "deserving" and "undeserving" poor. During this century, other terms were used. When I was in graduate school in the 1960s, the great debate was over a "culture" of poverty versus a structural explanation of poverty. The cultural explanation tended to be the dominant one, in the social sciences and in popular media as well. Oscar Lewis, an anthropologist who studied poverty in Mexico, first coined the term *culture of poverty*. Poor people were thought to have bad habits because they were exposed to environments that were very negative. There was a circular process going on whereby low-income people grew up in ghettos that had, as Kenneth Clark put it, a "tangle of pathology." Kenneth Clark, a Black sociologist, had done a lot of the work for the court decision of *Brown v. Topeka*. His argument was that ghettos bred a tangle of pathology that then caused people to lose the kinds of aspirations, habits, and capabilities that would enable them to become upwardly mobile. The cultural argument was a liberal one in that it argued against a "genetic" basis for failure. Proponents of the cultural argument said that it was not in the genes of low-income people to remain where they were, but it was their own fault in a sense because they created a culture that reproduced a set of characteristics that kept them mired in poverty. The war on poverty was premised, in many respects, on this cultural argument.

The war on poverty was not about restructuring society or redistributing resources, but rather it was an attempt to provide structures of opportunity within the ghetto. The premise was that if people living within ghettos felt that they had opportunities to move out of them, to improve their education, to work together to improve their community (that was the basis for the community action program), then their renewed hope would change their behavior. Thus, during the 1960s, the cultural argument led to demands of equal opportunity. The more recent debates since the late 1980s are framed more in terms of William Julius Wilson's concept of the "underclass." Wilson, a democratic socialist, attempted to provide a structuralist analysis of urban poverty, which saw the urban poor as people who were detached from the labor force. It was structuralist in the way it argued that jobs were geographically separate from the location of the poor and that the elimination of manufacturing jobs deprived minorities of what had been the ladder of upward mobility. However, the "underclass" explanation primarily emphasizes that low-income people are a population group that lacks role models who would enable them to acquire the necessary characteristics to become better educated and more capable of operating in the labor market of a technologically advanced society.

Ramsamy: During the sixties, we had broad-based coalitions for transformation that crossed ethnic, racial, and class lines. Why did these coalitions fall apart in later years? What happened to the visionary leadership of the 1960s?

Fainstein: The coalition of the 1960s was very short lived. Roosevelt's New Deal coalition really excluded Blacks; it was a working class White coalition that consisted of Southern agrarian populists and Northern working class people. Roosevelt was willing to sell out the interests of Black people, who were predominantly a rural population at that time, although the rural resettlement administration did set up Black towns in the South. The Roosevelt regime never seriously challenged Jim Crow. The armed forces remained segregated until after World War II. The South was maintained as a separate semi-feudal part of the country. One did not have a Black-White coalition until the short-lived Civil Rights Movement (about six or seven years) in which Blacks and Whites really worked together on a transformative agenda. Whites who participated tended to be young student types and the movement against the Vietnam War became their primary focus, rather than the Civil Rights Movement itself. As the CRM moved north and became a Black Power movement, Whites increasingly became excluded. Thus, a broad-based movement for civil rights really did not last very long or even at all. The Democratic Party, in a way, represented a coalition of Blacks and Whites, but it had great difficulty keeping the coalition together. As the scale of the Black presence grew, White working-class ethnic groups, who became known as the Reagan Democrats, felt that they were not being served by the program of the Democratic Party. Feeling that they were paying taxes but not receiving any benefits, they left the party.

Ramsamy: Did the situation improve under the Clinton administration?

Fainstein: Many leftists criticized Clinton for not making a special point of inner cities and minorities during his campaign. While this is true, I am not sure if this would have served any good purpose for him to have done so. The race card was played in previous elections but it did nothing but heighten antagonism. If one is results-oriented, one advocates an administration that can help the minority in the name of the majority. Clinton did have a conception of unity and was good at incorporating minorities and women into his administration. I think Clinton's style of being inclusive and not drawing issue lines that coincide with racial lines in the long run, improved the situation of minority groups. In this way, it is the opposite of identity politics. It is politics based on the premise that there is a common purpose and, to some extent, it is even a class-based politics. For instance, Clinton said that the Republicans' trickle-down economics had benefitted the wealthy. Under the Republicans, middle-class Whites tended to identify their interests with people who were much wealthier than they, simply because of the racial divide. If racial divides become less prominent, I think there can be much more of a coalition around economic interests for those people who are not part of the dominant economic class. But this means minimizing identity politics.

Ramsamy: Were the Los Angeles riots an isolated phenomenon or can we expect similar social crises in other major urban centers?

Fainstein: I think there is a reason why Miami and Los Angeles were the places where the riots took place. The rivalry between Blacks and Latinos there exacerbate conditions that existed in other places. In these cases, not only were people doing poorly relative to the rest of this society, but people at the bottom saw each other as rivals, making the situation worse. Riots were directly related to problems with the police in places where the police force did not effectively incorporate the Black community. Such places become particularly volatile. I think the major northern Black cities have been successful in incorporating minorities into the governmental structure, but in New York, the police are still 80% White, 10% Hispanic, and 10% Black, which signifies a potential for conflict like the one in Washington Heights.

Ramsamy: What is your analysis of the tensions that existed between the Dinkins administration and the police force in New York City?

Fainstein: New York does not have a residency law for police and Dinkins has experienced difficulty in getting one passed. A residency law requires police to live within the boundaries of the city. The effect of not having a residency law is that the majority of New York police live outside the city, predominantly in Nassau and Suffolk counties. These people then recruit their sons, daughters, nieces, and nephews into the police force, forming their own circles. The recruitment networks ensure that the police force is White and suburban, with parents and grandparents who were policemen, too. They then act as the overseers of a city that consists predominantly of minorities. Changing the residency law would help to change the composition of the police force, which may then offer the possibility of other reforms.

Ramsamy: The demographic makeup of the larger American cities has changed significantly in recent years due to the influx of immigrants from developing nations, often resulting in inter-ethnic conflict in urban areas. What are some of the reasons for this conflict?

Fainstein: The United States is experiencing almost as much immigration now as at the turn of the century. New immigrants are coming into urban areas that already have terrible job shortages. Although the defenders of immigration like to say that new immigrants do not take jobs away from native minorities, I tend to disagree. I think new immigrants, in a sense, are driving down the wage rate because they create a labor surplus. They are seen as docile workers, particularly illegal immigrants, who don't dare protest in any way. Because they can be exploited more than native workers, employers prefer to use them. Therefore, low-wage manufacturing is totally dominated by immigrants and the third world type informal market structure, which also tends to be dominated by immigrants, who are better able than native minorities to rely on family networks. This heightens tensions. It is my general feeling that the position of wage earners can be protected only when they are able to control the labor supply. The period when the United States working class was doing extremely well was when labor unions controlled the supply much better than they are able to do now. As a consequence of immigration and foreign competition from low-wage countries, the working class has very little power to control its wage, which leads to a depression of the wage rate. We have seen a declining wage rate in manufacturing and service industries in real dollar terms.

Ramsamy: What about Black-Jewish tensions?

Fainstein: There was a Black-Jewish alliance long before the 1960s in that Jews were always active in liberal causes. The current crises came, in part, from the suburbanization of the Jewish community and their greater identification with the attitudes of dominant White America as a whole. There is an antagonism toward Jews on the part of Blacks who see Jews as the people who run businesses in the ghettos and take away their money. Among people who have been repressed, depressed, and poor, there is a tendency to see everything as a conspiracy against them, and Jews have always been objects of conspiracy theory. If you listen to Black radio stations in New York, you hear very depressing kinds of statements that blame Jews for everything. People like Louis Farrakhan are demagogues and rabble rousers who exacerbate existing tensions in order to create a certain kind of appeal for themselves and to mobilize a following.

Ramsamy: The election of minority mayors has been a growing trend in many urban areas. What significance do you attach to this trend?

Fainstein: There has been a general consensus in the research on Black mayors that in terms of the general policy of cities, Black mayors have not made very much difference. Redevelopment policy is quite the same with Black mayors as it has been with White mayors. One of the positive aspects of Black mayors is that they have made a difference in determining who gets hired for city jobs; a lot more city jobs are now filled by members of minority groups. However, as long as inner cities have so few resources, minority mayors become totally dependent on the White business community in order to have any financial base at all. They are, therefore, unable to proceed with much autonomy or make very much difference. If you have a city of poor people, only so much can be done as long as we have a tax system where each jurisdiction has to support itself.

Ramsamy: Identity is increasingly becoming the mobilizing force for social movements within marginalized communities in the United States. How effective is identity politics in the struggle for empowerment?

Fainstein: While pride in one's culture and identity are very important, one of the things that radicals tend to forget is that they are a minority. As a poor minority, they can make a very logical argument as to why they should be abrasive and assertive. However, they forget that their opposition is going to be equally abrasive and assertive in response. They can easily be overwhelmed by their opposition. From a weak position, being very assertive about one's identity doesn't get one very far. It often gets one involved in a losing fight. It is politically more effective to be able to find common ground than it is to constantly take umbrage when there are very few resources at one's disposal to back up one's position. I also see identity politics as a mirror image and no better than the kind of abuse that minorities have always experienced. It is an eye-for-eye, tooth-for-tooth retaliation in many respects. It does not further public discourse in a productive way.

Chapter 52

Black-Asian Relations in the United States: Negotiating Globalization and Racialization

Kavitha Ramachandran

Introduction

Ask anyone about Blacks and Asians in America and invariably you will enter a discussion of the Los Angeles "riots" of 1992. All people can seem to remember are the enraged, gun-wielding shopkeepers; the screaming, scurrying looters; and the smoldering Asian corner store. No one seems to talk anymore about the rising and falling batons of the four White police officers who beat Rodney King with impunity. As that fateful episode unfolded in the City of Angels, no one noticed the panoptic gaze of White supremacy, that prime mover in American society that simultaneously authored this hyper-real drama, played a catalytic role in it, and remained the voyeur throughout, all unbeknownst to the public. The ubiquity of White power rendered it invisible while Blacks and Asians stood in sharp contrast to each other against the architecture of late capitalism in L.A.

Lamentably, these are the most memorable images in the album of Black-Asian relations in the United States, in spite of much contact and mutual cultural exploration between the two groups for nearly two centuries. The L.A. "riots," capture the popular imagination more than any other phenomenon and dominate even the academic study of Black-Asian relations in the United States. This is due, at least in part, to the American media's exploitation of the public's readiness to seize the "proprietor-patron" relationship as the metaphor *par excellence* for not only the riots, but all Black-Asian relations in general. My aim in this chapter is to inquire into this preoccupation and theorize what appear to be deep differences between Blacks and Asians. I believe that differences, especially structural ones, deserve closer scrutiny, but in a manner that does not fetishize them, because an exclusive focus on group attributes is liable to render those differences impervious to social change. Theories of identity and difference, in my opinion, ought to explain but also transcend the attitudes and prejudices learned all too well by living in the United States and negotiating its pecking order. Unfortunately, much of the discussion of identity, multiculturalism, difference, and "otherness" is abstracted from material reality and politics. The theoretical and practical concern about the materiality of life is made to appear obsolete in much current cultural studies discourse on identity politics in spite of its growing importance in a rapidly globalizing world. The effect of this bias, in my observation, has been to direct research away from the materiality of social control and exclusion in the United States.

In light of these considerations, I will examine some of the socio-cultural, economic, and spatial factors informing contemporary relations between Blacks and Asians in American cities. In the first part of the chapter, I provide a brief history of each group, respectively, in the United States. I then define and discuss the importance of the constructs "race" and "racialization" in shaping American thought and practice within the national "racial formation." In the second part, I examine how U.S. participation in the global economy translates into a conflict between native and immigrant labor in U.S. cities, thus making Black-Asian relations a quintessentially urban issue. In the third section, I describe how changing demographic patterns in American cities, resulting mostly from immigration, affect opportunity structures for native and immigrant workers who must negotiate racialization and globalization simultaneously for survival. I conclude the chapter with some comments on cooperation between Blacks and Asians to challenge their joint exploitation and manipulation by interrogating the American racial formation and the global economic practices that maintain it.

Note: When referring to peoples of Asian and African descent living in America, one may choose from a number of terms that are currently in use, each of which are preferred on various occasions for different reasons. *Black, Black American, African American, African, Asian, Asian-American,* as well as other hyphenated ethnic identifiers, such as *Korean-American,* or *Indian-American* are among the terms currently available. Since one of the purposes of this chapter is to highlight and describe the racialization of these peoples in American society, I deliberately use the collectively racialized terms "Black" and "Asian" in order to engage the visual rhetoric upon which the political and economic differences between these groups rest. I also employ these terms to illustrate how the American racial formation deliberately collapses the internal diversity of these groups in order to facilitate their manipulation and control by White, male-dominated capitalist society. One is also forced to work with these reductionist terms in order to access census and other data pertaining to "Blacks" and "Asians." While data collected with the aid of these labels may shed some light on "differences" between the groups, it is important to note that these racial labels do not capture the complexity of emerging global identities; in fact, they ultimately serve to entrench the racialization that produced them in the first place, as I shall argue later in the chapter.

Background

Racial "minorities"—that is, Blacks, Asians, Pacific Islanders, Native Americans, and Latinos—are growing more than seven times faster than non-Hispanic Whites, with much of this population explosion occurring in past two decades (U.S. Bureau of Census, 2000). In 1990, minorities nationwide accounted for about 61 million Americans, representing 25% of the country's total population. By 2000, these minorities numbered 84.5 million, or 28.6% of the total population. American demographers predict that the entire United States will have a "majority of minorities" by the year 2060. Given this plurality, multicultural dialogue (of which Black-Asian relations are a part) is more central to all aspects of American life than ever before, especially after the tragic events of 9/11. Yet, even as the United States grows more diverse and faces new challenges, its racial discourse remains trapped within the meta-narrative of "Black vs. White." This dichotomy has never been adequate for understanding the Asian, Latino, or Native American experiences, for example, let alone relations among these groups. In the ensuing section, I shall provide some background on Blacks and Asians, briefly discuss the racial formation of the United States, and identify the respective positions of these two groups within that hierarchy.

Blacks

The 35.4 million Black people in the United States are mostly descendants of Africans brought by force to the United States through the trans-Atlantic slave trade. They were the chief source of labor for Southern cotton, rice, and tobacco plantations and were sought for their superior agricultural skills and resistance to European diseases. Emancipation formally ended involuntary Black servitude but failed to make reparations for three centuries of dehumanization. Jim Crow laws made a mockery of three amendments to the Constitution intended to grant freedom, citizenship, and men's suffrage to Blacks; moreover, they were intended to prevent the integration of Blacks into the mainstream. Blacks were finally allowed to enter the Northern industrial labor markets during the Great Migration, but only to face institutionalized racism in a new urban context. The segregation and concentration of Blacks in racial ghettos deepened their inequality in White society but, ironically, urbanization presented them with new opportunities for organization and political representation through urban social movements. Also, the method of litigation allowed them to periodically challenge the unconstitutionality of certain laws in the nation's highest courts.

However, the systemic aspects of Black inequality were not confronted directly until the Civil Rights Movement of the 1960s. All the while, White backlash attempted to subvert the effective application of reparative measures. Since the 1960s, a sizable and influential Black middle class has developed as opportunity was created through affirmative action and other policies. However, so has a class of poor Blacks who remain spatially isolated, untouched by social policy, and de-linked economically and politically from the mainstream.

Their presence is acknowledged in the White world mostly through the pop-cultural art form of hip-hop and through negative, racially charged media coverage of welfare, crime, and other "inner city pathologies." While slavery itself has long been abolished, evolving institutions such as the prison industrial complex insure that as many as one in three Black men between the ages of 18 and 25 are incarcerated and living in a state of disenfranchisement harkening back to slavery (Human Rights Watch, 1995). Created in part by global economic forces that displace domestic labor, and in part by the racial formation of the United States, the Black poor are again marginalized by futuristic technological transformations and urban renewal that are all around, but do not include them. Furthermore, immigration over the past two decades of peoples from the African diaspora, both documented and undocumented, has increased competition for jobs, scholarships, and resources within the Black community while adding new dimensions to some fundamental questions about Black identity, citizenship, rights, and racial justice in America (Kelly and Lewis, 2000).

Asians

"Asians" are a pan-ethnic/racial "group" consisting of over 60 different nationalities originating in the continent of Asia, each with its own linguistic and cultural heritage, as well as its own political history. As the most rapidly-growing group in this country during the 1980s, Asians numbered more than 7.3 million in 1990 (U.S. Bureau of Census, 1990). By 2000, that number had increased to 11.3 million, constituting an increase of 45%, which is the highest rate of growth for any racial or ethnic group in that decade (U.S. Bureau of Census, 2000). Asian labor has been critical to American economic well-being and comfort for almost two centuries. For example, Asian workers in the garment and food services industries insure that Americans enjoy high fashion and good food at low prices. According to Espiritu (1992), for every Asian scientist or engineer, there is an unskilled or semi-skilled Asian worker earning less than minimum wage. The Asian population includes both the most and the least educated people in the United States (Espiritu, 1992).

Asians have also experienced a history of racism and oppression. As early as 1854, the California Supreme Court ruled that Chinese and Sikh men from India (the United States did not accept female immigrants at the time) who came to work on railroads and mines in the West Coast were not permitted to marry, own land, or testify against Whites. This ruling reveals that the United States had no intention of creating or franchising a permanent population of Asians in the country. In 1882, the Chinese Exclusion Act banned all immigration from China in order to arrest population growth and, in 1913, California prohibited aliens ineligible for citizenship from owning property. As Japanese immigration to the United States grew, discriminatory legislation was extended to them. For example, the 1924 National Origins Act excluded Japanese and most other Asians from immigrating to the United States. With the outbreak of World War II, 110,000 Asians (mostly Japanese) were relocated to "internment" camps in the Pacific Northwest regardless of their American citizenship. Only in 1952 were Asians born outside the United States permitted to become citizens through naturalization.

While the rampant bigotry and violence against Blacks is well-known and documented, violence against Asians, which accompanies each wave of xenophobia and nativism in American history, is not well-publicized by the American news media. A study by Kim (1998) indicates that a hate crime against Asians occurs nearly everyday in the United States. In the 1980s, a group of predominantly Latino youths called "Dotbusters" (named for the decorative forehead symbol or "dot" worn by many Asian Indian women) organized themselves to terrorize Asians of Indian descent in New Jersey. Also throughout that decade, a climate of Japan-bashing resulted in the violent murders of several Chinese, Koreans, Laotians, Cambodians, and Vietnamese who were assumed to be "Japanese." In late 1996, a White supremacist stabbed to death a young Vietnamese American college graduate because he wanted to show how easy it is to "kill a Jap" (Pham, 1996). A number of Asian women, some elderly and others young and pregnant, were pushed to their deaths onto the subway tracks in New York City (Kim, 1998). Such incidents show that even if current history is not marked by the blatantly racist laws of the past, Asian lives continue to be shaped by persistent phobic attitudes, discriminatory policies, and physical violence. Jaded stereotypes of Asian inscrutability, unfair competition, cultural unassimilability, and sexual perversity work the centuries-old doctrine of Orientalism (Said, 1979) and are applied to each new group of Asian immigrants during every new crisis. Refugees of U.S. wars in Southeast Asia find themselves being labeled "Chinks" and "Japs" as they step into a historical situation in America that they had no part in making. More recently, after the 9/11 attacks on New York City and Washington, D.C., the American public is more ready than ever to attribute terrorism to Asians, who were seen as foreign and alien all along.

For example, a Sikh man from India and a man from Pakistan were fatally shot in the aftermath of 9/11 because the attackers saw in their bearded or turbaned countenances an apparent "resemblance" to the notorious Osama bin Laden (*New York Times*, March 11, 2002).

Race, Racialization, and Racial Formation

However, neither the experiences of nor the differences between Blacks and Asians in the United States can be effectively explained without an understanding of the cultural logic of race, racialization, and racial formation, as defined here. *Race* is a social construct that collapses the range of complexions and features found in the entire human population into only three or four colors. By reducing the visual diversity of humanity to the crude labels "Black," "White," "Brown," or "Yellow," race translates "biological" difference into social stigma, liability, or privilege according to a historically given but continually modified color scheme. As a principle of social control, race, like gender and sexual orientation, regulates the representation, discipline, and manipulation of the self by inscribing racial rules upon the human body. The result is a regime of visual ideology and social practice that creates arbitrary but nevertheless real social identities, each with its own experiences, memories, and politics. The histories of racial identities are always plural, sometimes shared, and often conflicting, as race itself is in a given society. As such, race is simultaneously a tool of oppression and an agent of resistance, depending on who is using it and for what purpose.

In the United States, the racial category "Black" evolved with the consolidation of racial slavery into an institution. By the end of the 17th century, Africans, whose ethnic identities may have included Ibo, Ashanti, and others, were rendered "Black" by a culture of exploitation based on the racial logic described. With slavery, a new social hierarchy was established, resulting in the shaping of specific *racial* identities for the Black slaves and the White European settlers, respectively. Jordan (1977) has observed that "from the initially common term 'Christian,' at mid-century [sixteenth] there was a marked shift toward the terms 'English' and 'free.' After about 1680, taking the colonies as a whole, a new term of self-identification appeared—'white.'" Since then, "White" has contrasted with "Black" in American thought and practice, ascribing various socio-cultural, moral, and sexual meanings onto the relationship, with "White" always read as positive, dominant, or superior, and Black as its nemesis. This original racial hierarchical dualism dominates the discourse of difference in the United States such that it eclipses other aspects of identity including class, gender, or ethnicity. *Racism*, then, is the belief in and maintenance of such a ranking order by the subjects and institutions of a society, as well as the practices resulting therefrom. Yet, the systemic aspects and pervasive nature of racism in a given culture is seldom considered because of the perennial temptation to think of race itself either as an essence fixed in our genes, or as an empty illusion with no basis in fact. Instead, race and racism are better understood as unstable and de-centered constructs, a nexus of social meanings arbitrarily arrested, transformed, and deployed by political struggle within particular historical contexts.

The entry of immigrants of other races, such as Asians, or even the presence of hybrid identities of mixed race ancestry, for that matter, present anomalies for the "Black vs. White" model of race relations, on which much common understanding, scholarship, politics, and policy are based. Nevertheless, old binaries of race are applied to new "others" through a process identified by Omi and Winant (1994) as *racialization*. Racialization extends racial meaning to a previously racially unclassified group, social practice, relationship, or situation. The effects of this polarization on Asians is to cast their racial identities as shades of Black or White and wedge them into a mediating position between those two races. However, both processes obscure what Visweswaran (1997) terms *Asianization*, or the ways in which Asian groups become "Asian" as defined against, and in relation to, each other. By the same token, racialization also obscures internal differentiation within the racially homogenized identity "Black." As an evolving process, racialization is specific to each period in history even if it is based on pre-existing concepts and practices. It also refers to the manner in which the visuality of race is exalted as the primary identifier of difference in society. Because of racialization, Black or Asian "looks" become more important than other aspects of self-identification as the basis by which groups vie for resources, power, and social acceptance. As a result, class, gender, ethnicity, religion, language, and so on are of secondary importance in a society obsessed with racial appearance as the chief determinant of social position and striving.

As a racialized category, the term Asian is ubiquitous, although it is useful only in some contexts. While it embraces many identities, it universalizes the experiences of the dominant constituencies among Asians while obscuring the particular differences of subordinate members. Asians are not a group united by a common race, nationality, language, or religion in the way that Latinos share the Spanish language or Jews share a religion, for example. There is no single attribute that unites this disparate group or mends its internal lines of division. Consequently, the term *Asian* does not correctly identify or describe the groups it intends to name; nor does it lend itself to accurate comparisons with other groups, such as Blacks. Nevertheless, regarding "Asians" as a single group is both convenient and indispensable to Americans, including Asians themselves, for a variety of reasons. Identifiers such as "Asian" offer different kinds of political leverage within the United States, depending on the situation. They are used as functional categories by all those, including the government, who want a quick, easy grasp of racial identities that are neither White nor Black. On the other hand, in spite of its problems, widespread use of the term *Asian* has led Asians themselves to appropriate and transmute the label into a focal point of resistance, in much the same way that Blacks have done with "Blackness." "Asian" has thus become an organizing tool that connects the different Asian ethnicities and races who have experienced racism and exclusion in common within the American racial formation.

The signification made possible by the construct of race, as inflected by the process of racialization, extends beyond the boundaries of skin color, super-exploitation, social stratification, or discrimination into the realms of culture and hegemony. Thus, new racial "others" like Asians or Latinos, for example, find themselves racialized, incorporated into, and participating in the *racial formation* of the United States, which permeates every institution, identity, and social practice in the country (Omi and Winant, 1994). Furthermore, resistance to "racial projects" such as slavery, segregation, and so on is itself a product of the racial formation and bears its imprint (Omi and Winant, 1994). The racial formation of American society has changed over time and has employed various ideologies for its existence. For Blacks, rationalization of the racial formation may be less overt now, no longer supported by law, as seen in *Plessy v. Ferguson*. Nonetheless, their "place" in the racial formation continues to receive "scientific" justification through two popular arguments, namely the "underclass" and "IQ" theses. The former emphasizes environmental factors, while the latter stresses genetic ones in order to "explain" Black inequalities. Both, however, locate the socioeconomic problems of Blacks within race rather than class, further cementing the Black position in the racial formation. The underclass thesis roots the present unabated poverty and high rates of social dysfunction among many urban Blacks in the economic and social isolation of the "hyperghetto" (Wacquant, 1994; Wilson, 1987). Essentially a reprise of the "culture of poverty" thesis advanced by Lewis (1966), the underclass hypothesis does not blame Blacks directly for their situation but rather their lack of the attributes that would make middle-class Blacks or others willing to live with them. However, the problem with this perspective is that it still identifies the immediate cause of Black poverty in the traits of the Black poor and in the flight of upwardly mobile Blacks from inner cities instead of the economic inequality generated by the labor market practices, racism, and political decisions of mainstream society.

The IQ argument became attractive again in recent years with the publication of Herrnstein and Murray's book *The Bell Curve* in 1994. Although rejected by respectable scientists and reviewers, this book nevertheless received enormous publicity. It argues that intelligence is genetically transmitted, and that Blacks, in particular, lack the necessary genetic traits to produce intelligent offspring or qualify for good jobs. While it is unlikely that the book, which is riddled with statistical errors (see Gould, 1995) will persuade anyone not already convinced of its argument, its mode of framing the issue succeeds in focusing public attention on the presumed genetic characteristics of Blacks rather than their unequal relationship with White society. Thus, by resurrecting the ideology of biological determinism that many believed had been successfully refuted by luminaries like Gould (1981), *The Bell Curve* de-legitimates Black demands for justice by extending the prestige and credibility of science to racist theories of human difference.

For Asians, on the other hand, the "middleman minority" theory is often cited to explain their place in the racial pecking order (Bonacich, 1980). The Asian "middleman" is strategically positioned within the racial formation as the "buffer" between Black and White, and is said to profit from allegedly trafficking between the mainstream and the margins. These theories tend to target groups that are perceived to specialize in business or trade and concentrate in the petite bourgeoisie. As middlemen, Asians are marked as racially distinct from Whites or Blacks, supposedly poised to benefit from their intermediary position between the dominant Whites and subordinate others. However, this sandwiched positioning of Asians is strategically useful to Whites, who need a human shield from other subordinate groups' hostility to themselves. In addition to their own bigotry toward the middleman minority, dominant Whites foment the racist reactions of the subordinate groups and tweak existing tensions within the hierarchy to their own advantage. The middleman minority thesis is bolstered by the negative stereotypes of avarice, clannishness, or unscrupulousness generally attributed to Asians. The fact that these stereotypes originate in Whites' fear of economic competition is ignored by Blacks and other subordinate groups who find in Asians a scapegoat for their own predicaments.

A variant of the middleman minority thesis is the "model minority" stereotype, which often escapes criticism as a racist trope because of its seemingly flattering portrait of Asians. Conservative commentators like Sowell (1994) often point to the degree of economic progress and eventual social acceptance achieved by Asian immigrants, especially Asian Indians, Chinese, and Koreans. Influential media icons, writers, and policy makers (Will, 1994; D'Souza, 1991) herald Asians as the "model minority" and attribute the successes of these groups to their "superior cultures," work ethic, and family values, while denouncing Blacks and other "less-than-model" groups for supposedly lacking the virtues necessary for advancement. They praise the scholastic and material successes of Asians and offer numerous theories, the underclass and IQ arguments among them, to explain why such achievement is supposedly absent among Blacks. Curiously, in their accounts, Black immigrants are grouped together with American Blacks, while all Asians, on the other hand, are identified as immigrants, regardless of their citizenship status. However, by using Asians to uphold already problematic racist constructions of identity, and blaming Black economic failures on their own supposed lack of initiative, conservatives succeed in legitimating the neo-liberal, pro-market, anti-welfare economic doctrines that produce inequality in the first place.

Neither Blacks nor Asians realize that such a seemingly flattering characterization of the "model minority" poses several problems for the applauded groups as well as the "problem" groups, especially when the latter fail to emulate the former. If biological determinism degrades Blacks as genetically inferior, the dubious accolade of "model minority" artificially elevates Asian experiences through cultural determinism. It places all Asians into one category regardless of ethnic, linguistic, or class differences, because they are all assumed to have a common heritage or character. Asian poverty, exploitation, and despair are obscured in an attempt to chastise other groups for their own problems. Through circular reasoning, "Asian" values are inferred from success stories and then posited as the cause of success. As a corollary, Blacks' apparent lack of values is supposed to be inferred from their "failure" to match Asian success. The model minority label is often passed off as a benign compliment to "docile" and "hardworking" Asians but it is, in fact, invidious in its ability to deny "over-achieving," "over-represented," and therefore "undeserving" Asians access to opportunities. Simultaneously, it is used effectively to discipline the more "vocal" but "lazy" Blacks for their non-achievement. The paternalism inherent in the assumptions and usage of the model minority stereotype is debilitating to both groups but ultimately beneficial to the Whites who generated it. As in the case of the middleman minority theory, Whites watch surreptitiously as Asians receive the wrath and envy of others, especially Blacks, whose social exclusion and spatial isolation deepen as a result of Whites' hegemony in the world economic order, America's historic neglect of the Black plight, and continued racism.

For example, the various "explanations" of Asian "success" and Blacks' presumed lack of it predictably result in new immigrants imbibing negative caricatures about Blacks while being pegged by racist middleman stereotypes themselves. Thus, it is possible for newcomers of color "to develop, through theoretical and concrete experience, knowledge of how they are diminished by White Western racism, . . . but not always interrogate the way in which they automatically have greater status and privilege than individuals of African descent" (hooks, 1990). On the other hand, it is not surprising that the tables have turned after the 9/11 attacks, as "Arab-looking" people, especially immigrants, invoke the fear of terrorism in Whites and Blacks alike. Blacks, who were most commonly victimized by racial profiling as "criminals" until 9/11, are joined by "Middle-Eastern looking" Asians, Latinos, and others who are now cast as terrorists. Those fears are augmented by increasing levels of undocumented immigration, especially to the suburbs (*New York Times*, October 6, 2005). Thus, Americans have blamed immigrants and Blacks alternatively for degrading their cities, stealing their jobs, or hijacking their politics, depending on their latest worry: crime one day, economic competition the next, or terrorism the day after that. Blacks threaten from within by invoking fears of drug dealing, gangsterism, and welfare dependency, while Asians pose the threat of foreign economic domination, political disloyalty, and the theft of opportunities and resources. In other words, Blacks are regarded as a domestic but familiar menace, while Asians are always the outsiders, disconcertingly mysterious, and ultimately unknowable. In this manner, White racialization of the feared "other," is extended to new situations, then learned, internalized, and applied by all groups who participate actively in maintaining the social order.

Blacks and Asians: "Comparisons"

A common approach to the study of race relations is comparison, especially of the socioeconomic characteristics exhibited by the groups in question. However, given the different ways that groups such as Blacks and Asians are racialized into the American racial formation (discussed previously), any comparison is inevitably the product of that problematic process. In other words, most comparisons contain a built-in risk of error because they are uncritically based on existing racial categories, which are themselves derived through racialization. Thus, the groups being compared are twice racialized, once by White society itself, and again by methodologies of comparison. The outcomes of such racialized studies are, therefore, inherently power-laden and politically charged because they perpetuate, even if inadvertently, the racialization of groups in society. In this manner, comparative studies contribute toward maintaining the racial formation. For this reason, I argue that while comparisons of Blacks and Asians may be useful in *describing* certain group attributes, they cannot *explain* differences or predict groups' political behavior, as commonly assumed possible. What is often missing in such descriptive studies altogether is the background to whatever is apparent to the observer. The depth of context required is available only through socio-historical and political analysis.

For example, let us consider some differences identified by the noted Black scholar Manning Marable (1997) in his column, "Along the Color Line." While Marable's prolific works and presentations attest to the fact that he is very supportive of and dedicated to intellectual and practical efforts to foster Black-Asian cooperation, there are, nevertheless, a few methodological issues to be clarified in his comparisons of Blacks and Asians. These inconsistencies distort his interpretation of the respective socioeconomic status of Blacks and Asians and introduce the possibility of overgeneralizations. After reviewing some 1990 U.S. Census data, Marable (1997) determined that profound socioeconomic differences exist between Blacks and Asians:

- The median household income of Asian Americans was $36,000 compared to $30,000 for non-Hispanic White households, and $18,100 for African American households.
- According to the Census Bureau's *Survey of Minority-owned Business Enterprises*, the number of Asian American-owned businesses in the United States grew from 187,691 in 1982 to 335,331 in 1987—an increase of 79%, which means that in 1987, about 6% of all Asian Americans owned a business of some type, compared to 6.5% of all non-Hispanic Whites, and 1.5% of all Black Americans.
- Although African American college enrollments reached 1.4 million by 1993, the figure well underrepresented Blacks as percentages of the general population. Between 1976 and 1992, the number of African Americans who received both master's degrees and doctorates actually declined. Conversely, access to higher education for Asian Americans increased significantly during these same years. From 1976 to 1993, the number of Asian Americans enrolled in colleges and universities soared from 198,000 to 724,000. In academic year 1992–1993, Asian Americans were awarded more doctorates (1,580) than African Americans (1,350) and earned more professional degrees (5,160) than Blacks (4,100).

He then concludes, as many observers commonly do, that Blacks continue to be subjected to extreme economic and social discrimination, while Asians are not. However, I argue that such a conclusion might be premature, considering the data missing from this alternatively selective/overgeneralized profile of Asians. There is also a host of other questions that could have been asked about both Blacks and Asians but are not. Let us probe Marable's conclusion by considering a few geographical and statistical variables that were overlooked. For example, with respect to the median incomes quoted, one might ask whether household size was considered. Asians may have higher median incomes, but they are also more likely than Whites or Blacks to live in larger, extended-family households, as noted by Woo (1995). Also, median household income varies according to Asian ethnicity, and their particular opportunity structures, each of which ought to be considered separately if it is to be statistically meaningful (Woo, 1995).

It is also significant that Marable does not consider the spatial concentration of Asians in key cities when comparing household incomes, especially to Whites. One striking feature about Asians in the United States is that they are concentrated in a few areas, all urban. In 1970, about 80% of the total Asian population resided in five states—California, Hawaii, Illinois, New York, and Washington. Furthermore, 59% of Chinese, Filipino, and Japanese Americans were concentrated in only 5 of the 243 Standard Metropolitan Statistical Areas (SMSA) in the United States—Chicago, Honolulu, Los Angeles, New York, and San Francisco/Oakland. Immigration during the intervening decades has not only produced dramatic increases, especially in the Filipino and Chinese populations, but has also continued the overwhelming tendency for these groups to concentrate in the same geographical areas, especially those in California (U.S. Bureau of Census, 1990). What is often not realized by most observers is that such a pattern of residential concentration means that Asian median household incomes will be reported as higher than those of White households, who are more dispersed nationally. Also ignored by most observers is the fact that along with higher urban incomes in cities like San Francisco or Los Angeles come higher costs of living. When seen in relation to gender, again it is apparent that national income averages, which compare the income of Asian women with that of the more broadly dispersed White women, contain a systematic distortion not considered by Marable. In fact, if we compare women within the same area, Asian women are frequently less well-off than White women, and the difference between both groups of women pales when compared with White men, whose incomes are much higher than that of any group of women. A comparison of Black and Asian household incomes ought to at least reflect these geographic adjustments.

Next, it is possible that the preponderance of business ownership noted among Asians might be a selective response to limited employment and promotion opportunities in the United States by immigrants lacking professional skills or proficiency in English. These Asians might operate small businesses using large numbers of household labor and shared, rotating ethnic capital as an alternative to sweatshop employment (Kim, 1998). Noting that access to higher education is also unequal between the groups, Marable proceeds to speculate that this might be a reason why Blacks overwhelmingly support affirmative action programs and minority scholarships, while a large percentage of Asians do not. Again, such claims mask other realities that might be apparent if the questions were asked differently or if different questions were asked altogether. For example, if Asian ethnicity, class, and citizenship status were taken into account, inequality among Asians—such as poverty in Hmong communities, or high rates of delinquency and attrition among poor Vietnamese youth—actually mirror similar pathologies among not only impoverished Blacks, but poor communities in general, regardless of race. In the mainstream's uncritical view, gangsterism and addiction are not "supposed" to exist in a "model," "over-represented" minority. Data on Asians that universalize the experiences of the privileged to the entire population are often inappropriately used in comparisons with other entire groups, who might also have been homogenized and generalized.

Among Blacks, by the same token, it would be incorrect to generalize the experience of a middle-class Nigerian software developer, for example, to all Blacks just because both are identified in the United States as "Black." While racially categorized as "Black," this person might have little else in common with African Americans. An attempt to then predict the Nigerian's political behavior or beliefs based on his race would be regarded, justifiably, by Blacks and others as racist. Yet such presuppositions about Asians are commonplace and regarded as objective by all segments of American society regardless of repeated Asian attempts to point out this inconsistency (Aguilar-San Juan, 1994). To consider race alone is to ignore an individual's ethnicity, foreign educational attainment, native/immigrant status, or pre-migration access to capital and social networks, to cite a few other factors, all of which play a critical role in determining socioeconomic status upon arriving in the United States. Therefore, "comparisons" of Blacks and Asians based on racialized generalizations are liable to be contrived and likely to be flawed.

The examples given suggest that a statistical reassessment for the Asian and Black populations that accounts for internal diversity, geographic, occupational, and other variables is vitally needed if we are to gain a clearer picture of the "differences" between the two groups. However, I argue that even these corrections will, at best, still yield only slightly better descriptions, not necessarily good explanations. Descriptions, by definition, can answer only questions pertaining to "what," "where," "when," or "whom," whereas it is the domain of explanations to reveal "why" or "how." Comparative discourses often are based heavily on descriptive gradational constructs, such as "socioeconomic status" (SES), which tend to produce findings that are themselves graded. As such, they do little more than affirm an existing hierarchy or, worse, create a ranking system where one does not yet exist. Instead, I posit that relational constructs, such as "class," are better suited for explanation because they situate problems in relation to some context. It is more likely that a causal relationship might be discerned from a study based on relational constructs rather than gradational ones. Given the descriptive bias in contemporary scholarship, it is not surprising that most "comparisons" of Blacks and Asians do not contradict the premises upon which they were made. As functions of given American assumptions about race and the reductive formulas of racialization within which they are embedded, I contend that these "comparisons" reproduce the very structures of race and practices of racialization upheld by the racial formation.

Unfortunately, these "data," despite their flaws, are influential. They are splashed all over the news, text-books, literature, and popular culture, where they undergo a further spin cycle before aiding in the formulation and implementation of unjust public policy. Bearing a semblance of science, careless comparisons offer a convenient way to feed Blacks and Asians misinformation about each other and reinforce caricatures of Asian "businessmen" or Black "criminals." These stereotypes persist for two reasons: First, lapses in method-ological rigor often go unnoticed, as pointed out previously, because as participants in the American racial formation, most people receive prior preparation by that system to accept unquestioningly data presented along racial lines about other groups. Seldom do they inquire how "race" is constructed socially, whether race is even a legitimate biological category, given its innumerable inconsistencies, or how race is an ideological tool in the hands of powerful elites who can insist that one's social position is biologically and culturally, not politically, determined. Since living in a racialized society has habituated both Blacks and Asians to racism, it is all the more imperative that they identify and reject discourses that compromise on accuracy and lend themselves to social control. Secondly, one cannot overlook the fact that racist constituents within these very groups have a stake in maintaining the American racial formation. They leverage essentialist stereotypes of themselves and others and exploit narrow nationalist sentiments in order to redeem social or economic priv-ileges at the expense of those who are excluded.

In the remainder of this chapter, I shall try to provide some explanatory context for an alternative "com-parison" of Blacks and Asians as racialized subjects by exploring how globalization and employment shape class in the United States, while noting the fact that those who control these forces happen to be predomi-nantly White.

Deindustrialization, Reindustrialization, and Labor Migration: Contextualizing the Black-Asian Encounter

This section will consider some socio-spatial aspects of global capitalism that articulate with the racial for-mation of the United States and influence Blacks' and Asians' shifting relation to each other within that for-mation. Bearing in mind that global forces and local particularities must be considered concurrently, I shall examine how the United States' participation in the global economy visits upon Blacks and Asians as a con-flict between native and immigrant labor in American cities. I shall argue that the relationship between cap-ital flow and labor migration has changed demographic patterns in U.S. cities, making them more diverse, but it has also affected the opportunity structures relied upon by Black and Asian workers alike, as mediated by the American racial formation.

In examining productive organization and new spatial patterns in the context of rapid capitalist restruc-turing, it is possible to identify a central dialectic relationship: on one hand, the particularities of local places and cultures are transformed upon contact with the capitalist mode of production. On the other hand, spe-cific local traditions also actively co-produce and re-work the global capitalist system. Thus, capitalism may be theorized as capable of infinite variation, absorbing, combining, breaking down, and transforming every-thing in its path. Capitalism, according to the philosopher Karl Marx, contains an inexorable tendency to cri-sis given its inherent contradictions, which include its growth-oriented nature, its exploitation of living labor in production, and its technological and organizational dynamism. These crises, and the attempts to fix them, are always embedded in a local context, which then inform the reproduction of capitalism itself (Harvey, 1988). These factors set the American city as the stage upon which Blacks and Asians, as living labor, meet, interact, and compete.

In the contemporary phase of globalization, capital mobility has created new conditions for the mobil-ity of labor, the most important being the formation of a transnational space within which the circulation of workers can be regarded as one of several flows, including capital, goods, services, and information (Castells, 2000). As a result, Sassen (1988) identifies three important factors that play a role in labor migration to the major urban centers of industrialized countries such as the United States: 1) The development of production for export in several Third World countries through a massive increase of direct foreign investment and inter-national subcontracting and outsourcing by industrialized countries; 2) The development of major cities into nodes for the control and management of the global economic system; 3) The emergence of the United States as the major recipient of direct foreign investment in the world, after having been the main exporter of cap-ital for nearly four decades after World War II.

According to Sassen, foreign investment in developing countries contributes to the formation of a pool of potential emigrants as well as the emergence of emigration to the industrialized countries as an actual option. Secondly, transformations in the world economy have generated new or significantly expanded roles for major urban centers in the developed countries, thus restructuring labor demand there. The job supply is shaped by the growth of an advanced service sector, which includes finance and information technologies. It is also affected by the shrinking of traditional manufacturing industries and their replacement with a down-graded manufacturing sector and high-tech industries, both of which maximize sweatshop production. The result is an expansion of very high-income professional and technical jobs, on one hand, and a proliferation of low-wage jobs, on the other hand, both of which target immigrant workers. The latter is mostly a function of growth sectors but also of declining industries in need of cheap labor for survival.

Another source of jobs for immigrants is the immigrant business community itself. These jobs include not only temporary arrangements until a job in the mainstream society can be found; they also include a large array of professional and technical jobs that service the needs of expanding and increasingly income-stratified immigrant communities in the city. Finally, as global centers for servicing and managing a vastly decentralized manufacturing sector and for globalizing economic activity in general, cities like New York and Los Angeles are major recipients of direct foreign investment in banking and other advanced services (Fainstein, 1994; Soja, 1996). Decentralization of Western European and Japanese manufacturing and its subsequent re-location to the United States generated a need in the United States for centralized management and servicing. As a result, even more jobs became available. These three developments set the stage for labor migration to global centers. Immigration to the United States is in part a response to these conditions.

Immigrants to the United States have settled primarily in cities (Waldinger, 1989). From 1961 to 1990, more than 15 million legal immigrants entered the country, nearly half of them in the 1980s. During the same period, 4.8 million foreigners became naturalized U.S. citizens. They particularly gravitated to a relatively small number of metropolitan areas, with more than half of the 1990 total settling in only four metropolitan areas (LA/San Diego, New York, San Francisco, and Chicago), selecting those places that had experienced some economic expansion during the 1970s and 1980s (Steinberg, 1989). The highest numbers of immigrants from 1970 to 1980 came from Mexico, the Philippines, and South Korea, followed by China (Taiwan and People's Republic), India, the Dominican Republic, Jamaica, Colombia, and several Caribbean Basin countries, all of them filling particular niches in the U.S. labor markets. New entries and natural growth resulted in the pronounced expansion of the Asian and Latino populations in the United States from 1970 to 1980, 100% and 62% respectively. These growth rates were surpassed by some nationalities, notably the 412% increase of South Koreans (Sassen, 1988). The new Caribbean Basin and South-East Asian immigration, by far the largest share in the current immigration, is heavily concentrated in cities with high job losses in old industries and job growth in high-tech industries and specialized services (Steinberg 1989; 1995). As noted earlier, Asians have gone largely to the Los Angeles, San Francisco, and New York metropolitan areas, which have the three largest concentrations of Asians. Given the fact that Blacks are also primarily an urban population in the United States, Black-Asian relations are situated squarely within an urban context. It is not surprising, in retrospect, that the effects of the restructuring on domestic labor for over two decades in Los Angeles gradually set the stage for the 1992 uprising in that city. Those conditions are considered in following paragraphs.

Epidemic plant closings in the rubber industry and smaller firms, indefinite lay-offs, and deep pay cuts came as a severe blow to a segment of the labor market that was highly unionized and contained an unusually large proportion of well-paid Black, Latino, and female blue-collar workers (Soja, 1989). In Watts, economic conditions deteriorated more rapidly than in any other community within Los Angeles and did not improve since the riots of 1965. In the decade and a half following the Watts eruption, the predominantly Black area of South Central Los Angeles, the future setting of the 1992 riots, lost 40,000 in population, 20,000 jobs, and $2500 in median family income, which at $5900, fell below the city median for the Black population in the late 1970s (Soja, 1989). This selective deindustrialization crushed organized labor and significantly weakened many of the contractual gains achieved in the two decades following the World War II (*New York Times*, October 28, 2005). The concurrence of deindustrialization with a restructuring of the regional economy had a devastating effect on the Black population of Los Angeles.

Restructuring has been propelled by two key sectors since the 1960s: aerospace/electronics and apparel manufacturing. The aerospace/electronics cluster of industrial sectors in southern California, probably the largest urban concentration of advanced technology-based industry in the world, grew by 50% in the region during the 1972–79 period (Soja, 1989). The growth of the garment industry, on the other hand, ushered in another dramatic change in the regional labor market. Not only did the "high technocracy" settle in extraordinary numbers in LA; so did the largest pool of low-wage, weakly organized, and easily disciplined immigrant labor in the country. This still-growing labor pool has affected virtually every sector of the regional economy, but its imprint has been most visible, however, in the production of garments, especially in the "women's," "misses," and "juniors' outerwear" categories, which tend to be highly labor-intensive, difficult to mechanize, and organized around small sweatshops in order to adapt more efficiently to rapidly changing fashion trends. Of the approximately 125,000 jobs in this sector, perhaps as many as 80% were held by undocumented workers in the 1980s, with 90% of all employees being women. Unionization rates are low, while infringements of labor rights and violations of laws pertaining to minimum wage, overtime, child labor, and occupational safety are rife (Soja, 1989). Thus race, ethnicity, immigrant status, age, and gender cut across this economic landscape, accelerating the fragmentation and polarization begun with deindustrialization. As a result, Blacks and Asians compete in a regional labor market that is more occupationally differentiated and socially segmented than ever before. This, in turn, leads to shifting class relations between the two groups. In such a context, gradational comparisons based on fixed constructs such as socioeconomic status (discussed earlier) have little explanatory value.

Blacks and Asians: Negotiating Globalization and Racialization

Spatial segregation and social exclusion in America is generally seen as stemming from the ideological legacy and unstable interaction of two phenomena: (1) voluntary immigration, which created successive tides of newcomers, who were self-selected and who could eventually fade into the general population; and (2) involuntary servitude of a physically identifiable group, establishing a caste that even after emancipation could not escape stigmatization (Blauner, 1972). As a result, the social construction of "otherness" is thought to vary according to how the "other" is racialized within the dichotomy. However, while such a dichotomous characterization may be appropriate for capturing the historic difference between White and Black labor in America, it does not apply entirely to the experience of immigrants of color. Newly arrived workers from Asia or Africa, for example, may constitute voluntary labor (or involuntary labor, if one considers the labor rights violations mentioned previously) but still do not assimilate into American society. On the other hand, owing to their visible racial differences and apparently "outlandish" cultural practices, they find themselves socially and politically located at the margins of American institutional and personal spaces. The persistence of Chinatowns in American cities is a case in point. In addition, in the case of Blacks and Asians, it might be more useful to consider how the antagonism between native and immigrant labor, created by the global processes of capital and labor migration described earlier, becomes racialized within the U.S. national context which, in turn, articulates with emerging global racial identities.

In light of these problems, I propose an alternative conceptualization in which the conflict between "native" and "immigrant" labor is seen as an outcome of social and economic forces that produce two seemingly contradictory but dialectically related spaces: fixed spaces of place, on one hand, and mobile spaces of flows, on the other. Identities that manifest themselves within these spaces are subsequently racialized according to the logic of those spaces. Hence, both spaces include individuals who are visibly "Black," for example, but who experience racialization differently. These Black persons inhabit and enact that identity according to whether they are "natives" or "immigrants," rich or poor, men or women, among other factors. In fact, they may actually exhibit similar economic attributes and share common concerns with racial others who occupy their space, rather than with racial similars in the other space. Oprah Winfrey and an undocumented Dominican migrant worker working in a Florida citrus farm, for instance, may both look "Black" but have little else in common. On the other hand, Oprah's celebrity status and power in the entertainment industry places her in a social circle that includes Bill Gates and Lakshmi Mittal, the world's wealthiest men. As being Black or Asian in one space entails different social relations than in the other, appeals to primordiality become problematic and monolithic comparisons between the two groups get complicated. Therefore, the question is not how Blacks and Asians are different but, rather, how Blacks and Asians in spaces of flows relate to Blacks and Asians fixed in spaces of place.

Such a relational conceptualization, first of all, would permit the consideration of more identities than Blauner's dichotomy allows. For example, the identities of native Asians, such as fourth generation Japanese or Chinese, recent Black immigrants from Africa or Asia, as well as diasporan immigrants of Asian or African origin who had settled elsewhere outside of their "ancestral homelands" prior to emigration to the United States, might each be understood in their own right without being collapsed to fit into the dichotomy. More importantly, however, this perspective would allow for the fact that identities are not intrinsically fixed entities but fluid processes that may be arrested at will from time to time, for various political purposes, by those with power. In other words, the point is not simply to include more and more statically conceptualized racial identities in the hope of changing the dichotomy into a plurality but, instead, to improve one's understanding of the dynamic processes that produce identities and their shifting positions in the first place. From this perspective, it is apparent that the purpose of racialization as a political project is to obscure the processes that produce the two spaces mentioned previously and obfuscate the complexity of identities that result from them. The reductionism of racialization pegs Black and Asian identities as internally homogenous, but racially opposed, such that they are made to occupy alternative representational spaces that serve the material and psychic needs of those with the power to construct those spaces. These constructions are then linked rhetorically and practically with pre-existing essentialist paradigms of race in order to create a seemingly continuous reality for all racialized subjects. In the discussion below, I overview the result of this transposition as experienced by Asians and Blacks.

Although Asians have been in the United States since the 19th century, greater numbers, especially women, immigrated after the mid-20th century; notably, the specific recruitment of a female labor force intensified after the Immigration and Nationality Act of 1965 (Mazumdar, 1989). Since that time, along with Blacks and Mexicans, Asians, especially women, have constituted an important low-paid work force within the United States who are "occupationally ghettoized" in menial, domestic, and reproductive labor, textile and garment industries, hotel and restaurant work, and a current mix of mass production subcontracting and family-type firms (Glenn, 1993). Because of their material, gender, and racial differentiation from the abstract "citizen" recognized by the U.S. nation-state, Asians, even as citizens, are distanced from American nationalist narratives of representation. In other words, the racialization of "Asians" locates them at the cultural, racial, and political boundaries of the nation, which reinforces the ambivalent identification of both American-born and immigrant Asians with the nationalist discourse of "Who is American?" While the official narratives of immigrant inclusion propose to eventually assimilate immigrants as citizens, the conditions of undocumented Asian immigrants in the United States, especially women, directly contradict these promises of incorporation, equal opportunity, and equal representation. This is due, at least in part, to American immigration laws, which help to produce a racially segmented and gender-stratified labor force for the needs of capital. Thus, I argue that in addition to embodying the contradictions of globalization and its local ramifications, the "Asian" identity created by racialization entails a struggle for citizenship and recognition in a country that insists on identifying them as permanently "foreign." "Asians" must decipher and review not only their own experience of racialization within the U.S. national frame, but also interpret that of "Blacks" and other peoples of color who, along with "Whites," may constitute an already proletarianized, gendered, and nativist labor force, politicized to defend "their" homeland from the invading aliens of the East.

Black employment, on the other hand, has always been inversely related to immigration since Emancipation (Steinberg, 1995). The two brief intervals in the 20th century when immigration was at a low ebb marked the two major periods of economic and social advancement for Blacks. Between 1910 and 1920, the first decade of mass Black migration, there was a net migration of 454,000 Southern Blacks to the North, exceeding the volume of the previous 40 years combined. This migration corresponded with low immigration as a result of World War I. Again, when immigration was low between 1940 and 1950, 1.6 million Black workers migrated to the North and joined the predominantly White war-production workforce (Steinberg, 1995). Historically, when Blacks arrived in Northern cities, they encountered a far less favorable structure of opportunity than had existed for White immigrants decades earlier. First, these labor markets were historically captured by White immigrants who practiced a combination of ethnic nepotism and unabashed racism. Second, the occupational structures themselves were changing in the second half of the 20th century, due to the forces described in the previous section of this chapter. Not only were thousands of manufacturing jobs being automated out of existence, but a reorganization of the global economy resulted in the exportation of millions of manufacturing jobs to less-developed parts of the world. The fact that the technological revolution in agriculture lagged nearly a half-century behind the revolution in industry had fateful consequences at both junctures for Blacks, who were restricted to the agricultural sector throughout the 19th century—precisely during the most expansive periods of the American industrial revolution (Steinberg, 1989).

In light of this consideration, I contend that while Blacks eventually expressed their resistance to Southern agrarian and feudal culture through spatial mobility (by migrating to Northern cities during the 20th century) they arrived just as the manufacturing sector was beginning a sharp and irreversible decline, which suggests to me that Blacks' belated integration into Northern labor markets cannot be the result of race-neutral economic forces alone, as assumed by neo-classical accounts. At least as important is the racial formation that restricted Black workers' access to not only jobs in the declining industries, but also new jobs in the expanding service sector. Therefore, Blacks struggle with a form of racialization that concedes legal citizenship, but articulates with forces of globalization such that many of them are effectively excluded from emerging economies and locked into segregated places of economic immobility.

Some social scientists (e.g., Waldinger, 1989) argue that new immigrants do not compete with American workers, most of whom are in the primary labor market. Black Americans, as native workers, are said to spurn menial secondary market jobs performed by Black, Asian, or other immigrants at sub-minimum wages. Sweatshops are cited as a prime example of immigrants at work, followed by the claim that immigrants are hired because Black Americans and other native workers, including Asian Americans, will not submit to this kind of super-exploitation. However, such a claim contradicts accounts of Black youth lining up for full-time or seasonal jobs (Wilson, 1996). Not only are these jobs menial and low paying, but temporary and non-advancing as well. It is evident that even in the case of low-wage jobs, there is a clear preference for foreign workers who are regarded as more pliable and exploitable, especially if they are female and undocumented. One of the sad ironies of the Los Angeles riots is that unemployed Blacks eagerly applied to clean up the city, seeing it as a rare job opportunity, but their hopes quickly sank as Latino workers were employed instead (*New York Times*, June 10, 1992). Waldinger states that immigrants make numerous positive contributions to urban economies. He points out that had there been no immigration, New York would have suffered an even more severe economic decline. Out-migration of the White population from New York exceeded the outflow of jobs throughout the 1980s, leaving vacancies even in the face of employment decline. By tracing a sequence of events whereby the initial influx of immigrants replaces out-migrating native workers, Waldinger shows that this new, lower-wage labor force permits businesses to compete more successfully in international markets and increases the demand for locally produced goods and services. These outcomes, in turn, lead to the establishment of new business niches and support systems that increase the absorptive capacity of the local economy for additional immigrants. In a similar vein, Sassen (1995) notes that in addition to reinvigorating the formal economy, immigrants form the base of a developing informal sector that contributes to the further extension of global city functions, albeit often at the price of extreme self-exploitation.

Conclusion

The rapid influx of immigrants into American cities has been occurring in an era of deepening globalization, deindustrialization, privatization, and federal policies of disinvestment. In an effort to counter the increasing influence of foreign powers in global markets, U.S. corporations have attempted to maximize profits since the 1970s by advancing labor-saving technologies, closing down industrial plants, importing low-wage immigrant labor, and exporting manufacturing jobs abroad. As the United States became a society increasingly dominated by service-oriented high-tech industries, traditional manufacturing jobs in the steel rubber, auto, and non-defense aircraft sectors began to disappear from urban neighborhoods (*New York Times*, October 28, 2005).

This means poor Blacks and Asians face competition amidst chronic poverty, declining standards of living, underfunded schools, high rates of unemployment, and criminal activity in cities due to the noticeable absence of federal investment in civil society since the 1980s. The future of Black-Asian relations lies in both groups' ability to challenge racialization based on existing paradigms of fixed, immutable differences, so that they might form effective coalitions against the deleterious effects of global capitalism. Income polarization and status differences within and between the racial communities, described earlier, have created lines of division that further complicate Black and Asian relations. Notwithstanding this fragmentation, the diversity of the present-day American metropolis underscores the need to mobilize Blacks and Asians around urgent issues that stem from common life concerns. Furthermore, structures and ideologies of inequality that have been left unaddressed by the government and the public alike, inevitably will lead to conflict and destruction, as was demonstrated during the Los Angeles civil unrest of 1992. With these considerations in mind, scholars, policy makers, and the public must develop new strategies for bringing Blacks and Asians together as diverse constituencies in cooperation.

One significant obstacle, however, is the fact that the stagnation of class-based mobilizations has reinforced the economic disadvantage of people of color who have been marginalized or exploited by globalization. Also, since being economically disadvantaged in America can often be identified in racial and ethnic terms, Americans at all levels of the social hierarchy largely perceive the causes of poverty or wealth in terms of group traits rather than class exploitation or advantage, as argued earlier in the chapter. These perceptions are bolstered by essentialist identity politics based on appeals to primordiality that echo the very claims made by the American racial formation. In this chapter, I have attempted to identify some forces that govern exclusion and inclusion in U.S. cities and produce the multiple shifting positionings of Asians and Blacks in the American racial formation. In response to these forces, Asians and Blacks must jointly transcend the bifurcated paradigms that bind them both by recognizing the hybridities within their own identities. For example, an embrace of hybridity might enable many individuals of bi-racial Black-Asian ancestry to accept themselves as they are or gain approval in society without having to perpetually prove their racial authenticity to one group, often at the price of having to outwardly downplay the significance of the other racial identity(ies) in their lives, all while wrestling inwardly with their dual or multiple selves. Such conflicted states, among others, result from the internalization of essentialist notions of "self" and "other" within the American racial formation, and now effectively prevent both Blacks and Asians from confronting the real villains in the wake of LA 1992 and 9/11: White corporate power, class privilege, and patriarchy.

A transcendent politics might begin with an exploration of the shared history between Asians and Blacks in arenas such as political activism, the martial arts, music, and spiritual practice. Consider, for example, Korean pastors of Black congregations, Asian hip-hop artists, Tina Turner's conversion to Buddhism, Black sumo wrestlers, and Black experts in traditional Asian medicine. What is to be made of the fact that Yuri Kochiyama, a Japanese woman, cradled the dying Malcolm X in her arms after he was shot at the Apollo? Didn't Muhammad Ali speak out against the Vietnam War even if it meant going to prison? Do we take these examples as accidental tokens of fleeting trends in popular culture, or do they signify a deeper bond between Blacks and Asians?

On one hand, in these examples, I see great potential in popular culture's ability to defy the polarizing forces between Blacks and Asians. Pop culture can open up hybrid spaces of cultural production and consumption, and offer rich possibilities for theorizing identity where global and local converge. On the other hand, I believe this optimistic potential can be realized only if the study of popular culture moves beyond an exclusive focus on the racialization of the banality of everyday life to include an examination of the inequalities embedded in production and globalization, as well as other aspects of the materiality of contemporary culture.

References

Aguilar-San Juan, K. (1994). *The State of Asian America: Activism and Resistance in the 1990s.* Boston: South End Press.

Blauner, R. (1972). *Racial Oppression in America.* New York: Harper and Row.

Bonacich, E. (1980). "Class Approaches to Ethnicity and Race," *Insurgent Sociologist,* 10: 2.

Castells, M. (1989). *The Information City.* Oxford: Basil Blackwell Publishers.

Castells, M. (2000). *The Rise of the Network Society.* Oxford: Basil Blackwell Publishers.

D'Souza, D. (1991). *Illiberal Education: The Politics of Race and Sex on Campus.* New York: The Free Press.

Espiritu, Y. L. (1992). *Asian American Panethnicity.* Philadelphia: Temple University Press.

Fainstein, S. (1994). *The City Builders: Property, Politics, and Planning in London and New York.* Oxford: Basil Blackwell Publishers.

Glenn, C. (1993). "A Sociological View on Why Firms Differ," *Strategic Management Journal,* 14: 237–49.

Gould, S. J. (1981). *The Mismeasure of Man.* New York: Norton.

Gould, S. J. (1995). "Mismeasure by Any Measure," in *The Bell Curve Debate.* Russell Jacoby and Naomi Glauberman (eds.). New York: Random House.

Harvey, D. (1988). *Limits to Capital.* Oxford: Basil Blackwell Publishers.

hooks, b. (1990). "Postmodern Blackness," in *Yearning: Race, Gender and Cultural Politics.* Boston: South End Press.

Human Rights Watch. (1995). "Incarceration and Race," Available online at http://www.hrw.org/reports/ 2000/usa/Rccedrag00-01.htm.

Jordan, W. (1977). *White Over Black: American Attitudes Toward the Negro, 1550–1812.* New York: Norton.

Kim, E. (1998). "'At Least You're Not Black': Asian Americans in U.S. Race Relations," *Social Justice* 25 (3): 3–12.

Lewis, O. (1966). *La Vida: A Puerto Rican Family in the Culture of Poverty, San Juan and New York.* New York: Random House.

Marable, M. (1997). "Asian Americans and African Americans: Toward a Multicultural Dialogue." Available online at http://www.zmag.org/Marble/marable.htm.

Mazumdar, S. (1989). "General Introduction: A Woman-Centered Perspective on Asian-American History" in *Making Waves: An Anthology of Writings by and about Asian American Women,* Asian Women United of California (eds.). Boston: Beacon Press, 1–22.

Omi, M., and Winant, H. (1994). *Racial Formation in the United States.* New York: Routledge.

Pham, M. (1996). "Another Senseless Hate Crime." Available online at http://www.made/minority.com/ printout291.html.

Said, E. (1979). *Orientalism.* New York: Vintage Books.

Sassen, S. (1988). *The Mobility of Labor and Capital.* Cambridge: Cambridge University Press.

Sassen, S. (1995). *Losing Control? Sovereignty in an Age of Globalization.* New York: Columbia University Press.

Sassen, S. (1996). "Beyond Sovereignty: Immigration Policy Making Today," *Social Justice.* 23 (2): 9–20.

Soja, E. W. (1989). *Postmodern Geographies,* London: Verso.

Soja, E. W. (1996). *Thirdspace.* Oxford: Basil Blackwell Publishers.

Sowell, Thomas. (1994). *Race and Culture: A World View.* New York: Basic Books.

Steinberg, S. (1989). *The Ethnic Myth: Race, Ethnicity, and Class in America.* Boston: Beacon Press.

Steinberg, S. (1995). *Turning Back.* Boston: Beacon Press.

U.S. Census Bureau. (1990). *Statistical Abstract of the United States: 1990.* 120th ed. Washington, D.C.: U.S. Census Bureau.

U.S. Census Bureau. (2000). *Statistical Abstract of the United States: 2000.* 120th ed. Washington, D.C.: U.S. Census Bureau.

Visweswaran, K. (1997). "Diaspora by design: flexible citizenship and South Asians in U.S. racial formations," *Diaspora,* 6: 1–26.

Wacquant, L. (1994). "The hyperghetto as structure and practice," lecture presented at the Conference on New Conceptions of Urban Space, Columbia University Graduate School of Architecture, Planning and Preservation, October 14.

Waldinger, R. (1989). "Structural Opportunity or Ethnic Advantages," *International Migration Review,* 23 (1): 48–72.

Will, G. F. (1994). *The Leveling Wind, Politics, Culture and Other News, 1990–1994.* New York: Viking Press.

Wilson, W. J. (1987). *The Truly Disadvantaged.* Chicago: University of Chicago Press.

Wilson, W. J. (1996). *When Work Disappears: The World of the New Urban Poor.* New York: Knopf.

Woo, D. (1995). "The Gap Between Striving and Achieving: The Case of Asian American Women," in *Race, Class, and Gender in the United States,* Paula S. Rothenberg (ed.). New York: St. Martins Press.

Chapter 53

The Prong of Permanency, a Rant

Cheryl Clarke

This piece is written from my perspective as a dyke (a perspective I've been writing from for 25 years). I do not name each of the communities who have broadened and contributed to the gay and lesbian movement for liberation, i.e., bisexual, trans, questioning, ambiguously/ambivalently sexed and gendered people; for gays and lesbians are in the vanguard of this movement for marriage equality. Regardless of how our partnerships have enriched, restored, and rehabilitated communities all across this country, gays and lesbians are the focus of this critique. And so, I won't hold back.

Their Eyes Were Watching God, a foundational black woman's literary text written by Zora Neale Hurston in 1937, comes to my mind these days, especially the character Nannie. "Love is the very prong colored women gets hung on," Nannie tells her 16-year-old granddaughter, Janie, the novel's protagonist, whom she quickly marries off to a bachelor three times her age. Like "love" for black women, permanency for gays, lesbians, and other same-sex variants is the very prong we "gets hung on" when the arguments for marriage equality come up. We want that forever thing or the thing forever. We use the law, land, and furniture to make it so, don't we? Long demonized by/in the West, lesbians and gays long for longevity. "Longevity has its place," said Martin Luther King prophetically and critically, shortly before his untimely murder at the age of 39.

Admittedly, permanency has its place—replacing "promiscuity," the other, sexier p-word still applied to our communities. But let's not turn our whole movement over to the locking-in of the same-sex dyad. Need we dedicate our pride marches to marriage, as was the case in this year's New York Pride March [2004]? "We decided we had to attend the *parade* this year. We had to let people know we're here," said one 20–30-something New Paltz–married lesbian and her partner. First of all, young sister-dyke, it's a "march" not a "parade." Secondly, we've had a movement for 35 years, letting people know we're here. Can't help it if your pride was just born yesterday. This dangerous and ahistorical speaking and thinking burns me in our march toward marriage—or bust. This desire for permanency is driving us into state-sanctioned marriages. Same-sex folk want to be able to deploy marriage in as equivalent a way as opposite-sex folk do to bind each other to their relationships. Our pride marches could have been dedicated to ending the war in Iraq or the homophobic torture of Iraqi prisoners of war at Abu Ghraib, or to getting homeless youth off the streets, fifty percent of whom are queer, or lobbying against the cutting of funds to fight HIV/AIDS.

I am calling upon bulldaggers, dykes, faggots, feminist femmes, fierce sissies, and other outrageous progressive queers to have a major multicultural sexual liberation confabulation to take our movement back from liberals. Because marriage equality with its rhetoric of sameness is not why we came out of the closet in 1969 or before. We came out to dismantle marriage as an institution. (Yeah, like gays in the military; we shouldn't be prevented from joining because we're gay—but our whole movement shouldn't be contravened nor the lives of those queer service people endangered because liberal queers want to make political hay.)

Yes, I want permanency as much as the next queer. Who wants to risk being left when we're old and ugly. But must we sabotage our liberation just so that six-figure-salaried gay or lesbian elopes across the border to Massachusetts to lasso his/her six-figure-salaried lover into nuptial oblivion and tax shelters. And, yes, as I said above, lesbian and gay partnerships have changed the cultural, political, and material landscape of this country. But must we be married? And even if we are together 12, 17, 28, 32, 40 years as the lesbian and gay couples suing for marriage equality in New Jersey are—and I am full of admiration for them—we still want to lasso our partners into that vain institution, where the church and state converge and congeal.

Marriage Trivializes our Partnerships

Even though more than half of straight marriages in this country end in divorce, we still want leaving and taking up with the next same-sex lover with a SUV (or U-Haul) and a good dental plan to be just that much more difficult for our lovers. But according to the May–June issue [2004] of *The Advocate*, divorce attorneys are gearing up to handle gay and lesbian divorces. I am almost ready to agree with Double-Ya: get a constitutional amendment to preserve marriage for heterosexuals. Let heterosexuals have it. Marriage is a bankrupt remnant of the bondage of women and children. Remember also, marriage was denied enslaved black people, and was even denied interracial couples in many Southern states until the 1970s. Even heterosexuals, except those in Hollywood, think we're bonkers to invest in it.

Let us, the queers—and anyone else who wants to constitute a domestic partner relationship or civil union with whomever you choose, if it be your next-door neighbor—have those benefits that automatically accrue to married heterosexuals (and now married homosexuals in Massachusetts for the time being where institutions and corporations have rolled back domestic partner benefits for same-sex couples because we can get married now). And better yet, if we had universal health care, perhaps fewer of us would be so caught up in the marriage syndrome.

I tried out my premise of permanency on a dyke couple, I'll call Y. and B., who have been together for 19 years, are raising an 11-year-old daughter, own property together, and are both professionals with good insurance plans and politically against marriage. They laughed in all the right places when I read this piece to them, but Y. disagreed with my premise:

> *"I'll tell you why we want marriage," Y. proffered.*
> *"Yeah, why?" I asked.*
> *"Self-hatred."*

Chapter 54

Racial Desegregation and the Decline of Black Urban Landmarks

Robert E. Weems, Jr.

Introduction

During the early 20th century, urban Black America featured a number of impressive buildings constructed by African American entrepreneurs. At a time when African American consumers were denied equal access to "mainstream" insurance companies, banks, hotels, and restaurants, African American entrepreneurs provided these resources to Black urban residents. Moreover, when early 20th-century Black businessmen built such structures as the Chicago Metropolitan Assurance Company's home office complex, they constructed them to be as good or better than comparable White-financed edifices. Notwithstanding the intent of African American entrepreneurs to provide their fellow urban Blacks with *quality* insurance companies, banks, hotels, and restaurants, these Black-owned institutions became increasingly passé with the advent of racial desegregation. As African American consumers subsequently abandoned Black-owned, community-based enterprises in favor of exerting their new-found social and economic mobility, once-proud symbols of African American economic cooperation soon deteriorated (from lack of Black consumer support). Thus, the landscape of contemporary urban Black America is littered with long-abandoned, still impressive buildings whose historical legacy remains all but unknown to today's inner-city residents.

The Chicago Metropolitan Home Office Complex: A Case Study of the Decline of African American Urban Landmarks

Despite its current inactivity, the northeast corner of 45th and Martin Luther King (Jr.) Drive in Chicago was once one of the most talked-about spots within the historic Bronzeville* community. The site of the now-defunct Chicago Metropolitan Assurance Company's home office complex included the famous Parkway Ballroom and Dining Room; this area was a source of pride for both the company and the larger African American community. The subsequent decline of this Black Chicago landmark indicates that racial desegregation generated losses, as well as gains, for local African Americans.

Chicago Metropolitan's 1940 construction of a new, state-of-the-art, home office complex at 4455 South Parkway represented an important milestone in its history. Having outgrown its previously leased headquarters at 418 E. 47th Street, the company, then known as the Metropolitan Funeral System Association (MFSA), sought to graphically demonstrate its growth as an African American enterprise.

*Bronzeville was the popular nickname of Chicago's black community during the early 20th century.

Along with issues of race and corporate stature, the personal inclinations of company president Robert A. Cole and his chief lieutenant, General Manager Fred W. Lewing, also influenced the decision to build a luxurious home office complex. Both men, before their affiliation with the Metropolitan Funeral System Association, had extensive contact with mainstream American society. Cole had observed first-hand the amenities available to Whites during several years as a Pullman porter. Lewing, one of few African Americans during this period to grow up on Chicago's North Side, also knew of the superior goods and services available to European Americans in early 20th-century America. Thus, Cole and Lewing, in the tradition of the "Race Man" described by Horace Cayton and St. Clair Drake in their classic 1945 study *Black Metropolis: A Study of Negro Life in a Northern City*, felt compelled to provide Bronzeville residents with a multifaceted facility that compared favorably to those available to Whites. Ultimately, Cole and Lewing's attitude toward Black Chicagoans resulted in an enhancement of both the company's corporate image and profitability.

Once the MFSA decided to build a new home office complex, other Black Chicagoans actively monitored the progress of the then-Metropolitan Funeral System Association's 1940 undertaking. For instance, the Chicago *Defender* utilized weekly photo captions to keep its readers informed of the construction crew's activities. Moreover, as the winter of 1940 turned to spring, the *Defender's* coverage of this project likewise warmed from a matter-of-fact depiction to one of unrestrained enthusiasm. For instance, while the January 6, 1940, *Defender* featured 4455 South Parkway with a perfunctory photo caption entitled "Metropolitan Funeral System's New Home," the March 2, 1940, *Defender* described the MFSA's project with a photo caption entitled "A New Show Place of the South Side."[1]

The Metropolitan Funeral System Association's new headquarters formally opened on September 7, 1940. However, in late August, to generate even more community-wide interest in the company's new structure, Metropolitan Funeral System Association personnel relocated company operations in a truly dramatic fashion. Company agents marched from 418 E. 47th Street to 4455 South Parkway carrying MFSA records. During the agents' two-block march down one of Bronzeville's busiest streets, onlookers viewed the proceedings approvingly: some even cheered.[2]

A week-long open house celebration, held from September 7–13, continued the excitement generated by the agents' eye-catching march. The MFSA's new home, from an architectural standpoint, was ultra-modern. This building, constructed of white brick, mortar, and tile, was completely fireproof and air-conditioned throughout. Moreover, the first floor, which housed the company's administrative offices, featured the most up-to-date equipment and furnishings, including piped-in music.[3]

Although the Metropolitan Funeral System Association's stylish offices duly impressed open house visitors, the elegance of the Parkway Ballroom, located on the second floor, literally stunned Black Chicagoans. To reach the ballroom required climbing a winding staircase surrounded by marble walls. The September 7, 1940, Chicago Defender offered a description of what awaited visitors to this facility.[4]

> *The Parkway Ballroom is easily one of the finest ever built. Its air-conditioned walls are tastefully painted; its comfortable red leather chairs, and the entire scheme for seating make the place a literal palace. In the rear of the ballroom is a large bar well equipped to care for any number of guests and here the tables and chairs match the color scheme of red plush furniture.*

To assist open house guests in appreciating what the company called "A Monument to Bronze America," the Metropolitan Funeral System Association distributed a souvenir book which, among other things, advised:[5]

> *When you enter these exquisite buildings, look carefully around you. Every detail of efficiency and comfort has been provided. A pleasant air of cheerful modernity permeates you and those who serve you. . . . These walls are made for your contentment. Let their gracious colors talk to you. Here are the joys that delight the senses. All the wisdom of architecture waits you here. Revel in them, enjoy them. They are yours.*

Although this description appears a bit overdone, most observers considered the opening of the Metropolitan Funeral System Association's new home as an important event. The new MFSA home office was Chicago's first large-scale Black-controlled construction project since the hey-day of the old 35th and State Street Black business district.

The Parkway Ballroom quickly became the hub of Black Chicago's social life. Its presence filled a serious void in the lives of Bronzeville residents. In post-"Great Migration" Black Chicago, there existed a myriad of social and fraternal organizations. Yet, during the 1920s and 1930s, these groups were denied access to ballroom facilities in downtown hotels. Although there were approximately 75 public halls in Bronzeville that could accommodate at least 100 persons, most were in varying states of disrepair.[6]

When the Parkway Ballroom opened during the summer of 1940, it represented an important racial achievement. While it was not the first Black-sponsored attempt to bring recreational elegance to Bronzeville, the Parkway Ballroom represented Black economic self-determination at a time when Whites were gaining increasing control over Black Chicago's retail and entertainment economy.[7]

The Great Depression all but destroyed the historic Black-controlled 35th and State Street commercial district.[8] Consequently, the center of Bronzeville's economy (both retail and recreational) shifted to the White-controlled 47th and South Parkway (now King Drive) area. The construction of the Savoy Ballroom at 47th and South Parkway, by a consortium of White businessmen, exemplified this trend.

The Savoy Ballroom did provide Black Chicagoans a variety of activities, including dances, boxing matches, roller-skating, and big-band concerts. Still, the profits from these functions left Black Chicago.[9] Moreover, many white-owned Bronzeville night spots had a "Jim Crow" seating policy during the 1930s and 1940s. Whites were seated near the stage and Blacks sat in the rear. Thus, the Parkway Ballroom provided Black Chicagoans an elegant alternative to enriching absentee landlords or enduring racial insults.[10]

Many considered the Parkway Ballroom, during its heyday, to be the best Black-owned business of its type in the United States. Moreover, an informed source has asserted that during the 1940s and 1950s, the Parkway Ballroom was the finest ballroom in America (Black or White) that was not affiliated with a hotel.[11] Besides providing first-class facilities to Bronzeville's social and cultural organizations, artists such as Duke Ellington and Count Basie regularly appeared at the Parkway. With the decline of the White-owned Savoy Ballroom during the 1940s (partially caused by the Parkway's growing popularity), the Parkway Ballroom became the undisputed center of Bronzeville social activities.[12]

According to Clarence M. Markham, Jr., who founded *The Negro Traveler and Conventioneer* magazine in 1943, the Parkway Ballroom, during the 1940s and 1950s, was also a favorite of Black visitors to Chicago. At a time when downtown Chicago stood "off-limits" to African American travelers and conventioneers, the Parkway Ballroom represented a godsend to Black visitors seeking an elegant place to relax and socialize.[13]

The Parkway Ballroom's initial success contributed to the 1948 construction of an adjacent facility known as the Parkway Dining Room. This restaurant, completed in 1949, provided company personnel and Bronzeville residents a first-class eating facility. Noted for its extensive menu, which included filet-mignon, the Parkway Dining Room attracted especially large crowds on Sundays and holidays.[14]

Another popular aspect of the Parkway Dining Room was its courteous waiter service. Blacks in Chicago, similar to their brethren in other cities, were uncertain as to how they would be treated in restaurants. Black diners in White-owned restaurants frequently experienced slow service or outright verbal abuse. Unfortunately the majority of Black-owned eating establishments during this period could be characterized as "chicken shacks" or "rib joints." These facilities, while fine for a snack, were unsuitable for a formal dinner. The Parkway Dining Room, with its exquisitely dressed waiters, provided Bronzeville residents a means to enjoy the amenities associated with formal dining without having to risk insult.[15]

Although the Metropolitan Funeral System Association built its new home office complex to enhance the larger community, this building's primary purpose was to provide personnel and policyholders a luxurious place to work, transact business, and relax. Among the on-site benefits made available to employees were bowling alleys, a recreation room equipped with pool and billiard tables, a sauna, and a masseur. For policyholders, the company furnished the cashier's section of the facility with plush couches and chairs.[16]

The company's enhanced visibility, resulting from its new home office complex, had a positive impact on its profitability. In fact, the company's financial stature grew to the extent that in 1946, the Metropolitan Funeral System Association (a burial insurance company) evolved into the Metropolitan Mutual Assurance Company of Chicago, a full-fledged legal reserve insurance company.[17] It appears that activities associated with its new home office directly contributed to the company's growth. Bronzeville residents, who regarded 4455 South Parkway as an outstanding racial achievement, evidently became more amenable to company agents who sought their business.

Bronzeville's support for the company became even more pronounced in 1951 when the giant Metropolitan Life Insurance Company of New York sued the Metropolitan Mutual Assurance Company of Chicago over its use of the generic term *Metropolitan*. In its official complaint, Metropolitan Life claimed:[18]

> As used by the defendant, the defendant's name is deceptively similar to the name of the plaintiff and has given rise, and is likely to give rise in the future, to confusion in the minds of the general public, including policyholders, prospective policyholders, and borrowers, as to the respective identities of the plaintiff and the defendant.

Metropolitan Life's suit against Metropolitan Mutual, which the Chicago *Defender* aptly described as a "David and Goliath legal battle,"[19] was both bizarre and ludicrous. Especially, considering Metropolitan Life's long-standing refusal to hire Black agents (which the Metropolitan Mutual legal team cited in its official response to the Met Life complaint).[20] Nevertheless, in the ensuing months, both Metropolitan Mutual's legal team and Black Chicago newspapers waged a fight to defend the company's good name.

On March 13, 1951, the Chicago *Defender* published an article entitled "Metropolitan Mutual—Titan of the Business World," which gave a full-page account of the company's accomplishments. This article, among other things, revealed that Metropolitan Mutual had recently been rated as "excellent" and "worthy of public confidence" by Dunne's International Insurance Reports, the world's largest policyholders reporting service.[21] This evidence, not so subtly, sought to refute Metropolitan Life's questioning of Metropolitan Mutual's corporate integrity.

The July 7, 1951, issue of the Chicago *Courier* offered an even more complimentary assessment of Metropolitan Mutual. The *Courier*, which had become a strong competitor of the *Defender*, published a two-page feature entitled "Metropolitan Mutual: A Monument to Integrity." The *Courier*, after surveying the company's achievements, concluded:[22]

> A thrilling sight in its beautiful plant, the significance of Metropolitan Mutual lies even deeper than its stone and steel foundation—the significance is in the economic power that lies within the Negro race when men of integrity and business training take over the leadership of that power.

The subsequent trial basically upheld Metropolitan Mutual's defense. Still, it did substantiate Metropolitan Life's assertions that Blacks often referred to Metropolitan Mutual simply as "Metropolitan." A November 7, 1952, consent decree ultimately settled the conflict over the use of the term *Metropolitan*. This document ordered the Metropolitan Mutual Assurance Company to change its name to Chicago Metropolitan Mutual Assurance Company within one year. The court also directed Metropolitan Life to pay the Black Chicago company $6,000 to cover the legal cost of this move.[23]

Metropolitan Mutual personnel and policyholders hailed the November 7, 1952, consent decree as a victory. Not only did it deny damages to Metropolitan Life, but Metropolitan Mutual maintained the right to continue using the term *Metropolitan* in its company name. The widespread publicity given the trial, moreover, placed Metropolitan Mutual in the enviable position as a recognized fighter for African American economic progress.

Shortly after the company's substantive legal victory, the January 1953 issue of *Ebony* saluted Metropolitan Mutual's 25th anniversary. Noting the insurer's humble origins, *Ebony* proudly asserted:[24]

> Founded in a tiny, overcrowded basement office in 1927, Metropolitan is now housed in one of the most impressive structures ever built and owned by Negroes. Metropolitan's home office building on South Parkway has become one of the showplaces of Chicago's South Side.

Along with the Black media's favorable depiction of the soon-to-be Chicago Metropolitan Mutual Assurance Company, White publications also took notice of the company and its community-minded president. On July 9, 1955, the *Chicago Tribune* featured an extensive article entitled "200,000 Trust Robert A. Cole With Their Savings." The following excerpt conveys the tone of this piece:[25]

> The modern building at 4455 South Parkway, which houses this business stands as a testimony to a man who demonstrated vision and daring in the best rags-to-riches tradition. More important, Cole

operates one of the largest aggregations of private capital ever assembled in a single Chicago enterprise directed by a Negro.

By the mid-1950s, the northeast corner of 45th and South Parkway, indeed, appeared to represent "A Monument to Bronze America." Moreover, while such facilities as the Parkway Ballroom and Dining Room were a boon to Bronzeville residents, some White Chicagoans also applauded their presence. Because the Parkway Ballroom and Dining Room compared favorably to downtown establishments, some Whites hoped that Black Chicagoans would not be terribly concerned about desegregating Loop facilities. Still, Bronzeville residents, similar to African Americans throughout the United States, caught the desegregation fever generated by the U.S. Supreme Court's monumental May 17, 1954, decision related to the *Brown v. Board of Education* case.

The arrival of de-jure desegregation resulted in Black access to facilities previously closed to them. It also resulted in the deterioration of institutions that sustained African Americans before their increased social mobility. Racial desegregation's effect upon the Parkway Ballroom and Dining Room offered prime examples of this phenomenon.

Downtown Chicago hotels, beginning in the late 1950s, began to make their ballroom facilities available to Bronzeville social and cultural organizations. Although Black organizations were often charged higher rental rates than similar White groups, it quickly became "fashionable" to conduct Bronzeville's social activities downtown.[26] Meanwhile, the Parkway Ballroom and Dining Room's popularity declined. Thus, by the mid-1970s, both of these historic Bronzeville institutions were closed.

It appears that Chicago Blacks gradually abandoned the Parkway Ballroom and Dining Room partially because of the novelty involved with congregating downtown. Moreover, Bronzeville residents, after gaining access to previously "off-limits" facilities, sought to continually extend the boundaries of their new-found social mobility.

Just as racial desegregation contributed to the eventual demise of the Parkway Ballroom and Dining Room, it also contributed to the eventual demise of the Chicago Metropolitan Assurance Company. The late 1950s, besides generating new recreational options for Black Chicagoans, featured enhanced employment opportunities for African Americans. Black insurance agents, especially, quickly became sought-after commodities.

During previous decades, most mainstream insurance companies had either ignored Black consumers or charged them excessive premium rates. Prudential, Metropolitan Life, New York Life, and other industry giants began to actively seek Black clients as the African American standard of living began to rise dramatically during the 1950s. This development posed two distinct challenges to Chicago Metropolitan and other Black companies. First, many Black consumers, because they had been previously denied equitable coverage with industry giants, viewed prospective policies with mainstream companies as status symbols. Second, America's largest insurers decided to recruit Black agents from Black companies to service the African American consumer market. Thus, mainstream giants, with promises of financial reward, were able to secure many *trained* Black insurance agents.[27]

By the mid-1970s, Chicago Metropolitan, faced with increasing competition from White-owned insurance companies for both clients and personnel, was a company in trouble. One proposed solution to the company's woes was a joint venture between Chicago Metropolitan and the Black-owned Independence Bank of Chicago. Specifically, Alvin J. Boutte, Independence Bank's President, who joined the Chicago Metropolitan Board of Directors in 1977, proposed that Chicago Metropolitan move its home office from the historic 4455 S. King Drive location to a combination bank/insurance company building to be constructed in the 7900 block of South Cottage Grove Avenue. Although Chicago Metropolitan later financed a feasibility study for this project, it never to came to fruition.[28]

Numerous company employees and community residents applauded Chicago Metropolitan's decision to remain at 4455 S. King Drive. Many employees believed that leaving the northeast corner of 45th and King Drive would have been tantamount to dishonoring Robert A. Cole's legacy.[29] From the point of view of the company's immediate neighbors, Chicago Met's decision to remain on King Drive represented a vote of confidence in Chicago's inner city. Since the early 1960s, with the advent of Black residential mobility, many African American businessmen and professionals moved from central city locations to homes and offices further south. Consequently, 47th Street, once Black Chicago's main commercial district, became a rundown shadow of its former self, catering to Black Chicagoans financially unable to move. Thus, Chicago

Metropolitan's decision to remain in the inner city offered encouragement and stability to a neighborhood badly in need of both.

Apparently hoping to recapture some of the excitement (and increased business) associated with the 1940 construction of its home office, Chicago Metropolitan, in 1981, announced a multi-million dollar renovation of its historic headquarters. This project, completed in 1985, did, indeed, rejuvenate company spirit and reaffirm Robert A. Cole's legacy.[30] Unfortunately, the completed 1985 renovation of the Chicago Metropolitan's home office complex represented the *last* high point of the company's history. Continuing pressure from White-owned companies forced Chicago Metropolitan, faced with possible dissolution by the Illinois Department of Insurance, to undertake a dramatic corporate restructuring in 1990.

On November 9, 1990, the policyholders of the Chicago Metropolitan Mutual Assurance Company, held, perhaps, the most important meeting in company history. The purpose of this gathering was to approve the company's reorganization from a mutual insurance company (owned by policyholders) to a stock insurance company. In addition, Chicago Met policyholders were asked to approve the purchase of all subsequent stock by the Black-owned Atlanta Life Insurance Company, thus making Chicago Metropolitan a wholly-owned subsidiary of Atlanta Life. Chicago Metropolitan's Board of Directors, which approved the proposed reorganization at its August 15, 1990, meeting, unanimously urged Chicago Met policyholders to do likewise.[31]

On January 1, 1991, the Chicago Metropolitan Mutual Assurance Company ceased to exist. In its place, in accordance with the demutualization and sale of the company, stood the Chicago Metropolitan Assurance Company. Besides the name change, the reorganized company's Board of Directors assumed a new look. Out of 12 board members, only three former Chicago Met board members were retained.[32]

Between 1991–1996, Atlanta Life totally melded Chicago Metropolitan's operations into its own corporate structure. Moreover, because Atlanta Life had its own home office complex in Atlanta, Georgia, it had no need for Chicago Metropolitan's recently renovated home office complex at 4455 S. King Drive. Thus, the northeast corner of 45th and King Drive in Chicago, once referred to as a "Monument to Bronze America," quickly became a "white elephant" of no real use to its new owner. Sadly, besides former company personnel and Bronzeville elders, many contemporary Black Chicagoans have no idea of the rich historical legacy associated with the now deteriorating building at 4455 S. King Drive.

In closing, it appears unlikely that the excitement once generated at 4455 S. King Drive (and similar locales) can or will be recreated in a literal sense. Still, scholarly research and writing can, if only in a figurative sense, insure that historic African American community landmarks, such as Chicago Metropolitan's home office complex, will live forever.

Endnotes

1. Chicago *Defender*, January 6, 1940, p. 2, March 2, 1940, p. 6.
2. Interview, Mr. Donnie Jones, April 1, 1986. Mr. Jones, a former agent with the company began working for the MFSA in 1940, shortly before the agents' dramatic march through Black Chicago.
3. *The Metropolitan Opening* (Chicago: Metropolitan Funeral System Association, September, 1940), pp. 1–2; *A Monument to Bronze America Souvenir Book, 1940* (Chicago: Metropolitan Funeral System Association, 1940). This widely-distributed pamphlet commemorated the opening of the company's new home office.
4. Chicago *Defender*, September 7, 1940, p. 8.
5. *A Monument to Bronze America Souvenir Book* (Chicago: MFSA, 1940), p. 5.
6. Travis, Dempsey J. (1983). An *Autobiography of Black Jazz.* (Chicago: Urban Research Institute), 86–8.
7. Ibid., 36, 88–9. The Vincennes Hotel, located at 601 E. 36th Street, was the favorite meeting place of Bronzeville's elite from 1910–1940. Bacon's Casino, located at 49th and Wabash Avenue, was a converted garage that opened in 1940. When the Parkway Ballroom opened, the importance of these other facilities declined.
8. An important source of information about the historic 35th and State Street Black business district is *Black Metropolis Historic District*, a 1984 report (revised in 1994) compiled by Landmarks Division of the Chicago Department of Planning and Development.

9. Travis, Dempsey J. (1983). *Black Jazz*, 83–4, 93–110.

10. Ibid., 43.

11. Interview, Etta Moten-Barnett, December 8, 1985. Mrs. Moten-Barnett, the widow of Claude A. Barnett (the founder of the Associated Negro Press), was prestigious in her own right. She gained fame as a concert singer and actress. For instance, in 1942, she sang the lead in the Broadway production of *Porgy and Bess*. During her professional career, Mrs. Moten had the opportunity to travel extensively. Consequently, her assertion that the Parkway Ballroom was the finest ballroom in America not associated with a hotel must be taken seriously.

12. To determine the Parkway Ballroom's popularity, several long-time Chicago residents were interviewed at the William J. Dawson Nursing Home between November 11–December 30, 1985. On January 3, 1986, I interviewed my mother, Dolores J. Weems, herself a lifelong Chicago resident. I conducted another especially useful interview with the now-deceased Dr. Marjorie Stewart Joyner on May 28, 1986. Dr. Joyner, who lived at the same South Side location for 75 years, was a close business associate of Madame C. J. Walker and established a Chicago branch of Madame C. J. Walker's company at 47th and South Parkway.

13. Interview, Clarence M. Markham, Jr., February 19, 1986. Mr. Markham, along with four other Black railroad employees, established *The Negro Traveler and Conventioneer* because of their concern over the plight of Black travelers during this period. If a Black traveler, in mid-20th-century America, was unaware of a particular city's laws/customs relating to accommodations for Blacks, or if the Black traveler did not have relatives or friends in a particular locale, such African American travelers were often forced to sleep in railroad and bus stations. *The Negro Traveler and Conventioneer* served as a national directory service for Black travelers. Advertising revenue, secured from the Black-owned hotels and restaurants that appeared in *The Negro Traveler and Conventioneer*, kept the magazine afloat.

14. "Insurance Anniversary: Metropolitan Mutual of Chicago Marks 25th Year," *Ebony* (January 1958): 81; Clarence M. Markham, February 19, 1986; Jesse L. Moman, September 24, 1985. Mr. Moman, a long-time Chicago Metropolitan employee, coordinated the writing of a brief company history in 1977.

15. Interview, Edward A. Trammell, October 9, 1985. Mr. Trammell joined Chicago Metropolitan as an agent in 1951 and spent more than 30 years with the company.

16. Jesse L. Moman, September 24, 1985; company pamphlet, *Metropolitan Mutual Assurance Company*, 1950, no pagination.

17. *Illinois Department of Insurance Examinations of the Metropolitan Funeral System Association*, July 30, 1941, p. 24; October 1, 1943, p. 20; September 11, 1944, p. 20; June 24, 1947, 11; Minutes, Annual Meetings, Metropolitan Funeral System Association, January 15, 1945; January 21, 1946; Metropolitan Funeral System Association to the Illinois Department of Insurance, September 30, 1946.

18. Complaint against the Metropolitan Mutual Assurance Company of Chicago filed by the Metropolitan Life Insurance Company, Case # 51C-66, United States District Court for the Northern District of Illinois/Eastern Division, United States National Archives, Chicago, Illinois, pp. 3–4.

19. Chicago *Defender*, January 20, 1951, p. 1.

20. Metropolitan Mutual Assurance Company of Chicago's response to the January 12, 1951, complaint filed by the Metropolitan Life Insurance Company of New York, Case # 51C-66, United States District Court for the Northern District of Illinois/Eastern Division, United States National Archives, Chicago, Illinois, pp. 3–4.

21. Chicago *Defender*, March 13, 1951, p. 13.

22. Chicago *Courier*, July 7, 1951, p. 5.

23. Consent decree, November 7, 1952, Case # 51C-66, *Metropolitan Life v. Metropolitan Mutual*, United States National Archives, Chicago, Illinois.

24. "Insurance Anniversary: Metropolitan Mutual of Chicago Marks 25th Year," *Ebony*, 8 (January 1953): p. 79.

25. "200,000 Trust Robert A. Cole With Their Savings," Chicago *Tribune*, July 9, 1955, p. 8.

26. Jesse L. Moman, September 24, 1985; Edward A. Trammell, October 9, 1985. Mr. Trammell joined Metropolitan Mutual as an agent in 1951 and spent more than 30 years with the company. Ironically, John Seder and Berkeley Burrell's 1971 study, *Getting It Together: Black Businessmen in America* (an essentially positive depiction of African American economic development), contended that Black institutions such as the Parkway Ballroom and Dining Room declined because desegregation offered Black consumers an opportunity to escape their "captivity" to Black businessmen. Implying that desegregation "freed" Blacks from the oppressive grasp of Black businessmen is both historical and ludicrous. Black businessmen neither created or enforced America's segregation laws. See Seder and Burrell, p. 212.

27. Weathers Y. Sykes, April 15, 1986. Mr. Sykes joined Chicago Metropolitan in 1976 in the capacity of senior vice-president/Administration. He previously held a variety of administrative positions at the Black-owned Supreme Life Insurance Company of Chicago; Cleland Brewer, April 16, 1986. Mr. Brewer joined the company as an agent in 1959 and served in a variety of positions in Chicago Metropolitan's Agency Department; James S. Isbell, May 27, 1986. Mr. Isbell began working at Chicago Metropolitan in 1956 and served in a variety of positions in the Agency Department, including Agency Director; Lynn Langston, Jr., August 21, 1986. Mr. Langston joined the company as an agent in 1948 and was proud of the fact that he resisted the embellishments of White-owned insurers.

28. Minutes, Executive Committee Meeting, Chicago Metropolitan Mutual Assurance Company, March 14, 1977; Memorandum, Peter M. Cohen to Weathers Y. Sykes, July 11, 1977. Mr. Cohen represented the interior decorating firm of Richmond, Manhoff, and Marsh.

29. Louise Wood, April 22, 1986. Mrs. Wood began working for the company in 1947; Jesse L. Moman, February 11, 1986; Edward A. Trammell II, February 4, 1986.

30. Press Release, Chicago Economic Development Commission, May 1, 1981; Lucius Millender, "Chicago Metropolitan Gets a New Lease on Life," *Black Enterprise* 15 (June 1985): pp. 163–6. Chicago Metropolitan, because of its home office renovation, was designated as *Black Enterprise's* "Insurance Company of the Year" for 1985.

31. Proxy Statement, Special Policyholders Meeting, Chicago Metropolitan Mutual Assurance Company, November 9, 1990.

32. Josephine King to Robert E. Weems, Jr., July 6, 1993. King, who joined the company as a file clerk in 1959, ultimately became vice-president/Administration and a member of the Chicago Metropolitan Board of Directors. After the company's sale to Atlanta Life, she assumed the position of Chief Executive Officer of the soon-to-be totally dismantled Chicago Metropolitan Assurance Company; Proxy Statement, Special Policyholders Meeting, Chicago Metropolitan Mutual Assurance Company, November 9, 1990.

Chapter 55

AmeriFlora Comes to "Bronzeville": A Political Battle Over an Urban Landmark in Columbus, Ohio

Lewis A. Randolph

Ameriflora was nothing more than a reflection of the interests of the elites. It had nothing to do with the people; it had nothing to do with a flower show; it had nothing to do with building a community; it simply involved real estate. The hidden real estate agenda is now coming to light.[1]

Introduction

AmeriFlora was a unique economic development project for Columbus. Part international flora show and part Disneyland theme park event, it was expected to increase Columbus's exposure as a city both nationally and internationally. This type of dual event had never been attempted in the city by the local political and economic elites.[2] Given the uniqueness of the project, this research examines the progression of AmeriFlora and its role in fostering political conflict between the organizers and the Franklin Park (FP) Black neighborhood groups over spacial politics and access to a park that African Americans had historically claimed as their own.[3] The question that has to be addressed at this time is why did the African American community of Columbus claim FP as their own park?

FP is generally considered to lie within the boundaries of Broad Street, Wilson Avenue, Bryden Road, and Nelson Road.

The evolution of FP constituted a multi-tiered progression through four distinct periods. From 1842 to 1858, present-day FP was used by abolitionists to transport fugitive slaves along an underground railroad line that ran through the area rather than for recreational purposes. Bette Millat, in her unpublished manuscript "Underground Railroad Sites in Ohio, Especially Columbus and Vicinities," identifies some of the safe havens on the underground railroad in Columbus, including the FP area. "A black minister who led forty members of the Second Street Baptist Church at 186 N. 17th street continued the work of the Anti-Slavery Baptist Church which came from the First Baptist Church in 1824."[4] Although her citation does not directly identify FP as the location, 17th street is very close to FP.

The home of Mr. John T. Ward, a well-known and successful Black businessman and conductor on the Underground Railroad for 16 years, "was a well known station on the Underground Railroad which ran through Columbus and along its waterways."[5] He and his father provided food and shelter to fugitive slaves on their farm in Turo Township, now Whitehall, Ohio. One will quickly discover that Broad Street runs parallel to FP.

In addition, Broad Street runs directly into the Turo Township (i.e., Whitehall).[6] Although, Ward's house was located in Turo Township, Broad Street is a direct line along the Underground Railroad and ideal for moving fugitive slaves in and out of the city, making it a good drop-off and pick-up point for fugitive slaves. Moreover, the Second Baptist Church played a pivotal role in the Abolition Movement. The role of the

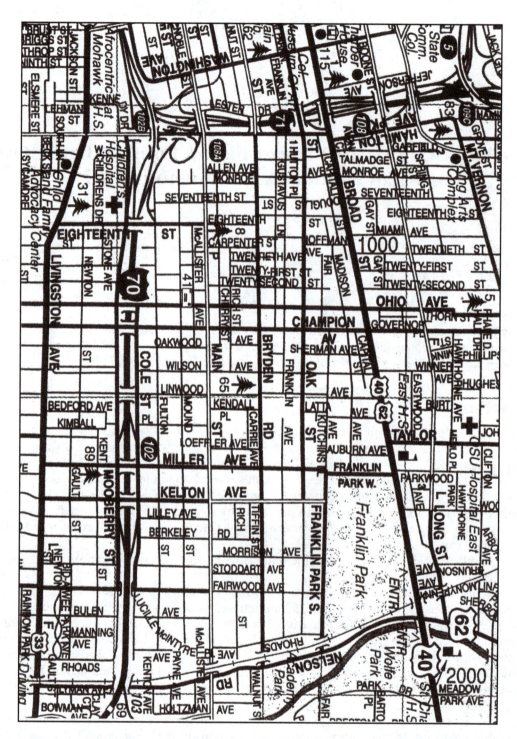

MAP 1 Seventeenth Street Baptist Church lies approximately somewhere along Seventeenth Street. Seventeenth Street is not far from what we know today as Franklin Park. The number "2" is placed above the words Seventeenth Street to locate that street on the map. The dark lines illustrate the approximate distance from Seventeenth Street to Franklin Park.

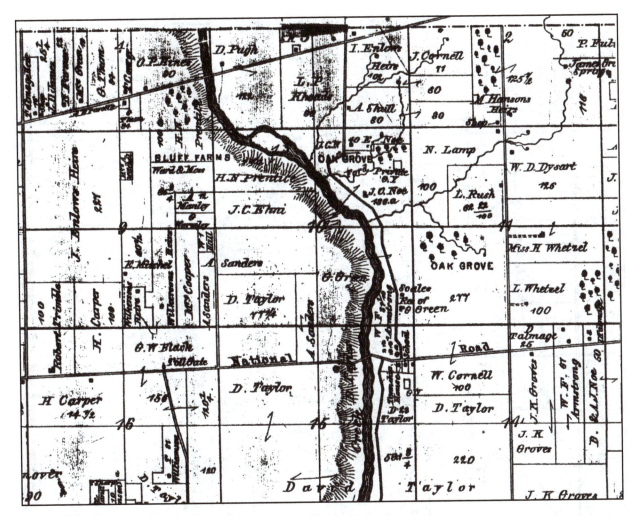

MAP 2   The Map was used to show where Mr. John T. Ward, an underground railroad conductor lived. The number "1" with a jagged line identifies where Ward lived in 1872. I used the 1872 map and not the 1842 map because Ward's residence and business address does not appear on the 1842 map. Ward's residence and business address is listed as "Ward & Moss." Thus, Ward's business and residence address were one in the same. Also, the "1" with small jagged line is being used to identify Ward's residence. Thus, I elected to use the 1872 map. Also, the reader will notice that the street that cuts through Franklin Park in 1872 was called the National Road. National Road today is Broad Street. Also, the area owned by D. Taylor is the present-day location of Franklin Park. The number "2" is used to identify the area that we know today as Franklin Park.

Second Baptist Church in the Abolition Movement is further documented in the history of the Second Baptist Church. For instance:

> *The African American members were dedicated to the abolition movement. So strong was their protest against slavery that they shared in the operation of the "Underground Railroad in the Franklin County Area. The Colored brethren of the Second Baptist Church sought an opportunity to work for the freedom of their race with the aid of many others who shared their feelings and dedication to aid, shelter, comfort, and escort the feeling slaves a safe place.*[7]

From 1852 through 1884, the FP area was designated as the Franklin County Fairgrounds, which were relocated in the late 19th century due to the eastward expansion of Columbus. The region was abandoned because of the remoteness of the Fairgrounds from the city.[8]

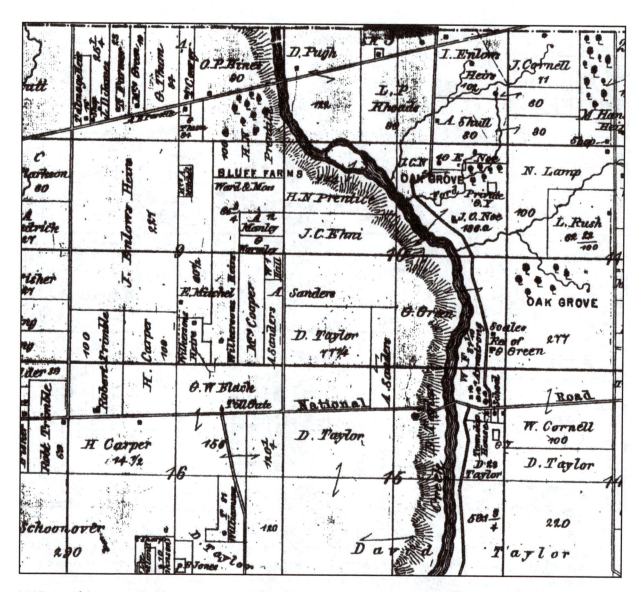

MAP 3   This map provides a visual illustration of the path that Mr. Ward may have taken when he transported the escaped slave along the underground railroad in Columbus, Ohio. Thus, based upon my discussion with a map archivist for the city map, we both deduced that Mr. Ward may have taken the following path to safely transport the escaped slaves to freedom. Thus, we believe that Mr. Ward probably started from point "1" (which is Franklin Park). Upon departing from Franklin Park, Mr. Ward may have turned onto the National Road. Next, he may have turned right onto the property owned by a Mr. A. Sanders and stayed on that particular course until he reached his property, and then turned right onto his property. Hence, Ward left with the escaped slaves from point "1," which was Franklin Park. Next, Ward may have passed by A. Sanders' property. Finally, Ward may have turned left onto his property. Thus, Ward's path in transporting the escaped slaves appears to be a plausible explanation of how the escaped slaves were transported from Franklin Park to Ward's home and eventually to freedom.

The Ohio General Assembly, realizing the social value of the 100 acre area, converted the location into Franklin County Park. During this period, the Park experienced numerous transformations that made it not only the largest park in Columbus but the most attractive. Impressed by the architectural beauty of the Botanical Conservatory at the Chicago's World Fair of 1893, Franklin Park officials decided to replicate it for Columbus. Thus, in 1895, Franklin County invested $24,000 and directed local architect J. M. Freese to reconstruct the Conservatory on the FP Property, making it the only park in the city to date to have such a monumental building on its grounds.[9] FP achieved national prominence in November 1910 when the Wright Exhibition flew from Dayton to FP, making it the first air freight terminal in the nation.[10]

Moreover, during this same period, a consistent Black cultural presence emerged in the FP that has generally gone unnoticed by the White community and was ignored in the recorded pamphlets written on the usage of FP by race. According to Mr. Leonard N. Napper, Sr., former Director of the Paul Laurence Dunbar Cultural Center, "African Americans have always perceived FP as their neighborhood park."[11] Napper, a lifelong resident of Columbus, supported his statement by revealing the following information: 1) as a boy he learned to drive in FP during the 1930s; 2) Black boy scouts held their camp/cook outs in FP; 3) Black Jr. High Schools kids used areas of FP to play football; 4) Black churches held Fourth of July picnics and religious celebrations in FP; and 5) young black males perceived FP as a place to cruise in their cars and meet young women. In other words, they used the park for male/female socialization purposes.[12] Likewise, Ms. Gwen Gardner, a long-time resident and homeowner in the FPA, stated that the Park was frequented in the past by African Americans to host cultural events.[13] Gardner pointed out that the old Paul Laurence Dunbar Cultural Center was originally located in Wolfe Park. If one examines Map 4, one will see that Wolfe Park (WP) is adjacent to FP and that there is an entrance from WP to FP. Moreover, Mr. Napper corroborates Ms. Gardner's story by stating that on many occasions, the Dunbar Center used FP for its cultural and festival activities.[14]

Thus, African American's usage of FP clearly established an historic and cultural/emotional bond to FP. Furthermore, the Black presence in FP is significant because the Black presence in FP parallels the historic Black presence in similar public spaces in three other cities. In the literature that has been written and that documents Blacks' usage of public spaces, Black usage of FP appears to be consistent with Black usage in: 1) Bell Isle in Detroit, Michigan; 2) Congo Square in New Orleans, Louisiana; and 3) Defremery Park and Recreation Center in West Oakland, in Oakland, California.[15] Moreover, over a period of time and during the life cycle history of FP, the Park eventually became identified as a "Black park" because of de facto segregation as a result of racial and demographic changes that occurred in Columbus. Galen Cranz makes this point in the book, *The Politics of Park Design*:

> . . . . we know from other sources that practices of segregation . . . was common. In theory the pleasure ground brought all different sectors of society, presumably including its racial and other ethnic components, together, but the practice of racial segregation was so unquestioned that officials did not need to call attention to it in any way.[16]

Despite not having been built for them, African Americans nevertheless perceive FP as their park and consider it a Black urban landmark.

During the latest transformation of FP from the 1950s to the present, the infrastructure of the Park and Conservatory received significant attention. As a result of the Park's 1974 acceptance on the National Roster of Historic Places, federal funds were made available for rebuilding and refurbishing. The late 1970s resulted in the addition of a new parking lot, maintenance to the Conservatory, the planting of new trees and plants, and the addition of a 12,000-square-foot garden center. However, with the construction of low-income apartments in the early 1970s, the Park began to deteriorate. Only within the recent years preceding AmeriFlora was a substantial private and public effort made to reverse the park's decline.[17]

In addition to this history of FP, the history of the Near East Side (NES) area surrounding FP is also significant. One of the oldest communities in the city, the NES covers approximately 2.5 square miles. Around 1890 the NES developed as a fashionable residential neighborhood that includes the prestigious section known as the Franklin Park Area (FPA).[18] Prominent local families such as the Wolfes (communications magnate) and Lazaruses (retail department store magnate) resided in the area at the turn of the century. Moreover, Franklin Avenue, which divides the FPA, was once known as "Judges's Row" because so many of Columbus's judges and lawyers lived there. Hence, the area was heavily populated by economic and political White elites as opposed to areas further away from the Park, where more from the lower White middle class lived. Around

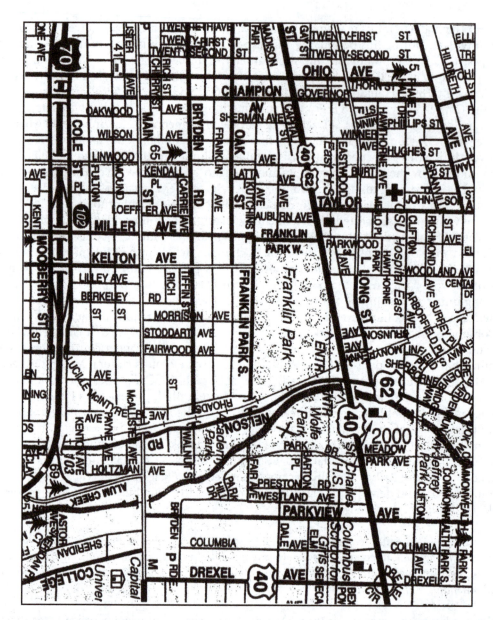

MAP 4 The map provides a visual illustration of the distance between Franklin Park and Wolfe Park. The significance of this particular map is that it provides a plausible visual image of how close Franklin Park and Wolfe Park were close to one another. Another significant point to Map 4 is that this map provides greater credibility to Ms. Gwen Gardner's point that the Dunbar Center used FP for their cultural laboratory and festival activities. Moreover, if one examines Map 4, one will notice that area of park the badge marked 62 actually divides the two parks and appears to reveal an entrance (ENTR.) into Franklin Park from Wolfe Park was in fact a reality. Furthermore, in Map 4, the Paul Laurence Dunbar is denoted by the letter x, which provides an approximate location of where the Dunbar Center may have been located.

1895, the FPA contained beautiful and expensive homes, some valued at $150,000 to $200,000, mansions for that era. But new developments in the small cities of Bexley and Whitehall later induced FPA residents to relocate to more sumptuous locations.[19]

Common urban problems after World War II also plagued the FPA. During the late 1950s, with the growth of suburbia, the FPA lost its affluent image as middle-class educated whites moved to the suburbs.[20] Simultaneously, the African American middle class gained access to the area, replacing the White middle class. African American middle class made initial inroads into the northwest area of the FPA, which was commonly referred to by its residents as "Bronzeville," for two reasons. First, classic studies conducted on urban African American communities by such preeminent African American sociologists/scholars as St. Claire Drake, commonly referred to the African American communities of urban African Americans as "Bronzeville."[21] Drake used the term Bronzeville, to denote the feeling of pride that African American held for their communities.[22] Thus, when the FPA of Columbus was referred to as "Bronzeville," it was symptomatic of what was transpiring in other urban Black communities across America. To this day, some older residents still call it "Bronzeville." Second, the area was referred to as "Bronzeville" because it was able to sustain a large African American population. For instance, this area was "complete with black owned stores, theaters, hotels, churches, and fraternal organizations."[23] From 1950 to 1980 the FPA became a predominantly African American community.[24]

Despite a venerable history of achievement by its initial Black residents, over the 1960s and the 1970s, the area's single-family dwellings were transformed into multi-family units. By 1990, 70% of the homes in the area were inhabited by more than one family.[25] As a result of this housing shift, the Park and some areas of the FPA became sites for crime and especially illegal drug activity.[26] Eventually the FPA was transformed from a community of homeowners to one of renters. Moreover, the social, economic, and demographic change in the FPA did not happen by accident. John A. Powell, in his article "Race and Space: What Really Drives Metropolitan Growth," reveals that,

> . . . economic and political isolation of poor minorities in the inner cities is caused by flight, or sprawl, and fragmentation. The movement further away from the central cities to the suburbs is sprawl. The effect of the creation of rigid boundaries, which separate municipalities from each other and more importantly from the central core is fragmentation. As a result of these forces, minorities find themselves in neighborhoods of concentrated poverty, where four out of ten of their neighbors (or they themselves) are poor. Of the more than 8.2 million people who live in these areas, more than half are black, a quarter are [Latino].[27]

In addition to social, economic, and demographic transformation in the FPA, other factors such as residential segregation and poverty deliberately affected Blacks. The frequent and persistent occurrence of concentrated poverty in areas such as the FPA from the 1940s to the 1980s was "perpetuated through government housing and transportation policies, institutional practices, and private behaviors. . . . Essentially, [governmental agencies such as] the FHA paid whites to leave the central cities and confined blacks to central cities, which in turn, were divested by the federal government and private capital."[28] A brief social and economic demographic profile of the FPA illustrates how these demographic changes shaped the current direction of the FPA.

Demographic Profile of FPA

As stated earlier, the FPA began as a predominantly White upper-income community that evolved into a predominantly black upper-, middle-, and lower-middle-class community. The area encompasses two and a half square miles, and in the 1990 census had a total population of 4,522: 84% African American, 13% White, and 3% other.[29] Females comprised 54% of the residents, and 72% of the population was under 44 years of age.[30]

There are 1,682 households in the FPA: 34% are owner-occupied and 66% are renter-occupied. The rental properties are predominantly multi-family dwellings in rehabilitated properties. The FPA has 1,026 families: 51% are headed by females; 40% are headed by couple parents; and 9% are headed by males.[31] The

FPA has a total labor force of 1,447 with 45% employed in service occupations; 26% employed in retail trade, finance, insurance, and real estate; 18% of the labor force is employed in industrial employment; and 9% in public administration or government. The area currently has an unemployment rate of 15.1%.[32] The average household income for the FPA in 1990 was $25,000. However, for the FPA, per capita income is much higher for Whites than for African Americans. The per capita income for Whites is $33,697; for African Americans it is only $6,815.[33]

The number of persons living below the poverty line in the FPA is 1,855. For the FPA, the percentage of the total population that is in poverty is 42.2%. Also, 37% of the residents have no high school diploma, and only 26% are high school graduates. About 16% have some college education but no degree; 8% have at least an associate's degree; 6% have obtained a bachelor's degree, and about 5% have graduate or professional degrees.[34]

A demographic profile of the FPA reveals that the area has a diverse economy. Most of the workforce is employed in the non-manufacturing sector. The FPA has changed significantly over the last 60 years and reflects a division: half middle- and lower-middle class people; half (40%) below the poverty level. The data also reveal a large economic disparity between the White and African American residents. The data reveal that the number renting is double the number owning homes. The political and social implications of this will be elaborated further in the analysis section of this paper. Thus, while most areas of Columbus enjoyed economic growth and consistent expansion, the FPA experienced highly uneven development.[35]

To understand AmeriFlora and the political conflicts between FPA residents and AmeriFlora organizers, city/state officials, African American elected officials, the larger Columbus community, and the residents themselves, one has to address six important questions: 1) What was AmeriFlora?; 2) What were the primary objectives of AmeriFlora?; 3) How and why was FP selected as the host site for AmeriFlora?; 4) Was the FPA community supportive of the event?; 5) Is FP a Black landmark, or is it an urban landmark that is housed in a Black neighborhood? 6) What lessons can be learned from this research? In this section of the analysis, the six questions will be used to generate plausible answers to these concerns.

Origins of AmeriFlora

According to R. Brent Dennis, former AmeriFlora design director and currently Executive Director of the Franklin Park Conservatory, the events that led to AmeriFlora can be traced to the city's unsuccessful attempt to host the 1992 World's Fair.[36] According to Dennis, during the early 1980s, there was much discussion in Columbus about what the city intended to do for 1992, which was the 500th anniversary of Columbus' voyage to the New World. Since Columbus was the largest city in the world named after Christopher Columbus, city leaders felt that something just short of hosting the Olympics had to occur during the quincentennial celebration. During the early 1980s Columbus was viewed as a city searching for an identity. Thus, city leaders felt that hosting the "1992 World Fair would be an appropriate thing to boast or hang 'our hat on' for the quincentennial celebration." The local leadership of Columbus exploited the idea of hosting the 1992 World Fair in order to showcase the city.[37] The city did submit an application to the International World Fair's Exposition committee, but the bid was eventually awarded to Chicago because it had hosted the 1892 World's Fair and some (including Dennis) felt that it would be granted the Fair again because it would be Chicago's centennial anniversary of the 1892 exposition.[38]

After Columbus lost its attempt to host the World's Fair, the city leaders searched for a replacement special event that could "propel Columbus into the rarefied heights of major league status."[39] The event that would be used to enable Columbus "to go where no city had ever gone before," was AmeriFlora.[40] AmeriFlora was the brainchild of Dr. John Peterson, former executive director of AmeriFlora, and former associate professor of the Horticulture Department at The Ohio State University. Dennis, Ms. Terrie H. TerMeer, former Community Affairs Coordinator, Director, and EEO/Affirmative Action, and currently Special Assistant to the Mayor of Columbus, and Mr. Michael D. Link, Chair of the Near East Area Commission (NEAC), all agree that it was Peterson who persuaded the downtown business community to support the project.[41] Peterson's idea was to host "the United States's first sanctioned International Horticulture Exposition, in 1992, as the centerpiece of a series of events commemorating the 500th anniversary of the discovery of the New World.[42] When Peterson obtained political and financial backing from the downtown business community for a floral show, AmeriFlora was born.

Although AmeriFlora was supported enthusiastically by downtown business leaders, the project was opposed by the horticulturalists of the United States. According to Dr. Edward Jennings, former President of The Ohio State University and a former advisory board member of AmeriFlora, horticulturalists opposed it because the United States has laws against the importation of flowers and vegetables because of potential diseases. But Jennings believed that the real motive behind the horticulturalist's objection was personal jealousy on the part of some in the horticultural community and because of the fear of economic competition from foreign countries.[43]

After Peterson secured local support for AmeriFlora, a proposal was submitted to the U.S. Christopher Columbus Quincentenary Jubilee Commission, which subsequently designated AmeriFlora an official Quincentenary project scheduled from April 20 to October 12, 1992. Dr. Randall W. Jackson, associate professor, Department of Geography at The Ohio State University, and President, Industrial Analysis and Marketing Models, and a former consultant for Ameriflora '92, stated that AmeriFlora involved two major events. The first event was the Grand International Horticulture Competition. Participants for this event would be international exhibitors representing their respective nations. Jennings concurred with Jackson's interpretation of the event. Jennings stated very clearly that "the flora show was going to be the centerpiece of the Christopher Columbus celebration." The second event was an "outdoor International Floral and Garden Festival."[44] According to Jackson, the event was basically designed to showcase cultural, artistic, and educational experiences and to appeal to "leisure-time and family activities."[45]

Using "leisure-time and family activities" was an attempt to capitalize on the success of the Disneyland theme format. For instance, according to Dennis, the initial plans for Ameriflora '92 did incorporate some Disneyland-type of events.[46] For example, the organizers planned to have "an array of entertainments— monorail swooping around a 260-foot Sky tower above more than 300 dazzling gardens. There are plans for a 'Grand Mallyway' of horticulture displays, a hands-on science and technology exhibit called Discovery Pavilion, a 3000-seat amphitheater, a performing arts complex, etc."[47] Although the Disneyland theme format was eventually dropped because of the costs involved, the AmeriFlora organizers continued to associate their event with Disneyland. The then-President of the Disney Corporation, Mr. Michael Eisner, along with some of the life-sized caricatures of Mickey Mouse, Goofy, and Donald Duck, were on hand for the opening celebration of AmeriFlora.[48]

The primary objectives of AmeriFlora were to make Columbus internationally visible; to provide an opportunity for horticulture and agriculture to showcase their new technologies and their best trees, shrubs, and vegetable products; to celebrate the discovery of the New World; and to promote travel and tourism. Ultimately, AmeriFlora was a high profile half flora show and half theme park, whose stated objective was to celebrate the city's anniversary, to promote tourism, and to increase the city's international visibility.

Franklin Park, The One!

Columbus initially selected the riverfront as the site for AmeriFlora, but this site was eventually rejected in response to the movement to save the FP conservatory. Dennis surmised that the organizers may have been influenced to give serious consideration to FP because holding the flora show there could stimulate the revitalization of the entire area. Financial costs of hosting a floral show in dual sites, FP and the riverfront, were simply too high. Moreover, Dennis surmised that during some of the private meetings between key city officials and the organizers, a joint decision was made to use FP instead of the riverfront. Dennis further suggested that FP was selected as the host site because the organizers wanted to use FP as a mechanism to expand improvements at the conservatory, and the organizers wanted to use Broad Street as a gardensquare. They wanted to replant trees along Broad Street that had died over the years, making it a more attractive area in which to live and shop. Close to downtown, FP was also the largest urban park in Columbus and possessed the spatial requirements for an international flora show of the scope of AmeriFlora. FP was also finally selected because the park's unique terrain was perceived by the organizers and consultants as an exceptional site for a garden festival.[49] FP's location, size, aesthetic value, and economic concerns contributed to the selection of FP as the site for the event.

From the organizers' perspective, supporting AmeriFlora was justified because they believed that it was a sound business venture in the best interest of the total community. However, according to Michael Link, and FPA activists Cornell McCleary and Richard Harris, and Mrs. Les Wright, former Columbus city councilperson, "the only time that the residents were involved in the process with the organizers, was after the decisions had been made."[50]

In fact, they concluded that the residents felt excluded from meaningful input into the decision making. Thus, when the organizers unveiled their $82.3 million dollar horticulture extravaganza in FP with the fanfare and hoopla of the groundbreaking ceremony, what awaited them was a small angry crowd of FPA residents who vocally expressed their displeasure with the AmeriFlora project.[51] The incident at the groundbreaking ceremony revealed that the FP residents did not trust the AmeriFlora organizers. The residents' lack of trust in the organizers may have stemmed from their previous experiences with them and from their perception that someone outside their community had made decisions for their community. From their perspective, their participation was limited to a brief photo session with the organizers for sound bytes for the local evening news.[52] Walter Cates, President of the Main Street Business Association and community leader from the NES, shared this perception because he publicly stated that "community leaders from the NES have apparently not been included in all of the planning events surrounding the exhibition."[53]

The groups ignored by the organizers subsequently were divided into two camps: one group which supported the project; and another group which opposed it.

Community Supporters

The origins of community support for AmeriFlora by some of the FPA community-based groups are complicated. The community support that was given to AmeriFlora was indecisive and weak because the community groups did not trust the AmeriFlora organizers. The community group's ambivalence toward AmeriFlora is illustrated when NEAC withdrew its support of the project in April 1990 because "organizational and community members felt AmeriFlora's leadership was ignoring neighborhood concerns. The commission representing more than a half-dozen other groups announced in City Council that they could not support AmeriFlora unless they were involved in the planning and decision making."[54] The community thought that the AmeriFlora organizers were ignoring their concerns of affirmative action and residential parking.

Affirmative Action Concerns

The management consultants hired by the AmeriFlora organizers as a human resource team were ex-Disney personnel officials who wanted to employ Job Corp training participants exclusively for AmeriFlora as they had when they ran the personnel park during the 1984 Olympics in the Watts community of Los Angeles, California. They assumed that since it had worked in Watts, a predominantly Black area, it should work in Franklin Park, another predominantly Black area. However, when TerMeer informed them that Ohio had no Job Corp program in this area, the management consultant team adopted a different strategy. They appealed to the suburban teenagers. But this employment strategy was ineffective because, as TerMeer explained, White college students from Columbus were not about to work for $5.00 an hour. Two months before the start of AmeriFlora, when the consultants realized that they were not going to achieve their hiring goal, they began to open up the process and hire some African Americans. Ms. TerMeer maintains that had she not sponsored a minority employment fair on the East side of Columbus, the management consultant team would not have met their employment goal. The initial employment strategy conflicted with the community's concerns. For instance, as early as July 12, 1992, the community had no affirmative action employment plan in place. The Black Leadership Coalition (BLC) "requested a delay in authorizing the $10 million for AmeriFlora '92 until issues raised by the coalition are satisfactorily resolved and a more equitable plan of black participation, inclusion, and benefit has been reached."[55] These same concerns were raised by the African American and Hispanic communities of Chicago during the 1992 Chicago World's Fair.[56]

Parking Illustration

Another illustration of how the concerns of the community were overlooked again by the organizers was the issue of parking. According to TerMeer, the FPA residents' primary concern was for a guarantee that they would be able to park outside of their own homes. As early as April 1989, Near Eastside citizens' groups expressed concerns about homes being razed to create parking for Ameriflora '92.[57] John C. Peterson, head of AmeriFlora at that time, assured the residents that "there will not be public parking adjacent to the park; I can assure that."[58] However, Link reveals that parking restrictions were eventually placed upon the residents. For example, the number of parking spaces available for guests of residents was limited to one person per resident. Moreover, before special parking decals were issued to residents of the FPA, residents frequently complained to NEAC about their cars being towed or ticketed for violating special parking restrictions.

Given the community's distrust of AmeriFlora organizers, groups that supported AmeriFlora initially often rescinded their support because the organizers broke commitments. An illustration of an organization that was constantly at odds with the AmeriFlora organizers was the NEAC. NEAC is a quasi-governmental community-based group established in 1979 by an ordinance of the City Council to address the needs of residents in the NEA and to solve problems in the NEA. NEAC is comprised of 21 members initially appointed by the mayor with the consent of City Council for 3 years; however, the members are currently selected by direct election.[59] According to its charter, NEAC has four primary responsibilities: 1) to identify and study the problems of the community; 2) to promote communication within the community and between the community and the city in general; 3) to review governmental departments for their effectiveness in the NEA; and 4) to review plans and applications for development and or demolition in the NEA. NEAC is the umbrella organization for all civic associations within the boundaries of the NES. Thus, although other groups inside the NEA compete politically with NEAC, it is still recognized by Columbus as the official political voice and representative of the NES.[60]

NEAC's position on AmeriFlora could best be described as indifference that could be attributed to the fact that the commissioners had not been held accountable by their constituents. The commission was no longer perceived by its residents as being a politically viable organization. Moreover, the leadership of NEAC reluctantly admitted that on some occasions it was difficult at times to find someone willing to run for a commission seat.[61] Yet another plausible explanation of why it was difficult to find candidates and the reason the FPA was plagued by apathy was that over 65% of the residents were renters, and only 35% were homeowners. The renters were not active in the political process, and they did not regularly attend NEAC meetings. Harris and McClearly corroborate this point by revealing that homeowners are much more involved in the political process and tend to dominate the NEAC. Furthermore, the renters' apathy allowed commission members to escape accountability and to pursue personal political agendas.[62]

Thus, if we accept the apathetic picture that has been portrayed regarding NES's Black poor, then the question that has to be raised is why are they apathetic? Perhaps the middle-class African American homeowners have neglected the interests of the Black poor, and instead pursued their own class interest.[63] The residents who supported the AmeriFlora project were middle class and had been homeowners in the FPA for at least 25 years. Furthermore, the Commission may have unwittingly attracted individuals who were not astute about neighborhood politics. Along with the political apathy in the FPA (individuals generally ran unopposed), the commission became complacent.[64]

An excellent illustration of the Commission's complacency was the Flowers' incident. Alice Flowers was the former chair of NEAC. During her tenure, Jim Barney, former director of Parks and Recreation, was led to believe that he had the Commission's blessing for the feasibility study on the FP. The problem with Barney's misperception was that it would lead to political controversy for NEAC. The political controversy erupted because Flowers, without the NEAC's approval, wrote a letter to Barney expressing her personal feelings that AmeriFlora could benefit the NES and that she thought FP was the best site for the event. The letter that was sent to Barney without the Commission's approval was interpreted by the Columbus Parks and Recreation Department as the Commission's approval for hosting the event.[65]

If the local neighborhood organizations were suspicious of AmeriFlora from the beginning, then one has to question why would some key community leaders nevertheless support a project about which they had strong reservations? To address this particular concern, I intend to provide several plausible and even painful explanations as to why the organizations, along with some key community residents, may have vacillated in their support for AmeriFlora. For instance, community groups like the NEAC, the Franklin Park Improvement Association (FPIA), the Eastgate Garden and Civic Association, and the Driving Park Area Commission were often at odds with AmeriFlora organizers because they didn't trust them. Consequently, their support for AmeriFlora was constantly in flux. However, in spite of their wavering stands on AmeriFlora, in the end the groups supported AmeriFlora because, as Link revealed to me during a personal interview, "We really had no other choice, because the event was going to happen with or without us."[66]

Community groups such as the Main Street Business Association (MSBA) wavered in their support of AmeriFlora because of personal gain. In fact, some community activists even asserted that Mr. Cates, President of the MSBA, was critical or supportive of AmeriFlora when it suited his personal interests. Mr. Cates vehemently denied the accusation.[67] Other individuals, such as African American elected officials and some religious ministers, were accused of supporting the event for personal gain. It was alleged that a former African American city council member, one African American state representative, and one African American state senator had supported AmeriFlora use of FP for personal gain involving specific projects in the Ohio General Assembly that were directly related to AmeriFlora. An illustration of this is the controversy of the alcohol issue in FP and the role of African American elected officials that ensued.

Alcohol in FP

Voters in Ward 55, Precinct E, which included FP proper, had defeated in November 1988 a request of an Oak Street business (the only business in the precinct) to allow beer sales. In accordance with the State's local liquor option laws, this issue could not appear on the ballot again for 4 years, not until November 1992. But House Bill 481, co-sponsored by state Representative Otto Beatty, approved by 86 to 10 in the Ohio House of Representatives on June 7, 1989, and amended and approved by the Ohio Senate on June 28, 1989, and signed into law by Governor Celeste,[68] permitted alcohol to be sold at restricted premises in the Park. The community was upset with Beatty because the FPA felt betrayed by their state representative.[69] In fact, when Beatty appeared at the Franklin Park Area Improvement Association (FPAIA) general membership meeting to explain his actions, "He stated that he supported the legislation because it was a way to allow AmeriFlora to sell alcohol in the Park and still maintain the 'dry' status of the rest of the precinct."[70] House Bill 737 was proposed by Beatty and another Black state Representative, Ray Miller, two years later to disallow the sale of alcohol in FP. As of the date of this writing, the bill has not passed the Ohio House. Although Beatty was reelected to office, there is growing discontent with his role in the controversy. Some residents as well as community leaders have stated in private that they will not support his reelection because they believe that he is too concerned with improving his political ties with the downtown business community instead of representing his constituents's interests.

One religious leader accused by McCleary and other community leaders of having "sold out" to AmeriFlora organizers is the Reverend Jesse Woods, pastor of the Love Zion Baptist Church.[71] Although Woods has publicly denied the allegation, rumors persist about his involvement with a local African American businessman who reportedly paid $30,000 to Woods in a parking lot venture during the AmeriFlora event. The controversy surrounding the parking lot venture was that the businessman complained to the NEAC that Woods had assured him that he could assist the businessman, for a fee, to obtain a temporary parking franchise from the city that would allow the businessman to charge a fee to AmeriFlora visitors to park in some of his vacant lots.[72] However, the license was never granted because the NEAC had already enacted a policy that prevented parking for visitors inside the community. Thus, Woods apparently misrepresented his influence.

Although some groups' support fluctuated, other NES groups and groups outside of the NES consistently supported AmeriFlora. For instance, groups such as the Old Towne East Neighborhood Association (OTENA), the Eastgate Garden Association, and an external group, the Long Street Business Association (LSBA) were very supportive of AmeriFlora. OTENA represents an area of Columbus that has undergone gentrification, and "it is quickly becoming populated by young whites" and may have been supporting AmeriFlora for economic reasons as well.[73]

The suggestion that OTENA's support may have been based upon an ulterior motive is plausible for the following reasons. OTENA has consistently been accused by FPA community activists of representing the interests of realtors and developers. The activists point out that this part of the NES is heavily populated by these interests, and the organization is controlled by them.[74] Another reason why the OTENA has been accused of representing the land interests is that the OTENA was part of a coalition that pressured the Columbus Planning Department to limit the number of multi-family dwellings in the NES. The political implication of the restriction is that it has negative consequences for African American renters. Furthermore, the long-term demographic implications of this kind of restrictive policy is that it could potentially displace the renters over a period of time, because the restriction would precipitate property owners to convert multi-family units into single units, thus reducing the availability of affordable housing for the lower-income population of the FPA.[75]

In addition to the concerns on the restriction to limit the number of multi-family dwellings, seasoned community activists such as Harris assert that the establishment of a review board is another measure that could negatively impact the African American community. A review board is set up in a particular area of a neighborhood to monitor potential housing blight. If an individual's home is found in violation of that area's housing rules, then he/she would be required to make the required repairs on their home. The costs of repairs along with other costs involved in the daily upkeep of a home could potentially force Black working-class families out of the FPA.[76] The restriction and review board housing improvement rules could alter significantly the African American population in FPA, and thus dilute their political base. Although there is no proof of the charge against OTENA, the perception that the OTENA is somehow conspiring against the Black population (especially the poor) is very much alive in the opinion of some community activists and residents.

Another group that was supportive of AmeriFlora was the Eastgate Garden Commission (EGC), which through its former president, Mr. Art Lee, perceived AmeriFlora as being a good idea for the community and FP. Moreover, he felt that the inconvenience of the construction and crowds was worth the price for a renovated Park.[77]

As has been explained, the FPA community groups initially opposed AmeriFlora, but later supported it. Although a community advisory group to AmeriFlora was established to solicit community input, support for AmeriFlora at best was weak because the advisory group did not trust the organizers who either ignored their concerns or consistently excluded them from key planning and decision-making processes.[78] Additionally, although some groups, individual community leaders, and some African American elected officials did support AmeriFlora, their motives were perceived by some residents and other groups as being personally at odds with the community's best interest. Even though the criticisms and perceptions of the groups' and individuals' motives for supporting AmeriFlora might be exaggerated, the perception lingers because of the political divisions exacerbated in the FPA as a result of AmeriFlora.

Having identified the groups that strongly or weakly supported the project, along with their possible motives, the discussion will now focus upon those groups that unequivocally opposed AmeriFlora.

Opposition

Based upon personal interviews with McCleary, the Harrises, and Mrs. Charlene Morgan, former President of the Columbus School Board, and current Board member at the time of this research, there really was no organized opposition in the form of one umbrella organization to AmeriFlora.[79] A majority of the opposition initially came from groups that eventually supported the event, and the most intense opposition to AmeriFlora came from groups outside the NES. The external groups were more organized and grassroots-oriented than the NES civic groups and associations. These forces were still opposing AmeriFlora during the final year of its use of FP, and their objections centered primarily around two interconnected issues: the residual plan for the park, and the battle to reclaim FP as an historical Black landmark.

The Political Battle over FP and the Residual Plan Meeting

The impact of post-AmeriFlora politics on the FP neighborhood and city politics was immediate. The city residual plan hearing on September 2, 1992, aired on the local government cable access channel.[80] The visual images that were seen by viewers following this event clearly revealed the deep-seated political and class divisions within the FPA and Columbus African American community. However, the Malcolm X Day Celebration in FP in 1971 was significant to the residual plan meeting in 1992.

On May 19, 1971, a group of community activists under the leadership of Nommo X, a long-time community organizer and activist, helped to organize a boycott of the public schools in Columbus, Ohio.[81] This particular protest was captured on film and was featured in the documentary film entitled *Claiming Open Spaces* by Austin Allen, which featured Nommo X.[82] According to Nommo, the initial crowd began with about 5,000 participants; however, as the protesters began their march towards FP, the number of marchers would eventually increase to about 10,000 to 15,000 participants. The march culminated with a gathering on a hill in FP, which mirrors the historic gathering of African Americans since 1901 to express their unity and engage in fellowship with other Blacks.[83] During the 1971 march, the participants attempted to rename FP after Malcolm X. Participants who were marching towards FP were already chanting the name of Malcolm X as the replacement name for FP. The march relates to the residual plan meeting in 1992 in two ways. First, the march was the first public attempt by Blacks in Columbus to publicly claim its ownership of FP by renaming it after the slain civil rights/human rights activist, Malcolm X. Second, the decision to celebrate the birthday of Malcolm X in FP was significant again because the African American community in Columbus was beginning the process of initiating a new kind of usage of FP. Thus, the protestors on May 19, 1971, were no longer using FP for cultural or social purposes, but they were now using FP for political and protest purposes. According to Nommo X, one of the key organizers of the Malcolm X Day celebration in FP stated in the Allen film that their march may have attracted some unnecessary attention from city officials. In other words, Nommo asserted that the city officials may have decided on May 19, 1971, to reassert their authority and control over FP as a result of the celebration and their public pronouncement to rename the park.[84]

Nommo's assertion that using FP for political purposes might lead to a "crack down" on groups using FP for political purposes in the future is not beyond the realm of possibilities because the idea that city officials might resort to restricting the use of public parks for political purposes can be substantiated by the following quote from Cranz:

> Discussions of politics and religion were heated and exciting, rallies and public meetings over religious and political issues were evocative of the city proper. As a result they were almost always kept out of park programming. Boston commissioners did not allow parks to be used for public meetings, and, in defending themselves, they reported that other cities were divided on this issue as well. Philadelphia allowed only religious meetings. The South Park system in Chicago forbade public meetings that would lead to crowds and speech making, and the West Side Park Department allowed no large gatherings for public meetings of any sort.[85]

Not only could the city begin the process of reasserting it legal control over FP, it could use FP to host the AmeriFlora event and assert their control over all city parks and FP in particular. Moreover, some of the same individuals who participated in the May 19, 1971, celebration may well have also participated in the movement to restore FP to the African American community and the residual plan meeting in September 1992. The residual plan itself will be discussed in order to explain it and later illustrate how this plan was used by activists to politically mobilize opposition to the city and to those political forces in Columbus that had a completely different agenda for the future use of the park.

The city's residual plan was an agreement among the NEAC, Columbus, and the AmeriFlora organizers. The agreement clearly listed the conditions under which the Park was to be returned to the community. For instance, when the organizers signed a lease agreement for FP in 1989, they promised to make certain improvements to the park that would become permanent fixtures and would remain at the site. The agreement also listed those improvements that would not remain on the site. Also, included in the plan was an agreement that 2 million dollars was to be placed in escrow for the purpose of implementing the residual plan. The organizers also entered into a lease agreement with Columbus representing the NEAC for the purpose of detailing the terms of how the Park was to be used and when the Park was to be returned to the community. The Park was leased in 1989 and was to be returned to the community on October 12, 1992.[86]

The issues that led to the heated September meeting were the removal of the fence that had been built around the entire Park during AmeriFlora, and the discussion of the new residual plan. These two issues were interrelated and reveal the community's frustration in working with the city and the organizers of AmeriFlora. The fence issue divided the FPA residents because some agreed with Parks and Recreation that the fence should remain. Their rationale was that the fence was an improvement made to the Park during AmeriFlora. The residents who supported this position were homeowners, especially those who lived close to the Park. In fact, some residents expressed concern that without the fence, they were afraid that the shootings, open drug use, and individuals driving their cars on the grass, might precipitate the deterioration of FP once again.[87]

In opposition to the fence were resident renters, some homeowners, and even outsiders who favored removing the fence because it reinforced the perception of their own powerlessness. They saw a situation in which they and their leaders were unable to prevent the invasion of their community by outside groups which took control of the Park, dictated the terms of its use, and fenced-out the neighborhood.

The fence also became a political symbol in the FPA to those residents who opposed its construction from the start, and supported its removal because they perceived themselves as reclaiming a part of their freedom as a neighborhood. In other words, the fence became a visible reminder of their community's oppression, and it had to be dismantled if they were to remain a cohesive neighborhood. The fence was also used as a politically mobilizing issue for groups from outside of the FPA. For instance, outside groups opposed to AmeriFlora were more organized than the FPA civic and associational groups. In fact, the "post-AmeriFlora" opposition did not emerge publicly until the City's Residual Plan Hearing in September 1992. The opposition to the residual plan at that meeting was comprised primarily of a group known as the "Coalition of Concerned Black Citizens" (CCBC).[88] Some members of the CCBC were actively involved during the negotiations with the city and the AmeriFlora organizers during the life of AmeriFlora; nevertheless, the group clearly revealed its political agenda during the September meeting. This organization can actually be traced to 1986 when it was formed out of concern that Columbus' schools were quickly becoming predominantly African American. Moreover, some of the members of the group eventually became involved in traditional groups such as the NAACP and the NEAC.

In fact, the group attained political creditability when it controlled the NAACP leadership from 1986–1988. During this period the organization became proactive on issues of importance to the African American community in Columbus. The positions taken by the NAACP leadership at the time often conflicted with the political agenda of the old Black political guard of Columbus. At the City's Residual Plan Hearing the CCBC dominated the meeting, not only by challenging the city officials' plan but also eventually by getting the city to modify the plan. Thus, in the short run, the Park was returned to the FP community. The fence was removed, and the Park remains attractively improved from its previous condition. In addition, the NEAC under Link's leadership was successful in getting representation on the newly created Conservatory Special District Board.[89]

Conclusion

Although, FP has a very special and historical significance to the African American community in Columbus, Ohio, FP on one level is a Black historic landmark and on another level it is an urban landmark that legally belongs to the city of Columbus. I arrived at this conclusion based upon the historic and cultural presence of African Americans in the park during the antebellum period in the United States. Moreover, even though FP, at one period in its history, was considered to be a "Black park" because of *defacto* segregation, FP still belongs to all the residents of Columbus. Finally, even though African Americans have been accustomed to thinking of FP as theirs and as a place where they could "cruise" and just be free, that feeling must be extended to all residents of Columbus as well.

There are three primary lessons for policy makers and event organizers of future urban events. First is the decision on the location of the event. From the experience of AmeriFlora (and other events) it seems that having the event in a residential neighborhood limits the success of an event in terms of urban economic development. This is especially true if neighborhood residents do not have a voice in event decisions. If organizers of future special events intend to utilize city neighborhood facilities as a host site for economic development-related activities, then they must communicate honestly and clearly with community residents and their leaders. Honest and clear communication with community residents and their leaders is essential to the success of an economic-related development activity at the neighborhood level because without it the activity will more than likely be unsuccessful. Second, citizen participation is crucial and should be the focus of all event decisions. Why? Because without citizen input and participation, future events like AmeriFlora will inevitably encounter opposition and receive negative publicity, which in the long run will most likely undermine their objectives. Third, community residents must hold their neighborhood leaders and elected officials accountable for the decisions that they make on behalf of their constituency. Failure to hold their neighborhood representative accountable might lead to another debacle involving a future chair of groups such as the NEAC.

Endnotes

1. Personal interview with Mrs. Joyce W. Harris and Mr. Michael Harris, residents of the Franklin Park Area, Columbus, Ohio, July 26, 1993.

2. Personal interview with Mr. R. Brent Dennis, former AmeriFlora design director and currently Executive Director of the Franklin Park Conservatory, Columbus, Ohio, July 21, 1993.

3. Millat, Bette. (2002). "Underground Railroad Sites in Ohio, Especially in Columbus and Vicinities," (unpublished Manuscript), Columbus, Ohio, pp. 2–3.

4. *http://www.eewardmovinq.com/tradition.htm*, (2003), p. 1 of 2; Millat, Bette. (2002). "Underground Railroad in Ohio." p. 3.

5. *http://www.eewardmoving.com/tradition.htm*, (2003), p. 1 of 2.

6. *http://thesbc.org/cgi-bin/index.cgi?action=printtopic$id=ourHistory+img=....*, (2003), part 1 of 2. According to this citation, by 1851 the initial Second Street Baptist Church was incorporated and built on 105–115 East Gay Street. The current Second Street Baptist Church is located at 186 North 17th Street.

7. Ibid., p. 1.

8. Personal interview with Mr. R. Brent Dennis, Columbus, Ohio, July 21, 1993.

9. Personal interview with Dr. John C. Peterson, former executive director of AmeriFlora and former Associate Professor of Horticulture at The Ohio State University, Columbus, Ohio, July 13, 1993.

10. Ibid.

11. Personal interview with Mr. Leonard N. Napper, Sr., former Director of Paul Laurence Dunbar Cultural Center (PLDC), Columbus, Ohio, May 19, 2003.

12. Ibid.

13. Personal interview with Ms. Gwen Gardner, life-long resident in the Franklin Park Community, and a former participant with the PLDC, Columbus, Ohio, July 13, 1993.

14. Personal interview with Mr. Leonard N. Napper, Sr., May 19, 2003; and personal interview with Ms. Gwen Gardner, Columbus, Ohio, July 13, 1993.

15. Cranz, Galen. (1982). *The Politics of Park Design: A History of Urban Parks in America.* Cambridge, MA: The MIT Press, 196; Allen, Austin. (1995). *Claiming Open Spaces: A Film.* [video recording/WOSU-TV] produced and directed by Austin Allen. Distributed by Urban Garden Films.

16. Cranz, Galen. (1982). *The Politics of Park Design: A History of Urban Parks in America.* 196–7.; Pitts, Dorothy Taylor McKinney, Sharon, Lacy. (eds.). (1993), Lydia Diane. A special place for special people: The Defremery story. Memphis, TN: Better Communications, 110–2.

17. Personal interview with Mr. R. Brent Dennis, July 21, 1993.

18. Personal interview with Dr. John C. Peterson, July 13, 1993.

19. Ibid.

20. Randolph, Lewis A. (1990). Development Policy of Four U.S. Cities. Unpublished PhD dissertation, The Ohio State University, Columbus, 104–6.

21. Drake, St. Clair, and Cayton, Horace R. (1962). *Black Metropolis.* New York: Harper Torchbook, 383–5.

22. Ibid., 385.

23. Personal Interview with Mr. Burrell Charity, Columbus City Official with the Columbus Planning Division, June 24, 1993.

24. Ibid.

25. Ibid.

26. Ibid.

27. Powell, John A. (1998). "Race and Space: What Really Drives Metropolitan Growth," *Brookings Review,* (Fall): 1998, 21.

28. Ibid., 21–2.

29. City of Columbus, Planning Division and Research, Columbus, Ohio, 1993. The percentages that were presented on pages 7 and 8, were obtained from the Columbus Planning Division. Moreover, the Columbus Planning Division converted the raw number into percentages. Furthermore, at the time of

this study this data was not available to the public or to researchers. Thus, the percentages that were used in footnotes 29, 30, 31, 32, 33, and 34 were obtained from the Columbus Planning Division.

30. Ibid.
31. Ibid.
32. Ibid.
33. Ibid.
34. Ibid.
35. Personal Interview with Mr. Burrell Charity, June 24, 1993.
36. Personal interview with Mr. R. Brent Dennis, Columbus, Ohio, July 21, 1993.
37. Ibid.
38. Ibid.
39. Paprocki, Ray. (1990). "Can AmeriFlora Work," *Columbus Monthly,* 16 (April); 36.
40. Ibid.
41. Personal Interview with Dr. Randall W. Jackson, August 8, 1993; Personal interview with Mr. R. Brent Dennis, July 21, 1993; Personal interview with Ms. Terrie TerMeer, Columbus, Ohio, July 12, 1993; Personal interview with Mr. Michael D. Link, Columbus, Ohio, July 16, 1993.
42. Personal interview with Mr. R. Brent Dennis, July, 21, 1993; Personal interview with Ms. Terrie TerMeer, July 12, 1993; Personal Interview with Mr. Michael D. Link, July 16, 1993.
43. Personal Interview with Dr. Edward Jennings, Columbus, Ohio, August 10, 1993.
44. Ibid.
45. Jackson, R. W. (1991). *Economic Impacts of the Columbus Metropolitan Area of AmeriFlora 92 Final Report.* Columbus, Ohio: Industrial Analysis and Marketing Models, l.
46. Personal interview with Mr. R. Brent Dennis, July 21, 1993.
47. Paprocki, Ray. (1990). "Can AmeriFlora work," *Columbus Monthly.* 16(April): 39.
48. Allen, Austin. (1995). *Claiming Open Spaces: A Film.* Urban Garden Films.
49. Personal Interview with Mr. R. Brent Dennis, July 21, 1993. Driving Park Community Newsletter, October/November 1989, vol. 1 Issue 3, p. l.
50. Personal Interview with Mrs. Les Wright, Columbus, Ohio, August 10, 1993; Personal interview with Mr. Michael D. Link, July 16, 1993; Personal interview with Mr. Cornell McCleary, a long-time FPA activist, Columbus, Ohio, July l6, 1993; personal interview with Mr. Richard Harris, July 16, 1993.
51. Paprocki, Ray. (1990) "Can AmeriFlora Work," *Columbus Monthly* 16, (April) 36. Allen, Austin. (1995). *Claiming Open Spaces: A Film.* Urban Garden Films.
52. Personal interview with Mr. Michael D. Link, July 16, 1993; Personal interview with Mr. Cornell McCleary, July 16, 1993; Personal interview with Mr. Richard Harris, July 16, 1993; and Personal interview with Mr. Burrell Charity, June 24, 1993.
53. Beaulieu, Lovell. (1990). "Commission wants more input on AmeriFlora," *Neighborhood News The Columbus Dispatch,* Columbus, Ohio, January 17, p. l.
54. Ibid.
55. Personal interview with Ms. Terrrie TerMeer, July 12, 1993; and Personal interview with Mr. Cornell McCleary, Columbus, Ohio, July 16, 1993.
56. Bentancur, John J., and Douglas C. Gills. (1993). "Race and Class in Local Economic Development," in *Theories of Local Economic Development: Perspectives From Across the Disciplines,* Richard D. Bingham and Robert Mier, eds. Newbury Park, CA: Sage Publications, 191–200.
57. Candisky, Catherine. "AmeriFlora fears aired: Director says no homes will be razed for parking," *The Columbus Dispatch,* Sunday, April 23, 1989, 6B.
58. Ibid.
59. Personal interview with Mr. Michael D. Link, July 16, 1993; Personal Interview with Mr. Cornell McCleary, July 16, 1993; and Personal interview with Mr. Richard Harris, July 16, 1993.
60. Ibid.

61. Personal interview with Mr. Michael D. Link, July 16, 1993; and Personal interview with Mr. Cornell McCleary, July 16, 1993.

62. Personal interview with Mr. Cornell McCleary, July 16, 1993; Personal interview with Mr. Richard Harris, July 16, 1993; and Personal interview with Ms. Gwen Gardner, July 16, 1993.

63. Ibid.

64. Personal interview with Mr. Michael D. Link, July 16, 1993; personal interview with Mr. Richard Harris, July 16, 1993; Personal interview with Mr. Cornell McCleary, July 16, 1993.

65. McCleary, Cornell. "Why AmeriFlora Outrages The Black Community," *Main Street Business Journal.* June 1992, 4–11.

66. Personal interview with Mr. Michael D. Link, Columbus, Ohio, July 16, 1993.

67. Personal interview with Mr. Walter Cates, Columbus, Ohio, July 16, 1993.

68. Franklin Park Improvement Association Newsletter (FPAIA), pp. 1–4. The FPAIA provides a chronology of events surrounding the alcohol issue in FP. According to the newsletter, "Voters in Ward 55, Precinct E, which includes Franklin Park proper, defeated a request of an Oak Street business (the only business in the precinct) to allow beer sales. In accordance with the State's local liquor option laws, this issue could not appear on the ballot again for four years—November 1992. . . . However, House Bill 481, which was co-sponsored by Rep. Otto Beatty (African American), is approved 86-10 by the Ohio House of Representatives. Section 4301.1403 permits alcohol sales at 'Exhibition Premises 'in Franklin Park." (Ibid.). Also, then Governor Richard Celeste eventually signed an amended version of Beatty's bill into law.

69. Personal interview with Mr. Cornell McCleary, July 16, 1993.

70. Personal interview with Mr. Michael D. Link, July 16, 1993.

71. Personal interview with Mr. Cornell McCleary, July 16, 1993.

72. Personal interview with Mr. Michael D. Link, July 16, 1993.

73. Ibid.; and Personal interview with Mr. Richard Harris, July 16, 1993.

74. Personal interview with Mr. Cornell McCleary, July 16, 1993.

75. Personal interview with Mr. Richard Harris, July 16, 1993; and Personal interview with Mr. Cornell McCleary, July 16, 1993.

76. Personal interview with Mr. Richard Harris, July 16, 1993.

77. Phone interview with Art Lee, July 20, 1993.

78. Personal interview with Ms. Terrrie TerMeer, July 12, 1993

79. Personal interview with Mr. Cornell McCleary, July 16, 1993; Personal interview with Mr. Richard Harris, July 16, 1993; and Personal interview with Mrs. Charlene Morgan; July 20, 1993.

80. Allen, Austin. (1995). *Claiming Open Spaces: A Film.* Urban Garden Films.

81. Ibid.

82. Ibid.

83. Ibid.

84. Ibid.

85. Cranz, Galen. (1989 or 1982). The Politics of Park Design: A History of Urban Parks in America. Cambridge, MA: The MIT Press, 23.

86. City of Columbus Residual Plan Hearing (video tape Part II). September 9, 1992.

87. Ibid.

88. Ibid.; Personal interview with Mr. Cornell McCleary, July 16; Personal interview with Mr. Richard Harris, July 16, 1993; and city of Columbus Residual Plan Hearing (video tape Part II). September 9, 1992.

89. Personal interview with Ms. Margaret Newkirk, August 10, 1993. Ms. Newkirk is a reporter for *Columbus Monthly Magazine.*

Chapter 56

Africana Studies, the Politics of Knowledge, and New Media Technologies

Gloria Harper Dickinson

Introduction

The concurrent growth and development of the information highway and new media technologies has profoundly changed the world's exposure to, and study of, African and diaspora people. The proliferation of websites, CD-ROMs and other new media resources has been both rapid and uncensored. As a result, even when difficult to determine whether or not materials are appropriate for academic use, hurried paradigm shifts have occurred. Moreover, since the 1960s, the ways in which knowledge about persons of African descent has been defined and disseminated has undergone rapid change. And as technocrats, the media, and the academy have engaged in new partnerships, Africana Studies scholarship has often lagged behind that of other humanities disciplines. Obstacles have included racial and/or gender-related technophobia, disparate resources in communities of color, and limited numbers of Africana Studies scholars with the opportunity/resources to participate in the development of the archival resources and research that would benefit the discipline.

This essay will explore the importance of new media technologies to the preservation, dissemination, and perpetuation of Africana Studies; digital resources suitable for academic purposes; the differences between commercial and academic websites; and strategies for evaluating websites and negative uses of the web.

The Politics of Knowledge

Global access to information about people of African descent has been manipulated and constrained throughout most of the modern age. Although documents, images and material culture reveal that European/African interactions were relatively free of bias before the advent of the Atlantic Slave Trade,[1] many studies reveal that the characterizations of people of African descent as "barbaric, uncivilized, and childlike" increase in direct relationship to the growing fiscal benefits garnered from Europe and America's "free labor."[2] Skewed and restricted access to information about Africana people remained the norm for over 400 years, and in recent times these restrictions have been explored in combination with the theory known as "the politics of knowledge."

Throughout the modern era, Western society's definition(s) of knowledge, structuring of educational institutions, publishing and media production decisions, and media imagery all have been shaped and informed by politics and power. Although discussions about "objectivity" have often been at the core of academic conversations, in reality a homogeneous group of privileged, male power brokers have defined knowledge. Moreover, the oft-heralded academic icons of "universality" and "objectivity" were often distorted by the biases of the very creators of the theoretical models.

However, post WWII paradigm shifts resulting from the GI Bill, independence movements among the colonized, the Civil Rights Movement, and the equal opportunity initiatives of the 1960s and 1970s fostered a more heterogeneous:

- student body
- graduate student body
- junior faculty
- arts community
- work force
- cadre of elected officials

As these multi-hued male and female "newcomers" challenged the validity of the countless theoretical "truths" of the academy, many pursued the research that allowed more inclusive global prototypes to evolve. These activists were in the vanguard of both academic and socio-political initiatives emphasizing inclusion, and many led the efforts to eliminate the perpetuation of imbedded disciplinary and interdisciplinary racial, gender, ethnic, sexual orientation, and religious stereotypes.

African Studies, New Media, and Shifting Paradigms

The Information Highway has been a great boon to the advocates of a more inclusive academy. Access to technology has dramatically reduced the "gate keeping" power wielded by editors, publishers, and producers. As mainstream technological access has increased, so too has information about the history and culture of people of African descent, making global access to information about Africana people more accessible today than ever before. But the flood of data presents a problem; the very absence of "gatekeepers" that has been so beneficial constitutes a double-edged sword. Inaccurate information can just as readily be posted on a website.

Even so, a very different (and far more accurate) 21st century Africana scholarship is certain to abound. However this digital revolution will demand more of users. Rather than relying solely on publishers and librarians, faculty, students, and researchers will be challenged to responsibly assess the quality and veracity of the digitized sources that they choose to utilize.[3] Consequently, it is incumbent upon those engaged in academic inquiry to acquire the skills needed to discern whether a website is commercial, academic, or personal,[4] since these criteria and numerous other factors will influence a site's appropriateness for a specific project.

Africana Studies professionals also need to keep abreast of teleconferencing breakthroughs because teleconferencing and real-time on-line conversations have the capacity to erode the fiscal constraints that heretofore have limited Pan-African research agendas. As African and diaspora students and faculty find instant contact more viable, certain research agendas will explode. For example, USA-based Afrocentric marketing classes wishing to work in a more global sphere need only log-on to collaborate with peers in Africa, Europe, and the rest of the Americas, eliminating many of the "filters" that may have hampered previous projects. In many instances the types of intellectual collaboration that Du Bois and Malcolm X envisioned will become feasible because lower costs, increased bandwidth, and high-speed access offer almost limitless opportunities.

In sum, new technologies will benefit both proponents of Africana Studies and advocates of new definitions of "The Politics of Knowledge." But they'll present challenges too. In fact, historian Chana Kai Lee notes that although

> . . . there is still considerable faith in notions like "objectivity." [she] can think of few new media sources that challenge this idea more fully than the web and secondarily CD-ROM. Any and everybody creates history on the web, and for me this raises some peculiar challenges, mostly because it hints at questions submerged more often than not: [i.e.] what is knowledge.[5]

As 21st century scholars face new challenges, great rewards will follow, for the explosion of Afrocentric new media marks the first time that a significant cohort of Africana scholars will control both the *production* and the *distribution* of intellectual property.[6] And since lack of control has been central to continuing myths, stereotypes, and misinformation, this technology has the potential to decrease their continuation by fostering an unprecedented upsurge of knowledge.

The late 1990s explosion of Afrocentric commercial and academic websites, and the simultaneous release of CD-ROMs like Encarta Africana and Art and Life in Africa offer clear evidence of this new Africana presence in cyberspace.

Unfortunately, most people of African ancestry still can't reach that presence. And as policy analysts discuss this issue, they urge governments and the private sector to make sure that Black people don't become "road kill" on the information highway.[7] Meanwhile, a 1998 study reveals another concern, for

> blacks were significantly less likely to be interested in articles about global news [but] did not exhibit a significant difference in whether or not they had ever purchased an item online or in the amount of money they spent during the last six months on online purchases.[8]

This means that even when Internet access is available, disproportionately larger numbers of students of African descent are likely to approach research about Africana Studies subjects less prepared because they've had less exposure to contemporary political, social, and economic issues.

Moreover, reviews of data about the "Digital Divide" and the differing resources in predominantly White and predominantly Black schools reveal additional reasons for concern because a combination of technophobia, inadequate funding, and lack of information continues to cripple many Black communities. In some instances there's very little money for hardware and software. In others, purchases have been made but the technophobia of teachers and administrators restricts student access to resources and new pedagogies. Additionally, in too many communities few parents and educators understand the innovative ways that the Internet and personal computers can be used to enhance student learning. Cutting-edge mergers of pedagogy and technology found in majority communities remain unknown in many communities of color. The sad result is that many students will have had limited access to the hardware and software that will shape and inform 21st-century research. They may be familiar with commercial sites, but because of the limitations of their schools they will have limited analytical skills and be ill-prepared to use on-line resources or produce digital research projects.

New Media and the Study of Africana People

Twenty-first century scholars will not be limited by the geographic boundaries of their predecessors. Virtual classrooms will allow instant contact with scholars all over the world. As primary source materials are digitized, many inquiries formerly reserved for "monied" graduate students will become the province of undergraduates.[9]

As more archival resources are digitized, post-secondary teaching and learning will also be enhanced. Increased access to primary source materials is already changing the nature of undergraduate learning and research. More and more students are becoming "novices in the archives" as the Internet gives students in Oregon, for example, access to primary source materials about the Underground Railroad in Lancaster County, Pennsylvania. Resources that a decade ago would have been limited to graduate students who would have required funding for cross-country travel is now available with the click of a mouse. Therefore, undergraduate use of primary source materials is altering the research and critical thinking skills associated with baccalaureate education. Africana Studies stands to be one of the greatest beneficiaries of this trend because so much of the material in the associated disciplines remains uncollected and unmined.

Instruction will change as the World Wide Web engenders a more learner-centered academy whose curricula compel students to take more responsibility. This requires familiarity with Africana Studies resources. Therefore, the next section will survey the myriad digitized materials that can enhance student learning. In addition to giving examples of different types of commercial, academic, institutional and organizational resources, examples of student constructivism (i.e., new media projects created by undergraduate learners) will also be highlighted.

Africana Studies New Media Resources—CD-ROMs

CD-ROMs are discs containing digitized information. They can hold text, pictures, music, video, and graphics. Some, like Ethnic Newswatch are text-based and are usually found in libraries. Others, like Encarta

Africana are interactive; they contain music, text, video clips, photos, and animation. Resources that will be beneficial to Africana Studies students include:

Interactive CD-ROM

- Encarta Africana
- Who Built America
- Art and Life in Africa
- In message from Taras

Two of the better known resources most often found in university libraries are:

- Ethnic Newswatch
- Black Newspapers

Africana Studies New Media Resources—Websites

The real explosion of information has been on the World Wide Web. Therefore, it is likely that Africana Studies students will spend more time "surfing the web" than working with CD-ROM and other new media. However, the proliferation of materials, the "quirks" of search engine programming, and racism can present obstacles.

One of the most egregious examples of racism is demonstrated by the difference in results generated by a search for "Black women" as opposed to a search for "African American women."[10] A search for "Black women" retrieves triple-x-rated and/or porno sites.[11] However, a search for "African American women" returns a totally different array of sites.

Other negative uses of the Web can be related to Africana Studies. In a January 5, 1998, "Front Page" article, *Philadelphia Inquirer* staff writer Sudarsan Raghavan explores negative uses of the Web. Noting that:

> ". . . much of the hate starts [on the web]. The internet is a hotbed of hate sites, particularly in Pennsylvania and New Jersey"

he opens a discussion of the many ways that representatives of "hate groups" have also used new technologies to recruit and proselytize.

Undoubtedly, it's VERY important for researchers to do some general reading before beginning a Web search. Recently a student preparing a paper on Affirmative Action Plans quoted statistics and conclusions taken from a site sponsored by an organization affiliated with former KKK leader David Duke. The student didn't do any research on the creators of the site, and ended up with very skewed findings.

Evaluating Websites

The most important skill that student users of websites can acquire is the ability to evaluate sites. When using websites, it is important to screen and evaluate your sources in the same way that you would with printed materials. Website quality and reliability varies in much the same way that publications do. In other words, "not all websites are created equal!"

The Milton S. Eisenhower Library at Johns Hopkins University in Baltimore supports a site known as "Milton's Web." Their guidelines are clear, evenly applied, and easy to follow. They list criteria for evaluating a website's applicability for academic work and advise assessing the authorship, publisher, point of view/biases, referral to other sources, and verifiability of data, *before* using sites for academic purposes. The URL for the Introductory Page of Milton's Web's evaluative guidelines is:

> *http://milton.mse.jhu.edu:8001/research/education/net.htm*

Of the five evaluative criteria listed in "Evaluating Information found on the Internet," detailed instructions for assessing authorship, publishing body and currency can be found at:

> *http://milton.mse.jhu.edu:8001/research/education/practical. html*

Commercial Sites

Africana Studies websites can be divided into many categories. Examples of commercial sites include "gateway" sites that lead to other related sites, encyclopedia, and sites for Black book clubs.

Gateway Sites

Netnoir *http://www.netnoir.com/* was the first Afrocentric commercial success. It began as an America Online (AOL) affiliate, but quickly established a site that could be accessed outside of the AOL network. Recognizing their success, many others followed suit. Among the best known is MSBET *http://www.msbet.com/*—a joint venture between Microsoft and Black Entertainment Television. Meanwhile, Melanet *(http://www.melanet.com/)* calls itself "the uncut Black experience" and is far more culturally nationalistic, and political, than NetNoir or MSBET. Not surprisingly, Melanet does not have the corporate support of the other two. Black publications such as *Essence* and *Emerge* maintain commercial sites, as do groups like *BlackFamilies.Com*. As website designers pursue niche marketing, it is important to remember that not all Afrocentric sites are appropriate for academic work and that evaluations are very important. Nevertheless, there is one commercial site that regularly compiles articles of value to academicians. The contemporary focus of *The Mining Company's African American Culture* site *(http://afroamculture.miningco.com/mbody.htm?terms=%22african+american%22&COB=home)* is an exceptionally helpful resource for students of culture studies and political policy.

Encyclopedia

Encyclopedia comprise another category of commercial sites. Brittanica *(http://www.eb.com)*; *Funk and Wagnalls Online Encyclopedia (http://www.funkandwagnalls.com/)*; and Microsoft's *Encarta (http://www.encarta.com/)* are three of the most comprehensive, but there is a fee to access their unabridged resources. The materials available for free are limited.

Black Book Clubs

Black book sales exploded during the 1990s. Black book clubs grew commensurately. The *African American Literature Book Club (http://aalbc.com/default.htm)*; *Quarterly Black Review of Books* (QBR) *(http://www.QBR.com)*; and *Black Issues Book Review http://www.bibook review.com* are publications that were launched amidst this growth. All are maintained companion websites devoted to keeping people abreast of new Black publications.

Academic Sites

Institutional Sites

In recent years, numerous institutions have digitized segments of their resources. Africana Studies researchers will find exceptionally rich on-line resources at the Library of Congress' American Memory Site, the New York Public Library's Schomburg Center for Research in Black History and Culture, and the Smithsonian Institute. Although smaller Black history museums like Detroit's African American History Museum and Philadelphia's African American History Museum have websites, they haven't digitized the types of primary source materials found at the major repositories.

Personal Sites

As 21st-century scholars break the yoke of dependency so long maintained by publishers, editors, and advertisers, personal web pages are certain to multiply. Robert Hill and Runoko Rashidi are two who have effectively used this strategy.

UCLA Professor Robert A. Hill has elected to use the Web in an innovative way. The Marcus Garvey and Universal Negro Improvement Association Papers Project is an NEH-funded research project of the James S. Coleman African Studies Center at UCLA. Their Garvey website *(http://www.isop.ucla.edu/mgpp/)* has excerpts from the Garvey manuscript collection. Scholars interested in the full collection can place on-line orders for the book while those pursuing less detailed projects can access the information on-line.

The site *http://www.saxakali.com/SaxakaliPublications/runoko.htm* informs readers that

> *Runoko Rashidi is an historian, writer and public lecturer with a pronounced interest in the African foundations of humanity and civilizations, and the presence and current conditions of Black people throughout the Global African Community. He is particularly drawn to the African presence in India, Australia and the islands of the Pacific.*

This personal page provides far broader access to a researcher whose work on the African presence in India, Australia, and the islands of the Pacific heretofore has not been readily available.

Bibliographies

Digital Librarian is a site maintained by Margaret Vail Anderson, a librarian in Cortland, N.Y. Among their numerous webliographies are two of great relevance to students of Africana history and culture:

Digital Librarian—Africana
ttp://www.servtech.com/~mvail/africana.html

Digital Librarian—African American
http://www.servtech.com/~mvail/africanamerican.html

These bibliographies are updated regularly; they are excellent resources when beginning research.

Gateway Sites

Africa

Africa South of the Sahara
http://www.sul.stanford.edu/depts/ssrg/africa/guide.html is maintained by the Electronic Technology Group of the African Studies Association, USA.[12]

The University of Pennsylvania site

(*http://www.sas.upenn.edu/African_Studies/AS.html*) is the oldest, and arguably most comprehensive, of all African Studies gateways. This site has national, regional, and international links to professional organizations, universities, professional organizations, curriculum resources, statistical data, multimedia resources, book reviews, and current events. It is constantly updated.

The Norwegian Council for Africa sponsors a searchable database at: *http://www.fellesraadet.africainfo.no/engindex.html*. Their Index on Africa contains more than 2000 Africa-related links sorted in categories by theme or country.

African Americans

Although History Matters (*http://historymatters.gmu.edu/*) was designed for U. S. History Survey teachers, it is particularly valuable to students. The site serves as a gateway to Web resources that focus on the lives of ordinary Americans. It emphasizes primary materials and is designed to actively involve users in analyzing and interpreting evidence. African American Issues Resources from Nerd World Media (*http://www.nerdworld.com/nw831.html*) and Voice of the Shuttle (*http://humanitas.ucsb.edu*) and the Crossroads African American Studies site (*http://www.georgetown.edu/crossroads/asw/afam.html*) are also gateways. The first is a collection of multi-disciplinary resources whereas the second is a Web page for Humanities Research. The last is a resource page for American Studies researchers. Any of these gateways would be appropriate starting points for academic work.

Carribean and Brazil

As Caribbean and Latin American Web access increases, the number of academic sites is bound to grow.
Brazilonline *(http://www.brazilonline.com/);* **World Area Studies Internet Resources– Caribbean** *(http://humanitas.ucsb.edu/);* and **Caribbean Cultural Center African Diaspora Institute** *(http://www.tmn.com/Artswire/www/caribctr/home.html)* are among the leading resources; however, the quality of the sites referenced is somewhat uneven.

Primary Source Materials

On-line Archives
The availability of ready access to archival materials is one of the Web's greatest assets, and two on-line archives of note feature materials on African American women and Black classical music.

Duke University's Digital Scriptorium is both a physical and "virtual" center in the Duke University Rare Book, Manuscript, and Special Collections Library. The URL for their collection featuring texts of the writings of African American women is *http://scriptorium.lib.duke.edu/collections/african-american-women.html*

Self-described writer, Web producer, and media producer Steve Mencher is the creator of the website Classical Music in Black and White *(http://php.indiana.edu/-afamarch/home.html)*. The site is hosted by the Indiana University Archives of African American Music and Culture and provides an assortment of resources by and about African American classical musicians.

U.S. Historical Census Browser
The United States Historical Census Browser can be found at *http://fisher.lib.Virginia.EDU/census/*.

This site is invaluable for the study of slavery, the great migration, and recent urban trends. It allows undergraduates to use primary source data that heretofore could only be accessed by graduate students with the financial resources to travel to cities with sites housing the data. Students can now look at slavery, the great migration, and recent urban trends by analyzing census data.

Slave Narratives
Excerpts from slave narratives, edited by University of Houston professor Steven Mintz, are located at *http://vi.uh.edu/pages/mintz/primary.htm*. Mintz has excerpted slave narratives and divided them into categories. Firsthand observations on enslavement, The Middle Passage, arrival, conditions of life, childhood, family punishment, resistance, flight, and religion can be downloaded.

The Duke University Special Collections Library Broadside Collection has digitized slave narratives whose pages are based on the exhibit catalog of a December 1995 exhibit of slave artifacts. The site, Third Person, First Person: Slave Voices From The Special Collections Library *(http://scriptorium.lib.duke.edu/slavery/)* offers first-hand accounts of plantation life from the vantage point of the enslaved.

Seconday Source Materials

Online Texts
Africana Studies has long been plagued by the whims of publishers. It isn't uncommon to find a book used during one semester out of print the next. Thus, the digitization of texts has been beneficial to many disciplines.

Survey Graphic: Harlem Mecca of the New Negro is a publication central to the study of The Harlem Renaissance. Yet it was often out-of-print. The hypertext edition *(http://etext.virginia.edu/harlem/index.html)* now makes this meaningful work readily available throughout the world.

Another resource is The University of Virginia's Electronic Text Center whose entire section of rare and out-of-print books is now available on-line. Their African American holdings *(http://etext.lib.virginia.edu/ subjects/afam.html)* include difficult-to-locate works by Booker T. Washington and W. E. B. Du Bois, as well as a digitized version of Harriet Wilson's *Our Nig*.

Journals
North Star (http://cedar.barnard.columbia.edu/~north/), published on the World Wide Web in association with the Afro-American Religious History group of the American Academy of Religion, provides information on

resources in the field of African American religious history. They also have links to works on the religious cultures of people of African descent.

Current editions of *The Western Journal of Black Studies* are also available on-line. They have volumes 18–23 archived. All can be located at *http://www.wsu.edu:8080/~wjbs/*

Supreme Court Decisions

A searchable site of Historical Supreme Court Decisions is located at *http://supct.law.cornell.edu/supct/cases/topic.htm*.

Information on affirmative action and desegregation cases can be obtained at this location.

Documentary Sites

PBS, The History Channel, The Biography Channel, and A&E have produced/aired exceptional Africana Studies documentaries. However PBS has been in the vanguard of website design. Their companion sites are particularly suited for academic use and the primary documents, contemporary interviews, and multimedia resources on their **Africans in the Americas** site *(http://www.pbs.org/wgbh/aia/)* comprise one of the richest on-line resources available to students of African American history and culture.

Stephen Speilberg's *AMISTAD* instigated an unprecedented mainstream awareness of slave rebellions. This, in turn, inspired an array of websites. However, the NEH funded Mystic Seaport Museum site, Exploring Amistad *(http://amistad.mysticseaport.org/main/welcome.html)*, is unparalleled. It is defined as a site designed to explore the Amistad Revolt of 1839–1842 and how we make history of it. The site's greatest strength is a library containing pages from over 500 primary documents. Amistad's compendium of court records, journal entries and newspaper stories offer a rare glimpse into the way in which history is "made."

The heart of the website is the Library that contains thousands of pages from over 500 primary documents including court documents, journal entries, and newspaper stories.

Virtual Museums

In 1998, museum professionals voted AFRICA: One Continent. Many Worlds *(http://www.nhm.org/africa/)* one of the best sites on the Web.[13] This is companion to a traveling exhibit by the same name, which is a collaborative project between The Field Museum, the Natural History Museum of Los Angeles County, the California African American Museum, and the Armory Center for the Arts. Its over 60 minutes of video, African and African American folktales, and photographs constitutes a rich resource for investigations of folk life and culture.

African Art: Aesthetics and Meaning

Benjamin C. Ray of the University of Virginia's Department of Religious Studies served as guest curator for this electronic exhibition catalog. UVA's Bayly Art Museum has been in the vanguard of electronic exhibitions, and this site also has examples of innovative student assignments using new media and the museum's on-line resources.

On-line Syllabi

One place to search for digitized sources and resources is on-line syllabi. Since search engines don't always retrieve these sites, it's often useful to use gateway websites that specialize in providing syllabi. Two gateway sites that are very helpful are the "Crossroads" American Studies site and the University of Texas "World Lecture Hall" site. Crossroads has numerous course listings that include Africana topics and resources. The Dynamic Syllabi at Crossroads URL is: *http://www.georgetown.edu/crossroads/webcourses.html*

The World Lecture Hall (World Lecture Hall at U Texas-Austin *http://www.utexas.edu/world/lecture/)* has another significant asset—it is searchable. Yet there are other valuable sites that may not show up on these gateways. Central Oregon Community College Humanities Professor Cora Agatucci's syllabus is a goldmine for students of African Literature. Her links on African film, African timelines, and specific authors like Chinua Achebe can save students hours of time with search engines. More important, since professors have often filtered out less reliable sites, links found in on-line syllabi are more likely to be appropriate for academic work. Yet you're most likely to find Professor Agatucci's, and other Africana Humanities sites, through H-net. H-net is sponsored by the National Endowment for the Humanities.

Student Projects

Using New Media to Enhance Your Research and Class Projects

This can be student-initiated or faculty-initiated. The depth of on-line writing makes it different and opens up many new options. *A word of caution:* This format should not be used if you're merely planning to present a traditional "two dimensional" paper. If you're going to use the strength's of the Web, then it's worth exploring.

Webliography of General Information Sites

Search Engines

For research purposes, Metasearch engines are most effective. These are resources that search 10 or more other search engines simultaneously. A metasearch engine sorts out duplicate answers, thereby making your initial inquiry much easier.

Alta Vista, Metacrawler, Dogpile, and Northern Light are among the better known metasearch engines.

Northern Light *(www.northernlight.com)* is an innovative search engine that manages to search both the Internet and its own special collection of over 1,800 premium sources of information not freely available elsewhere on the net *www.northernlight.com.*

Citing Electronic Sources

For guidance in properly citing electronic sources in papers/assignments, see *http://h-net2.msu.edu/~africa/citation.htm*

MLA Site—Modern Language Association guidelines for print and electronic data citations are found at: *http://luna.cas.usf.edu/~dwhisena/cite_examples.html*

Analyzing Documents

For guidance in analyzing documents, photos, cartoons, posters, and other media, visit the National Archives "Digital Classroom" site; *http://www.nara.gov/education/teaching/analysis/analysis.html*

PowerPoint Tutorial

http://commerce.ubc.ca/MBAcore/tutorials/powerpoint/ppt7.html offers step-by-step instructions for this presentation software.

British Library Catalogue

The British Library provides free Web access to its automated catalogues at: *http://opac97.bl.uk/*

General information on their Africana collections is available at: *http://portico.bl.uk/africa/*

Endnotes

1. For one of the most comprehensive account of Africans in Europe before 1918, see Debrunner, Hans Werner. (1979). *Presence and Prestige: Africans in Europe.* Basler Afrika Bibliographen, Basel.
2. For a full discussion of the progression of stereotypic images of Africa and Blacks in popular culture, see Pieterse, Jan Nedervee. (1992). *White on Black: Images of Africa and Blacks in Western Popular Culture.* Yale University Press.
3. For more guidelines on evaluating websites, see *http://thorplus.lib.purdue.edu/research/classes/gs175/3gs175/evaluations.html*
4. For an in-depth analysis of Afrocentric commercial sites, see *The Black World Today's* reprint of Jason Chervokas and Tom Watson's "Afrocentric New Media: Separate but Equal Hurdles" *http://www.tbwt.com/misc/nytimes.htm.* The original article was published in the May 16, 1998, edition of *Cybertimes,* the on-line edition of the *New York Times.* The on-line article includes links to all of the major Afrocentric commercial websites.
5. Personal correspondence with author.

6. In 1927, Dr. Carter Godwin Woodson created Associated Publishers with exactly this intent; however, the distribution options available via the Internet give today's scholars and academics a broader audience that Woodson and his collaborators could have imagined.

7. For a detailed discussion regarding issues of access and suggestions for using technology to empower Black communities, see Alexander's, Art. 1996 article, "African Americans and the Net: New Opportunities for Community Building" in *The Mining Company's* African American Culture section. A College of New Jersey course site entitled "Race, Class and Cyberspace" (*http://www.tcnj.edu/~set/cyber-1.htm*) has an extensive webliography of articles that explore many of the policy issues related to access and equity.

8. The 12/14/98 article "How Do You Surf the Net?—Are the habits of Black American Internet users different from those of others?" is located in the African American Culture section of *The Mining Company* website that is maintained by R. Jeneen Jones.

9. Digitized census data opens a world of possibilities to students who until recently would have had to travel to a city hosting a repository that had the data. Since the site also does mathematical compilations, students can rapidly obtain data that in the past would have required travel and days/weeks of "number crunching."

10. Always put the terms you're searching for inside quotation marks. A search for African American women will return sites with the words African, OR American, OR Women. This would obviously be hundreds of thousands of websites. "African American Women" in quotes will only retrieve sites where the words appear together and in that order.

11. The same thing happens with searches for "Chinese" women, etc.

12. ASA is the leading professional organization of African Studies Scholars. They reserve all rights to the site Copyrighted © 1994–1999 by Karen Fung.

13. See *http://www.archimuse.com/mw98/frame_best.html* for the poll results.

Chapter 57

Some Thoughts on Black Empowerment:
An Interview with Haki Madhubuti

Edward Ramsamy

Haki Madhubuti is the publisher and editor of Third World Press. He is also a professor of English and Director of the Gwendolyn Brooks Center for Black Literature and Creative Writing at Chicago State University. He was awarded the American Book Award in 1991 for the book *Black Men: Obsolete, Single, Dangerous?*, which remains one of the top 10 bestsellers in Black literature in this country. As a leader in the African American community, he is actively involved in promoting various African American social and cultural units that enhance the wholesome development of the community and its individuals.

Ramsamy: In your book, *Why LA Happened*, you mention that America is increasingly turning away from the race problem. Why do you think so?

Madhubuti: Well, as we know, the problem of racism has been around for a very long time, but it re-emerged quite openly during the Reagan-Bush era. During these 12 years, White conservatives have basically denied that race is an issue. As a result, they began to dismantle some of the gains we had made in the past. Appointing people like Clarence Thomas to powerful positions is, in effect, an attempt to neutralize our struggle. For 12 years, we endured the falsification of all kinds of events and information as well as the general belittling of the struggle that preceded the Reagan-Bush era. This was not unexpected; in fact, it was anticipated by those of us who got involved in the struggle. We knew that there was a very large right wing element that felt that Black people, people of color in general, were getting too much too fast. What many people don't realize is that this move on the poor of this country did not only affect Blacks. It affected poor Whites, too. We cannot continue to justify what is happening domestically to poor Whites as well as people of color.

Ramsamy: The United States is a class-stratified society. In addition, the gap between the rich and poor increased during the Reagan era. In spite of this reality, class alliances between Whites and Blacks remains an elusive goal. Why do you think this so?

Madhubuti: Generally speaking, the poorest Whites had always consoled themselves that they may be poor, but they are not niggers. The right wing has always played on that perception. That is how race became the primary factor, as far as I am concerned. Race will continue to be the number one factor. White supremacy helped to erase among poor Whites the notion that they have something in common with Blacks, that Blacks also struggle like they do. The supremacists fostered the idea that the concerns of Whites were the only legitimate concerns and that Blacks are to be blamed for White adversity. How else could it be justified that less than 9% of the world's population owns the world? There has to be a racial paradigm at work.

Ramsamy: Recent scholarship on the issue of race, as exemplified by K. Anthony Appiah's (Professor of Philosophy and African Studies at Harvard) book *In My Father's House*, propounds that race should not be the basis of political mobilization and that principles of non-racialism ought to be stressed. Do you see this as a utopian vision?

Madhubuti: First of all, we have to question why White supremacy exists. You are from South Africa and you know what it is like to live under White supremacy on a day-to-day basis. It is very clear that White folks are afraid of that which is not White. They see that when White mates with White, the result is White. But they also see that when White mates non-White, the result is non-White. I think this creates a great fear of genetic annihilation in them. Secondly, I don't think we can dismiss the power that White people, as a group, have. They dominate the world in so many ways, politically, economically, and so on. Let's take the example of Iraq. The United States would not have gone into Iraq if it were not for oil. The alliance against Iraq was basically a Western alliance, with Kuwaitis and Saudis coming on board. But basically, it is the picture of White folk sticking together. It happened in Panama and in Grenada. What's happening in Somalia? Did our country go to Somalia for primarily humanitarian reasons?

I don't think a class analysis alone is sufficient now: It has to be combined with race analysis. I think that one must also understand, especially if one lives in this country, that there is a class problem among Black folk as well. There is a privileged group of Black folk in this country who, for the most part, just wish that poor Black folk would disappear and then everything might be alright. Yet they, too, have gone through the same kind of brain mismanagement that most people of African descent have gone through in the world.

Ramsamy: In your work, you frequently call for educational reform that emphasizes an African value system. Could you please explain that?

Madhubuti: School or education is not some place you go to that separates you from your family or community. If we start with a value system that is child-centered and people-centered, not property-centered or profit-centered, we can begin to address the problem. We feel that, firstly, parents should not allow their children to be taught by people who do not love them, especially very young children who are so impressionable and vulnerable. We say that a child cannot be a part of our school unless his or her mother is intimately involved in the school in various ways. Secondly, we feel that as the child grows, we as teachers become the child's extended family, where the child would call a teacher "Mama" or "Papa" followed by the teacher's first name. This tells the teacher that he or she is responsible for the intellectual, psychological, and physical development of that child. We believe that although it takes a mother and father to have the child, it takes the village to raise the child and we see ourselves as the village. That's what we do in terms of education. We are also involved in businesses, health care, and other aspects of the social fabric of the entire community.

Ramsamy: Your emphasis on the relevance of an African value system has been criticized for presenting a very essentialized view of culture. Henry Louis Gates, Jr. (Professor of English and Chairperson of African Studies at Harvard) argues that this approach reduces pedagogy to self-esteem. Cornel West has characterized this view as "misguided" because of its "fear of cultural hybridization [and] . . . reluctance to link particular struggles to broader struggles for the common good." How do you respond to this criticism?

Madhubuti: I would disagree with that in a number of ways, especially when we are talking about Cornel West's book *Race Matters*. I think West is a theologian of the first rank. His first two books were groundbreaking in terms of a critique of mainstream theology and philosophy. *Race Matters,* on the other hand, is a "popular track" book for the lay person. In the first 15 pages, he lumped all the Afrocentrists together, which really bothered me. I wonder how Professor West can talk about Afrocentricity in a very negative way without giving examples or quoting directly from texts. I don't like labels. In our organization, we don't use "Afrocentricity." For the past 25 years, we have called ourselves an African-centered people. We know that Africa is not homogeneous. I have been many times to different parts of the continent, which is extremely diverse. It is a broad playing field. What we try to do is bring back the best. Coming from Africa, we are African-centered. This does not mean we deny Europe's validity or legitimacy. That would be stupid. What we are trying to do, as African-centered people, is to ask, "What have we contributed?" I don't think this perspective limits us in any way. Rather, I think the opposite is true. I was raised in a White setting. I have one of the best White educations in the world; I went to a White elementary school, White high school, and White university. I thought that I was culturally backward until I began to read outside of Western literature. That's when I began to see that there was more to the world than just Europe. This is what we are trying to teach our children. As a descendant of Africa one cannot bring to the table the same, worn over, imitated culture of Europe. Multiculturalism just becomes another term for integration if I cannot bring to the table anything different or new. So, in order to understand what an African-centered education means, I had to go outside of the western paradigm. I think that the Cornel West is seriously trying to grapple with these issues, but Gates, on the other hand, is an opportunist. He is being used by right wing elements disguised as liberals to promote their programs. For the past 25 years, the major proponents of Black studies and African studies, such as the National Council of Black Studies, have been persevering against great odds. My question to people like Gates is, "Where are you coming from?" All of a sudden, Gates seems to have all the answers. Well, he has the answers primarily because he does not want to face the challenge of the Eurocentric perspective in any significant way. He's just going to ride the same boat.

Ramsamy: Does that mean knowledge should be subjected to nationalism?

Madhubuti: I don't really see it as subjecting knowledge to nationalism. I see it as subjecting knowledge to truth. I think that we all come out of a cultural frame of reference. I am not speaking as a nationalist; I am speaking as a man who has been raised in a culture that denies him access to what is rightly his and what bound his people to a certain way of life. What I am looking for is a cultural paradigm. Culture becomes the defining factor, whether or not we have a culture that works for us. In this country, most certainly, Western culture and way of life has not worked for us. That is why we had to begin a search for our own cultures. In the south side of Chicago, there are no debates about these issues as there are here at Rutgers. They don't know who West is, or who Gates is, because they are just trying to survive, to be alive for another day. This is what informs our work. We want to find a cultural core that emphasizes life-giving and life-saving options. This is not simply an intellectual debate about whether Cleopatra was Black or White. That really doesn't matter to me. What I want to know is whether my children will be able to deal with the 21st century, from being computer literate to learning about our environmental crisis, to understanding the importance of languages. We feel that if we are anchored properly in a culture that works for us, then we can begin to communicate and interact with anybody on an equal basis. The problem is that we are not anchored yet. This gives rise to "Super Toms" who desperately want to be White because they can't understand the value of being Black or African, which remains a shame to them.

Ramsamy: During the 1960s, the central government made some efforts, albeit not enough, to address racial inequalities in the United States. The Kerner Commission, for example, acknowledged that economic and political structures create and perpetuate inequality in the United States. However, during the 1970s and 1980s the individual was blamed for his or her circumstances. Why did this shift occur?

Madhubuti: Around the turn of the century, this country was basically moving from being agrarian-based to being industrial-based. We then had the depression and moved into a war economy, which marked a very decisive change in the nature of the economy. It moved from being an industrial-based economy to being a service economy and an information-based economy. How did all these changes affect Black folk? Several things happened. The 1960s were the defining decade for us, because we stopped buying into the agendas of other people. We said we were going to develop our own agenda. What happened, especially during the period of the Kerner report, was that Black folk were becoming increasingly dissatisfied with how much they have been lied to. Many of us knew how hypocritical the Kennedys were although we didn't talk about it publicly. It's just coming out now. What happened was that we bought into integration and the words of the melting pot ideology, but we never melted or integrated. So King was shot, Malcolm was shot, and the cities began to burn because we began to see and feel that the disenfranchisement had moved to another level. What happened was that in the late 1960s, Black folk were pushed out of the economy while White women were taken in. The economy itself had declined to a level where one working White male alone could not support his family. Then Johnson brought in the "War on Poverty" and "New Society" federal aid to families with dependent children. The key to that move was that one could not receive aid if the father was at home. This caused Black men to hit the streets without jobs or benefits of any kind. Several things happened as a result. First, the money that we received from the federal government was not enough for anything, which encouraged corruption in thought, attitude, and actions in the families that received money in order to stay alive. Secondly, an underground economy developed. The underground economy was not anything unusual or new, because all new immigrant groups that came into the country developed some kind of underground economy to survive. The difference was that this underground economy was based on the dissemination of a new substance called "drugs," which were not manufactured in our communities. Drugs gave rise to a whole new cycle of dependency. Drugs fostered a culture of self-destruction. That is where we are today. We are still recovering today from the down period that began in the early 1970s.

Ramsamy: Movements built around the concerns of the Black community are much more localized now than they were during the 1960s. We no longer have large national coalitions as we did then. Is this a positive or negative change?

Madhubuti: There are real problems. There are now approximately 800,000 Black men locked up and about one-half of them are there for a drug-related crime. These men are between the ages of 18 and 29. These are the warrior years when a man gets ready to fight and seize opportunities. These men are denied that opportunity. What I have tried to do in my own life and my own work is to suggest very strongly that we cannot depend upon others outside of our community, our culture, to set us free. This does not mean that we can't form alliances, coalitions, and so on with sincere White men and women. However, we cannot depend upon them to be our saviors and lead us out of bondage. Therefore, we have to go block by block through our community and work on them. We work locally but think internationally. For instance, our publishing company is one of the largest Black publishing companies in the world. We are doing serious business, but we are locally based. The people we hire come from that community. It's the same with our schools. The people we hire in our schools come from our community. In our bookstore, we hire people from our community. We have about 64 people and we can easily double that number by next year. We all need to take this as a model and move on. At the national level, we work with other people. Ours is a multi-pronged movement with grass-roots leadership. What I call for is a national African American Congress where Black men and women from all backgrounds can be part of a common institution. The Black church is a major Black institution in this country. I think it is a shame that the National Baptist convention, which is about 8 million strong, is not talking to the National Council of Black Studies, for example. They are not talking to the National Association of Black Psychology. They are not talking to the National Association of Black Nurses. How do we get these structures to make and maintain contact with one another? If that becomes successful, then how do we begin to move representation from all these entities to a Congress where we can begin to plan 5-, 10-, or 15-year programs? Let me make myself clear on one other point. I live and work in the community. I am not talking from an ivory tower on a college campus. I teach in Chicago at an urban university. What we see in our community on a day-to-day basis is that our economic life is being eroded. The mom-and-pop stores are just about gone. Do you know who is occupying the mom and pop stores now? Palestinians, Koreans, and Middle Easterners who have discovered a new economic opportunity.

My question to Rutgers University is, "What happens to the Black students that come to the university?" Do they return to the community after they complete their education, or do they look for jobs in corporate America? Are these students asking themselves why they are not doing what the Koreans or Palestinians are doing? Why don't our students come back to the community to invest their skills and knowledge? That's a crucial question to me.

Ramsamy: In your writings, you emphasize that it is crucial to restore the Black family if the community is to deal with its numerous socioeconomic problems. Would you agree or disagree that your views seem to coincide with those of White conservatives who argue that a decline in family values is responsible for the crisis of Black Americans? Dan Quayle, for instance, remarked that children born out of wedlock and single-parent households played a role in creating instability and delinquency, which caused the LA riots. How is your position different?

Madhubuti: I live and work with the community. I see that over 50% of our households are Black women and children who are at the bottom of the economic ladder. In fact, the great majority of the children in our school come from single, female parent households. The call always has been, "Where are the men?" It is very clear to me that Black men are being removed from our community like sand in a wind storm. Black men represent a major threat to White male rule. At some point, we have to say, "enough is enough" and fight back. We have to take up a vision and fight to realize it. When most young Black men decide to fight nowadays, they are neutralized. When I was growing up in the lower east side of Michigan, it was not unlike Soweto, which you are familiar with. We lived in extreme poverty as a single parent household. My mother was an alcoholic; she died of an overdose when she was 35. Before she died, my sister had a child at the age of 14. My father was furious when he found out. As a result, his anger became my own, and I went to look for the man who had impregnated my sister. He was about 20 years old and I was 15 at the time. We fought and I was beaten badly. The point of this story is that we were ashamed. That was our belief then, that pregnancy should not occur without some commitment between the man and the woman. That's the way I think things need to be now, because otherwise, we will continue to have older men and younger women having many children. These children end up neglected in very serious ways. That's why we call for a child-centered world where our children become the reasons for our existence. I do not think that a single parent can raise a child in a wholesome way in today's economy. Women and men have got to learn to say "no." There has got to be some commitment beyond the bedroom. It is everyone's responsibility that his or her children go into adulthood having had proper nurturing, housing, clothing, security, and most importantly, love, so that they emerge as wholesome people. I don't want these children to go through what I went through. When I made a commitment to my wife, it was a commitment that we will withstand everything together. I just can't get angry because I am not happy anymore and then decide to leave. I can't do that because our children did not make the decision to come into this earth. We made that decision. Therefore, it is our responsibility to make sure that we can give them the ability to survive on their own.

I try to use my own life as an example. We realize that intelligent, independent-thinking Black women are not a threat to Black men, who are intelligent as well. My wife has a PhD from the University of Chicago. I don't have a PhD, but she is not a threat to me, because I am a productive and secure man. I am going to continue to be productive. She works at Northwestern University. We are partners. When a man and a woman are productive in their lives, then they don't have enough time to feel threatened by each other. I think that is the key. I have two daughters at Spelman College. We sent them there because we wanted to be sure that they had a cultural education. At the same time, we wanted to make sure that they were around women who were strong and independent. We wanted them to come out with minds of their own, without having to depend on men. This way, they will be able to compete in the world, but also understand that men and women have to complement one another. Men and women are equal, but different. That is why we have to complement one another. I think that patriarchal thinking exists for cultural reasons. My sons do not think that way. My sons can cook, clean, and take care of themselves.

Chapter 58

Hurricane Katrina: Winds of Change

Ben Wisner

The United States does not need higher levees; it needs another Civil Rights Movement.

What lessons can we draw from the human catastrophe of Hurricane Katrina in New Orleans, and small towns to the East along the Gulf Coast into the state of Mississippi into Alabama? There is a great deal to be learned about the complacency and hypocrisy of a national government that promotes itself as a model of technical and organizational efficiency. There were multi-layered failures to protect human life and to provide shelter and assistance with dignity. What one also learns is the depth of racial and class-based inequality in the United States. Mainstream America "discovered" poverty in the 1930s in the Great Depression. Again in the 1960s, Michael Harrington's book, *The Other America* (1962), shocked the White majority with its revelations of hunger in the midst of plenty, shattering another myth. Hurricane Katrina exposed, yet again, persistent poverty and official neglect. Elsewhere in this book the history of both malign and "benign" neglect has been fully set out. In this chapter we see the consequences in stark, concrete form.

Catastrophe: Domestic and International Solidarity

The scale of the disaster and its effects were enormous. However, we should not forget that in August 2005, when Katrina hit, 1.6 million people had been displaced in China by a typhoon and flooding, while only a short while earlier the megacity of Mumbai, India, was engulfed by monsoon rains that its drainage system could not handle. All of this came on the heels of the Indian Ocean tsunami catastrophe that killed 220,000 people in 11 countries in late December 2004, and just before an earthquake in Kashmir claimed the lives of 78,000. In all these cases, millions of people were made homeless, and lives and livelihoods were shattered. Before the 2005 Caribbean hurricane season was over, further thousands died in mudslides in Guatemala triggered by a storm called "Stan."

This is not to underestimate the human impact of Katrina. At least 1,200 people died in the storm and flooding. 600,000 people were displaced. Those displaced by the hurricane and flooding were spread over 20 U.S. states, where emergency declarations allowed a flow of special funds to the host communities from the federal government. Texas alone received over 200,000 people.

Sixty countries offered the U.S. assistance. It took 5 days for U.S. leaders to acknowledge this outpouring of compassion. Even then the offers of 1,100 doctors from Cuba and a million barrels of oil from Venezuela were spurned. Bangladesh offered $1 million in assistance and Afghanistan $100,000.[1]

Global sympathy for the United States following the Trade Tower disaster turned to ill ease and puzzlement when after 1, 2, even 3 years the U.S. government continued to project the image of a uniquely wounded polity. The President of Pakistan remarked that more aid had gone to the U.S. Gulf Coast following hurricane Katrina than was pledged for Pakistan's largest disaster in living memory.[2] Furthermore, the U.S. administration's narrow definition of "national interest" and monomaniacal focus on terrorism so weakened the U.S. Federal Emergency Management Agency (FEMA) that preparedness for and response to hurricane Katrina was fatally flawed.

Cause and Effect

Hazards are natural. Disasters are not. For a disaster like Katrina's landfall to take place, a people whose defenses and capacities for social and personal protection have been stripped away must be exposed to the hazard.

Along the Gulf of Mexico, people have been put at risk because of economic disparities and the priority given to the petro-chemical and casino development industries, as well as the retirement home industry. Destruction of the wetlands, greed-driven land use, location decisions in a laissez-faire environment, and disregard for the poor were all evident as Katrina made landfall.

The human tragedy taking place in New Orleans and in many other less-known communities along the Gulf Coast has deep roots in neo-liberal ideology that favors lax regulations and return to investment with no concern for the social and environmental consequences. Some 1,500 square miles (3,885 km sq) of wetland have been lost over the past 50 years. This wetland expanse would have reduced the height of the storm surge affecting New Orleans via Lake Pontchartrain. Experts estimate that one mile of healthy coastal wetland can reduce a storm surge by one foot. Much of the wetlands have been destroyed by criss-crossing them with access channels used by the petroleum industry, by oil spills, and by depriving them of silt from the Mississippi. Today the coast loses 25–35 square miles a year.[3] In addition, over a number of years, the budget for maintenance and extension of New Orleans' levee system had been cut. Programs for nourishing and rejuvenating the wetlands and for building artificial barrier islands offshore had not been funded. New Orleans has been known for decades to be a city waiting for a disaster, yet systems that should have protected it were neglected.[4]

In New Orleans, low-income, African American families lived trapped in poverty by the "downsizing" of the federal state. That meant less money for education, for small businesses, and for decent, low-cost housing and health care. "Workfare" reforms of the welfare system locked single mothers into minimum wage work at best, as grants for education are short-term and do not include money for day care and transportation. Thirty-seven million people live in poverty in the United States—up for the fourth year in a row in 2005. Many of these people live in the South, where the anti-union environment and less stringent environmental and land-use regulations have attracted chemical industries. The myth of idyllic seaside retirement has been sold to the elderly in the United States, and retirement homes have sprouted where more of the working poor serve as low-wage caregivers. Casino gambling has also added non-union, low wage employment—a desperate last resort for communities that are losing their traditional fishing-based economies due to overfishing and gross pollution of the Gulf of Mexico.

The foregoing describes day-to-day struggle for survival: a social and economic environment in which it is hard to mobilize neighborhood self-help and cooperation for self-protection, and where participation in elections—much less active lobbying for services and social protection—is sporadic and weak.

In short, the root causes of the catastrophe triggered by Katrina are deep.[5] In Latin America disasters such as Hurricane Mitch in 1998 are seen as the result of the accumulation over years of failed development and maldevelopment. The same must be said of Katrina's effects.

Race and Class in America

People have discussed the effects of a direct hit by a large hurricane on New Orleans since Hurricane Betsy in 1965 and Camille in 1969. In the aftermath of Camille, during which 256 people died in Mississippi, documentation of racial discrimination in the allocation of recovery resources was first documented, leading to a U.S. Congressional investigation.[6] Has the social, political, and economic situation changed since then?

Sixty-seven percent of the population of New Orleans was African American.[7] Twenty-eight percent of the city's population lived under the poverty line, and 35% of African Americans in the city.[8] Fifty-four percent of New Orleans residents were renters. There was low-educational attainment as well in the city, with 25% of persons older than 25 years having not graduated from high school.[9] The historical scars and racial tensions dating from the era of slavery and Jim Crow "reconstruction" still follow African Americans, especially in the Deep South. Black anger had spilled over into rebellion in several cities (Detroit and Los Angeles, for example) in the 1960s. Again in 1992 African Americans had rioted in Los Angeles in response to the acquittal of the White police that had beaten Rodney King. Did the authorities not expect a similar outpouring of anger in response to the obvious neglect and botched disaster response? Trust was clearly missing on both sides, and understandably.

The disconnect between Black lived reality in New Orleans and U.S. mainstream understanding was suggested by the plethora of erroneous and exaggerated reports of crime[10] following the hurricane. This frightened the military personnel sent to New Orleans who reacted with aggressive show of force, behavior guaranteed to create poor relations with the civilian population. Behind this reaction was a long history of racial mistrust and stereotypes of the "super predator" Black urban male. The media were slow to correct these false reports, for instance of numerous rapes and murders in the Superdome sports stadium that had become a shelter of last resort.

Despite the plethora of planning models and scenarios, New Orleans had no plan for the evacuation of approximately 120,000 families with no private automobile.[11] The year 2000 U.S. population census registered their existence. In fact, much was known about the poor, disabled, and elderly who were effectively abandoned as the hurricane approached. The U.S. Census lists 102,000 or nearly one-quarter of Orleans Parish as having some disability and 12% aged 65 and older.[12] Fleets of school buses sat in flooded parking lots. They could have been used to bring the people without transportation to safety in Baton Rouge or other inland cities. Likewise, the railway could have been used in the emergency.

Some of the dead in the storm were elderly people in private nursing homes. All these facilities were registered with the city and were supposed to have contingency plans for hurricanes. In some cases, however, the owners simply abandoned their charges. In others, it transpired that too many owners had negotiated contracts with the same few private bus companies and there was insufficient capacity. Proper oversight by city authorities could have avoided these failures of protection.

Faced with tens of thousands of people with no chance to escape a city filling with water, a huge sports stadium was rapidly opened as a shelter of last resort. Sanitary facilities were appalling, falling well below international standards.[13] The roof of the sports dome was ripped open by the hurricane wind. Air conditioning failed. Food and medical attention was sparse. This situation went on for four days while FEMA scrambled to provide assistance. Some displaced persons lived in these conditions for a week.

Besides the technical minimums specified by worldwide consensus through a Geneva-based organization, other international standards for humanitarian relief specify the following. It is questionable whether the FEMA complied with any of these during Katrina relief operations:[14]

- Respect and promote the rights of legitimate humanitarian claimants
- State the standards that apply in their humanitarian assistance work
- Inform beneficiaries about these standards and their right to be heard
- Meaningfully involve beneficiaries in project planning, implementation, evaluation, and reporting
- Demonstrate compliance with the standards that apply in their humanitarian assistance work through monitoring and reporting
- Enable beneficiaries and staff to make complaints and to seek redress in safety
- Implement these principles when working through partner agencies

Much of this loss and suffering would have been avoided if, at least a year ago, after the experience with Hurricane Ivan, authorities had taken the needs of the poor and indigent in New Orleans seriously.

Preparedness and Prevention

Hurricane Ivan in 2004 should have caused a re-doubling of precautionary planning. The night Ivan approached, low-income people without private vehicles sheltered in their homes below sea level. A direct hit would have drowned them. A U.S. Army Corps of Engineers computer simulation produced for a planning exercise after Ivan calculated that tens of thousands could die in the city, in the event of a direct hit by a slow-moving category 3 hurricane. By comparison, Katrina was a category 4 hurricane and had approached the city as a category 5 storm (winds more than 155 mph). Fortunately, Ivan veered away from the city at the last moment but still killed 25 people elsewhere in the South. Nevertheless, despite this close call, no public evacuation plan for low-income residents who do not own cars was developed. The authorities fell back on the questionable shelter and assured stress and humiliation provided by the "shelter of last resort," the Superdome.

As bad as Katrina was, things could have been worse. Because of a small westward turn that placed the dangerous northeast edge of the storm over Mississippi, winds and storm surge were not as great as they could have been. Will authorities finally get the message and do serious planning for the needs of the poor? Could Katrina be the beginning of demands from below for social justice in the face of the present social and spatial distribution of risk?

Time will tell, but with so much of the U.S. Federal Emergency Management Agency's resources devoted to planning for terrorism and with cities like New Orleans struggling with financial burdens that neo-liberal ideology leaves them to sort out on their own, optimism is hard to generate. An important part of the explanation for federal level disarray lies in the weakening of FEMA once it was absorbed by the super department created after the 9-11 terror attack. The Department of Homeland Security sees as its prime directive the protection of the "homeland" from terrorism. Commonplace hazards such as hurricane, flood, earthquake, and winter storm are treated in practice as secondary. In the new division of labor, part of FEMA's budget was transferred to other parts of the new superagency, and many senior FEMA staff resigned, retired and were not replaced, or were transferred. The emergency response agency that had performed very well from the Mississippi floods of 1993 and Northridge earthquake in 1994 was a shadow of its former self.[15] At its head was a director with no qualifications whatsoever in emergency management or disaster risk reduction. He had been appointed as a friend of a friend of the President.[16]

All the blame should not be laid at FEMA's door or at the national level. Louisiana state planning, as well as municipal preparedness and planning in New Orleans and elsewhere, were also deficient. However, under FEMA in the Clinton years, there was national-level support and encouragement of state and local planning and capacity building, for instance under programs such as Project Impact. National resources for such outreach and capacity building were cut by the current Bush administration even before 9-11.

So, across the board, planning for such a Gulf hurricane was insufficient, and money for the study, maintenance, and upgrading of New Orleans' levee system was cut in the years leading up to this disaster. National Guard troops in Mississippi and Louisiana and their heavy vehicles that could have helped with immediate search and rescue and relief were deployed in Iraq.

What Is to be Done?

Katrina was in no way an "act of God." In order to learn from this event, policy makers must admit the dead end into which laissez faire capitalism has led us all. Non-governmental organizations, faith communities, and activist groups need to mobilize the mass of the population in the affected area to see themselves not as victims of Nature, but victims of a late phase of globalizing capitalism, in this case superimposed on a history of racism. The affected people will then be in a position to see themselves as agents of their own well being and history and victims no longer as they demand social change. In concrete terms, we should focus on the reconstruction and recovery period as an opportunity for working people to "build back better" in social and political terms as well as physically.

But where will the recovery assistance come from? Six weeks after Katrina only about 1,000 of some 54,000 applications for Small Business Administration loans had been processed, and only 58 checks had been sent out.[17] Typically in disasters in the United States it is the small businesses that have the most difficulty recovering. While the official New Orleans commission advising on recovery uses the rhetoric of inclusiveness, the U.S. Secretary of Housing and Urban Development has stated that he expects there will be fewer African American people in the new New Orleans.[18] There are powerful economic interests that would like to see New Orleans rebuilt as a middle class, White city where casinos and other tourist facilities recreate a simulacrum of the unique culture centuries of historical struggle had produced.[19] In such an investors' and developers' paradise, service workers for hotels would probably be low-wage Hispanics. Some Black musicians would be tolerated, of course.

Few have been this explicit and crass—at least in public discourse; however, debate in the months following the hurricane increasingly turned around notions of triage and rationalization of land use. Commentators and politicians have openly questioned whether areas such as New Orleans' 9th Ward—formerly a vital community of African American homeowners and small business people—should be rebuilt since it is one of the lowest places in the city. There is certainly a double standard at work in such comments since Galveston Island off the Texas coast, where 8,000 lost their lives in a hurricane in 1900, should on that basis have been abandoned, not to mention Miami Beach, where hundreds of millions of federal dollars have been used to protect White real estate since 1924.[20]

The lines are becoming clearer. Grassroots activists such as those who founded Common Ground, an organization providing free health care and re-building assistance in the 9th Ward, clearly have a more democratic and participatory vision of recovery.[21] The emergence of this kind of activism is not surprising. All over the world there have been struggles to get recovery planning to occur in a participatory and inclusive manner. That struggle became very hot in Central America following Hurricane Mitch and in Indonesia after the tsunami. Women, in particular, are claiming a stake in recovery planning and insisting that their voices are heard. Survivors in the Peruvian town where anthropologist Tony Oliver-Smith lived refused to move after the 1970s catastrophe there.[22]

Women and people of color and people living with disabilities have a right to be part of the process in the post-Katrina situation. The impact of plans and investments need to be assessed through the lens of justice.[23] A multi-racial alliance of women struggled to get a place at the recovery planning table in Miami in 1992.[24] In May 2005, an International Recovery Platform was created in Kobe, Japan, with the purpose of pooling and making available the best of the world's recovery experience.[25] In its present unilateralist, passive-aggressive mood, the U.S. government is unlikely to avail itself of such recovery lessons from around the world, but nonprofits and people's groups on the Gulf Coast and their supporters certainly can.

In the end, however, recovery is not simply a technical or even only an economic matter. The deep roots of racism and inequality that divided and still divide the United States need to be exposed and removed. Katrina's impact is as much a case of environmental racism as any of the toxic releases that have been the focus of activists such as those associated with Robert Bullard's center in Atlanta.[26]

The United States does not need higher levees; it needs another Civil Rights Movement.

Endnotes

1. See "Disaster Diplomacy" *http://www.disasterdiplomacy.org/index.html.*
2. BBC, "Pakistan Postpones F-16 Purchases," 4 November 2005. *http://news.bbc.co.uk/2/hi/south_asia/4405818.stm.*
3. Public Broadcasting System (PBS), "New Orleans and the Delta," *Now,* 2 September 2005. *http://www.pbs.org/now/science/neworleans.html.*
4. See Barry, John M. (1997). *Rising Tide: The Great Mississippi Flood of 1927 and How it Changed America.* New York: Touchstone; Colton, Craig E. (2005). *Unnatural Metropolis: Wresting New Orleans from Nature.* (Baton Rouge: Louisiana State University; McPhee, John. (1989). *The Control of Nature.* New York: Farrar, Straus and Giroux. Wisner, Ben, Blaikie, Piers, Cannon, Terry and Davis, Ian. (2004). *At Risk: Natural Hazards, People's Vulnerability and Disasters.* 2nd ed. London: Routledge, chapter 7 on hurricanes.
5. An excellent history by Case Western Reserve historian, Ted Steinberg, digs deeply into these root causes: Steinberg, Ted. (2000). *Acts of God: The Unnatural History of Natural Disaster in America.* New York: Oxford, 2000.
6. Popkin, R. (1990). "The History and Politics of Disaster Management in the United States," in *Nothing to Fear,* A. Kirby, (ed.). Tucson: University of Arizona Press, 101–30.
7. U.S. Census Bureau *http://quickfacts.census.gov/qfd/states/22/22071.html.*
8. The Urban Institute, "Katrina: Demographics of a Disaster" 2 September, 2005. *http://www.urban.org/UploadedPDF/900835_katrina_factsheet.pdf.*
9. Oliver-Smith, Tony. "Forced Migration as an Index of Vulnerability in Hurricane Katrina," paper presented to the 2nd Meeting of the Expert Working Group on Vulnerability, United Nations Institute for Environment and Human Security, Bonn, 12–14 October, 2005.
10. Thevenot, Brian, and Russell, Gordon. (2005). "Rumors of Deaths Greatly Exaggerated," *Times Picayune* 26 (September). *http://www.nola.com/newslogs/tporleans/index.ssf?/mtlogs/ nola_tporleans/archives/2005_09_26.html.*

11. Ibid.

12. U.S. Census Bureau, *op. cit.*

13. SPHERE standards: *www.sphereproject.org.*

14. Humanitarian Accountability Partnership International, "Principles of Accountability," 24 October 2005 *http://www.hapinternational.org/en/page.php?IDpage=3&IDcat=10.*

15. Perkins, Broderick. (2001). "Bush Plan to Can 'Project Impact' Could Be Disastrous," *Reality Times* 8 (March). *http://realtytimes.com/rtcpages/20010308_impact.htm.*

16. On the destruction of FEMA by terrorism monomania of the Bush administration see Holdeman, Eric. "Destroying FEMA," *Washington Post*, 30 August, 2005, p. A–17. *http://www.washingtonpost.com/wp-dyn/content/article/2005/08/29/AR2005082901445.html.*

17. USA Today, "SBA Said to Be Probed on Katrina Help," 18 October 2005. *http://money.cnn.com/2005/10/18/smbusiness/sba_katrina/.*

18. Quoted in CBS News, "Will the New Orleans Poor Be Left Out?," 13 October 2005 *http://www.cbsnews.com/stories/2005/10/12/national/main938686.shtml.*

19. Davis, Mike. (2005). "In New Orleans: Ethnic Cleansing—GOP Style," *Mother Jones* 25 (October). *http://www.motherjones.com/commentary/columns/2005/10/gentrifying_disaster.html.*

20. Ted Steinberg, *op. cit.*

21. Common Ground Collective *http://www.commongroundrelief.org/.*

22. Oliver-Smith, Tony. (1986). *The Martyred City.* Tucson: University of Arizona Press.

23. Robert Bullard and Monique Harden, "Will "Greening" the Gulf Coast after Katrina Help or Hurt Blacks?" Environmental Justice Resource Center, 10 November 2005. *http://www.ejrc.cau.edu/greeningafterkatrina.html.*

24. Peacock, Walter, Morrow, Betty and Gladwin, Hugh (eds.). (1997/2002). *Hurricane Andrew: Ethnicity, Gender, and the Sociology of Disaster.* New York: Praeger; Miami: International Hurricane Center.

25. International Recovery Platform *http://www.recoveryplatform.org/top.html.*

26. Environmental Justice Resource Center *http://www.ejrc.cau.edu/.*

Chapter 59

The President's Initiative on Race: One America in the 21st Century, 1998

Struggling with the Legacy of Race and Color

Does race matter in America? During the Initiative year, this question arose over and over again. Time and again, the Advisory Board heard, "Yes, race matters." It became increasingly clear that America is still struggling with the impact of past policies, practices, and attitudes based on racial differences—what we are calling the legacy of race and color.

During the first meeting of the Advisory Board on July 14, 1997, Board members John Hope Franklin, Linda Chavez-Thompson, and Angela Oh began a discussion of the legacy of race and color, its implications for the future and achieving the goal of one America in the 21st century. Ms. Chavez Thompson initiated the discussion with her comment, "[T]he classic American dilemma has now become many dilemmas of race and ethnicity." Ms. Oh expressed her interest in having the conversation on race go beyond discussions of racism affecting blacks. She indicated: "We need to go beyond that because the world is about much more than that, and this [Initiative must look toward] . . . the next horizon." In response to Ms. Oh's comment, Advisory Board Chairman Dr. Franklin remarked:

> This country cut its eye teeth on racism in the black/white sphere . . . [The country] learned how to [impose its racist policies on . . . other people at other times . . . because [it had] already become an expert in this area.

> And I think that gives us the kind of perspective we need. It's not to neglect [others] . . . but it's to try to understand how it all started and how we became so proficient and so expert in this area [of racism].

This brief discussion was perceived by many as a split in the Board over whether the Initiative's focus would be on the past or future and whether the President's Initiative on Race would be confined to what many called "the black-white paradigm." The Board did not share this characterization of the discussion as dissension. Neither did the Board subscribe to the view that this preliminary discussion signaled an intent to ignore the growing racial diversity of the American people.

As the year progressed, we had numerous opportunities to read, think, and talk about these issues. We heard from many experts and individuals about the significance of the legacy of race and color and the way that legacy is manifested in current attitudes and behavior by both individuals and institutions. We have never been in doubt about the necessity of looking to the past to understand how America's history of slavery and racial exploitation has helped to set the stage for the framework of racial hierarchy, discrimination, and domination with which we now contend as a Nation. Appreciating this deep, historical root is fundamental, in our view, to understanding how the race issue has become a seemingly intractable part of our social life. In turn, this understanding is the platform upon which we will learn how to manage more effectively the increasing diversity and complexity of our Nation's ethnic and cultural present and future. In the words of Dr. Franklin at our first meeting: "The beginning of wisdom is knowledge, and without knowledge of the past we cannot wisely chart our course for the future." Nor was there any doubt that in looking to the future, we would seek to include those who are neither black nor white in our work.

In this chapter, we share some of the insights gathered during monthly Board meetings and at other events to which individual Board members were invited. Among the lessons learned is this: The absence of both knowledge and understanding about the role race has played in our collective history continues to make it difficult to find solutions that will improve race relations, eliminate racial disparities, and create equal opportunities in American life.

This chapter is not intended to be a recitation of the full history of every minority group in this country that has been subjected to discrimination. Nor could it be. It is an attempt to point to some of the more egregious examples of a long and documented history of racism and systematic discrimination in this country. For it is our history of denying rights and benefits on the basis of race that condition our present and potentially our future. This must be understood, but it is beyond this Report to provide that lesson in the detail that is necessary. Our point is that our history has consequences, and we cannot begin to solve "the race problem" if we are ignorant of the historical backdrop.

If we fail to devise effective solutions, we will, in turn, undermine our future as the world's most internally strong and globally competitive society. Educating the Nation about our past and the role race has played in it is a necessary corollary to shaping solutions and policies that will guide the Nation to the next plateau in race relations—at which point race no longer results in disparate treatment or limited opportunities and differences are not only respected but celebrated. We understand that this challenge is a formidable one. We also recognize the potential cost of not going forward and are heartened by the obvious enthusiasm of the many Americans who have participated in dialogues and meetings stimulated by the Initiative.

Understanding the Past to Move to a Stronger Future

At the dawn of a new century, America is once again at a crossroads on race. The eminent African American scholar W. E. B. Du Bois noted decades ago that the main problem of the 20th century would be the color line. Indeed, at the end of the 20th century, the color of one's skin still has a profound impact on the extent to which a person is fully included in American society and provided the equal opportunity and equal protection promised to all Americans in our chartering documents. The color of one's skin continues to affect an individual's opportunities to receive a good education, acquire the skills to get and maintain a good job, have access to adequate health care, and receive equal justice under the law. But now, more than ever, racial discrimination is not only about skin color and other physical characteristics associated with race, it is also about other aspects of our identity, such as ethnicity, national origin, language, accent, religion, and cultural customs. The challenge for America is to ensure that none of these factors continue to affect the quality of life choices so that we can finally treat each other with dignity and respect regardless of our differences.

The Board's work over the past year demonstrates that to meet this important challenge, it is necessary for all Americans to improve their understanding of the role of race in American history, including the history and contributions of all minority groups and the continuing effect of that history on race relations in America today. For example, few Americans realize that from 1934 to 1949, the Federal Housing Administration (FHA) used clauses mandating segregation in any housing development that used FHA financing, even after the Supreme Court invalidated such clauses in 1948. Segregation clauses were permitted until 1962. After that, racial segregation in housing originally financed by FHA remained entrenched based on custom and attitude. The concentration of public housing in cities is a similar example. Although discriminatory laws and policies may change over time, the long-term impact of these forces has been significant. Until all people regardless of race have equal opportunities, properly constructed and targeted programs such as race-conscious affirmative action are necessary tools that expand opportunity, increase diversity, as well as remedy past discrimination.

A critical component for a constructive and honest national dialogue about race and racism is a greater public awareness of the history of oppression, conquest, and private and government-sanctioned discrimination and their present-day consequences. Fundamental to this historical understanding is an appreciation of the ways in which the long history of slavery in this country has codified the system of racial hierarchy in which white privilege has been protected by custom and then by law. Even today many whites view African Americans and Latinos as less intelligent and more prone to violence than other ethnic groups. In addition, Dr. James Jones, at the second Board meeting, commented:

> We are influenced by our past in ways that are not always obvious. It is too much to claim that four centuries of bigotry and bias, institutionalized deprivation, and cultural oppression were eliminated by an act of Congress. . . . We have not by any means undone the legacy of racism.

Knowledge of the history of suffering experienced by minorities and people of color must also be supplemented by an understanding of their many contributions to American society.

Our History, Ourselves: Looking at America Through the Eyes of Others

From the first contact between the indigenous peoples and colonists from Europe to the latest hate crime in the evening news, our Nation has grappled with the tensions caused by interaction between peoples of different cultures and races. Our system of government has evolved from one in which rights and privileges were accorded only to those men of European heritage, whose physical attribute of white skin and whose ownership of property connoted superiority and privilege, to one in which a purported bedrock principle is that *every* American, regardless of race, color, national origin, religion, disability, age, or gender, is entitled to equal protection under the law.

The path toward racial progress has had a difficult, sometimes bloody history: Our early treatment of American Indians and Alaska Natives, followed by the enslavement and subsequent segregation of African Americans and then the conquest and legal oppression of Mexican Americans and other Hispanics, the forced labor of Chinese Americans, the internment of Japanese Americans, and the harassment of religious minorities is a history of which many Americans are not fully aware and no American should be proud. Even the language we chose to characterize these actions is likely viewed as too conciliatory—or kind—by those affected groups.

However, as difficult as it may be to acknowledge the darker side of our history, we strongly acknowledge and appreciate that at every stage of the struggle to close the gap between the promise of our democratic principles and our policies and practices, Americans of every race worked side-by-side to move the Nation closer to the realization of that promise. From the abolitionists of the 18th and 19th centuries to the migrant workers of the West and Southwest to representatives and constituent members of the Leadership Conference on Civil Rights at the close of the 20th century—all have fought to retain and expand civil rights protections. No racial group in America has been absent in these pursuits. Nor can it be so in the future if we are to succeed.

As we look back, we can see more than struggle and discrimination. Along the uneven path to racial progress, we have also witnessed great courage and extraordinary leadership by ordinary Americans. These are ordinary men and women who have recognized that race is often at the center of our challenge to close the gap between who we are and who we aspire to be as a Nation. Our continuing challenge is to understand fully what the struggle was about—making real the promise of America for all—and to identify and harness the energy and commitment exhibited by earlier generations of ordinary Americans of all races at critical points in our history.

Any analysis or description of a group—particularly as large a group as a race of people—has its limits and exceptions. No group is monolithic. Nevertheless, based on existing research and on what we heard and learned, there are some statements and conclusions about people in specific racial groups and their experiences in America that are valid more often than not. It is in that context, here and throughout the Report, that we offer our observations.

We begin the next section with a brief discussion of the experiences of the country's native, original populations with the system of racial domination. This is followed with a discussion of slavery and its aftermath, a discussion of Latinos and Asian Pacific Americans, and, finally, a brief reference to white immigrant and ethnic groups. These synopses are not intended to substitute for the comprehensive, complex histories of misuse, oppression, conquest, and slavery that many groups have experienced as they have voluntarily or by force migrated to this country. It is designed to highlight the long legacy of mistreatment that is so easy to forget while permitting us to the discuss the many contributions and positive changes that have occurred as racial and ethnic groups have adapted to and been assimilated into our society. Although there is a story of America that as a country has made great progress in racial accommodation, it is, we believe, essential to recall the facts of racial domination.

The events discussed are not treated in a comprehensive manner. Rather, they are meant to be signposts of historical episodes that have greatly influenced our attitudes about race. The very complexity of our task in this limited context highlights the very real difficulties of those who wish to engage constructively in racial reconciliation.

The American Indian and Alaska Native Experience Demonstrates the Complexity of Racial Relationships

Our understanding of America's racial history and its significance within the context of our larger history often is impeded by complex relationships and competing, sometimes contradictory, principles and values. The experience of American Indians and Alaska Natives is a powerful example of this complexity and contradiction.

We had a unique opportunity to meet with and learn from American Indian and Alaska Native tribal government leaders and members throughout the year. Board member Bob Thomas recently made this observation about American Indians and Alaska Natives:

> *Their history is unique, their relationship with our State and Federal governments is unique, and their current problems are unique. While not large in numbers, their situation tugs at my heart. I confess to being embarrassed this past year at my lack of knowledge of their overall situation. Embarrassed because I actually grew up and worked much of my life in geographic areas populated by Indian tribes, and I was oblivious to all but the common stereotypes. I suspect that most Americans are as equally oblivious, and believe a focused 'education' initiative [for] the American public is in order.*

On virtually every indicator of social or economic progress, the indigenous people of this Nation continue to suffer disproportionately in relation to any other group. They have the lowest family incomes, the lowest percentage of people ages 25–34 who receive a college degree, the highest unemployment rates, the highest percentage of people living below the poverty level, the highest accidental death rate, and the highest suicide rate.

American Indians and Alaska Natives have both a distinctive and extraordinarily complex status in the United States. They are the only minority population with a special relationship with the United States—one that has been developed over a 200-year period. It was crafted from an enormously varied set of indigenous societies, a massive European immigrant population, and the separate laws of each. The more than 550 American Indian and Alaska Native tribes are home to people who are both U.S. citizens and members of tribes that are sovereign nations.

Sovereignty as an independent political entity means that, like any Nation, they have geographic, land-based boundaries. No other racial minority in this country has a land base of over 56 million acres in mostly reservation land held in trust in the continental United States, with an additional 40 million acres in Alaska. Like any other nation, the relationship of tribal governments with the Federal Government is defined by the United States Constitution; treaties; executive orders; congressional acts; Federal, State, and tribal court judgments; and programs administered by all Federal agencies. Within reservation boundaries, American Indians are subject to tribal *and* Federal laws, but *not* the laws of contiguous States without tribal consent.

The significance of sovereignty to American Indians and Alaska Natives cannot be overstated. In a statement provided to the Board, tribal leaders of the Hualapai Indian Tribe described the importance of sovereignty and its relationship to race and racism:

> *[We] wanted to touch on a few key points for an understanding of how racism manifests itself against Indian tribes. . . . As Indian people, we have survived years of persecution—in what can only be understood today as a combination of racism and greed . . . we have survived as a Tribe. Our sovereign status is therefore not only a political status, recognized from the earliest days of European settlement in the United States, it is also key to our existence as Indians. Accordingly, the most virulent and destructive form of racism faced by Indian people today is the attack on our tribal sovereignty.*

Recently, Indian tribes have had to respond to questions about tribal sovereignty in the U.S. Congress. During the 105th Congress, Senate Bill 1691 was introduced that would provide, among other things, a waiver of tribal sovereign immunity. One tribe, the Pueblo of Laguna, has described this legislation as today's versions of the forced marches and allotments of years past because it attacked the foundations of tribal sovereignty and tribal Federal relations. The resolution of this issue promises to strain relations between the U.S. Government and Indian nations.

Few Americans have had an opportunity to learn about the indigenous people of America in a way that extends beyond the most simplistic, widely perpetuated stereotypes of Indians. Based on the experiences of the Board members during the year, it appears that little, if any, correct information about tribal governments is taught in most schools. This lack of understanding is particularly problematic when it involves those who are responsible for developing and implementing government policies and programs—at the Federal, State, and local levels.

Race and racism affect American Indian and Alaska Native communities in ways similar to their effect on other non-white and Hispanic minorities in America. Deeply entrenched notions of white supremacy held by European immigrants were applied to American Indians and Alaska Natives, who were regarded as inferior and "uncivilized." Therefore, access to opportunities has been limited, and American Indians and Alaska Natives have experienced exclusion and isolation from rights and privileges often taken for granted by most white citizens. They have become America's most invisible minority.

There have been some indicators of progress in redressing the shortfalls of history, such as President Clinton's 1994 reaffirmation of the Federal Government's commitments to operate within a government-to-government relationship with federally recognized American Indian and Alaska Native tribes, and to advance self-governance for such tribes. He also directed Federal agencies to build a more effective working relationship with tribes, consult with them openly and candidly, and fully consider their views prior to undertaking actions that may affect their well-being.

African Americans and the Unique Legacy of Slavery

Blacks have been subjected to long-term and systematic social and economic discrimination since their arrival on these shores. The African American experience is unique because of constitutionally sanctioned and governmentally enforced slavery and its legacy. However, discrimination directed against blacks began even before slavery was institutionalized. This discrimination reflected negative attitudes about race and color that were to remain in place from the 17th century to the present.

In many respects, the plight and history of blacks has commanded more attention than the history and treatment of other American racial minorities. This is true for a number of reasons. African Americans have constituted the largest American minority community for more than two centuries. An enormous body of thought was developed and propagated to justify their enslavement; out of this the negative stereotypes, myths, and superstitions about race were born. The only Civil War fought in the United States was over slavery and its economic importance to the Southern States.

For most blacks, the period following the Civil War and Reconstruction was a repudiation of the principles and values of the Constitution as they applied to Americans of African descent. Even as citizens, blacks were denied by law in the Southern States and by social custom in the North and West practically all the rights and privileges of American citizenship enjoyed by whites. This was accomplished in a systematic and complete way. In spite of the 13th, 14th, and 15th Amendments of the Constitution, the deeply ingrained ideology of white supremacy continued to impose upon black citizens the badge of inferiority and closed off most opportunities for them to assimilate as equals in American society.

Throughout the Initiative year, Board members frequently were asked if we would support a formal apology for slavery by either the President or Congress. Advocates for an apology maintained that this is a necessary step in the racial healing process for the country. We have given this issue considerable thought over the course of the year. We conclude that the question of an apology for slavery itself is much too narrow in light of the experience of blacks over the course of this Nation's history. Discrimination and racism directed against blacks have been unparalleled in terms of scope and intensity, not only during the period of slavery but also during the century following its demise. The period of slavery in this country represents a National tragedy from many perspectives.

Unless we take forceful steps to eliminate the consequences of this awful history of racism, they will continue to blight our Nation's future. The apology we must all make cannot be adequately expressed in words but in actions. We must make a collective commitment to eliminate the racial disparities in opportunity and treatment that characterize too many areas of our National life.

Perpetuation of the Badge of Inferiority

Latinos. Every minority group in America has a distinct and unique historical experience with racism and oppression. The early connections of American Indians, Alaska Natives, African Americans, Asian Pacific Americans, and Puerto Ricans and other Latinos to the United States are fundamentally different. Latinos trace earlier presence in the United States to either conquest or immigration. In 1848, with the end of the United States' war against Mexico, thousands of people living on land that was formerly part of Mexico became subjects of the United States. Similarly, Puerto Ricans became part of the United States by conquest in 1898. Puerto Ricans, like Mexican Americans, were bound by their language and culture and, although Americans by conquest, remained native to their geographical homeland. All groups, however, experienced marginalization and discrimination in the United States.

Hispanics are currently the second largest minority group in the United States; more than 1 in 10 Americans, or 10.7 percent, are Hispanic. Latinos are also one of the fastest growing populations and are expected to become the largest "minority" group by 2005. Latinos are now roughly 12 percent of the labor force and are expected to become almost 40 percent of new labor force entrants. About one in three Hispanics (30.3 percent) live in poverty, compared with 29.9 percent of blacks and 11.2 percent of whites as of 1990.

There have been a number of fundamental historical events which have helped shape the course of the relationship of the white population in the U.S. to its Mexican American neighbors. Foremost among them was the war against Mexico in the 1840s. In 1848, at the conclusion of the war, the U.S. and Mexico signed the Treaty of Guadalupe Hidalgo, in which the U.S. absorbed Texas, California, and the southwest. The U.S. occupied Mexico City in early 1848 and then ceded this territory for the modest payment of $15 million to Mexico. General Winfield Scott wrote at the time that during the war American soldiers "committed atrocities to make heaven weep and every American of Christian morals blush for his country." The former secretary of state of the Republic of Texas commented:

> The two races, the Americans distinctively so called, and the Spanish Americans or Mexicans, are now brought by the war into inseparable contact. No treaties can henceforth dissever them; and the inferior must give way before the superior race.

This experience of exclusion and discrimination has continued for other Hispanics who have come to the United States in large numbers since the late 1950s (Cubans) to the present record levels of immigration from Central American countries. It is critically important that the country be committed to including the historical experiences of Hispanics and other minorities within a comprehensive framework of our Nation's history if we are ever able to achieve one America. This is especially true with Latinos; according to the Census Bureau, they will become the largest minority group in America in the next century.

Asian Pacific Americans—The Perpetual Foreigners. The treatment of Asian Pacific Americans as non-white, non-European immigrants was similar to that of other non-white minority groups. For example, Native Hawaiians, following the conquest of the Hawaiian Islands in 1893, experienced the same type of racial and cultural subordination that Puerto Ricans experienced. Only in the past few years have the Native Hawaiian people gained recognition as a significant force in reclaiming their place in negotiations over such issues as land rights, cultural preservation, health care, and education in their native geographical homeland.

Although most Americans believe that Asian Pacific Americans are new to this country and have only recently affected the Nation's conversation and debate on race, Asian Pacific Americans have been shaping the discussion since the last half of the 19th century. Those who were immigrants were often thought of as a source of cheap labor. Discriminatory laws and in formal sanctions during those early years limited the economic opportunities of Asian Pacific Americans and excluded them from certain occupations. They were also prevented from establishing families and owning land in the early 1900s. The first Asian Pacific American immigrants thus were relegated to jobs as agricultural and factory laborers or owners of small businesses such as laundries, restaurants, and grocery stores that required little capital and few English language skills.

While discriminatory laws have limited economic opportunities for Asian Pacific Americans, America's long history of limiting the ability of Asian immigrants to become citizens and obtain the full benefits of citizenship has had an even more significant impact. These laws limiting citizenship and naturalization worked in tandem with seemingly neutral laws such as those that prohibited aliens from owning land to discriminate against Asian Pacific Americans. The internment of Japanese Americans was the most extreme of the discriminatory laws passed that treated Asian Pacific Americans as outsiders and foreigners who should be questioned about their loyalty. Even today new immigrants, many from other regions of Asia, such as the Phillippines, Vietnam, Laos, and Cambodia continue to feel the legacy of discriminatory laws against Asian Pacific Americans because they continue to be perceived and treated as foreigners.

Each of the minority groups discussed above share in common a history of legally mandated and socially and economically imposed subordination to white European Americans and their descendants. Such subordination has had powerful consequences for us as a Nation, which are manifested in the racial disparities discussed in Chapter Four.

However, our interaction with thousands of Americans of all races during the year has taught us that the blatant and egregious forms of prejudice and discrimination that were routine even three decades ago are not as frequent in contemporary society. Racial discrimination is still a fact of life—although it often is subtle. What clearly remain are significant barriers to opportunity. Barriers such as racially isolated and underfunded schools and deeply embedded racial stereotypes about the capacity, motivation, and ability of minorities have earlier roots deep in the past but have the capacity to shape our future unless we act as a community to eliminate them. Many Americans are searching for answers on how to achieve that result.

The White Immigrant Experience

Another experience that is important to the building of America is that of the white immigrant and the impact of ethnic difference on one's ability to assimilate into American society. For immigrants from countries such as Ireland or Poland, the process of assimilation often was fraught initially with discrimination in employment and disenfranchisement at the polls. After these groups gained some empowerment through the political process, social acceptance followed. For other groups with strong religious identification, such as those who were Jewish or Catholic, some degree of social exclusion, discrimination, and disenfranchisement was common, with social acceptance slower to follow. More recent immigrants, many of them Muslim, are only now undergoing the immigrant experience, and old world antagonisms fueled by new world rivalries slow the prospects for inclusion and acceptance of these groups.

The point is that any group that enters a new country has had to face a barrage of barriers, whether language or religion or unfamiliar customs. The greatness of the American experience has been the opportunity for immigrants from every other country to become active participants in our political process. However, we also recognize that race and color have added significantly to the difficulty of some groups to gain acceptance as Americans with full rights of citizenship.

Americans Hold Conflicting Views on Race and Racial Progress

While most minorities and people of color recognize the role of the legacy of race and color in their experiences, many whites do not. The Board found that the story of race at the end of the 20th century and into the 21st century is a story of conflicting viewpoints. Americans—whites, minorities, and people of color—hold differing views of race, seeing racial progress so differently that an outsider could easily believe that whites and most minorities and people of color see the world through different lenses. Whites and minorities and people of color also view the role of government in extremely divergent ways, especially with respect to the government's role in redressing discrimination.

Another element of contradiction, if not conflict, is the way in which America functions as a Nation of great optimism, tolerance, and inspiration focused on creating a more stable and diverse community, although discrimination, racial and ethnic oppression, and a smaller number of instances of outright racial evil persist. We are a country in racial transition; some of us welcome the change, others are unaware of or fear the change and its ramifications, while a few cling to an older order in which racism is so comfortably ingrained that it is simply characterized as "the way it is."

Differing Attitudes

According to numerous polls and surveys that we reviewed, most whites believe that much of the problem of racial intolerance in this country has been solved and that further investigation is unwarranted and inappropriate. Polls also show that most Americans have a distorted view of who we are as a Nation and are intolerant of some racial groups other than their own. A poll released by the Washington Post, Kaiser Family Foundation, and Harvard University revealed surprisingly uninformed views on the racial composition of America and the negative views that each minority group holds toward one another. A 1997 Gallup poll pointed out, "From the white perspective, there are fewer race problems, less discrimination, and abundance of opportunity for blacks, and only minimal personal prejudice." Another 1995 poll by the *Washington Post* revealed that only 36 percent of whites believe that "past and present discrimination is a major reason for the economic and social problems" facing blacks.

A contradictory image of race in this country is clearly held by a large majority of blacks and Hispanics. Numerous civil rights cases and social science reports carefully document this stark difference in viewpoints. Legal analyst Richard Delgado offered an explanation: "White people rarely see acts of blatant or subtle racism, while minority people experience them all the time." Research by psychologists echoes that conclusion:

> [W]e [white Americans] tend to see racism as not a problem and particularly not a problem for us. . . . However, from the perspective of the people of color . . . [t]hey experience the consequences of subtle biases on a daily basis. [T]hey see a discrepancy between what we say overtly, which is about fairness, and justice, and equality, and the subtle biases that pervade our society, and the way whites behave. . . . [C]reat[ing] a situation of distrust, where they don't believe whites and where they tend to see this bias everywhere.

Evidence presented to the Board makes it clear that many whites, in general, are unaware of how color is a disadvantage to most members of other groups. For example, at the September Board meeting, Dr. Lawrence Bobo of Harvard University observed:

> In many ways, the centerpiece of the modern racial divide comes in the evidence of sharply divergent beliefs about the current level, effect, and very nature of discrimination blacks and Latinos, and many Asian Americans as well, feel it and perceive it in most domains of life. Many whites acknowledge that some discrimination remains, yet tend to downplay its contemporary importance. . . . However, minorities not only perceive more discrimination, they see it as more institutional in character.

A number of experts raised the sensitive issue of "white privilege"—institutional advantages based on historic factors that have given an advantage to white Americans. To understand fully the legacy of race and color with which we are grappling, we as a Nation need to understand that whites tend to benefit, earlier unknowingly or consciously, from this country's history of white privilege. Examples include being able to purchase an automobile at a price lower than that available to a comparable minority or person of color; not being followed through department stores by clerks or detectives who seemingly follow almost all young Hispanic and black men; being offered prompt service while minorities and people of color are often still refused service or made to wait. White privilege can impact all aspects of life, as Dr. James Jones stated: "While whites are generally privileged or at least given the benefit of the doubt, too often persons of color are simply doubted." One of the lessons of our experience is the significant degree of unawareness by whites today of the extent of stereotypes, discrimination, and racism. One of our conclusions is the importance of educating all people of the continuing existence of prejudice and privilege. These invisible benefits need to be acknowledged by all as a vital and consequential feature of our society.

Moving in the Right Direction

If there has been a constant theme in our meetings over the year, it is this: Persistent racial disparities and discrimination remain. *Changing America: Indicators of Social and Economic Well-Being by Race and Hispanic Origin*, a report compiled by the White House Council of Economic Advisers, is being released in conjunction with this Report. These indicators of social and economic well-being by race present evidence that although progress has been made, significant racial disparities and discrimination continue despite more than 30 years of civil rights laws and some progress directly attributable to affirmative action and other programs.

Those who argue that there has been no change, however, and that racism is an unchanging fixture in American life are, in our observation, incorrect. Research revealed steadily improving racial attitudes, especially among whites, over the past four decades. It is fair to say that there is a deep-rooted national consensus on the ideals of racial equality and integration, even if that consensus falters on the best means to achieve those ideals. For example, local police and the Federal Bureau of Investigation aggressively pursued the investigation of the murder of James Byrd and death threats to 60 University of California at Irvine students with

Asian surnames, and there was a recent conviction obtained in the 30-year-old cases involving Klan-related murders of Medgar Evers and Vernon Dahmer.

Many tangible examples of racial progress exist, from the integration of the military to the numbers of minority-elected officials compared with 30 years ago, from the freedom of minorities and people of color to use public accommodations to the reduction of racial hostility when minorities and people of color seek to rent or buy homes, from the growing minority middle-class to the significant increase in interracial marriages. Discriminatory treatment still persists, but it is often, although not always, more subtle and less overtly hostile.

Too few of us have a real, or less than superficial, understanding of the forces that have resulted in the racial disparities that exist in educational and economic opportunity. Nor do we have a full or clear understanding of the way societal institutions currently manifest the vestiges of past discrimination and racist behavior. Many believe that racial discrimination is a thing of the past—the distant past at that. Yet, many also sincerely believe that racial inequality and racial disparities in education and employment are the result of lack of capacity, individual failing, poor family values, the influence of an environment in which personal responsibility is absent, or just plain bad luck. Although all of those factors may play a role with respect to specific individuals, the fact that minorities and people of color experience certain life conditions far more negatively than non-minority citizens offers powerful evidence that the consequences of a long history of discrimination, prejudice, and unequal treatment have not been adequately addressed in our society.

It is essential that we recognize the continuing impact of our history on today's world. We must be equally aware of the increasingly diverse Nation in which we live—which we discuss in Chapter Three—so that proposals for addressing discrimination and disparities reflect the issues and needs of a changing society.

The Changing Face of America

With few exceptions, the challenges and issues that the Advisory Board confronted in its meetings, dialogues on race, reports, and correspondence, while often complex, were not new. What has changed and will continue to change is the extent of our racial and ethnic diversity.

Thirty-three years ago, in 1965, President Johnson wrote in the foreword to a journal exploring the state of race relations:

> Nothing is of greater significance to the welfare and vitality of this Nation than the movement to secure equal rights. . . . No one who understands the complexity of this task is likely to promote simple means by which it may be accomplished. [The] . . . effects of deprivation [are interlocking]—in education, in housing, in employment, in citizenship, in the entire range of human endeavor by which personality is formed.

> If we are to have peace at home, if we are to speak with one honest voice in the world—indeed, if our country is to live with its conscience—we must affect every dimension of the [black American's] life for the better.

President Johnson and society's focus then was almost exclusively black/white. Sixteen years later, in 1981, President Johnson's 1965 statement about the plight of blacks was cited again in the same journal. However, in addition to confirming its continued relevance, the journal's editor noted that the issues raised by the President had grown even more insistent and complex. Importantly, the discussion in 1981 was expanded to include not only blacks but also American Indians and Alaska Natives, Mexican Americans, and Puerto Ricans; "four peoples—the 'victims' of conquest—men and women who did not choose America, who have long suffered exclusion and discrimination because of their origins, live overwhelmingly in conditions substantially different from those common to other groups in the United States."

In 1998, although we have made a great deal of progress, Americans are still divided by racial and cultural barriers. Our challenge is to see the barriers that remain as opportunities for learning, not as obstacles to common interests. We believe it is a challenge that can be met.

To be successful, however, we as a Nation first need to understand the changing face of America and the implications of the changes on how we think about race and race-related issues and how we improve race relations and become one American community in the new millennium. Trends indicate that as we move into the 21st century, we can anticipate an even more significant shift in the racial and ethnic profile of the American population, making reconciliation even more urgent.

A Nation in Racial Transition

From before its founding, through its expansion and colonization, and through immigration, this Nation has always had a diverse mix of races, cultures, and ethnic groups. This diversity is greater now than at any time in our history. America's native populations alone include more than 550 American Indian and Alaska Native tribes with distinct cultures, speaking more than 150 different languages—only a fraction of whom the Board was able to reach during its tenure. The Hispanic population comprises individuals of different cultures, national origins, and color. For example, people with family roots in Spain, Cuba, Mexico, the Dominican Republic, Argentina, and other Central and South American countries (e.g., Honduras, Columbia, Peru, and El Salvador) are considered Hispanic. Similarly, the Asian Pacific American category covers a large number of ethnic groups who also have distinct languages. Indians, Pakistanis, and Sri Lankans from South Asia are grouped together with Chinese, Japanese, and Koreans from East Asia. Also included in this group are Southeast Asians (such as Vietnamese, Hmongs, and Laotians) as well as Pacific Islanders (such as Fijians, Samoans, and Guamanians).

The black population is equally diverse. Although a majority of African Americans are native born, an increasing number of people who are considered blacks are immigrants from Africa and the West Indies. Of course, this heterogeneity within racial groups is not a new phenomenon. Whites have always included people of diverse ethnic, language, and national backgrounds. Europeans from different regions as well as people from the Middle East are classified as white for the purposes of data collection but obviously represent distinct groups.

During our meeting in September 1997, we heard from demographers who described the current United States population and the expected future racial composition of the population in the next 50 years. Today, as of the 1990 Census, the face of America is almost 73 percent white, 11 percent Hispanic, 12 percent black, 4 percent Asian Pacific American, and 1 percent American Indian and Alaska Native.

Census projections indicate that in the 21st century, America's racial landscape will continue to shift. In 2050, the population in the United States is projected to be approximately 53 percent white, 25 percent Hispanic, 14 percent black, 8 percent Asian Pacific American, and 1 percent American Indian and Alaska Native. (See "Racial/Ethnic Composition of the Population" at the end of the document.) Almost two-thirds of the U.S. population growth over the next 50 years most likely will come from immigrants, their children, and their grandchildren. Both Census Bureau and Immigration Naturalization Service (INS) statistics reveal that the overwhelming majority (almost three-fourths) of the new immigrants to the United States are Hispanic or Asian Pacific Islander.

According to recent Census Bureau reports, the United States now has, for the first time, more Hispanic children under age 18 than it does black children. Hispanic children have grown from only 8 percent of the population in 1980 to 15 percent in 1998. Census Bureau estimates that by the year 2020, 20 percent of all children under 18 years of age will be of Hispanic origin, while black children will constitute 17 percent of this age group. Another example of dramatic demographic change is that of Asian Pacific Americans, which was less than 1 percent of the total U.S. population in 1970. The Census Bureau estimates that this population will grow to 8 percent in 2050, representing the greatest percentage change of any racial group for that period.

Racial Designations Are Growing More Complex

The country's growing diversity will be influenced by the increasing number of intermarriages. Americans are marrying persons of different races at increasing rates. While second-generation immigrants often intermarry, third generation intermarriage is even more frequent.

U.S. Census 1990 data for people ages 25–34 indicate that almost 32 percent of native-born Hispanic husbands and 31 percent of native-born Hispanic wives had white spouses. Thirty-six percent of native-born Asian Pacific American men married white women, and 45 percent of Asian Pacific American women espoused white men. A majority of American Indian and Alaska Native men and women married white spouses and had the highest rates of intermarriage. In the 25–34 age group, 8 percent of black men and 4 percent of black women married individuals of another race. The percentage of whites intermarrying was smaller than that of blacks.

In our view, rates of intermarriage are important for two reasons. They measure social interaction between persons of different races *and* they complicate the way the offspring of these marriages may identify themselves by race. The U.S. Census has only recently allowed individuals to identify themselves by race using more than one racial category. It remains to be seen how offspring of racial intermarriage will identify themselves. This uncertainty casts doubt on whether the demographic changes predicted by the U.S. Census, based on the trends of previous years, will be fully realized. Indeed, the concepts of race and the language we use to discuss our diversity today may change as fast and dramatically as our diversity itself.

There are no easy metaphors or key slogans to describe what we are becoming. In the travels of the Board and through discussions with people across the Nation, it was apparent that people struggle to attach a new metaphor to the changing demography. The metaphors of a "melting pot" and "mosaic" are inadequate given what we know today. The melting pot suggests a loss of identity, and mosaic suggests that people will never come together but instead will maintain rigid separation. Instead, we are becoming a new society, based on a fresh mixture of immigrants, racial groups, religions, and cultures, in search of a new language of diversity that is inclusive and will build trust.

Searching for a New Language of Diversity

The changing face of America has serious implications for how we will talk about race in the future. We know, as Dr. James Jones stated during an early Board meeting, that race is a "social, not a biological construct," and that "race is a term whose use and impact is far more consequential to those who have been targets of hostile actions than those who have perpetuated them or been the incidental beneficiaries of their consequences."

There is no simple way to say what race or racial groupings mean in America because they mean very different things to those who are in and those who are out of the target "racial" group. At a Board meeting in San Jose, California, we were criticized for not including European Americans. When two Board members who are white indicated that they were descendants of Europeans, the critic denied that they were capable of speaking for European Americans, but when questioned was unable to explain with clarity why he felt that was so.

We have seen in our own lifetimes how social changes can influence the way we understand and talk about race. For example, most Americans have learned that it is inappropriate to use the terms "Colored" or "Negro" to refer to blacks or "Oriental" to refer to Asian Pacific Americans. It is also no longer an acceptable social norm to use derogatory racial epithets or caricatures, even though, regrettably, a few people continue to use them.

Further, many individuals want to identify themselves differently than society does. They bear the brunt of criticism by those who believe those individuals want to deny affiliation with particular racial groups. For example, Tiger Woods, the dynamic young golfer and the youngest player to win the prestigious Masters tournament, recognizes the contributions of both his mother's (Asian) and father's (black and American Indian) ancestors to his racial identification and has been criticized for searching for an alternative label for himself.

Racial groupings may be inadequate because individuals are uncomfortable with the breadth of the categories. For instance, many Americans of Asian Indian descent are uncomfortable with the use of the category Asian Pacific American to describe themselves or are uncertain if the term encompasses them. Cubans do not have the same culture as immigrants from Spain or El Salvador. Similarly, blacks who are immigrants from Caribbean countries or who have strong roots in the Caribbean are often more comfortable being described as Caribbean American than African American. In many cases, Arab Americans chafe at being labeled white, because this characterization ignores that Arab Americans are a diverse group of people. Even many members of white ethnic groups view the use of their ethnic origin in describing themselves (e.g., Italian Americans or Irish Americans) as an important aspect of who they are. Racial categories, although useful and necessary to track discrimination, often get in the way of both a clear analysis of facts and a clear-headed dialogue about what individual cultures offer to the community and country as a whole.

The country has moved toward new, as yet unsolidified, ways of thinking and talking about race and ethnicity. Yet there are still troublesome examples of racist activity: racially motivated hate crimes, the continued use of American Indians as mascots, and intimidation by white supremacist groups. The shifting characteristics of racial and ethnic groupings and their deeper meanings make it hard to have a concrete conversation about what race means to any one group.

Determining the Facts of Racial Diversity

In trying to develop a framework for the study and discussion of race during the year, Board members were aware of a number of reports and studies on the root causes of racial prejudice and its consequences. Two notable studies, Swedish sociologist Gunnar Myrdal's *An American Dilemma* and the Kerner Commission's *Report of the National Advisory Commission on Civil Disorders* described the history and systematic racial discrimination suffered by blacks. The Kerner Commission's dire prediction that we are a "Nation moving towards two societies, one black, one white—separate and unequal" chronicled the deliberate exclusion of Americans of African descent from full participation in American society. During the early months of the Initiative, despite our best efforts to broaden discussions and examinations of race, they seemed to veer almost inevitably to black-white issues. Until recently, most of the data gathered on race by government agencies compared black and white disparities. Searches on the Internet for data about racial categories and issues produce volumes on blacks and increasingly more on Latinos. But finding good sources of trend data beyond the black-white paradigm and recent data beyond Latinos is difficult. The major analytical reports on race in the past have focused primarily on blacks.

America's history of research obscures today's racial realities and issues. In his critique of the continuing and almost exclusive reference to the black-white paradigm in discussions of race, Professor George Sanchez of the University of Southern California made the following observation:

> The history of white on black racism blinds Americans from recognizing any other forms of interracial tensions. Racism against Asian Pacific Americans and Latin Americans is dismissed as either "natural byproducts" of immigrants' assimilation or as extensions of the white-black dichotomy. Moreover, when African Americans perform acts of racism, they are quickly ignored or recast except as a threat to the white dominated society.

America's racial conflict can no longer be confined to a discussion of white versus black. The concerns of Professor Sanchez must be included more often in the conversation on race and in the discussion of solutions. We can approach these issues more constructively if we acknowledge that the success of the modern civil rights movement is considered by many to have been a powerful influence on this country's consciousness about race, and it also helped to encourage more advocacy and activism among other minority communities. However, a more important factor influencing the expansion of the dialogue is the growing complexity and changing demographics of race since the 1960s.

Improve Data Collection

To understand fully the challenges we face in the 21st century, it is essential to improve reporting on America's less visible racial groups: American Indians, Alaska Natives, Native Hawaiians, and all of the subgroups that make up the big umbrella categories of Asian Pacific Americans and Hispanics. Board members often heard anecdotes about individuals feeling "left out" of the discussion because we failed to make appropriate distinctions and references. For example, the experiences of most Vietnamese Americans are different from those of Korean Americans or Japanese Americans. Yet, all fall under the category "Asian-Pacific American."

Puerto Ricans have experiences that are distinct from Cubans. Guatemalan Americans have a history different from Mexican Americans. In this case, all are Latinos or Hispanics in the demographic tables.

Steps are being taken to close the data gap. For the first time, a fact book has been published that documents differences in well-being by race and ethnicity in seven broad categories: population, education, labor markets, economic status, health, crime and criminal justice, and housing and neighborhoods. The book *Changing America: Indicators of Social and Economic Well-Being by Race and Hispanic Origin* was produced by the Council of Economic Advisers in consultation with the Federal statistical agencies in response to this Initiative. The information provides a benchmark for measuring future progress and highlights priorities for reducing disparities across racial and ethnic lines. It is only the first effort to identify such indicators; we hope they will be improved in the next few years. As we discuss in Chapter Five, these indicators can serve as the basis for a periodic report card on racial progress.

424 Section 5 Identity, Globalization, and Contemporary Struggles

In addition, the National Research Council, the research arm of the National Academy of Sciences, will convene a conference in October 1998 to examine past and emerging trends for different racial and ethnic groups in key areas, including health, education, employment, and the administration of justice. Researchers will submit papers summarizing social science evidence on these trends for whites, blacks, American Indians, Alaska Natives, Hispanics, Asian Pacific Americans, and others, and how the trends have been affected by public policy. The conference also will identify key gaps in research and data that need to be filled to promote a clear understanding of race-related issues.

The story of race in America is a story of transition. That we have changed and will continue to change is inevitable—how we make this transition is the story to be written and is within our control. Armed with more complete data, good will, and resources, we will be better able to identify problems, focus on our challenges, and establish our policy priorities. We also will be better equipped to learn and talk about our diversity in school, at work, and at home. We have good reason to know about all of America's faces because wherever we came from, and however long ago, we are moving into the 21st century together.

The next chapter is an assessment of the challenges we face and must meet if we are to sustain the forward movement of recent years in resolving the "problems of the color line" in America. Those challenges are not new, but they are more complex. As we have described, the face of America has changed and will change even more dramatically in the next half century.

We believe the recommendations that follow represent a downpayment on our future success as a multiracial, internally strong, and globally competitive democracy.

Forging a New Future

The recommendations in this Report to the President are intended to preserve the integrity of the principles that lie at the core of our democracy: justice, equality, dignity, respect, and inclusion. It is with these principles in mind that the Advisory Board acted on behalf of the President in this year-long effort. At times, we were met with doubt, distrust, and even disbelief. The negative reactions often seemed to draw more attention than the positive responses to our work. However, in most instances, our efforts were met with both enthusiasm and appreciation for the leadership and the willingness of the President to undertake this unprecedented initiative.

Literally tens of thousands of Americans shared in dialogues to weave our different, and common, experiences together so that paths toward deeper understanding might emerge. While many of the conversations allowed for greater insight and a shared sense of commitment to find ways to advance race relations, some conversations ended without resolution. But that is the nature of dialogue—a process that invites differing points of view and is open to possibilities yet unrecognized. Regardless of the outcome, we learned that there exists a genuine recognition by many people that the challenges presented by racial and ethnic divides in the country must be met.

This Nation has the capacity to meet these challenges affirmatively and the capacity required to incorporate positively the growing racial and ethnic diversity of its people into the planning for our future well-being and prosperity. We have the capacity to communicate with each other faster and over greater distances using the latest electronic technologies. Factual information about our history, race, and race relations can be accessed with ease, making possible a more constructive dialogue.

The Board further recognizes that the key to our ability to coordinate this communications and problem-solving effort is our capacity to harness the emerging technological advances to ensure that all Americans may participate fully in this unprecedented undertaking.

Mapping the Road to Racial Justice and Equality

If we are to succeed in the mission to create a more just Nation, the Initiative's work must continue. Not only must it continue in name, but it must continue in the spirit with which it began. This year's effort has been vital to laying the foundation for the larger task. We now describe the essential elements we believe must be considered in developing a meaningful long-term strategy to advance race relations in the 21st century. These elements include the following:

- A permanent structure to continue the work of the Initiative.
- A public education program using a multimedia approach.

- A Presidential "Call to Action" to leaders in community, corporate, religious, and government sectors.
- A focus on youth.

All Americans can and should have a role in building on the vision for one America in the 21st century. As part of our final observations and recommendations, we have identified 10 ways that people can participate in this national effort to strengthen our communities and bring all Americans closer together. The final observations that follow address the need for an approach that can capitalize on the work accomplished this year.

The President's Council for One America: Continuing the Work of the Advisory Board

The goal of creating a more just and unified society requires continued leadership from the Office of the President. The momentum that has been created must be guided by the vision of the President as public discourse about race relations continues to expand and public policy recommendations are put into action. The need for such leadership can be most effectively asserted by establishing the President's Council for One America.

Establishing this Council will demonstrate a long-term commitment to the mission of the President's Initiative on Race and will ensure that the work that lies ahead will be coordinated, focused, and productive. Creating a system of accountability in connection with these efforts is of concern to all those who have expressed interest in, and support for, the Initiative. In light of the fact that literally tens of thousands of people across the Nation have been involved in this first year of study and dialogue, with hundreds of programs having been identified as Promising Practices, the establishment of the Council will send a message that the Initiative has been a genuine beginning to a larger, more extensive and ambitious program with respect to the whole matter of race, racial reconciliation, and bridging racial divides.

No one viewed a 1-year time frame as sufficient to begin this conversation, to study race relations, educate the Nation, take action, and achieve concrete, long-lasting results. The more extensive and ambitious program that should be created will be multifaceted and will preserve certain aspects of the initial effort. For instance, future plans should support opportunities for sustained dialogue at all levels, continue to identify leadership being demonstrated in local communities, expand research to include the experiences and analyses of increasingly diverse populations, and continue to educate the public about the facts and myths surrounding racial disparities and the value of our racial diversity.

One way of accomplishing these objectives is to publish a "White House Monograph on the State of Race Relations in America at the End of the 20th Century." We envision the monograph as a set of volumes containing work from a wide range of disciplines. What will make this effort valuable is that it will continue the dialogue and build on the social science research that is currently underway. It will invite deeper examination about the possibilities of racial reconciliation and will permit the commitment and dedication of many individuals to contribute to the creation of an unprecedented, single piece of work. The White House Monograph could be presented to the American people at the end of this term, in the year 2000. It would be a unique, enduring, and unprecedented contribution to the body of literature concerning America's conversation about race relations at the turn of this century. It would also become the basis for public policymaking as we enter the 21st century.

The Council can be responsible for identifying contributing sources and coordinating the selection, reviewing, and editing of the articles to be included in the series. The final product will be of value to future generations of Americans who wish to study, understand, and gain insights about how race has influenced our history and the development of public policy and become a guide to future actions.

Although a substantial amount of the Council's work would be associated with the process of publishing the monograph, it would have several critical ongoing functions. The Council would coordinate and monitor the implementation of policies designed to increase opportunity, eliminate racial disparities, and would be authorized to propose policies that recognize the enormous impact that improving educational and economic opportunity will have on easing racial tensions. There is a tremendous need to continue dialogue about expanding opportunities because there are so many useful but underutilized strategies that can be pursued. The vital cross-sections among race, education, and economic status was emphasized by members of the public and experts who appeared before the Board during the year. Clearly, there is a need to support innovative and new research that takes into account our diverse population mix and the cost to the Nation of untapped and underutilized human resources because of discrimination and the vestiges of past discrimination.

Another primary function of the Council would be to promote and expand the work associated with Promising Practices, which includes the dialogue that is so critical to racial reconciliation. Many local efforts need assistance to find resources; to replicate, expand, or improve their programs; and to share their experiences with other communities. Moreover, the thirst for more and better dialogue about race must be met with a substantial effort to increase the number of people to conduct dialogues in other settings. The Council can play a valuable role by outlining a national plan that would expand racial reconciliation activities. Those activities would include identifying resources, providing a bridge to other Federal agencies, motivating community and sector leaders to become engaged, and helping to replicate successful models in different regions of the Nation. In pursuing the goal of expanding the number of people actively engaged in racial dialogue and other racial reconciliation activities, the Council can focus on creating greater opportunities to bring public, private, and nonprofit partnerships together. The desire to pursue more collaboration in this regard was heard frequently throughout the year.

Cabinet members, as well as public members who are not a part of the Administration, should be asked to serve. Bipartisan participation, similar to the model offered by the Glass Ceiling Commission, should be sought in selecting public members. Public members would be drawn from a wide range of sectors, including but not limited to: local governance associations, philanthropy, faith-based organizations, private business, education, and advocacy groups.

The priority of the Council would differ dramatically from those of the Civil Rights Division at the U.S. Department of Justice, the Equal Employment Opportunity Commission, and the U.S. Commission on Civil Rights, those units that already study, monitor, and ensure compliance with our anti-discrimination laws. In contrast, the nature of the Council's work would be to expand on the process started in 1997–1998. This work includes coordinating the White House Monograph; working with the White House and other Federal agencies charged with implementing policies disproportionately affecting racial minorities and carrying out comprehensive civil rights policies; taking the next step with Promising Practices identified over the past year by convening a national meeting; responding to the continuing requests for information about what the Federal Government knows about race in America; and initiating opportunities for greater inclusion in the dialogue that was started. The unique role that the President's Council could play would almost certainly provide added value to the work already being done at the Federal level and would further stimulate the creation of new partnerships between government and non-governmental entities.

Developing a Public Education Campaign Using a Multimedia Approach

The role of print and electronic media in shaping public attitudes, beliefs, and opinions about race is enormous. Despite having only one formal opportunity to discuss media and racial stereotyping, the Board had the benefit of a study conducted by Robert M. Entman on media images of the major racial and ethnic groups in the United States. Additionally, the Board heard repeatedly that more attention should be given to using media strategies in promoting greater understanding about racial diversity in America. Not only should there be a focus on news media, there should also be a focus on entertainment media, in which depictions of protagonists and situational vignettes can be developed in more inclusive and non-stereotypical ways.

A media campaign that has the capacity to effectively disseminate factual information and inspire creative expression should be explored. In addition, it is critical to develop a coordinated media campaign. Its focus should be to pay tribute to the many contributions of Americans from different racial and ethnic backgrounds to emphasize our common values and principles as a Nation and to highlight facts about our racial diversity.

A national "report card" on the progress we make toward improving race relations should be part of any media campaign. This effort could build on the publication of the Council of Economic Advisers' (CEA's) *Changing America*, on behalf of the Initiative. Many Federal agencies already gather information that illuminates areas where we have succeeded in reducing racial disparities and where improvement is needed. The report card will provide a single source for the data that demonstrates our progress. The data that are most compelling can be distributed and easily incorporated into local or regional campaigns involving public service announcements (PSAs), street flags/signs, airport terminal signs, and so forth. A separate strategy should be delivered to target our new citizens who, during their swearing-in ceremony, often view a film about becoming an American. That film should be updated to include a message about the strength of our nation being derived from our diversity and commitment to principles of our democracy. Presidential authority throughout this campaign, along with bipartisan support, would ensure a broad reach for this effort.

A Call to Action

The Board has only begun the process of advancing our commitment to embrace the multiracial and multi-cultural reality of our Nation. An essential part of any future plan must include, and perhaps even build on, leadership and commitment at the local level. A call to action should be sent from the President to the National Governors Association, U.S. Conference of Mayors, National League of Cities, and National Association of Counties. That call should seek input on how local governments can address the racial and ethnic divides in their communities. The local plans should include approaches that are being currently utilized, the identification of institutional efforts aimed at bridging the racial divide, and recommendations for appropriate Federal action to complement local action.

Because funding almost certainly will be one of the suggestions for appropriate Federal support, the call should incorporate a framework that invites recommendations that outline innovative ways in which grants or matching funds can be made available. Priority should be placed on promoting public/private/nonprofit partnerships that seek to close racial divides. The Council should consider designing a research project that documents and positively reinforces the different ways in which local governments have institutionalized their efforts to improve relationships across racial and cultural divides and, to the extent possible, measure the effectiveness of the different approaches.

As we have stated earlier, there is no single strategy, group, organization, political party, or religion that can single-handedly make racial reconciliation a reality. Creating a more just society must flow from the collaborative efforts of many and from the public will of our populace to give true meaning to the values we espouse. The Federal Government is in a position to promote coalitions that transcend racial and ethnic differences; to address complicated issues related to our domestic and international obligations; to provide moral leadership concerning the need to find common ground among diverse people; and to facilitate collaboration between innumerable organizations, agencies, and individuals working in both the public and private sectors. This call to action should be expanded further to build on the outreach efforts to educational corporate, and religious leaders described in Chapter One.

Focus on Youth

Young people represent our greatest hope for realizing America's promise in the next century. The next step in this process should include a plan to address the many opportunities to work with youth. We urge the President to identify entities that have a commitment to youth leadership development, violence prevention, educational achievement, and the creative arts. Special attention should be given to making sure that the experiences of young people with disabilities, immigrant youth, and high-poverty populations are included.

Other Critical Issues

Throughout this Report, we have made a series of recommendations on many important topics. In addition, there are many other difficult and challenging issues of race that we have been unable to address in the depth that is appropriate to their importance. These are the issues that we now discuss briefly to demonstrate why the dialogue begun by President Clinton must continue. Some of these issues arose during the course of our meetings. Other issues were raised by the public in correspondence received by the Initiative staff. Still others were identified by experts as issues that continue to divide Americans and on which common ground remains elusive.

Civil Rights

Affirmative action retrenchment. As a number of polls have shown, Americans of all races agree that equal opportunity is an important principle of our democracy, but that agreement breaks down over what further actions, such as affirmative action, we should take to resolve the problem of discrimination. Affirmative action, perhaps more than any other contemporary civil rights issue, continues to divide Americans. From its beginnings as an executive policy to level the economic and educational playing fields following civil rights legislation of the 1960s to its current status as a policy that generates resentment by many whites who believe their children are victims of reverse discrimination or by minorities who feel stigmatized by the policy, affirmative action has been controversial.

Public opinion polls show that a majority of Americans of all races still support affirmative action when it is described as a tool to reduce racial discrimination. Yet that support drops significantly when affirmative action is described as racial preferences or a racial spoils system. More recently, it has been used as a political wedge to polarize public opinion. The concept is rarely defined in neutral terms, thus generating inaccurate and misleading discussions of what type of affirmative action programs are still permissible under the U.S. Constitution.

Higher education affirmative action. Recently, the courts have sent conflicting messages on the permissibility of affirmative action in higher education. Since 1978, most colleges and universities have followed the Supreme Court's decision in *Regents of University of California v. Bakke* in designing their affirmative action programs to increase minority admissions. Programs could use race as one factor to promote the educational benefits of racial diversity on campus. In 1996, however, the U.S. Court of Appeals for the Fifth Circuit ruled in *Hopwood v. Texas* that the University of Texas School of Law could not use race as a factor in admissions to law school when white applicants with higher test scores than minority applicants were denied admission; the Supreme Court elected not to review this decision on appeal. Before California voters approved Proposition 209 in 1996, the Board of Regents for the University of California system had voted to end all race-based affirmative action programs in those colleges and universities. When asked to repeal legacy admissions to the State university system (i.e., students admitted because their parents were alumni), the Board of Regents refused to do so.

On the other hand, a Federal judge in Boston recently upheld an affirmative action plan at a popular magnet public school with a highly competitive admissions policy, which used racial diversity as one of its factors for admission to promote the educational benefits of diversity. A disappointed white applicant's challenge to the University of Michigan affirmative action plan also is expected to further cloud the issue of how race may be used to enhance the educational experience. The Michigan case and other appeals will help clarify whether the *Bakke* decision is still good law. The Board is alarmed by the significant drop in black and Latino admissions in elite graduate programs in California and Texas and urges the development of a public education campaign to build a deeper understanding of the value of diversity in higher education.

Voters in the City of Houston voted this year to retain affirmative action by the city government when they voted for Proposition A; a judge in Texas ordered a new vote after a challenge to the language that was used in Proposition A. Voters in the State of Washington will vote later this year on whether to retain affirmative action by the State government. Similar challenges may be expected in other States. The U.S. Court of Appeals for the District of Columbia recently overturned an affirmative action policy maintained by the Federal Communications Commission to ensure racial diversity in the workforce of media outlets; an appeal is expected. Many media firms responded by stating that they would voluntarily continue their affirmative action programs in light of that decision.

This is an area clearly in flux. Board members were repeatedly asked about our views on affirmative action. We support affirmative action as one of many vehicles to identify qualified minority candidates for admission into the Nation's colleges and universities. Affirmative action continues to be a critical and necessary tool for overcoming past discrimination, eliminating disparities in education, and moving us toward the goal of one America. During our November Board meeting, we discussed the value of diversity in higher education, recognizing affirmative action as one tool among many being implemented to promote such diversity on campus. In our corporate forums we discussed affirmative action in the context of employment and contracting practices. We found that many believed diversity in both the classroom and the workplace to be vital to America's future, especially given the growing racial diversity of the Nation. However, we found disagreements over the best ways to promote equal opportunity and to achieve more racial balance in higher education and the workplace.

Critics of affirmative action argue that 30 years of civil rights laws have leveled the playing field and that policies such as affirmative action are no longer needed. Still others argue that non-racial factors such as class or poverty should be used instead of race. However, the data we have reviewed demonstrates that for far too many minorities, a level playing field remains a mirage. It is for these reasons and others that the Board supports the Administration's current policy regarding affirmative action.

In sum, affirmative action will continue to serve as a proxy for the Nation's continuing debate over equality and racial reconciliation. Leadership is needed to forge public consensus on affirmative action. The challenge is to develop public understanding of its value as a tool to achieve racial diversity and improve the public discourse on affirmative action programs. Significantly, a comprehensive study was recently published that presents empirical data on the long-term consequences of considering race in college and university admissions. This represents an opportunity to dispel the myths and misinformation that often dominate the debate and make constructive dialogue difficult. This type of disciplined research must be encouraged in other areas as well. The President and the Council should support, encourage, and facilitate such efforts.

Federal sector employment. Since the 1960s, the Federal Government has had a more representative workforce than many sectors in private industry. More recently, a number of Federal agencies have developed model programs for the recruitment, training, and promotion of their minority workers. They are experimenting with alternative dispute resolution methods to identify and resolve problems before they rise to the level of an Equal Employment Opportunity Commission complaint. On the other hand, the high number of complaints of racial discrimination in Federal agencies suggest that the fact or perception of employment discrimination continues to hamper the career prospects of minority workers. To the extent that additional resources for the Equal Employment Opportunity Commission would allow more prompt resolution of such complaints, the recommendations we have made previously will assist in this process. The Federal Government must ensure that it models the conduct we are encouraging other public and private employers to demonstrate. This issue requires serious consideration, study, and action.

Police misconduct. One of the more emotional issues we confronted during the year was police-community relations. From California to New York, from the Southwest to the Northwest, we heard far too many harrowing stories from minorities and people of color about police misconduct. At the same time, we recognize that the vast majority of police officers perform their jobs with dedication and a commitment to protect all citizens with equal vigor. However, actions by those officers who abuse the civil rights of minorities overshadow the positive actions of dedicated public servants and poison police-community relations. Too often, minorities and people of color view police officers as their enemies rather than as their protectors.

Clearly, this Administration's efforts to institutionalize community policing programs have been extremely helpful in improving relations between the police and minority communities, but more must be done. Police officers need to understand better the communities they serve, and community residents need an opportunity to get to know the police officers who pledge to serve and protect them. Police-community dialogues on a broader scale would help to build a sense of mutual respect and understanding and would help to isolate those police officers who dishonor their badges with their racist behavior.

Dialogue alone will not reverse years of mistrust and violent confrontations. Minorities and people of color demand that law enforcement agencies take more drastic disciplinary action against those officers who consistently violate their civil rights. If officers may routinely abuse minorities in their custody without fear of any real punishment for their actions, then this situation will continue to undermine efforts to improve police-community relations.

Media and Stereotyping

Negative racial stereotyping emerged as a central issue to reducing racial tensions and divisions in America. As the Kerner Commission recognized three decades ago, the media as an institution has both the power to exacerbate such stereotypes or to eradicate them through its work. That Commission exhorted the media to undertake an immediate self-examination of its coverage of the black community and the lack of racial diversity at every level of media. While the media has certainly improved the number of minority reporters, newscasters, producers, and filmmakers since then, a major problem still remains regarding the representation, coverage, and portrayal of minorities on the news, on television, in film, and in other forms of media.

A major study on race and media by a noted expert on this issue made many important observations on the media's treatment of whites, blacks, Latinos, and Asian Pacific Americans that demand further attention, especially in light of the constraints of the First Amendment and the government's ability to address these concerns. We believe it is essential, however, to pursue strategies that could increase public understanding of the media's role in race relations and on racial attitudes.

Two other studies on media and race focused our attention on this area of inquiry. The Center for Living Democracy published a survey showing that the respondents felt that while the national media frequency contributed to the racial polarization in this country, those same media outlets were seldom initiators or supporters of interracial dialogue. In March, 1998, Children NOW released its survey of 1,200 racially diverse children entitled *A Different World: Children's Perceptions of Race and Class in the Media,* in which young people demonstrated their sophisticated view of media images. These children indicated their desire to see all races portrayed "more often, more fairly, more realistically, and more positively." If youngsters, who already watch more television than their elders and receive more political news and current events from television or the Internet than their elders, are not given the tools to distinguish between the transmitted images and reality, then the process of reconciliation will take much longer. These studies, taken together, demonstrate the importance of educating the public about the impact of the role of the media in race relations and on racial attitudes.

Lack of Environmental Justice

Communities of color generally experience increased incidence of health threats associated with toxic pollution and other environmental sources of risk. A 1993 report by the Environmental Protection Agency (EPA) documented significant disparities in exposures to toxics and pollutants, particularly with respect to lead and air pollution. These patterns of environmental risk are correlated with compelling data concerning public health threats to communities of color. For example, the occurrence of childhood asthma, which is closely linked to air quality, is almost twice as high for blacks and three times as high for Puerto Rican children as it is for whites. Further research is needed to understand the precise role of environmental risks as distinct from other risk factors, such as access to health care, prevalence of tobacco use, or other health factors, in these communities.

Perceived and actual disparities in environmental conditions may be part of a more general exclusion from the governmental processes by which environmental priorities, policies, and standards are set. Pursuant to Executive Order 12898, Federal agencies have made a concerted effort to understand and address these types of disparities, and the White House Council on Enviromental Quality (CEQ) has undertaken a series of meetings with communities to respond to the conditions that generate environmental justice concerns and develop better models of community participation in environmental decision making.

Angela Oh represented the Board at an environmental justice meeting on July 10–11, 1998, which was convened by CEQ and the Race Initiative. This meeting, which served as the main vehicle for the Board to learn about environmental justice issues, was held in South Central Los Angeles and focused on concerns in that community. It included presentations from community members as well as small-group meetings with senior policy officials from the U.S. Department, Interior, Justice, Transportation, and the Enviromental Protection Agency.

Community leaders and citizens presented compelling examples of environmental justice concerns and demonstrated that there are often divergent views among the relevant government agencies and even within affected communities about the nature of the problem and the appropriate response. These debates highlight the need for better models for involving communities of color in the process of setting environmental and public health priorities, policies, and standards. In many cases, Federal jurisdiction to address these issues directly will be limited, but Federal leadership to compel State and local governments to pay attention to these issues will be essential.

Education

Bilingual education. During the past year, the State of California, which has the largest population of non-English speaking residents, voted to end bilingual education. To the extent that this issue becomes further politicized, other States with high immigrant populations may elect to follow California's lead. The Board heard from parents in a number of communities with large populations of students with limited-English language proficiency who were concerned about the ability of their children to receive an education if bilingual educations programs are curtailed.

In many instances, students from first generation immigrant homes still need help in acquiring the English language. Almost every survey conducted among immigrant families reveals that acquiring English is a high priority. They understand that language proficiency is the key to success in America. Yet in too many political campaigns, voters are led to believe that immigrant families are reluctant to learn English. Bilingual education, when properly implemented, is a valuable tool that permits limited-English proficient students to study math, science, and other basic subjects in their native language. The Board is concerned that the rejection of bilingual education is another indicator of the growing backlash against newcomers to America and, as such, requires a closer examination of how to promote continued support for bilingual education.

This issue should not be about whether new immigrants should learn English. There is little disagreement about that. The issue is how they will learn it and whether we will leave it to the educators to determine the most effective way of teaching English to children of immigrants. Another way we can support English language acquisition is to provide more classes for immigrant adult students, given the long waiting lists for such classes.

Tracking. During our June 1998 meeting, the issue of tracking in public schools emerged as an important issue affecting race relations within multiracial school settings. This is the practice in which children are evaluated during the early years of elementary school in terms of their academic abilities and placed on an academic "track" such as gifted, average, or learning disabled. Parents of minority students believe that their children are not receiving fair evaluations of their abilities, but instead are disproportionately placed in lower tracks to the detriment of their children's academic careers. Some suspect that the ulterior motive behind tracking is not merely to teach children who are at the same level in separate classes (so that slower children do not hamper higher achieving students) but is really to maintain separate schools within integrated settings. This is an old problem that demands renewed attention resolution.

Emerging technology issues. Technology can be enormously useful in bridging the gaps between disparate communities, but it can also widen them if we fail to acknowledge the gaps in access to new technologies. The information now available and the rapidity with which it can be transmitted across the country (and around the world) can facilitate dialogue on race. Chat rooms on the Internet that allow people to communicate without ever knowing each other's racial backgrounds are but one example of how new technologies can overcome negative stereotypes. At the same time, however, the ease of communication also makes it easy for those who would instigate racial hatred to spread their poison as well.

Moreover, the speed with which information technologies are incorporated into every sector of American business and society suggests that the disadvantage minority children currently face will increase in the near future. Minority children who attend schools without computers already are behind their more fortunate counterparts before they even graduate from school. Being competent in math and sciences as well as knowing how to operate computers are just some of the skills high school graduates in the 21st century will be expected to possess. Those without such skills will be left behind in the information revolution.

The key to facilitating constructive dialogue, furthering education about race, and sharing Promising Practices in a coordinated, dynamic way is our capacity to harness these technological advances in communications. We recognize, however, that the issue of technology and race is one that clearly requires more study. We must develop ways to ensure that our new technology becomes an instrument to narrow racial disparities and unify people across racial lines rather than becoming another tool of racial division.

Conflicts Between People of Color

The perpetuation of negative racial stereotyping is not solely within the province of white America. The ability of the dominant society to translate negative racial attitudes into policies and behaviors that adversely affect minorities and people of color has been well-documented. However, people of all races tend to feel prejudice toward and harbor negative racial stereotypes about people who are different from themselves. Focusing all of the attention on stereotypes held by whites and on racist behavior engaged in by certain elements of white America certainly tells only half of the story. Negative racial attitudes between members of different minority groups is just as damaging to racial harmony as that between whites and minorities. However, we will not be able to overcome these negative attitudes no matter whom they are directed against until we are willing to confront prejudice wherever it appears.

International Human Rights

Other countries that are grappling with the challenges posed by increasingly diverse populations are looking to our Nation for leadership. In 1994, the United States ratified the Convention on the Elimination of All Forms of Racial Discrimination ("CERD"), which embodies international standards against racial and ethnic discrimination that are consistent with American laws, values, and goals. Promoting respect for CERD's principles can strengthen America's global leadership and help eliminate racial discrimination on a global basis. The Council should look for opportunities to reference this recognition of the international dimensions of racial and ethnic non-discrimination in resolving domestic race relations problems.

Building a New Consensus

As we noted in Chapter Two, one of the barriers to improving race relations is our lack of knowledge about our collective past. As Board Chairman Dr. Franklin told us at our first meeting, "the beginning of wisdom is knowledge, and without knowledge of the past we cannot wisely chart our course for the future." A common base of knowledge is essential to genuine racial healing. We do not presume to tell teachers how to teach history, but we believe it is vital to our future that the history we teach accurately reflects our history from the perspective of all Americans, not just the majority population.

Teaching a more inclusive and comprehensive history is just one of the ways we may begin to become more comfortable about our Nation's growing diversity. Today, too many people fear the demographic changes that are occurring and too few people understand the strength that our diversity has always provided. On the other hand, minority communities continue to grapple with issues of inclusion or exclusion, which are often expressed in terms of identity politics that seem to reject the notion of common values and ideals. During this delicate period of redefining the American policy, we must exercise extra caution so that we may better understand and value our differences and understand that those differences do not signal disunity but instead reflect an enhanced strength.

Reaching Beyond the Choir

We were quite successful, we believe, in energizing people who are already involved in activities designed to bridge racial divisions—the so-called choir. We do not minimize this accomplishment, because we believe that even the choir needs reinforcement, recognition, and inspiration to sustain their efforts. At the same time, even stronger efforts must be made to reach beyond the choir to—the vast majority of Americans who are people of goodwill, but who fail to recognize the importance to their individual lives and to the lives of their children of overcoming racial divisions and narrowing racial disparities. If America is to achieve her full potential and if our children are to have an opportunity to achieve the same standard of living we have achieved, we must, as Executive Director of the Race Initiative Judith Winston warned, "acknowledge the fact that most Americans are not, and do not consider themselves racist, but they have responses to people who are different than they on the basis of race, that suggest that they have internalized—we have internalized these racist concepts and stereotypes . . . we have to find a way of engaging people, helping people to become engaged in conversations that are not confrontational and that are constructive."

In the past 15 months, we have planted seeds of racial healing, seeds that can erase "the fault line of race." We have traveled to communities in every region of the country to discuss issues of race. While these issues are often laden with emotion, we have tried to move the discussion beyond the polarizing impact of debate to the unifying impact of reasoned dialogue.

For it is reasoned dialogue, and not divisive debate, that ultimately will ease the fault line caused by race and strengthen our resolve to work together to build an American community worthy of the principles and values we espouse.

Ten Things Every American Should Do to Promote Racial Reconciliation

One of the most striking findings from our work is that there are many Americans who are willing to accept that racial prejudice, privilege, and disparities are major problems confronting our Nation. Many of them told us that they would welcome concrete advice about what they should do. To fill that need, we offer a brief list of actions that individual Americans could take that would increase the momentum that will make us one America in the 21st century.

- **Make a commitment to become informed about people from other races and cultures.** Read a book, see a movie, watch a play, or attend a cultural event that will inform you and your family about the history and current lives of a group different than your own.

- **If it is not your inclination to think about race, commit at least 1 day each month to thinking about how issues of racial prejudice and privilege might be affecting each person you come in contact with that day.** The more that people think about how issues of race affect each person, the easier it will be for Americans to talk honestly about race and eliminate racial divisions and disparities.
- **In your life, make a conscious effort to get to know people of other races.** Also, if your religious community is more racially isolated than your local area, encourage it to form faith partnerships with racially different faith groups.
- **Make a point to raise your concerns about comments or actions that appear prejudicial, even if you are not the targets of these actions.** When people say or do things that are clearly racially biased, speak out against them, even if you are not the target. When people do things that you think *might be* influenced by prejudice, raise your concerns that the person or institution seriously consider the role that racial bias might play, even unconsciously.
- **Initiate a constructive dialogue on race within your workplace, school, neighborhood, or religious community.** The *One America Dialogue Guide* provides some useful ideas about how to construct a dialogue and lists some organizations that conduct dialogues and can help with facilitation.
- **Support institutions that promote racial inclusion.** Watch television programs and movies that offer racially diverse casts that reflect the real world instead of those perpetuating an inaccurately segregated view of America. Support companies and nonprofit organizations that demonstrate a commitment to racial inclusion in personnel and subcontracting. Write the institutions to let them know of your support for what they are doing.
- **Participate in a community project to reduce racial disparities in opportunity and well-being.** These projects can also be good ways of getting to know people from other backgrounds.
- **Insist that institutions that teach us about our community accurately reflect the diversity of our Nation.** Encourage our schools to provide festivals and celebrations that authentically celebrate the history, literature, and cultural contributions of the diverse groups that comprise the United States. Insist that our children's schools textbooks, curricula, and libraries provide a full understanding of the contributions of different racial groups and an accurate description of our historic and ongoing struggle for racial inclusion. Insist that our news sources—whether print, television, or radio—include racially diverse opinions, story ideas, analysis, and experts. Support ethnic studies programs in our colleges and universities so that people are educated and that critical dialogue about race is stimulated.
- **Visit other areas of the city, region, or country that allow you to experience parts of other cultures, beyond their food.** If you have an attitude that all people have histories, cultures, and contributions about which you could benefit from learning, it is usually not difficult to find someone who enjoys exposing others to their culture.
- **Advocate that groups you can influence (whether you work as a volunteer or employee) examine how they can increase their commitment to reducing racial disparities, lessening discrimination, and improving race relations.** Whether we are a member of a small community group or an executive of a large corporation, virtually everyone can attempt to influence a group to join the national effort to build one America.

Chapter 60

Black Blame, Barack Obama, and the Future of Black Politics

Melanye Price

Introduction

"Come on people," was both the pleading refrain offered by Bill Cosby during his national Call Out Tour and the title of his book with Harvard physician, Alvin F. Poussaint. In the tour (of mostly black churches) and the book, Cosby extended the narrative he initiated in 2004 at the 50th Anniversary of *Brown v. Board of Education* Gala, in which he called on particular segments of the black community (e.g., the poor, single mothers, and youth) to take responsibility for their destructive life choices and the negative life outcomes that resulted (Cosby and Poussaint 2007). During this speech, Cosby made clear his disappointment that these members of the black community had betrayed the hopes and hard work of previous generations of activists. According to Cosby, "the lower economic and lower middle economic people are not holding their end in this deal."[1] They were letting down the civil rights generation by engaging in a long list of dysfunctional behaviors such as poor parenting, misplaced financial priorities, criminal behavior, giving their children ethnic names, and problematic fashion choices. For instance, in one exchange Cosby offered,

> *in our cities and public schools we have 50% drop out. In our own neighborhood, we have men in prison. No longer is a person embarrassed because they're pregnant without a husband. No longer is a boy considered an embarrassment if he tries to run away from being the father of the unmarried child*

Although Cosby was not the first African American to use tropes of personal responsibility to explain persistent community problems, his initial outburst and subsequent reaffirmation reignited this debate among African Americans.[2] They questioned the veracity of Cosby's comments, whether he had enough moral authority to be the one making them, and whether or not these things needed to be said at all. Ted Shaw, then-director of the NAACP Legal and Education Defense Fund, rose immediately after Cosby to offer a counterpoint to Cosby's assertions. He noted that many of the problems faced by the black community were not of its own making and were the result of discriminatory policies beyond their control.[3] In contrast, Kweisi Mfume, former NAACP head, along with many other black journalists and commentators, agreed with Cosby and gave him credit for saying what needed to be said (Tucker 2004). According to them, Cosby engaged in a tough love conversation with black people, especially certain community members, that was long overdue.

Less than four years later, Barack Obama announced his intention to run for president and began traveling across the country campaigning. While doing so, he made several statements that can be read as Cosby-esque. Rather than reigniting the heated debate over both the message and the appropriateness of the speaker, Obama's comments went largely unchecked. To some extent Obama and Cosby occupied similar social spaces where both the strength of connection to the targets of their critique and their authority to speak to these particular community issues was fragile at best. Cosby's status as a crossover comic with a mostly white audience and Obama's status as a relative newcomer to the national black political scene created some social distance between them and most black people. The difference, however, was that at least with Cosby there was a debate. When the political stake of the presidency came into play, debate was largely silenced and unwelcomed.

The narrative used by both Cosby and Obama represented the most recent remix of an enduring debate over who is to blame for stagnant black progress. This debate is largely based on two points of contention between black blame and system blame (Price 2009). First, there are those who engage in system blame by arguing that persistent inequality is the result of the legacy of slavery and continuing racial discrimination experienced by Blacks that is difficult to overcome. Alternatively, Cosby, Obama, and others acknowledge the history of racism and persistence racial discrimination, but still engage in black blame by assigning the lion's share of the responsibilities to African Americans' dysfunction. That this debate is not new does not diminish its relevance to contemporary political questions. In fact, the question of who is to blame emerged as an important political signifier in the 2008 presidential election, and its employment had real strategic importance for Barack Obama and future black candidates. Its invocation in the 2008 presidential election and beyond also raises important questions about the future of black political mobilization. This essay provides a more detailed understanding of the meaning of black blame, examines Barack Obama's usage of black blame, and explores the political consequences of this usage as it relates to the black community and its political future.

There is no question that Barack Obama used personal responsibility tropes and characterizations of black behavior that qualify as black blame. Whether chiding Blacks for poor parenting, dysfunctional priorities, or being too apathetic, Obama made clear throughout the campaign that there was much work to be done by Blacks themselves to improve community outcomes. The work that he prescribed was not only necessary but a unique set of objectives for African Americans that he did not offer to other racial groups. Instead, he made pointed statements to Blacks about the need, to quote *Chicago Sun-Times* columnist Lynn Sweet (2008), "to shape up." I argue that Obama's use of black blame achieved two rhetorical aims—he demonstrated to ordinary black people that he was connected to them and understood their challenges while signaling to Whites his ability to serve as an objective critic of black behavior. He was able to do these two things simultaneously by invoking black blame as a racial insider at predominantly black events that before the 2008 election were essentially black safe spaces (or the producers of what Michael Dawson (2001) calls the black counterpublic). In black churches and at majority black events he dispensed black blame as if he was engaged in a conversation with a bunch of old friends who needed and didn't mind a good talking to. His rhetorical style and mannerisms took on the tone of a southern Baptist minister rather than a Harvard educated lawyer. He engaged the audience with call and response and other racialized cues. Simultaneously, he was speaking as a racial interlocutor who, like members of other racial groups, questioned the values and priorities of certain segments of the black community. This "talking to" was done within ear and eyeshot of non-Blacks who saw Obama admonishing Blacks for their bad behavior. They saw him telling Blacks to take responsibility for themselves and they knew that Obama understood the problems they see as endemic and widespread amongst Blacks. In short, he tapped into beliefs that are the foundation of modern racial resentment (Kinder and Sanders 1996).

Obama's deployment of black blame coupled with his deracialized campaign style and his characterization of the role of race in contemporary America presents real problems for black politics. During the campaign, he asserted that racism was largely in the past and invoked black blame to indict Blacks who pointed to continuing racism as an inappropriate excuse for failure. Additionally, he equated black reactions to racial prejudices with the frustration of Whites who are disenchanted with the policy and real outcomes of civil rights gains, especially affirmative. When black blame is coupled with this view of American race relations, Blacks and their advocates are placed in the impossible predicament of being marginalized as disgruntled holdovers who cannot release the past or people who are so myopic they cannot see beyond their own narrow struggles to coalesce with likeminded people of other races. Either way the combination creates a hostile environment for making race-specific claims for problems that continue to uniquely plague the African American community.

Defining Black Blame

African-Americans continue to lag substantially behind Whites on most social indicators. Currently, as the United States undergoes its greatest economic crisis since the Great Depression and the unemployment rate hovers around ten percent, African American unemployment rates stand at 16.3%.[4] African Americans are almost three times more likely to live in poverty than Whites, with 35% of Blacks living in poverty and only 13% of Whites.[5] The African-American high school dropout rate is more than double that of Whites.[6] As Blacks, and other Americans, attempt to reconcile core American values with persistent unequal outcomes, it is expected that they also look to assign blame. Who is responsible? Does the conflict between values and reality represent a flaw in the American democratic system? For example, Rogers Smith (1993) asserts that though America national identity is viewed as a prototypical example of a free and equal democracy, it is also steeped in a tradition of discrimination based on "ascriptive hierarchy." Thus, America's democratic tradition has been inextricably intertwined with a tradition of exclusion of certain groups based on their racial and gender characteristics. Blacks who hold this view of the American political system as inherently hostile to black interests, either intentionally or through more benign forms of racial privilege, are more likely to see the American government and its agents as responsible for racial inequality—in other words to engage in *system blame*. Alternatively, can contemporary inequalities be explained by poor choices by Blacks themselves? In the post-civil rights era, where Blacks have more access and opportunity than at any other time in American history, are the efforts of past activists being squandered by consistently misplaced priorities? Those Blacks who view other Blacks as having misused the political capital of the previous generation by making poor choices engage in a process of *black blame*.

The focus here is on black blame and its deployment in the 2008 presidential campaign; however, neither the conceptual framework nor the strategic uses of black blame represent a new development. Inherent in most pursuits of racial uplift has been the judgment (most often by middle class Blacks) that poorer Blacks are not living up to high moral or social standards (Gaines 1996). Even black nationalists who prioritize racial pride believe that most Blacks need to experience some kind of cognitive liberation process in which Blacks purge themselves of internalized standards of black inferiority. Nationalists argue that this false consciousness drives the destructive behavior of Blacks. Black blame or system blame are not mutually exclusive, and presumably, one can believe that the government enacts policies that are hostile to black progress *and* that Blacks (often poor Blacks are the culprit) make choices that also hinder progress. In my research, however, most often people emphasize one or the other and the direction of emphasis has an impact on policy preference and prescriptions they support (Price 2009).

While discussing what black blame is, it is important to also discuss what black blame is not. This examination of black blame does not suggest that its invocation represents some form of self- or community loathing. Nor does it suggest that individuals who use black blame believe that racism has been purged from American society. For instance, black nationalists who sometimes invoke black blame see the poor choices Blacks make as a residual impact of the psychological and social devastation of slavery and Jim Crow (Price 2009). Blacks make bad decisions, but this is, in part, because they have internalized negatives images and racist stereotypes. Once these views are internalized, Blacks make choices that are damaging to their lives and to the life of their community. This example of black blame suggests the opposite of loathing. Rather black nationalists recognize the role of personal choice in individual decision-making, but also see these decisions as part of a larger system of oppression. Additionally, people who use black blame almost exclusively are not ignorant to the existence of racism. They simply subscribe to alternative readings of the role of race and racism in contemporary society. One reading might be that racial prejudices are simply not as strong as they used to be. The goals of the Civil Rights Movement have been largely achieved, and to the extent that racial prejudice continues to be a challenge in American society, it is a view held by a minority of the population. So African Americans' failure to succeed is the result of some other factor and for individuals who invoke black blame, it is attributable to irresponsibility or other character flaws. Another reading acknowledges the existence of racism, but views it as one of many possible obstacles. All people have impediments to overcome, and rather than focusing on racism, African Americans need to focus on making successful life choices. There are more ways to parse this argument but the fundamental premise is that racism is no longer an overarching reason for a lack of black progress.

Discussions of the severity or absence of racial prejudice toward Blacks have garnered significant public attention since Barack Obama began his presidential bid in 2007. Indeed questions of racial authenticity in the black community, whether or not race trumps gender in individual voting calculus, and how one measures racial progress are questions that have been bandied about in the echo chamber of cable network news. Journalists and media personalities asked whether Barack Obama was black enough for black people. Or would black women focus on their gender and vote for Hillary Clinton or their race and vote for Obama? Or did the election of an African American to the presidency signal the transition to a post-racial period in

American society? Interestingly, while the public began a two year period of hyper-focusing on race, the Obama campaign focused on universal themes with a broad cross-racial appeal.

Barack Obama as a Deracialized Candidate

The historic nature of Barack Obama's presidential campaign and subsequent election created opportunities to debate the importance of electing a black president and electing this black man in particular. Obama's campaign was innovative on many fronts. His campaign was able to harness new technologies in ways never seen before and develop a sophisticated campaign machine using new media and social networking tools to disseminate information, recruit volunteers, and mobilize voters. Using this machine, Obama amassed a record campaign fund from more varied sources than any other campaign in history. His campaign raised well over seven hundred million dollars with nearly ninety percent in individual contributions.[7] Throughout the election season, the Obama campaign boasted frequently about the amount of money they raised from small and first-time donors and suggested that this phenomenon signaled a groundswell of grassroots support for his candidacy. By the general election in November of 2008, Obama had achieved rock star status, which was only magnified by the fact that there was a battalion of celebrities who were actively campaigning for him. In addition, young voters, like celebrities, were attracted to his "story" and turned out heavily to volunteer for his campaign and vote for him in the election. In 2008, turnout amongst young voters increased significantly and Barack Obama received nearly seventy percent of the under-30 vote.[8] According to the Pew Research Center young voters participated more broadly in 2008; they attended more campaign events and donated more money than they had in previous years. A major factor may have been that many more youth said they had been contacted by the Obama campaign with nearly a quarter of all youth saying they were either contacted in person or by phone by someone from the Obama campaign (Keeter et. al. 2008).[9] Ultimately Obama won the presidency with 53 percent of the popular vote, and a solid majority among women, first time voters, African Americans, Latinos, and Asians.

African Americans played a key role in the 2008 election. They were a pivotal Democratic voting bloc in southern states where the Democratic Party has largely been abandoned by Whites. As states continued to push their primaries to earlier dates in the election season, South Carolina became an important test of Obama's staying power after his unexpected defeat in New Hampshire. African Americans constituted a majority of Democratic voters in South Carolina, and a third of the voters were African American women (Seelye 2008). Though prior to the election Blacks were split in their support for Obama and Clinton, Obama won South Carolina with a 55 percent majority.[10] Blacks' decision to support Obama gave him a large share of the vote in the Democratic primary and allowed him to remain competitive against Hillary Clinton. It is no secret that Blacks consistently support the Democratic Party in general elections; however, unlike other presidential candidates, Obama received a near unanimous endorsement from African Americans by garnering ninety-six percent of the black vote.[11] Moreover, for the first time ever, African American women had the highest turnout rate of all groups (Lopez and Taylor 2009). African-Americans viewed this election as an important historical moment and were excited about the prospect of voting for the first black president.

An important discussion that emerged post-election centered on the racial meaning of Obama's victory. Almost immediately, the media began to discuss whether or not the country had entered a post-racial period, the suggestion being that the election of a black president demonstrated Whites' ability to see beyond race and simply vote for their candidate of choice. For many, Obama's victory signaled a transitional moment in American history in which its history of African enslavement and racial prejudice was replaced by a period of racial openness and true adherence to the American ideals of freedoms and equality. While his blackness portended much for racial tolerance, Obama's mixed race heritage was also seen as symbolically important. Watching footage of Obama's family and seeing his extended family on the campaign trail presented a portrait of a multiracial family that represented the American racial mosaic. He was the son of a white mother and Kenyan father, with a black wife and daughters and an Asian sister. The visual told a story of American racial progress that was powerful for many Americans and resonated with a cross-section of voters.

Of particular interest were the differences between Barack Obama and previous black candidates. He was portrayed as measured, disciplined, and even-tempered—Candidate Obama's public persona countered the archetypal black candidate nee' black man. Undoubtedly, he was viewed by all as charismatic, but unlike black politicians who took office in the period immediately following the Civil Rights Movement, Obama was not angry (Sinclair-Chapman and Price 2008). He was different from the insurgent mayoral candidates who offered blustery challenges to entrenched and discriminatory urban bureaucracies. He also differed significantly from the most serious previous black presidential candidate, Jesse Jackson. During the election there were endless comparisons and sharp contrasts between Obama and Jackson. Where Jackson was a firebrand preacher whose political skills were honed in the fight for civil rights, Obama was a product of the post-civil rights era where overt racial prejudices were understood as socially undesirable and inappropriate for public consumption. Where Jackson was a product of a Historically Black College and the Jim Crow south, Obama was an Ivy League-educated lawyer who spent his childhood in Asia and Hawaii. Jesse Jackson's 1984 and 1988 attempts to earn the Democratic nomination were rife with divisive racial politics. His campaigns ultimately resulted in a disappointed African American electorate who felt that, at least in 1988, Jackson had been slighted by the Democratic Party leadership (Tate 1991).[12] Additionally, Jesse Jackson's bids for president in the 1980s were the first serious run by an African American candidate and thus the expected model for future candidates. Obama refused to step into the role of "black candidate" in favor of a more universal campaign style that involved minimal race talk.

In contrast, Obama's campaign style was a new millennium taking on an older campaign style for black candidates. In their examination of the 1989 election that ushered in the first black governor, Doug Wilder (D-VA) and black mayors in New York City, Cleveland, Seattle, and several other majority white municipalities, McCormick and Jones (1993) highlight two important anomalies in this election cycle. First, the fact that these officials gained office in non-black districts was in clear opposition to cross-racial voting trends that demonstrated a clear reluctance on the part of white voters to cast their ballot for black candidates (Reeves 1997). More importantly, McCormick and Jones highlighted another anomaly in these election outcomes that is particularly relevant here. They argued that these candidates engaged in a campaign strategy called deracialization or,

> *Conducting a campaign in a stylistic fashion that defuses the polarizing effects of race by avoiding explicit references to race-specific issues, while at the same time emphasizing those issues that are perceived as racially transcendent, thus mobilizing a broad segment of the electorate for purposes of capturing or maintaining public office (76).*[13]

For these scholars, deracialization impacted three areas of campaign strategy—"political style, mobilization tactics, and issues." These new deracialized candidates were working against white voters' perceptions of black candidates as angry insurgent candidates like the first wave of black mayors. They had to exhibit a nonthreatening demeanor while refraining from making explicit racial appeals to the black community and avoiding those issues that are or could potentially be viewed as being race-specific. These tactics provided enough normative and policy distance from the black community to make the black candidate more palatable to white voters. Since the 1989 election, the number of black candidates who have taken on variations of the deracialized strategies and successfully gained elective office has increased significantly.[14] Barack Obama's ascendency to the White House is the most important endorsement of this electoral strategy.

The key to the effectiveness of more recent deracialized candidates is their "story." White House Senior Political Advisor David Axelrod who, prior to working for the Obama administration, specialized in consulting for black mayoral candidates highlighted the importance of the candidates' personal stories. In an article in *The Nation* in 2007, Axelrod suggested that the best asset of black candidates with whom he worked was "the direct, lived experience of the effects of injustice with a simultaneous faith that the injustice wasn't permanent, that it could be overcome (Shayes 2007)."[15] Black candidates by virtue of phenotype offer a constant reminder of America's history of racial injustice; however, deracialized candidates, through the symbolism of their story and the style of their campaign, render that history past and offer a hopeful view of the present. Barack Obama began framing his story on the national stage during his 2004 Democratic National Convention. In this speech, Obama, a relative political unknown, used a significant part of his speech relating his personal narrative. He presented this narrative not as introduction but as personification of the American dream: his life experience embodied the values enshrined by the Founders. Most importantly, he framed his narrative as universal (thus race-less). He told viewers in the venue and across the airwaves that his experience was "a part of the larger American story . . . and in no other country on earth, is [his] story even possible."[16]

Black Blame and Barack Obama

During the 2008 campaign Barack Obama deemphasized race, but he did, at times, engage in racial cueing and use racial rhetoric. One form of race talk he engaged in was black blame, and his use of black blame requires a contextual assessment of not only what he said but the conditions under which he said it. There are several examples, but here I focus on three specific occasions that are prototypical of speeches Obama made as he traveled across the country and met with predominantly black audiences.[17] First, I examine two formal speeches given in black churches. One speech was given at a church service commemorating the anniversary of the Selma Voting Rights March and the other was given on Father's Day. Second, I examine a less formal speech given before a majority black audience in the south while stumping during the primary. It is important to reiterate that these speeches were delivered in front of majority black audiences to rousing success. Many African Americans, in the audience, agreed with his assessments and that agreement was clearly expressed through applause and cheering. Although the immediate room where the speeches were delivered was overwhelmingly black, all of these speeches received major news coverage and the two formal speeches were broadcast live on cable news as well as rebroadcast on CSPAN. In all of the coverage, there was virtually no critique of his rebukes of African Americans; if they were mentioned at all it was mostly referred to as tough love conversations in much the same way that the Cosby statements were characterized. Coverage tended to focus on the more universal aspects of the speeches such as his positions on education or other policy matters. Taken less seriously by the media and the Obama campaign was an unplanned public admonition by Jesse Jackson, who made what he thought was an off-camera remark about Barack Obama "talking down to Black people." Interestingly, it also proved beneficial to Obama who was able to demonstrate another contrast between himself and the Jesse Jackson-types of the black community.

Selma Speech

In February 2007, veteran activists and ministers from the civil rights struggle came together to commemorate the 1965 Selma Voting Rights Marches, which were a series of three marches from Montgomery to Selma, Alabama. The first of these marches was dubbed Bloody Sunday because of the ruthless violence against the protesters. As the marchers attempted to cross the Edmund Pettus Bridge, they were met by a mass of state troopers who ordered them to disband and within seconds began to brutally attack the marchers. Many marchers were beaten bloody and injured. Two more attempts were required before the protestors were able to successfully complete the march. During the presidential campaign there was a media spotlight on the commemoration of this seminal Civil Rights Movement event after Obama and Clinton were both invited to participate. At this point in the campaign, which of the two candidates would receive the bulk of the black vote was still an open question.[18] The Clintons had deep and strong ties to the black community, especially during Bill Clinton's two administrations, and Barack Obama had only recently declared his intention to run. Ultimately Clinton and Obama delivered dueling speeches in separate churches in Selma.

After recognizing various dignitaries who were in attendance, Obama began by relaying his story as he did so often on the campaign trail. However, instead of equating his story with a universal narrative of American progress and promise, he connected directly to the civil rights struggle. Relatively new to the campaign trail and still being introduced to most audiences, Obama discussed the similarities between his black immigrant father's experiences with the British colonizers in Kenya and black experiences in the Jim Crow south. In this way, he established his racial bona fides and status as a community insider. For the rest of the speech he outlined the heroic efforts of the civil rights generation and the level of indebtedness all subsequent generations had to them for those efforts. Obama also engaged in black blame as he discussed the ways in which younger Blacks have failed to live up to the ideals of the Civil Rights Movement. According to him, they have lost sight of the values and moral priorities exemplified by previous generations. At one point he suggested that previous generations' commitment to public service and community empowerment have been replaced by greed and materialism. For Obama, this new generation of Blacks,

Thinks it doesn't have to make as many sacrifices. Thinks that the very height of ambition is to make as much money as you can, to drive the biggest car and have the biggest house and wear a Rolex watch and get your own private jet, get some of that Oprah money.

Further, he asserted that these misplaced values were not only in opposition to the values of the previous generations, but they were morally empty without some level of commitment to service. He offered,

> There's nothing wrong with making money, but if you know your history, then you know that there is a certain poverty of ambition involved in simply striving just for money. Materialism alone will not fulfill the possibilities of your existence. You have to fill that with something else. You have to fill it with the golden rule. You've got to fill it with thinking about others. And if we know our history, then we will understand that that is the highest mark of service.

> I can't say for certain that we have instilled that same sense of moral clarity and purpose in this generation. Bishop, sometimes I feel like we've lost it a little bit.

In subsequent paragraphs of the speech, Obama questioned a mentality among young Blacks that regard speaking proper English and reading as acting white. The previous example represented a very mild form of rebuke, but later in the speech Obama's usage of black blame took on a sharper and clearer tone. When discussing what he labeled as "complaining" about persistent inequality and the government's role in fomenting inequality, he acknowledged that government had a role but added,

> We understand [there are problems in the government], but I'll tell you what. I also know that, if cousin Pookie would vote, get off the couch and register some folks and go to the polls, we might have a different kind of politics . . . Take off your bedroom slippers. Put on your marching shoes.

His retort here received significant applause; consequently, little is said about the fact that he was suggesting that government failure to address problems of inequality was the result of political apathy in the black community. It is important to note that implicit in his assertion was a class critique as well. Presumably, Obama and middle class Blacks are not this "cousin Pookie" he spoke of; nor are they the ones wearing the bedroom slippers. Thus, this rebuke of the other was a reprimand of the destructive behavior of poor Blacks.[19] He went further when discussing the fact that so many black children live in poverty. He started by suggesting that this was a problem everybody should ashamed of and added, "but don't tell me it doesn't have a little to do with the fact that we got too many daddies not acting like daddies." In this exchange, Obama was channeling Cosby's arguments with one exception. Obama attributed some blame to structural and governmental inequality; however, any fault of the government was mitigated by internal community problems.

Father's Day Speech

On Father's Day 2008, Obama celebrated at a Pentecostal church on Chicago's predominantly black Southside. Unlike the Selma speech that was to commemorate a particular moment in American racial history, there was no reason to offer any race-specific commentary at this event. It could have just as easily been an opportunity to present himself as a positive family man and attentive father. He had just become the presumptive nominee and his campaign was stockpiling money. Yet, he delivered a speech about the absence and failures of fathers in the black community. The reprimand included the same basic components as the Selma speech, except he did not open by relating his story to the audience. Unlike the introduction offered in the Selma speech, there wasn't a long preamble before offering the rebuke. He immediately jumped into a discussion about absentee fathers and the cost of that absence in the black community.

Before offering black blame he outlined the pervasive problems that plague the black community. He talked about truancy, crime, and failing schools among other problems. The plight of black children was of deep concern to Obama and the congregation, and on Father's Day it was the absence of men that was being examined. As in Selma, he acknowledged that there was a role for government to play in addressing these issues, but ultimately African Americans needed to take collective and individual responsibility for their children.

> But [black people] also need families to raise our children. We need fathers to realize that responsibility does not end at conception. We need them to realize that what makes you a man is not the ability to have a child—it's the courage to raise one.

His rejoinder that fatherhood extended beyond conception was a reiteration of the point made in Selma over a year earlier. Even fathers who were present in households were addressed in this speech. Those fathers who hadn't physically abandoned their families were chided for not setting better examples for their children. Instead of being engaged and active participants in the lives of their children they had emotionally checked out. He lectured,

> *It's a wonderful thing if you are married and living in a home with your children, but don't just sit in the house and watch "SportsCenter" all weekend long. That's why so many children are growing up in front of the television. As fathers and parents, we've got to spend more time with them, and help them with their homework, and replace the video game or the remote control with a book once in awhile. That's how we build that foundation.*[20]

He spoke in the collective—one black father speaking to other black fathers. In this speech, he inserted his story in the middle of his address when he talked about single mothers who are left behind to care for their children alone.

He recounted the stories of how his mother, with the help of his grandparents, raised him without his father. The condition of single motherhood and the image of the long-suffering single mother who sacrifices for her children are iconic in the African American community. He played on this popular image while telling his story and fleshing out his use of the image illustrates how he sometimes muddled or manipulated racial rhetoric. He focused on the struggles of his mother and other single mothers, but he was comparing two distinct racial images. The black single mother in the mind of most is a woman with low skills, low pay, and minimal education. His mother, however, was a well-educated white academic. Though the challenges all of these women face may be similar, the realities of their experiences are quite different. Even he admitted that this childhood was not as "tough as many young people today." However, his conflation of the two has the effect of grounding him in a particular black experience he did not have, reaffirming his insider credentials, and legitimizing his use of black blame.

Texas Stump Speech

Thus far Obama's uses of black blame have taken on a very mild form. If it were not for the settings and the reference to "Pookie," these narratives would hardly take on racial overtones. Without the racial specificity, Obama merely offered prescriptions for good living that could garner widespread support among members of any group. But he was direct about the fact that he was speaking to unique concerns within his own community—the African American community. An example of a more stringent form of black blame came from accounts of a less formal stump speech while trying to win the Texas primary. He gave this speech before a mostly black crowd in the small east Texas city of Beaumont. This was more severe not because of the direct invocation of race, but because his characterization of black parenting resonates with popular negative stereotypes of Blacks. He also provided some insight that he understood he was treading a fine line because he mentioned that some people might be offended.

In this speech and similar to the Father's Day speech, Obama reiterated the need for parents to model the behavior that they want to see in their children. In this particular monologue, he accomplished this by instructing the parents on the kinds of things they need to do to increase educational achievement for black children—less television, a healthy diet, parental involvement, etc. It is very difficult for any parent or interested observer—black or white—to disagree. His prescription was one that makes for a successful student and healthy childhood. However, as he continued this speech and offered more advice his frame became less universal, more racially laden, and he characterized the people he was talking about as clearly pathological. Obama pointed out the difficulties of getting kids to eat a proper diet and continued,

> *"I also know . . . letting our children drink eight sodas a day . . . eat a bag of chips for lunch or Popeyes for breakfast. Y'all have Popeyes in Beaumont?"*[21]

A reporter from the *Chicago Sun-Times* noted that these statements received "raucous applause from the mostly black audience." The fried chicken reference alone should give one pause, but Obama seemed to have tapped into African American frustrations. As the racial collective (of which Obama is a part) searched for remedies, members of that collective were faulted or blamed. Not just any black was blamed. The people in the audience were applauding, so they probably did not see themselves as culprits. No, the worst offenders were those elusive others who failed to show up to the political and Father's Day events. They were absent but their choices weighed heavily on the possibilities of responsible Blacks. They marked the entire race. So Obama got applauded, black audiences were appeased and prevailing stereotypes remained intact in the larger society. Indeed, unquestioned infusions of these stereotypes into popular debate confirmed and bolstered the racial resentment of white listeners.

Beyond the words on the page, Obama's rhetorical style also changed. He converted to a more ministerial style than conventional politician. In an interview with NPR leading up to the Selma commemoration, a reporter asked Obama about the difference in the way he talked to black and white audiences. In response, Obama offered,

> There's a certain black idiom that it's hard not to slip into when you're talking to a black audience. Anybody who's spent time in a black church knows what I mean . . . it becomes a little more like jazz and a little less like a set score.

That Obama adjusted his style for particular audiences was not surprising. Paying attention to the mood and expectations of an audience accounts for why some public speakers are so much better than others. Changing linguistic forms from standard English to a more colloquial English, commonly referred to as code switching, is a common practice for many Blacks. That individuals speak differently in the company of intimates and other members of their identity groups is expected, as is speaking more formally in more public spaces. The dilemma presented by these public addresses is that Obama spoke as if he was only among members of his identity group, but he was not. He was on the national, even international, stage. He was, to use an old adage, airing the black community's dirty laundry in public, which is not generally seen as a good thing. Obama, however, is given a pass for this transgression.

Obama and the Race Problem

To understand the message imparted by Obama's use of black blame, one must put them in the context of his larger view of race relations in America. I argued earlier that in the 2008 election the impact of black blame, as a conceptual and political tool, could not be understood unless we also examine Obama's campaign strategies that kept racial politics at the margins and instead relied on more universal narratives. Interestingly, we did not learn very much about Obama's views on race because they were intentionally muffled. When others raised questions about the racial significance of his campaign, he responded in ways that suggested he, like most members of racial minority groups, was very thoughtful about it. He understood that this campaign was historic and held special meaning for Blacks in particular. However, he initiated a discussion about race only once, when he was in the throes of the Jeremiah Wright controversy and seemed to have no other choice. In early March 2008, footage of several sermons by Jeremiah Wright, pastor of Trinity United Church of Christ, was released to the media. In one sermon he gave shortly after September 11th he suggested that America had gotten what it deserved because of its problematic foreign policy decisions. In the most incendiary clip, he suggested that America had been attacked on 9-11 because God had damned America for its oppression of people around the world. For days, news outlets looped Wright saying, "God damn America," over and over. Though the entire quote is still controversial, it is important to offer some context. In discussing social ills in the black community, Wright lectured,

> "The government gives them the drugs, builds bigger prisons, passes a three-strike law and then wants us to sing 'God Bless America.' No, no, no, God damn America, that's in the Bible for killing innocent people," he said in a 2003 sermon. "God damn America for treating our citizens as less than human. God damn America for as long as she acts like she is God and she is supreme."

Beyond this particular statement, reporters began to comb through his sermons to find incidents where he criticized America for its injustices at home and abroad. Obama was asked to explain whether he knew Wright had made these statements, and if he did, why he continued to associate with someone with these beliefs. Reverend Wright had performed Obama's wedding ceremony to his wife, Michelle, and baptized his two daughters. By his own admission, the title of his second book, *The Audacity of Hope* (2006), was inspired by one of Wright's sermons. Obama at first said he was not present when the 9-11 statements were made; however, as more controversial statements by Wright were uncovered it became more difficult for him to claim that he was unaware of Wright's positions. Eventually, Obama and his family resigned their membership from his church, but it was not enough to quell debate over this issue. The firestorm around Wright threatened to destroy Obama's cross-racial appeal and dominated the news cycle for several weeks.[22] Wright claimed that the media brouhaha was a vicious attack on the black church and black culture rather than a personal attack on him.

On March 18, 2008, at Philadelphia's Constitution Hall, Barack Obama stood before the media and delivered his highly anticipated speech on race relations, entitled "A More Perfect Union." This speech was supposed to put the Wright debacle to rest and redirect his campaign back to other issues. In the speech, he clearly and unequivocally condemned Wright's statements. He also recounted how he came to be a member of Wright's church. He quoted extensively from his first book, *Dreams from My Father* (1995), which offered a detailed account of his decision to join the church. Interestingly, he also equated the possibility of completely shunning Reverend Wright with abandoning his racial identity or rejecting white members of his own family who harbored racial prejudices. For him, all of these choices were suboptimal because of the depth of connection he had to all of these people. Wright's controversial statements posed two dilemmas for Obama. First, he had to distance himself from what was being portrayed as anti-Americanism on the part of his pastor of twenty years. Second, he had to do this without alienating African Americans for whom the black church serves as a pivotal religious and social institution. To be sure African Americans were excited about the prospect of a black president, but the black church continues to hold a special place in the minds of many Blacks. Blacks continue to see their churches not only as religious institutions but also as social service agencies and sources for political knowledge (McDaniel 2008; Harris 1999; Calhoun-Brown 1996). Therefore, even Blacks saw the need to jettison Wright, but there was still a need to tread carefully. By all accounts he successfully navigated this dilemma and received widespread praise for the speech.

This response to the Wright problem was a crucial moment that Barack Obama addressed racial politics. There was no avoiding an implicit nod to racial politics every time he shared his story, but that same story was often situated in a context of American racial progress. In familiar form, he began by telling his racial history in tandem with America's problematic racial history. He spoke directly to America's history of racial discrimination from the Founders' conflicts over the morality of enslaving Africans to protest efforts to ensure black freedom. Additionally, he asserted that one of the missions of his campaign was to demonstrate Americans' capacity to unite in an effort to solve the nation's problems. Obama believed this unity was only possible because of his "unyielding faith in the decency and generosity of the American people" and "his own American story." His story, in this case, was that of a family representing a global village, and the possibility of this family was a uniquely American option. Acknowledging that many people wanted to "view [his] candidacy through a purely racial lens," he dismissed these efforts by offering his support from white voters as evidence. Next, he summarized the racial incidents throughout the campaign with vague references to Bill Clinton's comments before the South Carolina primary, the media's obsessive parsing of exit poll data on race, and questions about his blackness. After giving a full accounting of the events leading up to the speech, he addressed his vision of contemporary race relations. He outlined the challenges that Blacks and other minorities have overcome in the face of strident government opposition.

Most African Americans would agree with his version of history, though they might emphasize different aspects. When it came to his interpretation of the modern consequences of that racial history, he made several arguments that deviated from more popular frames of racial politics, especially those by black advocates. There are three particular aspects of his speech that are worth noting. First, he relegated any anger that Rev. Wright might hold because of his experiences with racism to that of a generational anger rather than a potentially rational response to ongoing racial hostility. For instance, he asserted,

> This is the reality in which Reverend Wright and other African Americans of his generation grew up. They came of age in the late fifties and early sixties, a time when segregation was still the law of the land and opportunity was systematically constricted.

> For the men and women of Reverend Wright's generation, the memories of humiliation and doubt and fear have not gone away; nor has the anger and the bitterness of those years.

In this way, Obama believed that Wright and like-minded members of his generation were reacting to static events that happened in the past rather than an ongoing (and current) racial reality that can impact Blacks of all ages. But what about people who are younger than Rev. Wright and who agree with his racial perspective? For Obama, they have no reason or legitimate excuse. According to his analysis, black people who were raised in the Jim Crow era or earlier were traumatized by their experiences of overt racism that narrowed their life possibilities. This racial regime existed in the past and it was the *memories* of these experiences that drove the Wrights of the world.

Second, Obama equated black frustration with continued discrimination with that of racial resentment by working class and middle class Whites. In his assessment, when African Americans take advantage of affirmative action programs that have been designed to redress centuries of racial discrimination Whites get angry about it.

> *In fact, a similar anger exists within segments of the white community. Most working- and middle-class white Americans don't feel that they have been particularly privileged by their race . . . So when they are told to bus their children to a school across town; when they hear that an African American is getting an advantage in landing a good job or a spot in a good college because of an injustice that they themselves never committed; when they're told that their fears about crime in urban neighborhoods are somehow prejudiced, resentment builds over time.*

This built-up resentment on the part of Whites is likened to black anger at the very discrimination affirmative action is meant to address. At best, these experiences are incongruent. At worst, they are in direct conflict. An alternative frame regards this white anger as subtle racism or racial resentment. For example, Kinder and Sanders (1996) suggest that most white Americans no longer hold overt prejudice based on assumptions of biological inferiority. Instead they hold anti-black sentiments based on beliefs that African Americans do not adhere to core American values and express this animosity through opposition to any programs that are perceived as beneficial to Blacks. If redress for discrimination against Blacks is the action that makes Whites angry, how can one advocate for Blacks and satisfy Whites simultaneously? These efforts are incompatible and when Obama equated the two, he provided a false possibility of racial unity. When this argument was coupled with his use of black blame he reinforced established views by Whites that Blacks lag behind because of their own behavior. In addition, black grievances were almost automatically rendered illegitimate.

Last, Obama proffered a way forward beyond the centuries-old racial morass. He addressed Blacks and Whites separately. African Americans must build coalitions with Whites and other racial groups to achieve bigger goals; however, these coalitions can only be viable if African Americans do not become "victims of their past." For Obama, the way forward was to connect to broad policies that appeal to "the larger aspirations of all Americans." Notably, he ended this direct appeal with a personal responsibility trope.

> *And it means taking full responsibility for their own lives—by demanding more from our fathers, and spending more time with our children, and reading to them, and teaching them that while they may face challenges and discrimination in their own lives, they must never succumb to despair or cynicism; they must always believe that they can write their own destiny.*

This particular iteration of the personal responsibility refrain resonates with all the other speeches examined in this chapter. He made a special plea to Blacks, which suggests that he believed that many Blacks were not in fact "taking full responsibility for their lives" and they were "succumbing to despair or cynicism."

After addressing Blacks, he addressed Whites and urged them to see "that what ails the African American community does not just exist in the minds of black people." He implored them to support government efforts to ensure fairness and justice for all Americans through the enforcement of civil rights laws and investment in public education. The actions he identified are really prescriptions for government action. Nowhere did he make individualized suggestions for Whites to "take full responsibility" for their personal prejudices. Only Blacks warrant a special note about personal responsibility and self-reliance.

CONCLUSION

To be clear, I am not assessing whether Obama was sincere in putting forward his prescriptions for the African American community or merely engaged in a campaign tactic that involved publicly excoriating African Americans to attract white voters. As previously stated, Blacks applauded his comments and Obama was generally described as a disciplined candidate who stayed on message. Beyond agreement and intentionality, the mechanics of using these kinds of rhetorical scripts were important in the 2008 election and have the possibility of impacting future elections. What are the consequences of using black blame and personal responsibility appeals for the candidate using this kind of rhetoric, for the targeted communities and for non-black listeners? It seems that engaging in racial distancing (either through black blame or other tactics) is crucial for black candidates wishing to be successfully elected to office in jurisdictions where Blacks are in the minority. This includes many major urban centers but also state and national elections. This racial distancing is likely to follow successful black candidates into office thereby decreasing the likelihood that they will be able to be strong advocates for vulnerable black constituents. How do African Americans and their advocates reconcile this paradox?

To answer these questions it is important to understand the costs and benefits for individual candidates and the black community, and discuss some potential outcomes for these political actors now that Obama is securely ensconced in the White House. First, Obama's actions demonstrate group connection. All identity groups have specific cultural interactions and Obama used cultural language and stylistic patterns when talking to black people. He used call and response, changed his oratorical style and engaged in black blame, but at what cost to the black electorate? Obama was able to maintain black support through superficial interactions without making any solid concessions or tangible commitments to the African American community. Second, Obama was an atypical black candidate but he was still black. Hence getting white votes was no easy feat. He had to demonstrate a certain level of independence from the black community. He accomplished this by drawing distinct and unambiguous boundaries between his political choices and his racial identity. When it came to dealing with racial issues, he was required to "genuflect at the altar of colorblindness" (Kim 2003; 89).[23] Because of his hyperfocus on race neutrality, anytime candidate and now-President Obama takes the side of black people, it will be seen as showing racial favoritism or hypocrisy. For instance, when black Harvard Professor Henry Louis Gates was harassed and arrested by a white cop for not producing identification on his own front porch, Obama made an offhanded comment that the cop had behaved stupidly. This comment received intense blowback from the mainstream media, police unions, and commentators and ultimately Obama softened his comments and invited Gates and the arresting officer to a now infamous "beer summit" at the White House (Cooper and Goodnough 2009). Beyond addressing the racism related to certain events, his capacity to make race-specific policy will also be hobbled. If his coalition attracts racially resentful Whites, they will not be happy with Obama championing racial policy. In his electoral coalition and in the Democratic Party, African Americans are a permanent fixture. They have no viable electoral options; alternatively, white voters can easily abandon the coalition for another candidate. This potential for mobility gives Whites more leverage, thus he has to be more attentive to their preferences. Admittedly, Obama was in an unwinnable position. If he wanted to be president he had to achieve it by assembling a broad multiracial coalition composed of groups with some consensus and many competing interests.

His strategy was obviously personally successful but it does not bode well for activists making claims on behalf of the black community. For Blacks and their advocates, making race-specific appeals to the Obama administration are all the more difficult. This difficulty stems from several unique political problems that arise from having a black president. First, Obama has already defined his political and governing style as universal, so all policies have to be couched in terms of broad appeal. He will deal only with the big issues and he has all but excluded combating racism and racial prejudice from that category. Organizations and activists will have little traction within the Obama administration unless they can find ways to frame black community needs in race-neutral terms. In Obama's own estimation, continued focus on racism signals an unwillingness to put aside the past and incapacity to subordinate special interests for the "larger aspirations of all Americans." Second, having a black president puts African Americans in the new position of deciding whether to use traditional insurgent tactics against one of their own. If the campaign is any evidence of future behavior, a protest/protection impulse will kick in within the black community.

This impulse represents a desire for African Americans to protect those members or segments of their community that they see as embodying the best of that community. This need to protect can be in direct conflict with the ability to critique or protest the actions of those who they have lifted up. It is a category that is often reserved for those African Americans who have achieved financial, athletic, or academic success. Cohen (1999) outlined the tensions, within the African American community, between the impulse to protect the image (at least counteract prevailing negative stereotypes) and the need to adequately address certain community problems that may carry social stigma or reinforce stereotypes. While racial problems will continue to exist, there will be a strong desire to preserve this historical moment by protecting Obama's image and refraining from making protest demands that may call for the upheaval of the status quo. This is particularly problematic given the fact that much of the political progress made by African Americans results directly from protest demands.

Indeed, most critiques—black, white, or other—of Obama during the campaign were seen as problematic in African American circles. The *Washington Post* reported, in the fall of 2008, that many African American commentators, protestors, and bloggers were chided by other Blacks for their critiques of Obama. One African American woman told the *Post* reporter, "'We can be black all day' after the election, said Griffith, the Houston executive. 'We've got to get there first.'" This woman suggested that there will be a future time when African Americans will be able to articulate their policy and opinion differences with Obama, but getting him elected (by not doing anything to embarrass him or call attention to his weaknesses vis-à-vis his race) were a higher priority. It was unclear, in her assessment and others, when that time will come. Though she spoke of it as an eventuality, the date of its arrival was ambiguous at best. Will African Americans be more open to exploring political differences now that Obama is firmly ensconced in the White House or will it be even more difficult to debate President Obama? I think the latter will be true.

Endnotes

1. http://www.americanrhetoric.com/speeches/billcosbypoundcakespeech.htm (accessed November 6, 2010).
2. Giddings' *When and Where I Enter* (1984), for instance, provides a detailed history of the Black Women's Club Movement whose primary focus was social service and community uplift. Beyond altruism, however, she finds that these women viewed their own progress as inextricably linked to the larger black community. She quotes Mary Church Terrell: "self-preservation demands that [black women] go among the lowly, illiterate and even the vicious, to whom they are bound to ties of race and sex . . . to reclaim them (97)." Social scientists have empirically demonstrated strong support for belief will later name this connection linked fate. (Gurin 1989; Tate 1993; Dawson 1994).
3. http://www.cbsnews.com/stories/2004/05/26/opinion/meyer/main619640.shtml (accessed November 1, 2010).
4. Bureau of Labor Statistics press release, available at http://www.bls.gov/news.release/pdf/empsit.pdf (accessed September 16, 2010) and Boyce Watkins, PhD, "Black Unemployment Rate Increases 700% more than White," on Black Voice at AOL at http://www.bvonmoney.com/2010/09/06/black-unemployment-rate-increases-700-more-than-white (accessed September 16, 2010).
5. http://www.statehealthfacts.org/comparebar.jsp?ind=14&cat=1 (accessed November 1, 2010).
6. http://nces.ed.gov/fastfacts/display.asp?id=16 (accessed November 1, 2010).
7. Information found at http://www.opensecrets.org/pres08/summary.php?id=n00009638 (accessed October 27, 2010).
8. http://www.cnn.com/ELECTIONS/2008/results/polls/#USP00p1 (accessed October 27, 2010).
9. Keeter, Scott and Juliana Horowitz, Alec Tyson. (2008). "Young Voters in the 2008 Election." Pew Research Center for the People and the Press, available at http://pewresearch.org/pubs/1031/young-voters-in-the-2008-election (accessed October 27, 2010).
10. http://cnn.com/ELECTIONS/2008/primaries/results/state/#SC (accessed October 27, 2010).

11. This was thirty percentage points more than any other racial group and more than Kerry and Gore got in the two previous elections. In 2004 Kerry got 88% of the African American vote and in 2000 Gore got 90%. Data found at http://www.cnn.com/ELECTION/2004/pages/results/states/US/P/00/epolls.0.html.

12. Tate found that Jackson's 1984 candidacy stimulated black electoral participation and his 1988 candidacy depressed it. She found that the negative effect was influenced greatly by the fact that Blacks felt Jackson had been poorly treated by the Democratic Party in 1988.

13. Emphasis added.

14. Contemporary examples would include Newark Mayor Corey Booker, Minnesota Congressman Keith Elison, and Massachusetts Governor Deval Patrick.

15. A brief list of Axelrod's clients include Dennis Archer (Detroit), Michael White (Cleveland), John Street (Philadelphia), and Lee Brown (Houston).

16. Obama, Barack. (2004). "Democratic National Convention Keynote Address." Boston, Mass. Available at http://www.americanrhetoric.com/speeches/convention2004/barackobama2004dnc.htm (accessed October 18, 2010).

17. A July 2008 article in the *New Yorker* points to more than a half a dozen incidents on the campaign trail in an article entitled, "Why is Jesse so Testy? Obama's Tough Love for the Black Community." This article was published after Jesse Jackson offered harsh critique of Obama on an open microphone that he believed was off. *New Yorker*, Daily Intel section, 7/10/08.

18. In a 2007 article, Gloria Steinem criticized media pundits for unnecessarily creating conflict between female and African American voters in the Democratic primary. She pointed to the fact that Hillary Clinton had a 40% margin over Obama in the African American community as evidence that the election was about highly qualified candidates rather than race or gender (Steinem 2007).

19. The text of the entire Selma speech can be found at http://www.barackobama.com/2007/03/04/selma_voting_rights_march_comm.php (accessed October 24, 2010).

20. A full transcript of this speech can be found at http://www.barackobama.com/2008/06/15/remarks_of_senator_barack_obama_78.php (accessed October 24, 2010).

21. Sweet, Lynn. 2008. "Obama tells Blacks to Shape Up," *The Chicago Sun-Times*. February 29. Accessed at http://www.suntimes.com/news/sweet/819177,CST-NWS-sweet29.article on October 24, 2010.

22. http://abcnews.go.com/Blotter/DemocraticDebate/story?id=4443788&page=1 (accessed November 1, 2010).

23. In her examination of the Red Apple Boycott in Brooklyn in the late 90s, Claire Jean Kim (2003) discussed the fact that newly-elected black mayor, David Dinkins, was forced to "genuflect to the altar of colorblindness. The yearlong boycott of two Korean markets in predominantly black neighborhoods incited not only the Asian community but Whites as well. They all perceived the boycott as unfair and the protestors as troublemakers. Any legitimate disagreements between the two communities were absent from discussions and Dinkins, who ran a deracialized campaign, received harsh criticism for not breaking up the boycott sooner and taking a more definitive stance against the protestors.

References

Calhoun-Brown, Allison. (1996). "African American Churches and Political Mobilization: The Psychological Impact of Organizational Resources." *Journal of Politics* 58, 935–953.

Cohen, Cathy. (1999). *Boundaries of Blackness: AIDS and the Breakdown of Black Politics*. Chicago, IL: University of Chicago Press.

Cooper, Helene and Abby Goodnough. (2009). "Over Beers, No Apologies, but Plans to Have Lunch." *The New York Times*, July 30, 2009.

Cosby Jr., William H. and Alvin F. Poussaint, MD. (2007). *Come On People: ON the Path from Victims to Victors*. Nashville, TN: Thomas Nelson.

Dawson, Michael C. (2001). *Black Visions: The Roots of Contemporary African-American Political Ideologies.* Chicago, IL: The University of Chicago Press.

Frymer, Paul. (1999). *Uneasy Alliances: Race and Party Competition in America.* Princeton, NJ: Princeton University Press.

Gaines, Kevin K. (1996). *Uplifting the Race: Black Leadership, Politics, and the Culture of the Twentieth Century.* Chapel Hill, NC: The University of North Carolina Press.

Giddings, Paula. (1984). *When and Where I Enter: The Impact of Black Women on Race and Sex in America.* New York, NY: Bantam Books.

Harris, Fredrick C. (1999). *Something Within: Religion in African American Political Activism.* New York, NY: Oxford University Press.

Hayes, Christopher. (2007). "Obama's Media Maven." *The Nation,* February 6th. Available at http://www.thenation.com/print/article/obamas-media-maven (accessed October 17, 2010).

Keeter, Scott and Juliana Horowitz, Alec Tyson. (2008). "Young Voters in the 2008 Election." Pew Research Center for the People and the Press, available at http://pewresearch.org/pubs/1031/young-voters-in-the-2008-election (accessed October 27, 2010).

Kim, Claire Jean. (2003). *Bitter Fruit: The Politics of Black Korean Conflict in New York City.* New Haven, CT: Yale University Press.

Kinder, Donald R., and Lynn M. Sanders. (1996). *Divided by Color: Racial Politics and Democratic Ideals.* Chicago: University of Chicago Press.

Lopez, Mark Hugo and Paul Taylor. (2009). Dissecting the 2008 Election: Most Diverse in US History. Pew Research Center Report, February 29, 2009.

McCormick, Joseph and Charles E. Jones. (1993). "The Conceptualization of Deracialization." *Dilemmas in Black Politics.* Georgia A. Persons (Ed.). NY, NY: Harper Collins.

McDaniel, Eric L. (2008). *Politics in the Pews: The Political Mobilization of Black Churches.* Ann Arbor, MI: The University of Michigan Press.

Obama, Barack. (1995). *Dreams from My Father: A Story of Race and Inheritance.* NY, NY: Three Rivers Press.

Price, Melanye. (2009). *Dreaming Blackness: Black Nationalism and African American Public Opinion.* NY, NY: New York University Press.

Reeves, Keith. (1997). *Voting Hopes and Fears: White Voters, Black Candidates, and Racial Politics in America.* Cambridge: Oxford University Press.

Seelye, Katherine Q. (2008). "In South Carolina, A Bid for Black Women's Votes." *The New York Times* January 14.

Sinclair-Chapman, Valeria and Melanye Price. (2008). "Black Politics, The 2008 Election, and the (Im)Possibility of Race Transcendence." *PS: Political Science and Politics,* 40(4), 739–745.

Smith, Rogers M. (1993). "Beyond Tocqueville, Myrdal, and Hartz: The Multiple Traditions in America." *American Political Science Review,* 87(3), 549–566.

Sweet, Lynn. (2008). "Obama Tell Blacks: Shape Up." *Chicago Sun-Times,* February 2008.

Tate, Katherine. (1991). "Black Political Participation in the 1984 and 1988 Presidential Elections." *American Political Science Review,* 85, 1159–1176.

Tucker, Cynthia. (2004). "Bill Cosby's Speech: His words sting because truth hurts." *The Atlanta Journal-Constitution;* Editorial, p. 15A. May 26, 2004.

Section 5—Study Questions

1. According to the Report of the National Advisory Commission on Civil Disorders, what caused American cities to erupt in the mid- to late 1960s?

2. Why are the Report's conclusions important?

3. According to Fainstein, what are the major trends in how the American government has addressed urban issues since the 1960s?

4. Briefly describe how Fainstein conceptualizes the war on poverty.

5. According to Weems, why have African American landmarks declined?

6. Describe the activities associated with Black-owned landmarks of Chicago during the first half of the 20th century.

7. What are some of the difficulties faced when attempting to compare Black-Asian relations in the United States?

8. List some of the socio-cultural, economic, and spatial factors that inform contemporary relations between Blacks and Asians in American cities.

9. Briefly outline the historical and cultural importance of Franklin Park in Columbus, Ohio.

10. What is Cheryl Clarke's perspective on current efforts to recognize and legalize same-sex marriages?

11. What were some of AmeriFlora's goals for the city of Columbus, Ohio?

12. How can the discipline of Africana Studies benefit from the usage and incorporation of new media technologies?

13. What are some of the challenges and obstacles faced by Africana Studies scholars seeking to utilize these new media technologies?

14. According to Madhubuti, why have white conservatives denied the problem of race in American society?

15. Describe Madhubuti's "African value system" and his call for educational reform.

16. What are some of the reasons that Wisner identifies for the failure of FEMA's preparedness and response to Hurricane Katrina?

17. What role did the social categories of class and race play in the preparedness and survival of the New Orleans victims of Hurricane Katrina?

18. Why did candidate Obama use the personal responsibility trope to characterize black behavior?

19. According to Price, what are the differences between system blame and black blame?